The Family

Second Edition

W. W. Norton & Company has been independent since its founding in 1923, when William Warder Norton and Mary D. Herter Norton first published lectures delivered at the People's Institute, the adult education division of New York City's Cooper Union. The firm soon expanded its program beyond the Institute, publishing books by celebrated academics from America and abroad. By midcentury, the two major pillars of Norton's publishing program—trade books and college texts—were firmly established. In the 1950s, the Norton family transferred control of the company to its employees, and today— with a staff of four hundred and a comparable number of trade, college, and professional titles published each year—W. W. Norton & Company stands as the largest and oldest publishing house owned wholly by its employees.

Editor: Justin Cahill
Project Editor: Caitlin Moran
Editorial Assistants: Erika Nakagawa and Miranda Schonbrun
Managing Editor, College: Marian Johnson
Managing Editor, College Digital Media: Kim Yi
Associate Production Director: Benjamin Reynolds
Media Editor: Eileen Connell
Associate Media Editor: Mary Williams
Media Editorial Assistant: Grace Tuttle
Marketing Director, Sociology: Julia Hall
Design Director: Hope Miller Goodell
Photo Editor: Travis Carr
Permissions Manager: Megan Schindel
Composition: Brad Walrod/Kenoza Type, Inc.
Art: Jouve International
Manufacturing: LSC Communications—Kendallville, IN

ISBN 978-0-393-61457-2

W. W. Norton & Company, Inc., 500 Fifth Avenue, New York, NY 10110-0017
wwnorton.com
W. W. Norton & Company Ltd., Castle House, 75/76 Wells Street, London W1T 3QT

1 2 3 4 5 6 7 8 9 0

The Family

Diversity, Inequality, and Social Change

Second Edition

Philip N. Cohen
Author of FamilyInequality.com

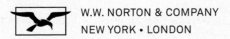
W.W. NORTON & COMPANY
NEW YORK • LONDON

Contents

1 A Sociology of the Family   2

2 The Family in History 34

5 Gender
156

6 Sexuality

7 Love and Romantic Relationships

8 Marriage and Cohabitation

9 Families and Children — 318

10 Divorce, Remarriage, and Blended Families

12 Family Violence and Abuse
436

13 The Future of the Family 476

About the Author

Philip N. Cohen, Professor of Sociology at the University of Maryland, is the founder of the blog FamilyInequality.com. He has published extensively on family structure, the gender division of labor within families, and inequality in the labor force. He has written for such publications as the *New York Times*, *The Washington Post* and *The Atlantic*, and has appeared on radio and TV, including NPR and MSNBC.

Preface

This book started with a question: Is "the family" an outdated institution, out of place in modern society, perpetuating inequality and irrational ideas; or is it a "haven in a heartless world" (Lasch 1978), a place of protection from the encroaching reach of the government and the ravages of the market economy, the last bastion of human loyalty—not to mention, love? As is often the case in academic careers, I spent some years working around the edges of this question and thinking of different ways to approach it. In my research I look at concrete but narrow questions I could address with data analysis. I study the demography of children and families, the division of housework between husbands and wives, the pattern of women's entry into the paid labor force, trends in divorce rates, and children's well-being.

However, publishing in academic journals, important as it is, can be a lonely business. To broaden the conversation, and expand my own focus to more general questions, eventually I took the project in two new directions: writing a blog (Family Inequality) several times a week, and writing a textbook over the course of six years for the first edition, and now a few more on the second. On the blog I wrestled with the daily stream of news, controversy, and conversation in a format that engaged students, teachers, and the reading public—a project that has now grown into a second book, *Enduring Bonds: Inequality, Marriage, Parenting, and Everything Else That Makes Families Great and Terrible* (Cohen 2018). And for this textbook I tried to fit my question within the much larger tradition of social science research on the family, using the best information I could find to shape a course around the most pressing issues. Eventually, I hoped, rather than answering the question I started with (which I never did), the project would give a new generation of students some information and tools they might use to ask their own questions on the subject.

The themes of this book—diversity, inequality, and social change—emerged as I moved back and forth between these streams of work: academic research, blogging, and exploring the massive body of family scholarship for the textbook. Here is how I see them.

- *Diversity.* The cultural, political, legal, and technological changes of our era lead to new family patterns. We face growing diversity in the timing of family events, the forms that families take, and the nature of intimate relationships. People in modern society probably have more family life choices to make than ever before, as seen in the demographic trends on everything from the timing of births to cohabitation and marriage, divorce, remarriage, and new family structures.

- *Inequality.* Even with all these choices, of course, everyone's options are constrained by various forces, but to very different degrees. Poverty, discrimination, and institutional restrictions are barriers to achieving family ideals. And because family structures and experiences have life-changing consequences for health, wealth, and well-being, growing inequality means the stakes are increasing. In the years since the first edition was published, one major constraint has been lifted, as same-sex couples are now permitted to marry in the United States—a change I've now integrated throughout the text.

- *Social change.* In the new modern era, people must justify their choices, to themselves and to others, because choice is how people frame diversity. In the absence of strong pressure for conformity, differences matter: we may get credit if things go well along our many different paths, but people will also judge us if things turn out badly. The elevation of personal choice to an ideal means everyone is held accountable for their family life, which is one reason many students want to take a course like this one.

As I pursued these themes throughout the book, the process was shaped by the unique combination of my training, work style, and theoretical approach. These have become pedagogical tools.

- In addition to my training as a sociologist, I also learned the tools of *demographic analysis*, and how to work with population data on children, families, family structure, and social transformation. As a result, I often investigate social change by analyzing demographic trends. That demographic perspective runs throughout the book.

- To figure out what's happening, and why, I produce many *graphs and charts*—comparing trends, contrasting the numbers for different groups, looking for problems and questions I haven't considered. The figures are both exploratory and illustrative. A selection of these figures appears in the book—much improved by the design work of Kiss Me I'm Polish's Agnieszka Gasparska and Rachel Matts—in a feature called the "Story Behind the Numbers."

- As I reviewed material for the book, looking for ways to organize it and explain it to students, I have come to turn frequently to the *theory of modernity* (described in Chapter 1). That means I ask questions about individual identity and institutional dynamics, personal freedom, and the need for self-definition in modern society. Whether students and instructors come to adopt this perspective or not, I have found it serves as a useful frame for translating the questions in the book into the language of personal experiences.

There are two other aspects of the writing I should mention at the outset. First, sometimes in academic writing we try to be comprehensive and provide citations to as many studies as possible that confirm a particular pattern of facts or explain the theory behind our work. That doesn't work very well for students who are approaching a subject for the first time. Instead, I have tried to provide specific references to the source of the information I used, and then, when making more general points, either to refer to a classic book or article, or to a recent study that exemplifies the point (and that includes within it many more references for background). A big part of revising this book for the second edition was adding hundreds of new citations—and removing many others—so these would be as current as possible. That includes the figures in the book, most of which have been updated with current data when available. So for those interested in digging deeper, I encourage you to follow the references to the subjects that interest you, to see what they wrote and what they read to get there. Second, with regard to data and figures, I have done a lot of my own calculations and analysis here. In those cases, there is no one place you can go to look up the numbers I use, but I have provided information about the data source.

To my amazement and extremely good fortune, hundreds of instructors and thousands of students picked up and used the first edition, enough so that we decided to revise the book. They also gave us their feedback, both informally and through in-depth reviews of each chapter. Taking their responses to heart, and working through the vast academic literature that appears every year (with the help of excellent graduate assistants), I was able to produce a substantial upgrade. Most noticeably, the book incorporates changes in the rapidly evolving legal, political, technological, and cultural contexts that surround the family.

To help with class discussions and inspire research projects, each chapter now includes a new "Trend to Watch" feature, each of which raises a question about the future—one that I can't yet answer, but that seems likely to be important as it unfolds. And in every chapter I have added content about aging and the family lives of older people, in response to requests from some instructors.

Here I'll mention some of the highlights of the new edition. Chapter 1 includes the proposed revision to U.S. Census family definitions, including same-sex couples, as well as an introduction to "big data," and a discussion of how political surveys failed to predict the winner of the 2016 presidential election. The history chapter (Chapter 2) has new material on the economic and social circumstances of older Americans, and the young adult children now more likely to live with them. Chapter 3, on Race, Ethnicity, and Immigration, includes changes to the race and ethnicity classifications used by the government, and expanded discussions of undocumented immigration and related policy changes. In Chapter 4, Families and Social Class, I tell the story of Donald Trump, Jr. (whose first, and so far only, job title is "executive vice president of development and acquisitions" for his father's company). And on the other end of the social class spectrum, we have a new discussion of the problem of poor families being evicted from their homes, and new poverty information for the elderly. The chapter on Gender (Chapter 5) includes new information on sexual diversity and intersex and transgender identities, including controversies over medical treatments and bathroom rights. Chapter 6, Sexuality, has a new section on sex at older ages, and a feature on pornography in the Trend the Watch feature. In Love and Romantic Relationships (Chapter 7), there are expanded discussions of the hookup culture on college campuses, the increasing role of mobile technology in finding partners for love and sex, older singles, and gay and lesbian relationships. Chapter 8 (Marriage and Cohabitation) spells out the political and legal transformation that brought marriage equality for same-sex couples—and the challenges we face in studying their experiences. In Families and Children (Chapter 9), I describe the consequences of the Great Recession, including delayed childbearing, and its implications for families in the future. Fittingly, the Trend to Watch in that chapter is about assisted reproductive technology. Chapter 10 (Divorce, Remarriage, and Blended Families) features new research on increasing divorce at older ages, as well as new data on blended families. In Chapter 11 (Work and Families), I have a new discussion of policies for work-family—or work-*life*—balance, including the growing importance of state and local policy innovation. For Chapter 12 (Family Violence and Abuse), I added new research on violence against older people, campus sexual assault, and the prospects of a society with less violence in the future. Finally, Chapter 13, on the Future of the Family, now includes information on the deportation of immigrants who have U.S.-citizen children, as well as a discussion of the "oldest-old" and testing the limits of human longevity.

Acknowledgments

I have a wonderful collection of debts to acknowledge, beginning with my original editor, Karl Bakeman. Karl persuaded me that I could write this book, and he was right, but only because of him. From the beginning of the first edition through the planning of the second, his insights, encouragement, and great humor made this project not only possible, but also interesting and even fun. I am deeply indebted to him. And now I am fortunate to have the company of editor Justin Cahill, whose expert guidance brought the second edition to this happy fruition. The rest of the team at Norton was helpful, diligent, and extremely supportive, including developmental editors Beth Ammerman and Harry Haskell, editorial assistants Miranda Schonbrun and Erika Nakagawa, media editor Eileen Connell, associate media editor Mary Williams, media editorial assistant Grace Tuttle, project editor Caitlin Moran, associate production director Ben Reynolds, associate design director Hope Miller Goodell, marketing director Julia Hall, text permissions manager Megan Schindel, photo editor Travis Carr, and sales specialists Julie Sindel, Roy McClymont, and Jonathan Mason.

I had the pleasure of working with four research assistants for the first edition: Amy Lucas, Emily Danforth, Rebecca Rodriguez, and Lucia Lykke. For the second I was joined by Joanna Pepin and Joey Brown. Each brought their own energy and perspective to make a valuable contribution to the process as well as the final project. At various times I consulted with, nagged, or bored a long list of colleagues. We shared questions about theories, sources, and data; false leads, tirades, and (my) personal angst; and the occasional celebration. They include: Syed Ali, Andy Andrews, Neal Caren, Anjani Chandra, Feinian Chen, Carrie Clarady, Dawn Dow, Claudia Geist, Jackie Hagan, Jessica Hardie, Amy Harmon, Amie Hess, Matt Huffman, Jeehye Kang, Meredith Kleykamp, Rose Kreider, Beth Latshaw, Michelle Janning, Heather Laube, JaeIn Lee, Jay Livingston, Kate McFarland, Melissa Milkie, Lisa Pearce, Rashawn Ray, Jen'nan Read, Cheryl Roberts, Virginia Rutter, Liana Sayer, Pamela Smock, Reeve Vanneman, Kristi Williams, and Moriah Willow. At key points I was the beneficiary of guidance and support from Andrew Cherlin, Stephanie Coontz, Paula England, Barbara Risman, and the members of the Council on Contemporary Families, on whose board I serve. Michael Hout and Emily Beller generously shared computer code. (Many more have contributed to helpful social media conversations.)

The wider network of family and friends can't be listed here, but first among them is my wife, Judy Ruttenberg, whose contributions and kindness I appreciate beyond words; and our beautiful children, Charlotte and Ruby (both now old enough to read it for themselves!). For supporting me in this and other things, I also thank my parents, Avis and Marshall Cohen, and: Ness and Heather Blackbird, Rhoda Ruttenberg, Miriam Ruttenberg and Peter Kraft, Daphne Olive and Dubi Paltshik, Ramsey Brous and Melissa Burress, Anne and Ira Brous, and Scott Matthews.

For each edition, the editors coordinated a rolling panel of reviewers providing feedback on the chapter drafts. These are experts in teaching this material, and their perspectives were invaluable as we shaped and reshaped the text:

Second Edition Reviewers

Richard Brinkman, Wenatchee Valley College

Marianne Jennifer Brougham, Arizona State University

Stacey L. Callaway, Rowan University

Caroline Calogero, Brookdale Community College

Wanda Clark, South Plains College

Jerry Cook, California State University, Sacramento

Raquel Zanatta Coutinho, University of North Carolina at Chapel Hill

Susan Crawford-Sullivan, College of the Holy Cross

Kathy Dolan, University of North Georgia

Melanie Duncan, University of Wisconsin—Stevens Point

Debra Edwards, Chemeketa Community College

Laura Evans, Penn State Brandywine

Katherine Everhart, Northern Arizona University

Patricia Gleich, University of West Florida

Peter Grahame, Pennsylvania State University—Schuylkill

Theodore Greenstein, North Carolina State University

Margaret Hagerman, Mississippi State University

Stephanie Hansard, Georgia State University

Jessica Hausauer, Minnesota State University Moorhead

Susan Holbrook, Southwestern Illinois College

Jennifer Hook, University of Southern California

Jessica Huffman, Old Dominion University

Robert Hughes, Jr., University of Illinois at Urbana-Champaign

Michelle Janning, Whitman College

Sarah Kendig, Arkansas State University

Uma Krishnan, California State University Northridge

Rachel Kutz-Flamenbaum, University of Pittsburgh

Lisa M. Lepard, Kennesaw State University

Bethany Letiecq, George Mason University

Carlos Lopez, Chemeketa Community College

Adriana Lopez-Ramirez, University of Arkansas at Little Rock

Gerald Loveless, Clackamas/Portland Community College

Emily Margolis, Towson University

Lorraine Mayfield-Brown, St. Petersburg College
Linda McCarthy, Greenfield Community College
Pamela McMullin-Messier, Central Washington University
Maegan Morin, University at Albany, SUNY
Katie Nutter-Pridgen, Santa Fe College
Sonia Oliva, College of Lake County
Jennifer H. Perry, Central Carolina Technical College
Carla A. Pfeffer, University of South Carolina
Michael Polgar, Penn State University
Daniel Poole, Salt Lake Community College
Jennifer Randles, California State University, Fresno
Janet Reynolds, Northern Illinois University
Elizabeth Riina, Queens College, CUNY
Mihaela Robila, Queens College, CUNY
Karen Sabbah, California State University, Northridge
Kelsey Schwarz, Georgia State University
Joann Watts Sietas, Serra College
Bahira Sherif-Trask, University of Delaware
Pamela R. Smith, Michigan State University
Rebecca Herr Stephenson, Loyola Marymount University
Mieke Beth Thomeer, University of Alabama at Birmingham
Beverly Thompson, Siena College
Kristin Turney, University of California, Irvine
Lisa Munson Weinberg, Florida State University
Sharon Wiederstein, Blinn College, Bryan
Brenda Wilhelm, Colorado Mesa University
Hyeyoung Woo, Portland State University

First Edition Reviewers

Ann Beutel, University of Oklahoma
Adrienne Bey, Wilmington University
Kimberly P. Brackett, Auburn University at Montgomery
Jessica Burke, Francis Marion University
Daniel Carlson, Georgia State University
Noelle Chesley, University of Wisconsin-Milwaukee
Jerry Clavner, Cuyahoga Community College
Lynda Dickson, University of Colorado Colorado Springs
Patricia Drentea, University of Alabama at Birmingham
Kathryn Feltey, University of Akron
Bethaney Ferguson, Cape Fear Community College
Anita Garey, University of Connecticut
Jean Giles-Sims, Texas Christian University
Anna Hall, Delgado Community College
Millie Harmon, Chemeketa Community College
Angela Hattery, George Mason University

Gesine Hearn, Idaho State University

Lisa Hickman, Grand Valley State University

Shirley Hill, University of Kansas

Carol Holdt, Portland State University

Erica Hunter, University at Albany, SUNY

Wesley James, University of Memphis

Barbara Johnson, University of South Carolina Aiken

Barbara Keating, Minnesota State University, Mankato

Traci Ketter, University of Missouri-Kansas City

Rebecca Kissane, Lafayette College

Amy Krull, Western Kentucky University

David Maume, University of Cincinnati

N. Jane McCandless, University of West Georgia

Renee Monson, Hobart and William Smith Colleges

Monika Myers, Arkansas State University

Michael Nofz, University of Wisconsin-Fond du Lac

Stacey Oliker, University of Wisconsin-Milwaukee

Sue Pauley, Wingate University

Gay Phillips, Tulsa Community College

Naima Prince, Santa Fe College

Victor Romano, Barry University

Daniel Romesberg, University of Pittsburgh

Louise Roth, University of Arizona

Linda Rouse, University of Texas at Arlington

Jerry Shepperd, Austin Community College

Jennifer Smith, University of Wisconsin-Green Bay

Susan Stewart, Iowa State University

Brooke Strahn-Koller, Kirkwood Community College

Jessi Streib, Duke University

Heather Sullivan-Catlin, SUNY Potsdam

Katherine Trent, University at Albany, SUNY

Ana Villalobos, Brandeis University

Elaine Weiner, McGill University

Debra Welkley, California State University, Sacramento

Alan Wight, University of Cincinnati

Sarah Winslow, Clemson University

Gilbert Zicklin, Montclair State University

In the category of people just doing their jobs, but in ways that helped me get through the day, finish the chapter, or solve a problem, I thank the workers at Weaver St. Market in Chapel Hill, the librarians and other staff at the University of North Carolina's Population Center, and the staff in the sociology departments at UNC and the University of Maryland, especially Karina Havrilla, Gaye Bugenhagen, and our chair, Patricio Korzeniewicz.

Since I started this project I lost two great teachers, and inspirational sociologists, who I knew from my days in graduate school: Harriet Presser, a professor at Maryland when I arrived, taught my Gender, Work, and Family seminar (which

I went on to teach); and Suzanne Bianchi, who was a teacher, collaborator, and mentor. I so wanted them to see this book completed, but I was lucky to work with them while I could; I hope they would be proud.

Looking back at these lists, I am amazed at how this project has enriched the web of social and intellectual interaction within which I work, now over more than ten years. As you, teachers and students whom I don't yet know, pick up this book, I hope you will help this conversation continue.

Additional Resources

For Students

InQuizitive
New to the Second Edition, InQuizitive, Norton's award-winning adaptive learning tool, personalizes quiz questions for each student in a game-like environment. Questions in each chapter activity help students master core concepts. InQuizitive activities for *The Family* incorporate many of the "Story Behind the Numbers" animations and figures to help students analyze the data and apply the concepts presented in the book. Assigning InQuizitive has proven benefits: in a recent study, when sociology students completed an InQuizitive activity prior to taking a summative quiz, grades increased by an average of 18 points. InQuizitive author Jessica Halliday Hardie is an assistant professor of sociology at Hunter College. She specializes in sociology of education, inequality, family, and the transition to adulthood.

FamilyInequality.com
The author's regularly updated blog shows students how what they learn about modern families applies to what's going on in the world around them.

"Story Behind the Numbers"
Narrated by Philip Cohen, these online animations are perfect for teaching online or in the classroom and are available on Norton's YouTube channel as well as in the enhanced ebook and Coursepack.

Ebooks
Same great book, a fraction of the price.

Norton Ebooks give students and instructors an enhanced reading experience at a fraction of the cost of a print textbook. Students are able to have an active reading experience and can take notes, bookmark, search, highlight, and even read offline. As an instructor, you can even add your own notes for students to see as they read the text. Norton Ebooks can be viewed on—and synced among—all computers and mobile devices.

For Instructors

Everything you need for your course is available at wwnorton.com/instructors.

Coursepack

Coursepack author Joanna Pepin is a Ph.D. candidate at the University of Maryland. Joanna specializes in the relationship between historical changes in families and stratification. *The Family*'s Coursepack offers a variety of activities and assessment and review materials for instructors who use Blackboard and other learning management systems. The Coursepack includes an optional ebook and features:

- A pre-reading quiz for each chapter

- Glossary flashcards and gradable glossary matching exercises

- A chapter review quiz for each chapter featuring multiple-choice and matching questions

- Gradable exercises on the "Story Behind the Numbers" animations

- 13 clips from the *Sociology in Practice: Thinking about the Family* DVD with accompanying multiple-choice assessments that connect each clip to key sociological concepts in each chapter

- Gradable activities based on familyinequality.com blog posts

- InQuizitive activities (optional)

Formats:

- Blackboard

- Angel

- Canvas

- D2L

- Moodle

Interactive Instructor's Guide

The Interactive Instructor's Guide author Patricia Gleich is an instructor at the University of West Florida.

New to the Second Edition, the easy-to-navigate Interactive Instructor's Guide makes lecture development easy with an array of teaching resources that can be searched and browsed according to a number of criteria. Resources include chapter outlines, discussion questions, suggested readings, and activities that encourage students to analyze the "Story Behind the Numbers" infographics.

Lecture PowerPoints

Joanna Pepin, University of Maryland

This fully customizable classroom presentation tool features Lecture PowerPoint slides with bulleted classroom lecture notes in the notes field that will be particularly helpful to first-time teachers. The Lecture PowerPoint images include alt-text, and the slides are designed to be used with screen readers.

Art PowerPoints and JPEGs

All of the art from the book, sized for classroom display. Alt-text is included, and the slides are designed to be used with screen readers.

Test Bank

By Lisa Lepard, Kennesaw State University and Kristin Ralston-Coley, Kennesaw State University

The Test Bank for *The Family* is designed to help instructors prepare exams. In addition to Bloom's taxonomy, each question is tagged with metadata that places it in the context of the chapter, as well as difficulty level, making it easy to construct tests. The test bank features approximately 650 questions, 25% of which are new to the Second Edition.

The Family

Second Edition

1 A Sociology of the Family

Americans have a long-standing interest in **genealogy**—the study of ancestry and family history—looking back through the generations for a feeling of connection to a larger family tree. They may search for links to early colonial settlers or immigrants, try to unearth the painful past of slavery among their ancestors, or maybe gain a piece of a long-lost family fortune. Traditionally, this involved research into family archives and public libraries, but recently such sleuths are using genetic tests to trace their family trees. Even when the link is literally microscopic, it can establish family ties across formidable social barriers. That was the case for Vy Higginsen, a Black woman who runs a Harlem school for gospel singers, and Marion West, a White cattle rancher from Missouri. The two discovered through DNA testing that they shared a distant common ancestor and celebrated their discovery at a reunion in Harlem. West, whose grandfather fought for the Confederacy in the Civil War, addressed his newfound Black family members, saying, "Dear God, thank you for this beautiful night and this great family we got here" (Kilgannon 2007:E3).

genealogy

The study of ancestry and family history.

3

The promise of a genetic connection is also how a 63-year-old woman named Derrell Teat ended up following a suspected descendant of her great-great-great-grandfather's brother to a local McDonald's, hoping to secure a piece of castaway DNA after he refused to give her a sample voluntarily. "I was going to take his coffee cup out of the garbage can," Teat said. "I was willing to do whatever it took" (Harmon 2007:A1). In both cases, the family connection was symbolic; the connection West, Higginsen, and Teat shared was meaningful to them because they believed that it was.

Through DNA testing, Vy Higginsen (left) and Marion West (right) discovered they shared a distant common ancestor.

To see how far you can take this symbolic form of family, consider the variety of virtual family members:

- People who have received transplanted organs from dying patients are increasingly becoming involved in the lives of their donors' families. For example, when Jeni Stepien married Paul Maenner, her father wasn't available to walk her down the aisle, because he had been murdered 10 years earlier. But the man who received her father's transplanted heart was there to do the honor. Arthur Thomas, whom the Stepien family had never met before the transplant, carried "a physical piece of my father" down the aisle with her, Stepien said—his new heart. And the wedding photographer snapped a picture of her placing her hand on his chest during the ceremony (Rogers 2016).

- For homebound elderly people, or those living in institutions, a company called GeriJoy sells a virtual "caregiving companion" service, in which a talking pet appears on an iPad app, interacting with its companion 24/7 under the direction of remote staff (who may be on another continent). The companion asks questions about relatives and flips through old family photos. And because the GeriJoy looks and speaks the same way even when it's operated by different staff members, clients can develop a personal relationship with it over time.

- Of course, in a country where more households have a dog (44 percent) than have children (31 percent), animals are an important part of family life, and they are often treated as family members (U.S. Census Bureau 2015a, Table H2; Humane Society 2016). On the Internet, for example, Americans have posted thousands of photographs showing off their "grandpuppies," referring not to the offspring of their dogs but to the dogs of their human children.

These examples of the many ways people establish family connections or develop relations that mimic families help illustrate the commonplace reality that our families are what we think they are.

Defining Families

We usually know what we mean—and whom we mean—when we use the word *family*. The clearest family connections are biological, as between parents and their children. Legal recognition binds people into families in the case of marriage or adoption. And emotional connections often rise to the level of family as well, as when people use the term "auntie" to refer to family friends who are not related by blood or marriage. In the simplest definition, then, **families** are groups of related people, bound by connections that are biological, legal, or emotional. As we will see, however, not everyone agrees about which biological, legal, and emotional connections create families.

families

Groups of related people, bound by connections that are biological, legal, or emotional.

Some people have families large enough to have reunions in city parks, while others live alone. Almost a quarter of American adults live alone or with people to whom they are not related.

Some family reunions are big enough to fill a city park pavilion, and few of those people know how everyone is related. But that is not the universal modern experience. For every sprawling family that includes hundreds of living relatives—distant cousins, stepfamilies, and in-laws—there are many others living as insular units of only a few people, either by choice or as a result of family dissolution, death, or isolation. Out of 242 million adults in the United States, 53 million live alone or only with people to whom they are not related (U.S. Census Bureau 2015a: Tables A1 & H2).

Usually, the label *family* signals an expectation of care or commitment, which is partly how we know who counts as a member of the family. That's why some people refer informally to a cherished babysitter as "part of the family." Family relationships are the basis for a wide range of social obligations, both formal and informal. For example, an illness or death in the family is usually accepted as an excuse for missing work or class (with no proof of a blood relationship required). People are expected to sacrifice their personal time, energy, and money for the well-being of their family members. That means waking up at night for a crying baby and spending your own money to send your kids to college—which is why college financial aid is affected by how rich or poor a student's parents are (Goldrick-Rab 2016). But caring is also the law, and failing to care for a family member—for example, by abandoning a child—may be a criminal offense. That differs from caring for members of society at large, a function that in the United States is mostly delegated to government and religious or charitable organizations.

If family relations imply caring, they also carry with them lines of authority. Challenging such authority can have unpleasant or even dangerous consequences. In the United States, many parents (or other caregivers) use moderate physical force against their children for discipline, and this is usually tolerated as a reasonable exercise of family authority; almost half of parents say they at least sometimes spank their children (Pew Research Center 2015a). Parents don't apply for a permit to spank their children; their discipline is informally approved based on common cultural understandings of family boundaries and relationships. Nonfamily authorities such as the police or social welfare agencies can also discipline children but only with legal permission, and generally not with violence (an exception is corporal punishment in some schools, where teachers and administrators are seen as extensions of parental authority). Thus, family authority is recognized both informally by common practice and formally by the law.

Biological or not biological, formal or informal—clearly, we don't all agree on a single definition of families. And rather than insist on conformity on the issue, I find it helpful to think of several types of definition: the personal family, the legal family, and the family as an institutional arena. Each of these conceptions is useful for different circumstances, and together they identify the subject matter of this book—the sociological approach to families. *Sociology* is an academic discipline that studies the nature and development of human society, in our case specifically the family. Often, that means looking at the same phenomenon from different angles, as we do with defining families.

The Personal Family

Any attempt to create a single definition of *family* from all the different ways people use the term runs the risk of being overly vague. For that reason, I define the **personal family** simply as the people to whom we feel related and who we expect to define us as members of their family as well. By this definition, a group of people who mutually define themselves as a family are a family, based on their own understanding of the concept *related*. Whom people choose to include in these groups changes from time to time and differs from place to place. Thus, over time it has gradually become acceptable to consider stepchildren and stepparents as bona fide members of the same family (see the discussion of *blended families* in Chapter 10). Because definitions of personal families follow common patterns, they are partly a product of the larger culture in which we live. In China, for example, some girls are informally adopted by families that do not have daughters and that may be prevented from having additional children under the country's restrictive fertility laws, and this is culturally consistent with ancient practices of informal adoption in that country. So even if our family choices seem highly personal, they reflect the interaction of our own decisions with all the influences we face and the practices of those around us.

As you can see, this definition is quite vague, but a more specific definition inevitably would exclude families as many people see them. In fact, most of us learn to recognize members of our own family before we are old enough to understand how the term *family* is defined. This personal family as we experience it in our daily lives sets the boundaries for our most intimate interactions from an early age.

According to child psychologists, understanding the difference between family members and others is an important part of our development in early

personal family

The people to whom we feel related and who we expect to define us as members of their family as well.

childhood. Young children who cannot "exhibit appropriate selective attachments" or who show "excessive familiarity with relative strangers" may be diagnosed with a psychological disorder that is usually associated with inadequate emotional or physical care (American Psychiatric Association 2000). Lack of family definition also causes many of the tensions in newly formed stepfamilies, which have difficulty establishing clear boundaries around units within the family or between the family and the outside world (Braithwaite et al. 2001). In short, defining our families is an important step in the construction of our personal identities, and the personal family is the definition we apply in that process.

The Legal Family

Most people don't judge the definitions others apply to their own families. We don't ask for proof that a student was emotionally close to her deceased grandfather before giving her permission to miss class for the funeral—that relationship is assumed. Increasingly, however, as families have become more diverse in their structure and as public rights and obligations have been tied to family relationships, the government's definition of families has grown more complicated. It also has taken on greater social and political importance. There is no universal legal definition, but the **legal family** is generally defined as a group of individuals related by birth, marriage, or adoption. This appears to be a straightforward definition, but in law the meaning of almost every word may be contested and subject to change.

Hannah Rocklein was adopted as a toddler from a Russian orphanage. Her adoptive parents later divorced. She now lives with her adoptive mother and siblings, stepfather, and dog.

legal family

A group of individuals related by birth, marriage, or adoption.

The most contentious term in this definition is *marriage*, which carries with it many rights and responsibilities overseen by the government. In fact, most debates over the definition of *family* in recent years have had to do with what marriage is (Powell et al. 2010). In 1996, when it first appeared that some states might start granting marriage licenses to same-sex couples, the U.S. Congress overwhelmingly passed, and President Bill Clinton signed, the Defense of Marriage Act. The law specified that the federal government would not recognize same-sex married couples as "married," even if their marriages were legally recognized by their home states. However, the Supreme Court ruled in *United States v. Windsor* (2013) that the federal government must recognize all marriages that are legally valid in the states, granting same-sex couples access to all federal benefits, from health coverage and Social Security pensions to the right to be buried in veterans' cemeteries with their spouses. Then, in the 2015 decision known as *Obergefell v. Hodges*, the Court went further, finally guaranteeing same-sex couples the right to marriage in every state. (We will return to this issue in Chapter 8.)

In 2015 the Supreme Court made same-sex marriage legal in every state, helping to change the definition of *family*.

Such official definitions clearly have implications for the distribution of limited resources. For example, until the *Windsor* decision, a same-sex couple married in Massachusetts, with one citizen and one immigrant spouse, could not use that marriage to gain citizenship for the immigrant spouse (J. Preston 2013). But many other aspects of life are affected as well. In New York State, for example, the official recognition of same-sex marriage affected some 1,300 statutes and regulations, "governing everything from joint filing of income tax returns to transferring fishing licenses between spouses" (Peters 2008:A1). The government's definition also lends credibility—or legitimacy—to some families and contributes to a sense of isolation or exclusion for those whose families do not conform.

In some cases, a legal definition of family relationships is enforced nationally, as in the federal tax code, immigration rules, or Social Security and the Medicare health insurance program. But usually the states apply and enforce their own laws regulating family life. Local legal definitions underlie many conflicts, ranging from adoption (who can adopt?) to residential zoning (how many "unrelated" people can live in one household?). Further, because the laws contribute to our personal definitions, and because legal definitions are inherently subject to political debate, they have gained symbolic importance, which may explain why so many people care how other people define their families. Even though local laws and definitions vary, the U.S. Census Bureau, which gathers much of the data on American families that we will examine in this book, uses the federal government's definition of the legal family (see Changing Law, "How the U.S. Census Counts Families").

How the U.S. Census Counts Families

The history of the U.S. Census offers important lessons about the definition of families. It also serves as an example of the emergence of individuality in modern society and the "institutionalized individuality" referred to by the modernity theorists studied later in this chapter (Beck and Beck-Gernsheim 2004).

The U.S. Constitution in 1789 ordered an "actual enumeration" of the population every 10 years, for purposes of apportioning political representatives among the population. A nationwide **census** has been carried out every 10 years since 1790. But the idea of counting everyone in the population is at least as old as the story of the Jews wandering in the desert after fleeing Egypt, in which God commanded Moses to "take the sum of all the congregation of the children of Israel, by families following their fathers' houses; a head count of every male according to the number of their names."

census

A periodic count of people in a population and their characteristics, usually performed as an official government function.

In all modern societies, the census plays a crucial role in the development of public infrastructure and the administration of services. These data collection efforts are large government projects, conducted at great expense. Even with use of online forms and mobile technology, the 2020 U.S. Census is projected to cost more than $13 billion and employ hundreds of thousands of workers visiting American households. The census also is one of the government's direct interventions into personal life, requiring the formal definition of all individuals' relationships and family boundaries. So the definitions that government officials use are important for how commonly accepted roles and identities are developed (Coontz 2010).

Until 1840, the U.S. Census recorded only the name of the "head" of each household, with an anonymous count of other people present (slaves were counted as members of their owners' families, though they only counted as three-fifths of a person for purposes of congressional representation). Starting in 1840, individuals were recorded separately, though still listed by household, under the "family head." At that time, census forms were filled out by enumerators, who knocked on doors and recorded information by hand. In 1870, confronted for the first time with large urban buildings that did not separate families into distinct households, the census defined a **household** as a group of people who share a common dining table. That idea stuck, and some variation of the concept of "live and eat separately from others" has been used to define households ever since (Ruggles and Brower 2003).

household

A group of people that lives and eats separately from other groups.

What Is a Census Family?

Today, the Census Bureau uses the legal definition of the family presented in this chapter, but with one qualification: a family lives together in one household. By the personal or legal definitions I presented earlier, members of the same family could live in different households. In fact, one person could be a member of any number of families. When it comes to collecting statistical data, however, that is not practical. So the Census Bureau limits each family to one household, and each person can only be counted in one place. That is why students living in college dorms are not counted as part of their families' households (which is also the case for military personnel abroad or on ships, prisoners, or people in nursing homes). With this definition—putting each person in only one household—the 2010 census showed that among the 301 million people living in 117 million households, there were 78 million families, or groups of people related by birth, marriage, or adoption who live together in one household (U.S. Census 2012a).

But how does the Census Bureau apply the legal definition of family? The task seemed simple at first. The 1880 census was the first to record information about each individual's relationship within the family. After listing the "head" of each family (always the husband in the case of married couples), the enumerator made a list of all other individuals in the household and made a note of the "relationship of each person to the head of this family—whether wife, son, daughter, servant, boarder, or other" (Ruggles et al. 2013). Those six categories now serve as a quaint reminder of a simpler time in family life.

Starting in the 1960s, as families became more complicated, the categories on the census form proliferated, and now people usually fill out the forms without assistance, choosing the category for each person in the household themselves. The idea of a "household head" came under attack from feminists in the 1960s, because they didn't like the presumption of male authority that it implied (Presser 1998). That pressure was successful, and by 1980, the census form dropped the category "household head" and now simply refers to a "householder," defined as anyone who legally owns or rents the home. That was one of many changes that followed. Figure 1.1 shows the relationship categories planned for the 2020 census, now including no fewer than 16 ways people can be associated with "Person 1," the householder.

Figure 1.1 **"Relationship" question planned for the 2020 Census**

How is this person related to Person 1? *Mark (X) ONE box.*

- ☐ Opposite-sex husband/wife/spouse
- ☐ Opposite-sex unmarried partner
- ☐ Same-sex husband/wife/spouse
- ☐ Same-sex unmarried partner
- ☐ Biological son or daughter
- ☐ Adopted son or daughter
- ☐ Stepson or stepdaughter
- ☐ Brother or sister

- ☐ Father or mother
- ☐ Grandchild
- ☐ Parent-in-law
- ☐ Son-in-law or daughter-in-law
- ☐ Other relative
- ☐ Housemate or roommate
- ☐ Foster child
- ☐ Other nonrelative

SOURCE: U.S. Census Bureau (2016a).

The historical concept of a "man and his family" has clearly been supplanted with a long list of individual relationships and identities. The most important recent change to this list is asking couples directly whether they are same-sex or opposite-sex, a question the Census Bureau did not ask before same-sex marriage became legal nationally in 2015. They further ask couples to identify whether they are married or "unmarried partners." Biological children are differentiated from adopted children, stepchildren, and foster children. In-laws and grandchildren are identified separately. You might notice another subtle distinction from the list in Figure 1.1. The categories "other relative" and "other nonrelative" appear toward the end. Although these are not defined on the form, their placement implies that the last two—housemate/roommate and foster child—are nonrelatives, while the rest are relatives. In fact, however, official statistics on families do not (yet) include those listed as unmarried partners as family members, even though many people in such relationships obviously think of themselves as being part of the same family. When society changes rapidly—as it is now with regard to family relationships—then laws, government policies, and cultural attitudes often contradict each other, which can provoke feelings of insecurity or conflict.

The Family as an Institutional Arena

Individuals define their own families. The state imposes a legal definition of families—"state" used in this way refers to the government at all levels. What about sociology? I can't tell you that sociology resolves the different or conflicting definitions of a family. But by stepping back and thinking analytically, we may be able to usefully frame the way families are defined. To do that requires the use of some terms and ideas that may seem abstract. But I hope that once we get over the hurdle of these abstractions, you will find that they help make your understanding of families more concrete.

Rather than identify certain groups of people as families or not, this sociological definition conceives of the family as the place where family matters take place. I will refer to that as an **institutional arena**, a social space in which relations between people in common positions are governed by accepted rules of interaction. In the family arena, for example, there are positions that people occupy (for example, father, mother, child, brother, sister). And there are rules of interaction, most of them informal, that govern how people in these positions interact. When a social position is accompanied by accepted patterns of behavior, it becomes a role. Family rules include obligations as well as privileges. For example, parents must feed, clothe, socialize, and otherwise care for their children in the most intimate ways. And children are usually expected to obey their parents. The **family arena**, then, is the institutional arena where people practice intimacy, childbearing and socialization, and caring work. Not everyone fits perfectly into these positions or follows these rules, but when they do not

institutional arena

A social space in which relations between people in common positions are governed by accepted rules of interaction.

family arena

The institutional arena where people practice intimacy, childbearing and socialization, and caring work.

conform—for example, when parents abuse or neglect their children—it only serves to reinforce the importance of the rules (Martin 2004).

An institutional arena is not a physical space with a clear boundary, like a sports arena, but a social place where a set of interactions play out. If you think of a game like soccer, there may be an ideal place to play it—a soccer field—but you can sort of play it anywhere. The rules are a little bit different here and there, and many of them are informal. You don't need lines on the ground or fixed goals. A great example of this is the common practice of widening or narrowing the space between the goal posts according to how many players are on the field. In the same way, the family is not a specific social arrangement or something that happens in one home or one type of home. Its rules and positions evolve over time and take place in the area of social interaction where intimacy, childbearing and socialization, and caring work are enacted.

These aspects of family life consume much of our personal, social, and economic energy and passions. But they do not encompass the domains of two other important institutional arenas that have direct interactions with the family: the state and the market. To understand the family's place in the society overall, we need to define these overlapping arenas.

The **state** includes many different organizations filled with people in many roles. But at its core, the state is the institutional arena where, through political means, behavior is legally regulated, violence is controlled, and resources are redistributed. The regulation of behavior is set out in laws and policies, and these are enforced with the threat or use of violence (from family court to the prison system to the armed forces). The state affects families directly through regulation, such as granting marriage licenses and facilitating divorces, and by redistributing resources according to family relationships. Redistribution takes place by taxing families and individuals and then spending tax money on education, health care, Social Security, welfare, and other programs.

The state also regulates the behavior of economic organizations and collects taxes and fees from them. In that way, the state has direct interactions with our third institutional arena, the **market**, which is the institutional arena where labor for pay, economic exchange, and wealth accumulation take place. All these activities are closely related to family life. For example, when parents decide whether to work for pay or stay home with their kids, they have to consider the jobs they can get and the costs of day care and other services. These decisions then affect family relationships and future decisions, such as how to divide labor within the family, how many children to have, whether to pursue advanced education—and maybe even whether to get divorced.

The key features of these three institutional arenas are shown in Table 1.1. Each arena signifies a certain type of social interaction, each is composed of organizational units, and each specifies certain roles for its members. Clearly, most people have roles in all of these arenas and take part in different organizational units. For example, a parent might care for his or her own children at home but also work as a nurse or day care provider in the market arena and act as a citizen on political questions, such as whether welfare programs should use tax money to pay for poor people's day care services. One way to look at such overlapping roles is to see them as interactions between the institutional arenas.

state

The institutional arena where, through political means, behavior is legally regulated, violence is controlled, and resources are redistributed.

market

The institutional arena where labor for pay, economic exchange, and wealth accumulation take place.

Table 1.1 **Modern institutional arenas**

	STATE	MARKET	FAMILY
TYPE OF INTERACTION	Law, violence, and welfare	Labor, exchange, and wealth accumulation	Intimacy, childbearing and socialization, and caring work
ORGANIZATIONAL UNITS	Legislatures and agencies	Companies	Families
INDIVIDUAL ROLES	Citizens	Workers, owners, and consumers	Family members

The interaction of institutional arenas is illustrated in the Story Behind the Numbers, which shows examples of overlapping roles. We can see the interaction of family and state arenas in the state licensing of marriages, and the interaction of family and market arenas in the role that commercial services such as day care providers make available to families. An additional interaction (not shown) is between state and market arenas, as when the state regulates the market by restricting companies' behavior. For example, under the Family and Medical Leave Act, the federal government requires large companies to give most of their workers (unpaid) time off from work when a child or another family member is sick. Finally, the figure illustrates one area where all three arenas clearly overlap: welfare policy. As we will see, state support of the poor is based on certain conceptions of family relationships (thus regulating family life), and market forces affect the ability of families to support themselves with or without welfare—even as family decisions affect the market arena (such as poor single mothers entering the labor force).

As we will see in Chapter 2, thinking about institutional arenas can help tell the history of the family. For example, Andrew Cherlin has argued that the growth of individual choice in family relationships signifies a weakening of marriage as an institution as its rules become more flexible (Cherlin 2004). Family history is also a story of changes in how different arenas interact. Returning to the example of parents punishing their children, the state intervenes when its authorities enforce laws against child abuse or acts of violence. The history of change in these two arenas is partly the story of how the line between parental and state authority has been drawn. The state's role also has evolved in the growth of public services in health care and education and in the changing state definitions of marriage, all of which alter the borders of the family arena and the roles of its members.

Throughout this book, we will use the idea of institutional arenas as a way to understand how larger forces interact with individuals and families to shape family life and how the family in turn contributes to larger social trends. Considering the relationship between individual experience and larger social forces is one of the main promises of sociology. And the family has been the subject of

The family is not an isolated entity.

Day Care

The market makes available—or not— the child-care services many parents need for their children.

Marriage Licenses

The laws and regulations of the state determine who can and cannot get married.

Welfare

All three arenas overlap in the welfare system, as poor families decide how to care for their children, with a mix of support from the government and income from their jobs.

People's roles in the family arena are strongly influenced by the actions of the other major arenas we discuss in this book, the state and the market. As these examples show, the services available in the market, and the policies of the government, all affect the way people make the most important decisions about family life.

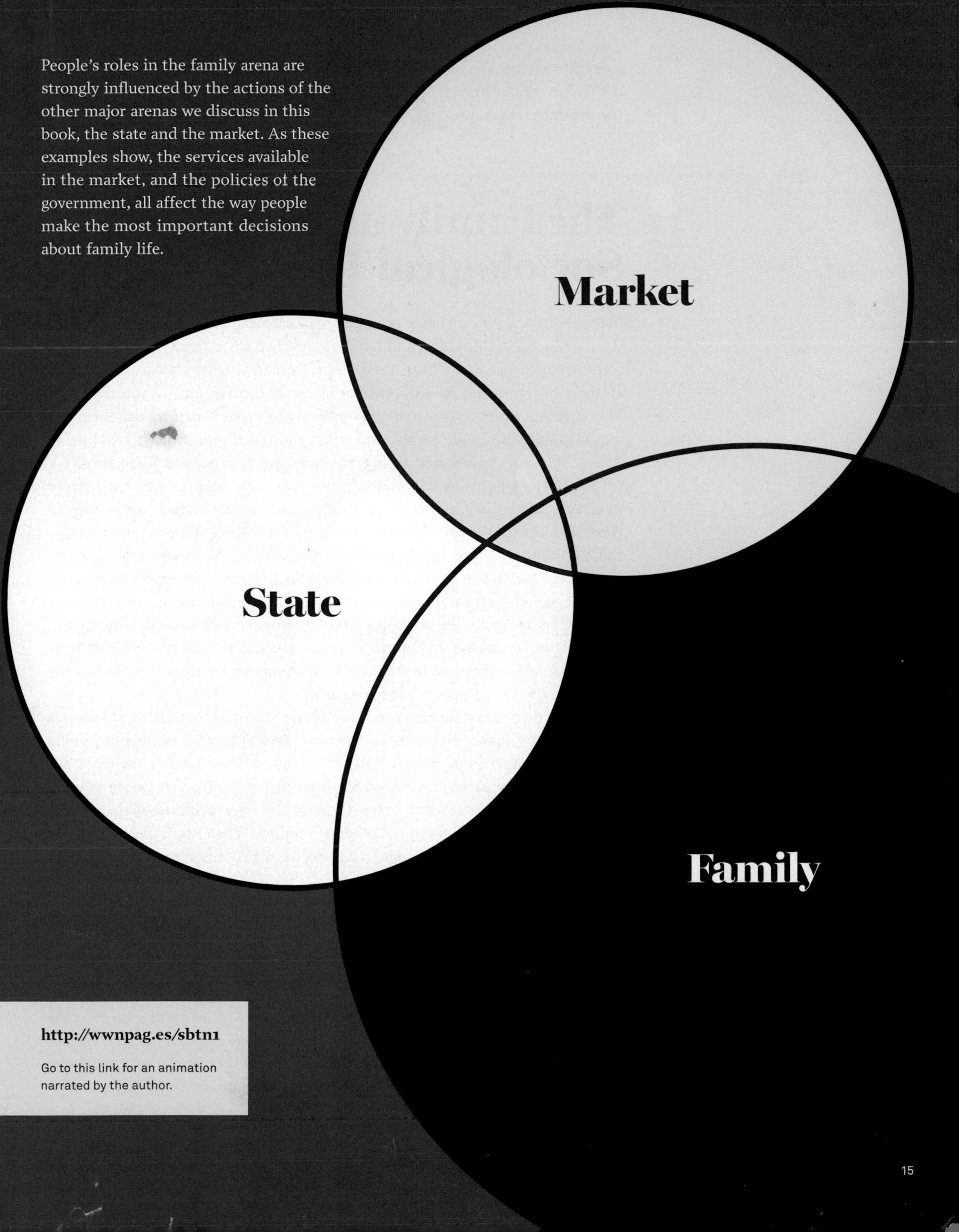

Market

State

Family

http://wwnpag.es/sbtn1

Go to this link for an animation narrated by the author.

sociological scrutiny throughout the history of the discipline. Therefore, before going further into the main subject of this book—the family as a diverse, changing feature of our unequal society—we will need to establish some additional theoretical background.

The Family in Sociological Theory

In this section, I present some prominent sociological theories and explain how they are useful in thinking about families and changes in family relationships. I want to emphasize that we are not necessarily marrying (to choose a metaphor) any one theory. Rather, we will consider a range of theories and perspectives that offer different kinds of explanations for the patterns we see. If we use theory to our advantage, we might be able to predict the future—or at least avoid being taken completely by surprise (Dilworth-Anderson, Burton, and Klein 2005).

In sociology, as in any other science, theory is a way to apply logic to a pattern of facts, to structure the way we think about our subject matter, and to help us generate ideas for research to enrich that understanding. Some factual descriptions of family life are widely known—for example, the modern tendency to leave home and live in a two-parent nuclear family after marriage, the growing practice of cohabitation outside of marriage, and the decline in the number of children per family in the last 100 years. (These and other historical trends will be discussed in Chapter 2.) But those are just facts, and there are different ways to make sense of them, to make them fit with our understanding of social life more broadly. That's where theory comes in.

Rather than choosing between theories, we may find that different theories work better to answer different types of questions. Some may seem more wrong or right than others, but most sociologists do not stick to any one theory, especially in family research (Taylor and Bagdi 2005). I will introduce two broad perspectives with deep historical roots—the consensus perspective and the conflict perspective—and tie them to the study of families. Then I will discuss several more recently developed theories to help us form a common understanding for the rest of the book.

Broad Perspectives

consensus perspective

A perspective that projects an image of society as the collective expression of shared norms and values.

Consensus The **consensus perspective** projects an image of society as the collective expression of shared norms and values (Ritzer 2000). This is an ancient view of society, with roots in Greek philosophy. It was also used to support democracy and the American Revolution, with the argument that society cannot work without the consent of the governed (Horowitz 1962). That doesn't mean that everyone agrees on everything, but rather that society exists as the enactment of social order. It means that most of us voluntarily get up in the morning (or thereabouts) and play our roles each day, instead of making the infinite other choices available to us that would lead to general chaos. This does not imply that society never changes or that there are no conflicts, but it does mean that order is the core of social life and that social change works best when it takes place in an orderly fashion; chaotic or rapid change is to be avoided.

In the tradition of this perspective, the dominant sociological theory is known as *structural functionalism*, which has roots in the work of French sociologist Émile Durkheim (1858–1917). It became the dominant theory in American sociology around the middle of the twentieth century with the work of Talcott Parsons (1902–1979). Although few sociologists today identify as structural functionalists, key elements of the consensus perspective remain influential. Researchers adopting this perspective in general examine some common pattern of behavior and ask, "What are the functions of this? What good is it doing that permits it to survive?" The theory often assumes that there is a good reason for things to be the way they are and tries to explain them based on this premise. As a result, the consensus perspective tends to focus on stability rather than change, in keeping with its harmonious image of society.

Examining American family life in the 1950s, when the dominant family structure was the **breadwinner-homemaker family** (an employed father, a nonemployed mother, and their children), Parsons mistakenly believed that major change was unlikely. That was good news to him, because he ardently believed that what he saw as the essence of families—the harmony created by the complementary roles of husband and wife—was essential to the preservation of the family as an institution (Parsons and Bales 1955). When Parsons looked at that family structure and asked himself why it worked, his answer was that it provided the basis for stability and cooperation. There was mutual compatibility between men and women, with each one performing a separate, necessary function. He called these functions *the instrumental role* of the husband and the *expressive role* of the wife. After studying different kinds of organizations (not just families), Parsons concluded that successful organizations had instrumental leadership that took charge of interaction with the outside world—for example, on questions of economics and trade. Balancing that was the expressive leadership necessary to provide emotional support, nurturing, and caring for the group (Parsons 1954). The division of labor within breadwinner-homemaker families, in which the husband works outside the home and the wife works inside the home, fit into Parsons's notion of a dichotomy between instrumental and expressive leadership. And maintaining this balance was essential to the success of the family as an institution.

To critics, all this looked like a long-winded rationalization of the male-dominated status quo, serving a conservative political agenda. In fact, the whole consensus perspective has been criticized as something people in positions of power use to justify the social structure that exists at any given time or place (Ritzer 2000). There may be some truth to that; we all have our biases. However,

Talcott Parsons

breadwinner-homemaker family

An employed father, a nonemployed mother, and their children.

at its best, this theory helps us understand the nuclear family as a model and how it might work as an ideal.

Conflict If structural functionalism starts from the premise that consensus and harmony form the basis of society, the **conflict perspective** takes the contrary view: opposition and conflict define a given society and are necessary for social evolution. Historically, this position has opposed the consensus perspective's tendency to portray the status quo as good and the forces of change as dangerously destabilizing. More specifically, in sociology this theory developed in reaction to the dominance of structural functionalism, suggesting that change, rather than stability, is the dynamic we need to explain. What came to be known as conflict theory drew on the work of Karl Marx (1818–1883; see Chapter 4) and others who believed that inequality and the conflict it causes are what drive history forward. In its moderate form, the theory argues simply that expressing conflict over differences is often the best way to arrive at positive changes in families, organizations, and society at large.

Conflict theorists focus on the competing interests of family members to understand family problems—for example, child abuse or divorce. Randall Collins, a leading writer in this field, believes that men use their greater strength to gain power in the family and achieve their own ends (R. Collins 1975). Some take a more expansive view of family conflict to describe the modern nuclear family as a tool for enhancing the profits of the rich at the expense of the poor. Connecting family inequality to Marx's theory of capitalism, they argue that the work that wives have historically done at home without pay—nurturing and caring, cooking and cleaning, raising the children, and so on—takes care of men, so employers don't have to pay them as much. In turn, husbands maintain domination within the family and provide stability to the system (Zaretsky 1976). Rather than see the different roles of men and women as harmonious and functional, conflict theorists see them as part of an unstable system ripe for conflict and change.

If structural functionalism can be faulted for projecting an overly rosy view of family relations, conflict theory may suffer from the reverse: an emphasis on opposition and power struggles to the exclusion of the many ways that family members truly love and care for each other. In fact, neither theory can explain everything, but both may be useful for understanding some elements of family life.

Contemporary Theories

The debate between structural functionalism and conflict theory raged in the middle of the twentieth century, when the breadwinner-homemaker family was the norm in the United States. It is no coincidence that the emergence of a new group of theories about the family coincided with the growing diversity of family life and the decline of the breadwinner-homemaker model. We turn next to these more recent developments.

conflict perspective

The view that opposition and conflict define a given society and are necessary for social evolution.

Feminism Feminism is part of the conflict perspective tradition, and feminists share many views with conflict theorists, especially a critical attitude about the breadwinner-homemaker model of family life. **Feminist theory** in general seeks to understand and ultimately reduce inequality between men and women. When it comes to the family, in particular, feminist theory sees "male dominance within families [as] part of a wider system of male power, [which] is neither natural nor inevitable, and occurs at women's cost" (Ferree 1990:866). The theory has a long history and many varieties; rather than explaining them all here, I will point out several recent contributions that have been most helpful to the study of the family (Baca Zinn 2000).

First, beginning in the 1970s, feminist researchers demonstrated that gender inequality is central to family life (see Chapter 5). In fact, one reason many of these researchers were reluctant to speak of "the family" is because the experiences of men and women (or boys and girls) may be so different. Feminists showed that if the family arena is where boys and girls learn to be boys and girls (and men and women), it is also where those gender roles are created unequal, with men in the dominant position, through the process of **socialization** (see Chapter 5). However, family dynamics also are important for how gender affects other institutional arenas, and the family is only one site of gender inequality. For example, as we will see in Chapter 11, one reason women earn less at paid work (in the market arena) is because their careers are more likely to be hampered by unpaid care work obligations within the family.

Second, feminist scholars have argued that family structure is socially constructed—the product of human choices rather than the inevitable outcome of natural or biological processes. Structural functionalists in particular

feminist theory

A theory that seeks to understand and ultimately reduce inequality between men and women.

socialization

The process by which individuals internalize elements of the social structure in their own personalities.

Drew Skinner's wife works long hours while he takes care of their young son. A small but increasing number of stay-at-home dads make it possible for their wives to remain in demanding jobs.

believed that the nuclear family is an expression of universal human tendencies; hence, nontraditional family structures are likely to be ineffective or unstable. To counter that view, feminists conducted comparative research (studying different cultures and time periods) to show the wide variety of family structures that have proved successful.

Later feminist theorists added a third important contribution. Just as early research had shown that the experience of family life differs dramatically for men and women, a subsequent generation argued that those gender perspectives are themselves not uniform. In particular, race, ethnicity, and social class all affect family life and gender dynamics in unique ways (see Chapters 3 and 4). For example, early feminists criticized the breadwinner-homemaker family as a structure in which men dominate women. But some contemporary feminists believe that in poor and minority communities, traditional family arrangements may be expressions of collective strength and resilience in the face of hardship, uniting men and women with a common purpose (Hill 2005). Together, these insights and findings from feminist scholars have contributed greatly to the work of family researchers, even those who do not share feminism's activist goal of reducing gender inequality.

Exchange

Exchange Conflict perspective and feminism tend to treat different roles within the family as reflecting unequal power, especially men's domination over women. On the other hand, the consensus perspective offers a more harmonious account of why men and women stay in families together despite their differences. Similarly, **exchange theory** sees individuals or groups with different resources, strengths, and weaknesses entering into mutual relationships to maximize their own gains. In this view, individuals are rational; that is, they consider the costs and benefits of their actions in making their decisions. When they cannot satisfy all of their needs on their own (and they rarely can), people enter into exchange relationships with others. As long as the relationship is rewarding, both sides stay engaged. If the exchange is not rewarding, and if the cost of leaving is not too great, either party may leave (Dilworth-Anderson, Burton, and Klein 2005). This theory is part of the consensus tradition because it assumes that patterns of social behavior are mutually agreed on.

These ideas are closely related to a model of the family proposed by the Nobel prize—winning economist Gary Becker, in which husbands and wives make joint decisions to maximize benefits that all family members share—for example, sending men into the paid labor force while women care for the children at home (Becker 1981). Many sociologists find that theory naive, because it seems to assume equality between men and women and harmony between their interests. Do men and women in families really make decisions and share rewards equally, and do they want the same outcomes for their families? Sociologists do not rule out the logic of exchange in family relationships. But rather than assume equality, they prefer to think of the exchange as a bargaining process in which individuals strike the best bargain they can, given the resources they have and the rules they have to play by. When the resources are unequal, as they usually are, the bargains struck reflect that inequality. In this way, exchange theory can

---

exchange theory

The theory that individuals or groups with different resources, strengths, and weaknesses enter into mutual relationships to maximize their own gains.

become part of the conflict perspective—viewing exchange as a process by which people act out their competing interests.

The division of housework between men and women is a common subject of research for exchange theorists. This is a classic example of bargaining relationships negotiated under conditions of inequality. Because of men's greater earning power, they hold a stronger bargaining position at the start of the relationship. Because women usually earn less money than men, they may accept an arrangement in which they are the weaker party and so take on the more onerous and time-consuming household tasks, such as scrubbing toilets and doing laundry. Not surprisingly, we usually find that couples share housework more equally when the individual incomes of both partners are more equal (Bittman et al. 2003). Of course, economic resources are not the only subjects of the negotiation; couples may also bargain over sex, children, friends, and so on (we will discuss some of these complexities in Chapter 11).

Symbolic Interaction Starting in the early twentieth century, some sociologists embraced the idea that we can understand what things mean to people only by studying their behavior. So actions, not words, provide the true basis for meaning, and meaning can only be understood by studying its relationship to action. The theory they developed, which came to be called **symbolic interactionism,** revolves around the ability of humans to see themselves through the eyes of others and to enact social roles based on others' expectations. The theory gets its name from the idea that social roles are symbols, which have real meaning only when they are acted out in relation to other people (interaction). People may adopt many social roles—for example, president, nurse, football player, husband, or pedestrian. But it is the act of performing a given role in

symbolic interactionism

A theory concerned with the ability of humans to see themselves through the eyes of others and to enact social roles based on others' expectations.

Steph Curry inhabits multiple social roles, including husband, father, and Golden State Warrior.

relation to others that gives it meaning. Human self-identity is formed through that action and from the reactions to our behavior that we expect and observe in everyone else (Ritzer 2000).

Defining, identifying, and acting on a social role requires a delicate give and take at the interpersonal level as people assess the effects of their actions on others and the expectations that others have. The intimate nature of this process makes the family an ideal setting for developing this theory. Because social roles do not exist in isolation, but rather only in interaction, we need to observe behavior within the family to see how family roles are defined and what they mean (Stryker 1968).

This theory has been especially useful for studying social change, when roles and the informal rules that govern behavior are not clearly defined. For example, being a parent means different things for people who are married versus those who are single, and the role of husband or wife comes with different expectations for men and women who are employed versus those who are not (Macmillan and Copher 2005). As single parenthood and dual-earner couples have become more common, we can see the new meanings assigned to the roles of parent and spouse only by observing how they are acted out in the daily lives of the people who occupy them.

Modernity

People often use the word *modern* to mean "contemporary," but in this book we will use it to refer to a specific period in history, from the eighteenth-century Enlightenment to the present. **Modernity theory** is very broad, but with regard to the family, it concerns the emergence of the individual as an actor in society and how individuality changed personal and institutional relations. Consider the scheme in Table 1.1 as a modern phenomenon. In the state arena, the individual emerged as a citizen, with the right to vote defining that role. In the market arena, the individual emerged as a worker, earning a cash wage to be spent on anything he or she chooses. What about the family arena? Here the individual emerged as an independent actor making choices about family relations freely, based on personal tastes and interests. Individual choice in the family had existed before modernity (more for some than for others), but only in this era did it become institutionalized, or expected of everyone (Beck and Lau 2005).

Modernity theorists break the modern era into two periods. In *first modernity*, up until the 1960s or so, there was gradual change in family behavior—for example, more divorce, a gradually increasing age at first marriage, fewer children in families, fewer people living in extended families (see Chapter 2), and more choice in spouse selection. These were only incremental changes, however. Even though people exercised free choice, the concept of a "normal" family remained intact as a social standard. Different family types or pathways—such as marriage much later in life, having children outside of marriage, remarrying after divorce, or marrying outside your race—existed, but they were on the margins of acceptability. In *second modernity*, since the 1970s, the chickens have come home to roost. Diversity and individuality are the new norm, and it's up to each person to pick a family type and identify with it. Thus, freedom from traditional restraints "brings historically new free spaces and options: he can and should, she may

modernity theory

A theory of the historical emergence of the individual as an actor in society and how individuality changed personal and institutional relations.

and must, now decide how to shape their own life" (Beck and Beck-Gernsheim 2004:502). The growth of family diversity is a major theme of this book.

Acting individually is supported (or even required) by other institutions, especially the state and the market, which increasingly have treated people as individuals rather than as family members. This is only natural once family ties such as marriage are considered voluntary, subject to divorce by either individual. For example, some welfare and health care benefits and taxation involve transactions between individuals and the government (although some programs are still geared toward families). And most employers don't consider it necessary to pay a **family wage** to male workers with stay-at-home wives, as they did in the past (see Chapter 2). Compared with the premodern past, this "institutionalized individualization" leads to a tremendous fragmentation of family identities and puts a big psychological burden on people. As a result, a sense of insecurity spreads through the population, driving people into the arms of expert identity fixers, especially therapists and self-help gurus.

If all of this freedom implies individual isolation and lack of direction, it also stands to revolutionize the nature of intimacy and family relationships, at least according to modernity theorist Anthony Giddens. In his view, relationships now may be truly based on personal choice and individual fulfillment. Free from the constraints of traditional rules, free from the need to reproduce biologically, and free to negotiate economic survival as individuals, people may now enter into the ideal "pure relationship"—and leave when it suits them—for the first time in history (Giddens 1992).

Demography and the Life Course
Two additional perspectives warrant attention here, which supplement rather than compete with the theoretical views already presented. Many family researchers study the family in relation to larger population processes. If a population is the number of people in a certain area or place, it may be seen as (a) the number of children who have been born, (b) minus the number of people who have died, plus (c) the number of people who have arrived in the past (minus those who moved away). Demography—the study of populations—therefore focuses on birth, death, and migration. Family researchers who take a **demographic perspective** study family behavior and household structures that contribute to larger population processes. They are especially interested in childbirth, but to understand that, they must study the timing and frequency of cohabitation, marriage, and divorce, as well as living arrangements in general (who lives with whom at different stages in their lives).

The demographic emphasis on timing contributes to an interest in the sequencing of events for individuals and groups in the population. The "normal" family structure of the past included a progression from childhood to adulthood that included marriage and then parenthood. As family life has become more diverse, the common sequences of family events, or family trajectories, have become much more complicated. Researchers using the **life course perspective** study the family trajectories of individuals and groups as they progress through their lives. One important goal of this research is to place family events in their historical context (Elder 1975). For example, if you want to understand attitudes toward family life among Americans who were in their 50s in 2010, you might

family wage
The amount necessary for a male earner to provide subsistence for his wife and children without them having to work for pay.

demographic perspective
The study of how family behavior and household structures contribute to larger population processes.

life course perspective
The study of the family trajectories of individuals and groups as they progress through their lives, in social and historical context.

The decennial census in the United States is a massive project that requires more than a million people to complete. Many are census takers, or enumerators, who visit households that have not submitted a completed Census questionnaire.

cohort

A group of people who experience an event together at the same point in time.

consider their history as a **cohort**—a group of people who experience an event together at the same point in time (such as being born in the same period). These people were born in the 1950s, when birth rates were very high, so they grew up in a youth-dominated culture. They were in their teens in the late 1960s, when much of the popular culture first embraced ideas of free love and uncommitted romantic relationships. Divorce rates shot up when they were young adults in the 1970s, which had immediate and long-lasting effects on their attitudes toward cohabitation and divorce. Rather than examining individuals at fixed points in time, life course researchers seek to gain a deeper understanding by considering life stories in their social and historical context.

Studying Families

We have seen how sociologists use theories to make sense of the facts they discover. But where do these facts come from? More important, how can we build a knowledge base to help us understand the reasons behind the facts? In principle, sociologists may gain information from any source at all. However, there are common methods of gathering information that have proved successful. Before examining these sources of data, I need to briefly describe a few of the challenges encountered in studying families.

To develop deeper knowledge often requires using more information than we started out looking for. For example, we know that African Americans on average are less likely to marry than Whites. However, to understand the reasons for that gap, we must look at a variety of factors, including not just individual preferences but also poverty and college attendance rates, income differences between men and women, and even incarceration and mortality rates. In other words, to understand the core facts requires knowledge of the context in which those facts occur.

Another issue we must contend with in research on families is the problem of telling the difference between correlation and cause. Many things are observed occurring together (correlation) without one causing the other. For example, a study of young children's vision found that those who had slept with the light on in their nurseries were more likely to be nearsighted. That is, light at night and nearsightedness appeared to be correlated (Quinn et al. 1999). The researchers suspected that light penetrating the eyelids during sleep harmed children's vision—that is, that light caused nearsightedness. However, a follow-up study determined that parents who are themselves nearsighted are more likely to leave a light on in their children's nurseries; it makes it easier for the parents to see. And since nearsightedness is partly genetic, it is possible that the nearsightedness of children who sleep with the light on results not from the light, but from the parents' nearsightedness being passed on to their children genetically (Zadnik 2000). In this case, despite the correlation of two facts, one did not cause the other. Researchers could only determine this by gathering contextual information about children's families.

Finally, although there are many sources of information, there are almost as many sources of **bias**—the tendency to impose previously held views on the collection and interpretation of facts. Consider an example: During the fall of 2016, the news for presidential candidate Donald Trump was not good: Polls from around the country showed he was very likely to lose the November election. One night the Fox News Network conducted an online poll of its viewers, asking them, "If the presidential election were held this week, who would win?" Despite the mountain of evidence to the contrary, the results showed that 86 percent of participants believed Trump would win. Because Fox favored Trump, and so did their loyal viewers, the poll produced a biased result—like an ice cream company asking children waiting in line at the ice cream truck what their favorite dessert is. Though that might be a good way to see how Trump supporters feel, it's not a good way to predict the winner of an election (even though it worked this time!).

We can't always eliminate bias, but we can increase accountability and transparency. That is why most sociologists prefer publicly funded studies, which make their data freely available and which in principle are repeatable by other researchers. That is, nothing is hidden about the way the information is collected and analyzed. And before results are accepted as reliable, a system of peer review is employed in which other scholars review the work anonymously,

How did researchers confuse causation and correlation in their study of night lights in bedrooms of nearsighted children?

bias

The tendency to impose previously held views on the collection and interpretation of facts.

checking for any sources of error, including bias, logical flaws, or simple mistakes in the analysis.

Sample Surveys

sample survey

A research method in which identical questions are asked of many different people and their answers gathered into one large data file.

The most common method of gathering data for sociological studies is the **sample survey**, in which identical questions are asked of many different people and their answers gathered into one large data file. By examining patterns among the responses to the questions we ask, we can find associations that help us understand family life. For example, if we ask people to tell us their gender and how often they do the dishes, we might find out if women do dishes more often than men.

Asking people for information about their lives and opinions is time-consuming and expensive, so we cannot study everyone. We need to find a method of choosing our study subjects. Consider a "quick vote" conducted by the CNN news channel, which asked the simple question, "Who does most of the chores in your household?" More than 30,000 people responded, and 60 percent of them chose "Mom keeps it all tidy," while 27 percent chose "Mom and dad split the work." (The rest were sprinkled across other categories.) (CNN 2008a). That is a big group of people, but how were they selected? Anyone who came to the CNN website was allowed to respond. We don't know who they were, but we might imagine some ways in which they were not representative of the general population—Internet users, people interested in reading websites about housework, people who like to click on website polls, and so on. We simply don't know from that survey if those responses represent the population as a whole.

Ideally, we would choose people by random selection, ensuring that each person in the group we want to study has the same likelihood of being interviewed in the survey. That is the best way to ensure that our results are not skewed by who is included or excluded. Students are sometimes skeptical about the principle of random selection. Is it really possible, for example, that the opinions of 500 people can accurately reflect those of 245 million American adults? If it's done right, the short answer is yes; the long answer has to do with probability theory. (If you don't believe me, consider this: When I have my cholesterol checked, why don't I have all of my blood removed instead of just a few ounces?)

We find the clearest evidence of the effectiveness of sample surveys when we can successfully use them to predict people's behavior, as has been done with many political elections. In the 2012 presidential election, for example, a careful analysis of the preelection polls allowed statistician Nate Silver to accurately predict for every single state whether Barack Obama or Mitt Romney would win in the actual election-day voting (M. Cooper 2012). On the other hand, in the 2016 election, although most analysts correctly predicted that Hillary Clinton would get more votes than Donald Trump overall, they were wrong about the vote in several key states that were decisive in the Electoral College. The sample surveys used in that election apparently did not successfully select voters at random (for example, Trump voters may have been more likely to hang up on the survey takers), or perhaps some voters didn't accurately report their voting intentions (maybe they were embarrassed to say they would vote for Trump). Although there are many ways that surveys can produce errors or lead to ambiguous results, the principle of random selection helps to ensure that we are not misled by research results from relatively small numbers of people.

In addition to random selection, we also make an important distinction between different kinds of surveys. As we have seen, the questions that concern us may involve interrelated sequences of events, such as the connection between nursery room lighting in infancy and nearsightedness years later. Still, although we are interested in events that occur years apart, most surveys are administered only once to each person. Others, known as **longitudinal surveys**, interview the same people repeatedly over a period of time. Tracking people over time is essential for answering questions about sequences of events. For example, researchers have long wondered whether the increase in divorce is the result of women gaining economic independence, so they don't "need" to be married. Or maybe it is the other way around, and women get jobs because they are afraid that a divorce will leave them out on a limb with little work experience (see Chapter 10). Only by carefully following families over time could researchers find that couples do divorce more often when women earn their own income, but marriage quality and satisfaction are even more important (Sayer and Bianchi 2000). Such surveys are time-consuming and expensive, since interviewees have to be tracked down again and again over a period of years, which is why the major longitudinal surveys are at least partly funded by the government, with many researchers sharing access to the data.

Even surveys in which each person is interviewed only once may be repeated at regular intervals, which allows us to track trends in people's answers over time. For example, the federal government has for decades conducted the Current Population Survey (CPS) every month, interviewing representatives from

longitudinal surveys

A research method in which the same people are interviewed repeatedly over a period of time.

Jackie, Sue, and Lynn are three of the subjects in *49 Up*, a 2005 documentary in the Up series that began in 1964 when they were seven years old. The series has revisited most of them every seven years since.

of households to generate such important facts as the national unemployment rate. And because the CPS also includes questions on family structure, we can confidently estimate, for example, that the employment rate of unmarried mothers fell from 72 percent to 68 percent over the decade from 2005 to 2015 (U.S. Bureau of Labor Statistics 2016a). Similarly, the General Social Survey (GSS) has been asking questions about American attitudes since 1972. From this survey we know, for example, that 36 percent of American adults considered sex before marriage "always wrong" in 1972, but that dropped to 20 percent by 2016 (Smith et al. 2017). These repeated surveys are essential for studying social change, another central focus of this book.

In-Depth Interviews and Observation

Sample surveys provide much of the basic knowledge we need to understand trends and patterns in family life. However, researchers often must make assumptions or speculate about the meaning underlying the behavior and attitudes measured by sample surveys. Even when we ask people directly about their attitudes, such as whether mothers or fathers should spend more time taking care of their children, the answers may be superficial, and respondents answer only those questions we think of asking in advance. Some researchers prefer not to be limited by brief answers to questions they bring to an interview.

One way to avoid this problem is to arrange much longer, in-depth interviews with a small number of people, usually those who share traits researchers want to study. For example, Sarah Damaske, for her book *For the Family? How Class and Gender Shape Women's Work* (2011), interviewed 80 women for several hours each to trace their employment histories and the reasons they gave for their decisions. She found that both working-class and middle-class mothers used a language of economic need to justify their decisions to work outside their homes, even though it was better-off mothers who were more likely to work steadily throughout their careers. Working-class women, on the other hand, were more likely to face difficult work-family tradeoffs that compelled them to move in and out of the labor force over time (see Chapter 11).

Even in-depth interviews, however, rely on the answers provided to the researcher. Sometimes, interpersonal dynamics and the subtleties of daily life are best studied through direct observation and interaction with the subjects of the research, known as ethnography. This was the method employed by Annette Lareau for her influential study *Unequal Childhoods: Class, Race, and Family Life* (2003). Lareau and her assistants inserted themselves into the lives of 12 families for about a month each, following them from place to place and taking copious notes on how the parents arranged their children's daily lives and interactions with the social world. Through this approach, researchers often learn things people would not reveal if asked, or may not even realize about their own lives (Jerolmack and Khan 2014). The results of Lareau's study revealed sharp contrasts in parenting style—and the meanings parents attributed to childhood—according to the social class of the family (see Chapter 4).

Time Use Studies

Most of what happens within families is informal. Unlike a job setting, there is no formal record of who does what, for which rewards, and who answers to whom. And there is no way of measuring how successful families are comparable to sales figures or profits reports in the private sector or services delivered in the government sector. Therefore, researchers studying families often rely on asking people in interviews to describe what they do or observing them firsthand.

To develop a more detailed accounting of what goes on within families, some researchers have produced **time use studies** that collect detailed data on how family members spend their time. Some of these studies are simply surveys in which the questions focus on how people spend their time. Others use time

time use studies

Surveys that collect data on how people spend their time during a sample period, such as a single day or week.

Theory and Evidence

Different theoretical perspectives and methods of gathering information can help us translate descriptions of particular family events or situations into more general knowledge about families and society.

- Brainstorm several examples of a family conflict, dramatic event, or daily occurrence. Try to think of situations that might be representative of a broader social phenomenon. For example, you might describe a family-related crime story from a TV drama, the changing family structure you or someone you know grew up in, or the real-life saga of a politician or celebrity in the news.

- Choose two theories or perspectives from the chapter that interest you. Describe how a theorist from each perspective might explain the examples you came up with. These do not have to be contradictory; they might simply provide alternative ways of looking at the situations in question or generate ideas about their underlying social causes.

- Select two methods of gathering data described in the chapter. Try to imagine how a researcher might use each method to gather information about the kind of situations or events you are trying to explain—for example, by collecting survey data or directly observing the behavior in question.

- Choosing one of your examples, combine one method and one theory that you think would most fruitfully develop your understanding of the social dynamics in question. Explain why you suggest this approach to turn your description of this case into more general sociological knowledge. What would you hope to discover from your study? How might your study change the way others think about this question?

diaries. Rather than asking people, for example, how many hours last week they spent watching TV or reading to their children, time diary studies ask people to record what they were doing, where they were, and who they were with for small increments of time over an entire day (Craig and Mullan 2011).

Time diary studies have been especially valuable in the study of work and families, as we will see in Chapter 11. For example, a large national survey in the 1990s asked men and women to estimate how many hours per week they did various household chores and other work. However, when researchers tallied up the hours spent on all the different activities, it often came to more than the number of hours there are in a week (Bianchi, Robinson, and Milkie 2006)! In contrast, when people are asked to fill out time diaries, recording their activities over the course of the day, the time estimates are more accurate. Recent time diaries show men spending just 10 hours per week on housework and women spending 16 hours per week (Bianchi et al. 2012). This method provides a window into the minute interactions that make up family life, but permits studying larger groups of people than is possible with in-depth interviews or observation.

Trend to Watch: Big Data

Big data research is increasingly common. Although there is not a single definition, we may define **big data** as data large enough to require special computing resources, and complex enough to require customized computer applications (Lazer and Radford 2017). Unlike surveys or Census data, big data usually were not generated for research purposes, but we can use them for social science research. Most often this research involves analyzing large volumes of text from online social interaction, such as social media sites. With billions of interactions occurring online every day, many of them leaving a digital trace, the potential to understand new forms of social behavior is exciting. For example, one study examined more than four billion tweets by 63 million users to measure patterns of happiness, finding that people send happier tweets on Friday and Saturday, and least happy tweets on Monday and Tuesday (Dodds et al. 2011). In another, controversial study, researchers at Facebook manipulated the posts that users saw, demonstrating that positive and negative moods spread contagiously among users, like diseases, even when people don't interact face-to-face (Kramer, Guillory, and Hancock 2014).

In addition to social media, big data analysts have also examined data from large databases of official records, phone records, and government documents (my own analysis of names, described in Chapter 2, is an example of such big data research). For example, a study of more than 40 million tax records for families over two generations found that children whose parents weren't married were less likely to escape lower social class positions when they grow up than were children whose parents were married (Chetty et al. 2014). The ability to mine sources of data like these, and finding new ways to analyze them, offers great potential for future studies of family life.

Billions of online interactions leave a digital trace that allows researchers to study social behavior in new ways.

Big data research requires powerful computers and advanced technical skills. It also raises questions about privacy and research ethics, since the people being studied have not consented to have their behavior examined—even though it may be in a public or semipublic space, such as Twitter or Facebook. And this research underscores the need for sociological theory to understand the patterns we see; just because we have a vast supply of data doesn't mean we can successfully explain social behavior. There's one big advantage, though: Big data research allows us to see people's actual behavior, rather than what they tell us they do or think, as is the case with sample surveys.

Moving On

In this chapter, we have seen that there are several ways of defining families, from a personal or legal perspective and through the lens of social institutions. Equipped with a clearer idea of what we are studying, we then added to our conceptual framework a set of sociological theories and perspectives, including the opposing views of the consensus and conflict perspectives and the contemporary theories of feminism, exchange theory, symbolic interactionism, modernity theory, and the demographic and life course perspectives. Finally, theories would ring hollow were it not for the factual foundations on which they stand. Therefore, this chapter also introduced a variety of methods that sociologists use to gather information, including surveys, in-depth interviews and observation, and time use studies.

Having completed our brief survey of family-related concepts, sociological theories and perspectives, and methods of collecting data, we are ready to delve deeper into the story of family diversity, inequality, and social change. The next step is to develop a common understanding of families in history and the emergence of the family as an institutional arena. We turn to that history in Chapter 2.

KEY TERMS:

genealogy   families   personal family

legal family   census   household

institutional arena   family arena

state   market   consensus perspective

breadwinner-homemaker family

conflict perspective   feminist theory

socialization   exchange theory

symbolic interactionism

modernity theory   family wage

demographic perspective

life course perspective   cohort

bias   sample survey

longitudinal surveys   time use studies

big data

Questions for Review

1. Define personal families, legal families, and the family as an institutional arena. Give examples of each, and explain how they're different from each other.

2. How has the Census's definition of a family changed over time?

3. When it comes to understanding families, how are structural functionalist and conflict theoretical perspectives different? Based on what you read in the chapter, contrast how the two theories might explain the breadwinner-homemaker family.

4. Describe three significant contributions of feminist theory to sociologists' understanding of contemporary families.

5. Why is exchange theory part of the consensus tradition of perspectives? Give an example of how an exchange theorist might explain housework.

6. According to modernity theorists, what distinguishes first modernity from second modernity? What are the implications for relationships?

7. What are some of the strategies sociologists use to avoid bias in their research?

8. What are the advantages of surveys, in-depth interviews, and time use studies? Why would sociologists pick one method over another to study families?

2 The Family in History

Families have been a part of human existence since the dawn of our species. But how people live in families has changed dramatically. This chapter will focus on the development of the family as an institutional arena—the social space where related people interact around commonly accepted roles and rules (see Chapter 1). The changes in family life discussed here must be understood in relation to four overarching historical trends:

- Most people today live much longer than in the past. In the Middle Ages, Europeans on average probably lived to about age 30, and as late as 1850 that had increased to only about 40 in the United States. At that time, an estimated 1 in 5 children died before reaching age 5 (J. R. Weeks 2011), but today more than three-quarters of Americans live to age 70 (Arias 2015). This increased longevity is the result of improvements in the standard of living, including better sanitation, medical care, and nutrition.

- People have many fewer children than they used to (see Chapter 9). A typical White woman in the United States in 1800 bore about seven children during her lifetime (Haines 2006). Today that number has fallen to less than two (Hamilton, Martin, and Osterman 2015).

- Family members perform fewer functional tasks at home (see Chapter 11). Such life-sustaining and nurturing activities as basic food and clothing production, education, and health care that often took place within families are now performed within newer institutional arenas, the state and the market. As work has moved out of the family, family relationships have come to rely more on emotional bonds than on economic necessity.

- In recent decades, families have become more diverse (see Chapter 13). The greatest change has been the decline of the two-parent nuclear family. That family type reached the peak of its dominance in the 1950s, but is now found

35

Think of your family members from two generations ago (or even more, if you have that information): How many children did parents have? What were the occupations for men and women? What level of education did they achieve?

in less than half of all American households. In its place, we have seen the rise of single-parent families, unmarried couples, and people living alone or in nonfamily group situations.

Each of these trends has changed the character of family life and the place of families in the larger society. We will keep these changes in mind as we trace family history through time, beginning with a brief foray into ancient history.

Early History

To establish some common background understanding, we will briefly discuss the early history of families, beginning with ancient times and then reviewing some early European history.

Prehistory: Cooperation and Survival

The Neolithic period isn't a big part of this chapter. But there is at least one story worth telling. It took place somewhere in central Europe about 4,600 years ago, during what is known as the New Stone Age, when disaster befell a small village. The young adults and older boys had apparently gone hunting. Someone attacked the village—we can't know who—and massacred the defenseless elders and younger children. Their skeletal remains still contain arrowheads and evidence that their bones were broken by the weapons used to overpower them. When the other villagers returned, they buried the victims. According to their custom, they placed food, tools, and weapons in the graves to nourish and protect the dead along their eternal journey. In one grave, they buried an older man and woman, along with two young children. DNA testing of the bones shows that the children were their biological offspring, making this the oldest DNA-confirmed **nuclear family** (see Changing Culture, "Family Types and Terms"). The villagers buried the family members facing each other, with their hands interlinked. Another woman was buried nearby with several other children (not her off-spring), this time facing away from each other (Haak et al. 2008).

Why the sad tale? Besides its dramatic appeal, the story shows that the ancient villagers recognized and honored different family arrangements, not just the nuclear family. They also buried stepmothers or aunts—older family members who were not blood relatives, according to the DNA analysis—in family graves with the children they cared for, but the graves were different. This is especially poignant because chemical analysis of their teeth showed that the women had lived in another region when they were children. So these women had married into the village from another group. But their family memberships were nevertheless considered eternal.

nuclear family

A married couple living with their own (usually biological) children and no extended family members.

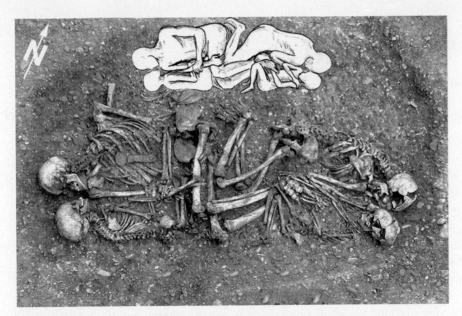

This Stone Age burial site contains the oldest DNA-confirmed nuclear family: a man and a woman (top left and right) and their two children (bottom left and right).

The archaeological record tells us that such flexible family arrangements have always been a crucial element of human social life. Although some people have lived in small, biologically related groups, others mixed and matched in ways that allowed them to survive. In fact, we now understand that the human species could not have survived without a system of family support, providing care for children who couldn't care for themselves. This isn't true of every species. Chimpanzees, one of our closest evolutionary relatives, do not have an extended period of childhood. Their mothers wean them (stop breastfeeding) when they are more or less ready to take care of themselves, at around 5 years of age. Among early humans, however, children were weaned at 2 or 3, an age when they were not able to fend for themselves (G. Kennedy 2005). As a result, the early survival of the species depended on adults caring for children through an extended period. Moreover, human mothers bore their children relatively close together in age, which meant that they couldn't carry them all around at once. The children could only survive with the help of additional adults beyond the mother (Gibbons 2008). These relationships, emerging at the dawn of our species, were the first human families.

The formation of relatively smaller, stable families—including some nuclear families of the kind described earlier—probably occurred only in the last 10,000 years or so, with the beginning of organized food production. The invention of agriculture allowed people to settle down in what are now known as the Americas, the Middle East, and China (Shelach 2006). The domestication of plants made it possible for hunter-gatherers to become farmers. During this time, larger social groups, which had been necessary for low-tech hunting, were augmented by more independent family units. Tiny one-person huts grouped around communal storage spaces were replaced by larger houses with room for four or five people and space for individual property (Flannery 2002). It appears that parents

Family Types and Terms

The prevailing family system is an important part of any society. And the many different kinds of societies have evolved around a wide variety of family systems. Those traditions help us understand how we came to be where we are today.

Today, most societies have a family system based on monogamy, the marriage of one person to one other person. Monogamous mating occurs in a few species of mammals (maybe 3 percent) but is more common among primates (10 to 15 percent [Fuentes 1998]). Because people are primates, and monogamy has been around for a long time, this has led some people to believe that monogamous marriage is the natural state of humans. But the history of human diversity suggests that it's not that simple. For one thing, different forms of marriage have often been practiced in one society at the same time. For example, polygamy, in which one person has several spouses, has usually occurred in societies where most people practiced monogamy—as is the case in some African countries, where polygamy was pretty common into the 1970s (Welch and Glick 1981). Although less common now, polygamy was the most prevalent form of marriage throughout human history. In prehistoric times, this practice may have given groups a biological advantage, since the more successful men could produce more children if they had multiple partners, while the weaker men had fewer children or none at all. Polygamy has almost always been practiced as men having more than one wife, reflecting the power of wealthy or influential men (Coontz 2005). Not surprisingly, polygamy is found in societies marked by great power inequality between men and women. In imperial China, for example, rich men often had multiple wives, and as a result, many poor men never married (Lee and Feng 1999).

When a monogamous couple live with their own biological children and no extended family members, it is known as a nuclear family. When a nuclear family is also functionally independent of extended family members, some social scientists call it a conjugal family. This is the modern ideal many people associate with the 1950s and 1960s, when new suburban homes, with trim lawns and picket fences, reinforced the image of the family as an independent (or even isolated) unit.

As we will see in Chapter 4, families are instrumental in accumulating and maintaining the wealth and status of those at the top of the social hierarchy. When wealth and power are transmitted from fathers to their sons, the family system is known as patrilineal (as opposed to matrilineal, from mothers to daughters). As we will see, many American Indians had matrilineal traditions, while European Americans were more patrilineal. That's why American wives and children usually take their surnames from the man of the family.

Suburbanization encouraged young couples to move away from their parents, but Americans had been a relatively mobile population since the westward expansion of the nineteenth century. In other societies, young couples often live with or near the husband's family home, in a living arrangement we call patrilocal, or near the wife's family (matrilocal). Contemporary societies are not usually rigidly gendered in this way, but in some cases strong traditions remain. In rural China, for example, it is still common for young women to move into their husband's household, where they play an important role in the family care system, especially in caring for the older family members. For this reason, having a son is more economically advantageous than having a daughter, because the son is likely to bring a wife/worker into the family, whereas a daughter may marry and leave her parents with no one to support them when they are old (Hvistendahl 2011).

Finally, we may speak of family systems as being either patriarchal, which means that power is wielded by men within the family, or matriarchal, in which women hold power. Although there certainly have been matriarchal families, truly matriarchal societies have been very rare in history; even in matrilineal American Indian tribes, for example, men usually had more power on questions of war (Eggan 1967). As we follow the history of families up to the present, we will see how men's power within society at large and their power within the family are mutually reinforcing.

Each of these terms represents whole systems or patterns of family life, different ways of acting and thinking from the moment we wake up till our heads hit the pillow (if we have one). Looking at all the different forms of marriage and family structure throughout history, and recognizing how successful those systems have been at maintaining their respective societies, it seems unreasonable to believe that there is one normal, or natural, family form ordained by God or evolution. There is simply too much diversity in the human historical record for that to be true.

As an aside, note that all of these terms have been used for families based on marriages between men and women. Now that the United States and many other countries permit marriage between couples of the same sex (see Chapter 8), we should have an appropriate adjustment of terms. Of course, marriage is marriage, and we don't always need to discuss the sex of the people involved. But when it is important to study, I have suggested that we call marriage of man to woman **heterogamy** and refer to same-sex marriage as **homogamy**—from the Greek hetero for "different," homo for "same," and gamos for "marriage" (P. Cohen 2011). But it's too early to know if this idea will catch on.

heterogamy

Marriage between a man and a woman.

homogamy

Marriage between two people of the same sex.

and young children lived together in these homes, along with grandparents if they were still alive (Steadman 2004). Still, even if prehistoric human societies formed nuclear families, they would not have survived if small families were responsible for all of their own needs. Cooperation beyond the immediate family was always essential.

From Europe to the United States

For most of this chapter, we will focus on the European origins of American family history. That's not because Europeans are more important than other groups, but because their traditions and practices dominated the legal, political, and cultural landscape in the early years of the country. Europeans were the

Edouard Victor Durand's *Whitsunday* (1888): What role (if any) does religion play in your family's life?

most powerful group in early American society; they not only set cultural standards but also enforced them by virtue of their political and economic power. Their model of the family was not adopted by everyone, however. In this chapter we will see how the historical experience of other groups diverged from the European-American story. We will return to this theme in Chapter 3, which examines racial and ethnic diversity in contemporary American family life through the intertwined stories of American Indian, African American, Asian American, and Latino families.

To help set the stage for American history, we will start with some themes pertaining to families in Europe (I have drawn from several sources, including principally historian Stephanie Coontz [2005]). The first is the important role played by the Christian (Catholic and Protestant) churches. Religious regulation of family life has varied considerably over the centuries, but from the time the Catholic Church consolidated its power throughout the Roman Empire in the late fourth century CE, Christianity set guideposts along the road of family life. With regard to marriage, state-established churches played the role held by government authorities today, determining the validity of marriages, presiding over marriage ceremonies, and allocating power and property among family members.

The second theme we see in European families is the extreme inequality and the separate family worlds of rich and poor. While rich families had elaborate marriage schemes—complex deals that involved land, armies, unwilling princesses, and domineering kings—the poor had no such luxury. They married and reproduced as matters of economic survival, often picking spouses based on whose family had a nearby plot of land or farming tools they needed for their crops. The children of the poor were workers in a family-based economy, not innocent cherubs sheltered from the harsh realities of life. To us, their lives would have seemed hard, bitter, and short.

Both rich and poor, however, shared a common third trait. Regardless of how marriage and family life were structured, family relations were not matters of personal preference or choice. Marriage was a political and economic institution that served important functions in society. For the rich it was necessary for maintaining their lineages and creating ties between powerful families. For the poor it was about arranging cooperation in labor, especially in working the land. In the countryside, survival depended on the division of labor between husband and wife. In those circumstances, marrying for love was far too risky a proposition to be practiced widely. In fact, being too passionate about one's spouse was highly suspect, raising concerns about social stability or even idolatry. Among Christians before the 1600s, the word *love* was usually reserved to describe feelings toward God or one's neighbors, not family members (Coontz 2005).

Finally, a pervasive theme through European family history and family structure is **patriarchy**, a system of male control over the family property and fathers'

patriarchy

The system of men's control over property and fathers' authority over all family members.

authority over the behavior of the family's women and children. That authority was not always absolute, but it was almost always present and acknowledged, both formally and informally. Each of these aspects of the European family system left a legacy that formed the backdrop for family life in the American colonies.

Origins of the American Family

To establish the background for modern American families, we set the stage with two periods: the colonial period before 1820, and the early modern period of the nineteenth century.

Colonial America (before 1820)

From the settlement of Europeans through the early nineteenth century, American family history was primarily the story of three interrelated groups: American Indians, White Europeans, and African Americans. In the passages that follow we will examine their stories separately, and consider how they intersected to create the complex set of family practices, dynamics, and traditions that emerged in the modern era.

American Indians: The Family as Social Structure The Europeans who founded the colonies that would become the United States encountered a vast and diverse population of what we now call American Indians (or Native Americans). Through a long, painful process (which continues to this day), the descendants of those indigenous tribal groups were incorporated into the fabric of the dominant European American society. We will investigate American Indians' contemporary family patterns in the next chapter; here we will consider their precolonial traditions.

Despite the diversity among American Indian groups, some historians have attempted to make generalizations about their family traditions. These include a strong respect for elders and a reliance on extended family networks for sharing resources and meeting essential needs. In most cases, family connections were the basic building blocks of social structure. Family relations were the model for nonbiological relationships, including those between members of the larger community and people's connections with the environment and animals (Weaver and White 1997). We know some of this from analyzing their languages. For example, Sioux Indians used family relationship terms for all members of the community, based on the nature of their cooperation. If a grown man moved into a community, he might be considered a stranger until an older

A tipi cover depicts scenes of traditional life, including hunting.

woman with whom he had a relationship started referring to him as her son, at which point he would become brother to her children, uncle to her grandsons, and so on (DeMallie 1994).

One common (although not universal) characteristic that set American Indians apart from Europeans was matrilineal descent, in which people were primarily considered descendants of their mothers rather than their fathers (see Changing Culture, "Family Types and Terms"). Among the Hopi Indians in the high deserts of the Southwest, families lived in clans following mothers' descent, with the oldest daughter inheriting the family home and living there with her husband and children. Because women were the property owners in the household, and men were relative outsiders surrounded by their wives' kin, women had greater authority within the clan (Queen 1985).

On the other hand, American Indians had some family traits in common with Europeans. Most practiced monogamous marriage—although their marriage bonds were not as strong as other relationships, and divorce was more common than among Europeans (Queen 1985). Like Europeans, American Indians also practiced a gender division of labor. For example, in groups that mixed hunting with agriculture, men did most of the hunting, while women grew and prepared food and reared young children (Gearing 1958). Even where matrilineal traditions increased women's power in the household, men usually had more political authority in the larger group (Eggan 1967). However, the relations between American Indian men and women in general remained more equal than they were among Europeans (Coontz 2005:42–43).

Colonial Americans: "So Chosen, He Is Her Lord" Coming from Europe, colonial Americans brought traditions for marriage and family life to the New World. Marriage for them was a practical arrangement that was considered necessary for civilization, not a source of love and affection. When in 1620 the English colonists in Jamestown, Virginia, showed signs of becoming undisciplined and unruly, a shipment of 90 intended brides was dispatched from the home country. The hope was to provide a stabilizing influence and encourage the male settlers to take a more mature view of the colonial enterprise. (The wives were also a valuable asset to the colonists, who were expected to trade 150 pounds of tobacco for each woman [Ransome 1991].)

Even if these early "mail-order brides" felt more like indentured servants than beloved wives, the male colonists endorsed the idea of choice in principle and rejected the Old World practice of arranged marriages. Still, colonial husbands' authority within marriage was virtually unchecked, and given the dependence of women on their husbands for survival, their choices were in fact very limited. As with the relationship between God and man under Protestant doctrine, the idea of free choice in marriage only served to reinforce the wife's duty to serve her husband. "The woman's own choice makes such a man her husband," wrote Massachusetts governor John Winthrop in the Founders' Constitution in 1645. "Yet being so chosen, he is her lord, and she is to be subject to him" (Winthrop 1853). In the Massachusetts Bay colony, local authorities were more likely to discipline husbands for failing to control their wives than for abusing them (Coontz 2005:141).

For the common people of colonial America—woman or man, free or slave, native or European—government was mostly a distant symbol when it came to family matters (Cott 1976). The system of marriage that prevailed in colonial times was supported by the Christian Church and by the power vested in local community leaders, who imposed their interpretation of Christian doctrine on marriage and divorce. Women could not vote, hold political office, or even serve on juries, so they had little choice but to comply with the marriage system. Their status as members of the local community—and often their survival—depended on conformity to the standards of the time. Once married, any property that a woman brought to the marriage, as well as the products of her labor, became her husband's. In fact, a wife's legal existence disappeared when she got married: under the legal doctrine of **coverture**, which lasted until the late nineteenth century, wives were incorporated into their husbands' citizenship.

coverture

A legal doctrine that lasted until the late nineteenth century, under which wives were incorporated into their husbands' citizenship.

Children and Families: More Work and Less Play

Colonial American families were large. The average woman bore about seven children in the course of her life, but one or more of them were likely to die at a young age. Children, like everyone else, played an economic role in the family, contributing to its survival and prosperity. Although this seems a shame or even a tragedy to us now—children growing up without a true childhood—the idea of childhood as a uniquely innocent stage of life was not common at that time. Most colonists held to the Calvinist view that children were guilty of original sin, and their evil impulses needed to be controlled through harsh discipline and hard work (Griswold 1993). Many families sent their children to live and work in the homes of others. Even rich parents did not spend much time interacting with their children (by today's standards). Because the bonds between family members in general were much less sentimental than they are now, these decisions did not provoke the kind of guilt or parental anxiety they would today (Coontz 2005).

Although couples had many children, most people did not live in large **extended families** under one roof. Households were mostly made up of nuclear families, plus any boarders or servants they had. Even though they didn't all live together, extended families played an important support role. Most people lived close to their siblings' families, and they shared labor and other resources. Among extended families, a **stem family** was the household formed by one grown child remaining in the family home with his or her parents. The favored child—typically the oldest son—would inherit the family home or farm, while the other siblings started their own households after marriage. This arrangement was common among farm families and those wealthy enough to leave an estate to their children (Ruggles 1994).

extended families

Family households in which relatives beyond parents and their children live together.

stem family

The household formed by one grown child remaining in the family home with his or her parents.

The colonial way of family life represented the first phase of a transition from the rural family, dominated by European Christian ideology, to the modern, urban, and industrial family system that was to come. As with all such transitions, the old ways were not completely left behind, but the pace of change in the nineteenth century would be so dramatic that many Americans felt powerless to understand, much less control, it.

African Americans: Families Enslaved

African families had gone through their own transitions, of course, of a particularly devastating nature. From the arrival of the first slaves in Jamestown in 1619 until the mid-1800s, Africans were forcibly removed from their homelands in western and central Africa and subjected to the unspeakable horrors of the Middle Passage aboard slave ships, slave auctions, and ultimately the hardships of plantation labor in the American South (as well as in the Caribbean and South America). Because they were thrown together from diverse backgrounds, and because their own languages and customs were suppressed by slavery, we do not know how much of slave family life was a reflection of African traditions and how much was an adaptation to their conditions and treatment in America (Taylor 2000).

But there is no doubt that family life was one of the victims of the slave system. The histories that have come down to us feature heart-wrenching stories of family separation, including diaries that tell of children literally ripped from their mothers' arms by slave traders, mothers taking poison to prevent themselves from being sold, and parents enduring barbaric whippings as punishment for trying to keep their families together (Lerner 1973). In fact, most slaves only had a given name with no family name, which made the formation and recognition of family lineages difficult or impossible (Frazier 1930). Slave marriage and parenthood were not legally recognized by the states, and separation was a constant threat. Any joy in having children was tempered by the recognition that those children were the property of the slave owner and could be sold or transferred away forever.

Nevertheless, most slaves lived in families for some or all of their lives. Most married (if not legally) and had children in young adulthood, and most children lived with both parents. This was especially the case on larger plantations rather than small farms, because slaves could carve out some protection for community life if they were in larger groups, and husbands and wives were more likely to remain together (Coles 2006). Even if they had families, however, African Americans for the most part were excluded from the emerging modern family practices described in the next section until after slavery ended.

A slave family in a Georgia cotton field, c. 1860.

The Emerging Modern Family (1820–1900)

During the Roman Empire (roughly 27 BCE–476 CE), the Latin word *familia* meant not just a man's wives and children but also his slaves and servants, who would bear his name after they were freed (Dixon 1992). In some ways, patriarchal power has been declining ever since. But with the spread of democracy and industrial capitalism, from the time of the American Revolution into the nineteenth century, new ideas, new laws, and the growth of the market economy hastened the erosion of fathers' absolute authority, bringing "profound changes in record time" (Coontz 2005:145).

Marriage: New Ideals, New Traditions Ironically, the period of rapid change brought about by democracy and industrialism also created a family characteristic that we often think of as "traditional": the sharply divided roles of fathers as breadwinners and mothers as homemakers. Even though most families still depended on the economic contributions of wives, the ideal of man as the economic provider became a powerful symbol in American culture. That ideal made men even more powerful and dominant within the family, even as women started embracing for themselves the growing ideology of individualism and personal freedom. The principle of autonomy for the country, as enshrined in the Declaration of Independence, also applied to individual citizens. As a result, individual free choice in marriage, as in democracy, was an ideal that was widely shared in the early years of the United States.

However, not everyone was happy with the idea that individuals, like colonies, had a right to independence and self-determination. A conservative backlash grew in the nineteenth century, led by those in positions of power who had used the language of independence during the American Revolution, but who grew increasingly uneasy with the spread of that idea throughout the population (even though slaves obviously were not included). These conservatives believed that women's freedom threatened the traditional family. And they had some success. In the decades after the American Revolution, most states went out of their way to pass laws denying women's right to vote, instead of merely assuming they were forbidden from doing so.

But it was too late. Independence, once promised, proved hard to revoke. The result was what Coontz calls "a peculiar compromise between egalitarian and patriarchal views" (2005:153). Women were still considered free, and the concept of male authority began to be replaced by the idea of men as "protectors" of women, while women cared for, loved, and nurtured their husbands. These gender roles came to be known as the separate spheres.

Meanwhile, with the recognition of individual rights and the spread of industrialization in the 1800s, the essential political and economic functions of marriage began to erode. That left young adults freer to consider the emotional aspects of their future marriages and to challenge parents or other authorities who tried to impose marriages on them for their own reasons. Companionship, affinity, love, and affection in marriage all began to grow more important in the minds of young adults—especially women—seeking a spouse.

John George Brown's *The Music Lesson* (1870) and *Courtship* (c. 1870) illustrate middle-class and working-class couples, respectively. Note the difference in their surroundings.

Not surprisingly, youthful ambition for happy marriages sometimes came into conflict with parental concern for economic or social status. The practice of **courtship** emerged as a compromise to reconcile these competing interests. Young couples themselves initiated courtship, which normally began with supervised contact in some public or semipublic place. Among the wealthy or middle class, that might mean a formal party or private social event. Despite having a choice at the outset, young people remained under their parents' watchful eyes. If the couple's interest persisted, additional meetings would take place in the woman's home, possibly leading to marriage if the parents approved. The system made it difficult for young women to act entirely against their parents' wishes, but offered some elements of free choice.

Among the poor and working class, parental control in spouse selection was less complete, but it was usually acknowledged that parents should approve their children's choices. Life at the low end of the income scale did not permit the luxury of shaping families around individual emotional desires. But the seed of the idea was planted, and whenever the standard of living permitted it, the poor would embrace the principles of choice and independence in family life. This would emerge as an important theme in the late twentieth century.

Children and Families: Fewer and More Tender One of the most monumental changes in family life in the nineteenth century was the drop in the number of children in each family. For White families, the average number was cut almost exactly in half over the century (see Figure 2.1). This was partly the result of couples learning how to prevent pregnancy. Mass production of condoms began in the mid-1800s (Gamson 1990), although most couples practiced withdrawal or limited the frequency of intercourse, as birth control information was not widely available in many places. But the declining birth rate was also the result of couples *wanting* fewer children. For one thing, many fewer children

Figure 2.1 **Children per woman, White women, 1800–1900 (average number ever born)**

SOURCE: Carter et al. (2006).

died after the mid-nineteenth century; the rate of infant deaths (those in the first year of life) was cut almost in half in just 50 years and has declined even more dramatically since 1900 (see Figure 2.2).

The emerging modern childhood also changed the logic of child rearing. During the nineteenth century, children's individuality emerged as a valued ideal, reinforced by the drop in the number of children and their greater likelihood of surviving. For example, children more often had their own rooms in the family home, with toys and books made especially for them. And they were less often named after their parents, helping to instill an independent identity. The prevailing view of children's morality also changed, as a new generation of experts declared that children were a blank slate of innocence, displacing the Calvinist notion that they harbored evil spirits that needed to be crushed. That change in thinking occurred as men started to work outside the home more often. So it was mothers who embraced the new, tenderer form of parenting, replacing the harsh discipline of fathers (Griswold 1993). Gradually, the parent-child relationship became more emotionally close.

Even between fathers and children—especially their sons—there were new emotional bonds. Instead of being tyrants with unchecked power, fathers took on the role of moral authorities who (ideally) led more by persuasion than by force. And children (again, especially sons) began to question fathers' domination in the family (Mintz 1998). As the historian Robert Griswold put it, "Hierarchy and order, the watchwords of older forms of paternal dominance, gave way to a growing emphasis on mutuality, companionship, and personal happiness" (1993:11).

Smaller families also meant that there were fewer adult children with whom elderly parents could live. As in colonial America, elderly parents mostly lived in their own homes with one of their grown children. However, most adults still

Figure 2.2 **Infant mortality, 1850–2014 (deaths per 1,000 births)**

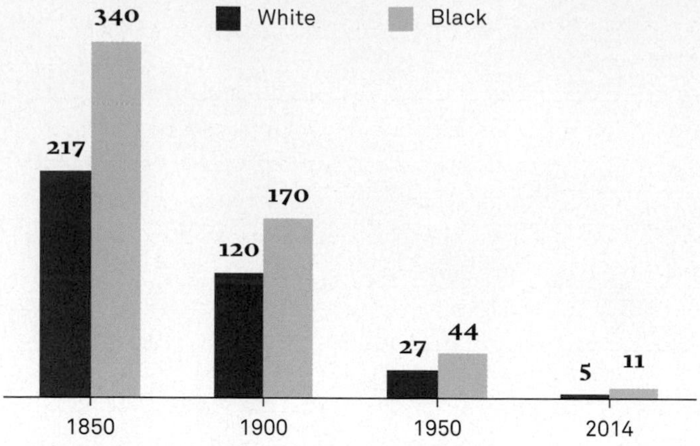

SOURCE: Carter et al. (2006), Kochanek et al. (2016).

did not live with elderly relatives, chiefly because there weren't many old people in the population. Only 4 percent of Americans were age 60 or older in 1850, compared with 21 percent today (U.S. Census Bureau 2016b).

Institutional Arenas In Chapter 1, we introduced the idea of three interrelated institutional arenas: the family, the market, and the state. These concepts help us understand the change in family form and function that has taken place over the last 200 years. Beginning in the nineteenth century, the market and state emerged as dominant features of modern society, and as a result, the family arena was transformed. I will briefly explain how the family lost its status as the center of the economy and began to be more directly regulated by the state. At the same time, the state started providing services that lightened the load on family care providers.

Family and Market: Men and Women, Separate and Together
In the nineteenth century, for the first time in history, "most people worked for someone else during their entire adult lives" (Katz 1986). Although that might not sound liberating, these workers were called "free labor" (as opposed to slaves) because their self-image was one of independently acting members of the new industrial economy (Foner 1995). That wage-labor relationship helped foster a sense of individual identity, reflecting American democratic ideals. Men's new identities—and the new workers were mostly men—were reinforced outside the walls of the family home in the factories and workshops of the industrial economy, where income-generating work took place.

Although there was no plan to make it happen this way, the industrial revolution also helped to reinforce the division of gender roles for men and women. Under the new doctrine of **separate spheres**, women were to make the home a haven, a sanctuary from the harsh realities of the industrial economy in which men worked for pay. This separation—women at home, men at work—was said

separate spheres

The cultural doctrine under which women were to work at home, to make it a sanctuary from the industrial world in which their husbands worked for pay.

to provide the balance necessary for social harmony (Strasser 1982). There were important exceptions, such as the hiring of young women to work in the early industrial mills of New England, but this only highlighted the rule that real workers were supposed to be men, because young women were expected to leave the workforce once they married.

Not surprisingly, the ideal of separate spheres was most strongly embraced among the expanding white-collar middle class in urban areas and promoted in new magazines targeted at that audience, such as *Harper's* and *Ladies' Magazine* (Mintz 1998). Men from these middle-class families, working at the growing number of desk jobs—wearing shirts with white collars—could be seen commuting on streetcars from suburban homes to their jobs in the central cities as early as the middle of the nineteenth century (Griswold 1993). Although separate spheres were not attainable by the great majority of working-class families, the ideal nevertheless was shared by men and women of most racial and ethnic groups and among the poor as well.

An important exception to these trends was farm families, many of whom continued to work in the older "family mode" of production. However, by the end of the nineteenth century, only 38 percent of the labor force worked in agriculture, while the proportion of the population living in urban areas (places with more than 2,500 people) climbed steadily to 40 percent (Figure 2.3). Further, the change in economic organization brought by industrialization was so pervasive that even farmwork increasingly operated along market principles, with workers leaving home to work for wages on a farm run as a business.

In the end, industrialism and separate spheres increased economic inequality between husbands and wives, with men's advantage growing. Because these new waged workers were men, the shift of economic power from the home to the workplace left men positioned to wield that power. And although women's

---

Figure 2.3 **From farms to cities, 1800–1900**

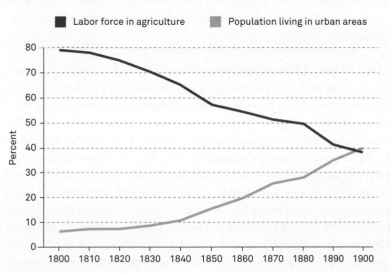

SOURCE: Carter et al. (2006).

labor in the home remained crucial for economic survival, the fact that it did not generate as much income as men's wage work created the impression that wives were dependent on their husbands.

But if these changes strengthened husbands' authority, they also strengthened that of wives. Although men wielded more economic power, women's influence over the children and household was enhanced. Emboldened by their newfound status as "managers" of the home, middle-class women especially sought recognition for the work they did. When that recognition was not forthcoming, many grew frustrated, steeped as they were in the cause of individual liberty and freedom. In 1869, for example, Harriet Beecher Stowe—who had published the sensational abolitionist novel *Uncle Tom's Cabin* almost two decades earlier—and her sister Catharine lamented men's high status, complaining that the "honor and duties of the family state are not duly appreciated" (Beecher and Stowe 1869:221). The two women listed the vast array of responsibilities burdening the typical (wealthy) wife:

> She has a husband, to whose particular tastes and habits she must accommodate herself; she has children whose health she must guard,...whose temper and habits she must regulate.... She has constantly changing domestics, with all varieties of temper and habits, whom she must govern.... She is required to regulate the finances of the domestic state, and constantly to adapt expenditures to the means and to the relative claims of each department. She has the direction of the kitchen.... She has the claims of society to meet, visits to receive and return, and the duties of hospitality to sustain. She has the poor to relieve; benevolent societies to aid; the schools of her children to inquire and decide about; the care of the sick and the aged; the nursing of infancy; and the endless miscellany of odd items, constantly recurring in a large family.

In the nineteenth century, the explosion of market relationships took families out of the center of economic life. However, it also reinforced the family as a separate social space, a place where a new kind of relationship developed. Less economic and more emotional, the modern family was emerging as a distinct institutional arena.

Family and State: "Monogamous Morality"

The family household under the principle of separate spheres was increasingly seen as a private place, caring for its members and raising its children instead of producing goods and services for public trade and consumption. In most cases, the state did not interfere with husbands' authority. Under coverture, a wife was incorporated into her husband's citizenship, under his name, and the husband was the family's representative when it came to interacting with the authorities or the law. Politicians generally believed that social stability required peace within the family. In fact, President Abraham Lincoln, warning against the conflict between slave-owning states and free states that was leading to the Civil War, knew that the public would understand him when he used the family as a metaphor, saying, "a house divided against itself cannot stand" (Cott 2000:77). Peace within the family required strong male leadership, just as peace within the nation required a strong federal government.

But if the government didn't interfere with male authority within the house-hold, it nevertheless became much more assertive about regulating who was married and under what conditions. In colonial times, most marriages had been blessed by local authorities alone, if at all, and there was very little civil regula-tion of family life. In the industrial era, however, the state's practical authority increased. For most people, the most powerful evidence of this authority may have been the spread of public education, which used local taxation to fund schools for most of the free population by the middle of the nineteenth century (Goldin and Katz 2003). In addition, such apparently simple functions as law enforcement agencies and the national postal service began reaching further into daily life.

The federal regulation of family life revolved around marriage and citizen-ship. Because a married man was the real citizen in the household, representing the rest of the family in the political arena, it made sense to insist that his mar-riage credentials were legitimate. In the name of safeguarding the character of the nation, then, the government began enforcing a sort of national "monogamous morality" when it came to family definition (Cott 2000:136).

Monogamous morality was not a new standard. It drew heavily from the Christian tradition, writing into law what had previously been religious or local custom. Rules for marriage included **monogamy** and a moral standard that required women to be faithful to their husbands (though not necessarily the other way around), while husbands supported their wives and children econom-ically. For example, when the government supported Civil War soldiers' widows, officials made sure they had not remarried, in which case the burden of support would pass to their new husbands (Cott 2000).

monogamy
A family system in which each person has only one spouse.

The reach of moral enforcement can also be seen in the Comstock Act of 1873, which banned shipment of "obscene" material in the U.S. mail. That meant not just pornography but also literature promoting birth control and even nonmo-nogamous relationships such as those advocated by some "free love" communes at the time. But monogamy itself was a key target of federal policy. Under the Dawes Act of 1887, a federal statute that granted individual landholding rights only to those male American Indians who were legally and monogamously mar-ried, Christian standards were effectively imposed over Indian family traditions (see Chapter 3). The enforcement of monogamy led to a long-running legal and political feud with the new Mormon Church, a feud that ended only after the Mormons officially renounced **polygamy** and Utah was permitted to become a state in 1896 (Cherlin and Furstenberg 1986). This burst of federal family regu-lation in the second half of the nineteenth century was mirrored by state laws and decisions at lower levels of government—for example, prosecuting and even jailing men who remarried after deserting their wives. In many ways, then, at the end of the nineteenth century, the government at all levels laid a much heavier hand on the family lives of its citizens than it had a century before.

polygamy
A family system in which one person has more than one spouse, usually one man and multiple women.

No Families: Widows and Orphans Families had become less cen-tral as sites of economic activity, but they remained an essential source of eco-nomic support for most Americans: Despite their inequality in the marketplace, husbands and wives were in fact dependent on each other, just as children were

The Sisters of Charity created the New York Foundling in 1869. It still exists today as a foster home and child welfare agency.

dependent on their parents. Yet in the new male-centered wage economy, many widows and orphans had no one to provide monetary support and joined the ranks of the chronically impoverished or the mentally or physically disabled. In this period, being short on family members often went along with being short on necessities.

In the past, people in these predicaments had been cared for by their extended families (if they got any care at all). But starting in the mid-nineteenth century, a new set of specialized institutions arose to provide for, or at least supervise, those who could not earn their keep in the industrial economy. This was a weak, disorganized patchwork of poorhouses, orphanages, penitentiaries, and almshouses, which often started out as charitable institutions before being taken over by local or state governments. There were two common features of this emerging welfare system. First, it isolated those in need of assistance from the rest of the population in residential institutions, sometimes for their entire lives. Second, the care provided was usually inadequate, since a lack of resources and ineffective or nonexistent government regulation made it impossible for institutions to provide a decent life for their wards (Katz 1986).

The plight of widows in particular was widely known. In fact, the federal government's ability to recruit soldiers for its army in the Civil War relied on the promise of widows' pensions, without which many soldiers would not have volunteered, for fear of leaving their wives and children destitute. The resulting bureaucracy was the precursor to our modern welfare system, providing federal support for hundreds of thousands of veterans and their widows (Skocpol 1992). This breakthrough made it possible for Americans without the means to support themselves—and without the support of employed family members—to survive under the care of the state. That made living without a family possible, a rare feat in the history of our species, although in the century to follow it would become increasingly common (Klinenberg 2012). Not everyone in need was able to benefit from early pension and welfare programs, which were selective in whom they assisted, but the modern state increasingly stepped in when people could not draw sustenance from the market or the family (Gordon 1994).

African, Asian, and Mexican Americans: Families Apart

Being without a family was one of many problems that confronted members of America's minority groups in the nineteenth century, whether African Americans emerging from slavery, Asian American immigrant communities, or Mexicans who found their lands annexed within growing U.S. boundaries. Each group developed its own family arrangements and practices in ways that were related to, but distinct from, those of Whites.

For African American families, the Civil War marked a decisive turning point. The abolition of slavery in 1865 did not mean their liberation from racial oppression; many African Americans entered into a new agricultural system of sharecropping in which they worked on land owned by Whites in conditions of desperate poverty, albeit not formal slavery. And in the South their very citizenship was far from guaranteed. But slavery's demise did make possible a family revival, allowing some former slaves to reunite with long-lost spouses and children and allowing many others to marry, have children, and live together in the manner of their choosing for the first time in America (Gutman 1976). For the first time, also, African American families could be legally recognized. In fact, the federal government, under monogamous morality principles, required legal marriages among those who qualified for federal relief provided to former slaves (Cott 2000).

The African American families that emerged in the late nineteenth century exhibited more gender equality, based on the greater economic role of women, than White families did. But their marriages also were more fragile, partly as a result of the persistent poverty and hardship they suffered, and ended more often in divorce or widowhood. On the other hand, African Americans developed stronger extended family networks of caring and cooperation. This was especially necessary for children, who were frequently cared for by extended family members and foster or adoptive parents (Furstenberg 2007).

The first large Asian group in the United States was the Chinese. These immigrants began arriving in significant numbers during the gold-rush years in the West, starting in 1852. Over the next few decades, several hundred thousand

An 1857 wood engraving that depicts Chinese miners living and working in California during the Gold Rush.

Chinese came to work in the mines and build the railroads of the growing western states, making up a substantial part of the manual labor force (Fong 2008). Almost all of them were men, most of whom had wives and children in China, where they eventually returned (Chew and Liu 2004). This arrangement—married workers spending years separated from their spouses—has been called the split-household family (Glenn and Yap 2002). In response to anti-Chinese racism in the West, Congress passed the Chinese Exclusion Act of 1882, which cut off most new immigration. As a result, few Chinese women could join the single men who remained. And because Chinese men were forbidden from marrying Whites (at least in California, where most of them lived), these men remained unmarried and childless. In the next chapter, we will see how the Chinese community—along with other groups from Asia—eventually flourished in the twentieth century.

Unlike the Chinese, who migrated to the United States in search of jobs, the first major group of Latinos in the United States were not immigrants. They were the descendants of Spanish colonists and Aztecs, and they became Americans when the United States won the Mexican-American War in 1848, laying claim to more than half of Mexico in what is now the American Southwest (Nostrand 1975). The new Mexican Americans were mostly poor farmers, but as large commercial farms began taking over their land, and as new railroads reached the territory, many traveled around the country for work. Like the Chinese and African Americans, then, family life for Latinos in early America often included long periods of separation, which required strong family bonds and extended family care relationships (Baca Zinn and Pok 2002). This experience contributed to Mexican Americans' *familism* (see Chapter 3), a strong orientation toward family needs and obligations that persists today (Landale and Oropesa 2007).

The Modern Family (1900–1960s)

During the nineteenth century, a number of forces had pulled men and women toward a nuclear family arrangement in which one employed man was stably married to, and economically supporting, one homemaking woman and their children. These included the cultural ideal of separate spheres, economic forces pushing men toward paid labor outside the home, and government attempts to enforce "moral" marriage. But most Americans couldn't live that way even if they wanted to. Most men didn't make enough money to "keep" a woman at home, and most families couldn't afford a home that provided the kind of privacy the ideal demanded.

By the middle of the twentieth century, however, the goal of the male breadwinner—female homemaker household was for the first time within the reach of most American families. Those who achieved that goal attempted to create a new kind of marriage, in which men and women were friends and companions as well as romantic partners. On the surface, by the 1950s the dream of the **companionship family** appeared to have become a reality. Beneath the surface, however, the foundation was decidedly shaky.

companionship family

An ideal type of family characterized by the mutual affection, equality, and comradeship of its members.

Marriage: Unequal Companions

Around the turn of the twentieth century, many young men lived independently, and many others lived with their parents or as boarders until they married in their late 20s. Women usually stayed in the family home until they married. In 1900, the typical man married at about age 26, the typical woman at 22 (see Figure 2.4).

Marriage was becoming more attractive to young people for cultural, economic, and political reasons. First, the nature of marriage—and the ideal of marriage—was undergoing a cultural shift that has been described as "institution to companionship." That was the subtitle of a textbook you might have

Figure 2.4 **Median age at first marriage, 1890–2015**

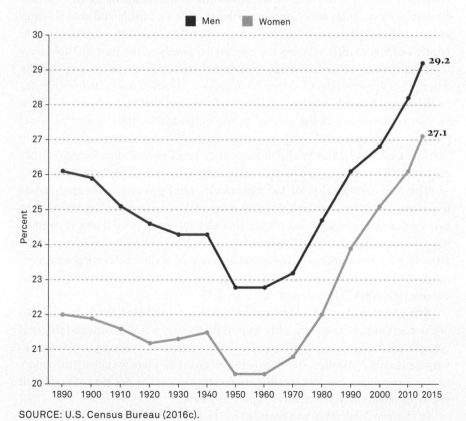

SOURCE: U.S. Census Bureau (2016c).

Table 2.1 **The companionship family ideal**

	PATRIARCHAL FAMILY	COMPANIONSHIP FAMILY
BASIS FOR CHOOSING A SPOUSE	Parental influence, social status, and economic needs	Self-directed motivation based on affection and personality
HUSBAND-WIFE RELATIONSHIP	Subordination of wife to husband	Equality based on consensus
BONDS HOLDING FAMILIES TOGETHER	Father's authority	Mutual affection and common interests
FAMILY SIZE	Extended	Nuclear
FAMILY GOALS	Duty and tradition	Happiness and personal growth

read if you took this course in the 1940s. The author, Ernest Burgess, saw a new, modern family type, which he described as "the companionship family, characterized by the mutual affection, sympathetic understanding, and comradeship of its members" (Burgess 1963:vii). I summarize the ideal of the companionship family and how it differed from the patriarchal family of the past in Table 2.1.

The companionship family ideal was just that—an ideal, not a reality. But the description Burgess offered shows the direction in which many people thought families were headed: smaller families, freely chosen, that make decisions based on mutual interests, in the service of the individual happiness and personal growth of husband and wife. It was an ideal shared by many Americans, especially (but not exclusively) the White, middle-class families that dominated popular culture, politics, and the business world in the mid-twentieth century (May 1988).

The core relationship of the new model family was the **companionate marriage**, which was a companionship, a friendship, and a romance, rather than being a practical platform for cooperation and survival, as marriage seemed to have been in the past (Cherlin 2009). The companionate ideal was especially attractive to men working in the growing sector of white-collar corporate jobs, many of whom, even if well paid, felt alienated and frustrated by their impersonal bureaucratic work (Mintz 1998).

The promise of companionate marriage also contributed to the breakdown of the courtship system—the old compromise between free choice and parental supervision in choosing a spouse. The independence of young people was no longer so easily controlled. In the growing urban areas, there was plentiful opportunity for unsupervised interaction, fueled by cash in the pockets of employed young men, and driven—at least in part—by cars.

In this way, courtship was replaced by the freewheeling system of **dating**, in which young adults spent time with a variety of partners, before making

companionate marriage

A view of marriage as a companionship, a friendship, and a romance, rather than as a practical platform for cooperation and survival.

dating

The mate selection process in which young adults spend time with a variety of partners before making a long-term commitment.

long-term commitments (see Chapter 7). The authority of parents was severely compromised in the process, replaced by the authority of young men, who now initiated and paid for dates. The companionate marriages that resulted from dating—despite their ideology of sharing—thus started off with a man in the driver's seat.

Beyond the symbolic importance of independence, however, the economic opportunity necessary for achieving the ideal—an employed man supporting a homemaking wife in their own home—became more accessible. For many years, American workers (and their unions) had demanded from their employers a **family wage**, the amount necessary for a male earner to provide subsistence for his wife and children without their having to work for pay. As American industry grew and the threat of labor unrest became more unsettling to employers, more companies started paying their workers enough to support a whole family. Ford Motor Company crossed a symbolic threshold when it dramatically increased pay, introducing the "Five Dollar Day" in 1914. That wage was intended to promote workforce stability, home ownership (and car buying), as well as worker loyalty (May 1982). And it succeeded.

The federal government also gave marriage a political boost in the early twentieth century, replacing the stick with a carrot. The strict moral tone of marital regulation of the nineteenth century gave way to a pattern of economic incentives for marriage (Cott 2000), including Social Security and Aid to Dependent Children (discussed shortly). These programs indirectly promoted marriage because women who never married or who got divorced were not eligible at first to receive their support. After World War II, the government provided extensive benefits to male veterans, especially low-interest loans to buy homes, which also had the effect of encouraging marriage (Cherlin 2009).

Taken together, all of these factors—the cultural shift toward the companionate marriage and away from parental authority, the economic opportunities for independence provided to men through industrial development, and the political incentives to marry offered by the government—increased the motivation and ability of young people to marry in the first half of the twentieth century. Because most married couples conformed to the separate spheres ideal, or tried to, some observers assumed that the family as an institution was stable and secure. Talcott Parsons, the sociologist most identified with the theory of structural functionalism (see Chapter 1), was one such naive observer, writing in 1955: "It seems quite safe in general to say that the adult feminine role has not ceased to be anchored primarily in the internal affairs of the family, as wife, mother and manager of the household, while the role of the adult male is primarily anchored in the occupational world" (Parsons and Bales 1955:12–14). That image might have applied to the 1950s, but it would not last much longer.

family wage

The amount necessary for a male earner to provide subsistence for his wife and children without their having to work for pay.

The companionate marriage made the combination of companionship, friendship, and romance between equals the new marital ideal; however, the companionate marriage still left the man in the driver's seat.

Children and Families: From Bust to Boom

On average, Americans married younger and younger over the first half of the twentieth century, but the birth rate continued to decline—an unusual combination. White women had an average of 3.6 children each in 1900, and that fell to 2.3 children by 1940, continuing the steady decline we saw in the nineteenth century (Carter et al. 2006). But all that changed—at least temporarily—from the end of World War II to the mid-1960s. The **baby boom**, which refers to the period of high birth rates between 1946 and 1964, reversed the long-standing pattern of declining fertility (see the Story Behind the Numbers), producing a huge population bubble of "baby boomers" who are now in their 50s and 60s.

baby boom

The period of high birth rates in the United States between 1946 and 1964.

To understand this seismic event in family history, we need to look at the experience of the cohort of adults who married in the 1940s and 1950s. There was a sudden drop in age at marriage between 1940 and 1950 as the young couples who would produce the baby boomers got married (look again at Figure 2.4). If you work back from marriages that took place in, say, 1945, you'll see that those couples were born in the early to mid-1920s and thus experienced childhoods marked by the deprivation of the Great Depression of the 1930s.

The economy revived and eventually soared as a result of American participation in World War II (1941–1945), when increasing numbers of women entered the workforce to replace men who were serving in the military. Even though millions of men returned to their jobs after the war (and women resumed their roles as homemakers), the nation faced a cumulative shortage of workers brought on by the decline in birth rates in the first half of the century. That shortage of workers, combined with the growing economy, produced a dramatic spike in wages beginning in the late 1940s.

Baby boom parents experienced a rare sequence of events, with severe economic depression and all-consuming war followed by sudden prosperity (Cherlin 2009). After difficult childhoods and a long period of uncertainty about the future, they embraced the prospect of stability. They married, and an unprecedented number of them bought homes, encouraged by a boom in housing construction in the suburbs (connected to cities by the new interstate highway system, begun in 1956) and made affordable (to Whites) through new federal mortgage guarantees (Freund 2007). The historian Elaine Tyler May writes that American families after World War II perceived an "intense need to feel liberated from the past and secure in the future" (1988:10). To achieve that feeling, they turned inward toward family life—and they had a lot of children.

Television shows from the mid-twentieth century, such as *The Adventures of Ozzie and Harriet*, showcased the ideal of the breadwinner-homemaker family.

In light of these long-term trends and the unique circumstances of the postwar years, it is clear that the 1950s were a highly unusual decade. Since that time, the 1950s have come to be seen as the pinnacle of the "traditional" American family, epitomized by the stably married and loving couple, headed by one male wage earner and made possible by a homemaking wife. And in fact, that model was never more prevalent than in the 1950s, but it was a tradition that was invented in the nineteenth century and it had very shallow roots. The traditional family had always been more an ideal than a reality. In fact, it seems most realistic to describe it as a myth (Coontz 1992).

New Family Diversity (1960s–Present)

There are many dimensions to the family changes that occurred after the 1950s, but I think they can best be captured by the concept of increasing family diversity. More individuals and families were arranging their lives and relationships in more different ways than ever before. The 1950s-style "traditional" family persisted as an ideal for many people. But as a reality it shrank further and further from its dominant position. In its place emerged a wide range of families and living arrangements, most prominently including individuals living alone (both younger and older adults), single parents (some of them divorced), blended stepfamilies, and unmarried couples. And now of course some couples include partners of the same gender, who may be legally married. Each of these changes will be featured in later chapters; but here I want to focus on the growth of family diversity itself.

Why did family patterns depart so dramatically from the 1950s ideal? Two institutional factors were important in the postwar period. First, market forces more than ever challenged some of the core functional tasks of modern families. With the growth of modern services, such as laundries and restaurants, and new technology, such as washing machines (see Changing Technology, "Laborsaving Devices"), much of the work that housewives did was taken over by paid service workers or machines. One government analyst went so far as to predict that "the final result might be virtually to eliminate the home as a place of work and housewives as a functional group" (Durand 1946).

The biggest challenge to the 1950s ideal was women's increased tendency to leave home for paid work. Women's employment had increased gradually from the beginning of the century into the 1950s. During that time, most employers only hired single women. But starting in the 1950s, as women married at younger ages and the growing economy needed more workers, there simply weren't enough single women to go around. Employers opened their doors to married women, and women responded eagerly (Goldin 1990). After 1960, employment rates for both married and unmarried women rocketed upward in a 30-year burst that would

Decline in birthrates, increase in women workers

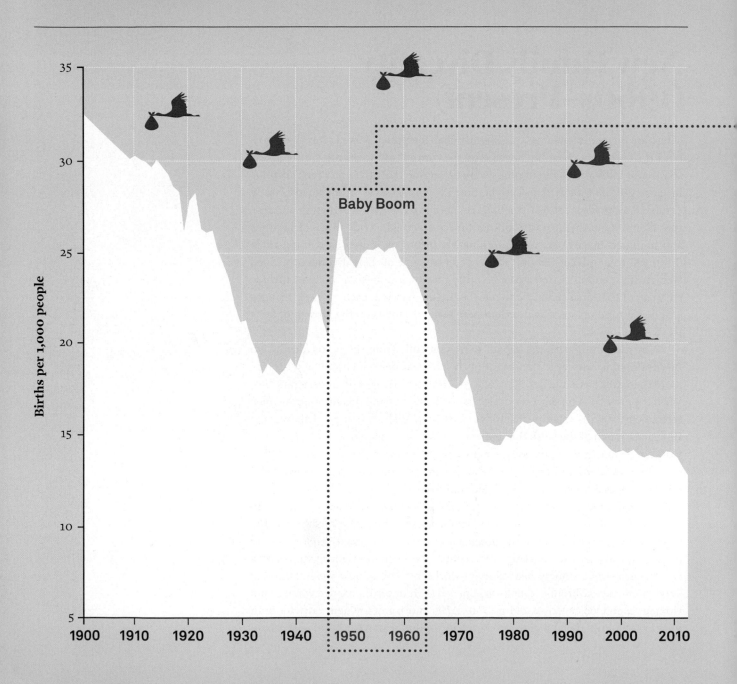

From 1900 to 2010 the birth rate dropped roughly 60 percent, from more than 32 births per 1,000 people in the population to 13. During that time, women entered the paid labor force in growing numbers, working everywhere from factories and restaurants to schools and hospitals. But the story isn't that simple. Starting at the end of World War II, in 1945, there was a huge increase in birth rates—the baby boom. Why? The children of the Great Depression (from the 1930s) found economic prosperity after World War II (in the 1950s). Men had good jobs, and the suburbs beckoned. They bought homes and married young at record rates, and went on to have a lot of children. But in the end, despite the baby boom, the big stories of the century were still falling birth rates and rising employment for women.

Sources: Vital Statistics of the United States, Statistical Abstracts of the United States, Current Population Surveys.

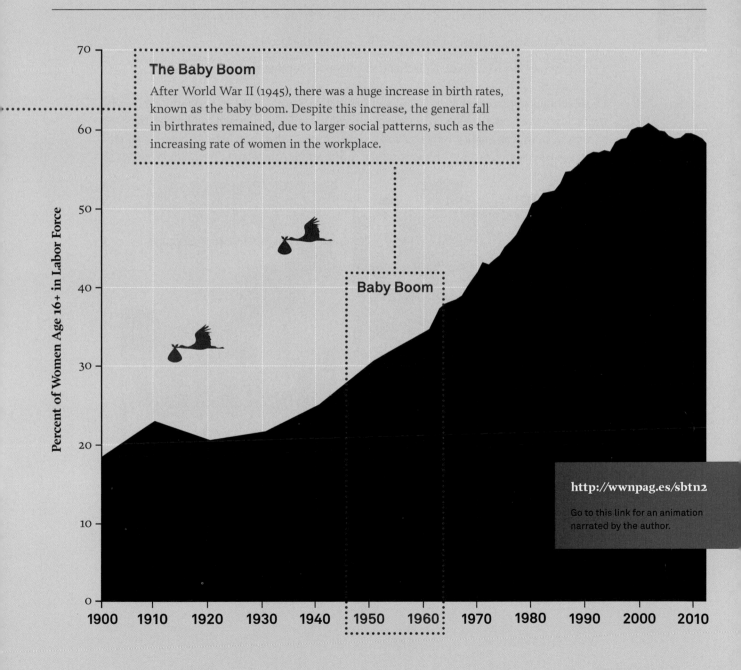

The Baby Boom

After World War II (1945), there was a huge increase in birth rates, known as the baby boom. Despite this increase, the general fall in birthrates remained, due to larger social patterns, such as the increasing rate of women in the workplace.

Baby Boom

Percent of Women Age 16+ in Labor Force

http://wwnpag.es/sbtn2

Go to this link for an animation narrated by the author.

Laborsaving Devices

The last 100 years have produced an "industrial revolution" in the technology used to do housework (Cowan 1976). In the 1920s alone, most middle-class families acquired the following inventions for the first time:

- Electric irons, replacing heavy irons (made of real iron) that had to be heated on the stove

- Hot and cold running water, reducing the need for pumping, hauling, and heating water

- Central heating, instead of heating the house with the kitchen stove

- Gas, oil, or electric stoves, replacing coal- or wood-burning stoves

These products greatly reduced the amount of labor necessary for keeping a family fed and warm. Over the next 50 years, a cascade of further inventions promised to increase the efficiency, as well as quality, of housework (Strasser 1982). Most notably, electric refrigerators, clothes washers, and vacuum cleaners spread to almost all American households (Figure 2.5).

Innovations in household technologies promised to reduce the labor involved in running a family, but such innovations did not lead to less housework for housewives. Who does the housework in your family?

Figure 2.5 **Households with key appliances, 1922–1977**

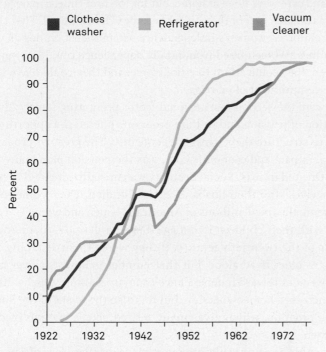

■ Clothes washer   ■ Refrigerator   ■ Vacuum cleaner

SOURCE: Author's calculations from Bowden and Offer (1994).

The majority of households also had blenders by 1970, clothes dryers by 1972, and microwave ovens by 1986 (Bowden and Offer 1994). Even canned and frozen foods saved additional time and labor (Cowan 1976).

Somehow, however, all this innovation did not lead to a reduction in the total work done by housewives. Studies of time use found that nonemployed women experienced almost no change in the hours of housework they did from 1900 to 1965—more than 50 hours per week. Since then, they've reduced their housework modestly, to about 39 hours (Ramey 2009).

Instead of hauling coal and wood, the modern, better-equipped housewife worked to ever-higher standards of hygiene—for example, sterilizing baby bottles (Mokyr 2000). She spent more time cooking balanced, nutritious meals, changing clothes and linens more often, and, ironically, shopping. And there was more to clean, including the bathroom, which didn't exist as a separate room in most houses before the 1920s (even when they were indoors, toilets were not in their own room).

To make matters more difficult for the middle-class housewife, many lost their household servants during the first two decades of the century. In 1900, there was one household servant or cleaner for every 9 households in the country; but by 1920, there was only one for every 15 households (Carter et al. 2006).

The reason laborsaving technology in the household usually does not lead to a reduction in labor is because housework is as much about relationships between people as it is about creating a product. So, within marriages, it "expands to fill the time available" (Cowan 1976:15). Technology does change what labor gets done and how onerous it is to do (Bittman, Rice, and Wajcman 2004). But what really cuts the time women spend on housework is getting out of the house and earning money. So the movement of women into the paid labor force did more to shrink their housework burden than any modern invention (Bianchi et al. 2006).

Utilities and appliances may make the labor easier, but it is social relations and work arrangements that change housework demands. Technology—and the availability of services—made it possible for families to cut down on the most onerous housework. That trend helped justify many women's decision to enter the paid labor force (Greenwood, Seshadri, and Yorukoglu 2005) but the machines alone didn't reduce the amount of housework people actually did.

radically change the foundation of marriage and family life in the United States (Cotter et al. 2004). Women's work finally moved primarily from the home to the market, following men's movement of the previous century. This didn't eliminate housework and care work done at home, but for the first time, a majority of women's work was done as part of the paid labor force (Thistle 2006). That shift to market work reinforced women's independence *within* their families as well as *from* their families. Women freed from family dependence could live singly, even with children; they could afford to risk divorce; and they could live with a man without the commitment of marriage.

State forces were the second institutional factor promoting family diversity. A combination of pension and welfare programs offered the opportunity for more people to structure their lives independently. The greatest program, in terms of social impact and economic cost, was the pension plan known as Social Security. Created in 1935, Social Security was initially intended to provide pensions to wives after their husbands retired or died. The income security it granted eventually freed millions of Americans—men and women—from the need to live with their children in old age (Engelhardt and Gruber 2004). At the beginning of the twentieth century, if they weren't married, only 1 in 10 people age 55 or older lived alone; but that number is now just over half. Some of that movement toward independence came from improving health at older ages, and increased homeownership, but it is also the result of the Social Security pension program, which gives many retired people enough income to live on their own.

For younger adults, growing welfare support made marriage less of a necessity, at least for poor women with children. The federal program known as Aid to Families with Dependent Children had been created as part of the Social Security Act to support widows and women who had been abandoned by their husbands. In the 1960s and 1970s, the program grew explosively, eventually supporting millions of never-married mothers and their children. Although it always carried a shameful stigma and provided a minimal level of monetary support, welfare nevertheless underwrote the independence of many poor single women, thereby increasing the options available to them (Mink 1998). Not all young adults shared this newfound independence, of course. Even as more people struck out on their own, there has also been a steady rise in the number of young adults living with their parents, especially in the last decade (see Figure 13.8).

The growth of women's employment was more striking among those with higher earning power, especially college graduates (Cohen and Bianchi 1999). Poor women, especially African American women, had long been more likely to work for pay, but their lower earnings did not offer the same personal independence that those with better jobs enjoyed. On the other hand, welfare support was a bigger factor in the growing independence of poor women. Thus, market forces increased the independence of middle-class and more highly educated women, while state forces increased the independence of poor women.

As a result of these trends, after the 1950s more people had more choices for how to live and arrange their family lives, and the diversity of family arrangements increased dramatically. One way of representing that change is shown

Figure 2.6 **Distribution of household types, 1880–2015**

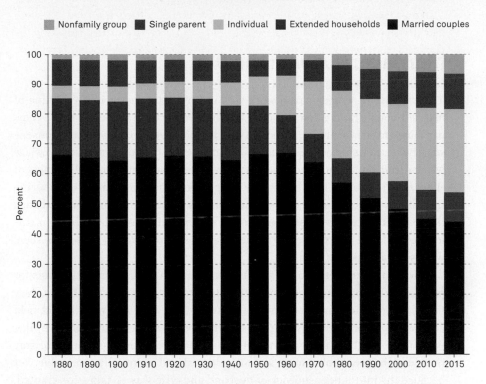

Note: Data for 1890 are not available; these are interpolated.

SOURCE: Author's calculations from U.S. Census data as compiled by IPUMS (Ruggles et al. 2016).

in Figure 2.6. Here I have categorized each household into one of five types and calculated what percentage of households were in each arrangement, from 1880 to 2015. The largest category is households composed of married couples living with no one except their own children. If there was any other relative living in a household, I counted it as an extended household. The third category is individuals who live alone. Fourth are single parents (most of them mothers) living with no one besides their own children. In the final category are households made up of people who are not related (including unmarried couples).

Figure 2.6 shows that the married-couple family peaked between 1950 and 1960, when two-thirds of households represented this arrangement. After that decade, the proportion of married-couple households dropped rapidly to less than half (44 percent) in 2015. The greatest increase during this period was in the categories of individuals and single parents, which together accounted for 39 percent of all households in 2015. Extended households are less common than they were a century ago, mostly as a result of the greater independence of older people (although their numbers have increased again in the last several decades). In sum, the chart shows that the dominant married-couple household of the first half of the twentieth century was replaced not by a new standard, but rather by a general increase in family diversity.

Marriage: Out with the Old

The increase in women's paid work was an important factor in the decline of married-couple family dominance. It highlighted a crucial weakness in the companionate marriage model. Although in principle based on equality and consensus, the relationship between husbands and wives in the companionate marriage was far from equal: husbands had more power because they earned all or most of the family's income. This became more apparent when women started pouring into the labor force, because they almost always earned less than their husbands in jobs that were less prestigious. So the partnership implied by the companionate ideal still bore the stamp of the separate spheres, which, as we have seen, were separate but not equal.

Modern marriages also had another fundamental weakness. If the basis for marriage truly had become mutual affection—rather than strict authority, duty to follow tradition, and economic necessity—then affection was all that held couples together. What if it turned out that couples didn't love, or even like, each other? Without strong bonds of tradition and economic pressures to stay married, divorce seemed more and more logical and eventually acceptable. Yet because the mutual dependence of husband and wife was so taken for granted, this weakness was not apparent even to the educated observer at midcentury. (If you used the Burgess textbook I mentioned earlier for this course, you wouldn't even find a chapter devoted to divorce and its consequences!)

Some critics say that popular respect for the institution of marriage has declined, as indicated by the rising divorce rate after the 1960s (see Chapter 10) and the increasing acceptability of raising children outside of marriage (see Chapter 9). But in fact the opposite may be true. Consider the fight for access to marriage by gays and lesbians, which was one of the most dramatic civil rights efforts in recent memory—a sign of the elevated cultural status of marriage. However, it is true that by treating marriage as a true love relationship, we raise our expectations, and any marriage that falls short of this emotional standard no longer seems acceptable. After centuries in which being single was not a genuine option—and love wasn't the principal ingredient of marriage—it's hardly surprising that when people finally have a real choice, more and more choose not to follow the traditional path. They live alone, marry later in life, divorce more, and have children whether they are married or not. All of these factors have contributed to the growing diversity in family life over the last half-century, but they don't necessarily signal a decline in respect for marriage.

Modern Relationships, Modern Identities By the end of the twentieth century, Americans on average spent much less of their lives within marriage than at any earlier time in the nation's history. As we have seen, this trend reflected cultural changes that made it more acceptable for adults not to be married, as well as changes in the state and market that made it more feasible to live independently (Coontz 2000:289).

For young women, the change in the last half-century has been especially dramatic. Before the 1950s, because women married young—and likely stayed in their parents' home until they got married—very few young women lived on their own. In 1960, only 3 percent of women between 25 and 34 lived in a household without a spouse or any other relatives (see Figure 2.7). In the ensuing decades, living independently (or perhaps with a romantic partner outside of marriage) became a normal part of young adulthood for women; as a result, that 3 percent had grown to 22 percent by 2015. For men, the trend over time is similar, but they had higher rates of living independently at the end of the nineteenth century, when many lived as boarders and worked away from home. And they are even more likely than women to be unattached today, with about a third living with no formal relatives.

Marriage is not the only traditional relationship to which Americans have become less attached. Between 1880 and 1990, the percentage of adults who shared a household with any child under 18 dropped by half, from 70 percent to 35 percent (Goldscheider, Hogan, and Bures 2001). With less time in marriage and less overlap with the lives of their children, today's adults, young and old,

Figure 2.7 **Percentage of adults, ages 25 to 34, living with no relatives, 1870–2015**

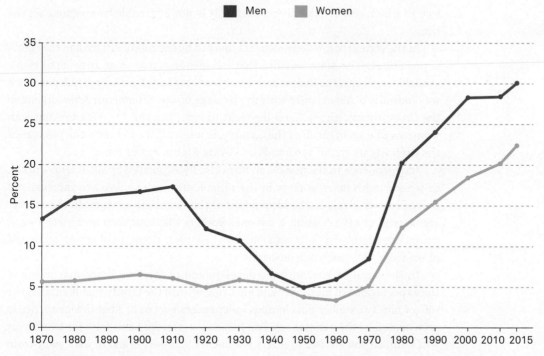

Note: Data for 1890 are not available.

SOURCE: Author's calculations from U.S. Census data as compiled by IPUMS (Ruggles et al. 2016).

experience more residential isolation from family over the course of their lives. That's not the same as not having a family, because most people have family relationships with people away from home. But increasing physical separation has both heightened family members' sense of independence and underscored the voluntary nature of contemporary family relationships (Klinenberg 2012).

I used modernity theory in Chapter 1 to explain how a sense of individuality has become the new normal state of affairs in contemporary families. In this chapter, we can see where that trend has led, with the decline of the traditional nuclear family and the rise of diversity in family arrangements. The longer periods of life spent living apart from family members increases people's sense of insecurity as they are forced to choose a family type, while increasing their sense of freedom at being able to do so.

Independence For marriage truly to be optional, it had to be possible to survive—maybe happily—without being married. As we have seen, the rise of women's employment was an essential element for that transformation. Another was the incorporation of single mothers into the major welfare programs—not just those who had been widowed or abandoned by their husbands, but those who had never married. In this way, the market (employment) and the state (welfare) made possible the transformation of marriage from a necessity to a voluntary arrangement. And that, in turn, changed the nature of the marriage relationship.

In each of the three institutional arenas that we are focusing on in this book—the state, the market, and the family—a form of independence is possible and becomes desirable for most people. That is, each arena includes an independent role to which people may aspire, even if it is not attainable by everyone all the time.

In the state arena, independence is marked by the role of citizen and the rights it prescribes. The state certifies that independent role as an individual right, available to all citizens in a modern democratic society. For women, independence was formally achieved only with the passage of the Nineteenth Amendment to the Constitution, giving them the right to vote, in 1919. For African American women and men in much of the country, it wasn't achieved until the passage of the Civil Rights Act of 1964 and the Voting Rights Act of 1965.

Independence in the market arena is chiefly expressed by the role of worker, as we saw with male workers in the nineteenth century. Women increasingly moved into that role in the second half of the twentieth century. In the market arena, everyone is a consumer, but only workers who have their own incomes can act independently in their consumption behavior, rather than acting on behalf of someone else (such as a husband).

In the family arena, with the development of the love-based marriage and the expectations of mutuality and affection within the family that it entails, the role of family member now implies independence as well. That independence is represented by the marriage choice. Just as you can vote and work for whomever you want, so you are free to marry whomever you want—and to walk away from a spouse whenever you want.

Independence in each of these arenas is, naturally, a double-edged sword. In

If I Could Change One Thing...

It might be hard to imagine yourself living in a different historical time period. If everything were different, you wouldn't be the same person anyway. But what if you could change just one thing? Imagine how just one aspect of your life would be different if it had taken place in a different time.

For example, Judy and I married after college and were together more than 10 years after that before we decided to have children. During that time, we lived in five different cities, we each earned two advanced degrees, and we experienced many aspects of independent adult life without the responsibilities (and joys!) of parenting. But such a decision would have been unusual 50 years ago and almost unheard of 100 years ago. The acceptability of "starting a family" so long after starting our family—just that difference—changed the whole structure of our lives. If we had felt more pressure to have children earlier, I could imagine a whole sequence of events—paths not taken—that would have changed everything.

- Looking at your own family history, identify a key decision point or event that shaped your family life in the years that followed. For example, it could be a marriage or divorce, the birth of a child, or a change in family structure.

- Make a list of family events and decisions that followed from that turning point—things that depended on that historical event: for example, how divorce set different family members heading in their own directions or how births changed a family dynamic.

- Using your imagination, relocate that turning point to a different historical moment. For example, consider the family living in colonial America, the Industrial Revolution of the nineteenth century, or the 1950s.

- In a short essay or even a brief outline, describe how the decision or event you selected might have been different in the alternative time period. How would cultural or economic pressures have led family members to make different decisions?

- In your essay or in a class discussion, try to spin out the implications of this imaginary scenario. What would be different for the family if that turning point had been reached at a different time in history? Your answers might help explain how historical context shapes the paths of our lives in ways we don't notice at the time.

the state arena, citizenship rights come with responsibilities that restrict our choices, from taxation to regulation to (at the extreme) compulsory military service. In the market, the freedom to contract our own labor also gives employers the freedom to hire and fire without regard for loyalty. In the family arena, the independence achieved in the twentieth century introduced a sense of instability that once was unfamiliar but now has become a way of life. As insecurity in the market and family arenas has increased—epitomized by job loss, falling wages, divorce, and single parenthood—some people argue that the state should provide additional protections to individuals (Saraceno and Keck 2011). This question is at the center of much of the policy debate we will explore in Chapter 13.

Children and Families: Emotional Bonds

As marriage has changed—becoming more emotional and less essential, more an expression of independence than of dependence—how have the relationships between parents and children changed? Falling birth rates, especially after the baby boom, mean that children have fewer siblings today than they did in previous eras, so the interactions between parents and their few children may have grown more individually intensive. The period of parenting also seems longer, as the typical young adulthood has been extended by more years of education, delays in starting careers, and later marriage (Furstenberg 2000). We will return to parenting attitudes and practices in Chapter 9.

Although multigenerational living has in general become less common (as shown by the declining number of extended households in Figure 2.6), some grandparents have grown emotionally closer to their grandchildren than they were in the past (Bengtson 2001). Grandparents live longer than they used to, enjoying more years in better health. And with fewer grandchildren to dote on, they may have longer-lasting, more emotional relationships with their grandchildren. On the other hand, the greater physical distances between family members and the financial independence of older Americans make those relationships more voluntary, and some people never develop them (Cherlin and Furstenberg 1986). For those grandparents, the greater independence mentioned above might also lead to loneliness, a growing problem among the older population.

This pattern of development—a growing emphasis on family relationships based on emotional bonds rather than practical need—may have occurred sooner among middle-class and affluent families, for whom the economic basis of marriage was less important. Nevertheless, thanks to its dissemination through popular culture and mass media, the ideal of the love-based marriage is now widely shared among poor and working-class families as well. One pattern that seems to be distinctive among poor families is a trend toward more direct caregiving by grandparents. This is partly because of the prevalence of single-parent families among the poor, especially those who are African American or American Indian. These families may rely on grandparents—many of whom are healthy, active, and under age 60—to help care for their children (Simmons and Dye 2003). Thus, the growing diversity of family arrangements includes an increasing support role for some grandparents and increasing independence for others. Although that independence is a welcome development, and most old people would rather live alone than with family members, it comes with the risk of isolation (Klinenberg 2012).

Meanwhile, among the middle class, some middle-aged adults are feeling a

What are some reasons grandparents might play an increased role in their grandchildren's lives?

care squeeze (Spillman and Pezzin 2000). Many adults (usually women) in their 40s find themselves raising adolescent children at the same time they are caring for aging parents. Even if all three generations involved are physically healthy, those in the middle, who have been labeled the "sandwich generation," may face conflicts managing the emotional, practical, and financial needs of their parents and children simultaneously, often while going through their own midlife crises (Roots 1998). The difficulties women encounter are exacerbated by their increased career commitments (see Chapter 11), even though they still do the majority of family care work, and the likelihood that they have few siblings to share the load.

What's in a Name?

I conclude this chapter with an example of how the family and identity choices we now face may be liberating even as they increase anxiety: the problem and opportunity of choosing names. Married people choose their own names, and parents choose names for their children. Neither decision was complicated 100 years ago, but both have grown much more so in recent decades.

Before the 1970s, it was very rare for American wives not to assume the family surname of their husbands. No laws regulated this practice one way or the other until the 1970s, when there was a sudden spate of laws either permitting women to keep their family name or, in some cases, requiring them to take their husband's name. Although this was resolved within a few years—no states now forbid women to keep their maiden name—the uptick in legal activity showed that the question had become a pressing issue.

In recent years, only 3 percent of married women over age 60 have had a surname that differs from their husband's, compared with 9 percent of those under age 30 (Gooding and Kreider 2010). With almost 1 in 10 couples choosing to have different surnames, this clearly is a question almost everyone must consider.

Naming children presents an entirely different set of options, opportunities, and potential anxieties. Modernity theory suggests that individuality emerged as a project in the twentieth century, and parents seem to have adopted that project with respect to their children. As noted earlier, many parents used to name their children after themselves. Some still do, but many more choose a name simply because they like it (one that sounds pretty, for example), because it signals a certain style (such as an old-fashioned name), because it represents the kind of person they hope their child will become (a popular political figure or celebrity), or because it shows their creativity (an invented name). This question has become important enough, and difficult enough, that there are many books, articles, and websites to help parents make this pivotal decision. There's even a book called *Baby Names for Dummies*.

The result of all these choices has been a tremendous increase in the diversity of names. Using a technique developed by Stanley Lieberson (2000), I illustrate this trend by showing the percentage of all girls born who were given the most popular names in each decade from the 1940s to the 2010s (Figure 2.8). As you can see, in the 1940s, the top 100 names for girls made up almost two-thirds of all names. Now the top 100 account for less than one-third. The five most popular names alone dropped from 15 percent to less than 5 percent of the total during that time.

Figure 2.8 **Top 100 girls' names as percent of all girls born, 1940s–2010s**

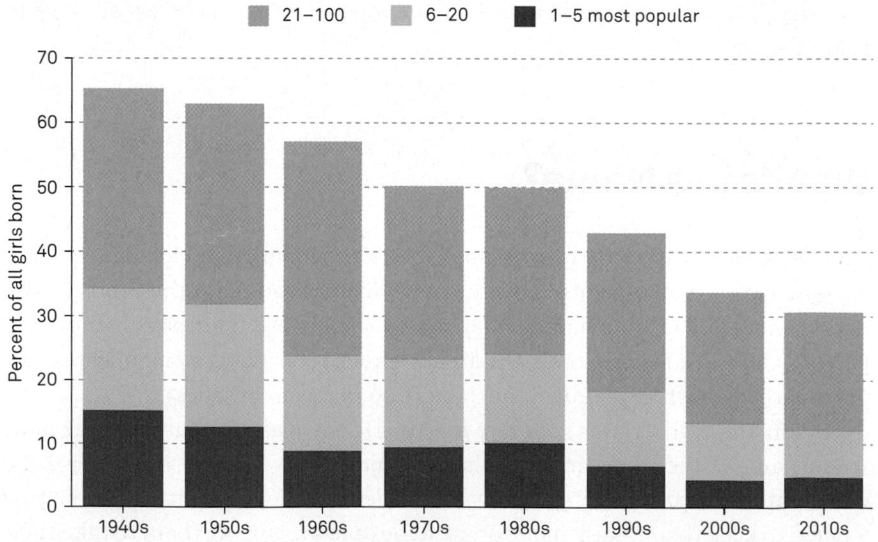

SOURCE: Author's calculations from Social Security Administration (2016).

Another way to view this trend is to focus on the most common girl's name, which was Mary in the earliest recorded records in this country all the way through 1961—probably 200 years (except for six years in the 1950s, when Linda topped the chart). Since then, no name has been in the number 1 spot for more than 15 years (Jennifer, 1970–1984). Emily had a chance, from 1996 to 2007, but her reign ended in time to fit the pattern of declining name dominance over time. In fact, Mary has dropped out of the top 100 for the first time, falling to 124th as of 2015, and now names like Rylee and Kayla are more popular.

We can't assume that these naming trends mean that people are just more individualistic or less conformist than they used to be—although they may be. Rather, the fact that people have to choose—to make an active choice, rather than follow a tradition—naturally leads to a greater diversity of outcomes. Family life in the last half-century reflects the same tendency. As people become *free* to make choices, they are also *compelled* to make choices. And when people choose, the outcomes are much more varied than when there are no choices to make.

This insight about the increasing diversity of personal names opens a window onto a different source of family diversity, as well as inequality and change: the racial and ethnic variations in the United States, both in the past and in the present. Building on the history of families told here, the next chapter will help us understand the story of family diversity.

Trend to Watch: Urban Transformations

In the early twentieth century a new generation of independent, employed young adults came of age in rapidly growing industrial cities such as New York, Chicago, and Detroit. They left home in the evenings—unsupervised—to socialize in the clubs, dance halls, and amusement parks that sprung up to serve them (Peiss 1986). Eventually, those cities would spawn the car culture that came to dominate the twentieth century, and with it the emergence of the dating system.

If dense urban environments helped create the new American adulthood in the 1920s, the suburban environment helped make the unique style of family life that emerged from the 1950s—living in single-family homes relatively isolated from each other. Their teenaged children were more likely to meet up at the multiplex movie theater than at a corner store or neighborhood coffee shop.

Today's cities are changing again. Young, single adults—especially women—are increasingly drawn to cities where the best new job opportunities are found (Traister 2016). Especially attractive are those areas where they can live close to work, walk and bike around their neighborhoods, and socialize in close proximity with like-minded peers. That dense social life allows people to use hookup apps like Tinder and Grindr to find partners nearby. As more cities encourage programs such as bike-sharing, car-sharing, and even sharing housing through apps like Airbnb, the appeal to young adults with few family commitments may grow more.

On the other hand, some older people—including those whose children have left the family nest, those who are single, and those who are widowed—are finding it easier to live in small apartments in urban areas, provided they have helpful and convenient amenities nearby. Smart city planners are responding to this demand as well (Klinenberg 2012). Urbanization transformed family life over a century ago. Now today's evolving family life is contributing to a new transformation of our cities. It's too early to tell what city life will be like for the next generation, but there is little doubt that the new family diversity is helping to shape that future.

KEY TERMS:

nuclear family   **heterogamy**

homogamy   **patriarchy**   **coverture**

extended families   **stem family**

courtship   **separate spheres**

monogamy   **polygamy**

companionship family

companionate marriage

dating   **family wage**   **baby boom**

Questions for Review

1. What are the prehistoric origins of family life?

2. Compare the relationship between men, women, and children in American Indian families, Colonial American families, and enslaved African families prior to 1820.

3. How did married life change during the nineteenth century? Why?

4. How was family life disrupted for many African Americans, the Chinese, and Latinos in the nineteenth century?

5. How is the companionship family different from the patriarchal family? What led to the emergence of the companionship family in the twentieth century?

6. Why was there a baby boom in the middle of the twentieth century?

7. Beginning in the 1960s, why did family patterns depart so dramatically from the 1950s ideal?

8. What factors led to the decline in the number of married couples in the late twentieth century?

9. How have the relationships between parents and children changed since the 1960s?

3

Race, Ethnicity, and Immigration

Before we can learn how race and ethnicity connect to questions of family diversity, inequality, and social change, we need to know what race and ethnicity are. Not surprisingly, this is a complicated issue, as the following example illustrates.

Kylie Hodgson and Remi Horder, a British couple who each had a White mother and Black father, had twins. The twins were fraternal, meaning they share many but not all of the same genes. Although both parents would likely be seen as Black (or African American) in the United States, the twins differ from each other by skin color. The genetic difference between them is very small. And yet if they had been separated at birth, they would likely have different outcomes in life—not because of the inherent differences between them, but because of how others would see them and how they would come to see themselves. (A couple with a similar experience is pictured on the next page.) Do they belong to different races?

Sometimes, as in this case, race appears to be a simple accident of birth. But the community we are born into—and the category we inhabit as we grow up and interact with our family and the wider world—are the result of much larger social forces. These forces have profound effects on everyone, directly and indirectly, through our families.

What Are Race and Ethnicity?

We begin with some terms and definitions that will help us make sense of the facts and stories that follow.

Sophia Greenwood's drawing of her family. Sophia's mother had Black and White parents, and Sophia's father is White. Through interracial marriage and adoption, Sophia also has close relatives from Costa Rica and South Korea.

Twins who look like they are of different races challenge social ideas of race and ethnicity. Dean Durrant, who is of West Indian origin, and Alison Spooner, who is White, have two sets of twins. In each set, the twins would probably be labeled as different races by strangers. How might they be treated differently?

Biology and Race

The surface differences between groups of people around the world led scientists in the eighteenth century to attempt to categorize people into "races," which roughly corresponded to populations of the different continents (Banton 1998). After Charles Darwin's theory of evolution gained currency, nineteenth-century scientists ranked the races in hierarchical order, believing that the more advanced (that is, richer and more powerful) populations were more evolved (Gould 1996). Now, however, biologists understand that the groups commonly called "races" do not fit the scientific criteria for racial classifications we see in other animals, where subspecies, or "breeding populations," are genetically more distinct from each other (Keita et al. 2004). That is because modern humans emerged from Africa quite recently in evolutionary time—probably just 50,000 to 80,000 years ago—to populate the other continents (Zimmer 2016). And even then they did not remain truly separate populations, but rather continued to migrate around and produce mixed children, preventing the formation of very different races (Cohen 2015).

Ironically, the difference on the surface—skin color—is perhaps the most important biologically. Among people who lived near the equator, dark skin was an important adaptation that improved survival dramatically. Because they were more likely to live long enough to become parents, dark-skinned people came to dominate the populations near the earth's equator. Other differences between groups, such as facial shape or hair type, do not appear to affect survival, so scientists now believe that they evolved randomly from groups living apart (Berg et al. 2005). After being separated for just a few tens of thousands of years, the worldwide remixing of human groups in modern society is further undermining genetic differences between groups of people.

Definitions

So *biology* doesn't support the classification of people into races. But deeply felt divisions between groups of people remain important *socially*. In the United States, the federal government collects information about race and ethnicity mostly to enforce civil rights laws against discrimination. According to the U.S. Census Bureau, the government's main statistical agency, the racial categories they measure are "not an attempt to define race biologically, anthropologically or genetically," but rather "reflect a social definition of race recognized in this country" (U.S. Census Bureau, 2012e). So how do we arrive at that social definition?

One important modern principle used in almost all data collection about race and ethnicity involves self-identification: the race and ethnicity you choose are up to you (or your parents, if you're too young to fill out the form). And you don't have to offer any proof to justify your choice. In practice, however, the definitions that people apply to themselves usually conform to how others see them as well. That means that self-identity is partly a social product. This quality—self-definition as a social product instead of a fixed, objective category—is one reason we say that race and ethnicity are *socially constructed*. The categories we use, and the assignment of individuals to categories, are the outcome of social interaction and beliefs; they change over time, and they differ from place to place.

The original American definition of *Black* is a good example of social construction. During the period of slavery, anybody who had any identifiable African ancestry, no matter how remote, was considered Black in the eyes of both the law and White society. That was the so-called one-drop rule, referring to one drop of African blood (also known as the rule of hypodescent). It was not based on a scientific understanding of race, but rather on the economic interests of male slave owners, who wanted to make sure that the children they fathered with Black slave women remained their property instead of becoming their heirs (R. Moran 2001). By this one-drop rule, a White woman could give birth to a Black child, but a Black woman couldn't give birth to a White child (Fields 1982:149). Although the U.S. Census included the racial category "mulatto" for mixed-race individuals for several decades after 1850 (see Changing Law, "How the U.S. Government Measures Race"), this peculiar rule has largely stuck (mostly informally) to the present day. That is why Barack Obama grew up with a Black self-identity and was labeled the first Black president, because his father was Black, even though his mother was White.

Race and ethnicity are both socially constructed, but the two concepts reflect different ideas. Racial identities reflect perceptions about biological traits. A **race** is a group of people believed to share common descent, based on perceived innate physical similarities (Morning 2005). Note that common descent and physical similarity remain a matter of perception, not biological certainty. Racial identity is usually passed from parents to children within families, and family interaction is the first site of racial self-awareness.

race

A group of people believed to share common descent, based on perceived innate physical similarities.

How the U.S. Government Measures Race and Ethnicity

The statistics in this book mostly rely on the race and ethnicity categories used in the latest Census, in 2010. The U.S. government at that time counted five distinct races—White, Black, American Indian or Alaska Native, Asian, and Native Hawaiian or Pacific Islander—and allowed people to identify with as many of these races as they like. It also counted, in a separate category, Hispanic or Latino ethnicity. These categories are established by the federal government and implemented by agencies across the country, the most prominent of which is the U.S. Census Bureau, which is mandated by the U.S. Constitution to conduct a count of the population every 10 years.

The racial identification question from the 2010 census form is shown in Figure 3.1. You will notice several confusing things about the question. For example, although Asian is considered one of the "race" groups, the form actually lists a series of national origins (e.g., Chinese, Filipino), and there is no check box labeled "Asian." That is because many people from these

Figure 3.1 **2010 Census race question**

What is Person 1's race? *Mark* ☒ *one or more boxes.*
- ☐ White
- ☐ Black, African Am., or Negro
- ☐ American Indian or Alaska Native — *Print name of enrolled or principal tribe.* ↗

☐ Asian Indian   ☐ Japanese   ☐ Native Hawaiian
☐ Chinese   ☐ Korean   ☐ Guamanian or Chamorro
☐ Filipino   ☐ Vietnamese   ☐ Samoan
☐ Other Asian — *Print race, for example, Hmong, Laotian, Thai, Pakistani, Cambodian, and so on.* ↗   ☐ Other Pacific Islander — *Print race, for example, Fijian, Tongan, and so on.* ↗

☐ Some other race — *Print race.* ↗

SOURCE: 2010 Census race question (U.S. Census Bureau 2010b).

groups don't express a racial identity beyond their country of ancestral origin. To make matters still more complicated, the Latino group, which is considered ethnic, not racial, is identified in a separate question altogether (not shown here). As a result of the multiple-race option ("one or more boxes") and the separate Latino identification, any one person may be a member of many racial and ethnic combinations.

The 15 possible check boxes on the 2010 census form represent only the latest attempt by the government to keep up with America's changing demography and culture. In fact, since 1880, the race and ethnicity categories on the census form have changed every decade. For example, the only Asian category in 1870 was "Chinese." The category for Americans of African descent was "Black" in 1850, along with "Mulatto"—used for those of mixed African and European descent. In 1930, both were dropped for "Negro," which became "Negro or Black" in 1970 and "Black, African American or Negro" in 2000 (Farley and Haaga 2005). Finally, in 2013, the Census Bureau announced it would drop the category "Negro" on future forms, leaving simply "Black or African American" (Yen 2013).

The most important recent change to this system of categories was the option to check more than one race identification box, implemented in 2000. This policy was a response to the growing presence of interracial couples, who resisted the instruction to impose one racial category on their children (Brunsma 2005). The change also was aimed at the millions of immigrants, most from Latin America and Asia, for whom the American system of racial classification was uncomfortable and often confusing (J. Lee and Bean 2004). For example, many Latinos consider themselves to be White but also another race, such as Indian (referring to the descendants of Central and South America's indigenous populations).

In practice, however, relatively few people identify as more than one race. From the 2015 American Community Survey, the Census Bureau estimates that a total of 10 million out of 321 million people in the United States identify as more than one race, and one-quarter of them were Latinos (see Figure 3.2). Nevertheless, this relatively small population of multiracial people is very diverse, representing many different combinations. Allowing them to choose more than one racial category has improved the identification process for them, even though it has complicated the work of demographers and government statisticians.

The categories have changed many times over the years, and they are now changing again (Cohn 2016). In 2020, the Census Bureau will probably begin using a new form. (This change is still in the proposal stage as I write in 2017, but I think it's on its way toward approval.) To clear up confusion many people have over the difference between "race" and "ethnicity," they propose combining the races and Latino ethnicity into one question, using general wording such as, "What category describes this person?" Then the form will offer the list of races, and Latino origin, all in one box. This is mostly because many Hispanic people did not know which race they should choose.

In addition, they are likely to add a new category, "Middle Eastern or North African" (MENA, for short). MENA is a geographic designation rather than a race or ethnicity covering roughly the area from Morocco in North Africa east to Iran, including the northern African countries of Algeria, Libya, and Egypt, the Arab countries of the Middle East (such as Syria, Iraq, Palestine, and Saudi Arabia), and Israel. Before now most of the people whose ancestry traces to these regions have identified themselves as White in the U.S. system, but often with some confusion—and many Americans don't treat Arab immigrants, for example, as "White,"

Figure 3.2 **U.S. population, by race and ethnicity, 2015**

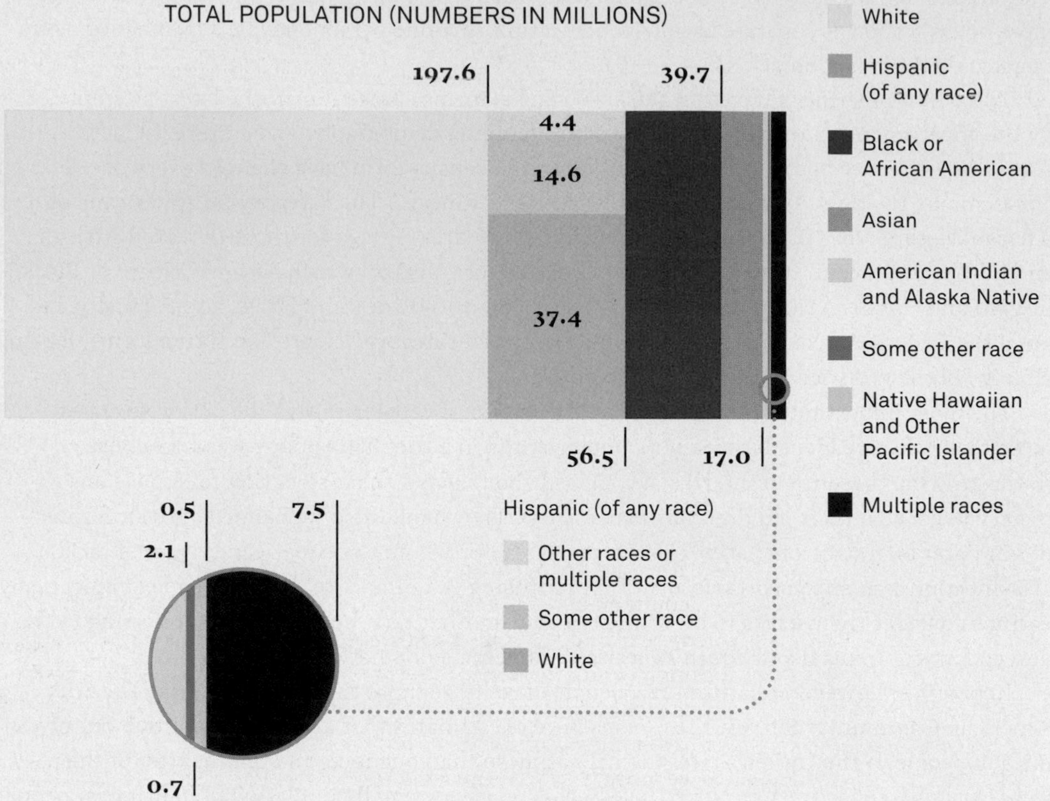

TOTAL POPULATION (NUMBERS IN MILLIONS)

White

Hispanic
(of any race)

Black or
African American

Asian

American Indian
and Alaska Native

Some other race

Native Hawaiian
and Other
Pacific Islander

Multiple races

197.6

39.7

4.4

14.6

37.4

56.5   17.0

0.5   7.5

2.1

0.7

Hispanic (of any race)

Other races or
multiple races

Some other race

White

Racial and ethnic identification are complex. Of the 2015 population of 321 million people, estimated by the U.S. Census Bureau, the largest group, non-Hispanic Whites, was 197.6 million. About 56 million were Hispanic, two-thirds of whom (37.4 million) considered themselves White as well. Most of the Black, Asian, American Indian, or Pacific Islander people only used one racial category. Finally, 7.5 million non-Hispanic people identified as more than one race.

SOURCE: Author analysis of American Community Survey data from Ruggles et al. (2016).

either. The MENA category will include Muslims, Christians, and Jews, and people speaking Arabic, Persian, Hebrew and other languages. There are an estimated 2 million people with MENA ancestry in the United States, about half of whom are immigrants (Jong and Batalova 2015). The Census Bureau believes that putting these groups into one category will reduce confusion, but time will tell.

For now, we continue to use the categories as shown in Figure 3.2, which provides a convenient way of handling the complexity of this system. In the column for total population, I have included each person in only one category, with all Latinos placed together (56.5 million) regardless of which racial category they identified. The main column also shows the 7.5 million people (not including Latinos) who chose more than one race. In most of the statistics in this book, however, I follow a common convention by including multiracial people in the largest non-White group they identify (for example, people who choose Black and White are included in the Black category).

One consequence of the option to choose more than one race is a weakening of the informal rule of "one-drop" identification of African Americans. Rather than simply identifying children of any Black parent as Black, an increasing number of interracial couples are identifying their children as members of both of their parents' races. Although their numbers remain relatively small, this may be an important historical development within families. In 2015, for example, the Census Bureau recorded about 67,000 children born to married couples in which one parent was White and one was Black, and in 73 percent of those families, the infants were identified as both White and Black on the Census form (American Community Survey 2015, via Ruggles et al. 2016). This simple response to the multiple-race option shows the symbolic power of a government category to alter such intimate details of individuals' lives as their racial identity.

On the other hand, ethnic identities are focused on cultural traits. An **ethnicity** is a group of people with a common cultural identification, based on a combination of language, religion, ancestral origin, or traditional practices. One important difference between ethnicity and race is the sometimes voluntary nature of ethnic identity. Ethnicity can change over a person's lifetime—for example, when a child grows up and leaves the family. It can even change from one social setting to another, as when we move from a group of friends to a family celebration. Racial identity is more stable.

In the United States, the concepts of race and ethnicity often overlap. Thus, many people use the ethnic term *African American* and the racial term *Black* interchangeably, because that group includes both perceived physical similarities and common cultural identification. On the other hand, Latinos (also known as Hispanics) are usually thought of as an ethnicity because of a shared cultural heritage. But in other ways they are thought of in racial terms, as when a person is said to "look" Latino. As a result, both African Americans and Latinos fit the combined concept of a racialized ethnic group, or a **racial ethnicity**, which is an ethnic group perceived to share physical characteristics. (To make it clear that I am referring to cultural groups instead of skin colors, as the names imply, in this book I capitalize *Black* and *White* along with other racial-ethnic groups.)

In light of such confusing concepts and categories, it is worth asking why sociologists and government bureaucrats go to the trouble of classifying people this way. I believe such classifications make sense for two reasons. First, many aspects of family and social life still reflect persistent separation between people along racial-ethnic group lines. Despite a remarkable loosening of the boundaries in this country, most people still live, marry, reproduce, and raise children primarily within their own racial-ethnic group. This practice of marriage and reproduction within a distinct group is called **endogamy**, and it is the most important

ethnicity

A group of people with a common cultural identification, based on a combination of language, religion, ancestral origin, or traditional practices.

racial ethnicity

An ethnic group perceived to share physical characteristics.

endogamy

Marriage and reproduction within a distinct group.

If you didn't know who this man was, would you describe him as "African American"? (He's Usain Bolt.)

way people maintain group boundaries from one generation to the next. (Marriage outside one's group is known as **exogamy**; both it and endogamy are discussed in Chapter 8.)

Second, the enforcement of these divisions in the past has stamped contemporary American society with long-lasting inequalities between racial-ethnic groups. Because of that legacy, many people still discriminate against members of other groups and maintain deeply held preconceptions about their nature and human qualities. As long as people mistreat others based on their racial-ethnic identities, these group definitions continue to matter. In other words, because our daily experience is partly shaped by our identification with racial and ethnic categories, both social scientists and government officials need to pay attention to these distinctions.

exogamy

Marriage and reproduction outside one's distinct group.

What about Whites?

Interestingly, as some researchers have discovered, Whites often do not identify themselves as a member of *any* racial or ethnic group (M. McDermott and Samson 2005). Of course, as I mentioned in Chapter 2, European Americans get a lot of attention in this book by virtue of their dominance of economic, cultural, and political life in the United States. But we should consider them as a distinct group as well.

According to racial statistics, Whites are the largest group in the United States, even if Latinos who also consider themselves White are excluded. This group today includes people from a wide variety of ethnic backgrounds, mostly from Europe. But they were not always seen as one race. In the nineteenth century, many people spoke of the creation of an "American" race made up of the different European groups that constituted the majority of the population. For example, the writer Timothy Wilfred Coakley said, "We have evolved the race of races, the American race," which he described as a "racial fraternity" of diverse Europeans—not including the many American Indians, Mexicans, Blacks, and Asians in the country at that time (Coakley 1906).

The concept of an American race mostly faded away in the twentieth century, replaced by the term *White* (although many people continued to use the erroneous term *Caucasian*). But not all Europeans were automatically considered White. The waves of immigrants from Germany, Ireland, Italy, and Eastern Europe in the nineteenth and early twentieth centuries each went through a period when they were excluded from the mainstream and considered outsiders (Ignatiev 1995). In successive waves, only as each group intermarried with other Europeans, improved their economic status, and moved out of immigrant ghettoes in the major cities were they widely accepted as White (Painter 2010).

Because these groups do not enforce strict boundaries to intermarriage, over time they have become combined in many different ways. Some White Americans have a strong ethnic identity associated with their European ancestry, while others do not. The Census Bureau offers blank spaces for people to write in their "ancestry," however they define it, and two-thirds of Whites wrote something in. Table 3.1 shows the most common responses offered. We should not consider

Table 3.1 **Ancestry of White, non-Hispanic Americans, 2015**

ANCESTRY	PERCENT
German	22.9
Irish	16.3
English	12.0
Italian	8.1
Polish	4.5
French	3.8
American Indian	3.2
Scottish	2.7
Norwegian	2.2
Dutch	2.1

SOURCE: Author's calculations from the 2015 American Community Survey data from IPUMS (Ruggles et al. 2016).

these to be strictly accurate counts of actual national origins, however, since many people leave the spaces blank, and those who do write something may be referring to either distant or recent ancestry and may be considering only some of their ancestors. In addition, some people write in terms that are not especially helpful at determining ancestry, such as *United States* or *White*. As with race, there is no enforcement of any particular definition; ancestry, too, is self-identified.

In the rest of this chapter, I will focus on minority groups: American Indians, African Americans, Latinos, and Asian Americans. In sociology, a **minority group** is a racial or ethnic group that occupies a subordinate status in society. Such groups are usually, but not always, smaller than the dominant group. Subordinate groups merit special attention in our sociological analysis because their status raises questions about rights and social justice, which are sources of conflict and change in society.

minority group

A racial or ethnic group that occupies a subordinate status in society.

The U.S. Population

The growing diversity in family structure (see Chapter 2) has coincided with a rapidly expanding diversity in the racial-ethnic composition of the population. The main factors behind U.S. population change are immigration, especially from Latin America and Asia, and higher birth rates among immigrants and their children than among the more settled groups in the population.

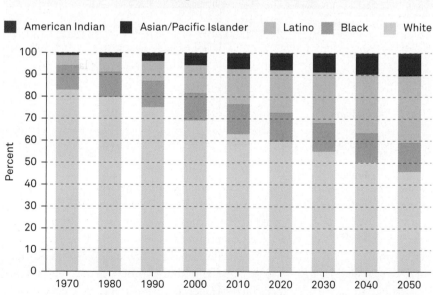

Figure 3.3 **U.S. race-ethnic composition, 1970–2050**

Data for 2020–2050 are projections. The figure includes multiple-race people in their minority-group identities.

SOURCE: Author's calculations from U.S. Census Bureau sources.

The White population is gradually losing its dominant numerical status, as you can see from Figure 3.3. The greatest growth is among Latinos, who in this figure are shown as a separate group regardless of their race. They have more than tripled their share of the population from 1970 to the present and, if current trends continue, will reach 30 percent of the total population by the year 2050. Although much of the Latino population growth results from immigration, high birth rates among Latinos also make a large contribution to the population. On average, Latina women today have about 2.1 children in their lifetime, compared with 1.9 for Black women, 1.8 for non-Hispanic Whites, 1.7 for Asian women, and 1.3 for American Indians (Hamilton, Martin, and Osterman 2015). The Asian population increase is mostly the result of immigration.

Chapter 2 described the growing exercise of choice in how people shape their family lives. In this chapter, we will see that some of the change in family structure has also resulted from a *lack* of choice, as people make family decisions in reaction to changing circumstances beyond their control. The trend toward more racial and ethnic diversity adds a layer of complexity to this story and makes it harder and harder to identify one dominant type of family.

American Stories

The history related in Chapter 2 is one of growing individual independence as a feature of modernity. But for many members of minority groups, the struggle for *collective* autonomy and self-determination remains a dominant theme in family life (P. Collins 1994). Therefore, we need to pay attention to the larger social issues affecting each race and ethnic group. Because we have not yet discussed in depth some of the topics we will cover here, such as marriage and childbearing, we will return to these topics in more detail in later chapters. For now, we will simply introduce each minority group as a building block in our larger story of diversity, inequality, and social change.

American Indians

The story of how hundreds of tribes that were once spread all across North America shrank to a tiny fraction of the U.S. population is one of conquest, genocide, oppression, and perpetual struggle. For American Indian families—many now living hundreds of miles from their ancestral homelands, in territories chosen by the government for their undesirable qualities—those harsh realities remain very real to the present day. On the other hand, the family life of American Indians has been crucial to their survival and persistence and gives meaning to the lives of many people who remain connected to the cultural traditions of their ancestors.

There is no way to know for sure, but by one authoritative estimate, there were about 1 million American Indians and 350 tribes living in the areas now covered by the United States around the year 1600, when Europeans arrived. By the start of the twentieth century, that population had been catastrophically reduced by two-thirds or more by disease and war (Snipp 2006). Since then, the numbers have rebounded, and by 2010, there were 2.5 million American Indians counted by the census. That number rises to 5.2 million if we include those who self-identify as American Indian as well as another race, reflecting the fact that this group has historically married, reproduced, and lived among the White and Latino populations at relatively high rates. Still, American Indians make up just 2 percent of the U.S. population (Humes, Jones, and Ramirez 2011). The largest tribes today are the Cherokee, followed by Navajo and Choctaw, who together account for 40 percent of those American Indians who specify a tribal identity (Norris, Vines, and Hoeffel 2012).

The rapid growth of the American Indian population over the last century—and the past 50 years in particular—is mostly due to the greater desire, or willingness, of those with mixed ancestry to express that identity (Hobbs and Stoops 2002). That mixed ancestry is part of a painful legacy in which many people left behind their ancestral traditions to become more successful in modern American society. In addition, for decades social welfare authorities forced many American Indian children into boarding schools, or placed them with White foster families, severing their ties with their families and culture (Sullivan and Walters 2011). Even today American Indian children are almost four times more likely than those in the general population to be living in foster families (American Community Survey 2014, via Ruggles et al. 2016). Figure 3.4 shows that those who self-identify as American Indian and another race are in some ways doing better than those who are only American Indian; they have higher rates of education, lower rates of poverty, and fewer children born to unmarried women. But both groups are much poorer, less educated, and show higher rates of single parenthood than the U.S. average.

The Oglala Lakota live on the Pine Ridge Reservation and ride horses as part of a centuries-long horse culture, but also because there is no public bus service.

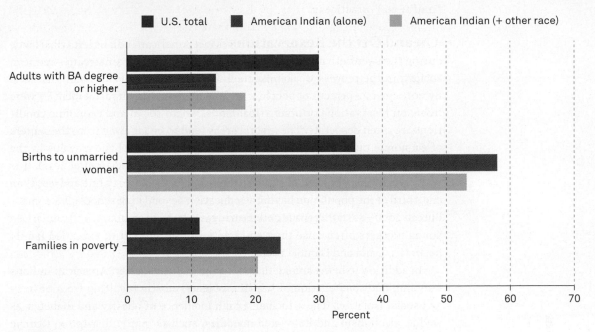

Figure 3.4 **Family profile, American Indians**

SOURCE: American Community Survey 2014 via American FactFinder 2016.

Traditional Family Life

As noted in Chapter 2, families were a central building block of social structure for American Indians before their contact with Europeans (Weaver and White 1997). Their societies frequently stressed the value of cooperation over competition, the well-being of the collective over that of the individual, and a spiritual orientation. Analysis of their ancestral languages shows that family boundaries were often drawn broadly. For example, among the Hopi, mothers' sisters were also called "mother," and maternal cousins were called "brother" and "sister" (Coles 2006).

Some historical practices among American Indians have gained the attention of social scientists, including the acceptance of informal same-sex marriage. In these couples, one of the members fulfilled the duties commonly performed by members of the other sex. Rather than being stigmatized, this cross-gender role was often a recognized status, constituting in effect a third gender identity (Coontz 2005). Also, some (but not most) American Indian tribes practiced polygamy; those men who had enough property to support multiple wives would marry them, and the women's labor would in turn support the larger family (Hoxie 1991).

These are just a few of the diverse family practices among American Indians. Some traditional practices today remain more prevalent on reservations or tribal lands, where they are sources of identity and pride. In these areas, for example, grandparents are more likely to be involved in caring for their grandchildren (Mutchler, Baker, and Lee 2007). However, the massive disruption of their social lives under pressure from the U.S. government and the encroaching non-Indian population meant that the traditional way of life for American Indians was radically transformed, to the point that it has become difficult to identify what a "traditional" practice is.

On and Off the Reservations Most American Indians left tribal lands during the twentieth century and worked their way into mainstream American society, in the process weakening the hold of traditional values and practices. By 2010, just 22 percent of people with an American Indian racial identity were living on reservations or other tribal lands, where social and economic conditions are often desperate. These rural areas tend to be far away from the centers of economic opportunity. The largest reservation, that of the Navajos in the Southwest, has about 175,000 residents (Norris, Vines, and Hoeffel 2012). It is very poor, with 44 percent of children living below the poverty line and less than one-third of the population having an education beyond high school (U.S. Census Bureau 2007–2011a). Teenage childbearing is relatively common, and unmarried young mothers often raise their children with the support of extended family networks (Dalla and Gamble 1998).

In addition to being among the poorest groups in society, American Indians face a unique constellation of health problems, mostly resulting from poverty and social isolation. These include a high incidence of obesity and diabetes, as well as alcoholism and its related maladies, such as family disruption (Sarche and Spicer 2008). They also experience high rates of accidental and violent death, including suicide, especially among young men, for whom suicide rates are more than three times the national average (Indian Health Service 2003). Recently, however, the gambling industry has provided an unexpected flow of increased income into American Indian communities, more than 300 of which now operate casinos in 29 states. Indian-owned gambling facilities in 2011 generated more than $25 billion in revenue, almost twice the level of a decade earlier (National Indian Gaming Commission 2013). These businesses have funded the expansion of social services and the development of new facilities such as schools and medical centers (while generating big profits for some operators). Whether this trend continues and whether it will lead to greater income and well-being for the majority of American Indian families remains to be seen.

African Americans

African Americans were prevented from exercising their family choices first by slavery and then by a series of direct and indirect forces in American society. These included discrimination, poverty, unemployment, high mortality, and segregation. As a result, African Americans have experienced important aspects of racial inequality through their family lives.

Slavery's Legacy There is no doubt that Black families were disrupted in every possible way under slavery (see Chapter 2). But what is the long-term role of slavery's legacy? Social scientists have long considered the impact of slavery on the fate of African American families, with some arguing that it has maintained a powerful presence in family life into modern times. But history also reveals Black family resilience as a recurring theme in the struggle for freedom and survival. These two lines of thought have framed much of the research on Black family life and family structure (S. Hill 2005).

Some early historians assumed that Black family structure reflected cultural traditions passed down from Africa. But early research showed that their families were shaped by slavery, discrimination, and poverty more than by cultural traditions (Frazier 1939). It is true that the families of slaves and their descendants were more fluid and less stable than those of other groups. That is, Black adults had more informal or common-law marriages (in which the partners lived together without the legal recognition of marriage) and higher divorce rates. Black children more often lived with foster or adoptive parents—formally or informally—and more extended family members were directly involved in child rearing (Furstenberg 2007).

With a relatively weak tradition of nuclear families, some people saw Black families as matriarchal, or female dominated. Compared with the White nuclear family—with its image of a strong, providing father and a caring, nurturing mother—this family structure was viewed as a problem for Black families, especially with regard to raising boys to be providers and leaders for their own families.

Those who saw the legacy of slavery as contributing to the contemporary plight of Black families were sympathetic, but their emphasis on family structure created the impression that family behavior, more than ongoing racism and poverty, was the principal cause of racial inequality. One such analyst was Daniel Patrick Moynihan, a sociologist and government analyst who later was a U.S. senator from New York. In what became known as *The Moynihan Report* (1965), he wrote: "A fundamental fact of Negro American family life is the often reversed roles of husband and wife. . . . The matriarchal pattern of so many Negro families reinforces itself over the generations." Because Moynihan (and others) attributed ongoing racial inequality in large part to the nature of Black family life, they appeared to be "blaming the victim" and contributed to racist stereotypes (Ryan 1976). In response, a different story came to dominate research, one that stressed the strength and resourcefulness of Black families.

Family Resilience Long after slavery, economic hardship continued to keep the "traditional" nuclear family out of reach for many African Americans, although it remained the goal most of them sought (Gutman 1976). Strong women's leadership was in part a necessary reaction to such hardships, as Black men alone were rarely able to earn enough to keep their families out of poverty. But rather than adopt the "blame the victim" approach, later scholars tended to see Black families as resilient and adaptive. In this view, Black families may have been more mother-centered, or matrifocal, than White families, but there was no "problem" of female domination (Billingsley 1992). This approach emphasized the economic and political oppression experienced by Black families and saw their fluid family structure as a useful reaction to, rather than a cause of, persistent poverty.

In fact, careful historical research has shown that most African Americans lived in nuclear families in the decades after the Civil War (Gutman 1975). Black women worked at home when possible, adhering to the same ideal of separate spheres for men and women embraced by most Whites (Jones 2010). The end of slavery made it possible to make decisions based on family well-being for the first time. Although those decisions were heavily constrained by the limited economic opportunities for African Americans, the family bonds that emerged from this struggle were uncommonly strong.

Even strong Black families, however, were often forced to separate as fathers migrated in search of work (Griswold 1993). Keeping families together was all the more challenging in the face of high death rates, especially among Black men. At the beginning of the twentieth century, about 4 in 10 Black wives experienced widowhood before they reached age 50. In fact, the uncertainty created by the ever-present threat of sickness and death may have contributed to the tradition of informal marriages among African Americans (S. Preston, Lim, and Morgan 1992). In summary, rather than slavery per se or traditions imported from Africa, it was poverty, lack of opportunity, and mortality that historically limited Black family structure.

Urban Poverty Hurt by the deterioration of the southern agricultural economy, in which many had worked as landless sharecroppers or tenant farmers, and seeking security in industrial jobs, Black workers and their families left the South by the millions between World War I and the 1950s, creating what has been called the Great Migration (Tolnay 1997). Despite new opportunities in blue-collar work, however, the transition was hard (Franklin 1997). In the decades that followed their migration, most African Americans in the North came to live in cities characterized by high levels of residential segregation, with Blacks and Whites living in separate neighborhoods. Often this was a direct result of business and government policies, such as redlining (the denial of loans and other services to people living in a defined neighborhood) and the preferential home mortgage programs for White families mentioned in Chapter 2. In the segregated inner cities where most Blacks lived, poverty and social isolation reinforced each other, even as racial discrimination blocked access to better jobs (W. Wilson 1987). Such patterns of residential segregation have persisted to the present day, as the example of Milwaukee, the most racially segregated city in 2010, illustrates (Figure 3.5).

In the United States today, there is a highly visible Black middle class, which includes many married-couple families (Landry and Marsh 2011) as well as a growing number of single people, whose education and job skills permit them to attain a higher standard of living (Marsh et al. 2007). Today's Black middle class also increasingly lives in suburbs outside of America's major cities (Lacy 2007). These middle-class families are led by workers with either college degrees or valuable technical skills,

Between World War I and the 1950s, millions of Black workers and their families left the South during the Great Migration. Most of them moved to urban cities such as New York City, Chicago, Philadelphia, and Detroit.

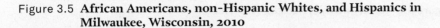

Figure 3.5 **African Americans, non-Hispanic Whites, and Hispanics in Milwaukee, Wisconsin, 2010**

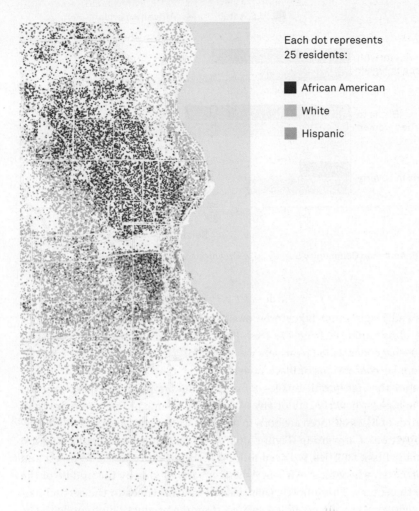

Each dot represents
25 residents:

■ African American

■ White

■ Hispanic

Each dot represents 25 residents: pink for African Americans, yellow for Whites, orange for Hispanics. You can see the almost complete separation of the Blacks from Whites into different parts of the city; Hispanics are heavily concentrated as well, but have more overlap with non-Hispanic Whites.

SOURCE: Author's map created from 2010 Census data accessed via Social Explorer on July 10, 2013.

generating enough income to cover their basic needs, and they usually own their homes (discussed further in Chapter 4).

The growth of the Black middle class has been a cultural event, partly because it represents a dramatic change from the historical dominance of first rural and then urban poverty among the Black population. As a result, popular TV has featured a string of celebratory shows. Most prominently, *The Cosby Show,* which ran from 1984 to 1992, featured a successful doctor married to a successful lawyer and their high-achieving children; it was the most watched series of the 1980s

Figure 3.6 Family profile, African Americans

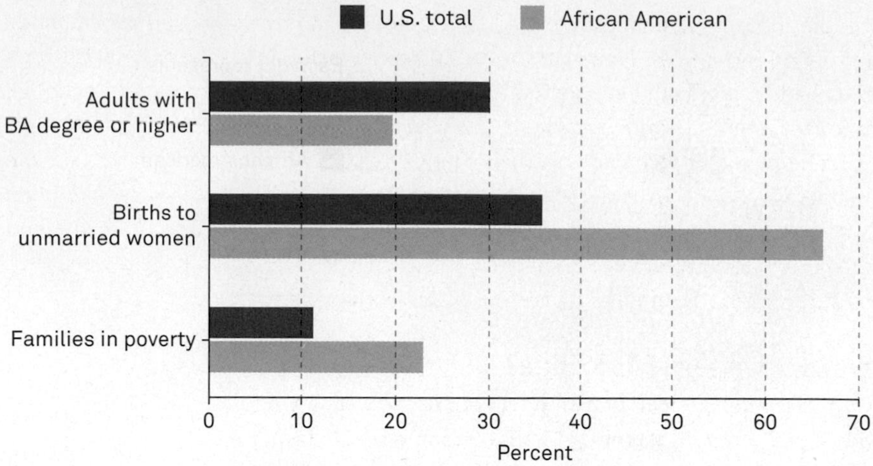

SOURCE: American Community Survey 2014 via American FactFinder 2016.

(Inniss and Feagin 1995). Like *Cosby*, most subsequent shows focusing on Black middle-class families—from *The Fresh Prince of Bel-Air* (1990–1996) to *Blackish* (2014–)—have focused on relatively wealthy families, highlighting the contrast with popular conceptions of Black poverty.

Despite the high-profile images of middle-class families, African Americans have the highest poverty rate of any major racial-ethnic group, and more than two-thirds of Black children are born to mothers who are not married—the highest proportion of any group (Figure 3.6). To understand the difficult situation of so many Black families, we need to look at the big cities in the Midwest and the Northeast, where most African Americans were living by the middle of the twentieth century. Those northern cities fell on hard times in the second half of the century when the economy shifted from the production of goods to the provision of services—from making steel, cars, and appliances, for example, to providing legal and financial services, health care, and insurance. This economic transformation came to be known as deindustrialization (Bluestone and Harrison 1982). And it was steep: the share of workers in manufacturing fell from a third in 1960 to one-fifth in 1990, and then to just one-in-twelve today (U.S. Bureau of Labor Statistics 2016b).

African Americans suffered the most in this transformation for several reasons. First, it was hardest on workers without higher education, especially men. Instead of working in a unionized factory job, as many high school graduates (or even dropouts) did in the 1950s, they were often stuck with poorly paid service jobs or no jobs at all. Second, the loss of jobs was greatest in the old industrial cities, where so many Black families had settled (Kasarda 1989).

As good-paying blue-collar jobs left the cities or disappeared, the concentration of poverty in inner cities became more acute. As a result, poor urban families not only faced unemployment or lower wages but also found themselves surrounded by neighbors in similarly dire straits—a situation exacerbated by rigid residential segregation (W. Wilson 1987). The concentration of poverty contributed to a breakdown in family and other social support systems. Poor people in poor neighborhoods had fewer employed family members or friends to rely on for help (K. Newman 1999). To make matters worse, local institutions that had traditionally supported Black families, such as churches and schools, also lost members and financial resources.

The rise of concentrated urban poverty had many negative effects on the people who lived in America's inner cities. One consequence may have been the most far-reaching family change among African Americans since the end of slavery: the rapid, deep decline in marriage rates, and with it the increase in children born to unmarried parents, which continues to the present.

Retreat from Marriage? In Chapter 2, we saw that married nuclear family households have lost their dominant place in American family structure. Certainly, the drop in marriage rates has not been limited to African Americans (as we will see in Chapter 8), leading some researchers to declare a general "retreat from marriage" (Kobrin and Waite 1984). Among African Americans, however, the trend has been much steeper. As a result, the difference in marriage rates between African Americans and the rest of the population has widened (see Figure 3.7).

There are a number of reasons Black family structure changed with the economic times (W. Wilson 2009). Job loss and economic stress contributed to increased rates of separation and divorce, rates of which have been especially severe among African Americans (R. Taylor 2000). But more important, joblessness also prevented marriage in the first place. Even if it sounds old-fashioned, it's still true that men without jobs usually do not make attractive marriage partners.

Other demographic and economic pressures also reduced the availability of men for Black women to marry (Lichter, McLaughlin, and Ribar 2002). Black men have higher mortality rates and higher incarceration rates than other groups. And most people still marry within their own race—especially Black women, who have the lowest intermarriage rates of any major group. Taken together, these factors have left many Black women facing a shortage of men to marry (Albrecht et al. 1997).

To demonstrate this pattern, consider four of our biggest metropolitan areas: Los Angeles, Chicago, New York, and Philadelphia (see the Story Behind the Numbers). Unmarried, young Black women outnumber unmarried, *employed* Black men in their age group by about 2 to 1 in these areas. The rest of the Black men are either

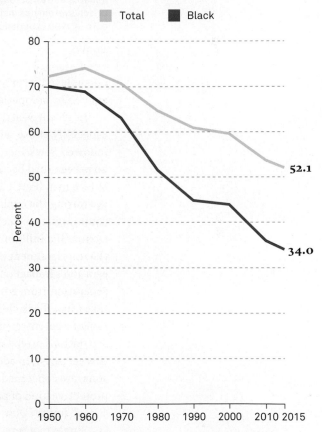

Figure 3.7 **Percentage of adults married, total U.S. and Black population, 1950–2015**

The prevalence of marriage among adults has declined for the whole U.S. population, but the change has been much greater for African Americans.

SOURCE: Author's calculations from U.S. Census data as compiled by IPUMS (Ruggles et al. 2016).

Inmates at New Jersey's Bayside State Prison making license plates. The expansion of the prison system has disproportionately affected Black families: A quarter of Black children born in 1990 experienced the incarceration of a parent at some point in their lives.

unemployed, in prison, in the military, no longer living, or already married. White women by comparison face a much smaller shortage of employed White men.

In recent years, the impact of incarceration on African American families, especially those who are poor, has been dramatic. A longitudinal study that followed Black men born in the late 1960s until they reached age 34 found that 20 percent had been imprisoned at some point, compared with only 3 percent of White men (Pettit and Western 2004). That was the first generation to come of age during the explosive expansion of the prison system, which hit urban Black communities especially hard (Alexander 2010). The number of prisoners grew from half a million in 1980 to more than 2 million by the late 2000s, driven by the imprisonment of more and more people for drug crimes (Lynch 2012). Incarceration's impact on families also extends to children, many of whom experience separation from a parent—usually a father—as a result. Recent research shows that 1 in 4 Black children born in 1990 at some point experienced the incarceration of a parent, compared to just 1 in 25 White children (Wildeman 2009). Those separations often lead to other hardships, including poverty, crime, and violence (Dwyer 2015). In addition to incarceration, Black parents, especially those with sons, are concerned about the threat of police violence. One response has been a protective kind of parenting that aims to keep sons from projecting a dangerous "thug" image (Dow 2016).

Single mothers, incarcerated parents, joblessness, health problems, and the threat of police violence all pose challenges for child rearing. In response, Black grandparents are more likely to live with their grandchildren than are those of most other racial-ethnic groups, as 12 percent share a household with their grandchildren (Ellis and Simmons 2014). Such extended households are a historical continuation of Black family resilience, easing the burdens of racial inequality by pooling social, economic, and emotional resources (P. Cohen 2002).

Latinos

At 59 million, Latinos are the largest minority group in the country (U.S. Census Bureau 2016d). Some Latino families have been in the country for many generations, but a greater number are relatively recent immigrants. Most are of Mexican origin (63 percent), followed by Puerto Ricans (10 percent) and Cubans (4 percent; Ruggles et al. 2016). Despite a common ancestry in the New World colonies of Spain, the circumstances under which different groups of Latinos entered the United States make for very different experiences for their families.

Culture and Diversity The original Mexican Americans were already living on land in the Southwest that was annexed by the United States after the Mexican-American War in 1848. But in recent decades, Mexican immigration has been dominated by poor workers with low levels of education seeking entry-level jobs. Puerto Rico was also annexed—first as a U.S. colony and later as a partly self-governing commonwealth—when Spain ceded the island to the United States in 1898. But the biggest influx of Puerto Rican migrants was in the two decades following World War II, when many poor workers came to New York and New Jersey. (As U.S. citizens since 1917, Puerto Ricans enjoyed automatic right of residency.) In contrast, the first Cubans to arrive in large numbers were fleeing the Cuban revolution of 1959. These were mostly well-educated professionals who were received positively in Florida by the government and assisted financially as political, rather than economic, refugees.

These three groups were joined by later waves of migrants, including growing numbers from Central and South America. Although sometimes poor and desperate, many were surprisingly well prepared for life in their new environs (Bean and Tienda 1987). The continuing flow of immigrants helps maintain a cultural continuity among Latinos, as recent immigrants are welcomed into the established immigrant community (Wildsmith, Gutmann, and Gratton 2003). That's why more than three-quarters of Latinos speak Spanish at home. Because of recent immigration (and higher birth rates), Latinos remain a very young group on average, with a median age of 27.5, which is 10 years younger than the national average (American Community Survey 2011, via American FactFinder 2014).

Since 1917, Puerto Ricans have been U.S. citizens by birth; therefore, they are not immigrants when they move to one of the 50 U.S. states.

Why are there so many single Black women?

http://wwnpag.es/sbtn3

Go to this link for an animation narrated by the author.

The drop in marriage rates has been felt by all groups, but it has been steepest for African Americans. One reason is the situation of Black men. In 50 large metropolitan areas, unmarried, young Black women outnumber unmarried, employed Black men in their age group by about 2 to 1. Many of the Black men are unemployed, in prison, or no longer living. As a result, Black women experience a shortage of men to marry. The economy, job discrimination, incarceration policies, and health disparities all combine to hurt the life chances of Black men and women, including their chance of marriage. For Whites the "marriage market" numbers are much more even.

Due to larger social forces—the economy, job discrimination, incarceration policies, and health issues—Black men under age 35 are:

6x
more likely to be incarcerated than White men

1.8x
more likely than White men to be poor

1.5x
more likely than White males to die before age 35

2x
more likely to be unemployed than White males

Sources: Author calculations from U.S. Census Bureau data provided by IPUMS.org (Ruggles et al. 2014); Glaze (2011); Hoyert and Xu (2012); U.S. Census Bureau (2012d); U.S. Bureau of Labor Statistics (2014b).

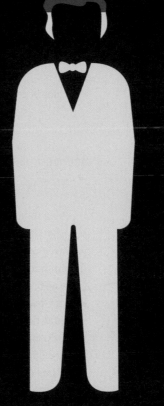

51.1 employed, unmarried Black men

100 unmarried Black women

92.8 employed, unmarried White men

100 unmarried White women

Four Largest Metropolitan Areas

| New York City | Chicago | Los Angeles | Washington, D.C. | New York City | Chicago | Los Angeles | Washington, D.C. |

| 53.4 | 100 | 39.8 | 100 | 52.9 | 100 | 60.1 | 100 | 90.5 | 100 | 94.1 | 100 | 97.3 | 100 | 94.8 | 100 |

Figure 3.8 **Family profile of Latinos, by national origin**

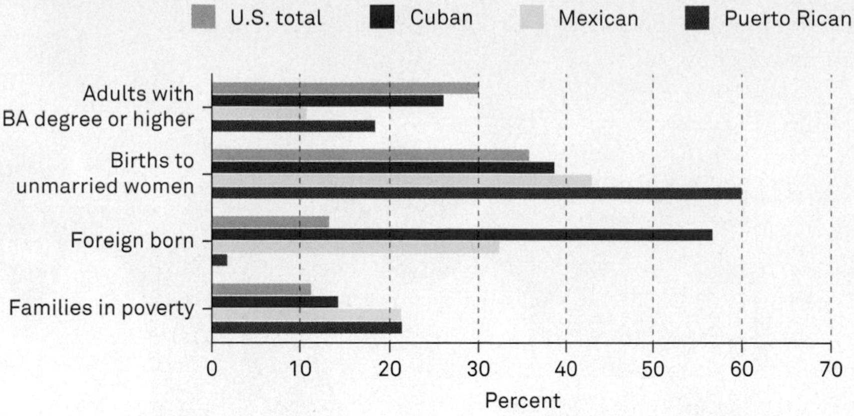

Legend: U.S. total · Cuban · Mexican · Puerto Rican

Categories (y-axis): Adults with BA degree or higher; Births to unmarried women; Foreign born; Families in poverty

X-axis: Percent (0–70)

SOURCE: American Community Survey 2011 via American FactFinder 2014.

As a result of their diverse origins and history, we should not generalize too broadly about different Latino groups (Baca Zinn and Wells 2000). For example, with regard to family structure, Mexicans and Cubans are much more likely to live in married-couple households than are Puerto Ricans, who have much higher rates of births to unmarried women (see Figure 3.8). Still, all Latinos trace their history back to Spanish-speaking countries dominated by a Catholic culture. In colonial days, these societies were generally more tolerant of cultural mixing with Europeans, African slaves, and native people than were the Protestants of the U.S. colonies (Coles 2006). Thus, language, religion, and less rigid racial divisions constitute common elements of Latino culture.

Familism One cultural trait that many observers associate with Latino culture is **familism**, a personal outlook that puts family obligations first, before individual well-being. Even if the extent of this attitude is sometimes exaggerated, family relationships—including strong intergenerational ties—play a central role in daily life for most Latinos. Latinos are two to three times more likely to live in extended families than most other groups. This is especially apparent among Latino immigrants, most of whom maintain close family ties back home. And many have joined relatives in the United States who migrated earlier, creating family chains of immigration (Carrasquillo 2002).

Although some critics believe that strong familism makes the Latino community inward looking and slows their integration into the American mainstream, there is no doubt that family cooperation has also helped immigrants survive and even thrive in their new American context (Sanchez 1993). In fact, if poverty and hardship drive families together for support, strong intergenerational ties among Latinos are probably as much a response to such challenges as they are a reflection of cultural tradition (Baca Zinn and Wells 2000).

Younger average age, more children per family, and extended households all make the average Latino family substantially larger than that of any other

familism

A personal outlook that puts family obligations first, before individual well-being.

major group (Figure 3.9). However, in many respects, Latinos exhibit the same trends followed by the rest of the country. In particular, they, too, have seen a decline in marriage at young ages and a rapid increase in the number of children born to unmarried parents (Landale and Oropesa 2007).

Asian Americans

In Chapter 2, we saw that the first large group of Asians in the United States was Chinese workingmen in the nineteenth century, most of whom did not intend to stay in the country. And because those who did stay were legally forbidden from marrying Whites, their numbers dwindled. However, in waves of migration over the twentieth century, immigrants from many other Asian countries eventually joined them (Takaki 1998). Thus, like Latinos, most Asians are within a few generations of their families' immigration to the United States. Today the U.S. population is 6 percent Asian American, and although still relatively small, they are the fastest growing minority group. The largest groups trace their ancestry to China (23 percent), the Philippines (17 percent), and India (19 percent). Asian immigrants today are mostly professionals, students, or the family members of previous immigrants. And because so many Asian families include immigrants, 70 percent of Asian Americans speak a language other than English at home (Ruggles et al. 2016).

Family Traditions, Modern Times Several features of Asian American families are common—although not universal—among the different national-origin groups. In some communities, especially among Chinese and other East Asians with a Confucian religious background, there is a tradition of striving for educational excellence. Historically, this derives from the ancient Confucian exam system, through which even poor children could achieve success through diligent study (Chao 1995). Parental support for education—some might say parental pressure, as represented by the figure of the "tiger mother" popularized by author Amy Chua (2011)—is one reason why less than 3 percent of Asian Americans 16 to 24 years of age are high school dropouts, compared with 8 percent of the total population (Ruggles et al. 2016).

Most Asian cultures also include strong imperatives to respect and care for elders. Although it is not safe to assume that cultural practices from their homelands are uniformly followed today, Asian Americans remain relatively likely to live in multigenerational households (Jeong and You 2008). Overall, 12 percent of Asian American grandparents live with one or more of their grandchildren (compared with 10 percent of the total population; Ellis and Simmons 2014). Related research has also shown that Asian Americans tend to be more authoritarian in their parenting style and place less value on their children's independence than do members of most other groups (Chao and Tseng 2002).

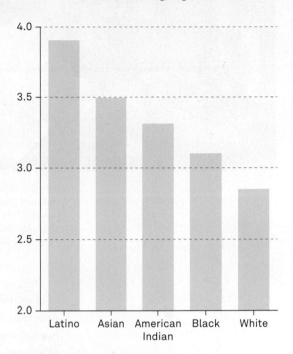

Figure 3.9 **Average number of family members living together**

SOURCE: Author's calculations from American Community Survey 2015 via IPUMS (Ruggles et al. 2016).

Amy Chua (left), a second-generation Chinese American who is a Yale law professor and Harvard graduate, wrote a book about the demanding standards for success she set for her children (2011). However, the diverse Asian-American population also includes many working-class families, such as Southeast Asian immigrants (Kelly 1986). Pictured at right is Ta Poh Poh, a refugee from Myanmar.

Besides cultural tradition, however, there may be other reasons for high Asian American educational achievement. For example, many Asian adults themselves immigrated with higher educational degrees or moved here to study for professional careers, both of which probably help their children do better in school (Lee and Zhou 2015). The common practice of multigenerational living partly results from successful Asian immigrants deciding to bring their elderly parents here to settle and live with them, which is permitted under family reunification laws (Treas 2008). However, while some of these older immigrants are well integrated and feel supported within their families—and provide assistance with child rearing—many others experience loneliness and isolation, having left behind the land of their upbringing as well as friends and other relatives (P. Brown 2009).

Inequality and Diversity As you can see from the profile of the three largest Asian American groups shown in Figure 3.10, members of these groups have higher levels of education, lower levels of unmarried childbearing, and lower poverty rates than the U.S. population at large. As a result, Asian Americans overall have relatively high incomes and occupational status; more than half of Chinese and Asian Indian workers are in managerial or professional occupations (P. Cohen 2012). However, among some smaller groups from Southeast Asia, poverty rates are high, and most adults work in blue-collar occupations (Reeves and Bennett 2004). These stark discrepancies reflect the conditions under which people from different countries came to the United States. The more recent waves of immigrants from Southeast Asia were political and economic refugees, fleeing desperate circumstances in the hope of a better future, usually without professional skills or education.

The success of some Asian immigrants has come at a high cost as well. Ever since the Chinese Exclusion Act of 1882 (see Chapter 2), some Americans have resisted what they see as competition from Asian workers. In one tragic

Figure 3.10 **Family profile of Asian Americans, by national origin**

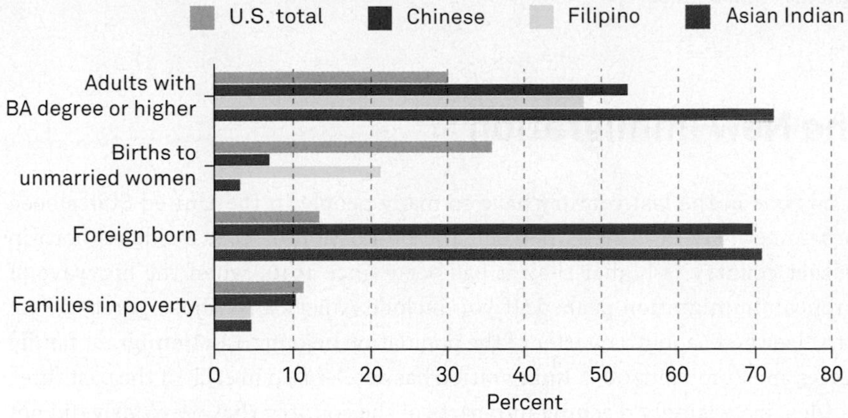

SOURCE: American Community Survey 2014 via American FactFinder 2016.

example, in 1983 a Chinese immigrant named Vincent Chin was beaten to death outside a bar by Detroit auto workers who mistook him for a Japanese man; they blamed Japan for the decline of the American auto industry. Less violent but more widespread, the stereotype of Asian Americans as successful students (the "model minority") may create hostility and cultural division as well as warping the expectations held by teachers and students themselves (Warikoo and Carter 2009).

The diverse origins of minority groups in the United States make it impossible to offer simple generalizations about their experiences. This is especially true among those who have immigrated in the last century or so, whose origins span the globe and whose fortunes are almost as variable. These immigration stories are a vital part of the history of American families—including my own.

Immigration

In 1921, the SS *Ryndam* sailed into Ellis Island, New York, with a cargo of 30 people destined for new lives in the New World. The youngest person on board was Sylvia Patinkin, or Cywja (pronounced "Tzivya") in her native Yiddish language. At age 7, my grandmother—who would live to age 95—was the youngest of seven children, all traveling with their mother. The family had been separated by World War I after their father had left for America. Sylvia's mother was 47 by the time she finally made the journey from Poland to Chicago, where Sylvia's father was waiting for them. Like so many families before them, and millions more since, the Patinkin family was first pulled apart and then put back together through the process of immigration. That journey left no part of the family unchanged—and the immigration of so many families from so many different cultures has had the same effect on this country. Their integration into the new society brings new influences to American families, but it also provokes rapid and sometimes difficult transitions.

The New Immigration

At no time in the last century have so many people in the United States been born somewhere else. At 15 percent, the proportion of U.S. residents born in another country is higher than it has been since 1910, when the big wave of European immigration peaked. If you include Americans whose parents were born elsewhere, about a quarter of the population belong to an immigrant family (Portes and Rumbaut 2005). Immigration has accelerated in each of the past three decades, increasingly reaching into parts of the country that previously did not have large immigrant populations, especially in the Midwest and Southeast. (My own suburban Montgomery County, Maryland, now has a population that is 33 percent foreign born [U.S. Census Bureau 2016e].)

The current wave of immigration dates back to 1965, when a reform of the federal laws allowed the immigration of any number of spouses, children, and parents of U.S. citizens (see Changing Law, "Immigration Uniting and Dividing Families"). This change in policy opened the door to family reunification through immigration, and most legal migration since that time has been family related. Without this principle, immigration would result in an influx of individual workers rather than families; under the law, whole immigrant communities have grown and thrived. Family-based immigration also ensures that immigrant communities are regularly "replenished," which helps the leading immigrant groups—such as those from Mexico, China, and the Philippines—continue to grow as families flourish around the first few members who move here (Waters and Jimenez 2005). On the other hand, a family-based immigration system may increase the social distance between immigrant groups and the rest of society by encouraging them to interact within their own community.

Current immigration debates are complicated by families whose members have different immigration statuses, with one or more undocumented parent and U.S. citizen children.

Generations

When people move from one society to another, they adapt to their new cultural environment through "a complex pattern of continuity and change" (Berry 1997:6). It's not

Immigration Uniting and Dividing Families

Immigration creates both opportunities and obstacles for families. The chance to lead a new life motivates many to move to the United States, but the resulting family dislocation and disruption bring bittersweet returns. Immigration is the journey from one country to another, but it also means crossing a legal border—whether legally or not—so changes in law and enforcement weigh heavily in the process. American legal history has been a seesaw of permissions and penalties for immigration, resulting in confusing patterns of family division and unification, depending at different times on race, ethnicity, national origin, and family structure. The following are a few of the changes that have affected the formation—and separation—of families.

1882: Chinese Exclusion Act

In response to virulent anti-Chinese sentiment among Americans in the West—including those in the White-dominated labor movement—Congress passed the Chinese Exclusion Act, barring Chinese from becoming citizens and blocking new immigration (Berlet and Lyons 2000). That prevented Chinese workers, almost all of them men, from bringing their families. In 1894, Wong Kim Ark, who was born in San Francisco, attempted to visit his parents in China. On his return, the authorities declared that under the Chinese Exclusion Act, he could not be a citizen because his parents were Chinese. But in an 1898 decision, the U.S. Supreme Court sided with Wong and declared that citizenship by birth was guaranteed under the Constitution. Even so, the act prevented most Chinese immigration until 1943.

In *United States v. Wong Kim Ark*, the Supreme Court declared that citizenship by birth was guaranteed under the Constitution. Although this decision is more than a century old, it is at the heart of the current immigration debate.

1924: Immigration Act

After decades of European immigration brought millions to America, Congress virtually shut the door with the Immigration Act of 1924, permitting only a few immigrants per year according to a country-based quota system—and completely shutting off immigration from Asia. As a result, immigrant communities were not "replenished," and their children's integration into mainstream society accelerated.

1945: War Brides Act

Tens of thousands of U.S. military servicemen married local women while serving in Europe or Asia during World War II. The War Brides Act permitted the immigration of their wives and children and later was extended to Korean wives of U.S. soldiers from the Korean War (1950–1953). The immediate welcome these women received was not always warm. Ruth Poore, who had married an American air sergeant in England, arrived in New York with almost 1,000 other women and children. "They had to lock the buses we were held in," she remembered. "We were being picketed by women who were mad at us" (Foley 2004:72).

1942–1964: Bracero Program

Faced with both the need for agricultural workers and popular resistance to full-scale immigration, the United States extended "temporary" work permits to millions of Mexican workers through the Bracero Program. Instead of preventing whole families from immigrating, however, the program opened a door that many families eventually went through. Repeated trips over the border often led to permanent settlement on the U.S. side, where many *braceros* (Spanish for "manual laborers") made the connections necessary to bring family members as well.

Catalina Corella and her daughter Margarita Flores in 1948. They joined Catalina's husband, Jesus Corella, when he worked on a ranch in the Bracero Program.

1965: Amendments to the Immigration and Nationality Act

Among the most important immigration laws of the twentieth century, these amendments to the original 1952 act (which was highly restrictive) lifted all numerical restrictions on the immigration of spouses, children, and parents of U.S. citizens. They also ended the country-based quota system. As a result, most immigrants now arrive as family members, and most of them are from Latin America and Asia.

2002: Homeland Security Act

After a decade of attempts at policing the United States–Mexico border to control illegal immigration, the newly created Department of Homeland Security took over immigration enforcement. Through fence building and patrols along the border, the government has made illegal crossing much more difficult and dangerous. The result, ironically, is that male undocumented immigrants, who used to travel back and forth between work in the United States and their families in Mexico, are more likely to establish permanent residence in the United States and bring their families here to live.

2012: Deferred Action for Childhood Arrivals

Acting without approval from Congress, the Obama administration in 2012 implemented a rule protecting people who had entered the country illegally as children (mostly brought by their parents) from deportation and allowing them to work. The rule was limited to children still in school, young adults who had graduated high school, and military veterans, as long as they were not convicted of a felony. Almost a million young adults were accepted into the program through 2016 (USCIS 2016). It only provided temporary protection, however, and did not grant the immigrants permanent status in the country. And because it was done without Congressional approval, any president has the authority to reverse it without approval, something Donald Trump promised to do during his campaign for the presidency.

a simple process, of course. Immigrants and their children learn the ways of their new homeland through **acculturation**, the acquisition of a new culture and language. For families, that acculturation may be *consonant*, when parents and children together gradually transition away from their home culture and language; or it may be *dissonant*, when children develop English ability more quickly and integrate into the new society more easily than their parents (Portes and Rumbaut 2001).

acculturation

The acquisition of a new culture and language.

Immigrants do not simply join the new culture, however, and leave the old one behind. New groups blend into American society to varying degrees through a process sociologists call **assimilation**, the gradual reduction of ethnic distinction between immigrants and the mainstream society. Both the immigrant group and the mainstream culture adapt to each other, moving toward the point—perhaps never fully reached—when the ethnic distinction is no longer recognized at all (Alba and Nee 2003). Unlike acculturation, assimilation is successful only when the host society accepts the new group (Gans 2007). In the United States, new groups have received very different levels of acceptance, depending on the timing of their arrival, the economic and social role they play, and the attitudes of the dominant group toward them (Portes and Rumbaut 2005). For example, some highly educated Asian immigrants have come as professional workers with good jobs waiting for them, while many less skilled Latinos have come as manual laborers (sometimes illegally), and most recently some Syrians have arrived as refugees from that country's brutal civil war (U.S. Department of State 2016a). Each of these circumstances leads to a very different experience of acculturation and assimilation.

Researchers refer to immigrants according to their relation to the family's migration. So the "first generation" is the immigrants themselves, the "second generation" is their children, and so on. Each generation has its own experience, and in some cases that fosters a strong self-identity. That was the case for Japanese immigrants, known as *issei* (first generation) and *nisei* (second generation). The original immigrants were cultural standard-bearers, and their children played the role of mediators between the old ways and the new society (Glenn 1986). As studies have become more detailed, researchers have discovered that the age at which people immigrate, not just their generation, has a major impact on their role in the family's acculturation (Rumbaut 2004). Table 3.2 shows some of the issues they face, using the terms for these partial "generations."

Generational change is evident among Latino immigrants on such key family indicators as age at marriage (or cohabitation), number of children, and overall family size. For example, Latinas overall average 2.1 children per woman (Hamilton, Martin, and Osterman 2015). However, Latinas born abroad have children at higher rates (about 2.3 per woman) than those born in the United States (about 1.9). So those who are removed by a generation from the immigration experience show family patterns more similar to the dominant culture. Conflicts can arise when the children change more rapidly than their parents, a pattern exacerbated by children's access to new technology, including online media, in addition to their quicker language acquisition. On the other hand, there are many cases in which children of immigrants choose to affirm their ethnic identity by showing their commitment to caring for family members and demonstrating loyalty to their families' collective needs (Pyke 2004).

One recurring theme in the conflicts that arise among immigrant families is the choice of marriage partners made by the young immigrants and those of the second and later generations. The barriers between groups—and the possibility of overcoming them—are perhaps never more clearly exposed than they are when two families view each other across the chapel aisle.

Table 3.2 **Immigrant generations**

GENERATION	AGE AT IMMIGRATION	FAMILY ISSUES
.5 generation ("point-five generation")	Retirement age	Joining their families in the United States at older ages, without command of English or regular employment, these immigrants may feel isolated and dependent on their children. But they provide a connection to their homeland for the grandchildren.
First generation	Working-age adulthood	These are the classic immigrants, whose fateful decision brings the family to the United States, usually for employment or a better future. Despite success at work, they may never feel fully integrated into the new society, especially if they do not learn English well.
1.5 generation	Childhood (especially ages 6–12)	Having learned to speak a different language first, this generation may speak English imperfectly, but they are often the most acculturated members of the immigrant family.
Second generation	Children of immigrants	Born and raised in the United States, but members of an immigrant family, they are the transitional generation, whose easier acculturation may lead to conflict with their parents.
Third generation	Grandchildren of immigrants	They may retain their identity as part of an immigrant family but come to see their ethnicity as family history rather than their own experience.

Intermarriage

Racial and ethnic groups can only exist if the categories they represent stay distinct in the minds of society's members. And the idea of separate groups can only persist as long as there is some actual separation between groups in daily life. For that reason, **intermarriage**, or marriage between members of different

intermarriage

Marriage between members of different racial or ethnic groups.

racial or ethnic groups, is the "litmus test" of racial and ethnic difference. We can use the frequency of intermarriage to measure the degree of integration between two groups. At the same time, the experience of intermarriage *creates* the integration of two groups. In the United States, the stiffest barrier to integration has been between Whites and African Americans.

Black and White

The first U.S. law prohibiting marriage between Blacks and Whites was passed in Maryland in 1661, and most African Americans lived under such laws until the 1960s (Moran 2001). During slavery, White male slave owners fathered many children with Black slave women, and the "one-drop rule" ensured that their children remained slaves, protecting the perceived integrity of the White race. But the possibility of Black men fathering children with White women remained an unacceptable affront to southern White public opinion.

Throughout the period of slavery and well into the middle of the twentieth century, many Whites were willing to resort to violence—legal or illegal—to prevent mixing between the races. Several thousand African Americans were the victims of lynching from the 1880s to the 1930s, and in more than a third of these cases, the mob sought to avenge an alleged interracial sex crime (Tolnay and Beck 1995). In the words of anti-lynching crusader Ida Wells-Barnett (1892), they acted on "the old thread-bare lie that Negro men rape white women." Within the legal system, the process was different, but the outcome was often the same: death. In the twentieth century, 455 Americans were executed for the crime of rape, and 89 percent of them were Black, mostly convicted of raping White women (U.S. Census Bureau 1996:table 357).

Laws against interracial marriage were common in the twentieth century and were on the books in 16 states when they were declared unconstitutional in the 1967 U.S. Supreme Court case *Loving v. Virginia*. (Loving was the name of the White man whose marriage to an African American woman led to their arrest, in their bedroom, by local police.) But old attitudes die hard. In 1973, President Richard Nixon was privately discussing abortion rights (which he opposed) when a hidden microphone captured him saying, "There are times when an abortion is necessary. I know that. When you have a Black and a White. Or a rape" (Savage 2009). That a Black-White pregnancy was at the same level of shame as one resulting from rape pretty well illustrates the strength of the taboo.

Since the 1970s, we've seen steady but slow growth in the rate of interracial marriage. You might say it's grown from "nearly non-existent to merely atypical" (Pew Research Center 2006). By 2015, some 8 percent of married African Americans were married to Whites. But because Whites are the larger group, that translated into less than 1 percent of married Whites (see Figure 3.11).

African Americans remain the minority group that is least likely to marry outside their own race. And it is even less common among Black women than it is among Black men, which is especially notable given the shortage of Black

Figure 3.11 **Black-White marriages, 1970–2015**

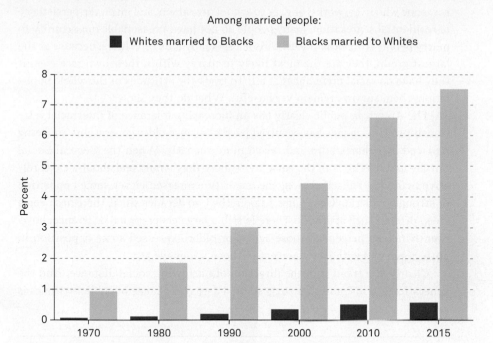

Among married people:

■ Whites married to Blacks   ■ Blacks married to Whites

SOURCE: Author's calculations from Decennial Census (1970–2000) and American Community Survey (2010–2015) via IPUMS (Ruggles et al. 2016).

men described earlier (Crowder and Tolnay 2000). On the other hand, some groups have high rates of intermarriage. In 2015, almost two-thirds of American Indians who married paired up with someone of a different race. The other minority groups were in between, with about one-third of Asian Americans and one-quarter of Latinos marrying someone outside their group (see Figure 8.6). From an ethnic perspective, it is perhaps not surprising that Asians and Latinos are much more likely to marry outside their specific national-origin group (for example, Chinese, Mexican) than they are to marry outside the larger racial-ethnic group (Waters and Jimenez 2005). (We'll have more to say about intermarriage between racial-ethnic groups in Chapter 8.)

The Future of Social Distance

The level of acceptance that members of one group have toward those of another has been called social distance. Some sociologists believe that intermarriage is itself a good measure of **social distance**, because it shows the breakdown—or lack thereof—of society's most rigid taboos (J. Lee and Bean 2004). In fact, because marriage rates reflect concrete actions toward integration, studying

social distance

The level of acceptance that members of one group have toward members of another group.

them may tell us more than we can learn from surveys in which people say what they think about other groups. However, because most people end up marrying someone who lives, works, or goes to school near them, and given the persistence of residential segregation, many people do not have a reasonable opportunity to marry people from other races. This is especially true of Whites, because as the largest group, they are the most likely to marry within their own race even if they have no racial preferences at all. To track the attitudes of the whole population, then, surveys remain very useful. What do they show?

The American public clearly has an increasing tolerance of interracial relationships. This change has occurred partly because older generations are being replaced by cohorts born and raised more recently. When the General Social Survey asked Whites in the early 1990s how they would feel about a close relative marrying a Black person, the majority expressed either some opposition or strong opposition (see Figure 3.12). In the two decades since, there has been a steep drop in such attitudes. There is still a large generational difference, however. Nineteen percent of those age 35 or older expressed some opposition in 2016, compared with just 7 percent of those under age 35.

Clearly, the trend is in the direction of narrowing social distance. And the generation gap in Figure 3.12 suggests that a greater change in public attitudes is

Figure 3.12 **Percent of Whites who say they would be "somewhat opposed" or "very opposed" to a close relative marrying a Black person, by age**

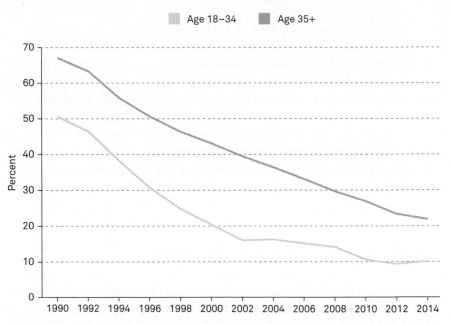

The lines are smoothed with a four-year moving average.

SOURCE: Author's calculations from the General Social Survey, 1990–2014 (Smith et al. 2016).

Social Distance

Research shows that attitudes toward relationships that cross racial and ethnic lines are often affected by the nature of the relationship and the social perspective of the observer.

		Your relationship with a member of _____ group			
		Close friend	Date	Live together	Marry
Would anyone disapprove?	You				
	Your parents				
	Your grandparents				

The table presented here shows four relationships, ranging in level of intimacy from close friendship to marriage and expressing different levels of social distance. Consider the attitude that you yourself, your parents, and your grandparents might take (or have taken) toward such a relationship between you and a member of a specific racial-ethnic group (or just write in "a different" group).

Perform this exercise on your own, in small groups, or as a class exercise: Use a photocopy or drawing of the table and insert comments reflecting the attitudes for each situation. You can also just mark an X in each spot where disapproval is likely or has occurred.

Does the level of disapproval you anticipate (or have experienced) depend on which group is considered? Do you think the views of your family members differ across the generations? If so, do you believe that those views simply reflect generational attitudes, or some other factor? Try to explain the pattern you find.

on the way. The generational pattern is also apparent among immigrants. Both Asians and Latinos are considerably more likely to be intermarried in the second or third generation after immigration, compared with those who immigrated themselves (Stevens, McKillip, and Ishizawa 2006). That was also the case for Italian and other European immigrant families in the first half of the twentieth century, which suggests that these newer immigrants could be on a similar path of social integration (Pagnini and Morgan 1990). With regard to the Black-White family divide, U.S. society may be moving in the same direction—at least toward a breakdown of the strictest barriers—but the pace of change remains quite slow.

America's increasing racial and ethnic diversity makes very visible the idea of different families enacting different traditions in their own way. Maybe that makes family diversity seem more natural or inevitable. But it doesn't eliminate the social conflicts that arise over the different forms and expressions of family life. In the remainder of the book, we will delve more deeply into the many forms of family diversity. And we will see that inequality is both a cause and a consequence of that diversity.

Trend to Watch: Undocumented Immigration

There were an estimated 11 million undocumented immigrants living in the United States in 2014, the most recent reliable estimates (Krogstad, Passel, and Cohn 2016). Undocumented immigrants are people who entered the country without permission, or who have stayed longer than they were permitted to under the conditions of their entry (such as a tourist or student visa). This population is now 5 percent of the U.S. workforce, and their children are 7 percent of K–12 public school students. However, the number of undocumented immigrants has fallen from its peak in 2009, as economic conditions and stepped up enforcement made entering the country illegally less attractive and more difficult. In fact, about two-thirds of the undocumented immigrants now have been in the country 10 years or more. And while the number of undocumented immigrants from Mexico and Latin America has fallen, the number from Asia has continued to increase (Pew Research Center 2016a).

An undocumented Mexican immigrant mother speaks with her three American-born children in their apartment in Colorado.

While some politicians (including President Trump) have demanded the expulsion of all undocumented immigrants, others favor a more selective approach. For example, the government could expel those with criminal records and grant others legal status to remain in the country, work, and—under some proposals—eventually become citizens. The debate is complicated by the fact that undocumented immigrants have millions of children who are U.S. citizens by virtue of being born here. Expelling those children would be unconstitutional, while expelling their parents would break up their families and cause great harm to the children.

With the decline of illegal immigration, the issue has changed. Although Donald Trump campaigned to chants of "Build the wall!" referring to his promised 2,000-mile wall along the Mexican border, the issue of undocumented immigration is less a matter of border security and increasingly a question of how to treat the immigrants and their families that have been living here for years. However, if the flow of undocumented immigrants increases again, the political debate could shift once more.

KEY TERMS:

race   ethnicity

racial ethnicity

endogamy   exogamy

minority group

familism   acculturation

assimilation   intermarriage

social distance

Questions for Review

1. How are race and ethnicity different from each other?

2. How has the U.S. government changed how it measures race? Why are these changes important to sociologists?

3. How have the racial and ethnic populations in the United States shifted in the twentieth century?

4. Describe three disruptions in American Indian family life that have occurred in the last century.

5. According to historians and sociologists, what are some of the legacies of slavery and the Southern agricultural economy that have shaped African-American families?

6. How have extended households eased the burdens of racial inequality for Black families?

7. What is familism, and how does it play a role in Latino family life?

8. Describe at least one source of conflict between parents and children in immigrant families.

9. How did the immigration reforms of 1965 affect families?

10. What are some of the factors behind the growing intermarriage rate in the United States?

4

Families and Social Class

Donald J. Trump Jr. is the oldest son of the billionaire real estate developer, reality TV star, and president whose name he bears. Like his father, he attended the Wharton School at the University of Pennsylvania and got an undergraduate degree in economics. And then—after a year off, in which he says he "lived as a vaga-bond"—Don Jr. started his first job out of college: executive vice president of development and acquisitions at the Trump Organization. That is the same job title later held by two of his younger siblings, Ivanka and Eric (*Washington Post* 2016). The man who would become President Trump inherited the real estate business from his father, Fred Trump, and eventually the empire will pass to his children. Although Don Jr. at first avoided the spotlight, because he didn't want to seem like "just Donald Trump's son, some little rich kid running around," he eventually embraced his place in the family business. "When I started working," he recalled, "I realized that there's an end goal, that I can use some of this. [Staying in the background] would be like having an advantage and not taking advantage of it. That's called stupid" (Williams 2006). By age 38, his personal net worth was estimated at $150 million, but it may ultimately be much more, if he inherits a share of his father's esti-mated $3.7 billion (Bankrate 2016; Wang 2016).

We all know that there are rich people and poor people and people in between. But for sociologists concerned with families, social class is more complicated than that. Within families, not everyone is in the same financial position: What about a doctor married to a nurse? We might also ask who controls the money and who inherits it when someone dies. As we saw in Chapter 1, even who belongs to a

A rise in long-term unemployment contributed to more families and working-class people going to food banks for help. Unfortunately, the 2000s recession reduced private donations and government funds to food banks.

Donald Trump Jr., a billionaire's son whose first job out of college was executive vice president of development and acquisitions for his father's company.

family is not always clear, since different people have their own definitions of family relationships and obligations.

It might seem intuitively obvious that the Trump family is not just exceptionally rich; they are in a different category from almost everyone else. That raises a fundamental question: Is social class experienced as a continuous gradation from poor to rich or as a set of discrete conditions? In other words, does social class refer to individuals or to groups?

Many people think of class as a ladder of economic resources, with richer people (and their families) climbing higher than those with fewer resources. But most sociologists—myself included—are interested in classes as *categories*, in which people share a common set of circumstances and perspectives (Tilly 1998). These two different views of social class are depicted in Figure 4.1, with the ladder climbers representing the continuum-of-resources view and the stacked boxes representing the discrete-groups view. Both views show people in richer-versus-poorer stations, but the ladder accentuates their status as individuals and their ability to move up and down. The boxes, on the other hand, highlight the shared positions of people in groups and also the barriers between groups that make it difficult to climb around. Which perspective captures the modern experience of class matters because it may reflect how people see themselves and how they behave in everything from marriage decisions to parenting styles to political action (Lareau 2011).

For our purposes, the difference between the ladder view and the boxes view is vital to understanding families—which are, after all, groups of people with a lot in common. To address this distinction more systematically and to understand its importance for modern families, we will need to revisit some of the sociological theories we introduced in Chapter 1, especially the consensus and conflict perspectives. And we will meet two new theorists: Max Weber and Pierre Bourdieu.

Theories of Social Class

Both the consensus and conflict perspectives provide important insights into the role of social class in modern society. But their assumptions about how society works lead to different interpretations of class and inequality. These differences regarding social class are best understood through the issue of **division of labor**, the social process of determining who does what work and

division of labor

The social process of determining who does what work and for what rewards.

Figure 4.1 **Two perspectives on social class**

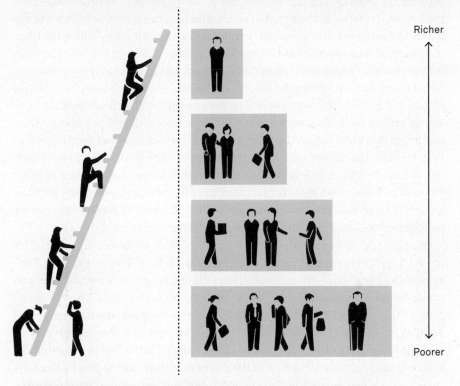

Richer

Poorer

A continuum of resources is shown on the left, with richer people above poorer people on the socioeconomic ladder. A set of discrete groups is shown on the right, with smaller, higher classes stacked on top of larger, lower classes and with the people in each box sharing a common set of circumstances.

for what rewards, a central concern from the early years of sociology (Durkheim 1893/1997).

Consistent with the precepts of functionalism, consensus theorists have worked backward logically from the prevalence of social inequality in all societies, albeit to widely varying degrees, to the assumption that inequality therefore serves an essential function. In a classic statement of this position, Kingsley Davis and Wilbert Moore (1945) argued that some jobs are more important and more difficult to do than others. Society therefore needs a way to find and train the most talented people for these jobs and motivate them to perform well. (Think of surgeons or airplane pilots.) The system that fulfills this need, they believed, is a pattern of unequal rewards that creates incentives for people to strive for the best jobs they can get. Unequal rewards, therefore, are necessary to entice people to seek the extensive training required for difficult and important work. In this view, social class is a continuum from lower to higher rungs on the economic ladder, with the different levels of reward determined by the kinds of jobs people have. And the inequality between those lower and those higher on the ladder is not only beneficial but also necessary to the functioning of society.

exploitation

The process by which the labor of some produces wealth that is controlled by others.

The conflict perspective, drawing especially from the work of Karl Marx in the nineteenth century, also takes the division of labor as the crucial element in defining the class system (Marx 1867/1990). But rather than seeing classes, and the inequality between them, as necessary and beneficial, conflict theorists see inequality as the result of economic **exploitation**, the process by which the labor of some produces wealth that is controlled by others. Scholars in this tradition believe that the fundamental class division is not one of skills and expertise, but one of ownership. In a capitalist society, capitalists—those who own and control property (capital)—dominate those who have no capital and therefore must subsist by selling their labor on unfavorable terms. Social classes are distinct categories, in this view, defined by their ownership (or lack of ownership) of capital. By extension, the classes are defined by their relationship to each other; capitalists and workers exist only in relation to each other. The class structure of modern societies has grown more complicated since Marx's time, especially with the growth of large middle-class categories (E. Wright 1997). However, the conflict perspective on social class still carries great weight in sociology.

Neither the consensus view nor the conflict view, as described so far, does much to explain the complication of social class for families. For example, consider college students, who may not have jobs or live off their own income and whose future class position may differ from that of their origins. To what social class do they belong? To address this, let's consider the work of another classical sociologist, Max Weber (1864–1920). Weber believed that the opportunity to succeed is crucial to the definition of class. Weber's work (Weber 1946) is the source of the sociological concept of **life chances,** defined as the practical opportunity to achieve desired material conditions and personal experiences. For Weber, it was not abstract freedom but the *practical* ability to achieve that defines a person's life chances. This concept is different from the conventional American view of opportunity, which focuses on the absence of formal obstacles to success. For example, in a capitalist economy, a person with few material resources or skills does not have high life chances, even if that person has the hypothetical possibility of becoming rich, because the practical chance of doing so is very small (E. Wright 1997).

life chances

The practical opportunity to achieve desired material conditions and personal experiences.

The concept of life chances helps explain how social class works within families. The job or income of a parent clearly affects the life chances of his or her spouse and children. (For example, children whose parents have high incomes are much more likely to complete college.) Similarly, the spouses of rich people have historically had the chance to live a lifestyle far more lavish than their own income or career would have permitted (although wives in such marriages often remain subordinate to their husbands). Thus, the income and other resources of those we are connected to influence the life chances of each of us and therefore our class position (Szelenyi 2001).

social capital

The access to resources one has by virtue of relationships and connections within a social network.

This brings us to the broader idea of **social capital**, the access to resources a person has by virtue of relationships and connections within a social network (Portes 1998). The French sociologist Pierre Bourdieu (1930–2002), who developed this idea (Bourdieu 1986), believed that families are only one such social network, but perhaps the most important one. Belonging to a group, such as a family or an exclusive club, makes it possible for people to draw from the

The Missoni family's fashion company is based in Italy and its zigzag pattern is famous worldwide. Founded by Rosita (center) and her husband, Missoni employs several family members in executive positions.

resources held by all of its members. For example, think of parents paying for college, an uncle getting someone a job interview, or the chance to meet potential spouses at an exclusive party. Ideas and knowledge can be thought of as resources acquired through a social network as well, such as learning how to act in different situations or being taught skills in certain kinds of work. Naturally, the resources of the group are not automatically shared equally with everyone. Instead, getting access to those resources depends on being a group member in good standing, which requires effort and upkeep. In family terms, that may mean offering one's own resources to other family members, protecting the family name and reputation, and obeying one's elders—or at least being polite at Thanksgiving dinner.

Social capital is not something that only rich people have. After all, poor people might get jobs from their uncles as well. But the amount of social capital—in addition to the amount of money in their pockets—is one of the things that divide those in lower classes from those in upper classes.

Families in Their Social Classes

To illustrate this divide more concretely, let's consider two very different extended families. The first is a wealthy family. I pieced together their story from public sources, such as wedding announcements, corporate biographies, alumni newsletters, and obituaries. The second is a snapshot of a working-class family drawn from Katherine S. Newman's book *No Shame in My Game: The Working Poor in the Inner City* (K. Newman 1999). These descriptions are meant to illustrate how a class may hold together through families and across generations.

Generations of Wealth and Privilege Audrey Winston has two sisters, Dorothy and Elizabeth (I've altered their names and a few details to protect their privacy). Their parents, William and Barbara, were White and wealthy. William had two engineering degrees from Columbia University; Barbara was a graduate of an Ivy League university as well and worked for an elite private high school. Two of the girls attended that same high school, whose alumni include a former U.S. president as well as many other prominent politicians, writers, scientists, and celebrities. The third sister went to a different New England private school. For college, the sisters went to Brown, Yale, and Skidmore College. This is an elite New England family, wealthy and well educated—the sort of family whose weddings are often reported in the *New York Times* (which is how I found them, in the wedding announcements). The family is diagrammed in Figure 4.2, with the Winstons shown in orange.

Two of the three daughters married, and those marriages give a further glimpse of the class to which they belong. Audrey married a banking executive, himself a graduate of an elite private high school and an Ivy League university. His parents were successful professionals. Dorothy married a lawyer, Robert Whittaker, also a product of prep schools and an elite private college, whose father was an Episcopal Church leader.

Figure 4.2 **An elite extended family**

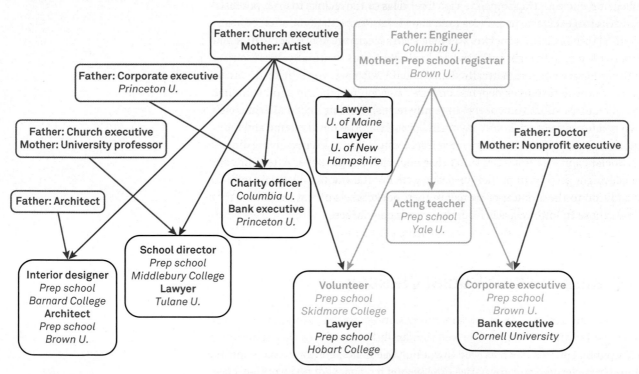

The Winstons (orange) and the Whittakers (pink), along with their in-laws (purple), formed a wealthy family network through marriages among their children. The couples are shown in boxes together. Most are graduates of prestigious private prep schools and universities, working in high-paid professional or corporate careers.

To look one step further, consider Robert's siblings (his family is shown in pink). His brother was a lawyer who married a lawyer; one sister married a lawyer, another married a banking executive, and the third married an architect. Between them and their spouses, they attended Barnard College and Columbia, Princeton, Brown, and Tulane Universities. The spouses' parents (shown in purple), in turn, were all college-educated professionals, including some who attended Ivy League schools and worked as corporate executives.

This is a small slice of the American upper class. Showing their interconnections is important for understanding that this class is not just people with very high salaries and professional jobs, but a *group* of connected families full of people with high salaries and professional jobs. Substantial wealth passes from generation to generation, along with the lifestyle, education, and social connections of their extended networks, enjoyed in their big houses (and summer homes) and private schools for their children. When they marry, they usually marry endogamously, that is, within their group. Although not formally named, like the aristocracies of old Europe, this class still uses family ties to forge a cohesive social group. And unlike the poor or working class, this is a very exclusive group, membership in which is closely guarded. As a class, they share common interests, experiences, and ways of looking at the world, which are reinforced in their selective schools and tightly connected social interactions (Khan 2011). And when they need a job or a spouse or a friend, they have a network of potentially like-minded people to whom they may turn—people who may be in their alumni association, school PTA, or yacht club. Their class membership is not just a result of inherited wealth, high-income jobs, and high education, but a result of a huge stock of social capital to which all members have access—and life chances that reflect these opportunities.

Identifying a friendship network is more difficult than tracing a group related by marriage, as I have done here, because friendships are not usually publicly recorded. However, I found one easy example: a short visit between Audrey and two of her college friends was reported in the gossip section of the alumni newsletter. The couple, who were married, stayed with Audrey and her husband while they were in town. This couple, I discovered, are not only Ivy League graduates but also successful corporate executives themselves, with MBA degrees. She was a commercial banker and marketing manager who left the workforce to be home with the children, while he was a managing director at one of the biggest financial firms in the country. Thus, friendship connections also appear to be highly selective.

Generations of Working Poverty Now consider a family from the other side of the tracks—an old phrase that refers to people from different social classes living on different sides of the railroad tracks, which have long been prominent physical and social barriers in American cities (Du Bois 1942). In her book, Katherine Newman details the struggles of the working poor—that is, people who often have jobs but are unable to achieve economic security or stability. She tells the story of Evie, a Black woman in her late 50s who works as a letter carrier (K. Newman 1999:164–165). She has seven daughters between her ex-husband, William, and her current partner, Harry, who is retired from a job parking cars.

Three of the daughters have jobs—as a medical secretary, a corrections officer, and a hairstylist. All seven daughters have husbands or partners, whose jobs include truck driving, bus driving, and construction work. Two of the men are military veterans; several of the families receive public assistance. Three of the daughters have children with former partners. None of the daughters has been to college, but a few of their children have started (and one granddaughter is attending law school after marrying an accountant).

As the family tree expands to include cousins and their families, we find that the adults have jobs as postal workers, fast-food workers, military service members, and clerical workers. College attendance is rare, while poverty and public assistance are very common. In the three generations represented, there is little evidence of movement out of the working class and its meager material conditions; only one of Evie's descendants has married or cohabited with someone who has a professional degree. What social capital they have doesn't provide the needed resources for much improvement in life chances.

Family Networks Drawing from the ideas presented so far and the examples of the two extended families—each of which has grown within its own social class borders—we can now bring in the idea of social networks (see Chapter 6). Like the Winstons and their affluent relatives, Evie's working-poor family is a network of people with similar class backgrounds and economic circumstances. Seeing families this way helps make sense of the relationship between family and social class. In the network diagram in Figure 4.3, each circle represents an individual in an immediate family, represented by the clusters of circles. When someone joins another family (usually through marriage), the clusters are connected with a dotted line. The clusters of families are separated into two groups by the railroad tracks, representing two different social classes.

In this scenario, most families have connections only to those within the same class, and only a few marry across the tracks (represented by the dotted pink lines). These groups are not just at different levels from each other; rather, they occupy distinct social spaces, and the barriers between them are formidable—like the railroad tracks that separate city neighborhoods. The clearest example is marriage patterns, such as those in the extended families just described. What is the chance that these two families would ever be joined by marriage? Exogamy that cuts across social classes is no less fraught with potential problems than the intermarriages between racial-ethnic groups that we discussed in Chapter 3 (Streib 2015).

Figure 4.3 is just an abstract representation; the true number and nature of the connections would need to be determined by research. Such research can take the form of case studies (like the ones considered here) or analysis of demographic data. For example, we will see in Chapter 8 that 4 out of 5 American marriages include spouses on the same side of the college/no-college divide—and that pattern has grown stronger in recent decades. In different societies or different periods in history, we might find looser or denser groups of families, with more or less contact across the tracks.

Thinking about families grouped into a social class helps us to understand a crucial aspect of class: **class identity**, which we can define as the awareness

class identity

The awareness of, and sense of belonging to, a specific social class.

Figure 4.3 **Families in social class networks**

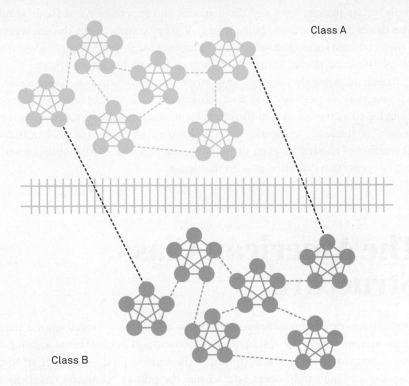

Class A

Class B

This diagram represents individuals (circles), families (clusters of circles), and social classes (orange versus blue), with social classes separated by a symbolic social boundary (railroad tracks). Dotted lines represent kinship ties through marriage. There are many more connections within each social class than there are across the tracks.

of, and sense of belonging to, a specific social class. If people did not have class identities, we might think of social classes as just statistical groups of people with similar economic profiles. But with class identity, they become familiar social settings with distinctive ways of life and patterns of interaction. Because social class involves intimate, lifelong family relationships, classes develop shared patterns of thinking and acting (Lamont 1992). These patterns are partly the result of similar economic circumstances and experiences, such as owning wealth and property (or not), working for others versus managing others at work, and so on (Kohn 1977). But they also follow from the everyday interactions their members have with each other, through which they socialize with each other and build a repertoire of expected and acceptable behavior, similar to the process that happens within families (Khan 2012).

The concept of class identity, in turn, helps us with another problem in figuring who belongs in which social class—the fact that many people have fluctuating incomes. For example, poorer families may see their incomes bobbing up and down around the bare minimum as they navigate between different jobs and income sources. Middle-class families experience fluctuations as well, even if they don't usually rise to the level of threatening the family's survival. Class identity, on the other hand, is more durable, persisting for years, if not generations (Roksa and Potter 2011). That is because people are raised and socialized according to their family's class perspectives and the behavior and expectations of those around them (Irwin 2009). Further, their social capital helps smooth out the unevenness in their circumstances from year to year: During good years they may help friends and relatives, and during lean years they may draw on help from others.

In general, when the barriers between classes are strong, class identity tends to be stronger as well, because it is reinforced by close contact among people belonging to a given class. On the other hand, when people flow easily between classes, the tendency to identify with their own class origins is weaker. In fact, the number of classes, or even the existence of discrete, identifiable classes, is not always certain. We turn next to that issue.

The American Class Structure

Combining various approaches to social class and the way Americans see themselves, and analyzing the distribution of income and occupations, sociologists have developed a common description of the contemporary structure of social classes (E. Wright and Rogers 2011). I use the phrase "common description" because it reflects the fact that most sociologists have given up attempting to precisely define social classes in modern society. Instead, we are satisfied if we can use concepts and measures that help explain the nature of social life and the problems we face, both individually and collectively (Lareau and Conley 2008). With that in mind, the following four categories provide a useful framework for learning about social class.

- *The capitalist and corporate managerial class.* This very small group is sometimes called "the 1 percent," although the actual number is not certain; "upper class" may be a more appropriate label. In the General Social Survey (GSS; Smith et al. 2015), 2.7 percent of American adults identify themselves as "upper class" (see Figure 4.4). They have an extremely high standard of living, as well as both economic and political influence far beyond their numbers.

- *The middle class.* This much larger group has historically had relatively stable jobs based on their higher education or technical skills and credentials. Although their standard of living is much more modest than that of the upper class, they are able to meet basic needs, including health care and education, and usually own homes. Somewhat less than half the U.S. population (42.4 percent) chooses this category to describe themselves.

- *The working class.* Although lacking the higher education or training of the middle class, this large group has a standard of living similar to that of the

Figure 4.4 **Percentage of Americans who identify as . . .**

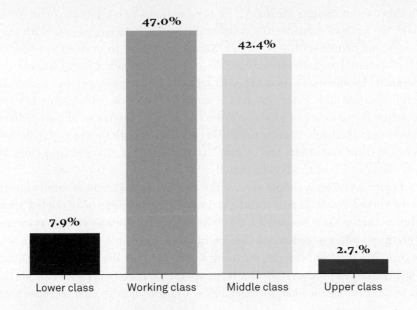

SOURCE: Author's calculations from the 2014 General Social Survey (Smith et al. 2015).

middle class, but with much less stability. Their jobs, once based in industries with strong labor unions or government protections, are less secure, and they more often experience economic shocks that threaten their way of life—as was painfully apparent during the recession of the late 2000s. In the GSS, this group is slightly larger, 47 percent.

- *The lower class.* Most people in this group do not have higher education or skilled jobs, so their families have low incomes and a high degree of economic insecurity. As their job situation fluctuates, they may experience periods of outright poverty, including lack of adequate medical care and housing. Among this group are the very poor, who are unable to compete for the jobs that might lift them out of poverty. They usually depend on government assistance for much of their food, medical care, or housing. Only 7.9 percent of the population identifies as "lower class" in the GSS, but based on their economic conditions, most sociologists believe that this group is larger. As we will see, the official poverty rate was 13.5 percent in 2015.

Clearly, social class categories and identity are important parts of family life, for better or worse. What we have not addressed explicitly to this point, however, is social class inequality. If classes represent higher and lower levels of economic status and security, then the distance between them is social class inequality. And one of the most important trends in U.S. history for the last half-century has been the growth of such inequality.

Increasing Inequality

To think about income inequality, we need to make two kinds of comparisons. First, we have to consider the relative difference between people with more money and people with less money. Second, we need to understand how the overall level of inequality in society changes over time. What seems like extreme inequality in one context may not be as severe in another context. (An additional, very important dimension beyond the scope of this book is inequality between societies; Korzeniewicz and Moran 2009.) As people view those who are richer or poorer than themselves, their perception is affected both by the social distance between them and others and by how that distance has changed over time. We will discuss each of these issues briefly.

Figure 4.5 offers a simple view of the current distribution of family income in the United States. Family income is the combined income of all related people who live in the same household. If you line up all families according to income, with the poorest on the left and the richest on the right, and add up their incomes as you move from left to right, the result will be the pink line shown in the figure. The highlighted points on the line help explain the pattern. The first shows that 26 percent of families had incomes below $37,500 in 2015, and together those

---

Figure 4.5 **U.S. family income distribution, 2015**

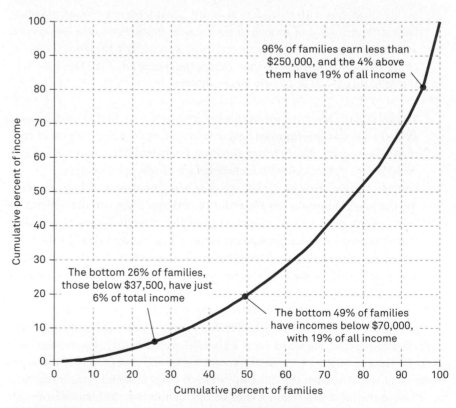

SOURCE: Author's calculations from U.S. Census Bureau (2016f).

Figure 4.6 Family income inequality, 1947–2015

The Gini index of inequality measures the extent of income inequality, with a score of 1 representing complete inequality (one family has all the income) and 0 representing complete equality (all families have equal income).

SOURCE: Author's calculations from U.S. Census Bureau sources.

families have just 6 percent of all family income. The bottom half of families were all below $70,000 each, and together they had 19 percent of all income. Finally, the top 4 percent of families all had incomes of $250,000 or more, and their share of all income was 19 percent.

If the top 4 percent of families received 19 percent of the income in 2015, is that "a lot" of inequality? One way to answer that is with a measure called the **Gini index** (Allison 1978). The Gini index is a score between 0 and 1, with 0 representing complete equality (all families have the same income) and 1 representing complete inequality (one family has all the income). The income distribution shown in Figure 4.5 has a Gini index of 0.45. When we compare that number in 2015 with the level of inequality in previous years, as I've done in Figure 4.6, it becomes clear that income inequality has increased dramatically, and almost continuously, since the end of the 1960s. To understand the reasons behind this trend, we need to consider changes that have affected those on the bottom, in the middle, and at the top of the economic ladder (Levy 1998).

- *At the bottom: keeping the poor from improving their lot.* Among the lowest earners, there have been changes in public policy and family structure that have kept their incomes from rising. For example, the legal minimum wage, which is set by the federal government (although some states set

Gini index

A measure of inequality in which 0 represents complete equality and 1 represents complete inequality.

theirs higher), has been allowed to fall as inflation eroded its value. From its peak in 1968, the minimum wage had fallen 35 percent by 2016, after inflation is taken into account. At $7.25 per hour, this translates into just $15,000 per year for a full-time job. (In response to the falling value of the minimum wage, some places have implemented "living wage" laws, as we discuss shortly.) Meanwhile, the growing number of single-parent families (see Chapter 9)—most with only a mother's income to live on— has contributed to the number of poor families as well (McLanahan and Percheski 2008).

- *In the middle: divergent fortunes.* In the middle-income ranges, some trends have pulled families down while others have lifted families up, resulting in a greater degree of inequality. On the one hand, the decline of the manufacturing sector in the face of global competition hurt many middle-income workers, who had previously been able to earn a good income without the benefit of a college degree (but with the help of labor unions that used to be stronger). Noncollege jobs now are likely to be low-wage service jobs (think of fast-food jobs). On the other hand, in the new service-oriented economy, those with higher education are doing much better (think of lawyers). Further, many women now receive higher earnings than they did in the past, but these gains have largely benefited women with more education. On top of these economic forces, the increasing tendency of people to marry at their own education level has exacerbated the split between families with two high earners and those with two low earners (Schwartz 2010).

- *At the top: the new superrich.* Finally, a new pattern of very high incomes has emerged, spurred by government policies that include the deregulation of the finance industry, reduced taxes on certain kinds of income earned by the very rich, and relaxed restrictions on corporate lobbying for those policies (Stiglitz 2013). This includes three groups: chief executives at major corporations, whose incomes include stock in the companies and huge bonuses; investment bankers and financial managers who handle vast sums of money; and celebrities and superstar athletes, whose growing audiences have propelled their incomes upward (Keister 2014). As a result, the richest 1 percent of individuals now earn more than 20 percent of all income in the country (Piketty, Saez, and Zucman 2016). (See Trend to Watch.)

These factors all contributed to increasing inequality between families (Allegretto 2011). As the gap between rich and poor has grown, the threat of slipping down from the upper class or the middle class has become a constant worry for many families. In fact, insecurity and instability are potential issues for all but the richest of American families. As we will see in Chapter 10, job loss and economic stress in general increase the likelihood of marriages ending in divorce. And sometimes an economic crisis threatens a family's class identity as well as its material well-being.

In the United States, where owning a home is often considered a marker of middle-class status, the breaking point may occur when the family is at risk of losing a house. Consider a working-class family described in a 2011 *New York Times* report (Tavernise, Deparle, and Gebeloff 2011):

> Jennifer Bangura works at Georgetown University Hospital as a cashier. Together with her husband, a driver for a catering company, their family income is just under $50,000, enough to pay a mortgage of $800 on a house she purchased in 1992. But after taxes, medical costs and the gas to get to work, they slip into the category of near poor. Their situation has been made worse by a second mortgage, taken out several years ago to raise money for their daughter's college tuition. The monthly payment shot up to $2,200, an amount she says is now untenable. "It's killing me," said Ms. Bangura, who is 50 and originally from Jamaica. She said she has been making payments for years and that "to lose it now would tear me apart."

Although this family's basic needs are not immediately threatened, they may have to choose between college and homeownership. A crisis of this type is more than just financially destabilizing. One of the young adults that Kathleen Gerson (2010:48) interviewed about their childhood experiences explained how her father's business failures shook up her parents' marriage as well:

> Things would look okay and then all of a sudden my mother would find out we were seven months behind on the mortgage. It felt like every time you made a step forward, you ended up getting hit with something else. The most obvious thing was the economic instability, but it created so much instability in the family 'cause we were so busy just trying to survive each day.

One of the most important questions about inequality, both for analysts and for those attempting to make policy, concerns poverty. What is poverty, who is poor, and what can and should we do about the problem? We turn next to that issue.

Poverty and Policy

The class categories described earlier are not official definitions. Still, social class is important for government policy, especially tax and welfare policy. Although the amount of government intervention is lower in the United States than in many other countries, the government does distribute income downward to assist the poor. To do this, it has to identify richer people to tax and poorer people to receive benefits. Toward this end, various laws establish dividing lines between those with higher and lower incomes.

The federal government uses income categories to set tax rates, so that rich families usually pay higher tax rates than poor families—a practice known as *progressive taxation*. In fact, a majority of the American public agree that the rich should pay higher taxes than they do now (McCarthy 2015). The rules are complicated, and there are a lot of exceptions, but taking all federal taxes and credits into account, the poorest fifth of households pay 3 percent of their income in taxes to the federal government, compared with 13 percent for those in the middle, and 26 percent for the richest fifth of households (Congressional Budget Office 2016). Other taxes (such as local sales taxes and gasoline taxes) are not progressive because everyone pays the same tax rate, but people with low incomes tend to spend more of their budget on such items.

In addition to setting tax rates, the government also defines poverty and uses that definition to determine who may get government benefits. In 2015, a family of four was considered "poor" if their combined income was less than $24,036. This is the official **poverty line**, the level of income below which the federal government defines a family or individual as poor. This definition was created in the 1960s based on a formula that simply multiplied a family "economy food plan" times three, because at the time food accounted for about one-third of a family's expenses. Since then, the poverty line has been adjusted annually according to the inflation rate (Iceland 2003).

If the intention of the poverty line is to identify those families that are unable to meet their basic needs, there are at least three problems with this measure (Short 2011). First, the price of food has risen more slowly than the price of housing and medical care, so living on a food budget times three is no longer adequate. Second, the calculation doesn't include important government benefits that some low-income families get, especially medical assistance and tax credits. Finally, it doesn't take into account the different cost of living in different places; that $23,283 might be enough to live on in a small midwestern town, but not a big coastal city. Nevertheless, although it is a crude measure, the benefit of the poverty line is that it allows us to assess the problem of poverty in a consistent way over time and for different groups (S. K. Danziger 2010).

poverty line

The level of income below which the federal government defines a family or individual as poor.

The feasibility of the "SNAP Challenge," in which participants try to eat an average of $4–5 worth of food a day, is hotly debated by Democrats and Republicans. Logistics aside, it is a question many fortunate people might not have to ask themselves every day: How much do your meals cost?

Research on poverty encompasses many research methods and data sources. It also involves difficult questions of politics and public policy as well as morality. Some people say that the government has no right to redistribute money from the rich to the poor. Others argue that those of us with money to spare must fulfill society's moral obligations to care for the poorest of the poor—and the government is our agent in that endeavor. One source of that perspective is Christianity. According to the Gospel of Matthew (25:31–46), Jesus promised salvation for those who met this obligation:

> Take your inheritance, the kingdom [heaven] prepared for you since the creation of the world. For I was hungry and you gave me something to eat, I was thirsty and you gave me something to drink, I was a stranger and you invited me in, I needed clothes and you clothed me, I was sick and you looked after me, I was in prison and you came to visit me.

For those who did not rise to the moral challenge of caring for the poor, Jesus instead promised "eternal fire."

Regardless of our moral or political perspectives, however, we need a basic understanding of the problem. To that end, I have organized some key facts about poverty in the United States:

- *Poverty increased dramatically during the 2000s.* In the years 2010–2012, the official poverty rate in the United States was 15 percent. That is, about 46 million people were living in families (or alone) with incomes below the federal poverty line. That was the largest number ever recorded and an increase of about 15 million from the year 2000 (see Figure 4.7). On a percentage basis, the poverty rate in those three years was as high as it had been at any time since the 1960s. The increase in poverty was caused by a combination of the factors that increased inequality (discussed earlier) and by the severe economic crisis that began in 2008. By 2015 the poverty rate fell slightly, to 13.5 percent, as the economy slowly recovered from the crisis, but it is still worse than at the beginning of the 2000s.

- *Poverty is concentrated by race/ethnicity.* We saw in Chapter 3 that poverty rates differ widely for various racial-ethnic groups (see Figure 4.8). In fact, American Indians, Latinos, and African Americans are all more than three times more likely to be poor than Whites. This long-standing pattern has been exacerbated by recent trends (Edin and Kissane 2010).

- *Poverty is closely related to family structure.* People who live in households headed by a single mother are much more likely to be poor than other groups in the United States. As we will discuss in Chapter 8, African Americans and people with less education are less likely to marry. And we know that women with less education have more children, on average (see Chapter 9). A single woman who lives with her children is especially likely to fall into poverty—or be unable to rise out of it. As a result, although there are many poor people living in married-couple families—12 million, almost as many

Figure 4.7 Percentage of U.S. population in poverty, 1960–2015, by family type

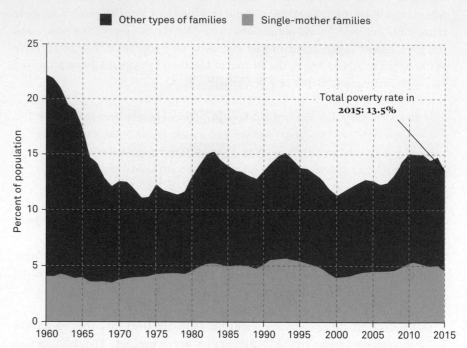

■ Other types of families   ■ Single-mother families

Total poverty rate in
2015: 13.5%

Percent of population

Note the large share of the poor who are in single-mother families (but the even larger share who are not).

SOURCE: U.S. Census Bureau (2016g).

as live in families headed by single women—the poverty *rate* for people in single-woman families is about five times higher (30 percent versus 6 percent). This is illustrated in the Story Behind the Numbers.

- *Poverty for old people has dropped dramatically since the 1960s.* In 1959 more than a third of people age 65 or older lived in poverty. At that time, old people were more likely to be poor than children. However, in the years since, as the Social Security program distributed more money to retired people, and people started working longer into old age, poverty rates plummeted. By 2015, only 9 percent of people age 65 or older lived below the poverty line, compared with 19 percent of children (U.S. Census Bureau 2016h). This trend has transformed old age for millions of seniors, making it one of the signature accomplishments of social policy in the last century.

- *People in poverty suffer from serious deprivation.* Even in a rich country like the United States, those at the bottom of the economic scale go without many of the things most people consider necessary. Sometimes such deprivation is episodic—it comes and goes—but it still looms large in the lives of the poor. For example, about half of the children in families below the poverty line experience at least one of these hardships in a given year: periods of

Figure 4.8 **U.S. family poverty rates, by race/ethnicity, 2015**

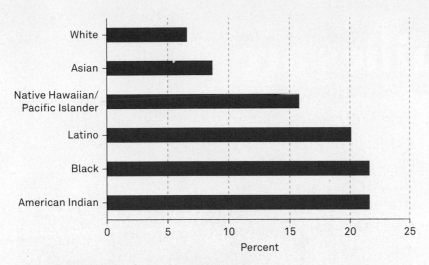

Families are defined by the race/ethnicity of the householder. Races are for those who specified only one race; White group excludes Latinos.

SOURCE: American Community Survey 2016 via American FactFinder (2016).

food shortage, overcrowded housing, being late on the rent or mortgage, and not going to the doctor when necessary (A. Sherman 2011). Not many people freeze or starve to death in the United States, but many do live in families that have to make painful tradeoffs to keep the heat on and put food on the table.

- *Housing insecurity is common.* About 600,000 people are homeless, that is, living in homeless shelters, on the streets, in cars, in abandoned buildings, or in other places not intended as dwellings. Although this is a lot of people, it is a small percentage of the population (about 0.2 percent). About a third of homeless people are living with their families, while the rest are alone. The problem has declined since the turn of the century because of concerted efforts by the federal government and local partners to identify and house homeless people. At the same time, however, about 7 million people in poverty are living doubled up in the homes of their extended families or friends, which is often a stepping stone toward homelessness (National Alliance to End Homelessness 2016). And still more face chronic housing insecurity, moving in and out of substandard housing, unable to pay both rent and utility costs, or facing eviction.

- *Many people move in and out of poverty.* We tend to think of how many people are poor at any one time. But poverty is an experience that many more Americans have at some point in their lives. For example, even though 15 percent of people are in poverty now, about twice that number experienced at least one year of poverty during the last 15-year period (Sandoval, Rank, and Hirschl 2009). That is because the number of people who are near the

Which families are in poverty?

48.5

Unmarried Female-headed Families

14.7 million people
(30% of this population)

http://wwnpag.es/sbtn4

Go to this link for an animation narrated by the author.

Single parents with children are much more likely to be poor than married couples with children. In fact, 30 percent of people in families headed by a single woman live below the official poverty line, compared with just 6 percent in married-couple families. But this does not mean that most poor families are run by single parents. There are fewer poor people in married-couple families (12.3 million) than there are in poor families headed by single people (17.6 million). That is because there are many more married-couple families in the population. Even if we eliminated poverty among single parents entirely, there would still be 26 million people living in poverty.

Source: U.S. Census Bureau (2016i).

Married-Couple Families

12.3 million people
(6% of this population)

191.3

59.0

18.3

Unrelated individuals

12.7 million people
(21% of this population)

Unmarried Male-headed Families

2.9 million people
(16% of this population)

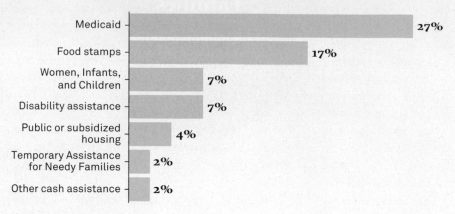

Figure 4.9 **Percentage of people in U.S. households where someone receives each type of federal assistance, last quarter of 2012**

SOURCE: U.S. Census Bureau (2016j).

poverty line—and at risk of falling below it in short order—is much greater than the number of poor at any one time. In fact, one thing that poor people and those at risk of poverty share—and something many more remember from their childhood—is the experience of uncertainty, of not knowing whether more serious hardship is right around the corner (Western et al. 2012).

Federal, state, and local governments operate many programs to assist people in need. The poverty line is often used as a guide for who should receive such assistance, but it's not a strict cutoff. For example, the federal Women, Infants, and Children program makes millions of low-income families eligible for nutritional support based on an income cutoff of 1.85 times the poverty line (Food and Nutrition Service 2013). Other programs that define eligibility in relation to the poverty line are Medicaid (medical assistance for the poor), food stamps, the school lunch program, and dozens of others (S. K. Danziger 2010). The most common poverty assistance programs are shown in Figure 4.9. They range in size from Medicaid, which supports more than one-quarter of the population, to Temporary Assistance for Needy Families (TANF), which supports mostly poor single mothers as they seek employment.

Despite the hardships that poor people experience, this patchwork of government assistance programs helps prevent many of the worst outcomes associated with economic deprivation. Some analysts have concluded that the various benefits reduce the number of people in real poverty by more than half (Ben-Shalom, Moffitt, and Scholz 2011). Still, even after taking into account government support, almost 1 in 6 Americans do not have the income necessary to support their basic needs (Short 2011). In terms of the social class categories outlined earlier, this would include the lower class as well as a significant portion of those in the working class who, even if they have jobs, do not command enough stable income to rise above a minimal standard of living.

Eviction While some middle-class families were losing the homes they owned—or were paying for—during the economic crisis, many poor families were losing their rented houses and apartments. Although some poor families live in federally supported housing, many more do not, either because they fail to meet the requirements of the housing program, or they prefer not to live in government housing ("the projects"), or—most often—because there is not enough subsidized or public housing available. As a result, millions of families that are legally eligible for housing assistance don't receive it. Their fate in a private housing market is difficult, and growing worse. As housing prices have soared in American cities, and legal protection for low-income tenants failed to keep up, the experience of eviction has become much more common. Sociologist Matthew Desmond, in his book *Evicted* (2016a), reported that most poor families in the rental market spend over half of their income on housing expenses, one in eight are unable to pay all of their rent in a given year, and millions are evicted.

Some evictions are legal, as landlords get court orders and sheriff's crews carry out the family's possessions. But more are informal "forced moves," as landlords pressure tenants to leave or threaten to evict them as a way to get them out. In Desmond's study, 11 percent of moves by renters in Milwaukee were forced. Sometimes informal eviction results from disputes over substandard living conditions. People answering his survey in Milwaukee, asked why they were evicted, gave answers such as, "We stopped paying rent because we had pest problems five different times." Another reported: "The landlord said that I was a nasty person and I didn't keep the house clean enough for her. She came to my house and fought me and my girls and that's when she proceeded with the eviction" (Desmond 2016b). These experiences are stressful for parents and disruptive for families—pulling scarce income from other important priorities—which compounds health, behavioral, and educational problems already too common among people who are poor.

Social Mobility and Class Persistence

We saw in the families described earlier that the children mostly followed in the social class footsteps of their parents, as indicated by the education and jobs they got and the people with whom they married and had children. Clearly, however, this is not always the case. How exactly the system repeats itself from generation to generation—or doesn't—is a major issue in sociological research (Beller and Hout 2006).

In sociological terms, this is the question of **social mobility**, or the movement, up or down, between social classes. The basic issue is people's class origin versus their class destination—that is, the social class status of their parents compared with their own class position in adulthood. Most Americans believe that we live in a society with a high degree of social mobility—a society in which

social mobility

The movement, up or down, between social classes.

anyone can rise from meager origins to achieve higher status or wealth (Ferrie 2005), as in the classic "rags-to-riches" stories popularized by Horatio Alger in the nineteenth century. And many people do rise—but many more do not.

In classical sociology studies, social mobility was studied by comparing the occupations of fathers with the occupations of sons (which made more sense when a father's income alone usually determined the status of a family). These studies produced a tool known as the "mobility table," an example of which I show in Table 4.1. This table shows men classified according to five job categories, ranked roughly from highest (upper professional) to lowest (unskilled and service). The numbers on the dark-green diagonal are the highest in the table, showing that sons are most likely to share their fathers' occupational category. Sons whose fathers were upper professionals are 2.2 times as likely to be upper professionals themselves, compared with sons whose fathers were in other occupations. (The pattern is similar for mothers and daughters.)

Is this a lot of mobility? Compared with most other wealthy countries, the United States has less social mobility. That is, American children are more likely to end up in economic situations similar to their parents' (Ermisch, Jäntti, and Smeeding 2012). This is particularly true of people at the opposite ends of the economic spectrum. Studies show that it is especially difficult to escape deep poverty and highly unusual to fall from extreme wealth (Beller and Hout 2006). In addition, the United States now has less upward mobility than we had in previous generations. For example, by the time they reached age 30, only half of Americans born in the early 1980s had incomes greater than their parents, compared with about three-quarters a generation earlier (Chetty and Hendren 2016).

We can think of the flip side of mobility as social class persistence—the

Table 4.1 **Mobility table of sons' occupations in relation to their fathers' occupations**

FATHER OCCUPATION	SON OCCUPATION				
	UPPER PROFESSIONAL	LOWER PROFESSIONAL/ CLERICAL	SELF-EMPLOYED	TECHNICAL AND SKILLED	UNSKILLED AND SERVICE
Upper professional	2.2	1.0	0.7	0.5	0.5
Lower professional/clerical	1.1	3.9	0.1	0.8	0.7
Self-employed	0.6	0.9	2.0	1.3	1.2
Technical and skilled	0.6	0.8	1.1	1.5	1.4
Unskilled and service	0.6	1.0	1.0	1.1	1.6

Numbers above 1.0 (shown in green) indicate that sons are more likely to be in the occupational category listed above if their fathers are in the category listed on the left; numbers below 1.0 (shown in yellow) mean that the outcome is less likely for sons.

SOURCE: The author's calculations from the General Social Surveys, 2006–2010 (Smith et al. 2014), using the categories from Beller and Hout (2006).

tendency of children to relive their parents' class status. The most obvious way for that to happen is for parents to pass their fortunes—if they have them—on to their children. Through inheritance, children of the rich may inherit wealth while children of the poor do not, resulting in a replication of the previous generation's inequality (E. Wolff and Gittleman 2011). Historically, inheritance taxes as high as 77 percent on the largest estates have mitigated this economic inequality. At its peak in the late 1970s, the federal estate tax was taken on the richest 7 percent of people when they died, but the limit has since been lowered so that now less than 1 percent of estates are taxed (D. Jacobson, Raub, and Johnson 2011). That change is part of what has made the tax structure in the United States less progressive, contributing to increased inequality.

Regardless of our individual efforts to succeed, then, the passing of wealth from one generation to the next adds a strong element of yesteryear's class structure into the present. In fact, by giving—or even just promising—money with strings attached, parents also may attempt to shape the values and behaviors of the next generation. For example, parents may withhold or withdraw financial support if they do not approve of their children's marriage choices. If such parents are successful, their children may inherit not only their assets but crucial aspects of their behavior and perspectives on society as well (Angel 2008:80).

Besides the money that passes directly from one generation to the next, I will discuss two important dimensions of family life that have consequences for the life chances of children in the next generation. The first is family structure itself, which can have cascading effects in many areas of children's development, and the second is parenting behavior.

Family Structure

In subsequent chapters, we will see a number of ways that family behavior differs according to social class. For example, people with lower incomes are less likely to marry (see Chapter 8). And people with less schooling have more children than those with higher levels of education (see Chapter 9) and have a higher risk of divorce (see Chapter 10). Combined with the forces that have increased economic inequality in recent decades, these trends mean that we now find children who live with married parents concentrated in higher-income families and those who live with a single parent (most often their mother) skewed toward the lower end of the income scale, often in poverty (McLanahan and Percheski 2008). This discussion is intended to prepare us for those later investigations.

The pattern of income and family type is shown in Figure 4.10. You can see that the most common situation for children of single mothers is a family income below $25,000. There are almost 9 million children of single mothers living in that income bracket. In contrast, the most common situation for children of married parents is a family income of between $50,000 and $100,000. If it is true that children are likely to remain in the same social class as the one in which they grow up, this would suggest that today's children of single mothers are most likely to dominate the lower and working classes of tomorrow.

Working and Poor

Consider the budget of a single mother living in Buffalo, New York (see Table 4.2). With two children, ages 6 and 3, her biggest expense is child care—more than $1,000 per month for a licensed, home-based center for her youngest and a small family care provider for her 6-year-old's after-school hours. After that, she needs about $700 for her rent, $500 for food, and $300 for transportation (maintaining, insuring, and fueling a car). Once the rest of her basic expenses are added up, she needs a total of $3,134 per month, or $37,602 per year.

But what does she earn? If she's a hotel housekeeper, she probably earns $20,000 per year (the median wage for a full-time, year-round housekeeper). A preschool teacher or nursing aide would make $24,000 or $25,000. If she had been working for a while and got promoted to manager in the food service industry, she could expect to earn $36,000—still not enough.

But the government helps. The housekeeper's salary—the only one below the official federal poverty line—would allow her to receive $2,000 per year in food stamps and free lunch for her 6-year-old in school. A teacher or nursing aide would qualify for reduced-price lunches. And then there are tax breaks—the Earned Income Tax Credit, a tax credit for each child, and a child-care benefit. But even with government support and tax credits, none of these jobs would bring her total income up to cover her basic necessities. What can she do?

In this exercise, breaking into groups for a discussion or working on your own, consider this woman's scenario and address these questions:

- Does the scenario seem realistic and/or reasonable?

- Looking over her budget, see where you might cut first or what you would do to make ends meet.

- Besides the budget, what else needs to change in this situation?

Then consider her children:

- How does the bare-bones budget affect their daily lives?

- What about their long-term development and future prospects?

- Besides monetary adjustments, what changes or adaptations can their mother make for them?

Finally, what—or who—is missing from this story? How might other family members, neighbors, community members, charities, or the government help (or hurt) the situation?

Table 4.2 **Budget worksheet: Single parent with children ages 3 and 6, living in Buffalo, NY**

EXPENSES	Annual	Monthly
Rent and utilities	$8,448	$704
Food	$5,691	$474
Child care*	$12,760	$1,063
Health insurance (employee contribution)	$2,609	$217
Out-of-pocket medical	$456	$38
Transportation	$3,821	$318
Other necessities	$3,817	$318
Total expenses	**$37,602**	**$3,134**

ANNUAL INCOME	Earnings	Food stamps	School lunch	Net taxes†	TOTAL	SHORTFALL Annual	Monthly
Maid/housekeeper	$20,000	$2,000	$471	$5,483	$27,954	$9,648	$804
Preschool/kindergarten teacher	$24,000	—	$403	$3,729	$28,132	$9,470	$789
Nursing aide	$25,000	—	$403	$3,413	$28,816	$8,786	$732
Food service manager	$36,000	—	—	-$674	$35,326	$2,276	$190

* Three-year-old in licensed, home-based care, 6-year-old in family-based care.

† Taxes include state and federal income tax and payroll taxes; credits include federal child-care tax credit, federal child tax credit, federal Earned Income Tax Credit. If net taxes are greater than $0, she gets money back on her taxes.

Source: Budget and tax estimates are from the National Center for Children in Poverty (2014); earnings estimates are from the American Community Survey 2010 (American FactFinder 2014); the value of school lunches is from the U.S. Department of Agriculture (2013); Earned Income Tax Credit estimates are from the Internal Revenue Service (2012).

Because of the stark contrast shown in Figure 4.10, much of the concern about family structure and social class focuses on single-mother families (Mayer 1997). Those growing up with a single parent face three kinds of scarcity that can make it more difficult to reach the middle and upper classes (McLanahan and Sandefur 1994):

- *Money.* The most important factor separating children of single mothers from those whose parents are married and living together is simply their lower incomes (Musick and Mare 2006). It may be difficult for these families to meet their basic needs, much less such benefits as better housing or private education. And the children in these families live with economic

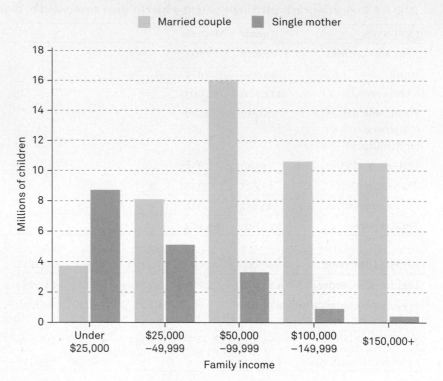

Figure 4.10 Distribution of children by family type and family income, 2015

Married couple ▪ Single mother

Millions of children

Family income

SOURCE: Author's calculations from U.S. Census Bureau sources.

uncertainty and insecurity, which increases their stress and threatens their self-confidence.

- *Time*. Single mothers have less time to spend with their children than do married parents (Vickery 1977). That is partly because there is only one parent, but also because of the time demands on low-income mothers who must work to support their families (Kendig and Bianchi 2008). In fact, some welfare programs exacerbate this problem by requiring mothers' employment, which tightens the time squeeze in single-parent families (Albelda 2011). The lack of parental time cuts down on the supervision and support for children as they mature. One result is that single parents, and poor parents in general, rely more on "media time" as a parenting strategy than do higher-earning parents (see Changing Technology, "The Digital Divide").

- *Social capital*. Closely related to the time squeeze is the frequent scarcity of social capital in single-parent families (J. Coleman 1988). Often starting with a smaller family network, children in single-parent families may have access to fewer resources from adults—especially economically successful adults—who can support them in various ways as they grow up (Lin 1999).

The Digital Divide

Beginning in the 1990s, the Internet spread rapidly, eventually reaching the majority of families in the United States. However, that spread occurred unevenly. High-income, high-education families gained access sooner, so that a digital divide—the social class gap between those with and those without access to current digital technology—opened up in the early years of the Internet (S. Martin and Robinson 2007). Even though the percentage of households with Internet access increased to 75 percent by 2012, fewer than 40 percent of those with less than a high school degree have access at home.

Figure 4.11 shows the percentage of families with children who have Internet access at home in relation to the education level of the householder. Notice that the families with less educated parents are slowly catching up. However, today's young adults were children in 2001, and those without Internet access in their homes then may still suffer the consequences today.

The gap in Internet access does not mean that children in families with less educated parents don't use electronic media, however. In fact, they spend considerably *more* time in front of screens. The biggest difference is in television watching, as the children of those with only a high school degree or less spend 25 minutes more per day watching TV than those whose parents graduated from college, and they are much more likely to have a TV in the bedroom

Figure 4.11 **Percentage of households with children who have Internet access at home, by parents' education, 2000–2012**

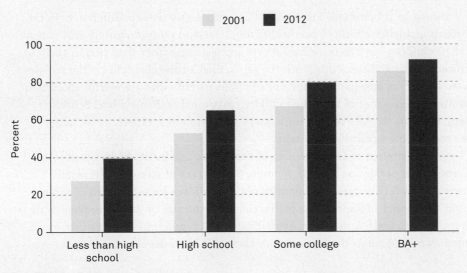

SOURCE: U.S. Census Bureau (2014a).

Figure 4.12 **TV use for children ages 0 to 8, by parents' education**

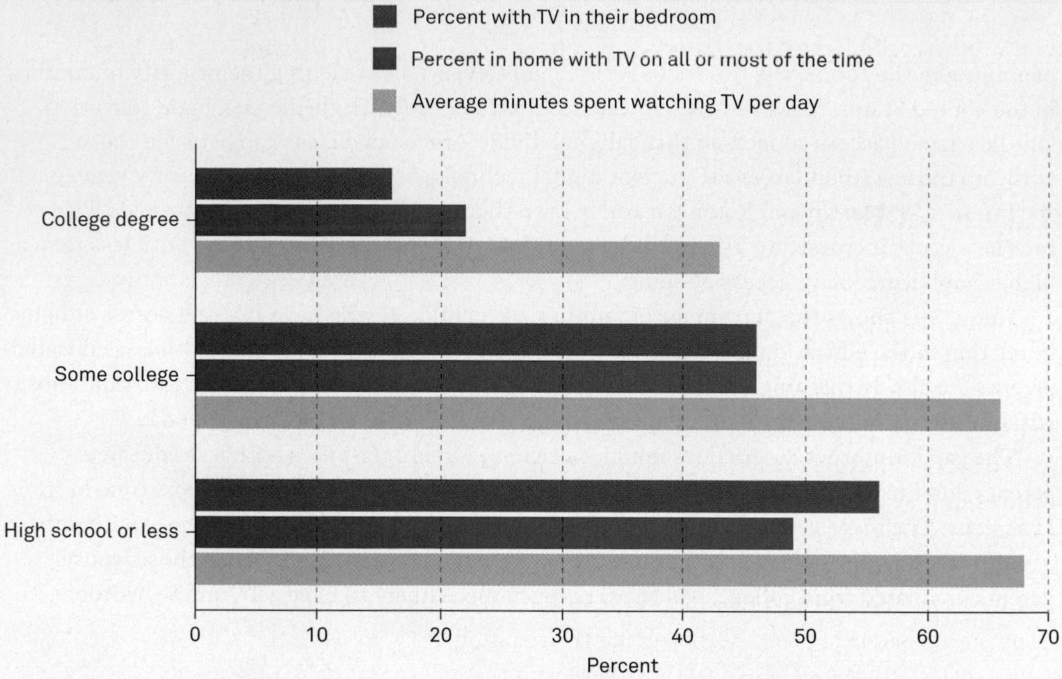
Percent with TV in their bedroom
Percent in home with TV on all or most of the time
Average minutes spent watching TV per day
College degree
Some college
High school or less
0
10
20
30
40
50
60
70
Percent

SOURCE: Common Sense Media (2013).

or have the TV always on at home (see Figure 4.12). This gap partly reflects differences in the approach to parenting; higher-educated parents are more likely to promote formal enrichment activities for their children, such as organized sports and lessons, rather than permit them to have unstructured free time (Lareau 2011). But the gap in media time also reflects the stresses and demands that lower-income parents face. For example, parents who are fearful about their neighborhoods limit the amount of time their children play outside (Kimbro and Schachter 2011). For others, the time squeeze of long work hours and commutes, especially for single parents, makes media time a practical necessity.

As social scientists attempt to trace the path of social class inequality from generation to generation, the digital divide has become an important subject of study. The research increasingly reveals that it is not just the quantity of time children spend in front of screens that matters, but the quality of their online interactions and the role of the technology in their lives (Roberts and Foehr 2008). And that makes digital decision making one more important area for parents to worry about as they try to guide their children's development.

Family structure clearly affects children's lives and their development in many ways. However, I should emphasize that the shape of one's family is not an isolated factor. Whether parents are married, in particular, reflects many influences, including the pool of potential spouses available to them. Often, these scarcities—of time, money, and social capital—merely exacerbate the challenges and hardships that children of the poor are going to face whether their parents are married or not.

Family Practices

In a *New York Times* investigation of the competitive world of raising adolescents, a 12-year-old girl named Lucy complained that "I barely even get to go outside when I get home." She felt burdened by the enriching activities, such as years of piano lessons, that her parents arranged for her. Another 12-year-old, Lauriston, said he took practice SAT exams and attended a private school for modeling. "I like being on stage," he told the reporter. "I like seeing people clap for me" (Wilgoren and Steinberg 2000). Busy and harried as they were, it seemed that these children, with their advanced skills and well-developed sense of confidence, were on the right track to succeed. Such activities might reflect good decisions by their parents to enhance their future potential. But they also require money (and time) to implement. So parenting is only one part of the equation. Money, parenting decisions, and time investments—and the experiences they make possible—all

Middle-class parents engage in "concerted cultivation," which includes providing their children with music lessons, sports lessons, academic tutoring, and travel experiences.

combine to offer some children both educational opportunities and the sense of accomplishment and ability that may contribute to their future.

Most American parents try very hard to help their children succeed. As economic inequality has increased, the win-or-lose nature of society has put more pressure on families to improve their life chances. This pressure isn't just economic; in fact, most parents at all income levels do not believe that the amount of money they have is the ultimate factor in determining their children's success. Rich parents can't (usually) just buy a promising future for their children. Instead, they use their money to help make it possible, and that requires a whole set of parenting practices, such as having their children participate in sports, providing lessons and tutors, arranging travel experiences, and activating the extensive social networks we discussed earlier. On the other hand, the children of poor parents aren't automatically destined for an impoverished adulthood. But the lack of resources in their families places obstacles between parents' efforts to propel their children upward and the achievement of social class mobility. Even when they do everything right, these parents may not succeed (see Changing Culture, "Educational Inequality"). We will return to parenting more generally in Chapter 9.

Without denying the importance of money itself, sociologists have long attempted to understand how parenting practices differ according to families' social class (Mayer 1997). In a classic series of studies, Melvin Kohn (1977) found that parents with jobs that required self-direction were more likely to raise their children to value that quality—to expect to make their own decisions and be in charge of their lives. On the other hand, those whose jobs required them to follow orders tended to raise their children to value conformity. By trying to prepare children for the future, then, parents ended up preparing their children to follow in their own occupational footsteps as well.

The sociologist Annette Lareau (2011) studied social class and parenting, taking into account increasing inequality, the growing importance of college education, and the rise of intensive parenting (see Chapter 9). Her in-depth study—following a handful of carefully selected families through their daily lives—eventually spanned more than a decade, and she describes major differences in the approach to child rearing between middle-class parents, on the one hand, and parents in the working class or in poverty on the other.

Middle-class parents practice *concerted cultivation*. The middle-class families Lareau studied took an aggressive approach to parenting, making constant efforts to develop their children's abilities. They filled up their children's schedules with age-targeted activities and made sure they actively stimulated the children's cognitive and social development. And, consistent with the Kohn study, middle-class parents taught their children to directly engage with the professional adults in their lives—such as teachers and doctors—rather than passively submitting to authority.

Working-class and poor parents practice the *accomplishment of natural growth*. The parents Lareau studied tended to see children's successful development as a natural outcome that would emerge if only their children were provided with protection, comfort, and care. Rather than schedule lots of formal activities, these parents permitted their children to play informally, spending more time

Educational Inequality

With economic and technological change increasing inequality in the United States, education has grown more important for separating people into higher and lower social classes. The best chance for children from poorer families to move up comes from the expanding higher education system (Breen 2010). But children from higher social classes are much more likely to make it through that system and emerge into a privileged class in adulthood. For example, as Figure 4.13 shows, children from high socioeconomic status (SES) families are four times more likely to complete a four-year college degree than those from low SES families (60 percent versus 14 percent). And those from low SES families are seven times more likely to finish only high school or less than those from high SES families (28 percent versus 4 percent).

How does this happen? The educational divide is apparent from the earliest ages. The living environments, resources, and parenting practices children experience vary dramatically. The

Figure 4.13 **Educational attainment by family socioeconomic status**

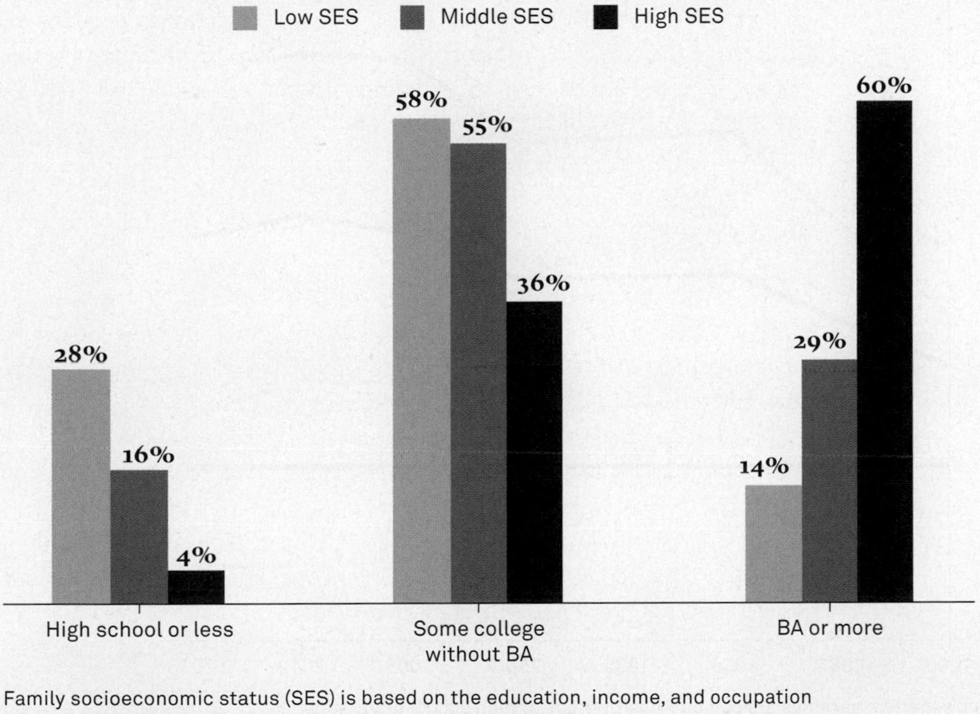

Family socioeconomic status (SES) is based on the education, income, and occupation of the parents of high school sophomores in 2002; educational attainment is for those high school students 10 years later.

SOURCE: National Center for Education Statistics (2015).

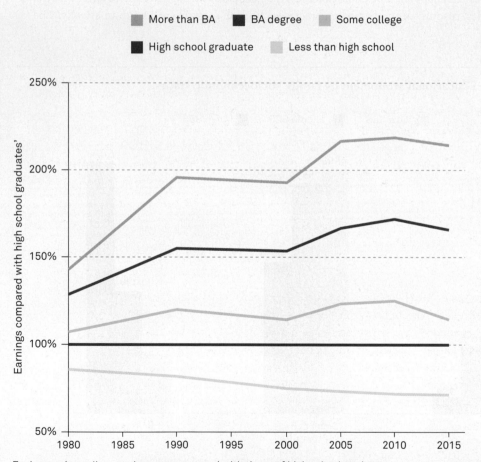

class differences that run through the lives of children are patterns rather than rules, and they aren't universal, but the result is clearly visible in the statistics we keep (Duncan et al. 1998).

Some of the social class gap results from parenting. For example, both mothers and fathers from high-income families spend considerably more time in hands-on caretaking of their children from infancy. That may be because they place a high value on such time and consider it important to their children's development. But rich parents also have more time to give—with fewer children to care for and (at least for women) fewer hours away from home at work (Drago 2009). By the time children reach kindergarten, those from more affluent homes are better prepared to succeed academically, in everything from math and reading ability to fine motor skills (Denton Flanagon and McPhee 2009). They also have fewer behavioral problems and are better prepared for school socially (Condron 2007).

Figure 4.14 Differences in earnings by education, 1980–2015

Each group's median earnings are compared with those of high school graduates.
Includes only people working full-time, year-round, ages 25–54.

SOURCE: Author's calculations from Decennial Census and American Community Survey data.

Middle- and upper-class parents also are more likely to understand how to work with—and get what they want from—the professionals in their children's schools, with whom they may share common experiences. Most teachers say that they want more parental involvement in the schools, and parents who are willing and able to provide that presence may improve their children's prospects in school (Langdon and Vesper 2000). At the college level, the cost of education and related expenses place an additional barrier to success before families and increasingly make completing college more difficult even for those who are able to attend. Of course, this barrier is much more difficult to overcome for students whose families are unable to help them cover the costs (Henretta et al. 2012).

These observable patterns in turn affect the expectations people have for their children, and that children have for themselves. A survey of high school sophomores found that 33 percent of those in low-income families expected to complete a four-year college degree; but when surveyed again in their senior year, only 25 percent expected to finish college. When those same students were followed up 10 years later to see if they had finished college, it turned out that their class background mattered more than their high school test scores. Rich high school students were more likely to finish college, even when their test scores were lower than those from families that were poor (National Center for Education Statistics 2015).

For a variety of reasons, then, children from higher social classes advance further in school, on average. As the benefits of higher education have increased—and the penalties for *not* getting higher education have grown steeper—the achievement gap between those from rich families and those from poor families has actually been increasing (Reardon 2011).

The consequences are serious and have grown more so since the 1970s. As Figure 4.14 shows, since the 1980s, those with BAs and higher degrees have been pulling away from workers who only completed high school, so they now earn about 1.7 times and 2.1 times more, respectively. This growing inequality increases the pressure on parents to help their children succeed in school.

in mixed-age groups of relatives or friends in the neighborhood. When it came to interacting with authority figures, working-class and poor parents were less assertive, and they tended to defer to the decision making of the professionals.

All the parents Lareau studied wanted to help their children be happy and successful. But for adults in different social classes, their own background of experiences—the nature of their daily struggles and joys—gives them a different perspective, which influences how they try to promote their children toward adulthood and independence. Lareau believes that the strategy of concerted cultivation provides important benefits for middle-class children. They are more likely to grow up with a sense of confidence and entitlement and to feel empowered to stick up for themselves in school and the workplace. For example, they are better prepared to choose an appropriate college and figure out how to get admitted to it (Lareau and Conley 2008). On the flip side, poor and working-class parents are more concerned that their children have fun and enjoy childhood. That's not a minor issue: many children as young as their early teens report feeling stressed when they have multiple activities scheduled outside of school hours and wish they had more free time (S. Brown et al. 2011). But by not aggressively cultivating their children's skills and talents, poor and working-class parents may miss opportunities for them to move up in the class hierarchy.

When we see the important role of parenting in determining the future social class status of children—and how access to money and other resources affects the odds of success in that effort—it's clear that parenting is not just about love. It's also about the unpaid work that mothers and fathers do within the family. The nature of that work, and how it is divided between men and women, is one of the subjects of our next chapter.

Trend to Watch: The 1 Percent

The United States has seen rising income inequality for the last several decades, as shown in Figure 4.6. However, this simple fact does not capture an important dynamic underlying that trend: the concentration of income and wealth among the very richest Americans. In the Occupy Wall Street protest movement that started in 2011, critics of inequality often declared, "I am the 99 percent!" in an attempt to unite everyone but the very richest under the banner of their cause (Gaby and Caren 2012). That wasn't just a handy political slogan, it also highlighted a very real trend. In 1980, the richest 1 percent of individuals earned 11 percent of all income; by 2014 that share going to the very richest had increased to 20 percent (Piketty, Saez, and Zucman 2016). On the other hand, now the bottom 50 percent of all earners pull in only 13 percent of all income. As in the case of the story of the Trumps that opened this chapter, the vast majority of individuals with incomes in the top 1 percent are White men (Keister and Lee 2014).

Will this trend continue, resulting in more and more money concentrated in fewer and fewer hands, and what does this mean for families who aren't in that very exclusive club? Economist Joseph Stiglitz (2013) has argued that the rise of the 1 percent is self-fulfilling, as these elite individuals increasingly gain control over high status positions and institutions—such as banks, law firms, and the upper reaches of government—that shape the rules and make accumulating more wealth possible. Further, this concentration of wealth may be harmful to the economy, if the richest people don't spend their money in ways that benefit regular workers and their families. On the other hand, the riches controlled by this group are a convenient target for policymakers who might want to raise taxes for social support and programs for families in need, such as health care or housing. So the democratic process could result in a policy change to tax the richest Americans more heavily. If not, we may find that more and more of us are working for the 1 percent, providing them with services and producing their luxury goods.

Questions for Review

1. Using the issue of division of labor, explain how functionalist and conflict theorists differ on the topic of social class and families.

2. What is social capital, according to Pierre Bourdieu? How does social capital distinguish poor families from wealthy families?

3. How do marriage, social networks, and inherited wealth allow families to maintain or improve their social class position across generations? Why is this a disadvantage for working-class American families?

4. Is inequality increasing in the United States? What evidence might you use to support your argument?

5. Why has poverty increased since 2000?

6. What are some of the social programs and policies enacted by U.S. lawmakers to help impoverished families?

7. What is the relationship between family structure and social mobility?

8. What is educational inequality? Why do students with wealthier socioeconomic backgrounds succeed in school at higher rates than children from less wealthy families?

9. What is class identity? What does class identity tell us about families that income does not?

5

Gender

After a few years of trying to get pregnant, in 2016 Chrissy Teigen and her husband, John Legend, decided to try in vitro fertilization (IVF), in which a fertility clinic uses his sperm to fertilize her egg in a petri dish, and the embryo is then implanted in her uterus for the pregnancy. And while they were at it, they chose a female embryo. Or, as she put it, "I picked the girl from her little embryo. I picked her and was like, 'Let's put in the girl.'" She added, "I'm excited…just the thought of seeing him with a little girl. I think he deserves a little girl. I think he deserves that bond" (*People* 2016).

Teigen and Legend's celebrity-couple story is a new twist on an old tale. For centuries, some people have attempted to influence the sex of the children they bore—but they usually had a preference for sons. That bias has diminished worldwide, but it remains most prevalent in East and South Asia today, where many people expect that sons will provide economic support to their elderly parents. The result is an incentive for parents to choose boys over girls, and a cultural bias in favor of sons (although this is weakening). And for those who cannot afford the IVF method, millions of people, most of them in Asia, have used sex-selective abortion—having an abortion after an ultrasound or other test reveals that the fetus is female (Hvistendahl 2011).

The practice of sex selection is secretive and not well documented, but the results are not hard to see in a number of Asian countries, where boys outnumber girls by a far greater margin than would be found naturally (Guilmoto 2009). In the United States, among some Chinese, Korean, and Asian Indian immigrant parents, there is still a preference for sons, most clearly apparent in the case of third children after the first two have been girls. In those cases, sons outnumber daughters enough to suspect some kind of medical intervention (Egan et al. 2011). However, most couples in the United States prefer a balanced

JeongMee Yoon's "The Pink and Blue Project" was inspired by her 5-year-old daughter (pictured), who could not get enough of the color pink. Companies that make toys, clothes, and other items for children make it easy to collect pink possessions for girls and blue possessions for boys, but usually not the other way around.

An unintended consequence of millions of "missing" girls in some Asian countries means that years later, men who want to marry will struggle to find eligible women.

family with one boy and one girl. Seven states have passed laws banning the practice (Guttmacher Institute 2016)—but the medical community is divided on whether sex selection that is not medically necessary (including by abortion) is considered unethical (Ethics Committee of the American Society for Reproductive Medicine 2015).

There are several ironies here. The technology and medical services available in the United States allow families to spend more than the annual income of the average Chinese family to realize their dream of having a daughter, while millions of Asian couples seek sons partly to provide them with economic security. Further, Teigen and Legend did not seek a daughter for traditional reasons—for economic gain, to carry on their family lineage, or to provide them with housework and child care. Instead, their motivations were internal and personal: to be the kind of parents and have the child they felt was important for them.

But can they, or any parents, be sure that the sex of their children will determine what kind of people they will grow up to become? In some ways they can; they can choose how to dress their children and do all the other countless things parents do to raise them as boys or girls. But as we will see, there is a lot that cannot be determined as well—many sources of uncertainty that modern families face with regard to sex and gender.

Sex and gender—what they look like and what they mean socially—have their origins in the biological union between egg and sperm. But their development and interpretation are achieved through the interaction between people in society and especially within the family. The differences we see between boys and girls, women and men, are often differences that we, not nature, create.

Sex and Gender

Sociologists commonly distinguish between sex and gender. Apart from its use to describe sexual acts, the term **sex** refers to one's biological category of male or female, based on anatomy and physiology. These categories are assigned at birth and remain influential throughout life as building blocks to the identities and behaviors we develop as children and adults and to the family relationships we create. **Sexual identity** refers to the recognition, or internalization, of a biological sex category. One's sexual identity usually matches one's sex category. That is, most people are identified by both others and themselves as either male or female. (We'll have more to say about sexual identity and sexual expression in Chapter 6.)

Although it's not quite this simple, you may think of sex as the "biological" category and gender as the "social" category, so that **gender** is the social realization of biological sex. Gender itself can be broken into two parts. **Gender identity** is the identification with the social categories boy/man or girl/woman. This identification is internal to the individual, although it is developed through interaction with others, primarily family members, at a very young age—and it remains a lifelong project even though the category to which people belong rarely changes. On the other hand, **gender expression** is a person's pattern of outward behavior in relation to common standards of a gender category—for example, through types of clothing or the use of a given name associated with one gender or the other. You could say that adopting a gender identity requires learning the behavior expected of a biological sex and then expressing it through individual action.

Usually, sexual identity, gender identity, and gender expression all correspond closely, so the simple term *gender* is sufficient to categorize people in most interactions. Sociologists distinguish between them for two reasons: first, because developing these parts of ourselves involves separate processes, so the different labels apply to different experiences and stages of development; and second, because there is a minority of people for whom sexual and gender identities do not correspond, and understanding the different forms of identity is important for understanding those situations. Using separate terms allows us to identify, for example, people who have a man's gender identity but display a woman's gender or those whose gender identity does not match their sex.

This description of people forming identities by learning roles or expectations and then expressing them through interaction with others is a useful simplification. But there are two important caveats. First, the content of those roles differs between cultural settings and time periods. That is, the roles of boys and girls are neither unchanging nor fixed by biology. Second, learning a role does not mean that people always perform according to its rules. In fact, people sometimes act out of a desire *not* to conform to the roles they are assigned.

The point of tension between conforming to accepted roles and expressing one's own sexual or gender identity is often where social change occurs. To use a historical example, many American women in the 1960s started dressing in

sex

One's biological category, male or female, based on anatomy and physiology.

sexual identity

The recognition, or internalization, of a biological sex category.

gender

The social realization of biological sex.

gender identity

The identification with the social category boy/man or girl/woman.

gender expression

One's pattern of outward behavior in relation to common standards of a gender category less "feminine" ways, sporting a mix of male and female clothes. One woman recalled, "In 1969 I even started to wear trousers to work (as a social worker). At the time this was certainly frowned on, yet two years later social workers were roaming the inner city in torn jeans, gym shoes and bra-less T-shirts" (E. Wilson 1990:72). This was a period of historic changes in gender patterns, partly caused by such individual acts of nonconformity.

Fashion is just one way we turn *biological* sexual identities into *social* gender identity and expression (Paoletti 2012). The way parents dress and interact with their children, thereby transmitting expectations and abilities from generation to generation, is at the heart of the socialization process—a topic to which we will return shortly. First, however, I will provide some context for thinking about gender and families, starting with the biological basis of sex categories.

How Different Are We?

Biology and sociology may appear to be adversaries in the debate between nature and nurture—the question of whether behavior is biological or social in origin. But the answer is rarely clear-cut. Human society has shown its capacity to intervene in the "natural" world from the cradle to the grave—from specifying the sex of fetuses, to using birth control and fertility treatments, to medically extending life in old age. And even when sex differences seem to come straight out of our genes—such as the anatomical differences between men and women—society always affects how such differences are interpreted and treated.

To explain this, a short description of the origin of sex categories may be helpful. The biological differences between males and females are based on anatomical and hormonal patterns that appear early during the fetus's development. Molecules of DNA, which contain the genetic information used to build a person, are arranged in long threads called chromosomes. Among human chromosomes, two are used to determine sex, the so-called X and Y chromosomes. A woman's body cells contain two X chromosomes (designated XX), and each of her eggs carries a single X chromosome. A man's body cells contain an X and a Y chromosome (designated XY), and each of his sperm carries either an X or a Y chromosome. If the sperm that fertilizes the egg carries a Y chromosome, then the fetus will develop into a boy (XY). During the pregnancy, the fetus will develop testes, which produce male hormones known as androgens (including testosterone); those androgens cause the fetus to develop male sex organs. But if the sperm that fertilizes the egg carries an X chromosome, then the fetus will develop into a girl (XX). With an XX fetus, there are no testes and therefore no androgens, so the fetus continues developing as it started, as female.

Sex differences are the basis for the observable, average physical differences between girls and boys, women and men. But a close look reveals that these are not "opposite" sexes. Male and female fetuses begin identically, and even after they develop, there is much more similarity than difference. In fact, early Western philosophers believed that male and female bodies were essentially the same, with the female being simply an inferior version of the male (Laqueur 1990). The

Women and girls in Tanzania carrying buckets of water on their heads. A gallon of water weighs roughly 8 pounds. If the buckets' capacity is a few gallons, the women could be balancing 8–24 pounds on their heads, and women often carry 40-pound loads.

view of the two sexes as opposites developed only in the eighteenth century—not coincidentally, perhaps, around the time the idea of "separate spheres" for men and women emerged (see Chapter 2). As is the case with race, the biological differences between the sexes acquire meanings that are socially constructed; they differ between societies and change over time. For example, although most Americans associate men with physically demanding work, in many African societies women have historically been responsible for the backbreaking task of hauling wood and water for their families every day (Cleveland 1991).

Sex Differences Made Social Compared with many other species, male and female humans are quite similar (Wade 2013). We exhibit a relatively low level of what biologists call *sexual dimorphism*, or physical differences between the sexes. For an example at the other end of the spectrum, consider the elephant seal. Male elephant seals are several times larger than females, and they could easily be mistaken for a different species.

Men's and women's bodies differ, but in relatively subtle ways, as shown by the iconic farm couple in Grant Wood's *American Gothic*. In fact, social practices often serve to enhance our perception of those differences, both visually and through patterns of behavior. Once we believe that people belong to one of two different groups, it's easy for us to make more of the differences we see and ignore the underlying similarities. That might be why audiences were not surprised by the extreme size difference between Moana, the latest Disney princess, and her demi-god companion Maui—compare her wrist to his big toe! (See images on the next page.)

But what difference does human sexual dimorphism make outside the sphere of reproduction? Consider the example of male athletic superiority. Half a century ago, the fastest male marathon runners finished their 26-mile race more

Why do people create extreme sexual dimorphism in visual works? Can you think of any male-female pairings in creative visual works (such as movies, comics, or video games) in which the woman is an equal physical size or larger? Male and female humans, like those shown in *American Gothic*, are much more similar than are male and females elephant seals. But in contemporary animated movies, like Moana, the difference is often extreme.

than 80 minutes ahead of the fastest female runners. It may have seemed that women were hopelessly weaker. But by 2010, the gap was down to less than 12 minutes, a mere 8 percent advantage for men (International Association of Athletics Federations 2014). Maybe the fastest man in the world will always be faster than the fastest woman, but this example shows that social intervention—such as the intensive training and encouragement of female athletes—can radically reduce such disparities. When feminist sociologists say that male domination is "neither natural nor inevitable" (see Chapter 1), they may be correct, even though some differences between the sexes are biological.

Height is one easily observable difference found in almost every family. The average American man in his 20s is about 6 inches taller than the average woman of the same age (McDowell et al. 2008). The average difference is substantial, but the overlap between the two groups is large as well. For example, the actor Daniel Radcliffe, at 5 feet 5 inches, is shorter than almost half of all U.S. women today; and at 5 feet 10 inches, Michelle Obama is taller than almost half of all American men. Figure 5.1 shows the height distributions of married men and women.

However, social behavior serves to enhance the difference in height between men and women rather than minimize it. The cultural expectation in Western

Figure 5.1 **Height distribution of married men and women, 2009**

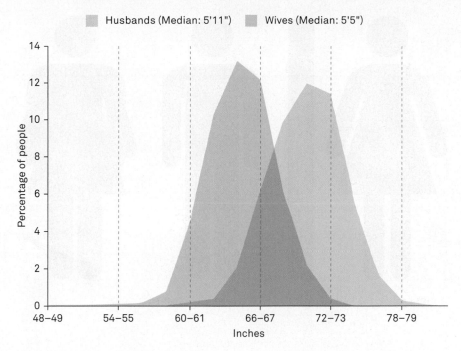

SOURCE: Author's analysis of data from the Panel Study of Income Dynamics (2009).

countries is that men pair up with shorter women (Fink et al. 2007). With the average man being taller than the average woman, this is possible to arrange—in fact, we could hypothetically require that every woman marry a taller man. That's almost what is already happening voluntarily. If you scrambled up the couples from Figure 5.1 at random, you would find that 8 percent of the men have taller wives. In reality, however, only 4 percent have taller wives. Thus, men and women go out of their way to conform to the taller-man expectation, and as a result even short men and tall women usually experience taller-man interactions in their daily lives and most intimate relationships (Stulp et al. 2013).

The taller husband conjures up images of the protective, dominant man ("Let me reach that for you") with a nurturing, supportive wife ("Can I fix you a sandwich?"). To choose a high-profile example, such an image was apparent in many official photos of Britain's Prince Charles and Princess Diana. They were actually very close in height, and he often looked shorter than her in candid pictures. But when they posed for portraits, he usually stood on a box or step, as in the picture for the stamp commemorating their royal wedding (Currie 1981).

The idea of women as the weaker sex corresponds to the pattern of male domination in modern society, as symbolized by the muscular male athlete and the taller husband. Consider also the common restroom symbols, shown in Figure 5.2. The icons for male and female may seem to be the same person, except that the female version is wearing a dress. However, on closer inspection, the overlay on the right shows that their bodies are subtly different. Although the

What would you estimate is the depicted height difference between Prince Charles and Princess Diana?

Figure 5.2 **Common restroom symbols**

SOURCE: AIGA, The Professional Association for Design (2013).

two figures are the same height, the woman's shoulders are narrower, her legs are thinner, and her arms point slightly outward, suggesting broader hips underneath her dress. Apparently, the symbols' designers did not merely rely on clothing differences, but also depicted variation in female and male body types consistent with the image of a stronger and larger man. This depiction is not inaccurate, but it accentuates rather than minimizes the differences between men and women.

Ironically, although everyone starts out as a female fetus before roughly half become male, the common perception still fits the eighteenth-century image of man as the basic "person" and woman as different in some way. This male-centric view has deep roots in Western religious traditions: consider the biblical Adam and Eve story, in which he was the original person and God created her to complement him. You may notice that something like the man on the bathroom sign is commonly used in graphic design to represent the generic "person." Similarly, in language, we often use male terms for the general person, as when we call a mixed-gender group "you guys" or refer to human products as "manmade." Such male-gender-based expressions show no signs of disappearing, despite the best efforts of feminists to eradicate sexist language.

But are women really the weaker sex? Strength may be measured in different ways, and the biology is more complicated than the restroom symbols imply. By some measures, in fact, men are weaker. For example, women live longer than men, on average, in 99 percent of all countries (United Nations Statistics Division 2012). In the United States, men are more likely than women to die at every age, as Figure 5.3 shows. Although men in their late teens and 20s are more likely to die from accidents and injuries they inflict on each other—so that at its peak the ratio of male to female deaths is 2.8 to 1—the pattern of natural deaths at all

Figure 5.3 **U.S. death rates by sex and age, 2014**

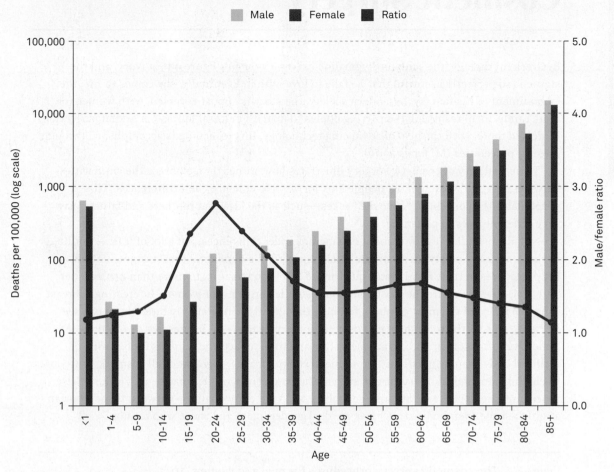

SOURCE: Kochanek et al. (2016).

ages favors females. Even male fetuses are more vulnerable than females: they are more likely to be born prematurely and more likely to experience complications during childbirth (Brettell, Yeh, and Impey 2008). The natural vulnerability may explain why humans evolved to produce slightly more male than female babies—usually about 106 boys for every 100 girls born. Thus, the stereotypical wife who needs to be protected by her (taller, stronger) husband often ages into the vision of a "little old lady"—who outlives the man. After a lifetime of higher death rates for men, the population over age 74 has four times as many widowed women as widowed men.

The image of women as the weaker sex persists, despite their greater ability to survive, partly because we exaggerate the differences between the sexes—by pairing women with taller men, putting more men in jobs that require more physical strength, and many other practices (such as women shaving their body hair). Perhaps the most extreme practices involve cosmetic surgery, which usually accentuates gender differences (see Changing Technology, "Cosmetic Surgery").

Cosmetic Surgery

In Greek mythology, the sculptor Pygmalion carves a woman's figure out of ivory, and the statue is so perfectly beautiful that he falls in love with it. Eventually, she comes to life, the embodiment of his fantasy. In modern society, the story is almost reversed, with women (or, more rarely, men) reshaping their living bodies to match a cultural fantasy of sexual perfection. More and more, with the help of advancing technology, this reshaping is accomplished through medical procedures (M. Jones 2009).

The popularity of cosmetic surgery illustrates how, rather than embrace the similarities between men and women, most people look for ways to enhance their differences. This perpetuates the concept of "opposite" sexes—such as the idea that mothers and fathers play very different roles in parenting.

Not all cosmetic surgery is about enhancing gender differences, but a lot of it is. According to the American Society for Aesthetic Plastic Surgery, the number of breast augmentation and lift procedures in the United States quadrupled from 1997 to 2015, to more than 450,000 per year. Together, those are the most common cosmetic surgeries for women. Interestingly, breast *reduction* is one of the most common for men (though it is still relatively rare, as you can see in Figure 5.4). Of the total spent on cosmetic surgery in 2015—an impressive $8.1 billion—$2 billion went for women's breast augmentation and lifts. In fact, the burdens (or benefits) of artificial body shaping mostly fall on women, who purchase 85 percent of all cosmetic procedures (including nonsurgical interventions such as the Botox antiwrinkle treatment). Because these procedures are expensive, they also contribute to a kind of inequality—between those who can afford to shape their bodies to achieve an ideal gender image and those who cannot.

Figure 5.4 **Top cosmetic surgery procedures for men and women, 2015**

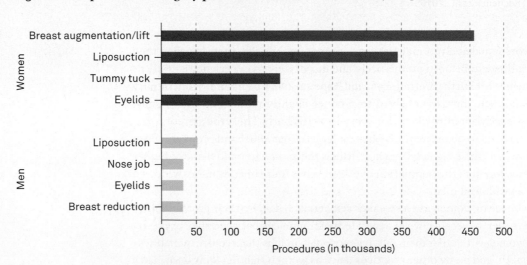

SOURCE: American Society for Aesthetic Plastic Surgery (2016).

These patterns have the effect of reinforcing the differences between men and women instead of their similarities, creating sexes that appear to be opposites instead of merely variations on a single human theme.

Sexual Diversity

To many people, the very idea of sexual diversity is perplexing, or even threatening. How is this an issue? Unlike the races, which are not logically defined according to biological criteria (see Chapter 3), two sexes can be clearly defined objectively, at least insofar as people's bodies are developed for one of the two different roles in sexual reproduction. But within those categories—male or female—people show great variety. There are differences in anatomy, reproductive ability, hormones, sexual orientation (see Chapter 6), and many other traits. How people are labeled and defined, and how those identities are applied, is socially constructed, and how to handle this diversity is a matter of some conflict. For example, in an attempt to satisfy its hundreds of millions of users, Facebook introduced the option to select up to 10 sex or gender identities out of more than 50, from (alphabetically) Agender to Transsexual, and then they added a further option to simply enter your own custom identity (Facebook Diversity 2015). As we will see, this increasingly complex process of social construction largely happens—or at least begins—within families.

The treatment of intersex people is an important instance of this social construction (Davis 2015). **Intersex** refers to a condition in which a person's chromosomal composition doesn't correspond with his or her sexual anatomy at birth, or the anatomy is not clearly male or female. These are part of a broader set of conditions that are clinically described as "disorders of sexual development" (L. Allen 2009). Intersex conditions are reported by doctors in about 18 out of every 100,000 births (0.018 percent), although they are probably undercounted, and the rates vary between different populations (Sax 2002). The most common disorder involves children who are genetically female but have a condition known as *congenital adrenal hyperplasia* that causes excess androgens in the uterus, leading them to develop ambiguous genitalia. (Remember, we all start the same, and males form male organs only after androgens flood the uterus.) This is the case with most hermaphrodites, an outdated term that comes from the mythological Greek figure Hermaphroditus, who was part man and part woman. In another condition, known as *androgen insensitivity,* children who are genetically male have a condition that prevents their bodies from using the male hormones, so they have female external anatomy but male internal anatomy (hidden testes instead of ovaries).

As noted earlier, a sexual identity is assigned to all children at birth, by parents or medical workers. In the past, that was usually as simple as someone declaring "It's a girl!" or "It's a boy!" although now the surprise is usually the result of an ultrasound procedure during the pregnancy (Shipp et al. 2004). The assignment of gender is not controversial for the vast majority of people, but it may be problematic for intersex children. Because adults are most comfortable when anatomy matches sexual identity, parents usually raise intersex children

intersex

A condition in which a person's chromosomal composition doesn't correspond with his or her sexual anatomy at birth, or the anatomy is not clearly male or female as girls if they have female or ambiguous appearance, even if they have male hormones (L. Allen 2009). Later in childhood, hormone treatments or surgical procedures may be applied to make children's body types more closely match the sex assigned to them by their doctors and parents (Thyen et al. 2006). Unfortunately, decisions to assign gender based on genitalia rather than hormones may result in psychological problems as children grow into adolescence and hormonal differences increase.

Finally, how we behave and relate to others is built up around the sexual identity we feel. **Transgender** people are those whose gender identity does not match the sex they were assigned at birth; that is, they do not behave socially in accordance with what is expected based on their body type. This crossover may be apparent through gender expression, such as wearing clothes associated with the other sex, but it does not necessarily indicate an attraction to people of the same sex. To some transgender people, their body feels—to them—at odds with their biological sex category (leading to the less-common term *transsexual*). They may use medical or cosmetic procedures, including surgery and/or hormones, in an attempt to bring their body into closer alignment with their sexual identity. Interestingly, while intersex conditions are often treated as a medically urgent situation, doctors usually urge caution and delay in their approach to medical transitions for transgender people (Davis, Dewey, and Murphy 2016). Still, while transgender identity used to be considered a psychiatric disorder, experts in the United States now consider it problematic only when it causes distress in a person's life, in which case it is known as *gender dysphoria* (Belluck 2016).

Despite these various forms of sexual diversity, there is an overwhelming tendency in modern societies to identify and label all people according to one or the other "opposite" sex. This applies strong, and sometimes oppressive, social pressure to those who do not conform to either identity. The flip side of that social pressure is a fascination with those who live outside the usual boundaries of sex and gender. In fact, paying inordinate attention to extremely unusual cases is one way that people reinforce their own feeling of being "normal." One recipient of such attention was Thomas Beatie, who was born female but had a male sexual identity; he was transsexual. He took male hormones, had surgery to deconstruct his breasts, and—after being legally recognized as male—married a woman. Then, when he and his wife wanted to have children but she could not become pregnant, they decided to impregnate him with donated sperm. That was still possible because of his female reproductive anatomy (and he stopped taking male hormones). He thus earned notoriety as the "pregnant man" and eventually gave birth twice, becoming the father to his children (Beatie 2008). Needless to say, the media were agog with the story.

The most famous person to make a transgender transition is now probably Caitlyn Jenner, who transitioned from her male identity as Bruce Jenner, an Olympic gold medal–winning athlete (Yahr 2015). Her popularity coincided with the rise of hit TV shows with transgender characters, such as *Orange Is the New Black* and the family drama *Transparent*. The protagonist in *Transparent*, like Jenner, transitioned from male to female in late adulthood. In fact, transgender transitions have become more common at older ages, often among people who

transgender

A term to describe individuals whose gender identity does not match their assigned sex.

are divorced or widowed, after their children have grown, or they have retired—reducing the difficulty of upending intimate relationships that often accompanies this change (Bernstein 2015).

Despite a shift toward accepting sexual diversity, however, transgender identities still present a problem for our strictly two-gender system (see Changing Culture, "Raising Androgyny"). Recent estimates suggest only about 1 out of every 200 American adults consider themselves transgender (Crissman et al. 2016). But in the last few years, the issue has exploded into the debate over public bathrooms (Schilt and Westbrook 2015). While some schools and local governments have embraced a new approach that permits people to use the bathroom that matches their gender identity, a backlash among conservatives has demanded that people be required to use the bathroom of the gender on their birth certificate. The legal and political debate over this question shows no sign of dying down (Human Rights Watch 2016).

There are many examples of cultural adaptations to transgender identity. In the Americas, many indigenous tribes once recognized a role for male-bodied people who occupied women's social positions (Trexler 2002). They dressed in both men's and women's clothes and participated in cultural rituals as women, and sometimes they married men. (Less often, female-bodied people acted as men in a similar way.) These people were essentially considered a third gender. Anthropologists once referred to them as "berdache," a term now considered offensive. In recent times, American Indian gay and lesbian activists have characterized them as "two-spirit" people, referring to the combination of male and female identity (Gilley 2006).

Caitlyn Jenner's public transition helped bring transgender issues into the public spotlight.

In modern societies, some countries have made legal moves toward recognizing gender diversity. For example, India, Pakistan, and Nepal have all enacted laws to grant rights to transgender people, including registration as "other" gender in addition to male and female for passports or voter registration (Godwin 2010). In the United States, there is some movement toward expanding options for legal gender identity. A judge in Oregon broke new ground in 2016, allowing a 52-year-old Army veteran named Jamie Shupe, who was born male and transitioned to female, to identify legally as "non-binary"—neither male nor female. Jamie, who now prefers to go by that name alone, said,

> "I was assigned male at birth due to biology. I'm stuck with that for life. My gender identity is definitely feminine. My gender identity has never been male, but I feel like I have to own up to my male biology. Being non-binary allows me to do that. I'm a mixture of both. I consider myself as a third sex." (Parks 2016)

Raising Androgyny

In 1974, a concerned parent wrote to the advice columnist Ann Landers: "Our daughter, age 9, is still playing Cowboys and Indians with the hat and holster set we gave our 7-year-old son for Christmas. He is playing with her doll. Do we have a problem?" The response from Landers, whom many considered a national expert on parenting, was not reassuring: "In all probability not, but it's too early to tell. Keep your eyes open, however. You might have TWO problems. If this pattern persists, particularly with the boy, I recommend that you have him evaluated professionally. Give it six months" (*Ms.*, December 1974).

Although today's experts would be more forgiving of a boy playing with dolls, parents still face dilemmas raising children. On the one hand, they might want their boys to be boys and their girls to be girls, according to the standards of their community or culture. Such children may benefit from a feeling of fitting in and normalcy, something many children crave. On the other hand, some parents see those gender types as unnecessarily restricting (Rahilly 2015).

androgynous

Neither exclusively masculine nor exclusively feminine.

They choose a more **androgynous** gender approach for their children—that is, one that is neither exclusively masculine nor exclusively feminine. Gender-neutral styles, activities, and interactions may give children the power to choose their own way and allow families to tap into talents that might otherwise be ignored. Children granted such freedom may develop a sense of flexibility in adult relationships, which advocates believe will lead to more egalitarian attitudes in the next generation (Witt 1997).

Although androgynous parenting seems like a modern idea, it might not have surprised American parents before the twentieth century—at least regarding the early years of life. At that time, boys and girls dressed much more similarly, up until at least age 5, with boys in dresses and long hair until they started school. (This sequence reminds us of fetuses in the womb, where everyone starts female before half become male.) The style changed around 1900, as boys were gradually dressed in pants at earlier ages. The famous feminist Charlotte Perkins Gilman was outraged. She wrote in 1910:

> The most conspicuous evil here is in the premature and unnatural differentiation in sex in the dress of little children...a little child should never be forced to think of this distinction. It does not exist in the child's consciousness. It is in no way called for in natural activities, but is forced into a vivid prominence by our attitude. (qtd. in Paoletti 1987:142)

Today, most parents happily gender-identify their infants from the day they are born, and in many ways—such as the division between boys' and girls' toys—childhood is more gender segregated than ever (Sweet 2014). But one couple who would have agreed with Gilman is a pair of Swedish parents who kept their child's gender a secret from all but their closest relatives until she or he was 2½ years old. "We want [the child] to grow up more freely and avoid being forced into a specific gender mold from the outset," the mother said. "It's cruel to bring a child into the world with a blue or pink stamp on their forehead" (*The Local* 2009).

Plenty of adults stop short of boycotting gender identification altogether but still attempt to rein in some of the more extreme forms of gender differentiation. For example, Abi and Emma Moore are sisters, each with their own children, who created an organization called Pink Stinks, which "confronts the damaging messages that bombard girls through toys, clothes and media." They write: "Girls' products overwhelmingly focus on being pretty, passive and obsessed with shopping, fashion and makeup—this promotes a dangerously narrow definition of what it means to be a girl. These 'Girly' products and concepts are marketed, for the most part, under the umbrella of pink" (Pink Stinks 2013).

The issue of gender identity in childhood is far from settled. When it comes to transgender teenagers and adults, most mental health experts now believe they should be supported in attempting to achieve the gender identity they want. But for younger children who identify with the other sex, there is no consensus. Some believe that therapy to "normalize" children's gender identity is warranted, while others support the social transition to the other gender, possibly leading to hormonal or surgical intervention (Dreger 2015).

Far more common than transgender identity is the routine adoption of androgynous styles and behaviors by children who are generally comfortable with their gender identity. Yet here again there are extremely different approaches. On the one hand, many parents routinely encourage children to bend gender stereotypes—like those children in the 1974 letter to Ann Landers. On the other hand, some parents (and authorities) enforce strict gender roles, even when there is no explicit question of gender identity at issue. For example, many schools maintain rules about hair length for boys, in essence requiring a difference in how the bodies of boys and girls are presented, even at young ages. One North Carolina school made headlines in 2016 for suspending a third grader for having hair that touched his shirt collar (Ochsner 2016).

Taylor Pugh, just 4 years old in 2009, was suspended from prekindergarten because his long hair violated his school's dress code. In the background are his brothers and best friend, whose short haircuts were allowed.

These examples help to illustrate how even something that appears to be biologically fixed—such as the existence of two and only two opposite sexes—may mask an underlying diversity that can be interpreted in different ways according to the dictates of different cultures.

Now that we have established some of the key concepts and controversies in the social science of gender, as well as the biology that lays the foundation for gender, we can turn to an overview of the most common perspectives sociologists employ in their research and teaching.

Perspectives on Gender

In Chapter 1, I introduced some general theories used in the sociology of the family. Naturally, there are also a number of perspectives adopted by researchers who study gender in families. As with the general theories, these approaches help us think systematically about the facts we see and structure our research to answer the most pressing questions we face. Here, again, we do not need to choose any one perspective; rather, we will benefit from different approaches as they relate to different issues in different circumstances.

Biological Perspective

Because gender is so closely tied to biological sex, some sociologists use the science of sex differences to explore or explain gender patterns in human society. For example, some sociologists see the tendency of men to be more promiscuous—and of women to invest more energy in child rearing—as reflective of the biological investments men and women have in their children. Because men's contribution may be limited to a single sex act, while women carry children through gestation and usually the early years of life, men may be less involved in parenting and show less commitment to child rearing than women.

Instead of asserting that "nature" rather than "nurture" has the final word, however, most of these social scientists seek to integrate social and biological explanations of gender (Machalek and Martin 2004). Most also recognize that human behavior with origins in our biology and evolution is not inevitable, unchanging, or necessarily socially desirable from our contemporary perspective (Rossi 1984). Thus, it is possible that men had an ancient evolutionary tendency toward promiscuity and away from child care, and women tended more toward monogamy and child rearing. But the great variety of social arrangements now and in the past—especially differences in mating systems, such as monogamy versus polygamy (see Chapter 2), or parenting relationships—means that our species is not tied to any one model of behavior (P. Gray and Anderson 2010). Just as animals react and evolve differently in different ecological contexts, people adapt flexibly in different social contexts rather than being guided by a single blueprint (Dawkins 2006).

Biological explanations for family behavior, especially those stressing different and complementary roles for men and women, are often inspired by a structural functionalist view of society (see Chapter 1). Working backward from observed behavior, such theorists as Talcott Parsons looked for reasons (one might call them justifications) for why current arrangements served the greater social good. And biological evolution provides a useful framework for that perspective. Most sociologists, however, find it more fruitful to study processes of social change and variation, rather than focusing on stability and those aspects of family behavior that may (or may not) have evolutionary roots.

Feminism

The themes from feminist theory described in Chapter 1 figure prominently in feminist explanations of gender and the family. Feminist scholars argue that gender inequality is central to family life, that family structure is socially constructed rather than natural, and that family experiences for men and women differ according to race/ethnicity and social class. Gender identity and gender inequality are core principles of social life. In particular, the visible identification of differences between men and women, and boys and girls, is a modern preoccupation that reinforces these inequalities. Rather than being biologically ordained or determined by evolution, these differences are the product of social interaction—interaction that reflects men's dominant position over women. In fact, it is this understanding that leads to the important distinction between (biological) sex and (social) gender, as defined earlier (G. Fox and Murry 2000).

Feminists have long argued that a system of rigid gender categories and roles serves male-dominated society; because men have more influence over social rules, they set the standards to serve their interests (G. Rubin 1975). And that, feminists argue, is why the image of the "weaker sex" persists. Because the family, probably more than any other institutional arena, is where sexual identity is turned into gender identity—and where gender expression is learned and practiced—some feminists have expressed strong criticism of family practices such as the division of child care and housework and how family decisions are made.

In addition, how the roles for men and women are defined sometimes reinforces other aspects of inequality—such as inequality by race and social class—by setting standards according to the practices of dominant racial

Do you think more fathers are doing childrearing tasks like changing diapers? If you know any parents of young children, who changes the diapers?

and class groups (D. King 1988). For example, when Daniel Patrick Moynihan identified the "reversed roles of husband and wife" among African Americans as a social problem (see Chapter 2), he was describing the Black community from a perspective common among Whites in the 1960s. The fact that Black families had different gender patterns than White families made them an easy target for criticism.

Partly because they view such images and ideals as important tools used to create inequality, feminist researchers have done extensive studies of gender in the popular media, such as TV, movies, magazines, and the Internet. One far-reaching conclusion from this research is that popular images portray a narrow view of female beauty, setting a standard that harms more women than it helps. An unrealistic or unhealthy standard—seen in dolls that are anatomically fantastical or "super" models who are devastatingly thin—can make young women feel inadequate about their bodies, encourage food and weight obsessions, and induce depression (Milkie 2002). The problems caused by such images are exacerbated by the tendency to depict women mostly in relation to men (as in modern princess fairy tales), while stories about men are more likely to be about their own lives and achievements (Rowe 1979).

Finally, some feminists have also pursued psychoanalytic theory, inspired by work on childhood development that explores the emergence of male and female identity in families. In the tradition of Sigmund Freud and others, boys are seen as growing to reject their mothers and denying their own female nature, while girls emulate the nurturing behavior of their mothers (Chodorow 1978). In this view, the tendency of mothers to take primary responsibility for child rearing appears to be the basis of modern gender identities, since this relationship establishes the idea in children that women are emotional caretakers, while men are rational (though emotionally distant) leaders. Once that idea takes hold, it establishes the foundation for wider differences between men and women throughout society. And because these identities are developed at such a young age, people tend to think that gender differences are inherent to human nature rather than a product of social behavior (Brody 1999).

Masculinity

As we have seen in our discussion of race in Chapter 3, close examination of the dominant racial group (Whites) has often been neglected in research that focuses on the trials and tribulations of subordinate groups, such as African Americans and Latinos. Similarly, much of the early research on gender was really about women. That made sense because studies of gender sought to expand the common perspective of men as representative of society as a whole.

However, in the last few decades, researchers have explored how rigid gender expectations take their own toll on men and male identity. It is now clear that masculinity also has its own history and development—that it, like femininity, is socially constructed (Connell and Messerschmidt 2005). Researchers in this tradition see multiple masculinities—that is, different constructions of what it means or requires to be a boy or man—in different cultural and historical settings (Pascoe and Bridges 2016). Because these ideas involve fatherhood, parenting, and relationships with women, they have become important to studies of the family (Doucet 2006).

Just as women's fashion permits more variation in choice of clothes than men's, expectations for men's behavior and identity in general are often more strictly enforced than are those for women. A narrow view of masculinity is perhaps hardest on gay men and others who do not fit the mold established by the dominant image. For example, among young adults who were "gender nonconforming" in childhood (in their play, fictional character preferences, and gender identity) men are more likely than women to report having been bullied when they were younger—and then suffering from depression in adulthood (Roberts et al. 2013).

Symbolic Interaction

If gender identity and behavior are indeed socially constructed, how is this achieved? The theory of symbolic interactionism (see Chapter 1) argues that complex social systems are maintained through elaborate patterns of interpersonal interaction. Only by enacting our social roles and receiving feedback from others who understand their meaning can we build and maintain our identities.

Each of us faces the task of turning our membership in a sex category into the accomplishment of a complex gender identity, a process that has been called "doing gender" (West and Zimmerman 1987). One way we do this is by enhancing those aspects of our body and personality that conform to the common image of our gender and suppressing those parts of ourselves that don't fit. Another way is through public displays of identity, such as choosing the bathroom that matches our gender. This theory is especially important for the study of families, because our performance of gender identity requires an audience, and the most important audience from an early age are the members of our own family.

I drew on this theory in my earlier discussion about the importance of height differences between men and women in marriage. The common practice of matching taller men with shorter women sets the stage for the performance of gender identities in which men are physically dominant over women. By application of this simple rule, lifelong patterns of interaction are replicated in almost every family home—which brings us to the issue of gender socialization.

Gender Socialization

How different or similar boys and girls are, and how they get that way, is the subject of much research and debate (C. Martin and Ruble 2010). The nature and extent of our differences are crucial, because how we create, interpret, and act on those differences is ultimately what determines the patterns of behavior we see in society.

socialization

The process by which individuals internalize elements of the social structure, making those elements part of their own personality.

These patterns develop through **socialization**, the process by which individuals internalize elements of the social structure, making those elements part of their own personality. Many people think of gender socialization as simply teaching boys to be boys and girls to be girls. But the reality is more complex. It is not only something taught or done to people; it is also something people do to themselves. This includes learning the norms, rules, and beliefs of the culture around them as well as ways to adapt their behavior to get along in that environment.

Because gender is an important part of self-identity and behavior, the socialization process includes learning to adapt to the ways that gender is organized. This is not as simple as learning a particular "gender role" but rather requires developing the capacity to act and react to the actions and expectations of others. Thus, socialization is not like a computer program or brainwashing; people do not always follow the rules they learn through the socialization process, even if they have learned the rules well. And it is not something experienced only by children but is a lifelong process by which people learn to act—and think—in consideration of what others do and expect.

Gender socialization is the outcome of countless interactions, starting with those between parents and children. At the youngest ages, of course, parents have the dominant influence over this process. But as children age, their socialization continues under a variety of influences, including their own personalities and their interactions with siblings, peers, schools, and the wider culture. In adult life, socialization more often occurs in the other institutional arenas that we focus on in this book, especially the market.

Parents

From birth through adolescence, parents do gender with their children in many ways. Gender identity is expressed in how parents decorate their children's bedrooms, the styles and colors of clothing they choose for them, the toys and games children are given, the household chores they are asked to do, and eventually the occupational roles they are expected to fulfill as adults (Witt 1997).

Although every parent is different—and many may feel they are reinventing parenting every day—social scientists have discerned clear patterns in how parents, on average, treat boys and girls differently (S. Raley and Bianchi 2006). Besides the highly visible differences, such as clothes and toys, the ways parents interact with boys and girls may be subtly different. For example, parents are more likely to employ parenting strategies that encourage personal autonomy and decision making with their daughters, while they are more controlling and directive with their sons (Endendijk et al. 2016).

In some ways, the most important outcome of these parenting patterns is the affirmation of gender difference itself. We learn we are different partly by acting differently and partly by being treated differently, depending on our gender. How we are different—the particular qualities of boys as opposed to girls—may be less important than the basic fact of difference, which for most people serves to anchor their gender identities (Blume and Blume 2003).

As an example, take the issue of pink versus blue. One study of two middle-class American preschools, in which researchers observed about 90 days of classes, found 61 percent of girls dressed in something pink each day, while no boys were ever seen wearing pink (K. Martin 1998). In college, incidentally, pink may be less common among women, but it's no more favored by men. My own survey of about 250 college students found that only 6 percent of women identified pink as their favorite color, but not a single man chose pink (P. Cohen 2013a).

Now step back a few generations, to 1918, when the popular magazine *Ladies' Home Journal* offered this advice to parents for dressing their children: "The generally accepted rule is pink for the boy and blue for the girl. The reason is that pink being a more decided and stronger color is more suitable for the boy, while blue, which is more

Among children, pink is almost exclusively a girls' color today, but a century ago parents didn't usually dress young children in different colors according to gender.

delicate and dainty, is prettier for the girl" (Frassanito and Pettorini 2008). The gender associations of pink and blue feel so automatic now that it seems odd that the logic of this choice would be reversed from what we expect today. In fact, at the time there was not a strong association of gender with any colors for children—the very idea was probably a recent innovation of clothing mass marketers—which is why the magazine editors felt the need to explain their choice (Paoletti 2012). Even as late as 1959, when the Walt Disney Studios released the movie *Sleeping Beauty*, the magical fairies argued over whether Princess Auro-ra's dress should be pink or blue (Do Rozario 2004).

The use of color to differentiate boys from girls seems necessary in part because boy and girl babies look so similar. But the socialization of boys and girls serves as training for adult positions that are not just different but unequal. As the feminist sociologist Barbara Risman asserts, "Unless we see difference, we cannot justify inequality" (Risman 2004:430). As an example of difference creating inequality, think of the emotional training children receive. Being successful in the more powerful positions held by men doesn't usually require much in the way of sympathetic emotion, so boys learn to minimize emotional responses—except those useful for domination, such as anger and pride. Girls, on the other hand, are more likely to end up in lower-status positions, where emotional traits such as nurturing, respect, and even shame are more necessary to succeed (Brody 1999).

Judged by these standards, it appears that parents are very effective socializers of their children. By the age of 3, there is a clear difference in the toy preferences between boys and girls. Girls on average prefer to play with toys that represent caring for others, such as dollhouses, food service, and other family-based toys. Toddler boys, on the other hand, tend to prefer impersonal toys, such as trains and trucks, and tools of power, such as weapons (Golombok et al. 2008).

How does the color of a baby's outfit affect your perception of his or her gender?

As children age, these differences translate into gendered task assignments within the family, with girls more likely to do more routine housework, such as cooking and cleaning, and boys more likely to help out in the garage or the yard (Raley and Bianchi 2006). That may set the stage for patterns much later in life, inside and outside the family. In the workplace, men and women usually work at different kinds of jobs (discussed shortly and in Chapter 11). And in the family, when elderly parents need their adult children to care for them in their later years, grown daughters are much more likely to step in and provide such assistance.

Siblings

Aside from parents, no one is closer to a young child than his or her siblings. The presence of an other-gender sibling fosters development of separate gender identities based on gender-typical behavior and is one way siblings differentiate themselves within the family. But when two siblings are of the same gender, one may adopt behaviors that are less gender typical as a way of building an individual identity. To further complicate matters, birth order matters as well, as brothers with younger sisters have been shown to hold more traditional attitudes about gender than other boys (McHale, Crouter, and Whiteman 2003). And when older siblings are charged with caring for younger siblings, which has been common especially among African American families, sibling influences are even more pronounced (Whiteman, Bernard, and McHale 2010).

Interactive Circles of Socialization

Moving beyond parents and siblings, we find that people internalize elements of gender through all their interactions in the wider world. After all, families do not exist in social isolation; their interactions always take place in a broader social context—within a community or a country, for example. Religion may be an especially important cultural influence (see Changing Culture, "Gender and Religion"). Another influence on children, naturally, is the way their own parents were socialized. Based on their own socialization, parents raise their children with an eye on how others see, or might see, their behavior. That includes people the parents respect as well as those they compete with, fear, or even despise. Parents also use their own upbringing as a frame of reference, for better or worse. Thus, even the intimate behavior of parents is a pathway in which wider social influences affect children's development. (And remember, although this section focuses on children, socialization is a lifelong process, so parents are doing it, too.)

I have created a graphic representation of these wider social forces in Figure 5.5. We see individual family members interacting within a family, according to gender and family relationships. How those interactions play out also reflects influences from the local environment—for example, friendship circles, schoolmates, and people at work—as represented by the dark background color seeping into the lighter family circle. The process is repeated at the larger cultural level, where what I've labeled "cultural context" colors both local and family interactions.

In reality, the world around individuals and their families could be represented by any number of such circles and layers. It is up to researchers to find and explain the specific influences and how they work. And indeed, they have made many fascinating discoveries. To convey the flavor of that approach, I will describe some of their findings.

Figure 5.5 **Multiple levels of social context for gender socialization**

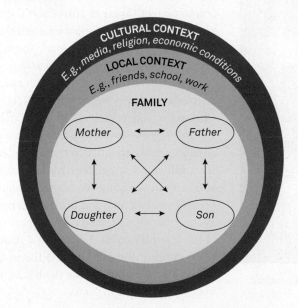

Individual interactions within families are influenced by the local content as well as by the larger culture around them.

Gender and Religion

As we saw in Chapter 2, Christianity, the largest religion in the United States, is a major source of cultural tradition. It shares with Judaism and Islam a theological legacy that goes back to the biblical Abraham, and thus they are sometimes known collectively as the Abrahamic religions. Together, these religious institutions continue to wield an important influence on gender and families. Today, building a modern identity includes shopping in the "spiritual marketplace" of religion—or choosing not to—and that choice partly reflects how people want to handle questions of gender and family (Roof 1999).

Religion's influence has important implications for families. People often turn to religion for guidance on parenting and pass on—or attempt to pass on—their way of life to their children. Usually, the influence of religion is conservative. That is, those who practice religion, as well as their children, express more conservative attitudes toward gender and family life, such as promoting the breadwinner-homemaker marriage ideal (Pearce and Thornton 2007). In fact, research comparing countries around the world finds that the more religious the population is, the more gender inequality there is in society (Schnabel 2015).

But the relationship between religious doctrine, personal attitudes, and family behavior is complicated. The expressed attitudes of religious conservatives do not always match their own actions, especially when it comes to making decisions about marriage and family (Denton 2004). Still, religious families are more likely to live in a breadwinner-homemaker arrangement. This is especially the case among Christian conservatives (Sherkat 2000) and those who place a high value on imparting religious and cultural values to their children in the home, such as Arab Americans (Read 2004).

It should be noted that when conservative religious women—such as Evangelical Christians, conservative Catholics, and Orthodox Jews—work in paid jobs, they often support gender equality in the workplace. But they still stand by gender divisions and male authority in the home (C. Manning 1999). That seems contradictory, but it makes sense to one Evangelical woman, who told an interviewer, "I think feminism has been a good thing in the work world....But it could be a threat to the family because it questions the headship of the man" (Gallagher 2003:168).

In 1972, Sally Priesand became the first ordained female rabbi in the United States.

Feminism within Religion

Significant feminist trends do exist within religious communities. For example, Orthodox Jews frequently separate men and women, calling for different family and work roles, clothing, and ritual requirements and even dividing the synagogue floor with a barrier to shield men and women from each other's sight. But Jewish feminists have adapted aspects of the religion in an attempt to satisfy both their feminist and spiritual needs (Dufour 2000). For example, some Jewish women have taken on Orthodox male requirements such as wearing the skullcap known as a yarmulke. In the Reform, Conservative, and Reconstructionist branches of Judaism, women are ordained as rabbis.

In the case of American Muslims, the practice of women wearing a veil, or hijab, has grown more common. The hijab may cover a woman's head or sometimes her entire body when she is outside the house or in the presence of nonfamily members. Those who support the veil believe that it protects a woman's virtue by shielding her from men's sexual gaze, while demonstrating a dedication to Islam. It also dramatically highlights the differences between the social roles of men and women and—in the traditional view—serves as a reminder that a woman's true place is in the home rather than in public. Not surprisingly, some Islamic feminists have spoken up, protesting that the veil displays women as submissive and subordinate to men (Read and Bartkowski 2000). On the other hand, still others appreciate the hijab as a visual critique of Western or American consumerism, which they believe turns women into objects of male sexual exploitation. And in Afghanistan, feminist organizers have even used veils to conceal their identities and actions as they build their movement in secret (Boone 2010).

The hijab is one of many elements of women's clothing that is loaded with religious, cultural, and political significance. Perhaps contrary to widespread images of the plain, black hijab, they can be stylish and colorful.

Religion in the Family

Christianity has long been associated with traditional, patriarchal gender relations in the family. Conservative Christian groups such as Promise Keepers and Focus on the Family promote the teaching of Ephesians (5:22) in the New Testament, which commands: "Wives, submit to your husbands as to the Lord. For the husband is the head of the wife as Christ is the head of the church." Husbands are commanded to love their wives but not submit to them— and there is no doubt in this theological tradition that man preceded woman and woman was created to meet his needs (Gallagher 2003). However, there is also a considerable feminist presence within Christianity, both informal and organized. For example, Catholics for Choice promotes abortion rights in the context of gender equality more broadly. And the Episcopal Church ordains many women as priests, including for a time its presiding bishop, Katharine Jefferts Schori.

Ironically, then, although the religions are older than modernity, their modern-day adherents include a mix of those who stick to "traditional" gender ideas as well as those who adapt their doctrines and beliefs to support more modern expressions of gender equality. There is no single influence of "religion" on the family. Instead, religion presents a veritable toolbox of ideological and practical devices available for shaping your own life.

In 2006, Katharine Jefferts Schori was elected the first female Presiding Bishop of the Episcopal Church in the United States. Her term ended in 2015.

School

For children, the primary location for nonfamily social interaction is school, where they are exposed to both the formal content of the school's instruction and authority and the informal curriculum of teacher behavior and expectations. One set of gender interactions around school concerns clothing. Parents usually send young children to school dressed in more or less gender-typical clothing. Teachers, partly reacting to how the children are dressed and partly imposing their own ideas about how children should act, in turn often treat children differently according to gender. For example, wearing dresses limits the physical behavior girls can appropriately do, sometimes leading to embarrassment and a heightened level of self-awareness of their bodies and clothes, and teachers often remind children of these limits (K. Martin 1998). Over the years, we can expect such gender differences to be reinforced in the children's personalities.

For older children, gender differences in school may be less focused on boy-versus-girl identification, but the gender differences are no less crucial to the future of men and women as adults. One common observation is that boys are more likely to pursue education and careers in mathematics-related fields, something that may be traced to high school, where girls are much less likely to take advanced math courses (DiPrete and Buchmanm 2013). Although some people believe that males have a biological advantage in math, this appears to be a case of strong influences from the social context. One study of 22 mostly wealthy countries found that high school boys scored higher than girls on math tests in every country but one. But the difference between their scores was quite small in some countries (including the United States) and very large in others. And the size of the difference was closely related to overall inequality between men and women in each society. The author concluded that if genetics is one cause of male math advantage, it is a relatively small part of the story (Penner 2008). Social inequality seems to be behind most of the difference—part of the web of social influences that affect what happens in schools as children develop.

Peers

In and around school and in the neighborhood, exchanges within a peer culture are also pivotal for children (Giordano 2003). In sociology, we think of **peers** as people in a similar social situation and of similar status with whom an individual interacts. For children, peers are generally about the same age, usually in the same neighborhood, school, or other social settings where children are together. Despite the strong influence of families and other institutions, peers are often the ones whose opinions matter most, especially for adolescents (Adler, Kless, and Adler 1992).

peers

People in a similar social situation and of similar status with whom an individual interacts.

Figure 5.6 **Girls and boys doing gender-typed activities**

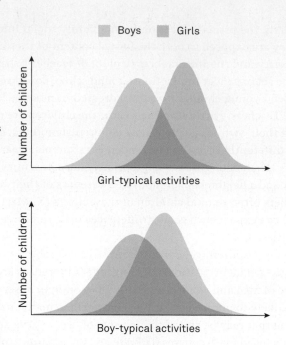

"Boy-typical" activities
Building model planes and cars
Using tools to make things
Playing sports
Playing video games
Things like washing the
 car and yardwork
Fishing or hunting
Horsing around and play
 fighting
Math and science

"Girl-typical" activities
Babysitting or looking
 after younger kids
Jumping rope or gymnastics
Shopping
Crafts
Tap dancing or ballet
Cheerleading
Making jewelry
Baking or helping in the
 kitchen

SOURCE: Author's calculations from Egan and Perry (2001).

Activities For children, the processes of choosing activities and friends are highly interrelated, whether the choices are made by themselves, their parents, or others. And they develop their gender identities through the activities they participate in, partly because of the other kids around.

One study helps us see the patterns of boys' and girls' activities (Egan and Perry 2001). Boys and girls in the fourth through eighth grades were asked how well they could do a series of activities. For example, interviewers read this statement to girls: "Some girls aren't good at using tools to make things . . . but other girls are good at using tools to make things." And they asked the girls which description fit them better. Then they broke the activities into "boy-typical" and "girl-typical" and counted how many girls and boys felt comfortable doing activities from each list.

As Figure 5.6 shows, boys and girls have different patterns of identifying with the two groups of activities. More girls are higher on the yellow "girl-typical" scale, and more boys are higher on the blue "boy-typical" scale. We could see this as indicating an extreme difference between the sexes, but there is also considerable overlap on each list (represented by the green areas in the charts), as boys express comfort with some items on the girl-typical list, and vice versa. (You might not agree with the activities listed for this study, which is more than 15 years old, but you can experiment with your own list in the Workshop activity for this chapter.)

Boys' and Girls' Activities

How did the men and women in your class today differ in their activities as children? Consider the list of gender-typed activities presented in Figure 5.6, and think back to your own childhood. What were some of your favorite activities?

You can use the activities featured in Figure 5.6, but it might be more interesting to generate your own. Pick an age—say, 10—and make a list of several activities you enjoyed at that time.

Here is a sample table for scoring up to 10 activities the class generates. Ask everyone in the class or student group to score each activity on a scale of 1 to 10, based on how much they participated in the activity when they were about 10 years old. Then calculate the average score for men and the average score for women for each activity.

Activity	Average woman's score	Average man's score
1.		
2.		
3.		
4.		
5.		
6.		
7.		
8.		
9.		
10.		

Consider these questions, either in discussion or as a writing assignment:

· What activities did you most have in common as boys and girls, and where is there least in common?

· Are other differences, such as race/ethnicity or age, apparent in your group?

· In your opinion, what is the source of the differences? That is, why did you do these activities? Can you tell what was your own choice versus something imposed by your parents, siblings, or others?

· What conclusions, if any, might you draw if this were a scientific study?

Alternatively, you can do a survey of people outside of class and ask them to rank activities according to their own childhood experience, either using the activities listed in the chapter or generating your own lists.

Ultimately, gender conformity may feel rewarding not because of what it tells us about gender but because it is a form of conformity, which produces a sense of belonging that many people desire. This is one more reason to pay special attention to the social context rather than focusing exclusively on the individual—one more reason, in other words, to think sociologically about gender.

Neighborhoods Sociologists have long been interested in neighborhoods as a social setting for interaction, partly because they are a source of peer influence (Rankin and Quane 2002). This is especially the case for poor African American families because their inner-city neighborhoods have undergone such a radical transformation, as we saw in Chapter 3 (M. Wilson 2009).

Peer influence in poor neighborhoods also tells us something about gender, however. Overall, young Black men and women have about the same high school graduation rates (Cataldi, Laird, and KewalRamani 2009). However, in poor neighborhoods—those with more low-income families, higher unemployment, and more people without college education—boys are less likely to graduate than girls (Crowder and South 2003). Why would boys be more harshly affected by distressed neighborhood conditions than girls? Research suggests that it is because adolescent girls tend to have more close social connections—a more supportive peer network. And they may be more closely supervised by their parents. As a result, they have more sources of support or protection from the difficult environment in which their families live.

This is a case where families—as well as neighbors, peers, and other local actors—interact differently with boys than with girls, leading to different outcomes. Outside of families, however, and especially for adults, the world of paid work—the market—is at the heart of gender interaction and gender inequality. (In this chapter, we focus on inequality in the workplace. But we revisit gender and work in Chapter 11, when we discuss the division of labor between men and women within families.)

Gender at Work

In Chapter 2, we saw that married women, including those with children, entered the labor force in greater and greater numbers from the 1960s through the 1990s (Goldin 1990). This broke down what was potentially one of the greatest barriers to equality between men and women—the divide between paid and unpaid work (P. Cohen 2004). In the process, women's independence dramatically increased. And although the change was greater for White women—as African American women especially had worked outside their homes in greater numbers in the past—among all groups of women the increase in employment was steep (Thistle 2006).

However, breaking down one barrier revealed more that remained to be overcome. Many forms of inequality and difference still exist between men and women in the United States. In keeping with the central theme of this chapter—how differences between women and men, girls and boys, are related to families—I will focus here on the division of labor between men and women in the workforce.

Former President Barack Obama's grandmother, Madelyn Dunham, worked in a bomb factory in Wichita, Kansas, during World War II (Remnick 2010). For a middle-class White woman, married and with a baby at home, working full-time in a blue-collar job was not considered normal just a few years earlier. But when push comes to shove, we often see the artificial nature of our social constraints. One of those times was during World War II, when the employment rates of married women shot up, especially for White women (Goldin 1991). What had once seemed improbable to many—the employment of married women with children at home—suddenly seemed much more normal.

Many of these working mothers were responding to economic hardship, as their husbands were off at war (as was the case with Dunham); others answered the patriotic call to serve the country; and still others seized an

World War II undermined the social construction of gender-separated work, as women built bombs, planes, and other supplies in factories.

opportunity to lead more challenging or independent lives. After the war, most women gave up their factory jobs (or were let go to make way for returning veterans), but the experience left an imprint on the workers themselves, as well as on their children, husbands, and employers. These women had shown that full-time employment outside the home could be an acceptable and even desirable part of a mother's life, even if she wasn't poor and desperate.

Education and Occupational Segregation

In the decades that followed World War II, many kinds of work became much more gender integrated—that is, done by both men and women. This was especially true in middle-class occupations such as real estate, bookkeeping, and high school teaching, where more than half the work is now done by women (Cotter, Hermsen, and Vanneman 2004). This change was possible partly because women devoted more of their lives to paid work and gained the experience and training they needed to move into new positions. But more important, the system of college education was increasingly open to women, and women responded by attending college at increasing rates. Women with college degrees had the credentials—and the incentives—to pursue new careers (P. Cohen and Bianchi 1999). In the early 1970s, among young adults (ages 25 to 34), there were just 70 women for every 100 men with college degrees. By 2015, women substantially outnumbered men in that category: 120 women per 100 men (see Trend to Watch).

How does gender affect the workplace?

Some of the most common occupations in the United States—truck driving, construction work, secretarial work, and nursing, for example—are almost completely segregated by gender. The same is true among some professions that require college degrees, such as engineering and elementary education. One reason for this is that the occupations women dominate are often in some way similar to the work women historically have done without pay at home for their families (such as child care), while men are more likely to do jobs that are not closely associated with domestic work (such as driving trucks). Some of this segregation is the result of men and women choosing different kinds of jobs. For example, boys grow up cooking, cleaning, and babysitting their relatives less often than girls do, so they may not want jobs doing that kind of work. But there are also sexist decisions by employers, and sometimes male workers try to keep women out of well-paying jobs. As a result, job segregation is an important part of the story of gender inequality in society.

Sources: Author analysis of 2016 Current Population Survey data via IPUMS (Ruggles et al. 2016).

http://wwnpag.es/sbtn5

Go to this link for an animation narrated by the author.

■ **Men (%)**   □ **Women (%)**

Male-dominated fields

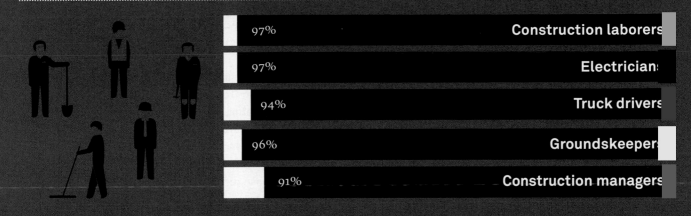

97%	Construction laborers
97%	Electricians
94%	Truck drivers
96%	Groundskeepers
91%	Construction managers

Relatively equal gender representation

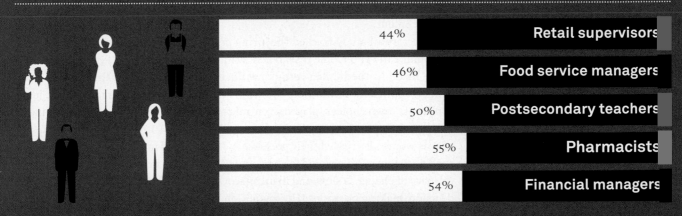

44%	Retail supervisors
46%	Food service managers
50%	Postsecondary teachers
55%	Pharmacists
54%	Financial managers

Female-dominated fields

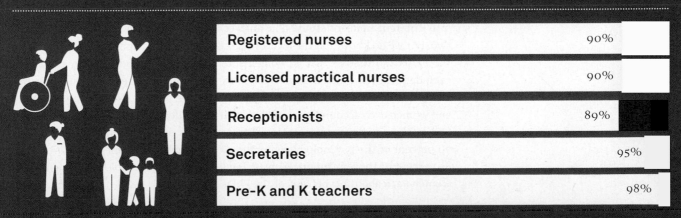

Registered nurses	90%
Licensed practical nurses	90%
Receptionists	89%
Secretaries	95%
Pre-K and K teachers	98%

Nevertheless, some of the most common occupations in the country—truck driving, construction work, secretarial work, and nursing, for example—are still almost completely segregated by gender, as you can see in the Story Behind the Numbers. And even in many professions that require a high level of education—such as engineering, law, and medicine—men still greatly outnumber women. There are several reasons for this persistent occupational segregation (see Chapter 11).

First, you will notice that the occupations women dominate are often in some way similar to the work women do—or did—without pay at home for their families. Child care, nursing, and teaching, for example, are jobs that were once done at home. On the other hand, men are more likely to do jobs that are not closely associated with domestic work, such as driving trucks and engineering (P. Cohen 2013b).

Do men and women simply choose different kinds of jobs? Yes and no. In some cases, job segregation does reflect worker preferences, based on likes, dislikes, and skills developed from childhood. For example, boys are less likely than girls to be called on to cook, clean house, and care for their younger siblings. But sometimes occupational segregation reflects the desire of employers, who have their own vision of what men and women should do, or of the male workers who dominate certain jobs and seek to protect them from what they see as women's encroachment.

One careful study tracked the hiring process in a single large corporation, a customer call center. The researchers wanted to see how employer decisions—those made in the human resources offices—affected the sorting of men and women applicants into different jobs. They found that job screeners, not just applicants' own choices, played a central role in the ultimate segregation of men and women in the company (Fernandez and Mors 2008). It is reasonable to believe that as women increased their presence in the ranks of managers and employers, such decision making would become more equitable. And that has happened, but the pace of change is slow, and in many workplaces women are absent from those decision-making positions (Huffman, Cohen, and Pearlman 2010).

The second source of continued segregation, which is more important for professional jobs, is the differences in what men and women study in college and graduate school. The same question applies to this process as to hiring: Is it individual choices based on socialization, or is it the decisions of those in positions of authority (such as teachers and admissions officers) that lead men and women into different fields of study? The answer is undoubtedly a combination of the two. But we do know that the level of segregation in education dropped rapidly in the 1970s and 1980s—that is, women entered fields they had traditionally been excluded from or steered clear of, such as math and science, business and law. However, after the mid-1980s, the pace of change slowed. Now, although men and women each account for about half of the PhD degrees awarded in the United States, the division into separate spheres remains pronounced. Women receive 70 percent of the psychology doctorates, for example, while men get more than 85 percent of those in engineering (P. England 2010). (In sociology, incidentally, women earn about 60 percent of the PhDs.)

Gender, Status, and Pay

The question of who has which job is very important for the gender bottom line at work: Who earns more? The short answer is that men do. Among full-time workers in all occupations in 2015, women's median earnings were just 81 percent of men's (see Figure 5.7). And the biggest reason for that disparity is that men and women work in different jobs. Within the same job at the same workplace, there is much less gender inequality, partly because it's illegal. However, laws requiring equal pay for equal work are notoriously difficult to enforce, and as recently as 2016, the U.S. Congress failed to pass a proposed Paycheck Fairness Act that would have strengthened protection for women in the workplace.

One important observation about change in the labor force in recent decades is that women have entered occupations formerly dominated by men much more than the reverse (P. England 2010). That is not surprising given that almost all jobs were male dominated half a century ago. But it is also true that jobs dominated by women have lower social status—and lower pay—than those men traditionally fill (P. Cohen and Huffman 2003; see Figure 11.4). As a result, men's jobs are more desirable for most people.

The question of job status and pay reminds us that difference is not just a matter of taste—like pink and blue—when it also leads to inequality. Most people agree that people in jobs requiring more training and skill or characterized by more difficult working conditions or more risks deserve greater rewards than others (although we may disagree over how much greater those rewards should be). But interestingly, even when jobs dominated by men or women are comparable in those ways, men's jobs pay more.

Figure 5.7 **The gender pay gap: women's weekly earnings as a percentage of men's, full-time workers, 1970–2015**

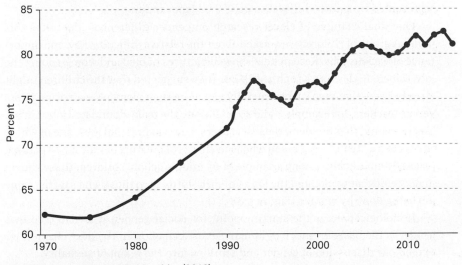

SOURCE: Hegewisch and DuMonthier (2016).

Figure 5.8 Male and female "tenics" at work

SOURCE: Artist's rendering based upon Liben, Bigler, and Krogh (2001).

A good example of this inequality is truck drivers (94 percent male) versus nurses' aides (89 percent female). Although the job training and demands are similar, full-time truck drivers make about 60 percent more than nurses' aides (U.S. Bureau of Labor Statistics 2016c). You may be surprised to learn that according to government estimates, the two jobs also require the same degree of physical strength, on average. To understand this, think back to the issue of taller men marrying shorter women. The constant association of men with greater size and strength—exaggerating differences that are real, of course—helps create the image of men's jobs as harder and more demanding, even when they're not. (Unlike nurses' aides, truck drivers at one time also had the advantage of being represented by a powerful, well-established labor union.)

One final example of clever research on gender differences illustrates this point. A group of children were asked about the relative difficulty, pay, and importance of various jobs. Researchers showed pictures of men and women doing the jobs (Liben, Bigler, and Krogh 2001). But they suspected that the children might already know that men's jobs generally pay more than women's—airplane pilots versus teachers, for example—and so might rate the male-dominated jobs higher. To get around that problem, the researchers made up fictional jobs, one of which they called a "tenic"—"a person who is in charge of creating handicapped parking places." Remarkably, among a sample of 65 middle school children, those shown male "tenics" at work rated the job as higher status than those who saw the same job being done by women (Figure 5.8).

If biological sex is the starting point for social gender, it is also true that gender is the basis for much of human sexual behavior. In the next chapter, we extend our discussion of gender and families into the realm of sexuality.

Trend to Watch: Women's Educational Advantage

With all the progress we have seen in the last half century, it is not surprising that some people assume we have reached—or even surpassed—the point at which men and women reached true equality (Cohen 2013b). In important ways, however, this is not the case: women have less income, wealth, and cultural clout than do men, and they are much more often the victims of sexual violence (see Chapter 12). And within families they remain subordinate to men much more often than the reverse. And yet, in one key respect, women have actually pulled ahead of men: completing college (Diprete and Buchmann 2013). In the age range 25 to 34, women are more likely to have finished a BA degree or higher education, 40 percent versus 34 percent as of 2016. In fact, women surpassed men's rate of college graduation in about 1996, more than two decades ago.

The movement toward greater educational achievement for women in the last few decades goes against the entire history of education, in which men dominated schooling at all levels. The traditional preference for sons, with which I opened this chapter, assumed that boys would be the ones to pursue an education and bring economic rewards to the family. As opportunities have opened for girls and women, and they have become more successful in school, parents have come to realize that investing in the education of a son has no better payoff than putting a daughter through school. In fact, most American parents would be offended at the suggestion that they should favor the education of their sons over their daughters—something that seemed obvious just a few generations ago.

So women's progress into higher education, and into many fields that were previously closed to them—such as law, medicine, and science—is one of the great achievements in human progress toward equality. But where will it lead? There are some who believe the modern education system, and the economy itself, are more oriented toward the "natural" talents of girls and women, from the ability to simply sit still at a young age, to working in teams, to empathizing with coworkers and clients in the professional workplace. But it remains to be seen whether women's advantage will continue to grow in the face of continued sexism, and whether it will expand into areas where they are still behind men, such as corporate management, engineering, and of course political power. After the 2016 election, in which Hillary Clinton lost to Donald Trump in the presidential race, just 19 percent of seats in Congress were filled by women, putting the United States in 100th place among countries of the world with regard to women's political power (Inter-Parliamentary Union 2016).

KEY TERMS:

sex   sexual identity

gender   gender identity

gender expression

intersex   transgender

androgynous   socialization

peers

Questions for Review

1. How are sex and gender different from each other?

2. What is an androgynous approach to raising children? Why might parents choose not to emphasize the gender of their children? What is the historical context for gender-identifying infants in the United States?

3. How have attitudes toward transgender and intersex people changed over time and between cultures?

4. Contrast biological, feminist, and symbolic interactionist theories of gender. How do they explain the real or perceived differences between genders?

5. What is gender socialization? Give examples to show how parents, siblings, peers, schools, and other institutions influence gender identity. Which ones do you think have the most influence? Why?

6. How does religion influence gender equality within families?

7. What are education and occupational segregation? What causes gender segregation at work and school? What are the consequences for men and women?

8. What is the relationship between occupational gender segregation and workers' pay and the prestige of the job? What explanations do researchers have for these gaps?

6 Sexuality

Sex and sexuality are important elements of interaction within the institutional arena of the family. For adults, families are a place where sexual behavior between partners is socially acceptable and expected, part of the special kind of intimacy that sets family relationships apart from all others. For children, families are where sexual identity (see Chapter 5) is first learned and where many hold their darkest sexual secrets, including rape and abuse (to which we will return in Chapter 12). The fundamental question of who we are often begins with sex: In English, we usually describe people with gendered pronouns (he/she) and nouns (boy/girl, brother/sister, man/woman) rather than neutral terms, such as "child," "sibling," or "person." Those core identities have a biological basis and are rooted in the beginning of all human life, but they are also subject to social change.

As we saw in Chapter 5, sexual and gender identity are building blocks of social interaction. But sexuality plays an important role in self-identity as well, a role that has become increasingly visible and explicit since the sexual revolution of the 1960s. Today, the phenomenon of celebrities "coming out," or revealing their sexual orientations in public, is not sensational, but this wasn't the case as recently as two decades ago.

In 1997, Ellen DeGeneres was a successful comedian with her own sitcom on national television. However, her "all-pants wardrobe," the "awkward chemistry" she had with male characters on the show, and the conspicuous absence of a boyfriend generated Hollywood gossip that she was gay (Handy and Bland 1997). In the face of such career-threatening rumors, rather than concoct a straight persona or slide out of the spotlight, DeGeneres decided to embrace her sexual orientation publicly. After some delicate negotiations with Disney, which

When we are children, the family is where we first learn about sexual identity. When we are adults, sexual behavior between partners is socially acceptable and expected.

What are some reasons for the large and rapid shift in acceptance of gays and lesbians in the United States?

owned the network, she wrote an episode for the show in which her character—also named Ellen—would eventually admit that she was a lesbian by accidentally speaking the line "I'm gay!" into an airport public address system. The episode was a huge ratings success. DeGeneres went on to become a popular daytime talk show host with a solidly mainstream audience, and by 2016 she was the fourth-most-admired woman in America (Gallup 2017a). When she married actress Portia de Rossi, their wedding video was proudly played on the equally mainstream *Oprah Winfrey Show* (Bruni 2009).

DeGeneres's story illustrates the growing acceptance of homosexuality (especially for women) in the United States (Fetner 2016), but it also represents a broader theme of this book. In the modern era, sexuality became part of the individual identity project, part of the expression of free choice that is now expected of everyone (see Chapter 1). DeGeneres made the proclamation of her sexual orientation part of her public, even commercial, persona. Since the 1990s, the news of celebrities coming out as gay has grown much less controversial. Still, partly because sex is such an integral part of what the entertainment industry sells, the sexual orientation of celebrities remains an issue (Healy 2012). There is now a tendency for individuals to include their sexuality in the image they present to others—millions of others in the case of celebrities, but the rest of us, too, on a smaller scale (Gamson and Moon 2004).

The new openness about sexuality, along with the feeling of uncertainty that comes with that growing individual freedom, plays out within the family arena. For example, how do people perceive appropriate family roles with regard to sex and sexual behavior? How will the law treat sexual diversity and family relations? And how will parents raise children in a world that often seems so different from that of their own childhood? These questions have been fueled by technological advances in areas as diverse as birth control and infertility and by political debates over a range of issues, from sex education to gay marriage. In this chapter, we will lay the groundwork for understanding and responding to these challenges.

Sociology and Sexuality

In the social science of sexuality, there are three major areas of study, which frame the discussion in this chapter. The first approach is to study *identities*. Central to these is gender identity, discussed in Chapter 5. Here we focus more on sexual identity and sexual orientation. Sexual identity is usually male or female, but for some people it is ambiguous or mixed. Just as there are many sexual identities, not just two, so sexual orientation covers a broad spectrum of homosexual and heterosexual behavior. Through interaction with others, we express ourselves in ways that reflect and reinforce our identities—and influence those around us.

Our identities related to sex and gender are closely related to human *biology*, which sets the stage for sex in the social realm. Some sociologists have taken on the task of integrating the biological and social sciences. An understanding of biology helps those who study human sexuality and evolution to understand the prehistoric origins of today's behavior patterns (Roughgarden 2004). More concretely, the biology of sexuality is important for studying social issues such as fertility and infertility, sexual disorders, and sexual behavior related to health, to which we will return later in this chapter (Walvoord 2010).

Our identity and biology are the building blocks of *sexual behavior*, which creates the social reality of sexuality that we see around us. Although studying intensely private behavior is challenging, sociology has a long history of trying to understand the type and quantity of sexual behavior through surveys and observation of social interaction (Brecher and Brecher 1986). These studies provide us with crucial knowledge of the who-does-what-with-whom variety. Such investigation naturally leads to questions about the social context of sexual behavior, such as changing attitudes about what is acceptable and desirable, images from the media, and legal restrictions on sexual conduct.

Sexual Identity and Orientation

Sexuality has become an increasingly important part of most people's identity in the modern era. Why? One reason may be that, partly because of medical technology, people now distinguish sex for procreation from sex for pleasure (Cocks 2006). That opens up sexual behavior to different meanings and purposes, depending on the social situation, and expands choices. Sex for pleasure has become an acceptable pursuit in a way that it wasn't for America's Puritan ancestors. And once self-satisfaction was recognized as a goal of sexual behavior, then differences in how to attain that satisfaction grew in importance. Eventually, finding one's way sexually became an important part of defining oneself not just to others, but even to oneself (Giddens 1992). That may be why, although homosexuality has existed forever in terms of sexual attraction and behavior, the word *homosexual* to describe a *kind* of person first appeared in the late nineteenth century (OED 2013).

As detailed in Chapter 5, sociologists define gender in terms of social categories and sex in terms of biological categories. The distinction is useful because social categories are more flexible, changing with the times, whereas sex categories reflect more unchanging biological characteristics (although human *interpretation* of the sex categories is not historically fixed; Fujimura 2006). We might say we are born with a biological sex, which usually creates a sexual identity, and we join a gender through our social interactions.

Gender and sexual identity help people figure out who they are. But people are also like a chemical element: Their nature is partly determined by what they are attracted to. **Sexual orientation** is the pattern of romantic or sexual attraction to others in relation to one's own gender identity. The pattern of attraction exists on a continuum that ranges from exclusively heterosexual to exclusively homosexual, with variations in between that represent degrees of bisexuality. Despite that variation, people commonly embrace a sexual orientation that is either heterosexual (*straight*) or homosexual (*gay*, for both men and women, or *lesbian* for women only). Bisexuality is not a widely recognized identity, partly because it is awkward for people with a single sexual partner to identify as bisexual, and also because people who identify as bisexual often find themselves excluded from both straight and gay social groups (Scherrer 2013). Finally, a small percentage of people—about 1 percent—have no sexual attraction to people of either gender and may adopt an asexual identity (Brotto and Yule 2016).

The common use of broad categories—gay and straight—obscures a lot of variation in the patterns of attraction within each group. One alternative is to use the term *LGBT* (lesbian, gay, bisexual, or transgender) or *queer* to describe all people outside the narrow norm of heterosexuality. These terms help avoid having to specifically identify or define each person's sexual orientation, but they run the risk of lumping together very diverse groups of people.

Sexual orientation itself is not the same as behavior. Some people who don't identify as gay or lesbian have sexual relationships with people of the same sex, so others may think of them as gay. For example, sociologist Tony Silva interviewed a number of rural White men, most of them married to women, who consider themselves straight (or bisexual) but also secretly have sex with men (Silva 2017). On the other hand, some people who think of themselves as gay or lesbian have heterosexual romantic or sex lives (Bauer and Jairam 2008). In recent decades, as gay and lesbian relationships have become more accepted, some people who were heterosexually married left their marriages and entered same-sex relationships. They may have "always been gay" but never expressed it, or they may have developed a new identity as a result of newfound attractions (Isay 1996).

Large-scale surveys of the population, capable of providing reliable data on sexual orientation, are relatively new. They may be able to answer some basic questions regarding sexual orientation, but we need to be careful as we study these patterns. Some sociologists have found that sexual orientation as an identity is not a fixed quality that people "have." Rather, it requires continual updating and "performance," and people's orientation can change over time as they age or move between different social situations (Gamson and Moon 2004).

Nevertheless, surveys to date have confirmed some basic patterns. Same-gender sexual attraction and behavior occur more commonly among women than among men. And this has grown more common in recent decades. For example, women born around 1990 are about twice as likely as those born a generation earlier to report having ever had sex with another woman, while there was no increase in same-sex behavior among men (England, Mishel, and

sexual orientation

The pattern of romantic or sexual attraction to others in relation to one's own gender identity.

Caudillo 2016) Still, exclusively homosexual behavior and identity are relatively rare, occurring in less than 5 percent of American adults (Copen, Chandra, and Febo-Vasquez 2016). The Story Behind the Numbers illustrates the frequency of homosexual or bisexual behavior, attraction, and identity among young adults.

Attitudes about Sexual Orientation

Complexity makes it hard to study human sexuality, but that challenge is even greater because of the stigma often associated with homosexuality. The sociologist Erving Goffman (1963) used the word **stigma** to describe an undesirable quality that sets a person apart from others in his or her social category. He called such qualities "deeply discrediting." Clearly, this is a socially constructed concept, so that what is stigmatized now might not be in the years to come. In the case of homosexuality, the stigma partly results from **homophobia**, which is the fear of or antipathy toward homosexuality in general and gays and lesbians in particular. That fear contributes to the stigma, creating a social cycle that has proved slow to change (Loftus 2001). It also makes sexual orientation difficult to study because it's difficult to talk about.

One thing that has changed dramatically, however, is the medical and scientific attitude toward homosexuality. Early in the twentieth century, doctors considered same-sex attraction a mental disorder or disease, a problem to be explained and treated (Risman and Schwartz 1988). Sigmund Freud thought that homosexuality was the result of abnormal sexual development or family relationships, so that, for example, boys could become gay because of emotionally distant fathers, and some might be "cured" by psychoanalysis (Puts, Jordan, and Breedlove 2006). Early supporters of what we now call gay rights countered that homosexuality should be considered an acceptable lifestyle choice.

In the last few decades, however, the debate has shifted. In 1973 the American Psychiatric Association removed homosexuality from its list of mental disorders (Bayer 1981). Scientists now understand that homosexuality (like heterosexuality) is a naturally occurring condition. Regardless of whether sexual orientation is the result of social or biological factors, both homosexuality and heterosexuality may be part of a healthy sexual identity (J. Weeks 2000). In fact, failure to come to terms with one's sexual orientation is now considered a potential mental health problem by many professionals (Isay 1996). In addition, some scholars have adopted a "queer theory" approach, which stresses the fluidity and diversity of sexual orientations and behaviors and rejects science's attempt to fit people into narrow classifications of sexuality (Gamson and Moon 2004).

As in medicine, most religious denominations in the United States historically saved their harshest moral condemnations for homosexuality, which was singled out for punishment in the founding texts of the Judeo-Christian faiths (Hasbany 1989). Even as the scientific consensus shifted, many religious Americans have remained opposed to homosexuality, and today people who are affiliated with a religion are much more likely to consider homosexuality unacceptable than those who are not affiliated (Pew Research Center 2015b). Some religious

stigma

A quality that is perceived as undesirable and that sets a person apart from others in his or her social category.

homophobia

Fear of or antipathy toward homosexuality in general and gays and lesbians in particular.

Sexuality between the genders

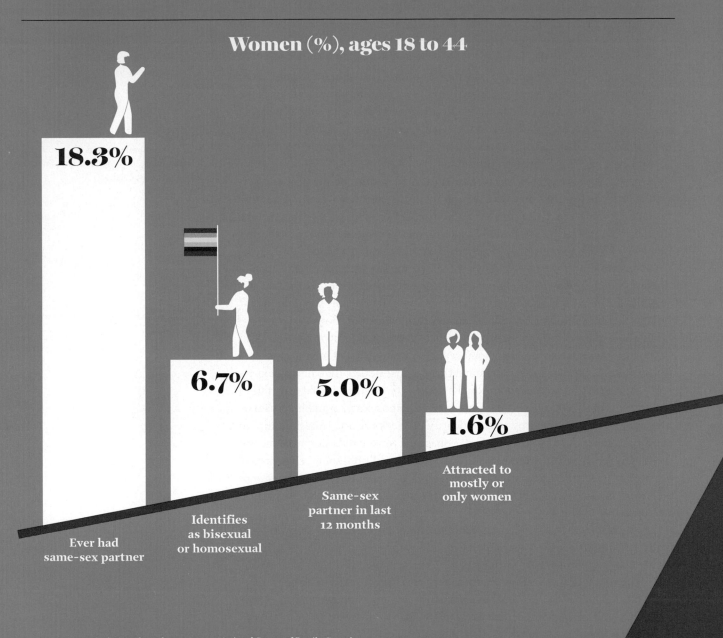

Women (%), ages 18 to 44

18.3% — Ever had same-sex partner

6.7% — Identifies as bisexual or homosexual

5.0% — Same-sex partner in last 12 months

1.6% — Attracted to mostly or only women

Source: Author calculations from the 2013–2015 National Survey of Family Growth.

In recent years social scientists have improved the research on sexual orientation. We can answer some basic questions confidently based on large federal surveys. First, same-sex sexual attraction and behavior occur more commonly among women than among men. Women are especially more likely to be exploratory than men, more frequently reporting isolated or past same-sex sexual experiences and romantic attractions. For example, women are more than twice as likely to have had a same-sex sexual partner in the past year. Second, exclusively homosexual behavior and identity are relatively rare, occurring in less than 5 percent of American adults. But the way we ask the question matters quite a bit— "have you ever had sex with a man?" is a very different question from "do you consider yourself gay?" This kind of complexity makes it hard to study human sexuality, but it is even harder because stigma and fear make the subject difficult for many people to talk about.

Men (%), ages 18 to 44

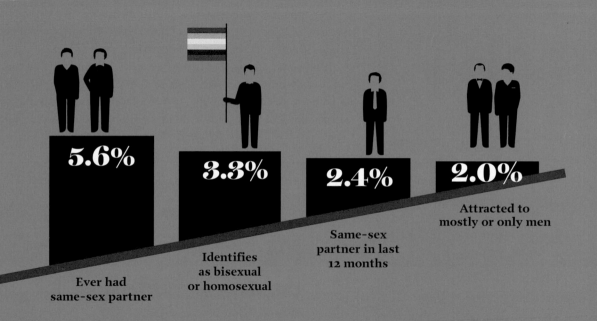

5.6%
Ever had
same-sex partner

3.3%
Identifies
as bisexual
or homosexual

2.4%
Same-sex
partner in last
12 months

2.0%
Attracted to
mostly or only men

http://wwnpag.es/sbtn6

Go to this link for an animation
narrated by the author.

groups and "family-values" conservatives treat homosexuality as a problem to be solved and attempt to change gays and lesbians "back" into heterosexuals, much as left-handed people were once forcibly retrained to use their right hand (Flentje, Heck, and Cochran 2013). The weight of such negative assessments—their stigma—contributes to the mental anguish that some gay people experience, especially those who are themselves religious (M. Wilcox 2003). However, further change may be on the way. One prominent Christian group that spent decades working to "free" homosexuals from their same-sex attractions, Exodus International, disbanded in 2013. Its leader, Alan Chambers, apologized for inflicting harm on gays and lesbians, some of whom committed suicide (Chambers 2013).

In the face of these countervailing scientific and ideological forces, the U.S. population is divided between those who think that homosexuality is wrong and those who don't. However, the proportion who feel that gay or lesbian relations are "morally acceptable" has risen rapidly in recent years, from 40 percent to 60 percent since 2001, as Figure 6.1 shows. This is part of a general trend toward greater tolerance of sexual and family behavior. But there is still less moral approval of homosexuality than there is of less controversial behaviors such as single parenthood, sex outside of marriage, or divorce.

It is worth noting that heterosexuality, the majority sexual orientation, is not usually studied or even discussed explicitly. It is as if there are "people" and then there are "gay people." For example, the great majority of mothers, when talking to their preschool-aged children, refer to adult relationships as if

Figure 6.1 **Percentage saying the particular behavior is "morally acceptable"**

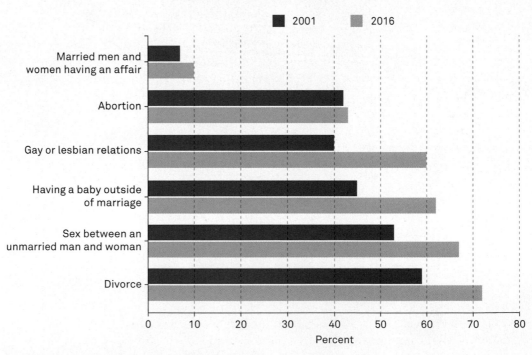

SOURCE: Newport and Himelfarb (2013); Swift (2016).

they are always heterosexual (K. Martin 2009). This reminds us of how Whites are ignored in studies about race (see Chapter 3), because what is seen as "normal" requires no explanation. In fact, that is part of the concept of stigma, the sense of being different rather than conforming. Taken together, the pressures to conform to the majority sexual orientation and the assumption that everyone is straight until proven otherwise have been referred to as *compulsory heterosexuality* (A. Rich 1980).

Interestingly, those who believe that homosexuality is something people are "born with," rather than a personal choice or an outcome of social environment, are much more likely to have positive feelings toward gay men and lesbians (Haider-Markel and Joslyn 2008). In this light, some researchers have examined early childhood experiences, looking for clues to the development of sexual orientation—perhaps inspired by Freud's speculations—but no factors have emerged as pivotal to that development (Risman and Schwartz 1988). That leaves the field to those who consider biological factors more important, a question to which we will return shortly.

Coming Out

The rapid pace of change in cultural attitudes toward homosexuality has left many families divided, with older generations holding more negative views than those who grew up in a more tolerant era. This generational clash has shaped many *coming out* experiences—so named in reference to the historical pattern of gays and lesbians keeping their sexual orientation "in the closet" before "coming out" to make their true identities known.

Coming out is the process of revealing one's gay sexual orientation to the significant people in one's life, a process that may unfold over years (Rust 1993). Consider the example of an anonymous woman who made her story public on the website gayfamilysupport.com. She had no ambition to shake up her family or take a political stand regarding her sexuality, even though her relationship, if exposed, could have put her girlfriend's career in jeopardy at a time before gays were permitted to serve openly in the U.S. military. (Under the policy known as "don't ask, don't tell," which lasted from 1993 to 2011, homosexual men and women could serve in the armed forces provided they kept their sexual orientation secret.) But eventually she felt she had to tell her parents. She related:

> So my family seems pretty normal, open-minded, relaxed. Then why did it take me until I was 22-years-old to tell my parents that I'm a lesbian?...I met someone. She is not just a girl, she is the love of my life. We've been "hiding" for over four years now. We live together, but because we are still young it still sounds OK for young girls to have roommates....I finally said, "Well enough is enough." One day I sat down with her and said, "Baby we are in our twenties, we have a house, we have cars, jobs, dogs, we pay taxes, and neither of us has told our parents we love each other?" So I went first. I pulled my parents aside separately and told them I was in love....My dad said, "Kinda' figured. I'm OK with it. I still

coming out

The process of revealing one's gay sexual orientation to the significant people in one's life.

love you just the same, but I do want grandkids." I assured him that we could still have kids, adoption probably. My mom, oh God. When I told her I started to cry immediately.... She blamed it on my friends, she said it was a choice.... She said she never really wanted to talk about it again. Meaning she was just going to pretend like I never told her. Pretty harsh, could've been worse.

This coming out story—posted online by a noncelebrity, involving only her own family—is a far cry from the Hollywood stardom version exhibited by Ellen DeGeneres. But both represent the reality that sexuality forms a core of the modern identity. Family relationships are often where such identities are formed and expressed. And when social change occurs, such as the increasing acceptance of homosexuality, intergenerational interactions show the friction between old and new attitudes. Clearly, modern openness about sexual identity has not completely eased tensions over the role of sexual behavior, within or outside of families.

The Biology of Human Sexuality

To understand human sexuality, we need to know something about its biology. That means knowing about sexuality and the human body, but it also means knowing how biological properties and processes influence social behavior and how actions in society may in turn change that biological playing field. We will begin by continuing the discussion of sexual orientation, a suitable issue for exploring the relationship between biology and sexuality. From there we will move to a brief discussion of evolution and its implications for family issues today.

Where Does Sexual Orientation Come From?

The determinants of sexual orientation remain poorly understood despite decades of scientific study. One serious problem is that the subject we are trying to explain is not clearly defined. Even with growing openness about sexuality, compulsory heterosexuality is still the rule rather than the exception, so we do not know the relationship between the underlying sexual orientation in the population and the identities we see in our studies (Igartua et al. 2009). Do all adults answering a survey today even know what their "true" sexual orientation is? As we saw in the Story Behind the Numbers, there are different ways to identify one's sexual orientation, which may reflect different points on the same scale. Which of those responses (or some others) should put someone in the gay or lesbian category in a scientific study? Despite such questions, researchers have pursued biological influences among both genetic and hormonal sources (Frankowski 2004).

With regard to genetics, it may be surprising to learn that no connection has been found between the sexual orientation of parents and the sexual orientation of their children (Patterson 1992). (Even if there were such a link, it could also indicate parental interaction, rather than genetics, as a cause.) Some studies of twins—another method used to investigate genetic effects—have found that pairs of twins are likely to have the same sexual orientation, but other studies are inconclusive. Reasonable scholars disagree, but I am inclined to believe the report that summed it up this way: "If same-sex romantic attraction has a genetic component, it is massively overwhelmed by other factors" (Bearman and Brückner 2002). Genetics is at most just a part of the story.

If sexual orientation is not genetic, it may still be "natural," or something people are "born with." That is because there are ways that hormone levels can be affected as a baby or child develops. In recent years research has focused on hormonal influences in the womb. One pattern that has emerged is that boys with older brothers are slightly more likely to identify as gay (Blanchard and Vander-Laan 2015). Although the theory is unproved, some scientists believe that a woman's body has some sort of immune reaction to the presence of male hormones in her uterus during pregnancy. When she has more pregnancies, the hormonal mixture in her womb changes. This goes along with some other evidence that hormone levels affect development in ways that influence sexual orientation (Frietson et al. 2010). Even if these hormonal influences are real, however, they, too, account for only a small part of the explanation, since most gay men and lesbians haven't experienced these effects (Francis 2008).

It may seem strange that such a basic question of human existence is so hard for us to understand. There are a few reasons for this. First, it may be that sexual orientation has too many variations and sources of influence for current science to fully understand them. Simply put, the biological causes of human behavior are not simple. Consider an example from another area of behavior, addiction (Goldman, Oroszi, and Ducci 2006). We know that there are genetic components to addiction—or addictions, since there are many—and they may or may not appear together in the same people. But there are also social limits on addictive behavior, which means, for example, that people can't be addicted to things that are not available to them (such as cocaine or pornography in societies that don't have these vices). In terms of sexual orientation, that means that any biological influence can only be felt within the limits set by the society in which people develop and live.

Remember, also, that most research has focused on explaining homosexuality rather than heterosexuality. Heterosexual attraction—or at least heterosexual sex—is assumed to be programmed into human instincts because it encourages reproduction and survival of the species. Homosexuality, which doesn't have an obvious evolutionary purpose, is the puzzle most research tries to solve, although it is only one end of the sexual orientation continuum.

Evolution and Human Sexuality

Once upon a time, a pair of male chinstrap penguins lived at the Central Park Zoo in New York City. They were a devoted couple, and eventually the zookeepers

In 2011, the Toronto Zoo's male African penguins Pedro and Buddy became famous for exhibiting homosexual behavior. Same-sex animal pairings often make headlines worldwide. What does that say about our society and media?

gave them an abandoned egg to hatch, which they successfully raised into a healthy female chick named Tango (D. Smith 2004). There are many pairs of male penguins in the wild, and they often seek eggs to hatch and raise (or they might simulate hatching behavior with egg-shaped rocks). This particular story became controversial because it was the subject of an award-winning children's book called *And Tango Makes Three*. For its positive depiction of two loving dads and their tolerant zookeepers, the book achieved the distinction of being one of the most controversial in public and school libraries around the country well into the 2010s (American Library Association 2016).

The story of Tango doesn't tell us much about human sexuality, but it does shed light on disagreements over how homosexuality should be regarded in the United States today. It also illustrates the well-known scientific fact that some members of hundreds of other species—from insects and spiders to birds, dolphins, and whales and a variety of monkeys and apes—display homosexual behavior, forming long-term bonds, performing sexual acts, or raising young together (Bagemihl 1999). The scientific attitude toward this behavior has changed, so what used to be considered evidence of disease or disorder is now understood as part of the complex evolutionary development of many species. It turns out that sexual acts and emotional attachments in animals, as in humans, are not always geared toward conceiving and producing new members of the species (Sommer and Vasey 2006).

Some social scientists have interpreted behavior that is widespread among humans as evidence that it represents an evolutionary adaptation—that is, something that helped (or still helps) the species survive and reproduce. For example, male aggressiveness toward females, together with female submissiveness, may have once enhanced the species by making it possible for stronger men to reproduce more, in the process spreading their aggressive genes. In response, feminists in particular have countered that human sexuality in modern society has symbolic qualities, cultural variation, and capacity for change that far outstrip its biological evolutionary purposes (Caulfield 1985).

It is also worth noting an interesting difference between humans and some of our closest evolutionary cousins. Unlike apes and monkeys, female humans don't have obvious physical displays to show off the fertile periods in their menstrual cycles (Pawłowski 1999). No one is sure how that difference came about, but some people interpret it as evidence that humans have more innate potential to make sexuality socially constructed, rather than being overwhelmingly driven by instinctive urges. (As we will see, the advent of modern birth control has removed reproduction even further from the motivations of many sexually active humans.) In a similar way, you might say that our capacity for complex language has made possible a symbolic level of reality that is unique among animals.

In general, sociologists (including me) argue against using an evolutionary perspective that assumes that human behavior is instinctive. After all, rape, murder, and infanticide are common among animals; although they have always been part of human society, we still hope to minimize these behaviors. We spend billions of dollars attempting to counteract other natural aspects of our biological existence as well, such as disease and even the aging process itself. Further, searching for the evolutionary roots of modern practices often seems like an exercise in explaining why the way things happen to be right now is "natural" or okay. From its inception, the idea of *social Darwinism*—evolutionary theory applied to human society—has been used to defend inequality between the haves and have-nots and between men and women (Hofstadter 1944). In that sense, this line of thinking is similar to functionalism, as discussed in Chapter 1, which proceeds from the assumption that the behavior patterns we see serve a positive function.

Despite these cautions, it is remarkable that we humans have the capacity not only to study behavior among other species but also to reflect about our own nature and development using evolutionary theory. And this is the source of many insights into our society. For example, some scientists believe that because women carry fetuses and breastfeed infants, they are more inclined to make personal investments in their children, while men are more interested in having many children—an inclination connected to men's greater number of sexual partners. If, indeed, such evolutionary forces helped shape our personalities, how do they work in modern society?

In fact, biological forces often operate in the background, exerting much weaker influence than contemporary social factors. As a final example of the interaction of social and biological influences, consider women's menstrual cycles again. For centuries, some women and their doctors have reported physical and psychological symptoms associated with the menstrual cycle (Stolberg 2000). In modern society, however, mood fluctuations based on the day of the week are greater than those based on the time of the month. Clearly, the social significance of different days of the week—and especially weekends—is a human creation, but it also contributes to wide mood swings, as people do more work (or attend classes) on weekdays and look forward to weekends as a time to relax

(McFarlane, Martin, and Williams 1988). We will see the interaction of social and biological influences even more clearly when we discuss medical conditions related to sexuality in the last section of this chapter.

Sexual Behavior

In most respects, sexual behavior is less constrained now than it was in the past, for at least four reasons. First, the potential to separate sex from reproduction through modern birth control has widened the possibilities for exploring partners without making long-term commitments. Second, the greater acceptance of sex outside of marriage has reduced the social penalties imposed on those who pursue such relationships. Third, the growing independence of young adults from their parents' supervision—including living on their own before marriage—has increased their sense of freedom and stimulated the pursuit of self-determination (Treas 2004). And finally, due to improving health, medical intervention, and changing expectations, sex at older ages—beyond the reproductive years—has become more commonplace. As a result, the pursuit of good sex as a personal goal has probably never been so widely accepted across almost all segments of society.

Modern Intimacy

In the modern era, sexuality became part of the new intimacy of family life. That occurred over the eighteenth and nineteenth centuries as the family came to represent loving informal relationships, in contrast to the economy, which became identified with competitive formal relationships (Cancian 1987:50). The distinction between loving and competitive relationships was anchored by the restriction of socially acceptable sex to the family arena. Of course, since the "separate spheres" idea relegated women's influence to the family home, this restriction of sexual behavior to within the family was more rigid for wives, and infidelity by husbands was more acceptable. In any event, over the twentieth century, as divorce became more common and questioning the value of marriage grew more acceptable, the quality of sexual intimacy joined the list of common criteria people used to evaluate their own marriages.

This increasingly explicit appreciation of sexual pleasure, along with the centrality of sexual identity to the modern self, did not always sit well with the guardians of traditional morality. For example, some traditionalists were (and remain) agitated about the question of male masturbation. Sexuality is not just a part of relationships with others, of course, but also a part of self-realization. And what better way to get to know oneself than to have sex with oneself? At least that was the fear expressed by moral leaders during the Victorian period of the nineteenth century, when there was a cultural panic over masturbation. Sexual self-gratification was seen as evidence of "the dangerous excesses of modern selfhood taken to a potentially unlimited degree" (Cocks 2006:1214). For women, masturbation was not yet an issue of public concern, probably because their sexuality simply was not taken seriously. In fact, some middle-class women in the nineteenth century visited doctors who treated their "hysteria" by bringing them to orgasm, a practice that apparently did not offend moral leaders (Coontz 2005). The results of the masturbation panic included such extreme (if rarely used) measures as the antimasturbation device pictured here. The episode only served to highlight the apparent powerlessness of religious and moral authorities to keep the widespread sexual awakening in check.

In the eyes of Victorian moralists, masturbation raised the possibility that inward-looking quests for satisfaction would eventually replace the need for family relationships altogether. Although the fear was overblown, it is just one of many cases in which the idea of uninhibited sexuality appeared to threaten traditional images of the family. Such fears have prompted opposition to many social changes, from the spread of mixed-gender college dorms to the availability of pornography.

Defensive reactions to social change regarding sexuality are exacerbated by the lack of concrete information about sexual practices, a subject that has sometimes been considered inappropriate for scientific study. Social science made a big splash in that regard with the reports by Alfred Kinsey and his colleagues at the Institute for Sex Research in the 1940s. Although Kinsey attempted to present "an accumulation of scientific fact completely divorced from questions of moral value and social custom" (Kinsey, Pomeroy, and Martin 1948:3), what become known as the Kinsey Reports were greeted with a firestorm of concern and even condemnation as the private sexual worlds of Americans came into the public eye. Although Kinsey's research methods have been questioned by many social scientists—they involved interviews with thousands of volunteers who were self-selected rather than being randomly chosen—some of the basic findings remain central to the study of sexuality discussed in this chapter. (The study and its director were memorialized in the Hollywood drama *Kinsey*.)

The study of sexuality is still fraught with controversy. Ironically, it was the need to understand sexually transmitted diseases, especially the AIDS crisis starting in the 1980s, that led to greater scientific attention to sexual behavior. (I call that ironic because the *lack* of understanding of sexuality contributes to the transmission of such infections.) The spread of HIV, the virus that causes AIDS (acquired immune deficiency syndrome), called attention to the details of sexual behavior, including condom use, anal sex, and the combination of sex and intravenous drug use. Thus, the crisis helped raise awareness of the need to understand the social nature of sexual behavior (Shilts 1987). That may be why more recent knowledge about sexual behavior comes from studies geared toward health, with major surveys on the subject having titles that include such phrases as "Health and Social Life" (Laumann 1994), "Adolescent Health" (Resnick et al. 1997), and "Family Growth" (Copen, Chandra, and Febo-Vasquez 2016). Although these research efforts cover subjects other than sexual behavior, collectively they have served to follow up and extend the original Kinsey Reports with more sound scientific methods and data.

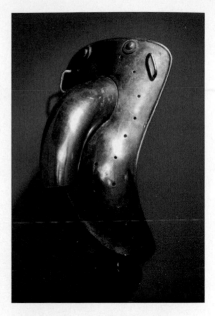

This antimasturbation device for men was invented around the turn of the twentieth century. A leather strap would have held it in place.

Sex before Marriage

As marriages were increasingly judged on the basis of their sexual qualities, nonmarital sex also grew more common and acceptable. Research in the last generation has established some common patterns of this behavior. Here are a few generalizations that serve to anchor our more detailed investigation:

- *Sex comes before marriage.* Beginning with the generation born in the 1960s, almost everyone—95 percent of Americans—has had sexual intercourse before marriage (Finer 2007). That is not so much because people are having sex at younger ages, but because they get married at older ages after having sex in their teens and early 20s. (Of course, some of these people are merely having sex with the partner they will eventually marry.)

- *Men have more partners than women.* The average age for first intercourse is about 17 for both men and women, but men on average increase their number of partners more rapidly through young adulthood. By the time they reach their late 30s, most men have had about seven sexual partners, compared with five for women (Figure 6.2).

- *Having many partners is relatively uncommon.* Despite the greater acceptance of sexual freedom, in the age range 18 to 44, only 4 percent of men, and 2 percent of women, report having five or more partners in the previous year. The majority report having had one sexual partner in the previous year—76 percent of women and 71 percent of men (Centers for Disease Control 2016a).

- *Sex without consent is relatively common.* Six percent of women and 5 percent of men, asked about their first intercourse, report that they "really didn't want it to happen at the time," and that is especially likely when it occurred at a young age (Centers for Disease Control 2016a). Among women ages 18 to 44, 20 percent report that they have been forced to have intercourse (National Center for Health Statistics 2016). As we will see in Chapter 12, rape occurs most often within families or between dating partners.

Although one of the major changes in sexual behavior has been the growth of nonmarital sex, most sexual activity still takes place between people who are in long-term relationships with an expectation of fidelity. People in married, cohabiting, or long-term dating relationships generally expect to have sex only with their long-term partner and expect the same commitment from him or her (Treas 2004). Before discussing such relationships, however, we will pause to consider how men and women are treated differently in the moral standards for sexual behavior.

The Sexual Double Standard A common assumption in our society is that women are more passive and inhibited sexually, while men are more

Figure 6.2 Median number of lifetime sexual partners

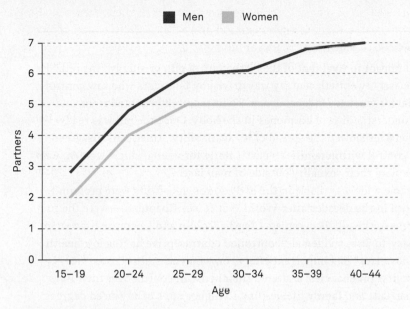

Data are for opposite-sex partners only and include oral sex, anal sex, and vaginal intercourse.

SOURCE: Author calculations from the 2013–2015 National Survey of Family Growth (Centers for Disease Control 2016a).

performance and achievement oriented (taking pride in having a large number of sexual partners, for example). That fits with the pattern of men having more sexual partners than women. However, because this belief is so culturally ingrained, it's hard to know the origins or causes of the pattern. As noted earlier, some believe that it is traceable to evolution; but its persistence today is surely the outcome of social forces.

Consider our language regarding sexual intercourse. Most of the popular terms refer to things men *do to* women, not the other way around. One of the milder of these terms—amazingly—is "hit." In Ray J.'s song, "I Hit It First," to choose one of many examples, he refers to an old girlfriend, now with another man, "She might move on to rappers, and ball players, but we all know I hit it first." It seems strange that an explicitly violent word such as "hit" would seem less offensive than the other terms available. (Referring to a woman as "it" is also worth questioning.)

That onesidedness—in which men are perceived as doing sex to women—contributes to a moral standard that punishes women for going against the norm of passivity. The **sexual double standard** refers to the practice of applying stricter moral or legal controls to women's sexual behavior than to men's. Historically, this meant that women must not only refrain from initiating sex but also generally limit their sexual behavior to monogamous marriage or else fall from grace. Men, on the other hand, were expected to be more promiscuous even

sexual double standard

The practice of applying stricter moral or legal controls to women's sexual behavior than to men's.

The Pill

Few innovations had a social impact to rival that of the birth control pill, or simply "the pill." Its scientific development in the early twentieth century was driven by feminists who saw control over reproduction as essential for women's independence. Their research benefited from, and contributed to, the growing understanding of hormones in the body. Once the pill was ready for use, however, political obstacles slowed the spread of its availability. Americans disagreed over the proper role of birth control within families—particularly for young, single women, who might feel new freedom to explore their sexuality outside of marriage.

When the pill finally became widely available in the early 1960s, its effects were profound. The baby boomers—those born in the decades after World War II (see Chapter 2)—were the first to come of age with easy access to the pill. Economists Claudia Goldin and Lawrence Katz write that "a virtually foolproof, easy-to-use, and female-controlled contraceptive having low health risks, little pain, and few annoyances" had important effects on women's status (2002:766–767). It didn't just delay their first pregnancies; it altered their sense of control over their lives and their expectations for marriage and family life, leading to higher rates of advanced degrees and more professional careers, as the average age at marriage spiked upward (see Figure 2.4).

The costs and benefits of the pill's dominance among American birth control choices have been debated ever since:

- The pill increased women's independent—and private—control over their own reproduction. But did that also lessen men's sense of responsibility for birth control and for the effects of their sexual behavior? Couples often don't discuss birth control until *after* their first sexual encounter, and the fact that the pill is widely available leads some men to assume that their partners are using it.

- The pill improved the effectiveness of contraception for millions of individuals and families. However, like all hormonal birth control methods, it does not stop the spread of sexually transmitted diseases. Does it therefore exacerbate the public health impact of these infections, including AIDS?

- Tinkering with women's hormones has subtle and complicated long-term consequences. Although the hormone doses used today are much lower than they were when the pill was introduced, researchers continue to find some health effects. In particular, long-term use of the pill may increase the risk of breast cancer while reducing the risk of some other cancers (Gierisch et al. 2013). However, just by being a more effective contraceptive, it reduces the harm many women experience from unplanned pregnancies and abortions (Kiley and Hammond 2007).

In popular culture, the freedom that women achieve by controlling contraception themselves is often depicted as a double-edged sword, jeopardizing their family lives even as it opens new

Smoking is less prevalent now than in the time period depicted in the show *Mad Men*—especially in doctors' offices—but battles over women's access to birth control still rage on today.

doors. In the TV series *Mad Men*, for example, set in the 1960s, a male gynecologist offers this advice to a single woman asking for the pill: "There's nothing wrong with a woman being practical about the possibility of sexual activity... [but] I'll warn you now: I'll take you off this medicine if you abuse it." He adds, "Even in our modern times, easy women don't find husbands."

On the other hand, in the 1983 movie *Educating Rita*, the heroine is a hairdresser who decides to continue her education at age 26 and falls in love with her professor. Her husband, who doesn't understand her ambitions, thinks she has stopped taking the pill, but she secretly keeps taking it, allowing her to postpone parenthood and follow her dreams. A quarter-century later, in the TV series *Big Love*, one of Mormon Bill Henrickson's three wives, Nikki, secretly takes the pill, leading the rest of the family to believe she is unable to conceive. In both cases, however, what looks like a boost for women's independence from the family comes at a cost. By secretly hampering their own fertility, they cast shame on themselves and highlight the loneliness of their individual goals (Geyer-Ryan 1996).

For better or worse, the majority of American women have now used the pill at some point in their lives. Of those ages 15 to 44 who have ever had sexual intercourse, 82 percent have used the pill (Daniels, Mosher, and Jones 2013). The path to that level of popularity was long, however, as the following timeline shows.

Timeline

1873: Comstock Act
Under the guise of preventing the dissemination of obscene material, Congress banned the shipment of birth control devices through the mail. Some states even banned the shipment of birth control information. The law was relaxed in 1936.

1914: *The Woman Rebel*
Feminist Margaret Sanger begins publishing her journal, *The Woman Rebel*, and coins the term "birth control." Her efforts helped spur development of the pill.

1937: Progesterone's role discovered
The hormone progesterone may be used to inhibit women's ovulation. For the first time, several synthetic hormones were manufactured in the 1940s.

1950s: Private hormone research
Without government funding or support, birth control advocates raised private money for research into hormone treatments to prevent pregnancy. The first tests on humans were conducted in 1954, with large-scale trials started in 1956.

1960: FDA approval
The Food and Drug Administration approved the use of an oral contraceptive pill for women—the first drug approved for a purpose other than treating a health problem.

1965: *Griswold v. Connecticut*
The U.S. Supreme Court overturned a Connecticut law that banned contraceptives, declaring that married couples have a right to privacy in birth control decisions.

1968: Papal opposition
Rejecting the argument that the pill is an extension of natural birth control methods, similar to the so-called rhythm method (in which couples restrict intercourse to times when the woman's fertility is lowest), Pope Paul VI declared the pill unnatural and its use a mortal sin. The papal statement titled *Humanae Vitae* (Of Human Life) warned that the pill would lead to marital infidelity and "a general lowering of moral standards." In particular, the Catholic Church was disturbed by the separation of sex from reproductive ends. A man using birth control "may forget the reverence due to a woman, and...reduce her to being a mere instrument for the satisfaction of his own desires" (Paul VI 1968).

1970: More sex within marriage
Among married White couples, 40 percent had sex more than twice a week in the previous month, compared with 30 percent just five years earlier. Couples using the pill had sex more often than those using any other method of contraception (Trussell and Westoff 1980).

1971: Twenty-Sixth Amendment to the Constitution
The amendment lowered the voting age nationwide to 18, and most states subsequently considered adulthood to start at that age, permitting access to birth control without parental consent.

1971: One-third of young American women use the pill
Even with some states still blocking access for unmarried women, in 1971, for the first time, one-third of 21-year-olds had used the pill at some point in their lives (Goldin and Katz 2002).

1972: *Eisenstadt v. Baird*

The U.S. Supreme Court overturned a state law that banned the sale of contraceptives to single people, which had been intended to keep them from having sex before marriage. The court ruled that married and unmarried people had the same right to privacy and access to contraceptives. That was the last major hurdle before the pill could become widely available to all women over age 18 nationwide.

1976: Sex before graduation

Among American women born in 1945, the majority—60 percent—were still virgins when they reached age 21. But for the group born 10 years later, who turned 21 in 1976, only 30 percent had not had sex by that age (Goldin and Katz 2002).

2000: Worldwide use

Worldwide, about 76 million married women (or those in marriage-like relationships) were using the pill for contraception, plus an unknown number of women not in long-term relationships. It remains more common in rich countries, where medical care and prescription drugs are more readily available (United Nations 2004). The pill is the most common birth control method among American women who use birth control (Figure 6.3).

2012: Insurance and the pill

The federal government required most private health insurance plans to cover contraception, including the pill, under the Affordable Care Act (Sonfield 2016).

Figure 6.3 **Percentage of women using various methods of birth control, ages 15–44**

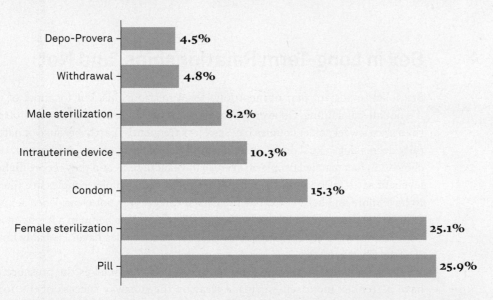

In 2011–2013, 62% of American women ages 15–44 reported using birth control. The pill and female sterilization are by far the most common. Note that some women use more than one method.

SOURCE: Daniels et al. (2015).

if they were married. Thus, for the same behavior that might earn a woman scorn or worse, a man might receive accolades or other rewards. The sexual double standard is apparent even among adolescents, as boys with more sexual partners experience higher levels of acceptance by their peers, while the opposite is true for girls (Kreager and Staff 2009).

This attitude has become less universal, however, as illustrated by widespread use of the birth control pill among unmarried women, which frees them to have sex without entering into traditional family relationships (see Changing Technology, "The Pill"). However, many people still apply the sexual double standard to lesser degrees. When single people do have sex, they expect the man to make the first sexual move, and men's sexual fulfillment usually comes first (Wade 2017). Moreover, when it comes to choosing a marriage partner (see Chapter 8), many men express a preference for women with less sexual experience—but they still prefer more experienced women for dating relationships (Crawford and Popp 2003).

The sexual double standard means that parents have traditionally tried harder to police their daughters' sexual behavior than their sons'. This may seem like an upper-class practice—protecting the chastity of daughters to preserve the family's reputation. But among the poor, the problem is not so much a lack of desire for control as the inability to protect their daughters from sexual exploitation (Treas 2004). Parents' protectiveness is reasonable as young women disproportionately bear the consequences of premarital sex—suffering from the stigma, as well as the possible emotional harm, of being seen as "fallen," not to mention the potential burden of single parenthood. We will return to teen sex shortly.

Sex in Long-Term Relationships, and Not

Sex is an important part of most long-term relationships, but for most of us it's not all-consuming. On average, married couples have sex a little more often than once a week; older couples have sex less frequently, partly because of naturally decreasing sexual desire. Although single people may appear to have more choices, in fact married people on average have more sex—and they report higher levels of satisfaction with their experience. Further, happier couples are likely to have more and better sex, but the causal direction is not clear: Does sexual satisfaction improve happiness within marriage, or does being in a happy marriage improve the quality and quantity of sex that couples have? Probably both are true (Byers 2005).

Over the twentieth century, sexual inhibitions declined as the pressure to have better sex increased—as made clear by the runaway success of the 1972 how-to book *The Joy of Sex* (Comfort 1972). As a result, sex within marriage became more adventurous, with more variety in sexual practices, more frank conversations, and higher expectations—all part of the growing importance of emotional expression within marriage, discussed in Chapter 2. These changes partly stemmed from increased access to birth control and sex education (as well as legal abortion), which freed people to experiment more. Married couples also have more privacy than they did before the mid-twentieth century, living in larger homes with fewer children and other relatives than in the past (Treas 2004). Just as children having their own rooms contributed to their sense of individuality (see Chapter 2), so physical separation from their children enhanced parents' freedom of sexual expression.

As for infidelity among married people, the best studies suggest that the numbers aren't as high as many people think. Among people who have been married, 21 percent of men and 12 percent of women in 2014 answered "yes" to the question, "Have you ever had sex with someone other than your husband or wife while you were married?"—and those numbers haven't changed much in the last two decades (Smith et al. 2014). Extramarital sex is most often motivated—or justified—by the desire for more or better sex, especially among men. Some social situations, however, are more conducive to extramarital affairs, such as when families are separated by travel or migration for work (Hirsch et al. 2009). As with all studies of private behavior, we can't be sure how accurate such reports are, but we have learned to administer sex surveys anonymously on computers, rather than face to face and in the presence of others, so we have some confidence in the results (Whisman and Snyder 2007).

Although condemnation of infidelity remains almost universal in opinion surveys, some environments more effectively encourage conformity to that standard. One of those is a religious community. Highly religious people often say that their faith helps them avoid infidelity within marriage (Dollahite and Lambert 2007). But it may be the informal social controls in such circles that keep people's behavior in check. That conclusion appears to be supported by surveys showing that people who attend religious services are less likely to have extramarital affairs, but the same is not true of people who merely express faith in God (Atkins and Kessel 2008).

Sex at Older Ages

There may be no better illustration of the separation of sexuality from reproduction than sex after menopause. Humans (along with two kinds of whale) are the only mammal species known to have a long lifespan after the end of their reproductive years, after menopause (Croft et al. 2017). The evolutionary reason for a woman to live so long after she can no longer bear children—in many cases more than half her life—at first was not clear to scientists. But we now believe that grandmothers caring for the young children in their families is more valuable to species survival than bearing more children would be, and the benefit is great enough to justify the resources needed to keep them alive. In addition to their family contributions, however, our long lives also include many years when sexual activity makes no contribution to reproduction, and yet it contributes to happiness and fulfillment for many people. In that way, older people are

Good health, access to healthcare, and a stable romantic partner, are all important to maintaining an active sex life in old age.

like modern younger adults who have sex using contraception. In fact, it is not uncommon today for a person to be sexually active for 60 out of 90 years, but only produce one or two children in all that time.

Research on sex in later life is still relatively sparse, but in recent years we have begun to develop more systematic information from social surveys (Lindau et al. 2007). The new research allows us to draw some conclusions (these were reviewed by DeLamater [2012]). Many people do remain sexually active into their 70s and 80s, despite age-related changes to their bodies. They may have sex within marriage, sex with nonmarital partners, or practice masturbation. For example, even among people age 70 or older, about half of men, and one-third of women, told a major survey that they had masturbated in the previous year. Lower numbers—43 percent of men and 22 percent of women—reported having vaginal intercourse.

We also know who is most likely to have an active sex life in old age. People who are in good mental and physical health, those with positive attitudes toward sex, and those who have a stable romantic partner are all more likely to be sexually active. The greater number of single women at older ages is a major factor in their lower rates of sexual activity. For those with medical conditions, including erectile dysfunction (see below), which can be linked to high blood pressure and diabetes, access to good medical care may be essential for maintaining an active sex life as well.

Sex beyond the reproductive years may not contribute to the growth of the species, but there is good evidence that it can contribute to health and happiness in old age. As the population ages (see Chapter 13), these issues will only take on greater importance.

Teen Sex

Because teen sex almost always implies nonmarital sex, some people are inclined to view it with alarm at all times. For example, one conservative advocacy group's report opens with the sentence, "Teen sexual activity remains a widespread problem confronting the nation" (C. Kim and Rector 2008). There are two reasons to take a closer look at the issue, however, regardless of your moral perspective. First, the facts are complicated. The proportion of teenagers having sex has fallen in recent decades, the nature of that sexual activity may have changed in important ways, and different behavior is concentrated in different groups. All that will be important for understanding the second reason, which is that the consequences of teen sexuality—positive or negative—often depend on the circumstances under which it is experienced, endured, or enjoyed. Studying who does it, with whom, and how is important for understanding the social impact of teen sex.

To begin this topic, I should note that the issue itself is poorly defined. Some teenagers are married, and for them "teen sex" is socially acceptable. On the other hand, some preteens are also sexually active or at least physically mature enough to be sexually active. And finally, some people in their 20s exhibit the same irresponsible sexual practices that cause concern among people worrying about "teen sex." Instead of focusing on "teens," we could think in terms of **adolescence**, which is the period of development between childhood and adulthood. A century ago, this concept referred to the age when sex was something young people could do but shouldn't—that is, between puberty and marriage (J. Moran 2000). But now that sex before marriage is so common, that original concept seems quite dated. For purposes of this discussion, I will refer to "teen sex" as sex involving unmarried people ages 13 to 18, which is the group most people have in mind when they discuss this issue.

Also, this discussion deals specifically with voluntary sex between teenagers, rather than rape or sex between teenagers and older adults. The latter may be illegal under age of consent (or "statutory rape") laws, which specify conditions under which a young person's consent cannot legally be given. In some states, unmarried people under a certain age may not legally have sex regardless of the circumstances. For example, you may be surprised to learn that in California, no one under age 18 may legally have sex unless the couple is married; the same is true in New York, but the age of consent there is 17. In most other states, the law is more complicated. In Pennsylvania, for example, teenagers may have sex between the ages of 13 and 16, but only if their partner is less than four years older (so an 18-year-old can have sex with a 15-year-old, but a 19-year-old can't—unless they're married, which is legal at age 15!).

Sometimes statutory rape is the lesser charge used by prosecutors if they can't prove that a forcible rape occurred, perhaps because the victim refuses to testify (Leonard, Ryan, and Smith 2009). This illustrates a tension in the law. Statutory rape laws in theory are intended to protect young people from more powerful partners who may coerce or force them into having sex. But in some states, young people can legally marry before they can legally have sex outside

adolescence

The period of development between childhood and adulthood.

of marriage (Goodman 1996). So preventing sex isn't the sole target of the law. Although the laws may protect the innocent, they also are part of the legacy of parents attempting to control their children's social lives and determine their eventual marriage partners.

What's Going On?

Even when it is not illegal, teen sex is one of those behaviors, like crime, that people tend to assume is always bad and probably getting worse. For example, a popular term paper website distributes a paper that opens with the claim, "The number of teenagers becoming sexually active, pregnant, and contracting sexually transmitted diseases are rapidly on the rise." But that doesn't fit the facts. The federal government carries out a major national survey every two years called the Youth Risk Behavior Survey, and the trend it shows from the early 1990s to the most recent survey is clear: Fewer high school students have had sexual intercourse, falling as low as 41 percent in 2015. Unfortunately, among those who do have sex, the percentage using a condom for protection has fallen in the last decade as well, which we will return to shortly (see Figure 6.4).

In many ways, teen sex is oriented more toward male than toward female desires. Among young teens, boys have a more positive sexual experience in terms of pleasure, popularity, and self-esteem, while girls are more likely to feel

Figure 6.4 **Teen sexual behavior, 9th to 12th grades, 1991–2015**

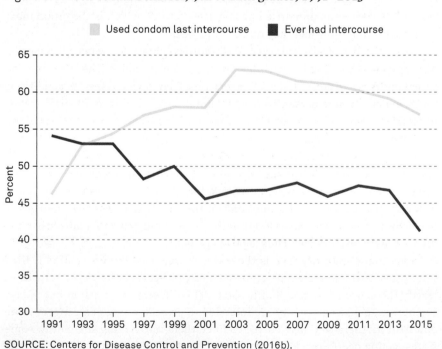

SOURCE: Centers for Disease Control and Prevention (2016b).

bad about themselves or feel as if they have been used (Brady and Halpern-Felsher 2007). And among college students, casual hookups (see Chapter 7) more often include orgasms for men only—largely because women are much more likely to perform oral sex on men (Wade 2017).

Sexual activity among teenagers—especially younger teenagers—is more common among groups that are socially disadvantaged by income, education, or race. The race differences are most pronounced among early teens from poor families, among whom Black adolescents have the highest rates of sexual activity (Akers et al. 2009). This may be partly because, for reasons that are not well understood, Black children on average reach puberty somewhat earlier than White children (Krieger et al. 2015). Still, it's important to remember that even among people from poor backgrounds, the majority of both boys and girls haven't had sexual intercourse before age 16 (Centers for Disease Control 2016b).

The generation gap in perceptions of teen sexuality—in which parents and other adults are more likely to view sex among adolescents as a serious problem— is not new. But it has been exacerbated in recent years by children's growing technological sophistication. Electronic media are an expanding part of all sexual communication, but the teen and young-adult sex scene has been particularly affected. Nationally, among teens age 16 to 18, about 10 percent report having shared sexual pictures of themselves in the previous year, but the numbers are higher in some areas than others (Ybarra and Mitchell 2014). These high-speed communications—and the easy availability of online pornography—contribute to what many adults view as a hypersexualized environment for adolescents (see Trend to Watch).

At What Cost?

Setting aside the question of whether premarital sex is necessarily a moral problem, sex among teenagers is a problem under much the same circumstances in which adult sex is a problem: when it's nonconsensual, when it leads to sexually transmitted disease or unplanned pregnancy, or when it has serious emotional consequences. Research clearly shows that people who begin having sex at earlier ages tend to have more sex, with more sexual partners, later in life (Heywood et al. 2015). And teen sex is more likely to lead to some negative outcomes, partly because of the poor emotional development of most teenagers and partly because of the lack of control over the resources that they need (including knowledge) to care for themselves. Nevertheless, by itself, the *number* of teenagers having sex is not a good indicator of the extent of these ill effects. For example, a study of six rich countries found that although teenagers in the United States start having sex around the same age, teenagers in the other countries have lower pregnancy, abortion, and birth rates, mostly because they are more likely to use birth control and to use it more effectively (Darroch et al. 2001).

Recognizing the importance of the context of teen sex and the relationships within which it takes place is crucial if parents are going to engage their children on this issue in supportive ways. In a fascinating comparison of middle-class

Dutch and American parents, sociologist Amy Schalet (2011) found that the Dutch parents were quite permissive in allowing their teenage children to have sex in their homes, while most American parents refused. Partly as a result, the Dutch parents ended up communicating much more openly with their children, allowing them to monitor the children's behavior and support them in positive ways, which helped them have healthy sexual relationships.

Of course, nonconsensual sex among teenagers has serious long-term consequences (and it is most often perpetrated by older adults). For example, when those girls later have voluntary sexual relationships, they are more likely to engage in risky behavior, such as having unprotected sex or multiple sex partners (Akers et al. 2009). Beyond these consequences, the problem also complicates our understanding of teen sexuality in general. For example, in describing the effects of sexual activity on teenage girls, those who willingly have sex with their boyfriends from school are often grouped together in studies with those who are raped by an older man. So it is sometimes hard to tell the difference between the consequences of voluntary and nonvoluntary sex for young people.

As with those who have been the victims of rape, adolescents who have sex at a young age may be acting in response to problems they already have—such as emotional weaknesses or lack of long-term perspective. However, careful studies have attempted to discern whether having sex at a young age further impacts adolescents, and how. One approach is to study teenagers from before middle school and see if those with early sexual experiences suffer negative mental health effects by the end of high school. It appears from such studies that teen sex doesn't harm boys psychologically. However, among girls, those who have sex early are at greater risk of depression (Sabia and Rees 2008). On the other hand, girls with depressive symptoms are also more likely to have sex earlier, so the question of cause and effect is not clear-cut (Spriggs and Helpern 2008).

Without a doubt, however, it is teenage pregnancy—specifically, unmarried teenage pregnancy—that tops the list of concerns with regard to adolescent sex. In fact, according to President Bill Clinton in 1995, it was "our most serious social problem" (Hoffman 1998). This problem was less of an issue before the 1960s, not because teenagers didn't have sex but because they got married younger. And teenagers who got pregnant were often expected to marry before giving birth (J. Gray, Stockard, and Stone 2006). After the mid-1960s, the tendency to marry during a pregnancy—so-called shotgun weddings—dropped dramatically due to the growing acceptability of single motherhood and the availability of legal abortion starting in the 1970s (Parnell, Swicegood, and Stevens 1994). As a result, teen pregnancy now more often leads to single motherhood, if not abortion.

However, the rates of teen pregnancy have declined rapidly in the years since a national crisis was declared. Figure 6.5 shows that the pregnancy rates for both younger and older

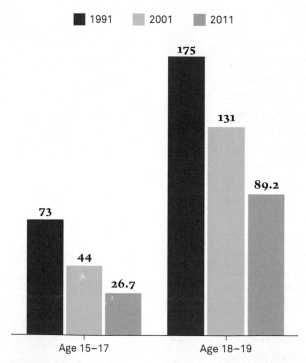

Figure 6.5 **Pregnancies per 1,000 teens, 1991–2011**

■ 1991   ■ 2001   ■ 2011

SOURCE: Kost and Maddow-Zimmet (2016).

teens dropped from 1991 to 2011. This change resulted from lower rates of sexual activity to some degree, as we saw above, but also from improved use of birth control (Guttmacher Institute 2006). (As discussed in Changing Politics, "Sex Education," efforts to encourage abstinence as a form of birth control have not been notably successful.) In addition, the negative effects of teen pregnancy were exaggerated in many early studies that failed to consider that those young women who got pregnant were already at risk for some of the problems they experienced, such as dropping out of school (Hoffman 1998). However, more recent studies have confirmed that having children early at least increases whatever obstacles young women already have to their educational progress (Sabia and Rees 2009)—as well as to their early career development—which is not surprising, given the time commitments of being a single parent (Levine and Painter 2003). Obviously, teen pregnancy remains a substantial concern. And the question of having children early is a part of a much larger set of issues, including the well-being of those children born to teen parents, a subject we will return to in Chapter 9.

Sexuality and Health

Sociologists who are concerned with health and illness usually study how social processes affect health and the way we perceive and act on health issues. That includes the way we communicate and interact with each other, as well as the dynamics of institutional arenas such as the state, market, and family. Two issues relating to health and sexuality will help to illustrate our focus: sexually transmitted infections and erectile dysfunction.

Sexually Transmitted Infections

Public awareness of sexually transmitted diseases (STDs) exploded in the 1980s, when the mysterious, incurable disease that came to be known as AIDS started striking some communities of gay men (Shilts 1987). Since its appearance, about 700,000 Americans have died of AIDS, and as of 2015, about 13,000 Americans die annually. The human immunodeficiency virus (HIV) that causes AIDS is usually, but not necessarily, transmitted by sexual contact. About two-thirds of new cases are the result of male-to-male sexual contact, with the rest coming from heterosexual sex or the sharing of intravenous drug needles (see Figure 6.6). Overall, 0.3 percent of all Americans are HIV-positive.

Since the 1980s, we have seen tremendous advances in treating HIV/AIDS. The result is that many people with the disease can live long lives, free from many of the symptoms that occur as the infection progresses, if they carefully follow an elaborate (and expensive) medical regimen including medications and checkups. Interestingly, because infection rates were higher in previous decades, and because people are now surviving longer with the disease, the greatest number of people living with HIV are now in their 50s (Centers for Disease Control and

Figure 6.6 Transmission categories for new cases of HIV, 2015

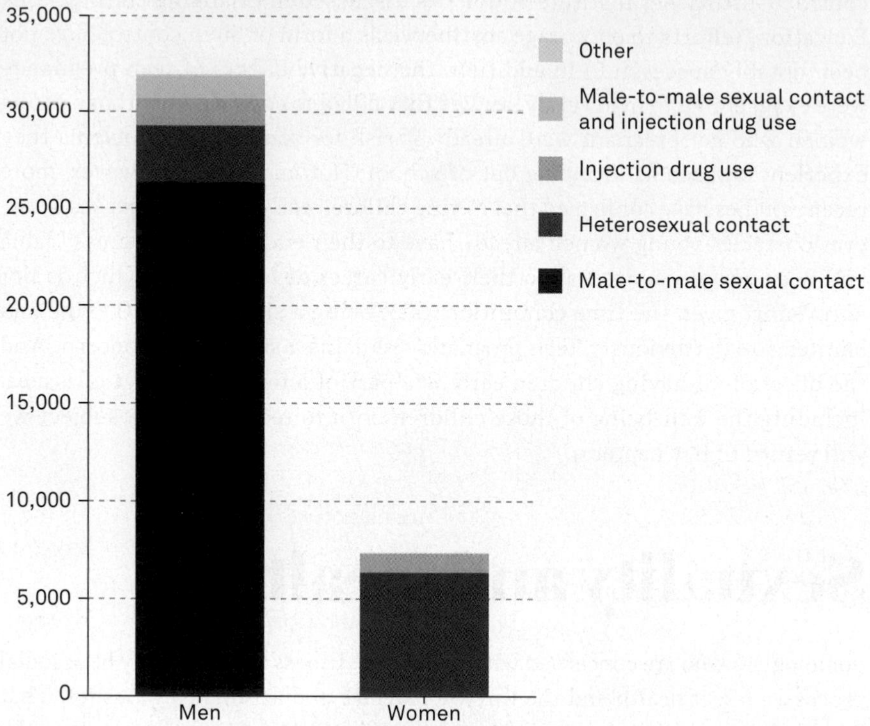

Most new cases of HIV, the virus that causes AIDS, result from men having sex with men. Among women, the greatest source of new cases is sex with men.

SOURCE: Centers for Disease Control and Prevention (2016c).

Prevention 2016c). Nevertheless, AIDS remains the most deadly of the sexually transmitted diseases, and the impact of the AIDS crisis on sexual behavior has been dramatic, highlighting the importance of health screening and the use of condoms during sex and leading many couples (and potential couples) to have explicit conversations they might not otherwise have had.

Despite the high profile and cultural impact of HIV/AIDS, a number of other STDs are much more common. In fact, a recent study of sexually active teenage girls found that more than a third had at least one sexually transmitted infection. The most common is human papillomavirus (HPV); although usually harmless, in about 10 percent of cases it persists, leading to an increased risk of cervical cancer (Forhan et al. 2009). An effective HPV vaccine has been developed, and it works if administered to girls before their first sexual intercourse. However, many parents object to the vaccine, believing that giving a sex-related vaccine to young girls will encourage them to have sex before marriage—a fear that is not supported by medical research (Jenna, Goldman, and Seabury 2015).

Educating for Sexual Health Three issues related to sexually transmitted diseases stand out from a sociological perspective. The first is the role of *sex education*, which is essential to help people take the actions necessary to protect themselves, such as using condoms when they have sex, limiting the number of their sexual partners, or not having sex at all. The education process involves young people, parents, teachers, the media, and public officials, all interacting to produce a system that works—or doesn't—to prevent diseases from spreading.

In addition to the schools, there are also local, state, and federal public health programs that attempt to shape sexual behavior. These efforts go beyond providing information, using marketing techniques to promote or discourage particular attitudes and behaviors in what is known as "social marketing." This may include combining educational materials with celebrity endorsement, corporate sponsorships, or—in the case of condoms—product giveaways (Friedman et al. 2016).

Backlash against HPV vaccines tends to fall into two (possibly overlapping) camps: (1) people opposed to vaccines generally and (2) parents who struggle with the idea of their preteen daughters having sex.

Public education and public health campaigns are opportunities to influence behavior on a large scale. For sociologists, they are also opportunities to study the intersection of institutional arenas. For example, although the family has a central role to play in educating and socializing children, state intervention through the schools often presents a challenge to family authority (see Changing Politics, "Sex Education"). Further, corporate interests, such as those selling medicines or even pornography, seek to alter public behavior around sex as well.

Social Networks The second way the sociological perspective stands out with regard to sexually transmitted disease is in the role of *social networks*. Infections can be thought of as tracers, marking the relationships between individuals who have sex. Most people are familiar with social networks from websites such as Facebook, which allow users to track their friends, friends of friends, and so on. Sexual infections work in much the same way. The diagram in Figure 6.8 shows part of an outbreak of chlamydia in a Colorado town in the late 1990s. Each dot represents one infected person, and each line represents a sexual contact between two people (Potterat et al. 2002).

For sociologists, a network diagram is useful for studying the pattern of relations between people. It also provides clues to how a particular disease infects a community. In this case, the dots highlighted in pink are individuals with the most sexual partners, responsible for a large share of all disease transmissions. The person represented by the green dot had four partners—not as many as the red dots, but enough to transmit the infection from one large group to another, possibly causing 15 infections in the group at the bottom. Each of these people plays a particular role in the community and in the spread of the infection.

Understanding the pattern of relationships between people in this way is useful for studying everything from disease outbreaks to phone calls to links on the Internet (Butts 2009). In the case of sexually transmitted disease, these patterns have shown us that a relatively small number of very active, centrally located individuals can have a big impact on the course of a disease. That can

Sex Education

Sex education is one of the most divisive issues in American politics—especially local politics, where passions run deep and small numbers of voters can have a big impact on school policies. The debate represents different worldviews over everything from the essential meaning of sex to the sacred nature of marriage.

According to sociologist Kristin Luker (2006), on one side are those who view sex as a normal part of everyday life that is harmful only if it's misunderstood, so education on the practicalities is essential. On the other side are those who see sex as sacred, a ritual performed in the service of God by two monogamously married adults who have never had sex with anyone else. They believe that teaching adolescents how to have sex safely just gives them tacit permission to have sex before marriage, undermining the moral teachings of their parents and churches.

Abstinence First, Abstinence Only

As talk about sex, and sexual imagery, became more and more common over the last hundred years, sex emerged as a growing factor in American politics. In the name of protecting children, conservative political activists successfully seized the issue of sex education, painting classroom instruction about sex as "radical, dangerous and immoral" (Irvine 2002). By the mid-1990s, partly fueled by the AIDS crisis and partly by the perception that youth culture was becoming more sexualized, a movement for "abstinence" education took hold at the local and state levels in many parts of the country. The premise of the curriculum is that abstinence must be taught as the only acceptable approach to adolescent sexuality, because to teach alternatives, such as birth control and condom use, would in essence give permission to children to have sex. In fact, supporters consider even discussing the details of sex with adolescents pornographic.

This "safe sex" poster illustrates condoms dressed as different career paths, such as doctors, writers, and teachers.

In reality, sex education in America is a patchwork of state and local policies, under a federal umbrella that cannot require a particular curriculum, but does offer money to states and school districts for some programs. The spread of what became known as "abstinence only" was rapid: since 1995, the percentage of adolescents receiving formal instruction on

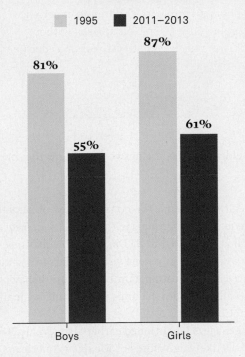

Figure 6.7 **Percentage of adolescents receiving instruction on birth control**

■ 1995   ■ 2011–2013

SOURCES: Lindberg, Santelli, and Singh (2006); National Center for Health Statistics (2016).

birth control methods has fallen drastically, as Figure 6.7 shows.

The federal government has played a big role in that development. From the mid-1990s to the late 2000s, Washington distributed $1.9 billion to states and districts to teach abstinence-only programs. However, rigorous studies of abstinence-only education have shown that they are not effective at influencing student behavior. Researchers have studied the number of sexual partners teenagers have, whether they use birth control or get pregnant, and the rate of sexually transmitted infections. None of these measures shows any effect that can be attributed to the abstinence programs. On the other hand, comprehensive sex education, which teaches specific practices and skills, is much more effective (Manlove, Fish, and Moore 2015).

To accompany abstinence education, at the urging of religious leaders, some young people took "virginity pledges," promising not to have sex until they were married. These, too, were ineffective; teenagers who took such pledges were no less likely to have premarital sex. However, if they did have sex, these students were actually *less* likely to use birth control. Remarkably, five years later, more than three-quarters of them denied having taken the pledge (Rosenbaum 2009).

As of 2017, about half of all states require that sex education classes stress abstinence as preferable for students. No more than 18 states require teaching contraceptive methods. At the extreme, 18 states require the teaching of abstinence but do not require teaching about contraception in their sex education curriculums. In addition, most states permit parents to pull their children from any sex education class they don't approve (Guttmacher Institute 2017a).

Preventing Social Chaos

Advocates for abstinence education have reactivated a historical fear in American culture that "sexual language will trigger social chaos" (Irvine 2002:3). Merely speaking the words, in some cases, is seen as a threat to morality. As a result, some rules strictly limit what teachers can discuss with their students. Ironically, according to sociologist Janice Irvine (2002:166), "although thousands of young people could watch Ellen [DeGeneres] come out on national television, many of them could not talk about it with their teachers the next day in the classroom."

Those who believe that children need comprehensive sex education see a different sort of social chaos. They see sexually transmitted disease and unwanted pregnancies among adolescents, along with the inequality that leads more poor and minority children to experience these problems, as the kind of social chaos that comes from young people having sex without the knowledge they need to protect themselves—that is, from neglecting to care for and educate children.

help educators or health care providers disrupt the network and slow the spread of infection.

Inequality As with most health problems, the consequences of sexually transmitted diseases are not felt equally by all groups in the population. *Inequality* is the third salient sociological issue related to STDs. Racial inequalities, in particular, have persisted or even widened in recent years. A person's sexual health reflects a combination of access to education, family structure, behavioral factors, and access to health care—all key issues driving racial-ethnic inequality in the United States, as we saw in Chapter 3.

The study of sexually active teenagers I mentioned earlier also revealed that Black adolescents are about twice as likely as Whites or Mexican Americans to

Figure 6.8 **Chlamydia outbreak diagram**

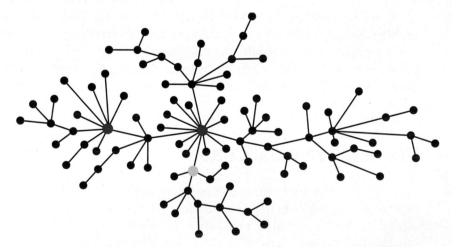

The figure shows part of an outbreak of chlamydia in a Colorado town in the late 1990s. Each dot represents one infected person, and each line represents a sexual contact between two people.

SOURCE: Potterat et al. (2002), with pink and green highlights added.

carry any sexually transmitted infection. That is partly because African American adolescents are more likely to be poor and to have had multiple sex partners (Forhan et al. 2009).

The case of HIV infection will help illustrate how that disparity occurs. As we saw earlier, 0.3 percent of all adults in the United States under age 50 are HIV-positive. But the rates are much higher among African Americans, at 1 percent (Centers for Disease Control and Prevention 2016c). Although those percentages reflect only a small minority of the Black population, the rates are much higher than for other groups, which has led some critics to accuse the government of neglecting the HIV/AIDS epidemic (Adimora, Schoenbach, and Floris-Moore 2009).

What causes this racial inequality? One set of causes has to do with sexual behavior—for example, having unprotected sex earlier and with more partners—and intravenous drug use. Although these causes may be within an individual's control, critics argue that better education and health care would help prevent such behavior. And that brings us to a second set of causes, the indirect result of poverty: the presence in a community of illnesses that are untreated (for example, herpes), which make people more susceptible to HIV infection. People who are poor have less access to health care prevention and treatment services and as a result are more likely to have infections of other kinds.

Finally, even if only a very small percentage of the Black population is infected—which is true—infections within the Black population may spread more rapidly. That is because of the great social distance and the low rate of intermarriage between African Americans and other groups (see Chapter 3). Because their "sexual networks" are quite concentrated, even a small number of sexually active men can spread HIV more quickly among the population if they have unprotected sex.

Erectile Dysfunction

In colonial America, *erectile dysfunction*—the failure of a man to achieve an erection—was considered a problem only insofar as it prevented a married couple from producing children. If there was no known medical reason for infertility (see Chapter 9), it was generally assumed that the "fault" lay in the woman's body. But in some situations, people understood that the deficiency was on the man's side. Even before medical experts had fully explained the biology of reproduction, they nevertheless understood that male ejaculation was a necessary part of the process. In principle, then, the failure to produce children could be attributed to the husband.

The Puritan religious authority Cotton Mather wrote that divorces should be granted in families where either spouse "utterly disappointed the confessed ends of marriage" because of "natural incapacities" or "insufficiencies" (Duberman 1978:396). In practice, however, it was very difficult for women to bring such cases. A review of eighteenth-century divorce proceedings in Massachusetts revealed only one woman who successfully had her marriage annulled because

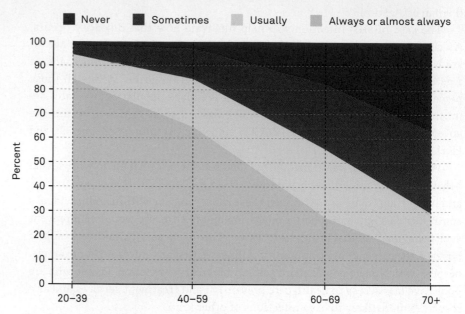

Figure 6.9 **Men's erectile function, by age**

■ Never ■ Sometimes □ Usually □ Always or almost always

The question asked was, "How would you describe your ability to get and keep an erection adequate for satisfactory intercourse?"

SOURCE: Selvin, Burnett, and Platz (2007).

of her husband's "sexual incapacity," and that required an act of the legislature (Cott 1976).

Erectile dysfunction (sometimes known as ED, presumably to make the term more acceptable in polite conversation) has probably always existed among people, although how common it was in the past we cannot know. As it became a medical issue that could be treated, however, its social significance was transformed. Describing ED as a medical condition instead of as a personal failure or physical defect has reduced the sense of shame associated with the problem and increased men's willingness to seek treatment. To make it seem more normal, some pharmaceutical companies have exaggerated its commonness (R. Moynihan, Heath, and Henry 2002). For example, the company that makes Viagra ran advertisements telling men, "Remember, you're not the first one to talk to his doctor about Viagra. 20 million American men have already had the Viagra talk." These companies also have enlisted men associated with strength and power, like race car drivers and military heroes, as spokesmen to endorse their products. The strategy seems to be working: Pharmacies filled more than 16 million prescriptions for ED drugs in 2014 (Russell 2016).

The primary cause of ED is undoubtedly age, with older men much more likely to report the problem. Above age 70, more than two-thirds of men meet the definition commonly used (Figure 6.9). However, there are also social causes, including smoking, lack of exercise, and diabetes. Men with lower levels of education are more prone to the problem as well, possibly because of poorer general health (Selvin, Burnett, and Platz 2007). As with infertility (discussed in Chapter 9), poor people are more likely to experience the problem, while the well-off are more able to treat it medically.

Erectile dysfunction is one of the most common disorders affecting sexual expression, one that has no doubt received more attention because it affects men—who are often the ones assumed to be "doing" sex—and because there is money to be made treating it. Doctors and therapists recognize that some women also have disorders affecting their sexual function and expression, but there is not yet a major drug available to address those problems (Brotto et al. 2010).

Sexual disorders reflect a combination of social and biological factors that prevent people from developing their sexual selves the way they want to—or the way others believe they should. In the next chapter, we turn to the relationships within which sex takes place.

Trend to Watch: Pornography

How is pornography affecting attitudes toward sex and sexual behavior? This is a difficult question to answer, partly because porn has become so common that its effects may be felt everywhere—even among people who don't use it themselves. The overall trend is clear: Today's young adults have been exposed to porn more than those of previous generations, for whom porn was more stigmatized, more difficult to access, and more expensive. Now that it's widely considered normal, and is easily accessed online for free, what effects will that have?

There is no one definition of pornography, but some common features have raised concerns about sexual health and behavior. For example, most porn does not include men wearing condoms, and college students who consume porn are less likely to use condoms themselves (Wright, Tokunaga, and Kraus 2016). A lot of porn is also violent and degrading, especially showing women apparently enjoying violent sex and sex oriented toward male sexual fulfillment (Wade 2017). Does exposure to these images alter how people think about healthy and enjoyable sex, encourage violence, and undermine the well-being of people's relationships? The short answer is yes, but the overall effect is not yet clear (Rasmussen 2016). There is evidence that pornography may contribute to conflicts within marriage (Perry 2016). And for some people it may lead to excessive or addictive behavior that causes problems not only with sex but with other aspects of social life (Wery and Billieux 2017). On the other hand, if used differently porn may also increase people's knowledge about and comfort with sex in positive ways (Doering 2009).

Even though pornography has become so common that it probably feels like a natural part of the social environment to most people, we should not assume that we know how it is affecting sexual behavior and relationships, or family life generally. This is something for future research to determine.

Your Sex Education(s)

Where do young people get the information they need about sex? A recent survey investigated how old children were when their parents broached various sex-related topics with them (Beckett et al. 2010). The study made headlines because it revealed that a number of "advanced" topics—such as how to use specific forms of birth control and how to handle the social pressure of a boyfriend who won't use a condom—were never discussed until after the teenagers had already had intercourse. Those in favor of comprehensive sex education in school took the results to mean that schools have to step in because parents often don't get the job done.

Of course, young people learn about sex—and other topics—not just from parents and schools, but from other sources as well, especially media of all kinds and their peers. For example, millions of teenagers were exposed to a negative portrayal of early pregnancy through the MTV reality series *16 and Pregnant*. There are many different paths to similar information, but sometimes the source makes all the difference.

This exercise aims to take advantage of the diversity of educational policies and practices experienced by today's college students. It can be done individually, in small groups, or as a classroom exercise. Using the following table to jog your memory, try to recall where and when you first learned about these topics (if you did). Then, in a short essay or group discussion, relate the content of the lessons. Consider these possible questions for starters:

- Did different sources or authorities give you different information? If so, whom did you believe, and why?

- Were you in a school that taught "abstinence-only" sex education, comprehensive sex education, or something else? What difference did that make to you?

- Which lessons were most important to you, and how did the source of the information matter to you?

- Was the education you received effective overall? Why or why not?

Topic	Age at first introduction	Source of information		
		Parent	School	Media	Peers/ other
Body development					
How babies are made					
Sexual orientations					
How sex spreads disease					
How birth control works					
How to use birth control					
Using condoms against STDs					
How to refuse sex					
Abstinence until marriage					

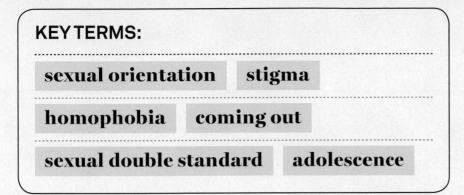

KEY TERMS:

sexual orientation   stigma

homophobia   coming out

sexual double standard   adolescence

Questions for Review

1. What is sexual orientation? How have attitudes toward homosexuality changed in the medical and scientific communities?

2. According to researchers, what is the role of genetics, evolution, and social environment in determining human sexual orientation?

3. What did masturbation mean to moral authorities in the nineteenth century?

4. What is the sexual double standard? What events, social movements, and technological innovations have challenged this attitude? Why?

5. Who has sexual intercourse more often and with higher levels of satisfaction: married couples or single people? Why?

6. How has technology exacerbated the generation gap in perceptions of adolescent sexuality? Why is this gap in understanding a problem for policymakers, parents, and teenagers?

7. Why have teenage pregnancy rates declined in the last 20 years?

8. Who is most at risk for HIV/AIDS infections? Why?

9. What does social network analysis reveal about the spread of sexually transmitted diseases? Why might sociologists find these data useful?

7

Love and Romantic Relationships

The night Jason first met Liz—they were in their mid-20s—he was immediately impressed. "Liz was tall, beautiful, and I could tell right away she was an unusual person who had her act together," he remembered. "And she made me laugh." A childhood friend had invited Jason to a party at Liz's apartment; he was looking for a job and later emailed Liz for contacts. What were the odds they would begin to date, hit it off, move in together, and marry three years later? On their first date, according to the *New York Times* wedding page, "they discovered they shared more than a sense of humor. He had played soccer at Princeton; she was on the water polo team at Penn." They were also both going to be doctors.

Was it a mysterious romantic spark that set off their relationship, beginning with her beauty and propelled by their joint passion for "helping others"? Or was it two young, White, single-and-looking, athletic Ivy League graduates with successful professional careers ahead of them, meeting at a party of people with similarly privileged backgrounds, and taking the obvious next step? We can't know for sure what attracted Liz and Jason to each other, but these questions highlight the sociological approach to love and relationships.

We are individuals, with our own experiences and outlooks on life. At the same time, we are embedded in a social world that shapes what goes on around us—and within us—in ways that we often don't recognize. The dynamic of that interaction between self and society—or, to put it another way, between biography and history—is the heart of sociology. As the sociologist C. Wright Mills famously put it, "No social study that does not come back to the problems of biography, of history, and of their intersections within a society has completed its intellectual journey" (1959/2000:6). There may be no better subject from which to learn this lesson than one as apparently intimate, personal, and individual as love itself.

What seems individual and personal, like dating and mutual attraction, is also shaped by larger forces in the social world.

237

Scripting Diversity

As we saw in Chapter 2, family structures have become more diverse over the past century. Similarly, the ways couples meet, form relationships, and build families have become more diverse as well. Rather than a change from one style of family formation to another, modern societies have moved from a dominant style to an abundance of approaches from which to choose. This freedom of choice—and the resulting pressure to choose—are prevalent features of our era, as discussed in Chapter 1.

Sociologists sometimes use the concept of scripts as a metaphor for the way people know how to interact in their differing roles (Simon and Gagnon 1984). A **social script** is a commonly understood pattern of interaction that serves as a model of behavior in familiar situations. Just as language has to exist before we can speak to each other, we often need scripts to at least get us going in a new social relationship (Laner and Ventrone 2000).

Recall a key insight from symbolic interaction theory: To interact successfully, people need to be able to see themselves through the eyes of others (see Chapter 1). For that reason, social scripts are a source of reassurance, letting people act on the assumption that their behavior is understandable and acceptable to others, without having to invent every situation from scratch. Naturally, scripts aren't step-by-step instructions that people follow to the letter. Rather, they serve to anchor or orient behavior—to help people locate their behavior in a social setting. And the *absence* of scripts can create a feeling of disorientation and confusion that may be quite powerful. Before you know how to act, in other words, you need to know what scene you're in and what role you're playing.

An example from TV may help illustrate the point. In a classic episode of the sitcom *Frasier*, Frasier attempts to set up his new boss with his single friend Daphne, but the boss (a gay man) thinks he's been invited to a date with Frasier. "That's a hell of a view," says the boss as he walks into Frasier's apartment and looks out the window, to which Frasier replies, "It's even better from the bedroom." What, seen from one perspective, is a casual comment with no sexual overtones—two straight male coworkers discussing an apartment—becomes an overt sexual approach when seen as the opening line of a date. The humor in the rest of the show stems from the repeated failure of the different characters to perform according to the scripts others are attempting to follow. (The episode, called "The Matchmaker," also won a special award from the Gay and Lesbian Alliance Against Defamation for its treatment of gay dating as noncontroversial.)

By the mid-1990s, when *Frasier* aired that episode, the "dating system" already had been declared dead (B. Bailey 1988). That doesn't mean people didn't go on dates anymore. In fact, most people still agreed on what a first date should be like—its appropriate script (Rose and Frieze 1993). But the rules were looking less clear.

By now it is safe to say that diversity reigns over conformity in how relationships are begun and built. As the TV show demonstrated, there are still scripts, but it's harder to know which one we're supposed to be following. Four specific developments underscore this overall change:

---

social script

A commonly understood pattern of interaction that serves as a model of behavior in familiar situations.

- The demise of the dating system as the dominant mode of relationship formation. Without a commonly understood series of stages from introduction to commitment—including the timing of sexual interaction—developing a relationship has become more variable and individualized.

- The increasing acceptance of living together as a common stage in relationships (see Chapter 8). With cohabitation now lasting anywhere from a short engagement to a lifetime, decisions about when, whether, and how to live together are a source of further uncertainty.

- The incorporation of divorced and older singles (many with children) into the mix of those looking for new relationships. This trend introduces still more variation in the assumptions and expectations for relationship behavior.

- The continual adaptation of communication technology to relationship dynamics, increasing the immediacy of interaction (M. Rosenfeld and Thomas 2012). The Internet has broadened the social world for many people, even as it has made it possible to meet and communicate with people based on very narrow specifications (for example, "29-year-old, tall, computer programmer Muslim male who likes cats but not dogs—and watching sports except football; willing to move to the West Coast").

You may be surprised that I did not include more sexual freedom or less relationship commitment in that list of trends. That's because, despite the perpetual concern that "kids these days" are leading the culture astray—a complaint that goes back at least to the Puritans of seventeenth-century New England—there isn't much evidence that young people exert that kind of influence in contemporary American society. While people born before the 1980s may be at a loss to understand "sexting" or "hooking up," these relative geezers (my age) are also pushing the dating scene in new directions, especially with sophisticated matching systems, and bringing apparently ever-more-complicated relationship histories and desires to that virtual first date.

Some people see a cultural landscape in crisis, in which "living by traditional moral virtues" has become an "alternative lifestyle," as two conservative professors complained (George and Londregan 2009). But I don't think the facts support the idea that American society has recently been dragged down the tubes by declining sexual morality and collapsing relationship commitments. As noted in Chapter 6, the proportion of high school students having intercourse has declined over the last few decades. As far back as 1976, 70 percent of 21-year-olds were no longer virgins. That seems similar to the late 2000s, when about three-quarters of college seniors reported having at least one hookup (Armstrong, England, and Fogarty 2010).

Almost three decades ago, an interviewer asked a sexually active 16-year-old about the future of her relationship: "Are we going to get married?" the teenager said. "The answer is no. Or will we be together next year? I don't know about that; that's a long time from now. But we won't date anyone else as long as we're together. That's a commitment, isn't it?" (Giddens 1992:10). Going back further, almost 100 years, a poet wrote, "Then should our love last but an hour / Need we turn from each other in shame?" (Hoyt 1923). The answer to that question probably depends on what one means by "love."

Love

Some scientists believe that humans developed the capacity—and the need—for love as part of the evolutionary apparatus of survival early in our development. Because human children require hands-on care for years, unlike most animals, children who were loved by their parents were more likely to survive. Because it made survival more likely, loving behavior became part of human nature (Lampert 1997). In fact, as we saw in Chapter 2, a broader sense of caring was necessary for human society to survive, as parents needed help from other adults to provide care for their offspring.

In a general sense of the term, **love** is a deep affection and concern for another, with whom one feels a strong emotional bond. However, that definition is not quite enough to answer the poet's question, "What is love more than a flame?" (Hoyt 1923). In the "flame" sense, we usually mean **romantic love**, which is the passionate devotion and attraction one person feels for another. According to sociologist Ann Swidler (2001), the modern version of romantic love is "mythical" because it involves an imaginary perfection. People elevate the idea of romantic love in their minds even if they know it is not always (or even often) attainable. That's why "the image of a couple walking hand-in-hand along the sea [is] more prevalent than the image of a man and a woman casually watching television" (Illouz 1997:5).

Swidler (2001) details four qualities of this romantic ideal. First, love is unambiguous and clear, as in "love at first sight." Second, love is unique, so there is "one true love" to be found for each person. Third, individuals seek both to prove and to demonstrate their true character by overcoming obstacles in the quest for love. These obstacles may be social, such as the barrier between the feuding families in *Romeo and Juliet*. Or the obstacles may be personal, as when a man gives up smoking or drinking to win over the object of his love. Finally, love is permanent, and a truly loving relationship is therefore eternal.

Clearly, this version of romantic love is an ideal, but it serves to animate and motivate many people in their search for happiness and satisfaction. And when real-life love falls too far short of the ideal—maybe just because a relationship has gone on for a few years and the "passion" is diminished—it may be doomed. Interestingly, as we will see in Chapter 8, the modern structure of marriage reinforces the ideal of romantic love by institutionalizing some of its elements. That is because adults, usually at a relatively young age, see themselves making a single, fateful choice to marry the one person who will be their partner in loving harmony forever.

The expectation that spouses would actually *love* each other was not common in Europe before the 1600s, but since then it has come to dominate the idea

love

A deep affection and concern for another, with whom one feels a strong emotional bond

romantic love

The passionate devotion and attraction one person feels for another.

The couple at left may be the ideal image of romantic love, but the family at right is probably more common.

of marriage (Coontz 2005). In recent times, anthropological research has found that some version of romantic love exists in virtually all existing cultures (Jankowiak and Fischer 1992). This supports the notion that love is inherent in our species, but we also know that the expression and interpretation of this ideal are culturally and historically specific.

Romantic love carries its own social scripts, which are useful for applying labels to our emotions in ways that help us decide how to act. For example, when (if) a couple reaches the moment in their relationship when one says to the other, "I love you," it is commonly understood to be a turning point. If the sentiment is reciprocated, the relationship is assumed to be going "to the next level." However, the meaning of such a moment has been subject to increasing uncertainty in recent times. Does it mean that the relationship is heading toward marriage? The moment still carries emotional weight—and demands a response one way or the other—but the next steps are often not clear, requiring further negotiation.

Making It Work

The negotiation and communication of modern relationships naturally take some of the romance out of romantic love. The spontaneous, irrational, passionate image of love weakens when people get out their calendars to schedule dates or compare prices for different brands of condoms. But that doesn't seem to weaken the idea of love, which remains central in modern relationships.

How is that possible? Swidler (2001) explains that there are actually two "cultures of love" in the United States, which exist side by side. Next to mythical, romantic love is a realistic or **utilitarian love**, which is the practical, rational dedication of one person to another based on shared understanding and emotional commitment. This version of love drives people to carefully consider the pros and cons of different partners and to look within themselves and try to identify what they really want from a relationship. People "work" on their relationships—often

utilitarian love

The practical, rational dedication of one person to another based on shared understanding and emotional commitment.

with the help of professional therapists or books by experts—to build love over time and maintain it through ongoing effort. The *New York Times* offered a clear example of this approach to relationships with an article titled "13 Questions to Ask before Getting Married," which included such seemingly obvious questions as, "How important is religion?" and "Will we have children?" (Stanford 2016). The watchword of utilitarian love is probably "communication."

Because utilitarian love is more rational, and romantic love is more spontaneous, some social theorists believe that utilitarian love is a reflection of modern culture. In that view, the shift from romantic love to utilitarian love parallels, for example, the growth of rational science replacing irrational religion as a way of explaining the world or the spread of democracy replacing monarchy (Lindholm 1998).

romantic relationships

Mutually acknowledged, ongoing interactions featuring heightened affection and intensity.

In this chapter, we are investigating love and **romantic relationships**, a general term that refers to mutually acknowledged, ongoing interactions featuring heightened affection and intensity (W. Collins, Welsh, and Furman 2009). Although romantic relationships need not be sexual, they usually include at least anticipated sexual interaction. Unfortunately, this definition can't be any more precise than the relationships themselves, which often have no fixed beginning or end and may not even be called the same thing by both partners.

Part of the uncertainty of modern romantic relationships stems from the coexistence of romantic and utilitarian love in many people's minds. As they move back and forth between these two ideals, people may start or end relationships—making demands on their partners or resisting them—based on whether they meet the criteria of either ideal of love. Because relationships are not as strictly regulated by family elders and other authorities as they once were, individuals no longer commit to relationships based on the expectations of others. The perceptions of other people—including family members, peers, friends, and employers—are still relevant. But our choices are now perceived as individual. If maintaining a relationship is a daily choice, love is one of the criteria people evaluate in making that choice.

As Anthony Giddens (1992) or other modernity theorists might say (see Chapter 1), the newfound freedoms of the late modern era set people up as lone individuals, without fixed directions to follow. If the love that results feels fragile—partly because it *is* more fragile and the underlying romantic relationships less stable than they once were—then its success should be all the more rewarding because it is based on personal choice and commitment. In that theory, such "pure" relationships are a hallmark of modern independence, along with all the uncertainties that it entails.

Relationship Rituals

In Chapter 2, we saw that the path to marriage evolved from the courtship system of the nineteenth century to dating in the twentieth. Since then, the dating system has become much less dominant (B. Bailey 1988). Although most people still date—and often use that term—it is not a clear and commonplace pathway from meeting to marriage.

We will begin by describing the form and function of dating. Then we will turn to the hookup scene, which causes part of the confusion over relationship-building scripts. As we will see, the bigger story is not hooking up per se, but instead the diversity of scripts available to follow (or create). That diversity is made more complicated by online dating, the increasing presence of older adults in the dating scene, and unique experiences for gay and lesbian couples.

Dating

To some students, it seems old-fashioned even to discuss dating in a college textbook today. "No one dates anymore" is a common refrain. But most people do still date, or do something similar to what used to be called dating. So despite changes in terminology, this remains an important area of study for sociology of the family.

When the dating system emerged in the early twentieth century, part of what made it so different from the older rituals of courtship was its widespread acceptance of overlapping relationships without commitment. It may be hard to understand how rapid and dramatic that change seemed to people at the time. For example, as late as 1948, an academic article reviewing college textbooks on marriage and the family complained that they didn't cover dating. "Today in most of the country," the author wrote, "especially in towns and cities, much dating goes on with no suggestion of marriage, either immediate or remote" (Lowrie 1948:90). He recommended that students take a course on the subject of dating in the last year of high school or the beginning of college.

On the other hand, it is also remarkable that the new system, in which young people met and socialized—sometimes sexually—with multiple potential partners, away from parental supervision, was so readily accepted (after a few decades of grumbling by the older generation). Rather than condemning the practice, Lowrie (1948) pointed out that dating seemed to improve young people's personality, life experience, personal poise, socialization skills, and preparation for marriage.

Dating was so accepted by the middle class that a 1956 survey of women entering college showed that they went on an average of about 12 dates per month (or 3 per week) with an average of about five different men (Kanin 1957). In fact, dating came to be seen as the "traditional," more formal system of getting to marriage. The dating system helped guide the transition from passionate romantic attraction—including lust—to the stable, mature love idealized in the established view of marriage. The social scripts associated with dating also served to regulate the acceptable timing of sexual intimacy.

By the time the rules of the dating system started to lose their grip on popular behavior, around 1965, its demise provoked fears of the "death of romance." Concerned elders now fretted that "in our search for freedom, honesty, love, and equality...we have found only meaningless sex, loneliness, and lack of commitment" (B. Bailey 1988:2). They were especially troubled by uncommitted sex. In fact, a recurring theme throughout modernity is that real love, together with social respectability, has been left behind in the traditional past by today's wayward young people.

Despite the decline of the dating system, several of its concepts and practices remain common. A "date" is a single event defined by the combination of goals pursued by the people involved, which generally include having fun, pursuing a sexual attraction, and learning more about the other person with an eye on a possible romantic relationship (Mongeau, Jacobsen, and Donnerstein 2007). In that way, a date is different from a simple sexual encounter or socializing between friends.

On the other hand, two people may consider themselves to be "dating" when they have formed a more stable romantic relationship or when they call the other one "boyfriend" or "girlfriend." That understanding, if shared by both partners, may trigger expectations. One teenage girl said that being a boy's girlfriend means he is making a commitment: "I'm gonna do this for you. I'm gonna buy this on your birthday. I'll take you out for dinner all these times. The word means a lot" (Milbrath, Ohlson, and Eyre 2009:339). That concept of dating is closer to the historical idea of "going steady," which implied being with only one person romantically (Bogle 2008).

In this discussion, I have attempted to avoid generalizing too much. If part of the lesson here is that diversity reigns over conformity, then it should be clear that people from different walks of life practice (or don't practice) dating in varied ways. Age, education, and marital status, for example, help shape people's social environments and expectations in ways that affect their romantic behavior and attitudes, as do race and ethnicity.

Because teenage relationships are largely shaped by a combination of family and peer influences, and peer groups are often racially or ethnically segregated, there are different patterns of behavior and expectations about relationships in different groups. In one local study, for example, African American and Mexican American high school students in northern California described romantic relationships in their own words. Their views showed many commonalities, such as the importance of maintaining one's status and reputation among peers and an idealized view of relationships. But there were differences as well. The Mexican American students were more likely to express appreciation for parental advice and guidance and to consider women's virginity an important moral value. African Americans, on the other hand, spoke more often about the skills needed to persuade others (using the term "game") and expressed a more practical approach based on an equal balance of expectations between men and women (Milbrath, Ohlson, and Eyre 2009).

Public and Private Dating Under the old courtship system, relationships moving toward marriage were contingent on decisions viewed as a public matter. Potential couples spent time together in private—usually in the woman's home in the case of affluent families, which is why the process was also known as "calling." But parents and the local community played a significant role in deciding which young people should be matched together. The private, personal considerations of the couple were less important.

On the other hand, even though dates take place in public settings, such as restaurants and movie theaters, the decision about whom to be with—and marry—is made much more privately by the individuals involved (B. Bailey 1988). In fact, many teenagers keep their dating relationships secret from their parents, even as they move about in public together, for fear of incurring their parents' displeasure (W. Collins, Welsh, and Furman 2009).

Further, unlike courtship, dating usually takes place in the market arena, often involving personal spending and commercial consumption, such as meals and movies. And dating involves spending the young people's own money—especially the young *man*'s money—which has a direct influence on the early interactions of the couple (Bogle 2008). Although that shift may seem subtle, it has important implications. For example, dating serves a vast commercial industry targeting single people directly, selling everything from clothes and cosmetics to meals and movies to dating advice. This commercial element further erodes family influence and enhances the power of market (or corporate) forces in the process of forming families.

The consumption aspect of dating enhances the public nature of the couple's commitment. In fact, the practice of dating was one of the most visible signs of the new twentieth-century mobility in which young men more and more commonly owned their own cars. Especially after World War II, cars became important visual markers of economic and social status (Whyte 1992). Whether in a car or not, however, to be seen by one's peers on a date is part of what makes a dating relationship real—acting out a social script that others can recognize and understand. And it makes dating appear more mutually respectful than an illicit relationship or casual sex.

In the words of one male high school student, when in a dating relationship the boy expects to "take her out somewhere. Go to movies together. Something you wouldn't do with any other broad." In a casual sex relationship, on the other hand, "you just meet her and take her to the house and do what y'all gotta do" (Harper et al. 2004).

Dating among Students
A lot of the research on dating has been directed at college students. That is partly because the growth of higher education and the tendency of people to delay marriage until their middle or late 20s have brought this population to the leading edge of the trends in dating. But this focus also reflects the simple fact that college students are easy to study, especially for researchers on university campuses. In any event, studies of college students have also provided some insights into larger social trends.

Students often socialize in mixed-gender groups. This provides a social setting for meeting and building friendships with a number of single people at once. And it differentiates these young people from most older people, especially those who are divorced, for whom simply meeting potential mates is a significant challenge (Mongeau, Jacobsen, and Donnerstein 2007). Together with the high concentration of single people, this feature of college life is part of what makes the dating scene there more efficient—more likely to produce more dates and more experience with a larger number of potential partners. And contrary to the notion that "dating" is over, one large survey at Stanford University found that more than 90 percent of students said they had been on at least one date, however they defined it (McClintock 2010). As an important exception, however, college students who commute to campus or attend part time often do not participate as readily in the campus dating scene (Risman and Allison 2014).

We have also learned that despite the spread of egalitarian beliefs—which promote equality between men and women—the majority of straight college students expect men to take the lead in formal date situations. That is especially the case for first dates (Lamont 2014). For example, most men as well as women believe that the man should extend the invitation, provide the transportation, open doors, cover expenses for the first date—and make the first sexual move if there is one (Laner and Ventrone 2000). And their hopes for the outcome of dates are often different. Research consistently shows that men in college are more likely than women to have a sexual goal, while women more often want a developing romantic relationship (Mongeau, Jacobsen, and Donnerstein 2007). (As we will see in Chapter 12, rape and sexual violence perpetrated by men are also most likely to occur in dating and romantic relationships.)

Ironically, because of the gains women have made in access to higher education—they significantly outnumber men on many campuses today—men benefit from being in short supply (Bogle 2008). According to informal accounts, the relative scarcity of men increases their bargaining power in the dating scene, both in terms of getting dates and in determining their outcome (A. Williams 2010). That is a stark contrast to previous generations, when men far outnumbered women. A study of students in 1950, at a school where men outnumbered women more than 3 to 1, found that women were twice as likely as men to go on multiple dates per week (W. Smith 1952).

On many college campuses in the United States, there are more female than male students. The rapid rise of women attending college is an impressive achievement; however, a potential unexpected effect of the gender imbalance could mean male students have more leverage when dating.

Hooking Up

Given the hookup scene's reputation for casual sex and noncommitment, it might seem odd to discuss it in a chapter on love and romantic relationships. Yet, as people move through the stages of their lives—whatever course they follow—these uncommitted sexual encounters are part of the basis for their later experiences and decisions. They help form the relationship history people bring from one encounter to the next, usually including dating, longer-term relationships, and marriage. And beyond individual experience, as sociologist Lisa Wade argues in her book *American Hookup* (2017), U.S. students live in a "hookup culture"—a social environment that affects them whether they engage in hookups themselves or not.

Without a fixed definition of **hooking up**, it is difficult to know how common it is. Still, it is safe to say that the term usually implies something casual rather than prearranged and without explicit commitment or exclusivity. Some people include all forms of sexual interaction, while others specifically exclude intercourse (Bogle 2008).

In college, a large study of students at 17 universities found that about three-quarters reported ever "hooking up" (Figure 7.1). (In this survey, the students used their own definition.) In follow-up questions, the researchers learned that many people had multiple hookups with the same person—which starts to look more like what might have been called a relationship at one time (Armstrong, England, and Fogarty 2010). In that case, the idea of hookups rather than dating seems to reflect a recognition that the relationships are not long-lasting or exclusively committed, and it might not be all that different from the era in which college students dated multiple partners in overlapping sequences.

A key difference between dating and hooking up, of course, is the expectation of sexual contact at the first encounter (see Trend to Watch). Wade (2017), who collected journals and interviews from groups of students at several colleges, describes a common heterosexual hookup script. It starts with "pregame" drinking before a party. At the party, intoxicated men and women "grind" on the dance floor, before one or the other initiates a hookup by turning to face each other. After some kind of sexual interaction in private—kissing, fondling, oral sex, or sexual intercourse—the next day hookup participants work to establish that the interaction was "meaningless." They do this by reminding themselves and their friends how intoxicated they were, and ignoring or avoiding the other partner (or at least avoiding the subject of sex in conversation with them).

"That's the hookup," writes Wade (2017). "A drunken sexual encounter with ambiguous content that is supposed to mean nothing and happen just once." The alcohol or

hooking up

A casual sexual or romantic encounter without explicit commitment or exclusivity.

Figure 7.1 **Number of hookups reported by college students**

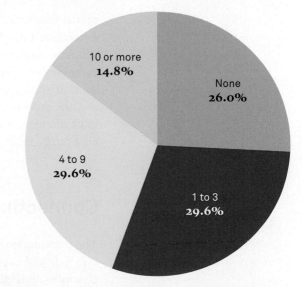

SOURCE: Armstrong, England, and Fogarty (2010).

drugs play a key role, allowing people to act uninhibited and justifying the decision not to get more seriously involved. People tend to view this lack of long-term involvement positively, both because they (especially men) want to hook up with different people and because they (especially women) don't want a serious relationship to develop, which might tie them down before they are ready in terms of their education and career goals. In fact, the students Wade talked to identify a special category—a different script—called "sober sex," which implies a potentially serious relationship with long-term potential.

I should stress that such general descriptions of sexual and romantic behavior, especially among young people, cannot capture the full range of emotional interactions that people experience. For example, although many men embrace the idea of casual sex with no strings attached, especially at a certain time in their lives, there are also a substantial number who are looking for, or at least open to, lasting relationships and emotional connections with sexual or romantic partners (Epstein et al. 2009). In addition, although it is more common for women than for men to abstain from hookups altogether, a substantial minority of both sexes stay out of the game. These young people are more likely to be religious in their orientation, but that is not the only path to abstinence (Burdette et al. 2009).

Finally, the risk of sexual assault is enhanced by the role of alcohol and drugs. In college sexual assaults, the assailants often believe—or say they believe—that the woman's use of drugs or alcohol was implicit permission for sex (K. Taylor 2013). That's what happened in the infamous rape case in which Brock Turner, a star member of the Stanford swim team, was convicted on three counts of felony sexual assault after being caught in the act of raping a woman with whom he had left a fraternity party. Both Brock and his victim were drunk; she did not remember the assault. A sympathetic judge (also a Stanford graduate) caused an uproar when he sent Brock to prison for only three months after Brock claimed the encounter was consensual and blamed the incident on their drinking (Stack 2016).

Whether or not "hookup culture" represents a dramatic change in American sexual and romantic behavior, it certainly seems from a distance (and across the generational divide in particular) that young people hook up with each other almost at random. However, the truth is more complicated. We know that most casual sexual encounters are anything but random, just as the selection of students attending a particular high school or college is not random. In other ways, too, the processes of partner selection and relationship building have become more discriminating, especially with the growth of online dating, to which we now turn.

Connecting Online

The combination of romantic ideals and utilitarian purposes can make for some elaborate and extended searches for the perfect partner. This is probably more true for older single people and those who are divorced or have children, for whom emotional and practical considerations appear to loom especially large (Whyte and Torgler 2017). That may have been the case, for example, with a divorced fourth-grade teacher in New Jersey named Kristen, age 33. She exchanged messages with 120 men in four months of online dating, talked to 20 on the phone, physically met 11, and went on multiple dates with 4 of them—but none of the relationships worked out (Harmon 2003).

The first major national singles database in the United States was Match.com, created in 1995. Match went on to become a multinational corporation that now owns Tinder and OkCupid, among other services (Cesar 2016). In the global competition for customers, Match and other online services have employed social scientists to develop their systems in a high-stakes race to profit from the singles market. That competition has produced many smaller sites providing matching by local area, as well as by race/ethnicity, age, body type, political affiliation, religion, and other criteria. As a result, the number of people using online dating sites has risen rapidly, now including one in four young adults (Smith 2016).

Internet dating sites provide easy opportunities to pursue romantic partners, sometimes more efficiently than in person, and allow some people to overcome social isolation in the search for a partner. But there are downsides and risks as well. Young Internet users risk exposure to unsavory or unscrupulous adults, who may openly or dishonestly pursue sexual relationships with children

"On the Internet, nobody knows you're a dog."

This 1993 *New Yorker* cartoon by Peter Steiner is still relevant more than twenty years later.

and adolescents. Each year, local and national law enforcement agencies arrest thousands of people who approach undercover agents online, thinking they are communicating with children. In rare cases, some children are recruited or even abducted for use in child pornography or child sex-trafficking operations (Pujazon-Zazik and Park 2010).

A much more common risk for adults is simply the rampant lying and misrepresentation on Internet dating sites. There is probably no way to know whether this is in fact more common than it is in the face-to-face dating scene, but there is considerable evidence of dishonesty online, some of it quite explicit. For example, a 79-year-old man who listed himself as being age 69 on Match.com complained to the *New York Times* that many women he considered overweight listed themselves as "slender" in their online profiles—although apparently he felt no remorse for his own misrepresentation (Harmon 2003).

In fact, a study of Internet daters' profile pictures, compared with how judges evaluated them in person, showed that about one-third of pictures were substantially inaccurate—for example, misleading in terms of age, weight, or skin condition. And consistent with the greater cultural pressure on women's appearance, women were more likely to use deceptive profile pictures than men. Interestingly, almost all the men and women reported that their pictures were accurate images of themselves (Hancock and Toma 2009). On the other hand, most people seem to assume that online profiles will include some deceptive or misleading information, with the attitude that "everyone lies on the Internet" (Drouin et al. 2016). It seems that online dating profiles may simply be another way of managing one's self-image, which usually includes some misrepresentation. Although such self-promotion is certainly not unique to online settings, the Internet increases the efficiency of such manipulation.

In addition to Internet sites geared specifically for dating and matching, of course, there are many ways that people looking for partners might find them online—through general social networking sites such as Facebook and Twitter, advertising sites such as Craigslist, specialized forums for people with particular interests, and through phone apps such as Tinder, Grindr, and Pure (among many others). A 2011 survey found that the number of people meeting their sexual or romantic partners online was increasing dramatically, both on dating sites and through other venues (M. Rosenfeld and Thomas 2012). As Figure 7.2 shows, 22 percent of relationships started after 2007 involved people who met online, and almost 10 percent started through online dating sites. At the same time, fewer people are finding their partners through family connections, school, the workplace, or their churches. The Internet has been especially important for gay and lesbian singles, who are less likely to meet mates at random because the pool of potential partners is smaller (McKie, Milhausen, and Lachowsky 2017). We'll return to gay and lesbian relationships shortly.

The Internet and mobile communications in general have accelerated interactions that once unfolded much more slowly. For example, as Aziz Ansari hilariously described in his bestseller, *Modern Romance*, the ability to respond immediately to text messages from a potential partner also raises the expectations and uncertainties associated with *not* responding immediately. After one make-out session with an old friend, Ansari texted her an invitation to a concert

Figure 7.2 **People who met their partner online, by year and type of Internet site (different-sex couples only)**

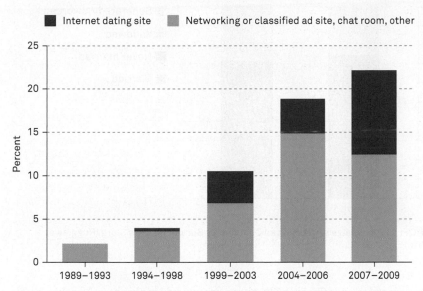

■ Internet dating site   ■ Networking or classified ad site, chat room, other

SOURCE: Author's calculations from M. Rosenfeld, Thomas, and Falcon (2011).

the next night—and then he waited, anxiously. As his distress over her nonresponse rose, he reflected on his predicament:

> "The madness I was descending into wouldn't have even existed twenty or even ten years ago. There I was, maniacally checking my phone every few minutes, going through this tornado of panic and hurt and anger all because this person hadn't written me a short, stupid message on a dumb little phone." (Ansari and Klinenberg 2016:5)

Many people similarly worry over immediate responses on social media, especially having to do with Facebook's "relationship status" (Toma and Choi 2015). For all the convenience and efficiency of contemporary communications technology, they have also added fuel to the dramas associated with love and romance, and the stresses those experiences entail.

Older Singles and Single Parents

Family studies from half a century ago concentrated almost exclusively on courtship and dating practices among those who had never been married and never been in a serious relationship—and had no children. Because more people are postponing marriage to later in life, and because more people are divorced now than were in previous generations, the population of people who are single and looking for relationships is both older and more diverse than it was

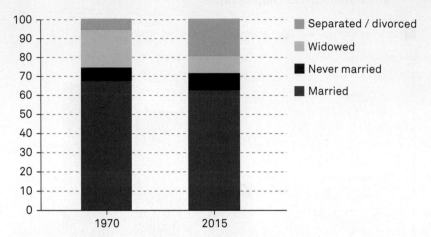

Figure 7.3 **Marital status of adults ages 55–75, 1970 and 2015 (percentages)**

SOURCE: Author analysis of American Community Survey via IPUMS.org (Ruggles et al. 2016).

several decades ago. Specifically, three groups of singles have become much more prevalent.

First, some singles are older than previous generations of daters, having deliberately postponed marriage, often to pursue education or their careers. These singles may be more highly educated, financially independent, and emotionally mature than younger daters. People in their 30s or 40s may have long-term goals for relationships from the outset, which set them apart from those dating in their teens or 20s (Sassler 2010).

Second, the rise in unmarried parenting has led to an increase in adults who live with children but who have never been married, many of whom are looking for partners. Some of these single parents—the vast majority of whom are women—are interested in marriage and creating a blended family. And they may have less time and energy for, or interest in, casual dating relationships than those without children. To make matters more complicated, many of the men they are dating have children from previous relationships as well (Edin and Nelson 2013). Not surprisingly, then, single parents with children are much more likely to end up with partners who already have children and thus may share elements of their outlook and lifestyle (Goldscheider and Sassler 2006).

Finally, divorced adults are a growing presence among singles. Those divorced parents who are still raising their children often bring complicated circumstances to dating or new relationships, especially when their own dating behavior has potential effects on their children's development and on parent-child conflicts (Whitbeck, Simons, and Kao 1994). And among older adults—those over 55—divorced people now dominate the population looking for new partners. Figure 7.3 shows that, among those in age range 55 to 75, most single people now are divorced or separated, which is a major shift from half a century earlier, when most single people in those ages were widowed. This illustrates the growing complexity of the dating environment for older adults.

Gay and Lesbian Relationships

The social environment for gays and lesbians has transformed radically over the last several decades, with a majority of Americans now telling pollsters they find gay and lesbian relations "morally acceptable" (see Figure 6.1). The experience of coming out and finding sexual or romantic partners has become less treacherous. Nevertheless, for gays and lesbians, finding mates and forming relationships can be difficult because of opposition from parents, religious leaders, teachers, or other authorities—as well as stigma in the culture at large (see Chapter 6).

One story helps illustrate these challenges and the progress toward over-coming them. In a rural high school in Florida in 2007, the principal became concerned about a "gay pride" movement in his school. He had seen students wearing rainbow paraphernalia or armbands with the words "gay pride" or just "GP." He took it on himself to interview about 30 students personally, asking them directly about their sexual orientation. One female student, who identified herself as a lesbian, was singled out. The principal urged her not to "go down the road" of being gay, because it was against the Bible. He forbade her from writing the words "gay pride" on herself or on any school materials and from wearing her rainbow-colored belt, under threat of suspension. (He actually prohibited all students from wearing rainbow patterns of any kind!) After a lawsuit, however, a federal court reversed his decisions, ruling that the school was violating their students' First Amendment rights to free expression (*Gillman v. School Board* 2008). Civil liberties advocates still use that court decision to protect student rights.

Heather Gillman was suspended from high school for being a lesbian and wearing gay pride items.

Gay and lesbian relationships reflect many of the same patterns as straight relationships (Peplau and Fingerhut 2007). However, same-gender relationships are complicated by negative social pressures that influence people's perceptions of who they are and whom they are attracted to as they gain experience and mature (Mohr and Daly 2008). Keeping in mind that much of this chapter is relevant to all groups of people, in this section we will briefly discuss some specific issues that affect same-gender relationships.

First, people often think of dating and romantic relationships as building blocks, or steps in the process leading to marriage. And as we will see in Chapter 8, the great majority of Americans do end up getting married (at least once). Because marriage between people of the same gender—although now legal—still generates opposition from many people, marriage may not be a clearly defined destination for gay and lesbian relationships. So even when such relationships are loving, stable, and long-lasting, marriage may not be taken for granted as it is for many straight couples.

In the terms used in this chapter, we would say that same-gender couples do not have well-established dating and relationship scripts to follow—or at least they must modify common scripts for their own purposes. If confusion about relationship scripts is a common feature of our era, then that lack of direction is especially pronounced in gay and lesbian relationships, which are often not socially accepted. The resulting experience for couples has been called "relational ambiguity," which increases stress and insecurity for many gays and lesbians (R-J Green 2010).

The official recognition of romantic relationships and their regulation by laws and government agencies reflect the interaction between the institutional arenas of the state and the family, as discussed in Chapter 1. Such recognition is not limited to marriage but extends to other settings, including public schools, where an official prom system facilitates relationship building among students (see Changing Law, "High School Proms"). How the state regulates romantic relationships as well as families is an outcome of legal and political processes that make family forms a matter of public debate, not just personal preference. We will return to the issue of gay marriage in Chapter 8.

The controversy over same-sex marriage is closely related to the second significant issue that differentiates gay and lesbian relationships: the social stigma associated with homosexuality (see Chapter 6) and the cultural opposition marshaled against it, especially from religious quarters. This in effect creates a social barrier to the pursuit of romantic and sexual interests. On the other hand, the lack of social recognition and support—including from family members, friends, and coworkers—may also strengthen gay and lesbian relationships, as partners come to rely more on each other for support and love (Peplau and Fingerhut 2007).

Among teenagers, those who are gay, lesbian, or bisexual tend to have their first "serious" relationships at older ages and are less likely to have active dating lives, especially in areas where few other people are visibly out (W. Collins, Welsh, and Furman 2009), partly because they have more difficulty meeting and identifying appropriate romantic partners. But they also may be bullied, harassed, or attacked by peers (Olsen et al. 2014). There are a variety of coping strategies, especially among teenagers, including staying in romantic relationships longer to avoid painful transitions or pursuing heterosexual relationships as a way of conforming (Glover, Galliher, and Lamere 2009).

Daily discrimination can take a psychological or even physical health toll (Russell et al. 2012). When it comes from people in positions of authority, it is especially threatening. Such discrimination has been shown to contribute to depression and suicidal thoughts, which are much more common among gay, lesbian, bisexual, and transgender high school students (Almeida et al. 2009).

Mate Selection

In Shakespeare's play *The Merchant of Venice*, Jessica says to her lover, Lorenzo, "Love is blind, and lovers cannot see." But while it may be true that lovers act impulsively, to the coldhearted social scientist, the patterns of human behavior suggest that even love is anything but random—and truly blind love is rare. (Although Shakespeare was fond of the idea of love at first sight, I should point out that Lorenzo had already judged Jessica to be "wise," seen her to be "fair," and knew that she had proved herself "true"—so he wasn't really blind, either.)

In fact, how and why people choose each other or end up together are central to our understanding of families and society and to broader questions of social change. Sociologists call this process **mate selection**. Understanding these first

mate selection

The process by which people choose each other for sexual or romantic relationships.

High School Proms

In the process of social change, different parts of society change at different rates. Behaviors that are formal (such as marriage) often change more slowly than those that are informal (such as dating). For example, friendships and dating across racial lines occur more easily than marriage because the resistance to change is less and the stakes don't seem as high to parents or other authorities who oppose racial integration.

Some practices fall somewhere between formal and informal—rituals that have a symbolic importance without a legal finality. One of these is the high school prom—the site of continuous legal and social conflict for decades.

Race

In 2004, the federal Departments of Education and Justice sent a letter to school districts around the country, advising them that racially segregated high school proms and race-specific senior honors (such as homecoming queens, most popular student, and so on) are violations of federal law and would not be tolerated (Marcus and Acosta 2004). The Fourteenth Amendment prohibits racism by government agencies, and the Civil Rights Act, passed by Congress in 1964, specifically outlaws racial discrimination by schools that receive federal money (Harrison 2007).

However, many high schools—mostly in the South—act as if the "separate but equal" legal doctrine formulated in the nineteenth century were still in place. They have continued to hold separate proms for Blacks and Whites, getting around the law by making one or both proms "unofficial" events held off campus without school funds (Lange 2003). Truly private events are not subject to antisegregation laws. But the private proms are supported by the schools' decisions not to hold official proms, decisions prompted by court orders to desegregate the student body (Harrison 2007).

In some cases, such as in Randolph County, Alabama, in 1994, the principal canceled the

In Montgomery, Georgia, interracial couples only began to attend integrated high school proms in 2011.

prom only after learning that mixed-race couples were planning to attend (*Lee v. Randolph County Board of Education* 1995). In Montgomery County, Georgia, White parents organized a segregated prom (Doyle 2009). But after a *New York Times* story brought national attention to the school district, officials eventually relented, and they now hold an integrated prom (Spencer 2015).

Sexual Orientation

The conflict over race looks a lot like the conflict over sexual orientation. When senior Constance McMillen asked the principal of her high school in Fulton, Mississippi, whether she could bring her girlfriend as a date to the 2010 prom—and wear a tuxedo—the answer was no: No girlfriend, no same-sex slow dancing, and no girl wearing a tuxedo would be permitted.

After McMillen protested, with the help of the American Civil Liberties Union, the district canceled the prom. A federal court reviewed the complaints and held that the district had violated McMillen's rights by canceling the prom. However, the court let stand the district's decision to defer to a private prom. Later, the parents who planned the private prom ended up discouraging McMillen and her date from attending anyway (*McMillen v. Itawamba County School District* 2010).

Although it was 30 years later, the *McMillen* case in Mississippi actually mirrored one from Rhode Island in 1980. In Cumberland High School, a gay male student was denied permission to bring his boyfriend to the prom, only to have the decision overturned by the courts. That decision, *Fricke v. Lynch* (1980), was the basis for Constance McMillen's case in 2010. As already noted, some social practices change more slowly than others in different parts of society. As late as 2015, the principal of a Louisiana high school told a lesbian student she couldn't wear a tuxedo to the prom—only to reverse his decision in the face of public backlash and legal intervention from civil rights groups (Hodges 2015).

Lines in the Sand

The symbolic power of the prom is sometimes confusing, especially in the case of race. Black and White students at some of the schools in question often socialize and especially play sports together with relatively little conflict. The dispute over proms occurs because parents and school authorities recognize it as an important stepping stone in what might be a long-term mate selection process. These older people are drawing from their own histories and recalling the prom scripts of their own youths, when prom dates often led to steady relationships and potential marriage.

One White high school senior in rural Georgia said, "I wanted to go to the Black prom, but my mom wouldn't pay. She doesn't like me talking to Black people anyway" (Doyle 2009). Parents may have trouble controlling the dating behavior of their children and whom they socialize with, but when it comes to an event with a formal role in relationship scripts, such as a prom or marriage, those resistant to change are more likely to dig in their heels.

steps—some of which form a path to family formation—is necessary for explaining at least three ways families influence the broader society.

- *Inequality.* If pairs of rich people form some families and pairs of poor people form other families, then there will be a very strong tendency for the lines of wealth and poverty to remain fixed through the generations. On the other hand, if people get together at random or actually seek each other out across the lines of social class or other divides, then inequality will be reduced over time. (Notice that this assumes that people transmit their social class background to their children, which we discussed in Chapter 4.)

- *Inclusion versus exclusion.* I concluded Chapter 3 with a discussion of "social distance," as reflected in the rates of intermarriage between Whites and members of minority groups. Although a growing proportion of Americans tell survey takers that they do not object to romantic relationships between people of differing race or ethnicity, the subject remains contentious (J. Lee and Bean 2010). Patterns of attraction and family formation are still gauges of the level of social inclusion or exclusion for members of different groups.

- *Family dynamics.* How families work together is partly the result of how couples choose each other and how those choices affect their relationships throughout adulthood. The stability of marriages, caring for children and other family members in need, and the health and happiness of family members—all these issues are related to the issue of mate selection.

In this section, we will discuss attraction and attractiveness, especially in relation to gender. Beyond physical attraction, romantic relationships emerge from emotional connections and common bonds that come from various sources. Finally, we will investigate how social boundaries between groups help to shape people's choices between partners.

Evolution

Interestingly, some of the research on the evolution of human sexual attraction has involved such cultural innovations as Barbie dolls, *Playboy* centerfolds, and the Miss America pageants—and ancient art and literature as well (Singh, Renn, and Singh 2007).

Scientists have attempted to piece together the evolution story by studying the historical record, by comparing people and tastes in different cultures, by studying the behavior and characteristics of nonhuman animals, and—more recently—by studying genes and their expression directly. Experts have different opinions, but my assessment of the evidence so far is that evolutionary forces operate in the background, while our preferences and actions flexibly adapt around, or even against, the forces of "nature" through social interaction. With regard to families in particular, sexual attraction is only part of what holds people together. The utilitarian aspects of couple relationships today are more important than any primal attraction in creating and maintaining real families.

There are complicated and sometimes conflicting forces at work in the process of natural selection, and social behavior is especially difficult to puzzle out. We know that specific traits might have emerged through evolution if they (a) increased the odds of survival, such as resistance to disease; (b) increased reproductive ability, such as healthy ovaries; (c) increased success in competition with other potential mates, such as big muscles (or good aim); or (d) presented some gimmick that fools potential mates into thinking one of the other good traits is present. Attraction to a particular feature of humans might have made evolutionary sense at one time, but we can't tell which attractions are evolutionary as opposed to cultural or a combination of the two. For example, it is common to assume that attractive features are those that are healthy, since mating with healthy people is good for survival. However, many of the traits considered attractive in modern Western societies bear no connection to health or reproductive fitness. Men with big chest muscles and thin waists aren't generally healthier than men who are thin all over (though they might win more fights). In women's case, however, some "attractive" features are related to good health, such as relatively low body fat and slim waists (Weeden and Sabini 2005).

Consider that last example related to female attractiveness: a slim waist, usually measured by the waist-to-hip ratio. Some scientists believe that when this ratio is low (that is, the waist is slimmer than the hips), it sends a signal to men that a woman is fit for childbearing. Over time, then, men who were attracted to that quality would be more likely to reproduce successfully (Barber 1995). Some studies have found that men in different cultures are attracted to this quality in a woman (Singh, Renn, and Singh 2007). And several researchers have analyzed *Playboy* magazine centerfold models and Miss America pageant winners (which list women's body measurements), finding that their average waist-to-hip ratio has been about 0.7, which is quite low.

However, a common beauty characteristic by itself isn't proof that the attraction to it has evolved biologically. And several pieces of evidence point in the other direction. First, there are considerable differences in what is considered attractive across time and place (Hergovich and Süssenbach 2015). For example, although ancient poetry and literature often mentioned slim waists as attractive, many writers didn't mention waists at all and focused their attention on other body parts (Singh, Renn, and Singh 2007). And evolution has also produced homosexual men, who might not be attracted one way or the other to women's waists.

A second piece of evidence is the trend in the last 60 years among pornography and fashion models toward unhealthy levels of thinness. From 1985 to 1997, for example, more than three-quarters of the women who posed in centerfolds were severely underweight by medical standards (P. Owen and Laurel-Seller 2000). And the trend over time showed that, as American women grew fatter, *Playboy* models grew skinnier (Gammon 2015). It seems implausible that evolution would drive men's attraction toward women who are so thin that they don't menstruate and are unable to conceive children. From these conflicting streams of theory and evidence, I conclude that although evolution played a role

From 1950 (left) to 1980 (right) to 1990 (middle), Barbie's body hasn't changed much.

in developing human beauty standards, these forces today are just some influences among many.

As an aside, when it comes to waist-to-hip ratio, no one beats Barbie. Well, almost no one: At last check, about 1 in 100,000 women matched her waist-to-hip ratio of 0.56 (Norton et al. 1996). Thus, Barbie might seem beautiful or attractive in some cultures, but it's not because she's a "natural" beauty. Still, more than 50 years after her creation in 1960, if we are to believe the doll's manufacturer, Mattel, 90 percent of young girls in the United States had at least one Barbie doll (Vaidyanathan 2009). Given the nature of "pretend play," it is obvious that many of these girls identify with Barbie at least in some ways. And that returns us to the gender issues we introduced in Chapter 5.

Gender

This discussion of women's body parts may seem unbalanced, or even sexist. But research on the evolution of sexual attraction has focused much more on women—assuming, perhaps, that the most powerful men (rich, strong, well armed) will "choose" the women they want, rather than the other way around. From a sociological point of view, this raises other questions. We ask not only why people want what they want, but also how people with power maintain their power. In other words, who gets to choose? Both questions are relevant to the issue of mate selection.

To address why people want what they want, remember that in Chapter 5 we defined *socialization* as the process by which individuals internalize elements of the social structure, making those elements part of their own personality. In the case of gender socialization, one of the most important outcomes is simply the differentiation of men from women. The low waist-to-hip ratio of a Barbie doll or *Playboy* model is a prime example of exaggerating a difference between the bodies of men and women; marking that trait as "beautiful" underscores the social value we place on such differences. If beauty is in the eye of the beholder, then the cultural beauty standard is a way of getting our brains to tell our eyes what beauty is.

Enhancing the difference between men and women doesn't just take place in our heads, of course. In Chapter 5 we examined cosmetic surgery. But one less dramatic social practice related to waists and hips is the wearing of high-heeled shoes, which most Americans seem to agree has a positive effect on women's sexual appeal. These shoes change a woman's posture to accentuate the movement of her pelvis, hips, and abdomen, thus calling attention to her waist-to-hip ratio (E. Smith and Helms 1999). In the process, unfortunately, high heels also undermine the basic functions of the foot's arch, causing all kinds of damage to the woman's body—in addition to more than 100,000 high-heel related injuries per year (Moore 2015).

From a socialization point of view, since almost everyone who wears them is a woman, high heels help establish the difference between men and women in the minds of children and reinforce it at all ages. And from the perspective of symbolic interaction, high heels help women "do gender" (West and Zimmerman 1987). They enhance those aspects of women's bodies that conform to the common image of gender and do so in view of the daily audiences that observe their bodies.

Feminist sociologists also are concerned with the high-heeled-shoe question, but from their perspective the question is: Why does it fall to women to alter *their* bodies to enhance gender differences, often risking their health and mobility in the process? One feminist answer is that men's power—political, economic, and cultural—affords them the leverage to demand submissive behavior from women. In fact, from this point of view, women's subordination is actually part of what men find attractive. High heels, then, don't just accentuate the hips; they also make women less powerful physically, which many men find attractive (MacKinnon 1991). To support this argument, I will mention a more extreme example related to feet and attractiveness: foot binding.

For about 1,000 years, some families in China—mostly wealthier families—bound the feet of their young girls, repeatedly tying them up as they grew and never releasing them as they aged. The bones of their feet became deformed, shorter and downward-pointing, causing permanent harm to their physical mobility (Cummings, Ling, and Stone 1997). The look was considered attractive, apparently, partly because it accentuated a family's class status (showing that their women didn't have to do manual labor) and partly because it conformed to a beauty standard of women as docile and weak. Also, it caused women to take short, wobbly steps that were considered feminine (resembling at least distantly the gait of women wearing high-heeled shoes). The practice grew less common

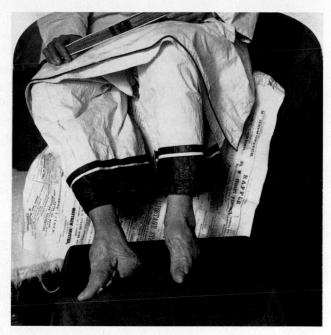

Left: American women in high-heeled shoes. *Right:* A Chinese woman with bound feet. Does manipulation of women's feet enhance their attractiveness or limit their physical mobility—or both?

in the early twentieth century before finally being banned by the Communists, who took power in 1949.

It might seem that foot binding and high heels have only a superficial resemblance, both involving women walking on their toes. After all, high heels are women's choice, not forced on them by men. But "choice" can be complicated. It was mothers, not fathers, who were responsible for binding the feet of their daughters, so although the girls themselves had no choice, the practice was enforced by women. And even in the case of high heels, some feminists would argue that the choice is only as "free" as women are in male-dominated society. Conforming to the dominant beauty standard is learned at an early age, and most women perceive it as necessary for success in love, marriage, and careers.

Race/Ethnicity

So far, we have only scratched the surface of questions related to romantic attraction. What if every person on earth could meet every other person on earth and freely choose a partner among them? Besides the obvious practical problems with this premise, there are two types of obstacles to achieving perfect choice. First, there are internal obstacles, which you may think of as mental or cognitive barriers to romantic attraction. Second, there are social and cultural boundaries that divide groups from each other. Of course, these types of obstacles may be closely related, so that social divisions in practice create the barriers in our minds.

homophily

The principle by which similar people have more of a given kind of contact than dissimilar people.

To understand the relationship between cognitive and social mechanisms for attraction and division, we will need a few more terms. Sociologists use the term **homophily** to describe the principle by which similar people have more of a given kind of contact than dissimilar people. Although its linguistic origin means "love of the same"—an ideal as old as the ancient Greek philosophers—we use the term for all kinds of interactions in which "birds of a feather flock together" (McPherson, Smith-Loven, and Cook 2001). Homophily may be found, for example, in patterns of casual contact, friendship, and worker collaboration as well as romantic relationships.

One useful feature of this broader concept is that it frees us to think of homophily as not just a question of personal preference but also one of practical limits. In the case of race, for example, one reason that "birds of a feather flock together" is that they tend to live in the same neighborhoods and attend the same schools, so they meet each other more and share common experiences.

Homophily may act in ways that are quite invisible to us. Returning to the example at the beginning of the chapter, Jason remembers being attracted to Liz because she was tall, beautiful, and had her act together. Was he also attracted to her because they were both White and had other similarities in their upbringing, perhaps so obvious as to go without comment? Or did the similarities in their backgrounds merely bring them together at the moment in which they were looking to make a match?

Endogamy In Chapter 3, we defined *endogamy* as marriage and reproduction within a distinct group. The most obvious case of this in U.S. society today occurs along the lines of race and ethnicity. However, various systems of endogamy have been practiced in all societies along the most important dividing lines of the day. In prehistoric times, exogamy—the opposite of endogamy—was an important means by which small bands of humans built connections between groups and extended their influence (as well as preventing the health problems associated with inbreeding, or breeding within small groups).

The ideal of utilitarian love, as we have defined it here, often reinforces endogamy, because forming families within a given group may reduce family complications and increase access to systems of social support (such as friends and extended family members). Romantic love, on the other hand, because it is based on individual desire rather than group affinity, challenges such a rational basis for love and has the potential to ruffle feathers between groups (Illouz 1997). For example, when family inheritance and status are at stake, people in positions of authority are usually more concerned with controlling the matching process, and they use that control to maintain the boundaries of their groups (Goode 1959). On the other hand, ruling classes throughout history have used exogamous "dynastic marriages" as a means of forging alliances between countries, families, and political regimes with competing interests.

To see how homophily and endogamy play out among young people today, we will return to the often-studied population of American college students. In Chapter 3, we saw that there has been a dramatic increase in the rates of racial-ethnic intermarriage in recent decades. During that time, the proportion of high school graduates moving on to college has grown, especially for African Americans. This has increased the rate at which Blacks and Whites meet and socialize together, especially in the more liberal environment of college campuses, where the stigma of interracial dating and relationships is less pronounced.

On the other hand, it is certainly not the case that bringing members of two groups together in one social space is all it takes to remove the barriers between them. When there is diversity in the backgrounds of students on campus, the dating system is selective—that is, romantic relationships are not assigned at random across the population. In fact, this is one of the earliest observations to emerge from studies of mate selection on American campuses. Going back to the 1920s, we know that students in high-status positions in the Greek (fraternity/sorority) system and with fathers in high-status occupations are more likely to be in relationships with those of similar status positions (Reiss 1965).

In the survey of Stanford University students mentioned earlier, researchers found that African Americans are the most isolated group in the dating scene (McClintock 2010). Asked about their most recent date (however each person chose to define that term), students revealed fairly strong racial-ethnic endogamy in their experience. In this chapter's Story Behind the Numbers, I have charted the relative frequency of dating matches between men and women of the four largest racial-ethnic groups. The chart shows the breakdown of dates for each group. For example, if people dated at random, 11 percent of dates would have involved one Black student. But Black students dated each other 46 percent of the time. Hispanics and Asians dated within their own groups about twice as often as they would have if dates were randomized. Thus, each group of men was most likely to go on dates with women from their own group. Dates between Blacks and Whites and between Asians and Hispanics were the least common. The chart shows that each group of men is most likely to go on dates with women from their own group.

Thus, even among students at an elite private university—where everyone is expected to emerge as a highly paid professional—the pattern of romantic attachments continues to reveal barriers along the lines of race/ethnicity (or attractions within these groups). This is all the more striking, the researcher notes, given that the student population is mostly young, well educated, geographically concentrated, racially diverse, and often far from the watchful eyes of their parents—all of which might be expected to encourage more adventurous romantic pursuits.

Additional evidence shows that racial ideas also are present *within* racial-ethnic groups. A study of several hundred African American students at historically Black universities found that a substantial minority preferred to date or marry someone with lighter skin complexion. Interestingly, men were twice as likely as women (about 35 percent versus 17 percent) to prefer matching with a light-skinned person (Ross 1997). This suggests that Black women are more subject to the White standard of attractiveness than are Black men (M. Hill 2002), which is consistent with my earlier observation that beauty pressures are stronger for women in general.

Endogamy Online It is still too early for us to know how the explosion of online dating will affect overall family patterns in the United States. However, several aspects of this technological approach might promote greater mixing of

Race and ethnicity divides college students' dating lives.

Person going on date is:	Person going on date is:
White	**Black**

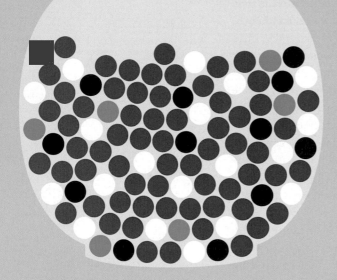

Chance of dating someone who is:

● White: **61%**	● Black: **6%**	● White: **31%**	● Black: **46%**
● Hispanic: **13%**	○ Asian: **20%**	● Hispanic: **17%**	○ Asian: **7%**

Source: Author's calculations from McClintock (2010).

You might think that at an elite school such as Stanford University, where all students are expected to emerge as highly paid professionals, race and ethnicity wouldn't be a major force in their love lives. But a survey of roughly 500 recent dates showed a strong tendency for the students to date within their own group. The illustrations show the breakdown of dates for each group. For example, if people dated at random, 11 percent of dates would have involved one Black student. But Black students dated each other 46 percent of the time. Hispanics and Asians dated within their own groups about twice as often as they would have if dates were randomized. This segregation is all the more striking given that the students are mostly young, geographically concentrated, and often far from the eyes of their parents.

In a totally random scenario the % chance of dating:

White: **55%** Black: **11%**

Hispanic: **14%** Asian: **20%**

Person going on date is:

Hispanic

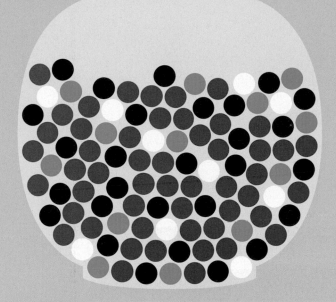

Chance of dating someone who is:

White: **50%** Black: **13%**

Hispanic: **28%** Asian: **10%**

Person going on date is:

Asian

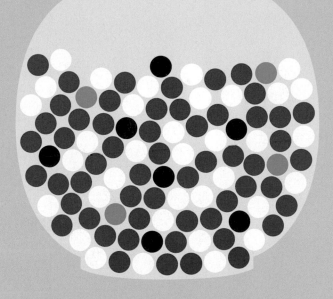

Chance of dating someone who is:

White: **54%** Black: **4%**

Hispanic: **7%** Asian: **35%**

http://wwnpag.es/sbtn7

Go to this link for an animation narrated by the author.

racial-ethnic groups. First, the systems may be based on true personality characteristics of potential matches—gathering and providing objective information—which should work against irrational boundaries that are based on stereotypes. Second, online dating has the potential to reduce geographical constraints that lead people to date only those who live or work close at hand.

Some early research confirms that racial-ethnic boundaries in fact remain an issue in online dating. For example, in one study, about 1 in 4 White men restricted their online searches to White women, much less than the two-thirds of White women who imposed such a restriction. As might be expected from the off-line studies, the most common restriction White men placed on their searches was against Black women (Feliciano, Robnett, and Komaie 2009).

The online dating site OKCupid has published some analyses of its users' behavior (see Changing Culture, "What's Your Sign?"). And that too shows persistent racial-ethnic divisions. Their analysis of half a million randomly selected users showed that White men were more likely than other men to receive a reply when approaching a woman for the first time, and Black women were the least likely to receive a reply from the men they approached (Figure 7.4).

Figure 7.4 **Percentage receiving replies to online dating messages**

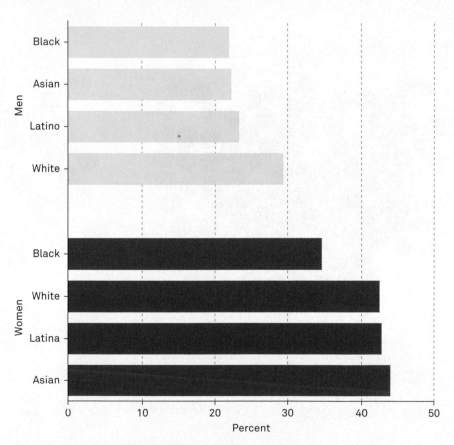

Note: Not all racial-ethnic groups are shown.

SOURCE: Author's graph from OKCupid research (Rudder 2009).

What's Your Sign?

Sometimes when things go just right between people, we say that "the stars were aligned" for their love. But can the stars really tell us what is in store for our relationships? That turns out to be one of the oldest scientific questions in the history of human society.

Even though ancient astrologers in Babylonia and Egypt didn't know that the earth and other planets revolved around the sun, they still could create a system to predict the alignment of the heavens according to calendars. And this ability gave them great power. The Greeks made astrology more mathematical in the last few centuries before Christ, giving us much of the system still used today (Svensen and White 1995).

By the thirteenth century, Italian astrologers did a brisk business advising people whom to marry, when to marry, and what kind of marriage was in store for them—all based on the alignment of the moon, planets, and stars. They were even called on to determine whether women were virgins before marriage and to resolve conflicts over who had fathered a child (Lemay 1984). These astrologers competed with the Christian church for authority, but the two systems were not so incompatible: Both involved deciphering the awesome and unknowable universe for lowly humans, while dispensing advice that served the interests of not-so-lowly humans (church leaders and rulers in the aristocracy).

Is that different from today? Although interest in astrology is declining, in 2009, one-quarter of Americans reported that they believed in astrology—that is, that "the position of the stars and planets can affect people's lives" (Pew Research Center 2009). Asked, "How often do you read your horoscope?" 12 percent of respondents in a national poll said they read it regularly, while another 44 percent read their horoscope "only if I happen to

Do you consult a horoscope for advice or consider the astrological sign of potential mates?

see it." Less than half of the respondents (43 percent) agreed with the firm statement, "Never, I don't believe in astrology" (60 Minutes/Vanity Fair 2011).

Why Do Fools Fall in Love?

How to find true love is the bread and butter of the astrology industry. In considering a relationship between, say, a Leo and a Virgo, one popular horoscope website tells the Leo, "Virgo is practical, prudent and conservative. You, dear Leo, are extravagant, sophisticated and spendthrift," and adds, "Virgo needs to be protected and asks for much from his/her partner. You demand the same amount of attention, so a conflict of interest will appear very soon." Sounds like a dicey match. If these descriptions really fit, the advice could be quite useful for finding a mate (eAstrolog.com 2013).

Truthfully, it's not that simple, as the in-depth analysis depends on which part of the month each person was born in—and professional astrologers can make a pretty penny deciphering the details. But before you pay for that detailed report, consider the research done by OKCupid, a free online dating site (Rudder 2009). Their system involves asking each user several hundred questions, as well as asking how their ideal partner *should* answer the same questions and how important each question is in their choice of a partner. This formula produces a match score for every pair of people in the database, based on how much they meet each other's expectations.

Taking a random sample of half a million users, the researchers at OKCupid measured the match scores for every pair of the 12 zodiac sign combinations, for a total of 144 different comparisons, with thousands of people in each group. What was the result? Nothing. Every single comparison produced almost exactly the same match score as the average for the entire site. In other words, knowing someone's zodiac sign tells you nothing about your potential to be a good match with that person.

According to the German philosopher and sociologist Theodor Adorno, who analyzed horoscope columns in Los Angeles in the early 1950s, astrology in modern industrial society preys on people's insecurity and teaches them not to question the social influences that really shape their lives. Adorno (1994) wrote that society presents itself to the individual as "rational"—governed by democratic laws, free markets, science, and technology, rather than the whim of rulers or the power of gods. But people still cannot really see or understand all the larger forces determining their fates (we trust that planes can fly, for example, even if we don't really understand how). That makes astrology seem potentially reasonable as the logical, complete system of explaining all-powerful, invisible forces.

The two ideas—rule by law and science, on the one hand, and the mystical effects of stellar constellations on the other—both appear to affect an individual's fate. But while one system may be baffling and too complex for most of us to understand, the other is just a series of random declarations told in a convincing way by people out to make a living off our insecurities.

In this chapter, we have reviewed the expanding diversity of scripts and relationships as well as some of the origins and workings of love and romance in modern U.S. society. From the Internet to college campuses to single parents with children, there clearly is no single dating scene or uniform set of rituals practiced by those who are pursuing romantic relationships outside of marriage. Romantic and utilitarian love coexist in sometimes uncomfortable tension, nevertheless forming the emotional bonds that may lead to marriage. As we will see in Chapter 8, marriage itself—and the unmarried cohabitation that precedes or sometimes supersedes it—present no simpler a picture.

Trend to Watch: Sex before Relationships

Sex outside of romantic relationships certainly isn't new. What is more unique to this period of history is that so many long-term relationships start with sex. Sociologists Kathryn Edin and Timothy Nelson, in their book *Doing the Best I Can*, describe relationships among young adults in Philadelphia who meet, have sex, and then maybe pursue a more serious relationship—sometimes spurred by a pregnancy. As a result, they may end up parenting with a person they don't know that well, and aren't that compatible with, and the relationship is at risk of failure before they get married (a risk compounded by the stresses of race and class hardship). Among college students, Lisa Wade (2017) reports that some serious college relationships start out as hookups—complete with the "competition over who can care less"—before the participants realize they have a potential long-term match.

If more relationships—marriages, parenting couples—are starting with sex, how does that change them in the long run? Maybe this is just part of the "sexual revolution" that we date to the 1960s, in which sex and sexual satisfaction became a much more explicit criteria for relationship fulfillment and success. If or when sex becomes less compelling to these couples, it may hasten the demise of the relationship. This may already be contributing to the rise of divorce at older ages (see Chapter 10).

On the other hand, maybe sex before relationships will help people make better decisions about whether to get into a serious relationship. Having had experience with other partners, and seen the relatively uninhibited sexual side of a potential serious partner, maybe today's young adults are in a good position to know more about what they want and to exercise their options to meet their own needs. In fact, this could be contributing to the delayed entry into marriage, which we will explore further in the next chapter—and maybe result in lower rates of separation or divorce.

Relationship Scripts

Twenty-five years ago, two researchers published the results of a survey of mostly White, straight, traditional-aged college undergraduates about dating scripts (Rose and Frieze 1993). They asked students to identify elements of both a hypothetical first date and an actual first date between a man and a woman. They also asked who would perform each action, the man or the woman. The results showed a fair degree of consistency in the expectations among men and women, with an especially strong agreement that men should take the initiative on most aspects of the date. I created the simplified list below based on their findings.

Either alone, in small groups, or as a class, compare this list with your own ideas of what you would expect on a first date and what you expect others would expect.

Before you say, "No one dates anymore," look over the list. If you don't call it "dating," do you or your friends do something that includes these activities or others like them? What about the gender balance? Would you expect a man to take the initiative on these or other aspects of a date? Why or why not?

Feel free to modify this activity, to include same-gender dates—whether or not you think this would lead to a different script—or to develop scripts for other stages or types of a relationship, such as online dating, group dating, or hooking up.

Finally, in class discussion, small groups, or independent writing, interpret your lists. What makes yours different from the list below? Consider the historical period and the social context (type of school, age or race/ethnicity of students, and so on). Is such a script useful, harmful, or even relevant today?

College Student First-Date Script, circa 1993

- Pick up date*

- Leave together

- Confirm plans

- Talk/joke/laugh

- Go to movie/show/party

- Eat

- Drink alcohol

- Take date home*

- Ask for another date*

- Kiss goodnight*

- Go home

*Items expected to be done by the man.

Questions for Review

1. Explain how social scripts (or their absence) affect our interactions with others.

2. Contrast the dating experiences of men and women at various ages: younger teenagers, college students, and older adults.

3. How do you define "hooking up"? How do your friends and classmates define it? Does the definition vary by age, regional background, or other life factors?

4. How do same-gender couples negotiate dating and relationship scripts differently from different-gender couples?

5. Describe three groups of singles that have become more prevalent recently.

6. Explain how schools and parents work around antidiscrimination laws to hold segregated proms.

7. Why might societal ideals of physical attractiveness no longer be related to health or reproductive fitness?

8. Can you see patterns of homophily in your friends and romantic partners?

8 Marriage and Cohabitation

Kristin Perry had a problem: At the time, she couldn't legally marry her long-time partner, Sandra Stier. "I'm a 45-year-old woman," she said. "I have been in love with a woman for 10 years and I don't have a word to tell anybody about that. [Marriage would tell] our friends, our family, our society, our community, our parents . . . and each other that this is a lifetime commitment . . . we are not girlfriends. We are not partners. We are married" (*Perry v. Schwarzenegger* 2010:12–13). It seems that the symbolic power of marriage is so great that without the recognition it provides, Perry and Stier couldn't express the true meaning of their relationship *even to each other.*

Perry's story, which she told during a federal lawsuit for same-sex marriage rights, illustrates the social value of marriage in American society. But it also shows the power of the government in bestowing that benefit through its legal recognition. (Recall our discussion of the legal definition of marriage in Chapter 1.) That sense of acceptance was one of the central motivations behind the drive to legalize marriage between people of the same gender, which finally resulted in victory before the Supreme Court in 2015 (as we discuss below). Paradoxically, many people who always had the legal right to marry don't seem to appreciate the weight it carries, treating the distinction almost casually. One man in a long-term, live-in relationship with a woman told an interviewer, "For credit card applications or for medical, we wouldn't say we're married. But to get a reservation at a restaurant, or if someone were to ask me at work if I was married, I would say yes. . . . Everyone at work thinks we're married" (P. Cohen 2010b).

This contrast in attitudes illustrates an important feature of marriage. On the one hand, it is a *symbolic* status, with emotional value, that sends a strong signal to others about our relationships. On the other hand, it is a *legal* status, which brings tangible benefits and protections to those who receive it. Together, these two features of marriage contribute to the culturally and politically charged nature of the debates over marriage; the value placed on marriage contributes to the notion that its perceived decline represents a cultural crisis.

Sandra Stier (left) and Kristin Perry (right) taking their case to court. The institution of marriage and the "married" label carry enormous power in society.

273

What does marriage mean in the United States today, and how does that differ from even the recent past? How does the growing practice of unmarried cohabitation alter the meaning of marriage or how marriage is lived by couples? To answer these questions, we need to familiarize ourselves with the trends and patterns underlying the changing structure of families and the relationships they comprise. First, however, I will pause to consider how this chapter reflects the overall themes of the book.

Diversity, Inequality, and Social Change

The pivotal subject of cohabitation and marriage provides a good opportunity to revisit our central themes: diversity, inequality, and social change. The trends and patterns in cohabitation and marriage—unions between adults that create families—reflect each of these themes.

Diversity

Even as marriage remains a very common, although not universal, event in the family lives of people in the United States, the pathways to marriage are quite diverse:

- About two-thirds of people who marry have lived together (cohabited) first. And many have children outside of marriage, either with their future spouse or with one or more other partners.

- Marriage and cohabitation between people of the same gender, although a relatively small minority of relationships, have become increasingly common and accepted in both mainstream culture and law.

- Many American marriages are remarriages for one or both partners. That's partly because we have high divorce rates but also because remarriage is common and acceptable as well. (We'll return to this subject in Chapter 10.)

Inequality

With the diversity of cohabitation and marriage experiences comes a pattern of inequalities as well, for both adults and children:

- Couples increasingly pair up according to education level and earning potential. Moreover, marriage is now more common for people with college degrees and less common for those without. All this means that there are more couples sharing two high salaries—and more singles scraping by on one low wage.

- Partly because marriage usually combines incomes from two adults, married couples are much less likely to be poor than single adults, especially single parents. In fact, single mothers and their children have poverty rates about five times those of married couples with children (Chapter 4).

- The recognition of same-sex marriages by the government and private entities, such as insurance companies, employers, and service providers, remains a contentious issue. Even with same-sex marriage and adoption now legal, gay and lesbian couples often face discrimination, and the laws providing for their protection are inconsistent.

Social Change

The nature of cohabiting and marriage relationships changes along with other major aspects of society, including culture, law, and state policies. Relationships between individuals within their families reflect these larger forces outside the family:

- The growth of individualism and the goals of individual fulfillment and self-expression have weakened the ties of marriage. But some analysts believe that the relationships that survive, when breaking up is so easy, are emotionally stronger (Giddens 1992).

- Over the last half-century, the law increasingly has treated people as individuals—whether they are married or not—rather than treating families as legal entities in themselves. For example, the rights and obligations of parents are often the same whether or not they are married (Cherlin 2009).

- Modern identities—how people think of themselves and explain their lives— have grown more diverse, paralleling the increasing complexity of family structures and relationships. For some people, families are central to their identity; for others, family life is only one situation among many that define who they are.

Through most of this chapter (unless otherwise specified), when I refer to "marriage" and "cohabitation," I mean couples involving a man and a woman. Although there are many thousands of gay and lesbian cohabiting couples in the United States, we do not yet have the data and research to incorporate a full discussion of these families (Zrenchik and Craft 2016). In this chapter, we will discuss how couple relationships fit into modern families and identities. But first we turn to the patterns and recent trends in cohabitation and marriage.

Who Gets Married

Because we discussed long-term trends in Chapter 2, in this section I will present information about the period from the mid-twentieth-century heyday of American marriage—in terms of its frequency at least—to the present. The major features of these trends are straightforward:

- Marriage rates have fallen dramatically since the 1960s. That means that the chance of a typical unmarried adult getting married is lower. The decline results from two trends at once: most people are marrying at older ages than they did in the past, and an increasing number of people never marry (although the great majority of people still eventually do).

- Marriage rates have fallen faster for some groups than for others. The most dramatic differences appear between racial-ethnic groups, with African Americans experiencing a more rapid and pronounced decline in marriage rate than any other group.

- Marriage is increasingly concentrated among those with higher education and incomes. For the first time, young people with college degrees are more likely to be married than those who did not graduate from college.

I will discuss each of these trends in turn, attempting to explain the reasons behind them and what they mean for families today.

The Decline of Marriage

The post–World War II boom in marriages (and babies) was followed by a rapid and equally startling decline. The phrase "retreat from marriage" first started appearing in family research in the early 1980s (Kobrin and Waite 1984), and as you can see from Figure 8.1, marriage rates have continued to drop steadily ever since. In 1970, for every 1,000 unmarried women, there were 77 weddings. By 2015, that number had fallen by more than half, to 34. (Such statistics were originally collected about women, so we often continue to report them that way today for historical comparisons.)

The marriage rate in a single year cannot tell us how many people will eventually enter into marriage. That is impossible to predict with certainty. However, despite the decline, among today's 50-year-olds, more than 80 percent

Figure 8.1 **Marriages per 1,000 non-married women, 1950–2015**

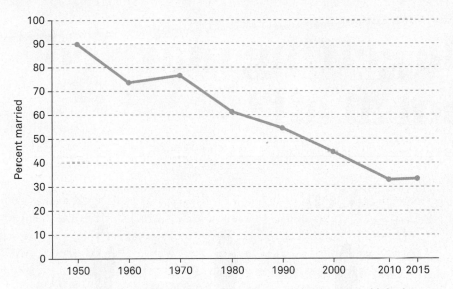

Marriage rates have fallen by more than half since 1970 and by about two-thirds since 1950.

SOURCE: Cruz (2013); National Center for Health Statistics (1968), AmericanCommunity Survey 2016 via FactFinder (2016).

have been married at some point in their lives, so it is safe to say that marriage remains extremely common (see the Story Behind the Numbers). The difference is that with later marriages and frequent divorces (see Chapter 10), married life now occupies a smaller portion of the adult lives of Americans than it did half a century ago. One way to look at that difference is to ask how much of our adult lives is spent in marriage. An average American living in 1960 could expect to be married for three-quarters of the years between ages 18 and 55, that is, 29 out of 37 years. By 2015, that number had fallen to 18 years—only about half of those 37 years. Crucially, those years of marriage occur not only later in life than they did in previous eras but also less continuously, as many people experience divorces and extended periods of being single. Thus, marriage now fills a smaller—and less dominant—place in the lives of American adults than it did in the past.

Consider the role of delaying marriage. In the 1950s, the average American woman got married at age 20 and the average man at age 23. In 2015, those ages were 27 and 29, respectively (see Figure 2.4). The extra five or six years of delay for those who get married occur at a crucial stage in the development of adulthood (Rosenfeld 2007). During that time, young adults tend to complete their education and embark on their careers; many also become unmarried parents and live in cohabiting relationships. Thus, marriage arrives later in the sequence of major life events.

There is no single reason for such a complex and far-reaching change as the decline in marriage (Smock 2004). However, by comparing people who marry

Are people getting married later, or not at all?

http://wwnpag.es/sbtn8

Go to this link for an animation narrated by the author.

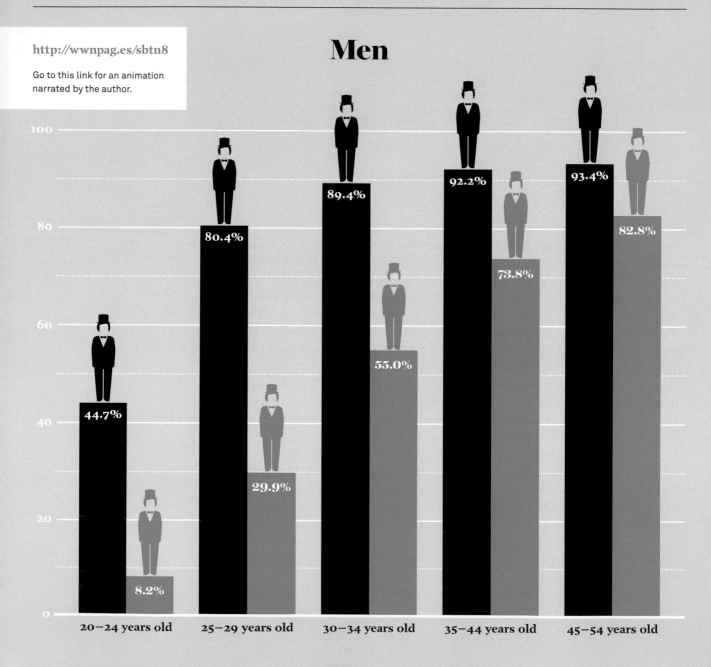

Men

- 20–24 years old: 44.7% / 8.2%
- 25–29 years old: 80.4% / 29.9%
- 30–34 years old: 89.4% / 55.0%
- 35–44 years old: 92.2% / 73.8%
- 45–54 years old: 93.4% / 82.8%

In the U.S. in 1970, 45 percent of men and 64 percent of women married in their early 20s. Those numbers have now plummeted to 8 percent and 14 percent, respectively. Despite the decline in marriage, most people still get married eventually. More than 80 percent of people have been married (at least once) by the time they reach their fifties.

Source: Author's tabulation of U.S. census data.

Percentage of Americans ever married, by age

■ 1970   ■ 2015

Women

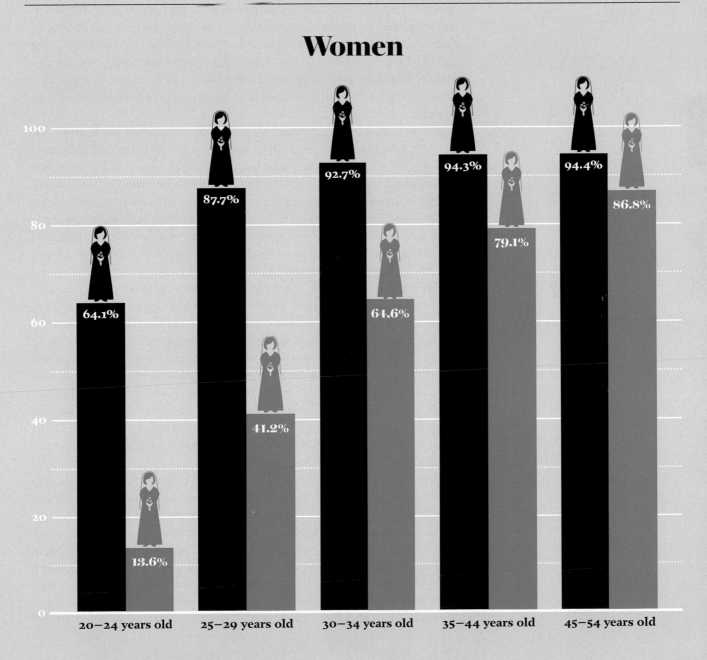

	20–24 years old	25–29 years old	30–34 years old	35–44 years old	45–54 years old
1970	64.1%	87.7%	92.7%	94.3%	94.4%
2015	13.6%	41.2%	64.6%	79.1%	86.8%

with those who don't, by studying how the behavior of married and single people has changed, and by comparing different societies at different times, social scientists have been able to sketch the broad outlines of this story (G. Lee and Payne 2010). I will break the types of explanation into three categories: culture, economics, and demography.

Culture The worry that people in modern American society are excessively individualistic, or self-oriented, is very old (Baumeister 1986). Recently, some social critics have argued that individualism is the underlying cause of decaying American institutions, weakening the bonds that hold people together (Putnam 2000). With the rapid decline of marriage that argument took on new urgency, especially for those who believe that a cultural change lies behind the "retreat from marriage." For example, the sociologist David Popenoe famously concluded more than 20 years ago: "Quite clearly, in this age of the 'me-generation,' the individual rather than the family increasingly comes first" (1993:538). In this view, the fact that young people today are less likely to marry implies that they simply care more about themselves—and less about others—than they did in the past.

But is a change in young people's attitudes toward marriage and family—and especially a growing devotion to self-interest—really behind the decline in marriage? Yes and no. Marriage does seem less important to many people than it once was. For example, a growing minority of Americans—36 percent in 2010—agree with the statement, "The present institution of marriage is becoming obsolete" (Pew Research Center 2010). One middle-aged African American woman recently expressed this ambivalence on a social networking website, writing, "If I ever get married, fine. If not, I will not spend one day trying to get a ring from every guy I meet and miss out on enjoying each day."

However, in many ways, marriage appears to be as important as ever. In fact, some researchers suggest that Americans hold marriage in such high esteem that they feel that neither their lives nor their potential spouses can meet their ideal of marriage. So they postpone marriage not because they don't *want* to marry, but because they want a *better* marriage than they feel they can achieve. That ideal may include the wedding day itself, which most people consider a once-in-a-lifetime affair worthy of great expense (see Changing Culture, "Weddings—And the Price of Perfection"). One 20-something single mother told an interviewer, regarding her boyfriend, "Right now we're getting our credit straightened out, paying off any debts. . . . Then we'll start saving money for the wedding" (Edin and Kefalas 2005:115).

Especially among the poor and working class, however, wedding bells may be postponed by a sense of insecurity that undermines the notion of marriage itself (Edin and Nelson 2013). Marriage is by its nature a long-term proposition, and the more uncertainty people have in their lives, the more difficult it is to act according to long-term goals and ideals. Consider a 20-year-old woman, living in poverty with her extended family. She had two children with her boyfriend—a man with a history of drug addiction and incarceration—and wanted marriage, but because too much in their lives was unsettled, she couldn't feel secure about the future. "I mean, I love him to death," she told researchers. "But marriage

Weddings—And the Price of Perfection

How much do you think a perfect wedding would cost? $5,000? $20,000? $50,000? More? What does the price of a wedding tell you about the value of marriage?

A wedding may be a religious or civil ceremony, marked by a consumer spending binge, or just a party with friends and family. Even if it is preceded by weeks or months of planning and followed by a honeymoon, it might not seem obvious that it changes people and their social roles fundamentally. But the interactions during this intense sequence of events carry the kind of symbolic weight that helps people recognize and adjust to a new, married identity.

The new practices begun after a wedding, as apparently trivial as starting to use a complete set of dishes for the first time, beginning to use married names, or sleeping in the same room while visiting relatives, may help create a new conception of oneself as a married person. They also reinforce the idea in others that the couple's relationship is different, that their family is undergoing a transformation. In short, weddings are part of how people *socialize* themselves into their new roles (Kalmijn 2004). All this may help explain why weddings remain so important for so many people. In fact, their social significance may have increased even as the marriage rate declines (Cherlin 2004).

The cost of hosting an ideal wedding is itself a barrier to many people considering marriage, especially those who will be covering the costs themselves. In one study, a 36-year-old carpenter who lived with his girlfriend said they had discussed getting married at the courthouse instead of having a church wedding, but his girlfriend wanted a "big ceremony with my mother by my side." His response was, "We just can't afford it, your mother doesn't have any money. It's not like she's going to pay for anything. I'm going to pay for this and we can't afford it....So, no, we can't do it" (Smock 2004:969). As marriage rates diverge between rich and poor, it's worth considering how every lavish wedding seen on screen or in the neighborhood reinforces the difference between those who can and those who cannot afford one.

Figure 8.2 **The cost of a wedding with all the trimmings and 141 guests: $55,654**

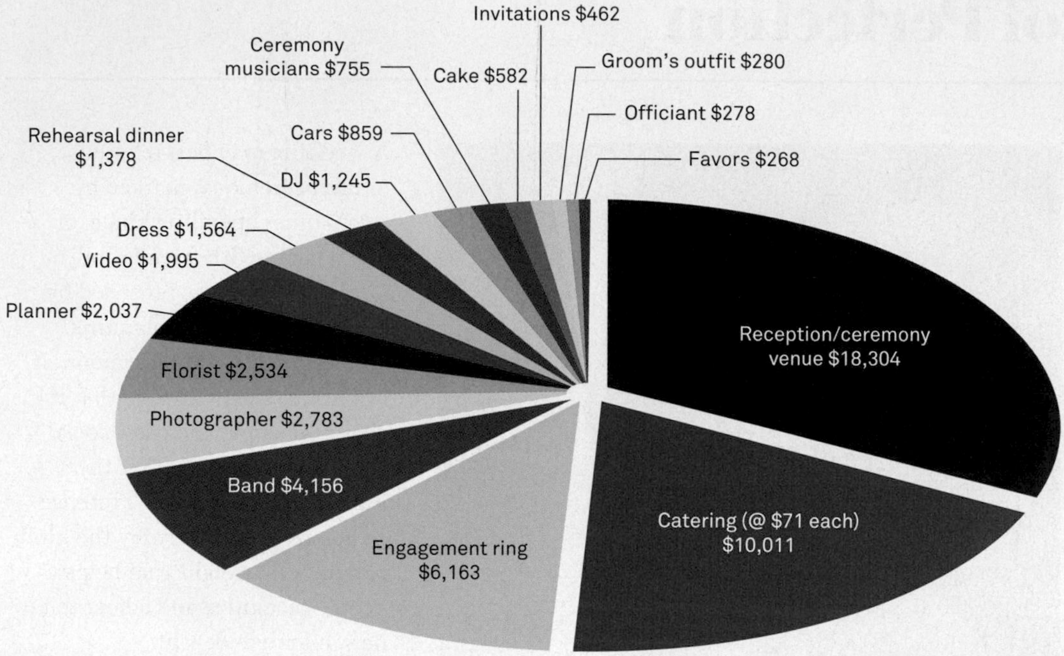

Invitations $462
Ceremony musicians $755
Cake $582
Groom's outfit $280
Officiant $278
Rehearsal dinner $1,378
Cars $859
DJ $1,245
Favors $268
Dress $1,564
Video $1,995
Planner $2,037
Florist $2,534
Photographer $2,783
Band $4,156
Engagement ring $6,163
Reception/ceremony venue $18,304
Catering (@ $71 each) $10,011

These are the average amounts spent on each item by those who bought them.

SOURCE: Seaver, 2017.

And the cost of weddings has mushroomed over the past century. In 1939, sociologist B. F. Timmons (1939) lamented, "there is little information about the cost of weddings in this country." So he set out to find the answer, and his Midwestern, middle-class students surveyed 154 friends and relatives who had recently married. On average these weddings cost $313, or $5,500 in today's dollar value (excluding honeymoons). In comparison, a leading industry group now puts the cost of an average wedding at $35,000 (Seaver 2017). In the 1930s, families in the study spent just $750 each for all costs associated with the reception, which today is the bulk of wedding costs, including the venue, catering, and entertainment—totaling thousands of dollars on average (see Figure 8.2).

Even rich families used to spend less than many middle-class families spend today. In 1945 the *Saturday Evening Post* featured a detailed account of Horace W. Osborne's daughter's wedding and how much "the whole shebang . . . set him back." His expenses, adjusted to today's dollars, were just about $30,000, less than today's average. But his family was quite rich: For example, the champagne he served cost $73 per bottle in today's money, and the reception was at their country club. So if today's average couple spends more than he did in 1945, we can conclude the average wedding has grown much more expensive. Further, the Osborne family had no DJ, rehearsal dinner, wedding planner, or videographer. When you include all the trimmings in a wedding today—all the frills shown in Figure 8.2—at the national average size of 141 guests, the total cost is about $55,000.

Of course, some people are critical of what Chrys Ingraham calls the "wedding industrial complex" (2008). In fact, the industry statistics I present here may be biased by an organization trying to convince people they *should* spend a lot on their weddings. Maybe the critics prefer a simple wedding, as more authentic or less stressful. Or they just don't want to spend their money to support the advertising, jewelry, and fashion industries—all while reinforcing traditional notions of marriage to which they might not subscribe.

On the other hand, the "wedding industrial complex" can serve the needs of modern families in many ways. For example, in some circles, both partners in an engaged couple now wear engagement rings, to express their love and their equality—and maybe to flaunt their ability to buy rings (Shattuck 2010). Once again, the shape of the wedding, like the shape of the marriage itself, is up for negotiation. And the choices we make about this present an image of ourselves and our families to the people we know, and even to ourselves.

is a bigger step. Being together eight years, we might as well be married. . . . I wouldn't trade him for anything, but I don't think I'm ready for marriage yet" (Garrett-Peters and Burton 2015). Before the 1960s, the social pressure on such a couple to get married would have been much stronger.

Ironically, there probably has been both a falling appreciation for marriage among some people and a rising ideal of marriage among others, with both contributing to declining marriage rates. As marriage has become less of a requirement for many aspects of adulthood—including intimacy, sex, living together, and becoming a parent—it appears to have become more of a symbolic achievement rather than a practical necessity (Edin and Reed 2005). And if marriage is a status symbol, then it makes sense that many people set a higher standard for what makes an acceptable spouse. That raises the importance of economic factors, as we will see.

Economics If changes in the culture seem to be contradictory, with some people discounting marriage and others elevating it to an unrealistic standard, economic factors are also complex. There are at least two major issues to consider: how economic independence frees people from a need to marry and how economic insecurity undermines people's prospects for marriage. Let's look at each of these issues separately.

On the one hand, some people have large enough incomes that they don't have (or perceive) a need for marriage as a means of economic support and security. This is especially the case among women, whose increased earning power boosts their potential for independence. Women's independence also reduces the incentives for men to marry, since it means that a man cannot count on his wife to devote herself exclusively to the job of caring for the family (Oppenheimer

1994). However, despite the declining economic need for marriage (for women) and the dwindling supply of free labor that marriage used to imply (for men), both men and women with higher incomes are *more* likely to marry than are people with lower incomes.

Why? There is an interesting paradox here. Although people with higher incomes don't have as much economic need to marry, they are also more sought after for marriage. Thus, they have more choices in the "marriage market," and this apparently tips the balance in favor of getting married. The well-off might be able to afford being single, but for the most part they don't seem to want to be single—at least not when they see their appealing prospects for marriage. And, especially for women, independence within marriage is an important goal, and those with higher incomes are more likely to feel confident that they won't be stuck in a bad marriage because of economic dependency. That may be why, for example, women with substantial student loan debt are less likely to get married (Bozick and Estacion 2014).

On the other hand, among those with lower incomes—who you might think would benefit the most from the cooperation of a marriage—marriage often seems like a commitment that brings more burden than benefit. As some poor single mothers conclude, "I can do bad by myself" (Edin and Kefalas 2005:81). Although poor people might prefer to be married, either they are not persuaded by the prospects they face or they do not find potential spouses to choose from (L. White and Rogers 2000). And many poor fathers, who see a future with limited career prospects, feel ashamed at their inability to meet the cultural ideal of a provider husband (Edin and Nelson 2013).

In fact, for some people, the numbers are simply not in their favor when it comes to finding a marriage partner. And that brings me to the third category of explanation for the decline in marriage: demography.

Demography The math of marriage may seem simple: 1 + 1 = 2 (or, in the even simpler romantic version, as The Who once sang, "one and one make one"). But in reality, the equation is much more complex. If every man wanted to match up with exactly one woman, and vice versa, and if there were no other rules or considerations, then just about everyone could get married. But circumstances, preferences, and social pressures intervene to limit people's options—and skew the math.

Sometimes, one restrictive condition can make a very big difference in marriage rates. For example, remember the number of men and women of different heights (see Figure 5.1). If an American man who is 5 feet 4 inches tall decides he will only marry a shorter woman, his choices will be limited to less than half of all women. In American society today, the primary restrictions that people apply to their marriage partner choices include race/ethnicity, education level, and religion. We'll discuss these choices shortly, but first I will provide a short description of demographic effects on marriage rates in general, focusing on two examples: the "marriage squeeze" experienced by women of the baby boom and the imbalance in the numbers of African American men and women in U.S. urban areas.

As you may recall from Chapter 2, the baby boom involved a prolonged spike in birth rates from the mid-1940s through the early 1960s, caused by the post–World War II surge in prosperity and the cultural celebration of breadwinner-homemaker families. Little did those millions of couples realize, apparently, how demography would affect the marriage choices of their children 25 years later. Because women usually married men who were about three years older, those millions of baby boomers looking for husbands discovered that they were a few million men short—that is, the supply of 22-year-old women greatly exceeded the supply of 25-year-old men. On the flip side, that relatively small number of 25-year-old men encountered an oversupply of 22-year-old women. This imbalance, called a *marriage squeeze*, ended up lowering the marriage rate for women and contributing to delays in marriage for the baby boom generation overall (Schoen 1983).

A different sort of marriage squeeze also affected women in the 1970s and 1980s, helping to lower marriage rates among poor and African American women. As industrial manufacturing jobs became scarcer in the big urban centers of the Northeast and Midwest—such as Chicago, Detroit, Cleveland, and Philadelphia—men without college degrees had a harder time finding steady work (W. Wilson 1987). As a result, if poor, urban women—mostly Black women—wanted to marry men with decent jobs, their chances of finding such a partner were reduced (R. Raley 1996). And men without steady employment or income potential found themselves shut out of the marriage market. In the last few decades, this shortage of marriage partners for women has been exacerbated by high rates of incarceration among urban Black men in their young adult years, driven by the "war on drugs" (Pettit and Western 2004). In this way, economic and social trends have created a demographic pressure that reduces the number of Black women who can marry, especially among those who are poor (see Chapter 3).

Both of these examples of demographic pressure reducing marriage rates involve the marriage prospects of women. However, demography also affects men's marriage chances. For example, Asian American women are more than twice as likely to marry non-Asians as are Asian men (see Figure 8.5). Partly as a result of such imbalance in intermarriage, Asian American men are less likely to get married at a young age (Passel, Wang, and Taylor 2010). Further, some immigrant groups have experienced sharp sex imbalances that limit their marriage options (such as the nineteenth-century Chinese discussed in Chapter 3). And in societies that practice polygamy, in which some men marry multiple wives, other men (usually poor men) may never have a chance to marry at all (J. Lee and Wang 1999).

Race/Ethnicity

The cultural, economic, and demographic forces just described have produced sharp differences in the marriage patterns of different racial-ethnic groups in the United States today. As Figure 8.3 shows, Asian American women are the most

Figure 8.3 **First marriages per 1,000 never-married women, 2015**

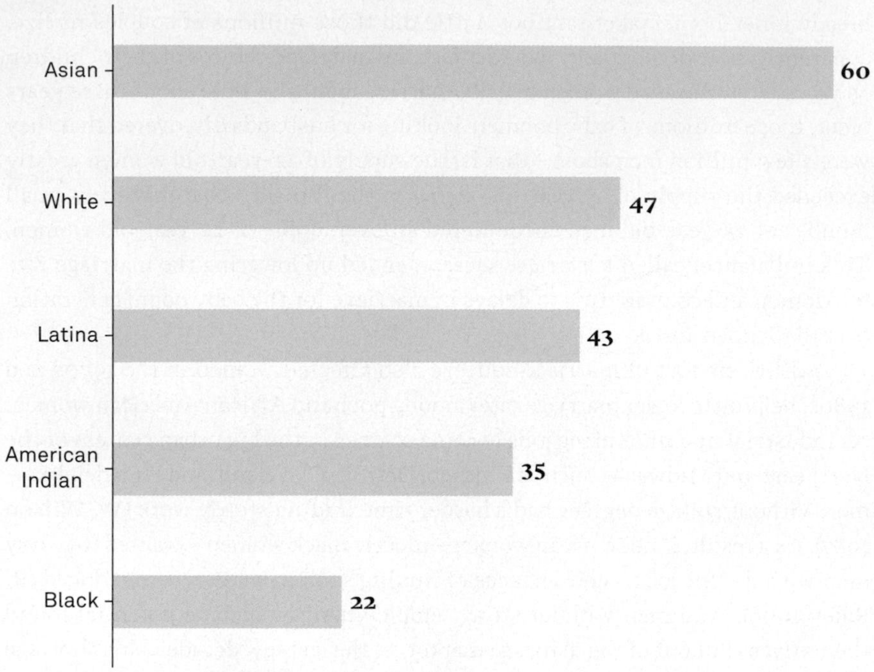

Black women have the lowest marriage rates, less than half those of Latinas, Whites, and Asians (Whites include only single-race women).

SOURCE: Author's calculations from 2015 American Community Survey data provided by IPUMS (Ruggles et al. 2016).

likely to get married for the first time in a given year, followed by White, Latina, American Indian, and then Black women. These contemporary differences reflect historical patterns of culture, economics, and demography.

In the case of African Americans, the marriage rate gap with Whites has grown since the 1950s. Although marriage has become less common—and more fragile—among all groups since the 1950s, the drop among African Americans has been fastest. As Figure 8.4 shows, in 1950 Whites were slightly more likely than Blacks to be married. But the gap has widened dramatically since then. What is the cause of these disparities? Economic and demographic factors have played the greatest role (Burton and Tucker 2009). Black men have been especially hard hit by employment problems as the country's manufacturing base has shrunk and moved away from large inner cities (W. Wilson 1997). And the sex imbalance in those cities is pronounced for African Americans. As we saw in Chapter 3, for example, in many cities there are less than 50 employed, unmarried male Black partners for every 100 unmarried Black women (see that chapter's Story Behind the Numbers).

However, there is also a cultural component to the lower Black rates of marriage (Tucker 2000). Researchers have found that Black women have no less desire to marry than White women, and the great majority of both groups also

Figure 8.4 **Percentage of American adults ever married, by race, 1950–2016**

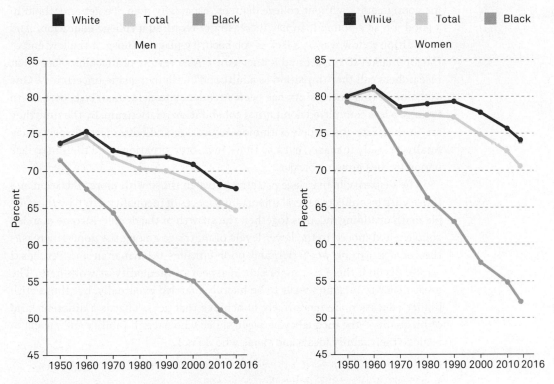

The gap between the Black and White percentages has increased dramatically since 1950. (White and Black include only single-race people after 2000; based on the civilian non-institutional population.)

SOURCE: U.S. Census Bureau (2017a).

expect to marry some day (Edin and Reed 2005). But there are other attitude differences. Research shows that African Americans are more committed than Whites to the ideal of *both* men and women being "good providers" to be "ready for marriage" (Pew Research Center 2010). If that means that African Americans set a higher economic standard for marriage, the result would be delaying or forgoing marriage, especially given the reality of economic insecurity in their communities.

Education

On the surface it appears that marriage patterns for those with more education and those with less education are growing more similar. The tendency of those in college or graduate school to delay marriage while they finish school and establish their careers means that marriage for them occurs later in life (Cherlin 2010). And in the last few decades, those with less education are increasingly delaying their first marriages as well, until their late 20s.

But the reason for the change among those with less education shows that their situation is quite different. Economic insecurity has become pronounced for young adults without college degrees, especially men. To get a foothold in a good job as a young man has increasingly required a college education. And in addition to low wages, a lack of job security plagues those at the low end of the job market (Danziger and Ratner 2010). As a result, young adults face what researchers call the "transition to adulthood" with increasing uncertainty. One outcome of this uncertainty has been a tendency to delay marriage, perhaps in favor of a less committed nonmarital cohabitation relationship. By the time they are in their late 30s, people with more education and better job prospects may finally be ready to marry, even as those in poorer situations find their marriage opportunities growing bleaker.

The disparity in marriage patterns between those with more education and those with less affects several important aspects of inequality. First, by the simple math of adding incomes together, the growth of the double-income married couple—juxtaposed to the lower levels of marriage among the poor—increases the income gap between rich and poor families (McLanahan and Percheski 2008). Second, there is a more subtle aspect of inequality at work here. The great majority of adults want to be happily married eventually, but those with higher education are more likely to achieve that goal. That is a different kind of inequality—the inequality between those who have the ability and means to achieve their family ideals and those who do not.

Why Do People Still Get Married?

After several pages devoted to a discussion of the decline of marriage, it is worth noting that there remain a variety of compelling reasons *for* people to get married. True, some of the reasons have eroded in recent decades. For example, most Americans do not feel they need to get married before having sex, living with a partner, or even raising children. And because so many marriages end in divorce, a wedding does not necessarily signify a lifelong commitment either. All of this contributes to what sociologist Andrew Cherlin (2004) refers to as the "deinstitutionalization of marriage." By that he means that the formal and informal rules of marriage—its social *norms*—have become weaker, leaving marriage itself more optional and behavior within marriage more negotiable.

And yet the great majority of Americans end up getting married. Why? One way to answer that is to use Cherlin's concept of the marriage institution. Although the institution is weaker, it still provides reasons to marry (Lauer and Yodanis 2010). We can put the reasons to marry in three categories:

- *Incentives.* A variety of rewards steer people toward marriage (or penalize them, relatively speaking, for *not* marrying). For example, state and federal governments offer rights and benefits to married couples. These include social protections, such as parental rights over their children and access to immigration for a spouse, and financial benefits, such as tax breaks and

Social Security pension funds. Market actors also contribute incentives, such as employers and insurance companies that offer insurance benefits for married couples.

- *Social pressure.* Because many people are aware of the real (or perceived) benefits that marriage provides, young couples often encounter advice and pressure to marry. Some advice comes from the media's packaging of social science research, which is generally positive about the benefits of marriage (Parker-Pope 2010). Or it may come directly from family experts and professionals, such as counselors and social workers. Other sources of pressure to marry include family members and religious leaders, although these have weakened in recent decades (Tucker 2000).

- *Imitation.* As noted in Chapter 2, modern society offers many more choices about family life now than it did decades ago. Because choice also implies responsibility, however, we feel we have only ourselves to blame if something goes wrong. In that situation, the "crowd" can serve as a reassuring presence in support of our decisions. Ironically, then, the more choices people have, the more they may seek to imitate others around them as a way of narrowing their options. That might affect smaller decisions, such as naming one's child after a celebrity, but it also helps lead people into marriage. Thus, although young adults may delay or experiment with alternatives (such as cohabitation), in the end most people choose to conform to common behavior patterns.

Clearly, with the pronounced decline in the frequency of marriage we have observed, these various reasons to marry are not as persuasive as they once were. Nevertheless, marriage remains one of the dominant experiences in the lives of most adults. The desire to marry, however, can only be realized if people can find suitable partners. And as with any of the family choices we discuss in this book, what seems most personal is often shaped by forces that are larger than any one person.

Who Marries Whom

In the previous chapter, I mentioned that I don't frequently pry into strangers' relationships. But there are two specific examples I would like to focus on for illustration—public figures whose stories are already well documented.

When Barack Obama and Michelle Robinson met, they may have been the only two Black lawyers at their firm in Chicago (Remnick 2010). They were also both Harvard Law School graduates, both tall and athletic, and as a couple they had the usual height and age spreads—he being a little taller and a little older than she. So in some ways they were even more similar than the couple I described at the beginning of Chapter 7. However, the fact that she was a successful

Is marriage a market? What can we learn from Barack Obama and Michelle Robinson (top) and Donald Trump and Melania Knauss (bottom)?

professional—and even his superior at the law firm—is a sign of how standards have changed as well.

Compare that now-former First Couple with an extremely different First Couple: Donald Trump and Melania Knauss. When their marriage began in 2005, he was a twice-divorced 58-year-old real estate tycoon worth hundreds of millions of dollars, and she was a 34-year-old model who had emigrated to the United States from Slovenia with just a high school degree in her 20s. The age and wealth difference between them was extreme compared with the Obamas, but in some ways their marriage conformed more closely to the traditional breadwinner-homemaker model. Is there a sociological story here?

Some researchers conceive of the spouse-matching process as a marketplace, in which people offer something of value for sale while they shop for what they like (and can afford). Most people probably don't like to think of their own marriage this way, but Donald Trump has contributed to this impression by speaking of Melania in ways that make her seem like a product. Defending the First Lady in 2017, for example, he said, "She was always the highest quality that you'll ever find" (Associated Press 2017). The marketplace concept was advanced by the economist Gary Becker (1973), whom we met in our discussion of exchange theory in Chapter 1. To define marriage as a market, like the market for cars or bubble gum, he made two assumptions. First, marriage must be *voluntary*, meaning people only marry if and when they think it will improve their lives (like buying bubble gum). And second, there must be *competition* for spouses (like shopping around for the right price on the right car). If those basic conditions exist, Becker theorized, then we can think of marriage as a market process.

The market concept fits with a long-standing popular view of certain patterns, or stereotypes, that people observe in American marriages (M. Rosenfeld 2005). For example:

- Rich men marry women who are poorer, yet beautiful (like the Trumps; Mclintock 2014).

- Men choose wives based on their potential as mothers, while women choose husbands for their potential earnings.

- Members of lower-status groups (such as Black men) marry members of higher-status groups (such as White women) when the latter have less money or education than themselves (Torche and Rich 2016).

In each case, people are seen to be using the assets they have to win the qualities they want in a marriage partner. Put another way, those with higher status in one respect, such as education, exchange that with a partner who has a higher status in a different realm, such as race.

Many sociologists find Becker's notion of market principles in marriage to be naive or idealistic. To us, social life seems more chaotic and conflict ridden than Becker's tidy supply-and-demand formulas imply, as if buyers line up for spouses who are auctioned off in order from best to worst, according to careful assessments of their "quality." Specifically, sociologists have described three problems with the idea (Illouz and Finkelman 2009). First, people making marriage decisions have desires that may be in conflict, such as sexual attraction and economic potential. Second, people often make bad decisions, especially in the realm of love and romance, so we cannot assume that marriage choices are "rational." And third, in real life, people shopping for a spouse do not have as many choices as, say, someone shopping for a car or bubble gum, so it's not reasonable to assume that spouses reflect a conscious choice from among many alternatives.

Despite such sociological skepticism, however, the marriage market concept has been very influential, and the term is widely used in research (Kalmijn 2010). Without accepting all the assumptions of exchange theory, in this book I use **marriage market** to mean the social space in which people search for potential marriage partners. Often we think of that space as simply the local area—the neighborhood, campus, or city, for example—but it need not be strictly geographical. With online dating, for example, the social space may be a group with some common interest or quality (for example, Christian vegetarians). In the study of marriage markets, we do consider economic factors. But sociologists focus further on two related sociological issues: the construction of personal preferences and the drawing of boundaries between groups.

Returning to the Obamas: First, why would two African American, Harvard-educated lawyers have a *preference* to marry each other? Maybe rather than making an exchange to get something they don't have, perhaps their common experience growing up to become liberal Black students at elite universities, exceeding expectations, and becoming highly successful in the face of long odds, all the while learning—being trained—to see the world in a similar way, made them susceptible to each other's charms and ways of thinking.

That interpretation calls to mind the discussion of socialization in Chapter 5. If socialization is a way to internalize elements of the social structure into our own personality, then it makes sense that our choice of a marriage partner might reflect that process. In other words, people bring their life stories—embedded in their personalities—to the marriage market. Note also that the Obamas' story follows the description in Chapter 7 of homophily ("birds of a feather flock together"). Such patterns, in which similar people end up together, are caused by both personal preferences and practical limits.

And that brings us to the second sociological aspect of marriage markets: *boundaries*. As we will see, race, education, and religion are the most resilient boundaries carving up today's U.S. marriage market. Those divisions are created by cultural or traditional practices (such as attitudes against interracial marriage) as well as more structural barriers (such as residential segregation).

marriage market

The social space in which people search for potential marriage partners.

How did preferences and boundaries shape the Trumps' and the Obamas' market of potential matches? We cannot know the intimate details, but there are some suggestive facts. The Trumps met at the Kit Kat Club in New York City, where a modeling agency owner was hosting a party. Having arrived at the party with another woman as his date, Donald was apparently struck by Melania's physical and social attributes, and by what she would add to his brand (Collins 2016). On the other hand, the Obamas went through a process with much more equal matching. By my calculation, in the Chicago area in 1990 (about the time they met), there were almost a quarter-million never-married adults between the ages of 25 and 34 (their age range). That's quite a large selection from which to "shop." But practically speaking, it was divided up into many different groups. For example, among all those young unmarried people, there were probably fewer than 200 Black lawyers—almost few enough to all know each other. The process of sorting out and winnowing the large population of a marriage market down to the magic number two may include the kind of economic motivations that Becker examined, but it surely goes beyond the simple rules of supply and demand as well.

Endogamy

American marriage markets are informally but sharply divided along the lines of race/ethnicity, religion, and social class. Thus, endogamy, or marriage and reproduction within a distinct group, is prevalent in the United States today, as it is in other modern societies. The opposite of endogamy—known as exogamy—was an extremely useful invention by early humans and ancient civilizations. This not only helped prevent war and conflict by facilitating interaction and trade between groups, it also promoted cultural innovation and diversity by promoting the exchange of ideas. And exogamy reduced health problems associated with close inbreeding (Coontz 2005). By ancient standards, we have a high degree of exogamy; that is, most people don't marry known relatives or people from their own village, so to speak. However, in terms of race/ethnicity, religion, and social class, endogamy is more the rule than the exception. And this practice helps maintain the existence of these groups from generation to generation (C. Kim and Min 2010). In fact, sociologists have long recognized that for better or worse, if people were to marry (and raise children) without regard to each others' backgrounds, it would undermine the existence of distinct cultural groups (M. Gordon 1964). This is most clearly the case with regard to race and ethnicity.

Race and Ethnicity

At a glance, marriage across the lines of race and ethnicity appears to have exploded in the last half-century. In 1960, just 2 percent of marriages in the United States involved people from different major racial or ethnic groups (Passel,

Wang, and Taylor 2010). By 2015, that figure had increased to 17 percent, more than eight times the rate of 50 years earlier. But is 17 percent a lot of intermarriage? That depends on how you look at it. During the last half-century, the American population has become much more diverse, especially with the growth of the Latino and Asian groups, as we saw in Chapter 3. As a result, by my calculation, if you could scramble up today's unmarried population and marry them off at random, about half of marriages would involve people from different racial-ethnic groups. So clearly, despite dramatic change, substantial divisions remain. And an intermarriage rate of 17 percent is still low compared with the potential for intermarriage in our society.

As we saw in Chapter 3, intermarriage between Blacks and Whites has increased slowly since the laws against it were overturned half a century ago, in the 1967 Supreme Court case *Loving v. Virginia* (Foster 2016). Figure 8.5 shows that Whites are the most likely to marry someone from their own group, with 89 percent of White men and women marrying other Whites. At the other extreme, only one-third of American Indians marry other American Indians—which poses a substantial threat to the future of a separate American Indian population. Intermarriage rates usually correspond to the size of the group: Members of larger populations (such as Whites) are less likely to marry outside their group, while

Figure 8.5 **Racial-ethnic patterns of marriage**

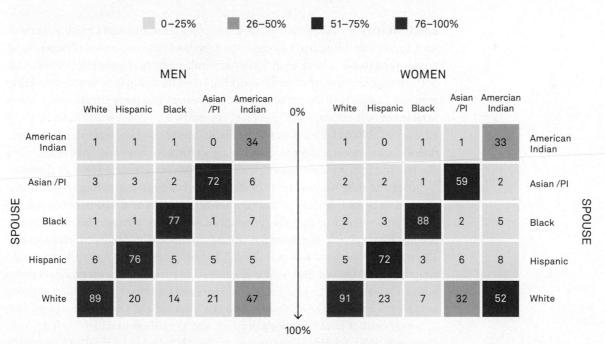

Among people who married in the last year, percentage of men and women who married someone from each of the five major racial-ethnic groups. Note that "PI" refers to Pacific Islanders.

SOURCE: Author's calculations from 2015 American Community Survey data provided by IPUMS (Ruggles et al. 2016).

those in smaller groups (such as American Indians) are more likely to out-marry. It is logical that people in larger groups would be more likely to find mates inside their own group. However, African American women, who are almost as numerous as Latinas, are much less likely to out-marry. And when members of the other groups do marry exogamously, they rarely marry African Americans. For example, White men are much more likely to marry Asians than Blacks, even though the Black population is much larger.

Relatively high rates of intermarriage for Asian Americans and Latinos reflect a number of factors, including where people live around the country, how divided different groups are between neighborhoods, and their levels of education (Qian and Lichter 2007). However, racial attitudes remain important. Those who don't identify as Black or African American are least likely to express acceptance toward a member of their family marrying an African American, compared with their attitude toward other groups (Passel, Wang, and Taylor 2010). Because of the highly symbolic nature of marriage—which is a source of family approval and recognition—such attitudes can have a strong effect on marriage decisions (Thornton, Axinn, and Xie 2007). Interestingly, as we will see, attitudes that serve as a social barrier to marriage may end up encouraging cohabitation as an alternative among couples that cross traditional dividing lines.

Although race and ethnicity remain potent issues in American marriage markets, suggesting the persistence of historical prejudices, there are also signs of modernization in marriage decisions. Chief among these are the increasing importance of education and the decline of religion as a factor in marriage.

Education Racial prejudice has a bad reputation in mainstream American society (Bonilla-Silva 2013). Even people who hold negative views of other racial groups tend to describe their attitudes as resulting from the qualities or behavior of the group, because irrationally disliking an entire group is frowned upon (Tarman and Sears 2005). On the other hand, choosing a spouse of the same education level is not only common but expected, especially for people with higher levels of education. If Barack Obama (or Michelle Robinson) had chosen to marry someone without a college degree, chances are many people would have questioned the purity of their motives (as they did when Melania married Donald Trump).

Over the past half-century, in fact, there has been a growing tendency for spouses to be matched according to education level. The division between high school and college is especially pronounced, with few marriages between college graduates and people who have not at least attended some college (Schwartz and Mare 2005). How severe is this divide? In 2016, there were 63 million married couples in the United States. If you categorize people into two groups—those with and those without a bachelor's degree—you find that in 49 million of those couples (78 percent) the spouses are on the same side of the divide—32 million in which neither have bachelor's degrees, and 17 million in which both do (U.S. Census Bureau 2016k). When you consider this divide in light of the trends in marriage rates discussed earlier—with marriage declining more among the poor—it is clear that the family lives of Americans are growing increasingly different, depending on their social class position.

Educational matching also reflects the modern ideal of marriage as a companionship of equals, with compatible tastes, pursuing individual goals (Cherlin 2004). Among those with college education, moreover, the compatibility between husbands and wives often extends to career aspirations as well. Men with high earning potential now usually expect a wife to bring in her own earnings; women usually prefer to have a career that enhances both their standard of living and their sense of independence in the marriage. (That sense of independence also provides security if the marriage should end.) These choices and expectations have contributed to closer income equality between husbands and wives (Sweeney and Cancian 2004).

Religion For most Americans before the mid-twentieth century, religious intermarriage was a greater practical concern than interracial marriage or marriage across social classes, if only because it was more of a practical reality. Since then, there has been a pronounced decline in religious endogamy (Cherlin 2010). This trend fits with the idea of individual choice and self-determination in modern society and the decline of traditional authorities such as the church (Myers 2006). Unfortunately, our detailed knowledge of religious trends is limited by the difficulty of identifying religious affiliations and because federal agencies don't collect information on Americans' religious beliefs. Nevertheless, we can draw some conclusions from a variety of sources (M. Rosenfeld 2008).

More than 90 percent of Christians are still married to other Christians (Pew Research Center 2011). The decline in religious endogamy has mostly been the result of changes in the behavior of the large population of liberal or moderate Protestants (such as Presbyterians, Episcopalians, and Methodists), who are now more frequently intermarrying among themselves as well as with non-Protestants. In contrast, more conservative groups—such as Catholics, Mormons, Baptists, and Pentecostals—have not changed as much. For example, according to the General Social Survey, the percentage of Catholics married to other Catholics fell only slightly from 1991 to 2008, from about 80 percent to 73 percent—partly because of rules within the Catholic Church regarding marriage to non-Catholics. The divide between Catholics and conservative Protestants remains especially sharp (Sherkat 2004).

For some groups with substantial immigrant ancestry, such as Jews, increasing intermarriage is partly the result of ethnic assimilation over the generations. Despite being a very small group, Jews have a relatively high rate of endogamy, with about 60 percent married to other Jews. But as Eastern European Jewish communities integrated into mainstream American society, intermarriage increased (Philips and Fishman 2006). The same pattern of assimilation may be true for Muslims, many of whom are immigrants. About 80 percent of American Muslims are married to other Muslims (Pew Research Center 2011). However, a national survey found that about 60 percent of American Muslims said it was "OK" for a Muslim to marry a non-Muslim (Pew Research Center 2007b).

Interestingly, we know relatively little about the growing population of Americans with *no* religious affiliation—now 20 percent of the population. But many people feel that belief in God is a necessity in a marriage partner. Only one-fourth of adults said that they would "be fine with" a member of their family marrying someone who doesn't believe in God (Passel, Wang, and Taylor 2010).

Sex Finally, remember that all of the research described here about who marries whom has examined couples comprising a man and a woman. Marriage also may involve two people of the same sex. Obviously, even if "birds of a feather flock together," the vast majority of people select spouses who differ from themselves on the vital characteristic of sex.

Now that same-sex marriage is legal in the United States (see Changing Law), we are slowly gaining knowledge about the selection of partners, and the dynamics of interaction, in these families. Unfortunately, we do not yet have reliable data on same-sex marriage. There is no national record of marriages; instead, official statistics come from the states. Most states (including some of the biggest: California, Texas, and Florida) do not collect data on the sex or gender of people getting married—it's not even recorded on the marriage license. Other states vary. For example, in New York entering the sex of the spouses on a marriage application is optional. The federal government collects data on marriage through surveys, but these do not yet provide a reliable account of same-sex marriages (Kreider and Lofquist 2015). As a result, although we can be sure that hundreds of thousands of same-sex couples have married since they were granted the right to do so, we don't know their exact number, or many other details about their experiences.

Cohabitation

cohabitation

Living together as a sexual or romantic couple without being married.

While we study changes in marriage patterns—who gets married and who marries whom—it's ironic that one of the biggest changes in marriage in recent decades has been something that happens *outside* of marriage. Defined as living together as a sexual or romantic couple without being married, **cohabitation** has rapidly become an expected stage in relationships for the majority of couples. Cohabiting couples may have a strong informal commitment to their relationship, and they may or may not be engaged to marry, have children, or be sexually exclusive. Naturally, in modern societies, all of that is up for negotiation.

As you can see in Figure 8.6, cohabitation has become much more common in the past several decades for Americans at all levels of education. Overall, about two-thirds of women under age 45 have cohabited with a man at some point in their lives. By changing the pathway to marriage, the experience before marriage, and the alternatives to marriage, cohabitation has radically changed the experience of marriage itself (Smock 2000).

Although the increase in cohabitation is broad, as Figure 8.6 shows, we also see that cohabitation is more common—and has increased faster—among women with less education (these figures are for women because they were originally collected in a government survey about women's health and family planning). Combined with what we have learned about marriage patterns, we now see that cohabitation is part of the social class divide in family experience. Those with less education are less likely to marry but more likely to live together. Thus, we should not conclude that they have no partners, but rather that their relationships are less stable and committed, on average, than those who have a higher level of education and therefore more economic security. As the age at which people get

Figure 8.6 **Percentage of women ages 19 to 44 who have ever cohabited, by education, 1987–2013**

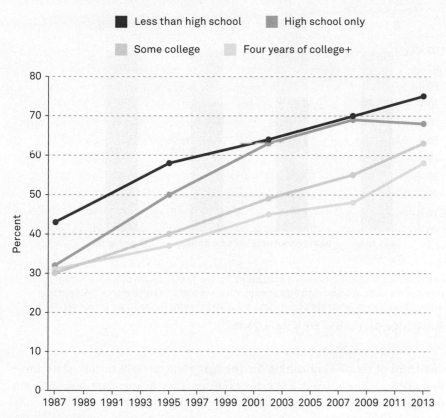

Cohabitation rates have increased rapidly, but the increase is fastest, and the levels are highest, for those with less education.

SOURCE: Hemez and Manning (2017).

married has risen—especially for racial-ethnic minorities and people with less than a college education—their single years have been partly filled by time spent cohabiting with partners outside of marriage (Manning, Brown, and Payne 2014).

Unfortunately for researchers, cohabitation is not always a clearly defined status (W. Manning and Smock 2005). First, some people live together only some days of the week or some weeks of the year—or "off and on," depending on the ups and downs of the relationship. So "living together" may be hard to pin down. And second, informal romantic or sexual relationships—without marriage or some other legal recognition—do not have clear start and end dates. The individuals involved sometimes do not even agree between themselves on the nature of their relationship. All of that makes cohabitation difficult to study—but does not make it less important to try.

Although most Americans will experience cohabitation at some point in their lives, it occurs at different ages, under many different circumstances, and for different lengths of time. On average, however, cohabitation is not a long-lasting relationship (Musick and Michelmore 2015). As Figure 8.7 shows, fewer than

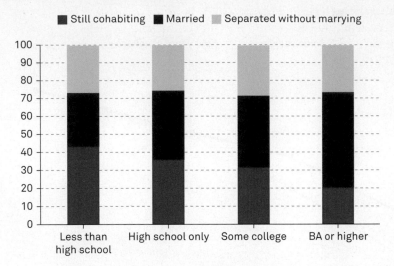

Figure 8.7 **Relationship status 3 years from the start of a first cohabitation, by woman's education level**

■ Still cohabiting ■ Married ■ Separated without marrying

About a third of people who start cohabiting for the first time are still cohabiting three years later. Women with higher education are more likely to marry their partner within three years, while those with less education remain cohabiting for longer.

SOURCE: Copen, Daniels, and Mosher (2010).

one-third of couples cohabiting for the first time are still in that state three years later, as some marry and others split up. Clearly, there are very different outcomes for these relationships.

Family instability among cohabiting families has been especially worrying to those concerned with children in low-income families (Graefe and Lichter 1999). About 40 percent of cohabitors live with children, and one in five of those families lives in poverty. For children whose mothers live with several men over a period of years, a series of changes in family structure—with the conflict those changes may entail—is a source of stress in their development (Fomby and Osborne 2010).

When we think about these experiences of cohabitation, it is helpful to break them into three conceptual categories: before marriage, instead of marriage, and after marriage. I say "conceptual" categories because we cannot cleanly separate couples into these three groups. But the elements of each kind of relationship— the people involved, their motivations, and the consequences for them—are worth examining.

Before Marriage

Living together before marrying is the most common form of cohabitation among younger adults. For these couples, cohabitation is a proving ground for the relationship—a chance to experience living as a couple without making a public, legal, or religious commitment. Cohabitation is now a widely expected stage in the relationship process, and about half of young women say they are engaged or have "definite plans" to marry when they move in with a partner (Vespa 2014). Most people believe that this arrangement—once commonly known as "living in sin"—is the right thing for a couple to do before marriage.

But living together without marrying—even with the expectation of marrying—is not just an experiment in a vacuum; it has effects on the relationship that may be permanent (Kuperberg 2014). These may be positive, such as the tendency to share housework more equally (Batalova and Cohen 2002). But there are also risks. Ironically, one risk is that couples who move in together may get married out of "relationship inertia"—the momentum of a lesser decision (moving in together) making a more important decision (marrying) easier to fall into carelessly (Stanley, Rhoades, and Markman 2006). Couples may end up living together under imperfect conditions, without making clear or informed decisions that take into account the long-term consequences of their actions (W. Manning and Smock 2005).

Among poor and working-class couples, cohabiting often reflects a plan to marry once they have more money. For example, one 28-year-old fast-food manager, already living with a woman and their child, told researchers, "We need to be financially secure [before we can marry]. We need to be able to support ourselves, you know?" If that doesn't happen, such couples may never marry, or financial strain may break up the relationship along the way. In other words, they may view their cohabitation as a step toward marriage, but economic reality often intervenes to block their desire from being realized (Gibson-Davis, Edin, and McLanahan 2005).

Financial pressures also drive some people into living together in the first place. For example, during the recession in the late 2000s, there was a large increase in the number of younger, low-income cohabiting couples, with many moving into already crowded households, suggesting that their decision to move in together was motivated more by a financial crunch than by a romantic ideal (Kreider 2010).

Instead of Marriage

A smaller group—not as well understood by researchers at this point—chooses cohabitation instead of marriage (Thornton, Axinn, and Xie 2007). Some of these couples are ideologically opposed to marriage, with its traditional image and expectations, but this is relatively rare (Rhoades, Stanley, and Markman 2009). Others make their relationship commitments without the help of religious or civil authorities, choosing to express their bonds independently (Elizabeth 2003).

But the choice is not always freely made. Nontraditional couples face obstacles to marriage even if they desire to marry. For example, their families may oppose the marriage, their religion might frown on it (in the case of interfaith or same-sex couples), or they may face condemnation on the basis of race/ethnicity, age, or social class differences. In such cases, couples often end up cohabiting to avoid the choice between confronting that opposition and ending their relationship. As a result, cohabiting couples are more likely to have bigger differences in educational attainment or different racial-ethnic backgrounds (Blackwell and Lichter 2000).

Finally, we should not assume that both parties in a couple see things the same way. When one partner wants to marry and the other doesn't, cohabitation may be a compromise. And some cohabiting relationships do not result in marriage because the couple can't make it work. For example, among women with a history of being abused as children, the difficulty in forming or maintaining intimate relationships may translate into a series of unstable cohabiting relationships without a marriage (Cherlin et al. 2004). For a minority of cohabitors—about 1 in 4—living together with a series of partners is an alternative to marriage, voluntary or not (Vespa 2014). This pattern is most common among the economically disadvantaged (Lichter and Qian 2008).

After Marriage

For people who have divorced or become widowed, cohabitation after marriage provides a path to a new family life that often seems less fraught with risk, especially when they have children. Cohabitation is increasingly common among older adults, and most of them have been divorced or widowed (Carr and Moorman 2011). As Figure 8.8 shows, for example, almost two-thirds of unmarried

---

Figure 8.8 **Marital status of unmarried cohabitors, by age**

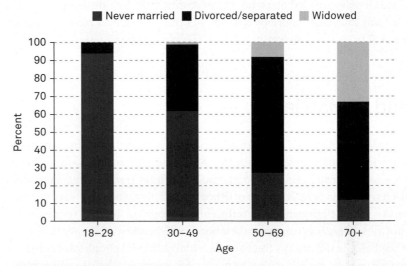

Most young cohabitors have never been married, but after age 50 the majority are separated, divorced, or widowed from a prior marriage.

SOURCE: Author's calculations from 2015 American Community Survey data provided by IPUMS (Ruggles et al. 2016).

cohabitors ages 50–69 are separated or divorced. Although some do end up marrying, they often see their arrangement as a long-term substitute for marriage, rather than as a chance to explore compatibility before eventually marrying (V. King and Scott 2005).

As the baby boom generation has swelled the ranks of the middle-aged, for the first time many of today's divorced and widowed people themselves cohabited before their first marriages. Their experiences of both divorce and premarital cohabitation contribute to an acceptance of living together without marrying their new partners. Age and stage in the life course make a profound difference in these relationships. Rather than maximizing the financial benefits of marrying, older people may be more interested in protecting their assets (maybe for their older children's inheritance) by not marrying. Research shows that divorced cohabitors usually keep their finances separate (Hamplova and Le Bourdais 2009); only after they have been together for a long time are they likely to pool their accounts, unless they are raising younger children together (Klawitter 2008).

Finally, recall that at advanced older ages, the number of women starts to exceed the number of men dramatically. This produces a different kind of demographic squeeze. When single women outnumber men, those few men may not feel compelled to risk a marriage, given their other options in the marriage market. And those many single women may feel pressured to accept cohabitation as a compromise, even if they would prefer a marriage, because they have few men to choose from. Nevertheless, cohabitors in the older population are in most respects as emotionally satisfied with their relationships as those who are married (S. Brown and Kawamura 2010).

The Modern Married Individual

As you can tell from the foregoing discussion, sociologists have spilled a lot of ink over the decline of marriage. And there is little doubt about this fundamental trend. Yet, for the people who are married—or those intent on getting married— there is no doubt that the experience is one of the most important aspects of their lives (Thornton, Axinn, and Xie 2007).

We will devote a good deal of attention later in the book to elements of married family life, including bearing and raising children, divorce and remarriage, work and families, and issues of power and abuse. To help prepare for those discussions, here I will describe some ways that marriage fits into the broader questions about modern identity introduced earlier. Then we will briefly investigate the benefits of marriage (and their limitations). In the final section, all of that will come together in a discussion of the political response to marriage decline and the debate over extending marriage rights to same-sex couples.

Marriage as a lifelong commitment to another person seems like a paradoxical ideal in a modern era defined by individualism. One explanation is that this contradiction is exactly *why* we have seen a decline in marriage and a rise in divorce—individualism and marriage don't mix. However, it's helpful to think that such a deep commitment to another person can still be a personal choice—an individual choice. Most people today do have more choice in their family lives than did people in the distant past (Klinenberg 2012). But perhaps as important, explaining this choice as a personal one has become expected of everyone (Beck and Lau 2005). To resolve the apparent paradox, then, think of it as a social expectation to strive for individual success at love (Lamont, Kaufman, and Moody 2000).

The expectation that we can explain love and commitment in individual terms appears in many contemporary romantic stories when one partner in a relationship demands to know *why* the other wants to get married or be together. This question was probably rarely asked before the 1960s, but today the answer—or failure to answer—can be a clear sign that the relationship is in trouble. Men have given good answers to variations on the question "Why do you love me?" in some movies, for example. In *Sweet Home Alabama*, the man's answer is, "So I can kiss you anytime I want." In *My Big Fat Greek Wedding*, he says, "Because I came alive when I met you." In the classic "I love you" speech delivered by Tom Cruise in *Jerry Maguire*, he explains, "You complete me." All of these answers—which the filmmakers clearly want us to see as the right ones—are completely self-centered, of course.

Many people pursue marriage for individualistic reasons—to fulfill their own goals, to raise children, to make themselves happy, and so on. In fact, maybe meeting those goals for both partners is just what makes a modern marriage successful. Consider what researcher Tera Hurt (2010) found when she interviewed 50 Black men about their marriages. The descriptions of what marriage meant to these men—80 percent of whom said that they were happy in their marriages—fit into four categories, each illustrated here by a comment from the interviews:

- *Lifelong commitment*. "Without my wife—I really don't know how to live without my wife. She has been there my whole life."

- *Success*. "I strongly believe that my wife is the key to my success. She keeps me grounded."

- *Emotional support*. "Friendship, meaning my wife is a person who I can sit down and talk with and would come to me and talk about things and we know it's between us."

- *Security*. "It means that you won't be lonely when you get old, for one thing, and you can live in the joy and the comfort of knowing that when you get old or dreaming that when you get old, you're going to have a friend."

These responses are mostly individualistic in that they are benefits for the men themselves. But they also imply mutuality. How could these men expect to continue receiving these benefits if they were not returning the favor to their wives? The theme of mutual support is one of several that run through studies of marriage's benefits and (less often) its costs—to which we now turn.

The Benefits of Marriage

A growing number of people—especially young women—have begun to publicly express the sacrifices that marriage entails. In her book *All the Single Ladies*, Rebecca Traister (2016) described her own path toward marriage:

> I saw more people every day when I was single than I do as a married person. I went out more, I talked on the phone with more people, knew more about other people's lives. I attended more baseball games and concerts; I spent more time at work, and certainly engaged more with colleagues and peers. When I met my husband, we turned in toward each other and our worlds got smaller.

Traister's research showed that this turning inward can make married people lonelier than being "single." And yet ultimately most people end up deciding that the benefits outweigh the costs, as Traister herself did.

People rarely explain their reasons for marriage by describing how it will save them money on rent or taxes or make them look good to their bosses at work or to their parents. And they don't usually say that they might need someone to help them get to the bathroom in the middle of the night when they are old and sick. But when sociologists study the benefits and costs of marriage, these are some of the issues they investigate. I will return to those bread-and-butter issues, but first, the not-so-simple question of happiness.

Happiness

There are two kinds of studies of marriage and happiness. The first kind asks whether people are in happy marriages—that is, whether the marriage is emotionally healthy. The second is about whether people who are married are emotionally happy in general. Naturally, these issues are linked.

With regard to happy marriages, the number of married people who tell the General Social Survey that their marriages are "very happy" has remained at just over 60 percent since the 1970s, with less than 5 percent choosing the worst option, "not too happy" (see Figure 8.9). It is perhaps surprising that marriages haven't grown even happier, because fewer people are married now, and it has become much easier (and more acceptable) to leave an unhappy marriage. So we might expect the *remaining* marriages to be happier. In fact, because marital satisfaction tends to decline over the life of a marriage, we might expect marriages to be getting happier simply because there are more short-term marriages now (Lavner and Bradbury 2010). However, the total numbers mask two important differences. First, Whites describe their marriages as happier than Blacks and others. Second, men say their marriages are happier than women do (Corra et al. 2009).

If you have ever been caught in the middle of a conflict between spouses, you probably won't be surprised to learn that men and women often describe the same marriages differently. In fact, many couples do have significant differences

Figure 8.9 Percentage describing their marriage as "very happy," 1973–2016

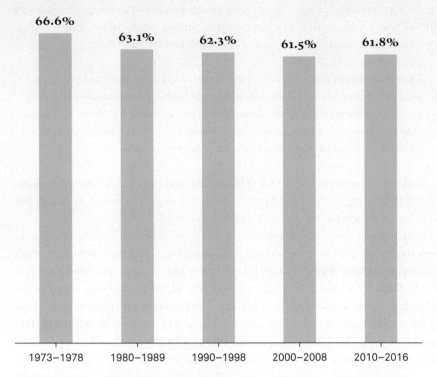

66.6%	63.1%	62.3%	61.5%	61.8%
1973–1978	1980–1989	1990–1998	2000–2008	2010–2016

The question was, "Taking all things together, how would you describe your marriage: very happy, pretty happy, or not too happy?"

SOURCE: Author's calculations from the General Social Surveys, 1972–2016 (Smith et al. 2016).

of opinion over how happy the marriage is—and it is usually the wife who has the more negative view (Schumm, Webb, and Bollman 1998). These gender differences fit with the longstanding view that marriage is more beneficial for men than for women, which led one sociologist to declare that every marriage is really two marriages—his and hers—that are often worlds apart (Bernard 1982). However, the differences overall are not as great as that statement implies. Probably more important is the simple fact that richer people are happier in their relationships, whether they are married or cohabiting, because they have less stress over economic insecurity (Hardie and Lucas 2010).

Unfortunately, we do not have comparable studies of gay and lesbian couples (Biblarz and Savci 2010). There have been some attempts to compare happiness and satisfaction in straight versus gay/lesbian couples (usually focusing on cohabiting rather than married couples). And the evidence so far suggests that cohabiting gays and lesbians are about as happy as cohabiting straight people (Wienke and Hill 2009). But these are mostly small studies that can reach only tentative conclusions (for example, Schumm, Akagi, and Bosch 2008). When we have enough information to make those comparisons, we might learn more about the nature of relationships between men and women as well.

With regard to the happiness of married people, there is enough research to say that, on average, married people are happier than those who are not married—and this applies to both men and women (Wienke and Hill 2009). However, there also are good reasons to suspect that happiness makes people get and stay married as much as marriage makes people happier. That is, happier people may be more attractive as marriage partners, better at developing relationships, and better at keeping the marriage from breaking up (Mastekaasa 1994). In fact, careful research that tracks people over time has shown that getting married does lead to greater happiness on average (H. K. Kim and McKenry 2002). An important caveat to these conclusions is that people in very unhappy marriages are usually not as happy as single people. We will return to the question of what makes relationships more happy or less happy when we discuss divorce in Chapter 10.

Health and Wealth

If happier people are more likely to get married, so are richer people, as we have seen in this chapter. So it is not surprising that married people—and married couples—have more income, more property, and more education than unmarried people. When we study the effect of one condition (such as marriage) on another (such as wealth), social scientists say there is a **selection effect** when the cause being studied has already been determined by the outcome that is under investigation. The best way to solve such puzzles is with longitudinal studies, to see the sequencing of events (see Chapter 1). Through such studies, we know that marriage does bring benefits to its participants, even though privileged people are more likely to marry in the first place. I see marriage benefits stemming from three sources: behavioral changes or responsibility, cooperation, and social status.

selection effect
The problem that occurs when the cause being studied has already been determined by the outcome that is under investigation.

Responsibility More than 100 years ago, Émile Durkheim (1897/1951) argued that married men were less likely to commit suicide because of their strong social ties and the people who depended on them (J. Smith, Mercy, and Conn 1988). Modern evidence confirms that married people have lower suicide rates than those who are not married (Luoma and Pearson 2002). In fact, married people are less likely to die from a variety of causes, even when we compare people at the same level of income and education (N. Johnson et al. 2000; Manzoli et al. 2007).

Most young adults see marriage as a sign of greater responsibility, which leads them to behave more cautiously (with less binge drinking and marijuana smoking, for example). The close presence of a spouse who depends on them (or keeps an eye on them) also encourages this development (Duncan, Wilkerson, and England 2006). In general, the productive routine, sense of responsibility, and obligations that people take on when they are married seem to promote healthier (and more lucrative) behavior (Umberson, Crosnoe, and Reczek 2010).

Cooperation Families can save money and effort by sharing their assets and abilities. Extra hands—and minds—working and living together can increase the efficiency of everything from paying rent and buying food to managing child-care arrangements and taking care of sick relatives. In economic theory, these benefits are maximized when the two spouses bring different skills and assets to the marriage (Becker 1981). For example, one of the reasons married men earn more than single men is that some of them have wives at home lightening their housework and child-care burdens, which economists call "specialization" (Bardasi and Taylor 2008). However, even though husbands and wives have grown more similar in terms of their skills and work behaviors, cooperation itself brings benefits. This surely contributes to the health advantage of married people noted earlier, as well as to differences in income and wealth accumulation. For example, 80 percent of married-couple households own (or are buying) their homes, compared with 63 percent of households in general (IPUMS-CPS 2016).

Status Although less tangible than health and wealth, social status is also a reward for marriage. For example, a classic study of professional workers concluded that married men received higher salaries because their managers thought they deserved to be paid more (Osterman 1979). This earnings advantage for married men persists today (Cheng 2016). The flip side of that is that even though married women—especially mothers—are celebrated by their peers and popular media, they may find that employers believe that they "deserve" lower wages (Correll, Benard, and Paik 2007). Even worse, some women who have not married feel a stigma from others in their social circles or a feeling of failure and loss that takes a toll on their happiness and even their mental health (Sharp and Ganong 2007).

Religion

One clear difference that sets married couples apart is their tendency to participate in religious observances and practices. Married people attend religious services more often than singles, as you can see in Figure 8.10. When husbands and wives share the same religious beliefs and attend religious services together, this tendency is associated with greater marital happiness. However, while religious beliefs remain common and strong among Americans, the institutional authority of religious leadership has declined. Even religious people are now more likely to pursue the individualistic goals of self-fulfillment and self-determination than they were in the past. The growing independence of spouses and especially the trend toward equality in men's and women's employment have weakened the traditional religious presence within marriage (Myers 2006).

It is perhaps no wonder that marriage is so advantageous. Why else would rich, healthy, well-educated, and powerful people be more likely to get married? However, should this be taken to mean that marriage is *inherently* good? Not necessarily. Rather, given our current society and its cultural expectations, marriage is a means to social advantage. Consider the findings from a study of 30 different countries. Overall, married people are happier and more satisfied with their lives than cohabitors, and both groups are happier than single people. However, the "marriage advantage" is smaller in countries where cohabitation is more common (Soons and Kalmijn 2009). If American society did not structure its rewards around the ideal of married family life, as we'll see in the next section, then perhaps the disadvantages of *not* being married would be reduced.

The Politics of Marriage

Marriage has not historically had a merely symbolic role in society. In her review of the place of marriage in many different cultures, Stephanie Coontz (2005) points out that whether, and to whom, people were married have determined everything from the "legitimacy" of children and the mutual obligations of husbands and wives to the orderly distribution of property from one generation to the next. In premodern Europe, marriage also served to bind families to the church, since Christian authorities regulated marriages. And in the United States, it brought families under the jurisdiction of the state. The historical decline of marriage, then, has brought about a lack of formal regulation over couple relationships.

Of course, in modern society, many aspects of individuals' lives—including things they are required to do (for example, care for their children) and are prohibited from doing (for example, commit violence)—are regulated outside the realm of legal marriage. And that is what makes marriage seem more symbolic now. But rather than cooling the debate, this symbolic character seems to heighten the emotions in the politics of marriage and its future.

In the sweep of history, some aspects of the decline of marriage clearly are beneficial. For most people, especially women, individual freedom has increased while repressive authority has weakened. Even married people are made more free by the loosening of restrictions on marriage and the right to divorce. Consider the practice of women taking their husband's family name, as most still do (Gooding and Kreider 2010). Few people realize it is a remnant of an older system

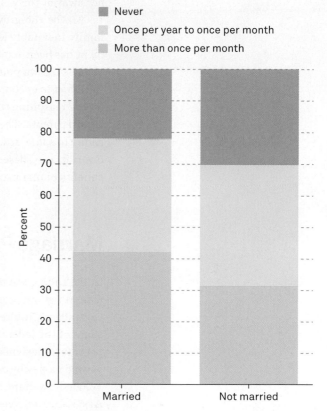

Figure 8.10 **How often adults attend religious services**

■ Never
■ Once per year to once per month
■ More than once per month

Married people attend religious services much more than unmarried people.

SOURCE: Author's calculations from the 2014 General Social Survey (Smith et al. 2016).

in which women became the property of their husband's family upon marriage. That legacy is still visible in the traditional practice of the bride's father "giving" her away at the wedding (Coontz 2005:76).

Maybe the growth of individual freedom in the institutional arena of the family inevitably led to fewer marriages or to more divorces. But this development has been—and remains—highly contentious. We conclude this chapter by discussing two political movements on behalf of marriage in society. The first is the effort to encourage marriage among poor people—especially parents—based on the reasoning that children benefit from the care of married, preferably biological parents. The second is the legal and political campaign to extend marriage rights to same-sex couples, which finally won a decisive victory at the Supreme Court in 2015, based on the demand for equal access to the symbolic and practical benefits of marriage for gay and lesbian couples.

Marriage Promotion

In the 1990s, the majority of legislators in the U.S. Congress believed that the federal welfare program in effect since the 1960s, known as Aid to Families with Dependent Children, was not working (Sidel 1998). Although it cost only a tiny share of the federal budget, conservative political activists had argued that the program—designed to help support families without breadwinner husbands—wasted money by essentially paying poor women to remain single (Murray 1984). When the welfare system was reformed in 1996, Congress created the Temporary Assistance to Needy Families (TANF) program. TANF established two major goals: to provide assistance to poor families (although less than in the past) and to "encourage the formation and maintenance of two-parent families" (Bush 2004).

With the Personal Responsibility and Work Opportunity Act of 1996, the federal government entered a new era of marriage promotion. TANF was designed to promote the well-being of children under the assumption that they would be better off living with married parents. The opening passage of the legislation declared, "Marriage is the foundation of a successful society" (P. Cohen 2014a). To further this goal, the law essentially gave poor mothers a stark choice: get a job or get married. Cash assistance was made temporary, and recipients were expected to have or seek a job. And, using funds from that welfare program, the federal government spent hundreds of millions of dollars—most of it distributed to state agencies and nonprofit groups—to encourage poor people to get married and to help them make their marriages more successful (Randles 2016).

For example, the Oklahoma Marriage Initiative received millions of federal dollars for "marriage and relationship training." It held thousands of workshops and counseling sessions and also trained people to repeat the training program elsewhere (Heath 2012). Supported in part by federal welfare grants, religious organizations, marriage counselors, and family advocates of various stripes have operated programs to promote and strengthen marriages (Nock 2005). Although they are not legally permitted to perform religious services with government money, religious organizations have used the federal grant program to pay for education programs that offer advice on "healthy" marriage habits such as, "Pray for your spouse, out loud, face-to-face, and holding hands," and, "A happy marriage is good, but it's more about holiness than happiness" (O'Brien 2015).

From the beginning, however, there were serious concerns about marriage promotion. First, some experts immediately were concerned that government money would be used to encourage people in abusive or unhealthy relationships to stay together, creating even greater harm than not marrying in the first place. The federal program showed its awareness of this concern by referring to itself as the *Healthy* Marriage Initiative, with the goal of "increasing the percentage of children who are raised by two parents in a *healthy* marriage" (emphasis added).

Second, because the "retreat from marriage" has been the result of widespread cultural, economic, and demographic changes, marriage experts were skeptical that the trend could be reversed by simply teaching individual behavior changes to poor people. This objection also reflects a basic concern that poverty and economic insecurity are the main problem for children, as these conditions deter marriage, rather than single parenthood creating poverty (Baker 2015). Critics argued that rather than promote marriage through training, counseling, and other programs championed by "family-values" conservatives, the federal government should pursue broader policies that help poor people earn a living wage, such as tax law changes, an increase in the minimum wage, and child-care support (Coontz and Folbre 2010).

Whether or not we like the idea of the federal government promoting marriage, it does not appear to have worked. For example, the federal Supporting Healthy Marriage project provided marriage education to low-income couples, through months of workshops, as well as educational and social events. Then they studied more than 6,000 couples, half of whom got the services and half did not. Careful evaluation of the results after 30 months revealed no difference at all between the two groups—those who received the services and those who did not—in terms of how many were still together (Lundquist et al. 2014). More broadly, in the 15 years after the national program began operating in every state, the percentage of young adults (ages 25 to 34) without college degrees who were married fell by 18 points, from 58 percent to 40 percent—much faster than it fell in the previous decade. Especially among those with less education and lower incomes, the retreat from marriage continues.

Marriage Rights

Meanwhile, the political movement for gay and lesbian rights was not retreating but rather advancing toward legal marriage. Before the 1970s, there was no major controversy over the gender of people getting married (Eskridge 1993). But in that decade, the gay population became more visible and, eventually, politically organized. The movement was energized by police crackdowns on gay bars (since homosexuality was illegal). The most famous occurred at New York City's

Stonewall Inn in 1969, which resulted in a riot as the bar's patrons fought back (Armstrong and Crage 2006).

In 1988, the General Social Survey asked U.S. adults whether they agreed with the statement, "Homosexual couples should have the right to marry one another." Seventy-three percent disagreed and only 12 percent agreed (the rest were unsure). But marriage was not a prominent issue in the gay rights movement until the 1990s. Originally, most members of the gay and lesbian community were not interested in marriage rights, and some feminists joined them, arguing that marriage is "so deeply flawed" as to be "unworthy of emulation" (Card 1996:2). But in 1993, President Bill Clinton allowed gay and lesbian recruits to join the U.S. military, as long as they held their sexual orientation secret, under the policy known as "don't ask, don't tell" (which was eventually repealed in 2010). The controversy that resulted, including major protest marches for gay rights, helped bring same-sex marriage as an issue to the fore (M. Warner 1999).

Ironically, opposition to gay rights became a bigger—and, for a long time, more successful—political movement. As public debate over the issue of marriage grew, many states specifically banned same-sex marriage, which had not been explicitly illegal before (Soule 2004). And at the federal level, Congress passed the Defense of Marriage Act in 1996 to ensure that if any states did legalize same-sex marriage, the federal government—including agencies such as Social Security and the Internal Revenue Service—would not recognize those marriages. In 2013, the U.S. Supreme Court overturned that statute and ordered the federal government to recognize same-sex marriages legally performed in the states. Then, in 2015, in the *Obergefell v. Hodges* case, the Supreme Court finally ordered all states to allow same-sex marriage (see Changing Law, "Same-Sex Marriage").

For some people—mostly political conservatives—the debate over marriage rights itself represents a sign that marriage is losing. Even if it means more people may get married, the new diversity represents a retreat from tradition. For those who support extending marriage rights, on the other hand, "marriage equality" has come to symbolize tolerance and acceptance of individual choices. The trend in public opinion is toward a growing majority in support of same-sex marriage, as shown in Figure 8.11 (Fetner 2016). Opposition is now concentrated among evangelical Christians and older political conservatives (Pew Research Center 2016b).

That brings us back to the symbolic importance of marriage with which we opened this chapter. Those who believe that marriage rights should be extended to gay and lesbian couples stress both the practicalities of inheritance, pensions, and taxes, on the one hand, and the priceless value of social acceptability on the other. And yet, I cannot help noticing that in the study of what Black men value about their marriages that I cited earlier (Hurt 2010), none of them mentioned the *recognition* of their relationship—either by the government or by their peers— as an important benefit of marriage. It is just that taken-for-granted nature of marriage that has come under scrutiny in recent years.

In the next chapter, we will move on to a set of issues that, if possible, are even more emotionally charged than the nature and decline of marriage: the parenting and well-being of children and the families in which they live.

Same-Sex Marriage

When I finished the first edition of this book in 2014, 17 states and the District of Columbia permitted same-sex marriage. On the other hand, 35 states had laws specifically *prohibiting* same-sex marriage (National Conference of State Legislatures 2013). In all, just 38 percent of the U.S. population lived in a state that permitted same-sex marriage. The change that followed over the next year was breathtaking, until at last, on June 26, 2015, the U.S. Supreme Court, in a deeply divided 5–4 decision, ruled that same-sex couples have a constitutional right to marriage (Liptak 2015). As a result, all states and the federal government now have to recognize the marriages (and divorces) of same-sex couples performed in any state, with all the rights, privileges, and responsibilities accorded to married people in state and federal laws.

The decision, known as *Obergefell v. Hodges* (2015), was the stunning culmination of a movement that changed the national landscape on the issue of gay and lesbian rights in what seemed like just a few short years.

The Legal Landscape

The federal government provides many benefits to married people. However, after the late nineteenth century, when the federal government intervened to regulate marriage among American Indians and Mormons (see Chapter 2), it has mostly been up to individual states to decide who is legally married. A crucial exception occurred when the U.S. Supreme Court ruled in *Loving v. Virginia* (1967) that state laws prohibiting interracial marriage were unconstitutional. Now again, as with interracial marriage in the 1960s, with same-sex marriage the federal courts faced a situation in which states could not agree on which marriages were legally recognized, and the right to equal treatment under the law was at stake.

Starting in 2004 some states had begun changing their laws to permit same-sex marriage. The first of these changes were made by state judges. Then several state legislatures voted to permit same-sex marriage. The federal court case *Perry v. Schwarzenegger* (2010), with which I opened this chapter, proved to be an important step in the legal march toward gay and lesbian marriage rights. The decision by the U.S. district court in that case overturned California's voter-approved ban on gay marriage. The judge writing the decision, Vaughn Walker, ruled that the state had no legitimate reason to deny marriage rights to couples of the same sex. Because the law no longer differentiates between the male and female partners in a marriage, he reasoned, the state could not justifiably require one partner to be male and the other female. Instead, given the benefits of marriage—both symbolic and practical—he determined that denying gays and lesbians access to those benefits was a form of discrimination that was not justified. (Some forms of discrimination are legally justified, such as denying blind people drivers' licenses or denying gun permits to convicted felons.) Subsequently, starting in 2012, a series of states passed same-sex marriage referendums by popular vote, representing the clearest expression of majority support for broadening marriage rights.

As the *Perry* case was making its way through the courts, eventually becoming the U.S. Supreme Court case known as *Hollingsworth v. Perry* (2013), so, too, was a case involving the federal government's Defense of Marriage Act, or DOMA. That law, passed by Congress in 1996 and signed by President Bill Clinton, forbade the federal government from recognizing the marriages of same-sex couples, even if they were legal in a specific state. And it released states from their obligation to recognize same-sex marriages performed in states that allow them. The federal aspect of that law—by which the government would not honor the marriages of some states in such policy areas as the tax code, Social Security, and military benefits—led to a U.S. Supreme Court challenge in the case *United States v. Windsor* (2013). The Supreme Court decided both cases in the summer of 2013, in the process almost, but not quite, creating a constitutional right to legal marriage regardless of sex.

In *United States v. Windsor*, Edith Windsor, who married her wife, Thea Spyer, in Canada in 1997 after a 40-year engagement, protested the federal government's refusal to recognize their marriage. The cost of that refusal was tangible: Windsor had to pay more than $600,000 in taxes when Spyer died (Applebome 2012). The estate would not have been taxed if Spyer or Windsor were male and the marriage was considered valid by the federal government. In the decision, Justice Anthony Kennedy wrote that denying legally married couples federal benefits harmed those couples without any justification. He declared that denying federal recognition to married couples created a system of "second-class marriages" for no other reason than to "impose inequality," that it "humiliated tens of thousands of children now being raised by same-sex couples," and "made it even more difficult for the children to understand the integrity and closeness of their own family and its concord with other families in their community and in their daily lives." At the same time, the U.S. Supreme Court let stand Judge Walker's decision allowing same-sex marriage in California.

The result of the two court cases—and the successful state marriage referendums—was to shift the national balance in favor of same-sex marriage. The court did not go so far as to overturn the state bans on same-sex marriage that remained in effect. But by the end of 2013 a federal judge—using the precedent set in the *Windsor* decision—overturned the state of Utah's ban on same-sex marriage, which had been approved by the conservative majority of its voters (Eckholm 2013), and a series of similar decisions followed.

After a string of decisions consistent with *Windsor*, however, by early 2014 one of the federal appeals courts had ruled that a ban on same-sex marriage *was*

President Obama welcomed the Obergefell decision, granting same-sex couples the right to marry in all 50 states, by lighting up the White House in rainbow colors.

constitutional. In that case, James Obergefell sought to be named the surviving spouse after his husband, John Arthur, died. The couple had been married in Maryland, but Ohio refused to recognize their marriage because of the state's same-sex marriage ban. With one federal court contradicting the others, that provided the conflict necessary for the Supreme Court yet again to intervene. The result was the *Obergefell* case decided in June 2015.

By the time of the Supreme Court decision on June 26, President Barack Obama—who had only three years earlier officially become a same-sex marriage supporter—said the decision marked one of those moments when "justice arrives like a thunderbolt." The Supreme Court, he said, had "reaffirmed that all Americans are entitled to equal protection of the law, that all people should be treated equally, regardless of who they are, or who they love" (Associated Press 2015). And that night the White House was bathed in rainbow lights—the unofficial colors of the gay rights movement.

What Marriage Means

The *Obergefell* case illustrates both the legal and symbolic importance of marriage, with which I opened this chapter. Legally, the case broadened the definition of liberty and equality, those treasured qualities defended by the U.S. Constitution (Chemerinsky 2015). In the case, the Supreme Court had to decide whether those states that prohibited same-sex couples from marrying were denying gays and lesbians equal protection under the law. The Court had established in previous cases that the right to marriage is a fundamental right, even though it is not specifically listed in the Constitution. That's why, for example, they ruled in *Loving v. Virginia* (1967) that the ban on interracial marriage was unconstitutional. But the question remained whether denying same-sex marriage was a reasonable restriction on that right. The argument for restricting marriage to man-woman couples was that marriage exists to support procreation and child-rearing in stable families. But the Court, with Anthony Kennedy again writing for the majority, determined that this doesn't justify excluding same-sex couples from the institution. Crucially, many man-woman couples cannot (or choose not to) have children, and many same-sex couples have children (through assisted reproductive technology or adoption) whether they are legally married or not—so procreation is not a defining element of legal marriage.

Symbolically, the *Obergefell* case—and the entire marriage equality movement—represents the deepening social recognition of family diversity. Just as the acceptance of divorce and remarriage, cohabitation and single parenthood all reflect the inclusion of more diverse family structures and practices within the mainstream, the legal victory for same-sex marriage rights stands as a symbol of social change in the family arena. That is why passions were so high on both sides of the case: The future definition of the family appeared to be at stake (we return to this debate in Chapter 13).

The Court was lifted by very favorable political winds. In 2010, when the case that opened this chapter, *Perry v. Schwarzenegger* (2010), was decided, more Americans opposed legal same-sex marriage than supported it. By 2015, 55 percent favored permitting gay and lesbian marriage, 16 points higher than the 39 percent who remain opposed (see Figure 8.11). In fact, one of the judges who opposed the *Obergefell* decision, Chief Justice John Roberts, argued that the

Court should stay out of the way and let the movement wage the struggle for equality in state legislatures and elections, where they seemed likely to prevail eventually.

But every day that same-sex couples were denied the right to marriage, the Court majority argued, was an unacceptable burden on their rights as Americans. Not only were gay and lesbian couples (and, especially, their children) denied the symbolic legitimacy of having their families recognized by the state, they were also denied the practical protections and support that the state grants through the recognition of marriage. Gay and lesbian couples were not truly free—free to move from state to state, to protect their children as married couples could, even to have legal protection in their divorces—as long as their second-class status was enforced with regard to marriage. In the end, legal scholar Erwin Chemerinsky (2015) wrote, June 26, 2015, will be remembered as a "historic step forward in advancing liberty and equality . . . an important advance to creating a more equal society."

The conflict over same-sex marriage in the United States is part of a global debate. As of 2017, same-sex marriage is legal in 22 countries, including the United States, the largest of which are Brazil, France, England, South Africa, Spain, and Argentina. Along with the United States, these countries have a population of about 1 billion, or just 15 percent of the world's population.

Figure 8.11 **Support and opposition to same-sex marriage, 2001–2016**

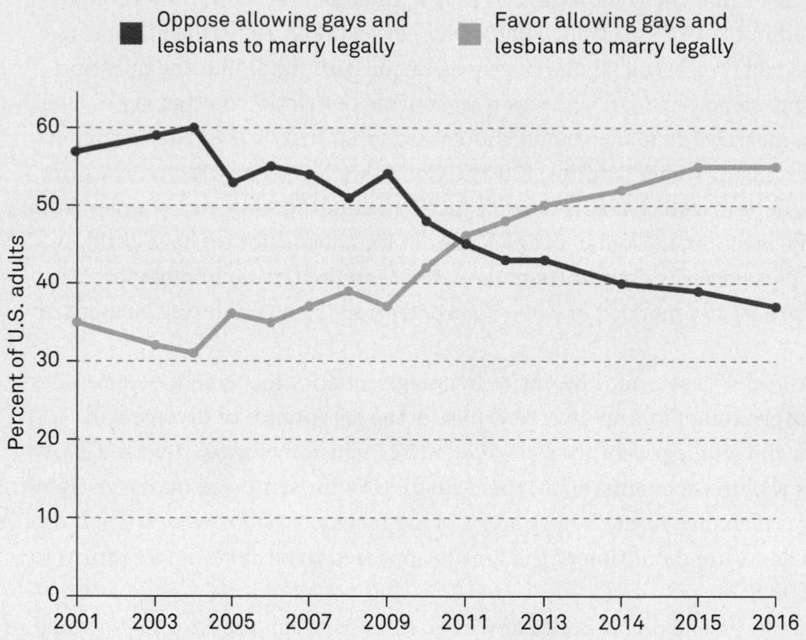

■ Oppose allowing gays and lesbians to marry legally   ▓ Favor allowing gays and lesbians to marry legally

Since 2012, the majority of people in a national survey have expressed support for legal same-sex marriage.

SOURCE: Pew Research Center (2016b).

Trend to Watch: Cohabitation

When I first started out doing demography, one of my first tasks was to figure out how many cohabiting couples there were in the United States—a question the government was just beginning to ask (Casper and Cohen 2000). Now, as we have seen, cohabitation has become much more acceptable. And the United States is not alone. In the socially progressive countries of Scandinavia (Sweden, Norway, Finland, and Denmark), more than one in four couples that live together are not married, and those relationships are often very similar to marriages (Noack et al. 2013). In some parts of Latin America cohabitation is more common than marriage (Esteve et al. 2016). But what this means for the future of family life is not clear.

Consider two possible futures. First, it may be that the continued decline of marriage leads to a gradual erosion of long-term, committed relationships. In that case, even if cohabitation becomes more common, it may take place in a society that increasingly doesn't expect permanent couple bonding, including for couples with children. In this scenario, the large number of couples cohabiting tells us the same thing that we learn from the falling number of people that are married: Individualism and individual autonomy are replacing strong couple commitments, for better or worse.

On the other hand, maybe cohabitation will increasingly replace marriage, representing a new system of commitment, one that doesn't rely on legal attachment or traditional ceremonies. In this second scenario, people continue to pair up in long-term couples, especially when they have children, but they do so without legal or religious regulation and authority. Maybe such relationships would not be as long lasting as marriages were in the old days, but they might still bring predictability and stable attachments to family life. Which scenario comes to pass—or whether something else emerges altogether—will depend on a combination of social and economic forces we cannot yet foresee.

YouTube Wedding

As I write this exercise, within the last 16 minutes, someone uploaded a wedding video on YouTube, showing the climactic moment of an orthodox Jewish wedding—when the groom slides the ring on the bride's finger, repeating the words of a Hebrew blessing. The next speaker addresses the couple, telling them that their parents and grandparents are proud of them and that their ancestors, too, should be honored: "The rabbis tell us that all of your ancestors are here together with you both." Hundreds of people are there. Another couple, a young man and woman, just posted a simple "wedding slideshow," showing themselves in various casual settings—at a park, on a beach, fishing, on vacation—set to a song called "I Love You." An hour earlier, someone uploaded "Camilla & Sarah's Lesbian Wedding." There are millions of videos with the word "wedding" in the descriptions.

For this workshop, you can work in groups or individually. Using YouTube or another public video website, choose the video of a noncelebrity—someone you don't know—and watch at least 10 minutes of it. On YouTube, you can search for "wedding" or particular variations, such as "Maui wedding," and then sort your results by upload date to see the latest video to appear. Or just browse for something interesting.

What can you learn about the couple, their families, and their family ideals from the wedding and the way it is presented? Consider:

- *Wedding size:* How many people are there?

- *Cost:* Is it in an expensive venue or casual? Can you see other indicators, such as flowers, a band, or bridal party outfits? Is the video professionally produced?

- *Family:* What family members are present or featured? Do children, parents, grandparents, siblings, or others have central roles?

- *Traditions:* Does the wedding follow a dominant tradition with which you are familiar? Or is it a mix of traditions? Or nontraditional? How can you tell?

In small groups, class discussion, or individual writing, share your interpretation of the video you watched. Consider the major themes of this chapter: diversity and inequality, who gets married, who marries whom, modern relationships, and the politics of marriage. Does the video you watched add to or challenge any of the themes presented here?

Questions for Review

1. What have been some of the major trends in marriage rates in the last 50 years?

2. What is the wedding industrial complex? What purpose does it have in society?

3. Explain the paradox of people with higher incomes marrying more than people with lower incomes.

4. What are various reasons for the lower Black rates of marriage?

5. Why do many sociologists critique Gary Becker's idea of the marriage market?

6. Why might there be a selection effect when studying the effects of marriage on wealth?

7. What factors affect a couple's decision to cohabitate or marry?

8. Explain why a manager might believe a married man should get paid more than a single man or married woman.

9 Families and Children

In Chapter 6, we saw celebrity Ellen DeGeneres make her sexual orientation part of her public image on national TV. Later, Ellen married the actress Portia de Rossi. As a married couple, it might seem obvious that the two had become a family. Rossi even legally changed her last name to DeGeneres. And yet when rumors spread that they were going to have a child, the headlines were all about whether they were ready to "start a family" (Berman 2009). And that's not just because they're a lesbian couple; the phrase "start a family" is commonly used to refer to couples that are having a first child. The often unspoken assumption is that childless couples somehow add up to less than a family.

As we learned in Chapter 1, Americans have long debated which biological, legal, and emotional connections create families. That debate has intensified as family patterns have become more diverse. Most of the concern focuses on whether *other* people's situations really count as families. For example, it might seem obvious to the people involved that "two women living together as a couple with one or more of their children" constitute a family. But when that description was read to Americans in a national survey, only 55 percent of respondents agreed that such a group should be considered a family (Powell et al. 2010). The persistence of the common euphemism "start a family" shows that children are a vital part of the cultural image of family life. But the fact that a lesbian couple with children might not be considered a family shows that the context in which families raise children is also part of that popular image.

Another example helps illustrate the way that having children completes the picture of a family for so many people. In an interview with researcher Diana Parry (2005:281), a woman named Heidi explained why she and her longtime boyfriend got married only after they decided to have children: "We probably wouldn't have gotten married if we hadn't decided to have kids. We had a great relationship, we'd been together for six years, we had owned a house together

Do you consider Specialist Alexis Hutchinson and her son, Kamani, a family? Her childcare plans fell through just before deployment, and she chose her son over her military commitment, for which the Army arrested and later discharged her.

for three years, everything was going fine and there was no real reason to make that next step except kids." Before having children, in other words, Heidi and her boyfriend were not a family, even though they lived together for years in a committed relationship. But having children called for a more complete family identity, one that included marriage.

In this chapter, we will investigate who has children and who doesn't as well as how the children are raised, or—as many Americans now might say—how they are "parented."

Childbearing

A glance at national statistics tells us that most American families have one to three children, with two being the most common. This is much lower than in the distant past, as family sizes declined for most of the twentieth century. (The exception was the baby boom period of 1946–1964, when most families had three or four children; see Chapter 2.) But that simple history glosses over a vast and growing diversity of family experiences. In the last few decades, several changes in particular have complicated this picture. Probably most important, more children now are born to parents who are not married. In 2015, 40 percent of births were to unmarried women (J. Martin et al. 2017). The trend toward single motherhood is commonly recognized, but some other recent changes are less so:

- Half of the women who aren't married when they have their first child are actually living together (cohabiting) with a male partner (U.S. Census Bureau 2015b).

- While fewer parents are married now than in the past, that doesn't mean children always have fewer parents. Many children are involved with *more* than two parents. That is because a growing number of families include stepparents and siblings from parents' previous relationships. In fact, among parents with two or more children, one in five have had children with two partners or more (Monte 2017).

- The number of women reaching age 45 without having any children has doubled since the 1980s. And because more families are having their first children at older ages, there are more adults—singles and couples—spending much of their lives without children (Abma and Martinez 2006).

Each of these facts suggests that the organization of American family life is changing markedly in ways that increase the diversity of family experiences (Smock and Greenland 2010). For those who have children, the structure of their families and the relationships around them reflect a broadening range of practices. And the growth of childless families—and families with fewer children, born later—has moved children out of the center of family life, at least for some adults.

Before we delve into these patterns, we will need to establish some terms and concepts for the study of families and children. I will use the informal expression "have children" to mean either biologically producing or adopting children. When someone "has" a child in either of these ways, he or she becomes a **parent**, an adult intimately responsible for the care and rearing of a child. We may identify **biological parents** as the adults whose bodies produce a child, including the father's sperm and the mother's egg. (If a different woman carries the fetus to term before it is born, as in the case of surrogate parenting, she is not considered a biological parent.) **Adoptive parents**, on the other hand, are parents to a child they did not produce biologically. In the United States today, adoption is usually a legal arrangement, with rights and obligations enforced by government authorities; but it may be informal as well, as with some stepparents or partners of a biological parent.

You may notice that this definition of parents is not restricted to a mother-father couple; in fact, it does not include either a specific number of parents or their genders. In many families, the parenting roles are more fluid than that, especially when the law does not set the rules, as in the case of same-sex parents in some places (which is one reason many same-sex couples tried so hard to make their marriages legal). The most common example of this ambiguity occurs in the case of stepparents interacting with biological parents and their children—the "blended family" situation to which we will return in Chapter 10. And it is even more complicated when the adults involved are not married but have only informal relationships (Edin, Tach, and Mincy 2009).

Individuals who are able to produce children biologically are commonly described as "fertile" (as opposed to those who experience infertility). But when I speak of **fertility**, I use it in the sense of the number of children born in a society or among a particular group. There are several ways of quantifying fertility, which we need not describe in detail here (Weeks 2011). When possible, I use a number that is simple to grasp: the **total fertility rate**, which is the number of children born to the average woman in her lifetime. For example, the U.S. total fertility rate in 2016 was 1.82. That means that the average woman would have almost two children over the course of her reproductive years if birth rates stayed the same.

Fertility rates are generally measured for women—mothers—rather than men because the information comes from birth certificates, which do not always specify the father (even though fathers remain legally responsible as parents). This social science custom is unfortunate because it neglects the importance of fathers (Guzzo and Furstenberg 2007).

Besides being relatively easy to understand, the total fertility rate is also useful for thinking about populations as a whole, such as countries or ethnic groups. If a country has a total fertility rate of more than 2.1 or so, the population will usually grow; if the rate is lower than that, it will eventually start to shrink. That is because if each woman bears two children, they "replace" herself and her partner in the population. Because some people don't survive to produce children, demographers refer to a total fertility rate of about 2.1—rather than exactly 2.0—as "replacement fertility" (in places where death rates at young ages are higher, more births are needed for "replacement" [Preston, Heuveline, and Guillot 2000]).

As mentioned earlier, the most common number of children for American

parent

An adult intimately responsible for the care and rearing of a child.

biological parents

The adults whose bodies—including the father's sperm and the mother's egg—produce a child.

adoptive parents

Parents to a child they did not produce biologically.

fertility

The number of children born in a society or among a particular group.

total fertility rate

The number of children born to the average woman in her lifetime.

Figure 9.1 Number of children born by the time a woman reaches age 45

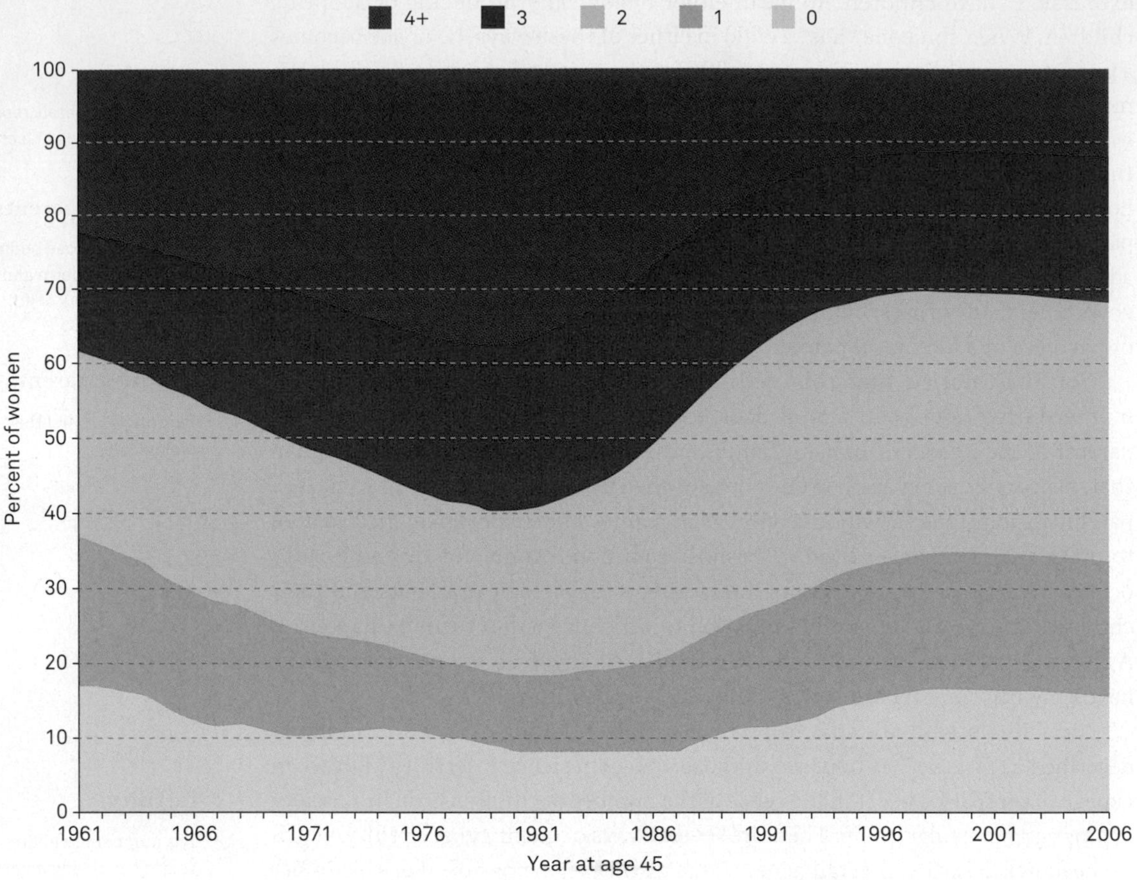

SOURCE: National Center for Health Statistics (2010).

women to have is currently two; as Figure 9.1 shows, about one-third of women have borne two children by the time they turn 45 years old. Still, one-third have had three or more children and one-third have had only one or none by the time they turn 45. And as recently as the 1980s, as the parents of the baby boom were reaching the end of their childbearing years, the most common number of children was four. More than a third of baby boom mothers had four children each. By 2006, only about 12 percent of women turning 45 had that number of children. In the remainder of this section, I will discuss some recent patterns of childbearing relating to marital status, race/ethnicity, education, and economic trends.

Unmarried Parents

As noted earlier, 40 percent of all children born in the United States are born to parents who aren't married, up from 28 percent in 1990 (see Figure 9.2). This trend is closely related to the decline of marriage that we observed in Chapter 8. That is, since the 1980s, marriage has declined more than childbearing, causing an increase in the number of unmarried parents. However, within this trend, there are people who become single parents in different ways:

- Young adults, either alone or with a partner they are not ready or willing to marry. These families are more likely to be poor than most other families (McKeever and Wolfinger 2011).

- Older women who are single—by chance or by choice—who decide to have children as single parents even though they might have preferred to be married first. Rather than wait for a marriage that might not occur, they adopt a child, use a sperm donor, or get pregnant with a man they're not planning to parent with (maybe even a man they live with). These families are less likely to be poor (Hertz 2006).

- Divorced people who have not remarried. One in eight women over 40 who have a baby are separated or divorced. Some of these new mothers are living with a partner they will eventually marry, but for some the divorce experience and the complications of the previous marriage are holding them back (S. Brown 2000).

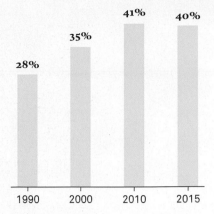

Figure 9.2 **Percentage of births to unmarried women**

SOURCE: U.S. Census Bureau (2011d); J. Martin et al. (2017).

Race and Ethnicity

We saw in Chapter 3 that single parenthood is much more common in some groups than in others. This is especially true among American Indian, Black, and Puerto Rican families, for whom more than half of all children are born to parents who are not married. However, there also are differences in how many children members of the major racial and ethnic groups have, as Figure 9.3 shows. The total fertility rates indicate that Latina women on average have 2.1 children, African Americans have 1.9, while Whites, Asians, and American Indians have the fewest.

The relatively high fertility rate among Latinos partly explains the growth of their population in the country as a whole, although immigration has played a major role as well (see Chapter 3). There are several reasons for this pattern (Landale and Oropesa 2007). First, most Latinos are descended from relatively recent immigrants—people who came from Latin American countries where fertility rates are higher than they are here. In their communities, having more children is a cultural expectation, and it's encouraged by the Catholic Church (Cutright, Hout, and Johnson 1976). (Catholic authorities actually prohibit the use of birth control, and although most Catholics today do not follow that rule, they still tend to have more children than average.) Not surprisingly, therefore, first-generation immigrants tend to have more children than those whose families immigrated in earlier generations. Second, groups with lower levels of education, such as Latinos, usually have higher fertility rates. And third, the

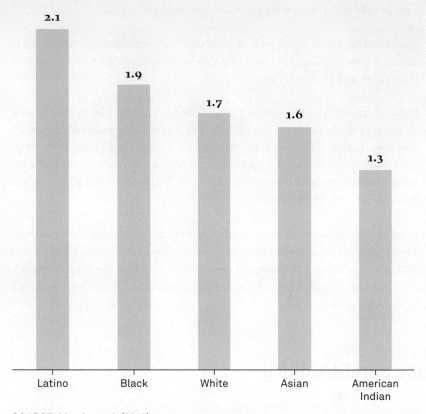

Figure 9.3 **Total fertility rates, by race/ethnicity: expected lifetime births per woman, 2015**

SOURCE: Martin et al. (2015).

immigrant Latino population includes many young, healthy adults—those who were most ready and able to move to a new country in search of better employment opportunities—who also tend to have large families.

Education

The long-standing pattern, not just in the United States but around the world, is that women with lower levels of education have more children (Kravdal and Rindfuss 2008). If you check the number of children for women in their 40s, when most are done with childbearing, the difference is substantial. Women who did not finish high school have an average of 2.8 children, compared with 1.8 or fewer among those with bachelor's degrees (see Figure 9.4). This is partly because some women stop their education after they have children—whether out of choice or necessity—while others postpone childbearing until they have finished school. As a result, those with higher education have children later in life (when they have fewer remaining childbearing years), while those with less education start having children younger and end up having more. Perhaps more important, however, once they have higher education, women face the prospect of giving up higher incomes and career status if they decide to have more children. This is known as an **opportunity cost,** the price one pays for choosing the less lucrative of the available options. In contrast, those whose lives are more devoted to child rearing in young adulthood—rather than advanced education—have less to lose (financially, at least) by having additional children.

However, careful planning is not always the rule. Almost half of all pregnancies are identified as "unintended," meaning the woman was not trying to get pregnant at the time, though she may have wanted to at some later time (Finer and Zolna 2016). An especially large portion of births among people with less education are unintended (England 2016). In fact, if we only count those women who had children only when they fully intended to, the education differences in the number of children mostly disappear (Musick et al. 2009). The high frequency of unintended births, especially among women or couples with less education or economic resources, partly results from their lack of access to good quality medical care, including effective contraception and health education.

opportunity cost

The price one pays for choosing the less lucrative of the available options.

Figure 9.4 **Average number of children ever born to women ages 40 to 44, by educational level, 2014**

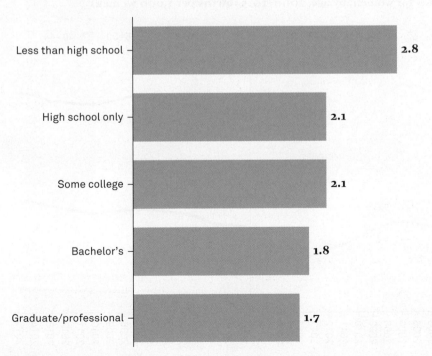

SOURCE: U.S. Census Bureau (2015c).

Economic Trends

Even though decisions about childbearing aren't perfectly planned, when we step back and look at larger trends we can see that childbearing patterns do show people responding to their economic conditions (Schneider and Hastings 2015). Clear evidence of conscious birth planning emerged during the recession of the late 2000s, when birth rates fell sharply for women under age 30 but rose for those who were older (see Figure 9.5). The trend toward having children at older ages was already underway in 2007, when the Great Recession began, but the economic shock accelerated the trend. As millions of people lost jobs, lost their homes—or faced profound economic uncertainty as such misfortunes befell their neighbors and coworkers—it appears that many younger people deliberately postponed having children. On the other hand, women who were nearing the end of their childbearing years had no such luxury, deciding to have children even though it might mean difficult economic sacrifices. However, the decision to put off having children, or having more children, will probably lead to fewer children eventually being born as a result of the recession, as some people lose the opportunity or end up permanently changing their plans (Currie and Schwandt 2014).

We cannot conclude from this recent history that hard economic conditions always lead to lower birth rates. Of course, in the long run rising standards of living have brought about lower birth rates, as we saw in Chapter 2. And it is still

Figure 9.5 **Birth rates for women, by age, 2000–2015 (births per 1,000 women)**

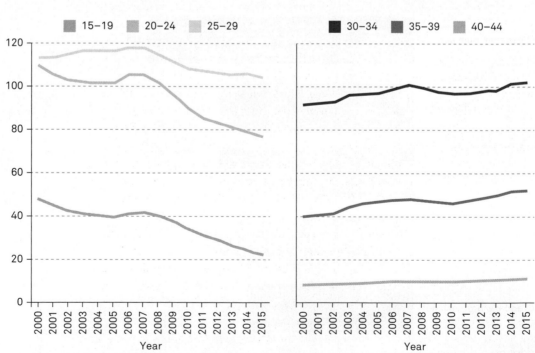

SOURCE: Martin, Hamilton, Osterman, et al. (2015).

the case that richer societies have lower birth rates than poor ones (Bongaarts 2015). But sudden threats to living standards, which make people uncertain about their plans and undermine their confidence in future economic gains, seem to lead families to postpone, or even forgo, having children.

Adoption

Half a century ago, most adoptions were secretive. Private agencies tried to match adoptive parents with children who were as similar to them as possible—especially racially. And children with medical or developmental problems were almost always shunned in the process (Herman 2008). Most parents did not want their adopted children to know of their origins, and there was little or no contact between the adoptive family and the birth family (usually a single mother). Since then, adoption has become much less common, but it is so much more open and acceptable that we probably discuss it more (Fisher 2003).

The main reason adoption became less common after the 1960s is the falling number of babies relinquished by birth parents. Because the stigma associated with unmarried motherhood has declined, unmarried young women are more willing and able to parent their own children. At the same time, with the growing availability of birth control (discussed in Chapter 6) and the legality of abortion, those women who are not willing or able to be parents are less likely to bear children. And fertility treatments offer an alternative to more parents who can't conceive on their own. Currently, only 2 percent of U.S. children—about 1.5 million—live in adoptive families.

On the other hand, adoptions have become much more open. This is partly because there are more interracial adoptive families—mostly White parents adopting children internationally or minority children from the United States—and these families are easily recognizable. The attention to these highly visible families, who also tend to be richer than average, sometimes obscures same-race adoptive families, such as Black parents adopting Black children, who are generally less wealthy (Kreider and Raleigh 2017).

Almost all adopted children now know that they live in an adoptive family. And most adoptions today include an agreement to put the children in touch with their birth family at some point (Vandivere, Malm, and Radel 2009). Research shows that by the time they reach adolescence, the great majority of adopted children say they are glad they got to know their birth parents. Child development experts believe that this is helpful for their sense of identity and security. One teenager's story illustrates how such "open" adoptions have helped reduce the stigma of adoption: "I remember in, like fifth grade, this one girl was like, 'I feel so sorry for you because your parents, like, gave you up,' and I'm just like, 'You know it's not like that. I've met my birthmother and know the whole story, and she loved me and still does and did me a favor letting me be raised, you know, in a better situation'" (Berge et al. 2006:1024).

Adopted children today can be divided into three categories (Raleigh 2016).

A national survey in the mid-2000s found that 37 percent of adopted children were adopted through the foster care system, which provides temporary care of children whose parents or other family members are unable to care for them. Another 38 percent were born in the United States and adopted through private services, usually as newborns. Finally, 25 percent were internationally adopted—that is, born in other countries and adopted by American parents (Vandivere, Malm, and Radel 2009). Children adopted through private services, rather than internationally or through the foster care system, are most likely to have contact with their birth parents (Brodzinsky and Goldberg 2016).

International adoption is a complicated and sometimes contentious issue. And it has a high public profile, partly due to adoptions by celebrities such as Madonna and Angelina Jolie. But these adoptions also attract attention because they usually create multiracial families, which are easily noticeable in the American social environment (Kreider 2007). From the early 1990s to the mid-2000s, it appeared that there was an ever-increasing flow of children adopted into the United States to be the children of American parents. At the peak in 2004, when almost 23,000 children were adopted abroad, the largest numbers were coming from China, Russia, South Korea, and Guatemala (see Figure 9.6). However, since that time the number has dropped dramatically, as the flow of children from each of those countries shrank. The decline was part of a worldwide trend in which international adoption was more closely scrutinized for ethical and legal

Figure 9.6 **Children adopted into the United States from other countries, 1990–2015**

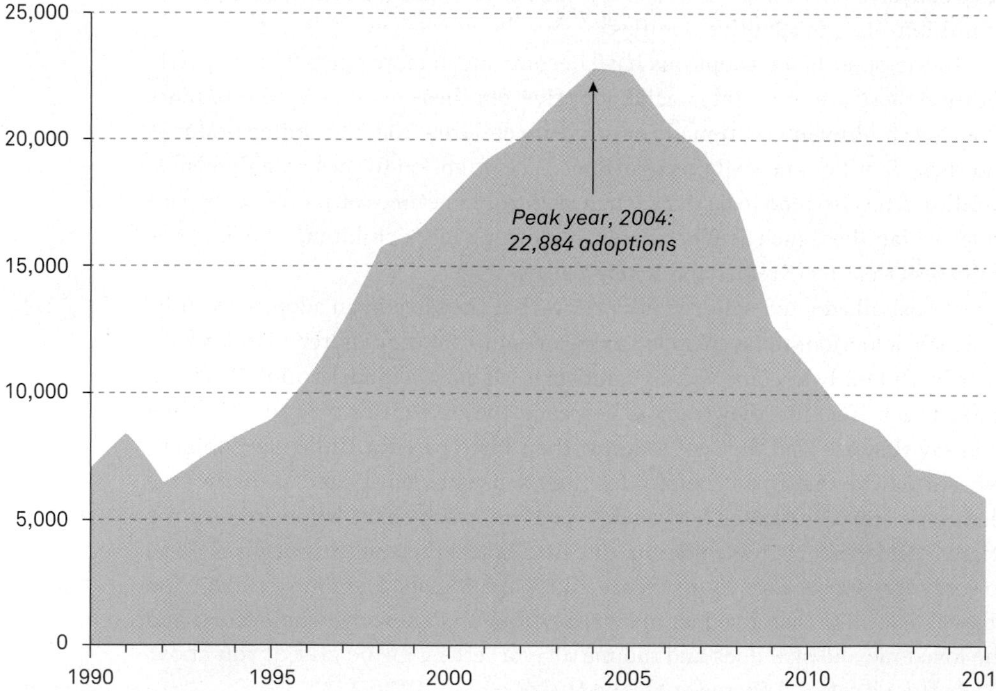

Peak year, 2004:
22,884 adoptions

SOURCE: U.S. Department of State (2016b).

violations. In the case of Guatemala, for example, adoptions to the United States were halted entirely when the U.S. government decided that the legal system in that country was not adequately safeguarding the poor women and their children who were entering the system.

To facilitate the complicated legal relationships involved in international adoptions, many countries, including the United States, have joined the Hague Adoption Convention (Bureau of Consular Affairs 2014). The convention is an international agreement that seeks to facilitate adoptions in the best interests of children who need families. One of its goals is to ensure that efforts are made to find adoptive families in a child's home country before placing the child into an international adoption. And it attempts to strengthen protections against the sale or trafficking of children. In fact, one consequence of this international effort appears to be a decline in the number of international adoptions, but advocates hope it will also improve adoption practices around the world.

Although adoption generally has become more open and less stigmatized, most couples experiencing infertility do not try to adopt children. That suggests that they do not consider adoption as valuable or rewarding as having a child through infertility treatments or deciding not to have children at all (Fisher 2003). On the other hand, research shows that those parents who do adopt make unusually large investments in their children's well-being, in terms of both time and money, even after accounting for their relatively high levels of economic resources (Hamilton, Cheng, and Powell 2007).

Why (Not) Have Children?

It would be useful to be able to characterize neatly the reasons people have children. Unfortunately, parents and potential parents are usually quite vague in their explanations. Consider Jack, a White 33-year-old who was living with his girlfriend when she became pregnant (Augustine, Nelson, and Edin 2009:110). Age 19 at the time, he remembered: "I was young, but I was ready. I thought I was okay, 'Let's start this family.' I was excited. I was a little scared. I loved her. She was my best friend. We could do this together."

Among the poor people interviewed in that study, the majority of pregnancies were not planned, but not completely unexpected either. More than having a reason *to* have children, they lacked the motivation to *prevent* it. In hindsight, however, the event takes on the full meaning of a life story. A 48-year-old Puerto Rican named Carlos said, "If I didn't have kids right now, I probably would have been dead. I have friends that died from overdoses of drugs, AIDS, alcoholic seizures and all kinds of stuff and most of those guys were those that didn't have children and I would have ended up like one of them, like a bachelor type guy with no kids and a heavy kind of addiction problem and dead by now" (Augustine, Nelson, and Edin 2009:110).

Before the development of a social safety net for old people—pensions, Social Security, and government-subsidized health care for the elderly—having children was an important part of most people's long-term survival plan. Even after children's labor stopped being a prime motivation for fertility, which was mostly the case in agricultural settings, parents hoped that their adult children would care for them in their retiring years. Now, however, raising children is a major expense, an investment that is expected to pay off not so much economically as emotionally and symbolically (Schoen et al. 1997).

Among the well-off, parents hope that their children will be a source of pride and achievement, bringing them happiness and satisfaction—and maybe showing off the family's successes to the wider community. And among the poor, having children serves as an important source of meaning and accomplishment that is not possible through economic means. In a stressful, unstable world of economic uncertainty, many poor people—especially women—hope that their children will provide a loving center to their lives (Edin and Kefalas 2005).

On the other hand, there are plenty of good reasons why people *don't* have children. In some cases, this reflects a deliberate choice on the part of the couple. In other cases, the decision is forced on them by circumstances or by nature. But whether voluntary or involuntary, the decision not to have children can be as life changing as the decision to "start a family."

Abortion

Approximately 900,000 abortions were performed in the United States in 2014, each reflecting the decision of a woman (and perhaps her partner) who was not ready, willing, or able to bear a child at the time of her pregnancy (Jones and Jerman 2017). This represents 19 percent of pregnancies (not including those that end in miscarriage). The vast majority of these abortions (92 percent) take place in the first three months, or trimester, of pregnancy (Jatlaoui et al. 2016). The reasons for terminating a pregnancy may be as complicated as those for having a baby. Sometimes, the pregnancy must be terminated for medical reasons related to either the fetus or the mother. But the most common reasons offered refer to time and resource constraints, such as the need to finish school, the costs of caring for a child, or the need to care for other family members, including older children (Finer et al. 2005). As noted in Chapter 5, there are some sex-selecting abortions in the United States, but this practice remains quite rare in this country.

Not surprisingly, the groups of women more likely to have unintended pregnancies—single (or cohabiting) women, those with low incomes or education, and Black women—are also more likely to have abortions (Jerman, Jones, and Onda 2016). The breakdown of birth and abortion rates by marital status clearly shows the difference in abortions (see Figure 9.7). Among women ages 15–44 in 2014, those who weren't married were less than half as likely to have a birth as married women, but about four times as likely to have an abortion.

Despite the Supreme Court's ruling, in the 1973 case known as *Roe v. Wade*, that a woman's right to abortion is protected as a private decision under the Constitution, the issue remains a divisive one in American politics (Luker 1984).

Figure 9.7 Birth and abortion rate (per 1,000 women), by marital status

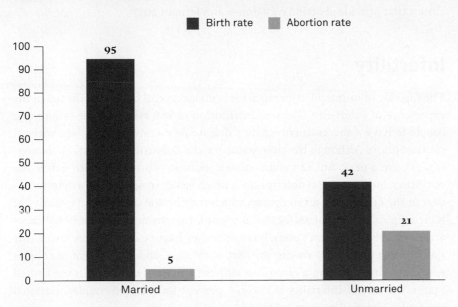

■ Birth rate ■ Abortion rate

SOURCE: Author calculations from 2014 National Center for Health Statistics and Guttmacher Institute data; includes women ages 15–44.

The Gallup poll, which since the early 1990s has been asking Americans whether they consider themselves "pro-choice" (in favor of abortion rights) or "pro-life," shows the population evenly split. That reflects a slight shift against abortion rights over the last decade. However, only 19 percent agree with the statement that abortion should be "illegal under all circumstances" (Gallup 2017b).

With the right to abortion protected at the federal level by the courts, opposition has taken a variety of forms (McBride 2008). Rather than challenge the Supreme Court's decision directly, opponents have worked successfully to prohibit the government from spending public money on abortions for poor women and to restrict the practice as much as possible at the state level. For example, states have limited insurance coverage for abortions, imposed waiting periods before an abortion can be obtained, required women to view antiabortion pamphlets—or even an ultrasound image of their own fetus—and required parental involvement when the woman is below a certain age (Eckholm 2014). In other cases, anti-abortion legislatures have sought to impose onerous regulations targeting the routine practices of abortion providers in an attempt to force them to shut down (Guttmacher Institute 2017b). At the extreme, some abortion providers have been attacked, and several have been murdered. Needless to say, no other medical procedure has been subjected to such a degree of political scrutiny.

This political campaign may have contributed to a downward trend in abortions. The rate at which American women obtain abortions has fallen for several decades. At the peak of abortion rates, in 1980, there were 29.3 abortions for every 1,000 women of childbearing age. By 2014, that number had fallen to 14.6, a drop of 50 percent. The decline is mostly the result of couples' increased use of contraception, but it also reflects reduced access to abortion services for many women. By one national estimate, 39 percent of women live in a county with no clinics that provide abortion care (Jones and Jerman 2017).

Infertility

infertility

The failure of a couple to have a successful pregnancy despite deliberately having sex without contraception.

The flip side of unintended pregnancies is unsuccessful ones, as reflected in the experience of infertility. The usual definition of **infertility** is the failure of a couple to have a successful pregnancy despite deliberately having sex without contraception. Although the time frame for the definition is arbitrary, demographers use a period of 12 months of sex without contraception to define the condition. Such a general description is much easier to apply than a determination of the cause for a given couple, which may be the quality and quantity of their reproductive gametes (eggs and sperm), the physical and hormonal characteristics of the woman's body, how often they have sex, and so on. Using this rather crude definition, we can say that worldwide, about 9 percent of couples experience infertility in a given year (Inhorn and Patrizio 2015). In the United States, the rate of infertility is lower, 6 percent for married couples (National Center for Health Statistics 2017).

The causes of infertility are many. People who are older and in poorer overall health are more likely to experience infertility. Smoking, obesity, and a history of sexually transmitted infections also increase the problem. But a certain incidence of infertility appears to be inevitable even among people who are young and healthy. In the United States, the pattern of infertility is consistent with other kinds of inequality: Black women are the most likely to experience infertility, followed by Hispanic and White women; and women with the lowest levels of education have the highest rates of infertility (see Figure 9.8). These patterns are probably the result of poorer overall health among Black women and those with less education.

Historically, failure to produce children cast shame on the wife. As far back as the stories in the Jewish Torah (Old Testament), both Abraham's and Jacob's wives, after years of infertility, offered up their maidservants to produce children (Genesis 16:1; 28:30). Infertility, in other words, justified infidelity. It was the woman's failure to reproduce that was to be overcome, and no one blamed the husband for having sex with the maidservant. Today, we know that male or female medical conditions are equally likely to cause infertility (so perhaps Abraham and Jacob could have tried providing their wives with a manservant instead).

With medical advances, infertility has come to be seen as a treatable problem, and an expanding number of methods are available (see Trend to Watch). Treatment is something of a mixed blessing, however. For some families, the path of medical treatment draws them into a long, expensive, physically taxing process that keeps the spotlight on their intimate lives and puts pressure on their mental health, their finances, and their marriages (Whiteford and Gonzalez 1995). Because most treatments are more invasive to the woman than to the man, the burden that women historically felt in some ways persists. In fact, the stress associated with the infertility treatment itself—especially for

Figure 9.8 **Infertility for 12 months, by race/ethnicity and education of married women**

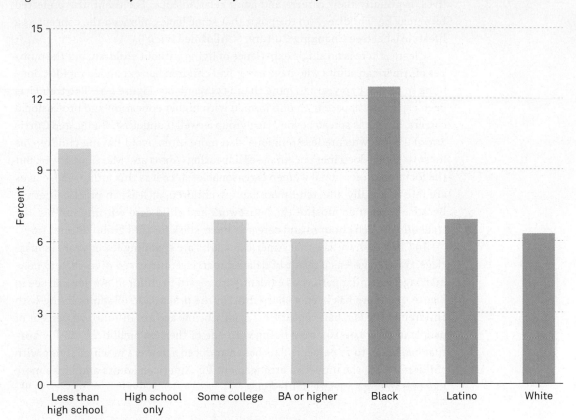

Note: Women ages 15–44; percentages are adjusted for age.

SOURCE: Author calculations from 2013–2015 National Survey of Family Growth.

the woman—is a growing area of concern among psychologists (Cousineau and Domar 2007).

In summary, although infertility is a natural part of the human sexual experience, there is a social reality to the problem that is more than medical, including living conditions and behavior that contribute to the problem and the different ways people perceive and address it. Advances in medicine have increased options for families, but only some people have the resources to take advantage of them. And the medical practices that might alleviate the problem also create a new set of problems, especially for the women who are most directly affected.

Living without Children

Are people who don't have children "childless," or are they "childfree"? For those experiencing infertility—sometimes spending years and thousands of dollars on fertility treatments—the answer is probably "childless." Others deliberately postpone or avoid having children, either because they are not interested in having children or because they place a higher priority on other aspects of their lives, especially their careers and adult relationships. For them, the preferred term may be "childfree," to the point that some have embraced the concept as a lifestyle label (see Changing Culture, "Childfree Living").

Clearly, there is no single experience of living without children, but the number of American adults who have never had children has expanded rapidly, doubling in the past 30 years to more than 15 percent (see Figure 9.1). The trend has been especially apparent among women with higher education and professional careers, but it has spread beyond that group as well (Lundquist, Budig, and Curtis 2009). People who are less religious also more often avoid having children, as most religious doctrines encourage childbearing (Abma and Martinez 2006). But the focus on professional women is reasonable, since it is this group whose lives are most radically affected by not having children, at least in practical terms. Because women do most of the housework and child care within families, the tradeoff between children and career is most stark for this group (Stone 2007).

In Chapter 8, we saw that American adults are spending fewer years in marriage, on average—as a result of delayed marriage, increased divorce, and non-marriage. A similar pattern is evident with regard to children. As you can see in Figure 9.9, there has been a sharp drop in the proportion of adults living with children in the last half century, especially below age 40. In 1960, 70 percent of people in their late 20s were living with one of their own children, but by 2015 that had fallen to 27 percent. This has introduced a new era in which living with children is less the universal arrangement for American adults and looks more like one among a variety of lifestyles.

Figure 9.9 **Percentage of adults living with at least one of their own children, by age, 1960 and 2015**

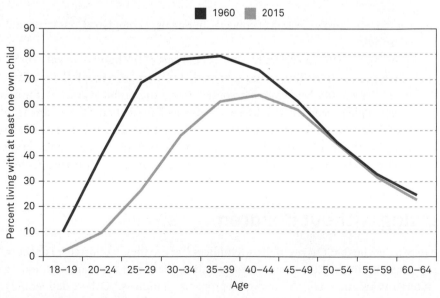

SOURCE: Author analysis of U.S. Census Bureau data.

Childfree Living

In an intensive-parenting culture, do people need to be "childfree" to enjoy adult social lives?

The website for Childfree Life bears the slogan, "A safe haven in a baby-crazed world." There, one finds a virtual community of people who seem more and more comfortable in their childfree state with every day that the culture of parenting grows more intense.

In the discussion areas, one person described the reasons she "never wanted kids": "The loss of self, how your life is no longer about YOU, it's about the kid(s). What's the point of me being here if I can't be who I want to be? Having kids would have destroyed any chance of that and turned me into a bitter, resentful, joyless person. Soooo glad I never did it."

Another chimed in: "When you have kids," she said, "you lose who you are, you can't be yourself or do the things you enjoy anymore because your whole world is expected to revolve around a child. I have too many books to read and crafts to do for that crap. Even without a kid I doubt I'll reach the bottom of my pile of books or get all my craft projects done, but at least I'll be able to get through some."

The passion of the childfree movement is motivated partly by backlash against the culture of intensive parenting. The recurring theme in these discussions is that people (especially women) who have children give up their individuality, their freedom, and their time. But if parenting were not such an intensive enterprise, their resistance to parenthood would not be so great.

Perhaps because a childfree person in a consumer society is considered an easy target for marketing (what else would they spend their money on?), there is a raft of books appealing to those who choose to be childfree. These include titles such as *Two Is Enough, Baby Not on Board, 40 Good Reasons Not to Have Children,* and *Beyond Motherhood.* The cover illustration for *Childfree and Loving It!* by Nicki Defago, a British journalist, shows only the torso of a slender woman, giving the impression that being childfree also keeps a woman young and thin.

Beyond the market appeal, however, the Internet meeting places and books for sale also underscore the fact that choosing childfree living remains a minority stance. In the context of family diversity, such a choice is among the widening array of acceptable options. But making that choice requires reason, justification, and a story to tell. And just as parents have a limitless supply of parenting advice from which to learn—and to use as justification for their parenting decisions—those without children apparently value the opinion of experts who back up their decisions as well.

Children's Living Arrangements

In recent years, sociologists have developed a growing understanding of family change, not as a step-by-step march of society moving from one stable period to another, but as a dynamic—and messy—process that takes place within families. This is especially important to understand for children, who often see the most profound social changes taking place within their own families and homes, even as they progress through their most important developmental years.

In her study of young adults "coming of age in a new era of gender, work and family," sociologist Kathleen Gerson (2010) describes children growing up in families in which "while the actors did not change, the play did." The same people play different roles as the historical context changes and the family grows. Gerson cites the case of a young man named Josh, whose stay-at-home mother kicked out his emotionally distant, substance-abusing father. Then she got a job to take care of her kids. But then the father "cleaned up" and came back a new man, now actively and emotionally involved with the children. And his mother was a new woman, with a greater sense of self-confidence and independence that came from her career success and from running the family on her own. In a sense, a new social era emerged within Josh's immediate family—but Josh was the same person, living through social change as he matured into young adulthood. This kind of story shows why it is complicated to understand (much less predict!) how the broad trends we study will affect the lives of those swept up in them.

A lot of adults affect the life of any one child. However, the adults who live with them have the most direct influence, provide the most care and supervision, and supply the most resources necessary for survival and development. For that reason, the study of child rearing often begins with an investigation of children's living arrangements. The changes in family structure and marriage patterns over the last half-century (described in previous chapters) are reflected in the lives of children today. Marriage rates have declined, divorce rates have increased, and the family relationships of adults have grown more diverse. More adults live alone—some not (yet) married, some divorced—and more are cohabiting without being married. The social, economic, and cultural behavior and decisions of adults have profound effects on the lives of children as well.

Figure 9.10 shows the living arrangements for White, Black, and Latino children from 1960 to 2016. These snapshots of family change again offer evidence of the themes of this book: diversity, inequality, and social change:

- *Diversity*. The dominant household structure for children 60 years ago was a household with two married parents. In every group since then, this dominance has given way to a greater diversity of arrangements. Beneath the broad categories shown here, there is still more diversity, moreover, including extended families, same-sex parents, and informal cohabiting relationships.

Figure 9.10 Living arrangements of children, by race/ethnicity, 1960–2016

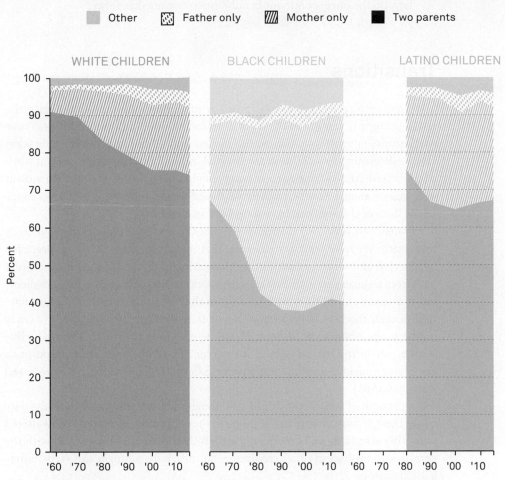

These groups include the great majority of children. (Data on smaller groups are available in Chapter 3.) Data for Latinos were not available for the decades before 1980 (when the Latino population was much smaller than it is today).

SOURCE: U.S. Census Bureau (2017b).

- *Inequality.* The scale of the family transformation is quite different across these groups, with African American children in particular seeing a much faster shift toward single-mother families. This represents inequality because such families have much lower incomes and other resources, on average, than two-parent families. And the children in single-parent homes are much more likely to experience disruptive family transitions (Rosenfeld 2015).

- *Social change.* Growing diversity and the inequality it has fueled are the product of the broader changes in society during this period. Most prominent are the economic trend toward a service economy, the declining fortunes of major industrial cities and rural areas, the growing economic independence of women, and the increasing cultural acceptance of family structures beyond the once-dominant breadwinner-homemaker form.

Transitions

Like Josh in Kathleen Gerson's (2010) study, many children experience the social changes of our era in the form of transitions within their families. These transitions—almost as much as the before-and-after situations that bracket them—determine how children are affected by family circumstances. Even when a family transition is from a worse condition to a better one—the end of a violent marriage or a move to a better neighborhood—sudden or unpredictable change in the lives of children can have long-lasting effects.

Transitions involving the romantic relationships of the adults are especially important. We have seen, for example, that most marriages today are preceded by a period of living together. Rather than think of that cohabitation as a direct path from engagement to marriage, with a short period of living together, remember that many children are born to couples that are living together but not married. If their mothers (with whom they usually live) get married, it may or may not be to their biological fathers. Thus, the life stories of the children who live with a cohabiting parent—about 40 percent of all children at some point in their lives—include multiple transitions in family composition (S. Kennedy and Bumpass 2008).

As a result of family transitions, children build relationships with adults only to see them change or end. In the process, they may also have to adjust to altered parenting standards and practices. Further, their lives are intertwined with the comings and goings of other children—siblings, half-siblings, and stepsiblings (Cherlin 2009).

Finally, family transitions always have an economic component. Either economic troubles can contribute to a transition (for example, by harming the parents' marriage), or they can be the result of a transition (as when a family loses one parent's income). This complex set of possibilities has been the subject of intensive study, motivated by the concern that the rise in family transitions generally is adding stress to children's lives (S. Brown 2006).

Beyond the changes in parents' romantic relationships, many families experience changes in household composition that include extended family members. This is especially the case during economically challenging times, as families pull together—or fall apart—in the face of a shifting balance between needs and resources. For a growing number of children, living in the home of a grandparent is part of their experience growing up, as shown in Figure 9.11 (Hayslip and Kaminski 2005).

A century ago, multigenerational households (those with three or more generations) usually included dependent senior citizens turning to their adult children for help. Now it is often the tight finances of the younger generation

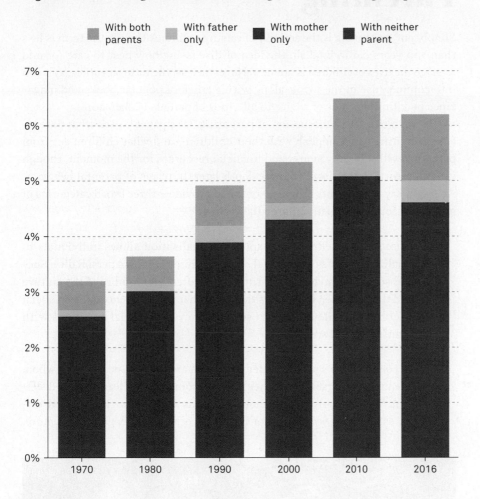

Figure 9.11 **Percentage of all children living in the home of a grandparent**

Legend:
- With both parents
- With father only
- With mother only
- With neither parent

SOURCE: U.S. Census Bureau (2017b) and author calculations from Current Population Survey data for 2016.

that lead to extending the family (Kahn, Goldscheider, and García-Manglano 2013). The increase in single mothers—especially those who are young and poor—drives many families to this option. One way we know that the trend toward children living with grandparents reflects economic hardship is that this practice is more common during hard times and among poor and immigrant families (Landale, Thomas, and Van Hook 2011). That is exactly what we saw during the economic crisis of the late 2000s; you can see in Figure 9.11 that children were most likely to live with their grandparents in 2010, when the recession was at its peak. Even when the move is for the better, however, remember that a child moving into her or his grandparents' house because the family has trouble paying the rent is experiencing a transition that may add stress to the child's development.

Parenting

parenting

The activity of raising a child.

Simply put, **parenting** is the activity of raising a child. Although the term is less than 100 years old in English, the idea of discussing how best to care for and manage the lives of children is not new. Nevertheless, the term *parenting* exploded into common use in the 1970s, along with a crush of popular books and magazines peddling all kinds of advice to all kinds of parents (Cohen 2018).

As we move into a discussion of parenting, let's pause to ask what parents are attempting to accomplish with their children—and what children get from parents. I will skip over money and financial resources for the moment, though we will return to that issue in more depth later. In terms of parental behavior, we might say that parents provide—or try to provide—three broad categories of skills or resources to their children (Lewis 2012):

- *Socialization.* As defined in Chapter 5, socialization allows individuals to internalize elements of the social structure into their own personality. Successful socialization is not just turning children into mimics of the culture around them. Rather, it prepares them for what they will encounter in social interactions and allows them to see how they fit in social situations with less confusion and stress.

- *Social bonds.* As we saw in Chapter 2, parents are the first people with whom children build the stable bonds they need as a foundation of learning and development. Without early, strong emotional bonds with adults, children have difficulty establishing secure relationships with others as they grow and mature.

A deluge of parenting books that both reflects and exacerbates parental anxiety.

- *Social networks.* An obvious example of social networks is parents helping their children get a job with a friend or colleague. But the networking that parents do with their children is much more extensive and subtle than that, and it starts much earlier. Deliberately or not, parents usually facilitate an entire web of friends and neighbors, relatives, potential mentors, teachers, and peers that shapes the social environment of their children. Naturally, such a network provides a mixture of positive and negative influences, so that maintaining and supervising it is a central part of parenting.

Parenting, then, is made up of many different parts and many relationships that all take place in a changing social environment that varies greatly from place to place. As parents develop a mental map of their goals and resources, they start with an image of childhood—who children are and what they need and deserve. As we will see, that mental image is a product of the historical moment.

The Meaning of Childhood

Before thinking about today's American children, consider briefly their ancestors in two historical periods. First consider the chimney sweeps of the early industrial cities in the United States, United Kingdom, and elsewhere. Orphans—children whose parents were either dead or too ill or too poor to care for them—worked as "apprentices" to thousands of chimney sweeps. Their masters would send the (mostly) boys as young as 4 years old into the long, hot, narrow shafts to sweep out soot left behind by burning coal (Mukherjee 2010:237–239). This was necessary to prevent the soot from catching fire. In the United States, the masters were usually African Americans, both slave and free (Gilje and Rock 1994). The children suffered egregiously from this practice, sometimes becoming trapped and either getting burned or suffocating, sometimes contracting various illnesses, including cancer. Over the course of 100 years, a series of laws raised the minimum age at which children could work in chimneys, until the practice eventually died out. What had once seemed an acceptable practice to most people in the cities eventually looked like an appalling abuse of innocent children.

Decades later, in the American cities of a century ago, children appeared to be everywhere. They roamed the streets as delivery boys and girls, vendors, or shoe shiners. In the afternoons and evenings they played in the streets by the thousands—not in the parks, ball fields, playgrounds, malls, gymnastics studios, or playrooms where many play today. In the structure of urban life—the streets, buildings, workplaces, and even homes—children seemed to be an afterthought; except for the schools, there was no place for them. Even their bedrooms were often shared with adults, some of whom were unrelated renters.

On January 4, 1911, the *New York Times* reported that almost 200 children had been killed in street accidents in the city the previous year by cars, trolleys, and wagons. Not only were children killed by street vehicles, they also were

Headlines like this, in the *New York Times*, January 4, 1911, called attention to the perils of modern urban life for children.

routinely crushed by freight trains that passed through the poor neighborhoods of the city. One official said, "Something will have to be done here soon to force tenement mothers to keep their children off the streets and on the sidewalks" ("Killed in Streets," 1911).

The uproar that followed these deaths, which included protests and marches, reflected the growing clash between old and new visions of childhood. Following the laws prohibiting children being sent up chimneys, the city eventually implemented traffic safety laws and regulations and went on to expand public parks and playgrounds, the infrastructure of modern childhood we know so well today (Frost 2010). What happened? Now just 7 pedestrian children per year are killed on the city's streets, even though the population has almost doubled (Centers for Disease Control and Prevention 2016d).

As we saw in Chapter 2, the number of children surviving to adulthood increased dramatically over the nineteenth century, and partly for that reason, parents started having fewer children. Children's usefulness as laborers also decreased. From farm labor to chimney sweeping to factory work, children's labor was once everywhere. But as the new industrial workplace increasingly demanded workers with higher skills and at least a minimal education, a 17-year-old who could read and write was eventually much more useful than an uneducated 10-year-old. And growing concern with child safety contributed to a period of vigorous policy reform during the Progressive Era of the early twentieth century (Hindman 2002). According to sociologist Viviana Zelizer (1985), American children—fewer of them and more precious—were in the midst of a transformation, losing their *economic* value while achieving a newfound *emotional* value that was considered "priceless."

That development was apparent in the treatment of children without families. In the nineteenth century, if such children could be sold to foster families, they might escape the dangerous and miserable life of an orphanage. This system was not based on the need for children to be cared for, but on the premise that children should work for their upkeep—which is what they did for their foster families (who paid for them). Only toward the end of the century did advocates for children start asserting their rights to have a loving family free from exploitation. By the early twentieth century, public policy had shifted to favor foster care or adoption whenever possible—not so the children could work for their foster families, but so they could have something like a family life. The moral ideal of families and childhood had shifted.

The paradox of priceless childhood is how expensive it is. Setting aside all the public costs associated with raising children—education, medical care, product safety inspectors, and so on—the costs for a family are daunting. The parents of a typical family with two children today can expect to spend between $175,000 and $370,000 to raise each child up to age 17, depending on how rich the family is (see Story Behind the Numbers). Those are not just the costs of food, clothing, or even private schools. People with children also spend more on things like housing—extra bedrooms, bathrooms, or a yard—translating into a cost of almost $100,000 per child for families in the high-income group. Much of this spending represents a desire on the part of today's parents to give their children whatever it takes to stay ahead in a world filled with uncertainty.

Competition and Insecurity

In the last few years, child well-being experts have found it necessary to advise parents to let their children *play* more. It might seem odd that such experts are trying to convince parents to provide more play time rather than more time studying or competing in organized sports, for example. But such is the state of American parenting in an era of busy, competitive parents raising few children per family (often born when their 30-something parents are in the middle of their careers), cutthroat admissions procedures (and skyrocketing costs) for education from preschool through college, and a self-conscious culture that pressures people to justify their parenting decisions to themselves and others.

In 2007, the American Academy of Pediatrics issued a report expressing alarm that children had less time to play than they used to. This disturbing trend, the report concluded, was the result of parents' "hurried lifestyle, changes in family structure, and increased attention to academics and enrichment activities at the expense of recess or free child-centered play" (Ginsburg 2007). The heavily scheduled lives of children, driven largely by parents' ambitions—and, perhaps, by their insecurities—might be backfiring. The negative consequences of not enough play, the pediatric doctors warned, might include increased risks of anxiety and depression in adolescence.

Parenting advice has been a booming industry for more than a century and has come increasingly under the purview of social scientists (Beatty, Cahan, and Grant 2006). One reason parents turn to published advice now more than in the past may be that they have grown up with fewer siblings—so they have less experience with children—and they have smaller extended families, which were a traditional source of parenting wisdom and advice (Clark-Stewart 1978). However, despite a century of parenting advice published by an increasing number of professionals, parents' anxiety about the quality of their parenting—and its effects on their children's futures—has if anything only increased (Hulbert 2003).

A certain level of insecurity among parents is almost inevitable, since every child is different and parents are naturally inexperienced at raising them. However, there is also reason to suspect that parents' insecurity has increased in the last few decades for two reasons. First, because parents have fewer children, their investment in each one has grown—so parents today spend more time and money on each child than they did in the past. Second, the growing perception of economic insecurity, together with the increasing necessity of advanced education for success in adulthood, means that the stakes for parenting seem very high to today's parents (Waldfogel 2006). On top of these concerns, fears about crime, terrorism, and accidents—although real threats—are irrationally prominent in the minds of many parents, occupying a space in their thoughts greater than the real risks justify (Nelson 2010b).

In some cases, the proliferation of expert opinion has introduced problems for parents to worry about (and then turn to experts to help solve). One example is "sibling rivalry," a term made popular in the 1930s to describe the conflict that arises out of jealousy between siblings. It quickly became a matter of considerable concern to parents, as experts warned that the problem resulted from parents

At a suburban playground in North Carolina, a parent stands near each playing child.

The high, and highly unequal, cost of raising children

Low Family Income (<$59,000)   High Family Income (>$108,000)

http://wwnpag.es/sbtn9

Go to this link for an animation narrated by the author.

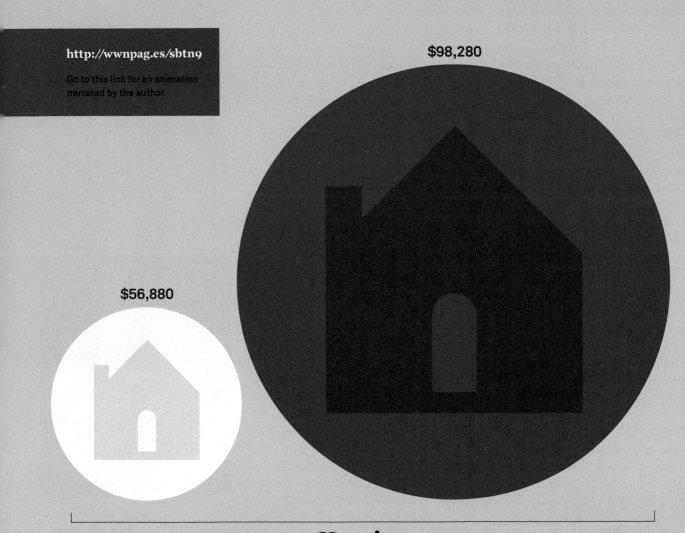

$98,280

$56,880

Housing

Children are so precious that they are priceless. At the same time, of course, they are also very expensive. For a family with an income of less than $59,000 per year, a married couple with two children can expect to spend about $175,000 to raise each child up through age 17. A family with an income over $108,000 can expect to spend much more — up to $370,000. Expenses for those whose children go to college — or continue living in the family home after age 18 — add even more to that bill.

People with children spend more on food, clothing, and education, but they also spend more on amenities like extra bedrooms and bathrooms, or a yard. Rich parents spend more, which means rich children cost more. It also means more consumption by children of the rich, and that illustrates how much inequality is experienced by children.

Source: Lino et al. (2017).

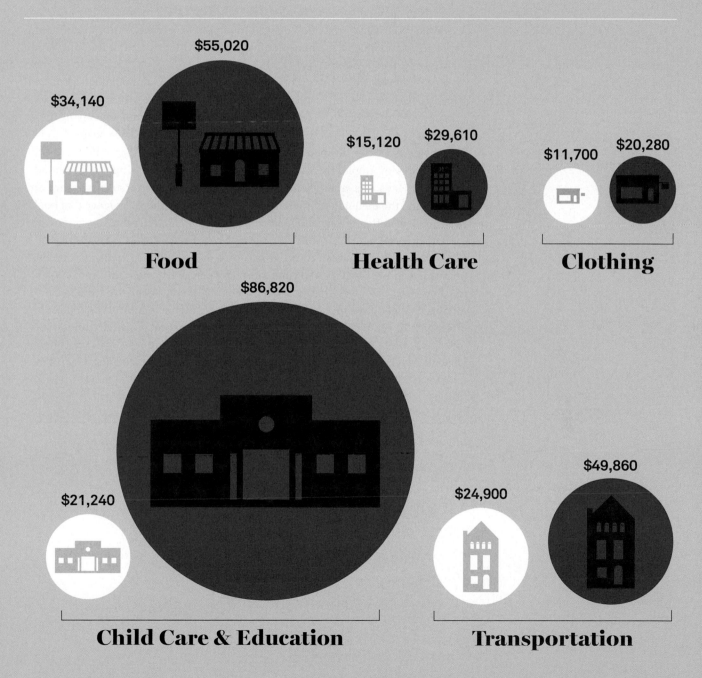

$55,020

$34,140

Food

$15,120 $29,610

Health Care

$11,700 $20,280

Clothing

$86,820

$21,240

Child Care & Education

$24,900 $49,860

Transportation

playing favorites among their children and could lead to trouble in adulthood (Stearns 1990). Of course, such conflicts have probably always existed, but applying a label to the problem and broadcasting advice to parents about it served to heighten the anxiety inherent in parenting.

Insecurity has also been fueled by the explosion of consumer culture, which not only sells advice to parents but also provides seemingly infinite opportunities to buy one's way out of the problem—from developmental toys and games to learning materials and clothes—in search of the perfect childhood (Cross 2004). Part of the advertising of childhood-related products and services is a strategy to promote feelings of insecurity and fear among parents—a common ploy in advertising generally (see Changing Technology, "Freedom and Constraints for Children"). This has contributed to a growing belief in the frailty of children, replacing what was once a more confident view of their natural durability and hardiness (Stearns 2003).

In her book *The Cultural Contradictions of Motherhood*, sociologist Sharon Hays (1996) described an ideology that she called **intensive motherhood**, a cultural pressure on women to devote more time, energy, and money to raising their children. As Hays pointed out, it was ironic that this pressure seemed to be increasing as women seemed to have less time available for their children due to higher rates of employment as well as more divorce and single parenthood. Although Hays was concerned primarily with the effects of such pressure on women and the inequality between women and men, in the years since that book was published, the term *intensive parenting* has emerged, referring to pressure on parents in general (Cha 2010).

Remarkably, from the 1960s to the 1990s—a period when women's employment rates grew rapidly—the time mothers spent with their children actually did increase. How was that possible? It seems likely that many women's priorities changed in response to the pressures of intensive motherhood or in an attempt to keep up with the unending stream of parenting advice and stress over children's success. Mothers compensated by doing less of other things, especially leisure and adult recreational activities, and by sleeping less (Bianchi 2000).

intensive motherhood

Cultural pressure on women to devote more time, energy, and money to raising their children.

Figure 9.12 **Children with selected health problems**

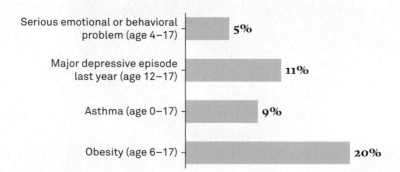

SOURCE: Federal Interagency Forum on Child and Family Statistics (2016).

Freedom and Constraints for Children

The modern attitude toward children as priceless and unique, together with the smaller family size of today's era, naturally leads to increased protectiveness on the part of parents. In some ways, children are freer than ever, thanks in part to technology that gives them access to more information more quickly—and puts them in touch with more people—often free from adult supervision. But modern development and technology have also created new constraints on children's freedom. The fear of crime in urban areas and the car-oriented layout of suburban areas have made children more dependent on adults to drive them around. And parents intent on monitoring—or controlling—their children's actions have access to a rapidly growing arsenal of technological tools to use toward that end.

That tension between freedom and constraint fits with how parenting practices changed over the twentieth century (Rutherford 2009). In keeping with the growing appreciation of children's emotional value—and emotional development—parents now try harder to foster their children's sense of autonomy and self-expression. For example, children have more freedom to decide how to dress themselves, and they're given more freedom to talk back to their parents.

Mobile phones give children more freedom but also give parents more surveillance. How old were you when you got your first mobile phone? If your parents bought it for you, did they put any parental controls on it?

On the other hand, parents have increased the constraints on children's physical movements outside the home.

Technology facilitates both trends in modern parenting: freedom and constraint. By 2014, about three-quarters of children ages 13 to 17 reported having a smartphone (Lenhart 2015). That clearly could enhance the freedom of children to communicate with others and express themselves, as well as gather information, find their way, and do all the other things smartphones enable. But phones also may enhance parental control in a variety of ways—and the most common reasons parents gave for giving their children a phone were safety and keeping track of the children's whereabouts. Sociologist Margaret Nelson, in her book *Parenting Out of Control* (2010b), considers the technology that parents use. She breaks it into three categories:

- *Connection.* From baby monitors to smartphones to social media accounts, parents may gather information about children when they aren't together. But they don't inherently constrain the children's behavior—and they enhance children's communication with others.

- *Constraint.* As children gain access to new technology, some parents are engaged in a continuous search for ways to keep their children within established boundaries. One national survey found that 40 percent of parents have tried to use blocks or filters to monitor or control their teens' online activities. Beyond that, 20 percent have specifically used parental controls on their teens' phones (Lenhart 2015).

- *Spying.* Secret devices, such as those in a phone or hidden in a car, can track children's movements. Besides alerting parents when speed or neighborhood limits are broken, for example, these may allow parents to keep secret records of children's movements. Further, computer keystroke recorders can tell parents what children have been typing (including their passwords). Basic tracking devices that use GPS technology with names like "Buddy Tracker" and "Mommy I'm Here" are available for less than $50. And then there are more invasive technological interventions, such as home drug tests.

Of course, many parents can't meet the expectations that they—or others—set for ideal parenting. Naturally, all children are different, and the contexts in which they grow up are infinitely variable as well. Many conditions that make life difficult for parents—such as poverty, unemployment, family disruption, illness, and insecurity—also make it harder for them to practice parenting as successfully as they would like (Dreby 2010). Children's health poses one set of challenges for parents, introducing financial costs, time demands, and emotional stress (see Figure 9.12). This is especially difficult for parents whose children have "invisible disabilities," such as attention deficit hyperactivity disorder, mood disorders, or the less obvious forms of autism (Blum 2015). Another daunting task is protecting children from racism or violence, including—especially for the parents of Black children—police violence (Dow 2016).

The goals of modern parents include investing more in fewer children, valuing them more highly as priceless individuals, and monitoring their progress at every step to encourage their success. How to secure the child's cooperation with this plan is another story. And that raises the question of discipline. When children don't do what their parents want, parents have wide leeway in how to respond. Consider spanking. In 2016, 68 percent of American adults agreed with the statement, "It is sometimes necessary to discipline a child with a good, hard spanking." However, that attitude actually represents a substantial change in the last three decades, as Figure 9.13 shows. In the 1980s, more than 80 percent agreed that spanking was sometimes necessary. In fact, only 45 percent of parents say they actually use spanking as a form of discipline, although that number is higher among African American parents and those with lower levels of education (Pew Research Center 2015d).

Public opinion on an issue like spanking reflects a combination of traditional beliefs and contemporary attitudes, and those attitudes are partly shaped by the advice of experts—doctors, teachers, social workers, and, more than ever, the media. And, as we saw in Chapter 4, parenting practices and ideals differ according to social class (Lareau 2011). Although there is a seemingly infinite supply of advice for parents—some good, some bad, and much irrelevant—careful social science has produced some verifiable results (Crosnoe and Cavanagh 2010). When

Figure 9.13 **Adults agreeing or disagreeing with the statement, "It is sometimes necessary to discipline a child with a good, hard spanking"**

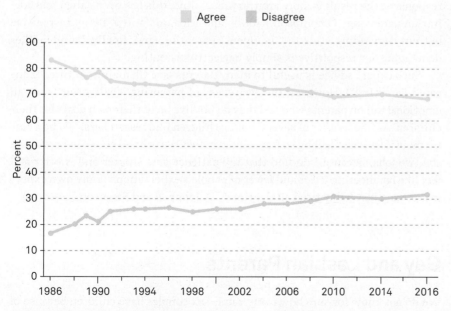

SOURCE: General Social Surveys, 1972–2014 (Smith et al. 2016).

it comes to children's success in three major dimensions—being happy and well adjusted, doing well in school, and staying out of serious trouble—some aspects of parenting have proved beneficial (Amato and Fowler 2002):

- *Supportiveness.* Supportive activities include spending time with children, working on homework or playing together, having private talks, and being accessible when needed.

- *Monitoring.* Useful rule setting establishes an environment for healthy development, especially for adolescents. Examples include not allowing children to be home alone, knowing where they are and what they're doing, and setting rules for TV or screen time.

- *Discipline.* When used in a consistent and proportional way, discipline helps develop a sense of security in children. On the other hand, most research shows that corporal punishment—the use of force, such as spanking—is not good for children (Afifi et al. 2012). In fact, spanking appears to increase aggressive behavior in children (Altschul, Lee, and Gershoff 2016).

Some child development experts divide the qualities of parenting into two dimensions, according to whether parents are responsive and whether they are demanding (Maccoby and Martin 1983). When parents are demanding they hold their children to high expectations. If they do so while being responsive to the needs and feelings of their children, it is known as "authoritative" parenting, which has been shown to produce good results in areas such as health behavior (Sleddens et al. 2011). This is similar to the ideal of "concerted cultivation" described in Chapter 4. On the other hand, when parents are demanding but not responsive, the result is more arbitrary discipline; this has been called "authoritarian parenting" (Thompson, Hollis, and Richards 2003). Being responsive but not demanding leads to "indulgent" parenting; and, finally, being neither demanding nor responsive is simply neglectful parenting.

Such expert advice is useful to many parents (see Changing Culture, "Educated Parenting"). However, the awareness of parenting ideals itself takes an emotional toll on parents who feel they do not live up to their own goals for their children. As one mother of several young children told researchers: "I'd be a better mom if I weren't feeling so fragmented between work and home. In particular, the two jobs, because I do find that my patience gets shorter and shorter as I feel like I'm meeting fewer and fewer of people's expectations or my own expectations and just being tired all the time" (D. Johnson and Swanson 2006:514).

Gay and Lesbian Parents

We do not know for sure how many same-sex couples have children because of our inadequate national data collection system. However, the number of children living with same-sex parents is probably less than 1 percent (Payne 2014). That

Educated Parenting

If you have children, will reading this book make you a "better" parent? However that is defined, I hope it's true. But the question raises a larger issue, which is whether parenting has improved as the education levels of parents—especially women—have increased.

Just as higher education correlates with lower fertility, we know that parents with higher levels of education do parenting differently from those who have spent less time in school. For example, they spend more time with their children and more money on their children's wants and needs (Bianchi et al. 2004). In some ways, certainly, children of parents with more education are better off. Consider a few examples.

Even at the preschool ages, childhood obesity is a growing problem. And the problem is much more common among the children of mothers with less education (S. Anderson and Whitaker 2010). This has to do with the tendency of these children to watch more TV and not get enough exercise or sleep. Figure 9.14 shows that children whose mothers have less education are more likely to be obese at ages 10–17. But we can't simply attribute the problem to the decisions that parents make. The circumstances they face—such as poverty, long work schedules, family stress, and their own health conditions—affect the daily routines of their children as well. Whatever the reason, parents with higher levels of education spend more time doing what researchers call developmental activities with their children (Altintas 2016).

Figure 9.14 **Obesity among children ages 10-17, by mothers' education**

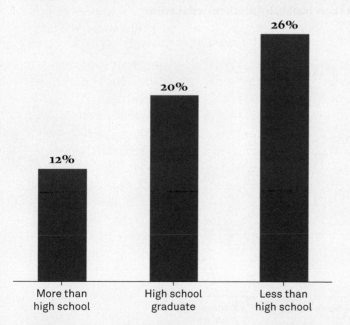

SOURCE: Author analysis of data from the National Survey of Children's Health. Percentages are adjusted for age.

Figure 9.15 **Breastfeeding infants at age 6 months, by mothers' education**

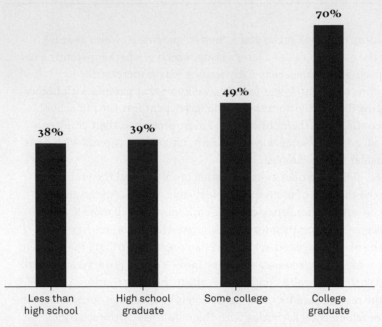

SOURCE: Centers for Disease Control and Prevention (2016e).

Figure 9.16 **Infants put to sleep on their backs, by mothers' education**

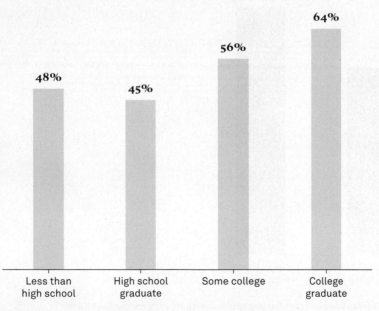

SOURCE: Broussard, Sappendfield, and Goodman (2012).

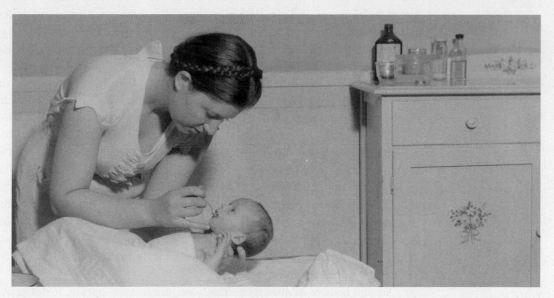

A woman caring for one of the "practice babies" in the Cornell University Home Economics program. They were known as "Domecon babies," short for "domestic economy."

Doctors and the government are engaged in a major campaign to increase breastfeeding among the mothers of infants, which has very important health benefits for children (Centers for Disease Control and Prevention 2013). However, breastfeeding is not always easy or possible, and there are many practical barriers to overcome. These include inflexible work schedules, long commutes, problems with child care, and the availability of medical support and advice. All of that—in addition to the lack of awareness among less educated women that breastfeeding is important—may explain why the practice is most common among women with the highest levels of education (see Figure 9.15).

Finally, consider the "back to sleep" campaign. Doctors have discovered that infants put to sleep on their backs are less likely to suffer sudden infant death syndrome, known as SIDS. A national effort has attempted to educate parents to the importance of putting infants to sleep on their backs—rather than their stomachs or their sides—as a way to reduce SIDS. The campaign has had some success, especially among mothers with more education. Research on new mothers consistently shows that those who have higher levels of education are more likely to follow the "back to sleep" advice—or at least to report that they do (Colson et al. 2009). Figure 9.16 shows the results from one such study conducted in Florida.

In the first half of the twentieth century, women who went to college often learned "home economics," which included the latest scientific information on parenting practices. At Cornell University, for example—an elite Ivy League school—women in the home economics program were taught child care using real babies, obtained from orphanages and child welfare associations. After a year of care by the student mothers in a special home, the babies were available for adoption. The program lasted until 1969. We don't use that system of training mothers anymore. But the education received by parents still seems to be an important piece of the story of how children fare in the care of their families—and of how some children have advantages over others.

number has grown rapidly in recent years, as gay and lesbian couples achieved the right to marry, and more are pursuing child-rearing options. And perhaps because of the long-running political debate over the marriage rights of gay and lesbian couples (see Chapter 8), the quantity and quality of their parenting have come under scrutiny as well.

Unfortunately, in addition to their total number, there is much else we do not know about the dynamics of gay and lesbian couples and their children. Research on the subject is complicated because of their evolving legal status, which means that direct comparisons are often impossible to conduct. It is difficult to compare, for example, the well-being of children raised by long-term, committed—but not married—gay or lesbian couples with the well-being of children raised by cohabiting straight couples who have chosen not to marry. In addition, many children living in same-sex parent families now have experienced a divorce or breakup of one parent, with the stress that such transitions might entail (Rosenfeld 2015). Nevertheless, despite concerns expressed by those opposed to same-sex marriage, the limited existing research shows no systematic difficulties for their children (Biblarz and Stacey 2010).

Gay and lesbian couples increasingly are pursuing adoption, foster care, or assisted reproduction together as couples. They may use donor sperm insemination in the case of lesbians or surrogacy in the case of gay men. Interestingly, perhaps in part because of the legal, technological, or financial obstacles they must overcome to have children, same-sex couples have been shown to be unusually committed to parenting (Biblarz and Savci 2010)—as we saw in the case of adoptive parents in general. That may be why, for example, they spend more time in "quality time" activities with their children than do different-sex couples (Prickett, Martin-Storey, and Crosnoe 2015).

Fatherhood

After what may seem like many pages in this chapter focused on mothers, it is fitting to devote some attention directly to fathers. That has been the attitude among family researchers in the last two decades, as they have turned their investigative lens toward the men who are parents (Marsiglio and Roy 2012). To get beyond the "traditional" father, however, has required considerable research effort. That's because of the complications that arise when studying men who may have had only a short relationship with the mother of their children—men who are not married to or living with those women and who may have moved on to "start" other families (Edin, Tach, and Mincy 2009). Our approach to studying families has usually involved those who live together in households. However, only 3 percent of children live with a single father. That means that the growing attention to single-parent families has ended up focusing almost exclusively on single-mother families. Nevertheless, whether they are stably married and living with their children, are parenting on their own, or have only a fleeting relationship with their children, fathers have an impact on their children's lives.

The study of fatherhood has found a pronounced shift in the cultural views of what makes a good father. From the period of separate spheres (see Chapter 2) until the 1960s, the **male provider ideal** of fathers was the dominant American conception of what a father should be, based on the father as an economic provider and authority figure for his children. In this model, successful employment—making career the priority—is the sign of a good father (Coltrane 1996).

A number of historical events undermined the dominance of the male provider ideal. The increase in women's employment cast doubt on how inherent and insurmountable differences in the roles of men and women are within families. And as family structures became more diverse, the assumption that a single earner supporting a stay-at-home wife with children was normal and natural gradually unraveled (we will discuss fathers staying home with their children in Chapter 11). Finally, recall that children in the twentieth century were increasingly seen as emotionally, rather than economically, valuable (Zelizer 1985). As a consequence, the emotional development of children came to be seen as more important, and child development experts started promoting the emotional bonds with mothers *and* fathers as beneficial—some would say necessary—to children's well-being. Eventually, the **involved father ideal** became dominant in American culture, defining the father as an emotional, nurturing companion who bonds with his children as well as providing for them.

The involved father ideal is now nearly universally accepted, and when men are asked to describe a father's responsibilities, their answers match this ideal

male provider ideal

The father as an economic provider and authority figure for his children.

involved father ideal

The father as an emotional, nurturing companion who bonds with his children as well as providing for them.

Figure 9.17 **Minutes per day spent in developmental childcare activities, for parents with children under age 5**

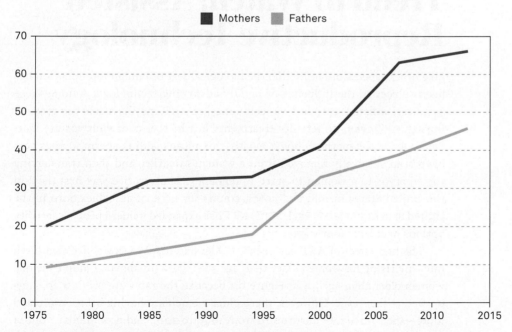

Average minutes per day among those who spent any time in developmental activities, such as reading to children, helping with homework, or attending educational events.

SOURCE: Altintas (2016).

quite closely. Most new fathers embrace the involved father ideal completely: They reject the suggestion that their economic role is more important than spending time with their children, and they believe that fathers must be as involved as mothers in their children's development (Lewis 2012). And despite the middle-class provider image that many people hold up as a model, many poor fathers have eagerly embraced the involved father ideal (Edin and Nelson 2013). Asked to choose the most important task for a father, almost two-thirds of fathers choose "show the child love and affection," while only 6 percent cite financial provision (Avenilla, Rosenthal, and Tice 2006). These shifting attitudes seem to have contributed to measureable changes in parenting behavior, as Figure 9.17 shows. Fathers (at least those who live with their children) have increased their daily time spent in developmental activities—such as reading to children, helping with homework, or attending educational events—from about 10 minutes per day to 45 minutes per day. And research confirms the positive effects of father involvement with their children (Carlson 2006). Mothers still do more of the care for and rearing of their children than fathers do, but parenting is not as one-sided as it was a few decades ago.

The involved father—as an ideal and as an incipient reality at least—has become a prominent feature of the American family's cultural landscape (Livingston and Parker 2011). As we will see, however, another important aspect of that tableau—divorce and remarriage—has played an important part as well.

Trend to Watch: Assisted Reproductive Technology

Like other aspects of family life, the biological feat of human reproduction has been subject to the influence of rapidly advancing technology. Among these advances, assisted reproductive technology, or ART, may have had the greatest impact. ART refers to fertility treatments in which eggs or embryos are handled outside the mother's body; mostly this means adding sperm to eggs that have been surgically removed from a woman's ovaries, and then transferring the embryos to a woman to start a pregnancy. The practice was first used in the United States in 1981 and now accounts for 1.6% of all babies born in the United States (Sunderam et al. 2017). ART has expanded modern people's fertility options in at least four ways.

The first effect of ART has been on older parents. We saw above that birth rates are rising for women older than age 30 (Figure 9.1 above). I didn't include women older than age 44 in Figure 9.1 because the rates are too low to show up well at that scale. However, these older women are having babies more and more—their birth rate quadrupled from 1990 to 2015, and now almost 1 out of every 1,000 women ages 45–49 has a birth each year. This reflects changes in the timing and ordering of people's family lives and careers, leading more people to "start a family" (or another family) at later ages. However, these choices

Parenting Advice

Sociologists who study the way people raise their children have often turned to published parenting advice as a source of information. For example, when the question is historical, it may be easier to find published advice than to figure out what parents really did. But advice isn't the same as parenting behavior. How might they differ?

Here's one example of parenting advice gone very wrong, as told by the women's rights activist Elizabeth Cady Stanton (1898[1993]). In the mid-nineteenth century, she decided to read up on parenting, because, as she remembered, "having gone through the ordeal of bearing a child, I was determined, if possible, to keep him." Some friends of hers, however, had a terrible experience at the hands of an "expert":

> They had been so misled by one author, who assured them that the stomach of a child could only hold one tablespoonful [of milk], that they nearly starved their firstborn to death. Though the child dwindled, day by day, and, at the end of a month, looked like a little old man, yet they still stood by the distinguished author. Fortunately, they both went off, one day, and left the child with [his aunt], who thought she would make an experiment and see what a child's stomach could hold.... To her surprise the baby took a pint bottle full of milk, and had the sweetest sleep thereon he had known in his earthly career.

For this workshop, let's consider the pros and cons of expert advice and the source of that advice for parents.

First, select a parenting topic to research. Examples include spanking, TV, exercise, diet and nutrition, potty training, and gender and play. The possibilities are endless. If you are working in groups, each group can take a different subject.

Second, develop a list of three or four advice sources. These could be from a simple Internet search, from a parenting book, or from a historical source in the library.

Third, compare the advice received. Consider these questions:

- What is the original source of the information? For example, was it a research study, personal experience, or a doctor?

- To whom is the advice aimed? Does it seek to advise mothers, fathers, people with higher or lower levels of education, or a particular racial-ethnic group?

- How effective is it likely to be, and for whom? Can anyone follow the advice or only some parents—such as those with jobs, lots of money, or helpful relatives?

- What are the motives of the group or individual offering the advice? Are they selling a product, book, or service? Promoting a particular ideology?

Finally, in your group, individual report, or class discussion, consider the outcomes that you think might result from people following—or not following—this advice. If the advice is helpful, what might be done to expand on its approach? If it is not helpful, how can we improve the method used or information presented?

run up against the rising risk of infertility at older ages. For all the older people having children, there are many others who want to but can't. ART has changed that equation, making it more possible for people to achieve their goal of having a baby, provided they are medically—and financially—eligible to take advantage of this technology.

The second effect of ART has been to facilitate more diverse family arrangements, including same-sex couple parenting, surrogate parenting (in which one woman carries a pregnancy for another woman and her family), and sperm-donor embryos. These are all ways of producing children in a process separated from sexual intercourse. Third, ART has enabled people to have children who might otherwise not have been able to for health reasons. In addition to the many causes of infertility, there are also times when, for example, a man in the military, or a man preparing to undergo sperm-damaging medical treatments, arranges for sperm to be available for his partner if he dies or his sperm becomes unviable. Finally, ART allows for possible genetic selection or manipulation of sperm, eggs, or embryos, to produce a child with traits the parents choose. The most common of these may be gender selection, but it also makes possible selection of embryos that are not afflicted by some genetic conditions or—more fancifully, at this point—other physical or behavioral traits. This may develop into the most controversial application of the technology, allowing, for example, parents to choose children based on their likely height, skin color, personality, type, and so on. As this technology advances, the consequences of these choices for parents and their families—and the new kinds of family relationships they create—remain to be seen.

KEY TERMS:

parent   biological parents

adoptive parents   fertility

total fertility rate   opportunity cost

infertility   parenting

intensive motherhood

male provider ideal

involved father ideal

Questions for Review

1. What configurations of people count as a family to you? Do you think your parents and grandparents would agree?

2. Describe the factors that cause some women to have more children than others.

3. Explain why the reasons for having children can differ between people who are rich and those who are poor.

4. Describe the three categories of skills or resources that parents provide to their children.

5. What are some ways people become single parents? How do financial and legal considerations affect their children?

6. Explain the different connotations in the words *childless* and *childfree*.

7. Using the issue of child labor, explain how the idea of childhood changed from the nineteenth century to the twentieth century.

8. According to Margaret Nelson, what are the three ways that parents use technology to supervise their children?

10 Divorce, Remarriage, and Blended Families

The performer Miley Cyrus described why she broke up with her fiancé, Liam Hemsworth, at the age of 21, this way:

> I was so scared of ever being alone, and I think, conquering that fear, this year, was actually bigger than any other transition that I had, this entire year . . . I don't ever want to have to need someone again, where you feel like, without them, you can't be yourself. (Effron 2013)

Are individualism and marriage the oil and water of modern relationships, unable ever to fully mix together? If people pursue marriage primarily to make themselves happy and then judge the relationship on the basis of their own happiness, then marriage will be unstable, always facing the risk that one partner or the other will feel unfulfilled and turn away. In fact, that may be why divorce has become a prominent feature of the relationship landscape.

Maybe that's not a bad thing. If it means that the relationships that do survive are built on genuine mutual happiness or satisfaction, then the modern family order may be an improvement over the past. But if the experience of divorce, or the threat of divorce, looms large in modern families, then we all live under a cloud of family uncertainty. Individual freedom is a cherished value for most people. But uncertainty comes with risks, especially for children, who are the most vulnerable to the stress of family transitions (Cherlin 2010). This is the central dilemma of divorce that we confront.

For the Children's Sake

Of course, there is nothing wrong with loving oneself if that means recognizing and respecting one's own needs and desires. But how is individual happiness to be balanced against family commitments, including marriage? This is as much a moral question as a practical or psychological one. In the face of such a quandary,

The critically acclaimed film *The Squid and the Whale* follows a couple's acrimonious divorce and its effects on their two sons.

many people evoke the principle of making decisions in the best interest of children rather than adults. Some parents try to prevent or delay divorce for the children's sake—to spare them the disruption, potential financial loss, and even shame of a family breakup. Other parents, however, *want* a divorce for the children's sake—to keep them from living under the cloud of constant bickering or to remove them from the care of an irresponsible (or even abusive) spouse.

And then there are the children themselves. Their parents' breakup may be the first time they seriously face the need to evaluate, in moral terms, the behavior of adults. For better or worse, in the words of researcher Carol Smart, divorce "shatters the taken-for-grantedness of family life." She quotes a 12-year-old girl whose parents divorced:

> I can remember some arguments and I can remember thinking "Oh my god my parents hate each other" but now I don't think they hate each other; they are friends. But if you argue in front of your children they will think you hate each other. You need to split up or at least give yourselves some space until you've thought about it because that is what is best for them. (Smart 2006:167)

Through the unhappy experience of her parents' conflicted marriage and eventual divorce, this girl learned something about how to apply ethical standards to adult behavior and came to believe that her parents made the right decision.

Divorce, perhaps more than most experiences in life, drives home the lesson that there are many sides to every story. Just as there are different angles to the story within a particular family, there also are many ways to see the social phenomenon of divorce. What to some people seems like the liberation of unhappy spouses (and children) from a life unfulfilled—or worse—to others seems like another step down the road toward the collapse of the family as an institution.

The long-term increase in divorce and remarriage in American family life raises several questions linked to our three overarching themes in this book. Clearly, the proliferation of different family arrangements contributes to *family diversity*. Further, the trend in divorce has been to widen social class *inequality* in family life, as we will see that divorce has become much less common among those with the highest levels of education. Divorce also highlights the *social change* toward an individual orientation in family life and decision making. You might link all of this to an overall trend toward selfishness on the part of adults, especially in relation to the well-being of children. But the weakening of those bonds—informal or legal rules and obligations that keep people together even when they don't want to be—might also be a sign of personal liberation and enhanced social freedom.

Although there are various ways of assessing U.S. trends in divorce, there is no dispute that divorce is vastly more common today than it was a century ago. Furthermore, the everyday nature of divorce has changed the institution of the family for everyone, even those who never themselves divorce. Children's lives and relationships are clearly affected when their parents break up; for example, many people whose own parents divorced react by limiting themselves to informal relationships—or by avoiding living with another person altogether—partly out of aversion to the possibility of divorce (Klinenberg 2012).

The expanding diversity of family arrangements leads to different kinds of life stories that sociologists seek to understand and explain. In this chapter, we will review some history and recent trends regarding divorce—the who, when, and why of couple breakups. Then we will consider some of the causes and consequences of divorce for women, men, and children. Finally, we will discuss the remarriage and blended family arrangements that follow divorce for most people, which raise a further set of questions and issues for modern families.

As in the case of marriage generally, although almost all studies and statistics about divorce relate to heterogamous couples—those with one man and one woman—gay and lesbian divorce and relationship dissolution are a part of the family landscape as well (Rosenfeld 2014). We don't yet have much systematic information about how and when such breakups occur, but what we do have so far reveals little difference in the patterns for straight versus gay and lesbian couples (Manning, Brown, and Stykes 2016). In most of this chapter I discuss research on couples without regard to their gender.

Church and State

The history of divorce in Western societies shows the state as an institutional arena, its leaders, laws, and regulations increasingly encroaching on the Christian church's authority with regard to the family. The family that emerged in the modern era is much more under the control of state authorities than of religious authorities, with deference to religious authority now usually seen as a conscious choice rather than a requirement. But before I tell that story, let me define a few terms.

Divorce as a legal event is only part of what concerns social scientists with regard to couple breakups. When marriages end, we refer to it as **marital dissolution**, the end of a marriage through permanent separation or divorce. We use that term because some couples who separate never get a legal divorce. **Separation** refers to the formal or informal separation of married spouses into different households. In some cases, this is a legal agreement, and in some states, separation is required before a divorce can be granted. Finally, **divorce** is the legal dissolution of marriage according to the laws of the state. (In the United States, marriage and divorce are administered by the state level of government, but because that is not the case in other countries, I use the term *state* to mean whatever government has authority over families.) I should add that researchers sometimes refer to any couple dissolving as "relationship dissolution," even when they have not been married. Especially when these families include children, the process is closely related to divorce. In this chapter, even though I mostly use the terms *marriage* and *divorce*, much of what we discuss is relevant to committed couples whether married or not.

Divorce is as old as marriage, although the rules and customs surrounding how marriages end have varied drastically. Most American Indian cultures permitted divorce, and it was more common for them than it was among the European

marital dissolution

The end of a marriage through permanent separation or divorce.

separation

The formal or informal separation of married spouses into different households.

divorce

The legal dissolution of marriage according to the laws of the state.

In this letter from 1530, English noblemen demanded that Pope Clement VII annul Henry VIII's marriage to Catherine of Aragon. More than 80 wax seals are attached below the lords' signatures.

annulment of marriage

A legal or religious determination that the marriage was never valid.

settlers who encountered them (Queen 1985). Likewise, ancient Jewish laws permitted divorce. Divorce was quite common among upper-class couples in the Roman Empire. But by the time of early Christianity, religious authorities introduced strong rules against divorce, with the Bible intoning, "what therefore God hath joined together, let not man put asunder" (Coontz 2005:86). In practice, however, the Catholic Church did not begin to enforce strict limits on divorce for common people until the eighth century. By the twelfth century, divorce was virtually impossible under Church doctrine. People could separate by mutual agreement (or, more often, one could desert the other), but they couldn't legitimately remarry unless they were granted an annulment, which was almost unheard of.

That history is what makes annulment important to understand. **Annulment of marriage** is a legal or religious determination that the marriage was never valid. After an annulment, the marriage is treated as if it never occurred. The logical distinction between annulment and divorce is what made it possible historically to prohibit divorce but still let some people (usually powerful men) take spouses. Religious annulment remains an important issue, mostly for Catholics. Under the doctrine of the Catholic Church, remarriage is permitted only if the marriage is annulled by the Church—that is, judged to have been invalid and therefore not binding on the spouses. Although this might seem like a convenient fiction, many Catholics who divorce do seek annulments so they can remarry and remain within the Church. The vast majority of annulment applications are accepted, but to help Americans maintain their ties to the Church, Pope Francis has said he wants to make annulments cheaper, faster, and easier to get (Yardley and Povoledo 2015). As a legal procedure, annulment exists in the United States today but is very rare, occurring only in cases where spouses were not legally permitted to marry when they did (Abrams 2013).

As the issue of annulment suggests, the controversy around divorce has always involved the problem of remarriage. Ending a marriage has never been as controversial as remarrying afterward and especially producing "legitimate" children—those whose parents are legally married—in a subsequent marriage. This tension is one source of the historical conflict between religious and state authorities, which long competed for the power to regulate marriage and divorce. This tension exploded in the sixteenth century, when England's King Henry VIII wanted an annulment so that he could take a new wife. The Roman Catholic pope's refusal to grant that annulment helped convince Henry to leave Catholicism and form the independent Church of England, with himself as its head. (Unfortunately for his new wife, Anne Boleyn, she bore a daughter and then had a series of miscarriages without giving birth to a living son, so Henry executed her before marrying again a few days later.) Although that split with the Catholic Church did not end the power of religious institutions in the realm of marriage and divorce, by placing family regulation under the control of the state it marked a significant historical step toward separating religious from civil authority over family law in Western societies.

Still, as we saw in Chapter 8, despite the separation of church and state enshrined in the U.S. Constitution, the conflict persists between some religious and legal rules and customs governing marriage. Recent debates over "marriage rights" have concerned same-sex marriage. But in the late nineteenth century, a similarly heated debate revolved around the right to marry for people who had been divorced. At the time, few Americans believed that the "guilty" party in a divorce should be permitted to remarry, but the accusing spouse—often the victim of abuse or abandonment—was seen more sympathetically. Still, conservatives feared that loosening the laws regarding remarriage would open up society to the rule of "free love," encouraging people to swap partners casually without regard for the sacredness of marriage (Cott 2000). In one case, a Catholic bishop in Nebraska declared that anyone who *attended* the wedding of a divorced man would be excommunicated (barred from the Church). Marriage rights advocates defended the principle of divorce and remarriage as a moral choice. As one radical journalist wrote, "It is dishonor to remain in a state of marriage wherein the soul cries out in agony of despair, and the bondage robs life of all its sunshine" (Harris 1906:393).

As divorce entered the twentieth century, it occurred with greater and greater frequency, even in the absence of physical abuse or abandonment. Although it remained quite rare by today's standards, the American public was riveted by the family dramas of celebrities and socialites, especially once the voices of the neglected spouses could be heard in the press (see Changing Culture, "Divorce, American Style").

Divorce Rates and Trends

As a family sociologist with an expertise in demography, I have frequently been asked, "What is the divorce rate?" This is really two questions. First, what do we *mean* by the divorce rate? And second, what is the number itself? I will try to avoid a long, technical answer, but each of these questions deserves a little attention.

There is no single definition of "the divorce rate." To see why, consider a few numbers. In 2015, there were an estimated 1.1 million divorces in the United States. I have to say "estimated" because there is no official count of divorces: five states, including the biggest (California), do not participate in the federal government's collection of divorce data. So that estimate is calculated from a large survey, the American Community Survey (which, fortunately, provides high-quality data from all states).

But what is the meaning of 1 million divorces? From the total number, we can

Divorce, American Style

Charlie Chaplin with Lita Grey during the making of *The Gold Rush*, which she was to have starred in.

From King Henry VIII to Miley Cyrus, the divorces (or breakups) of the rich, famous, and powerful have contributed dramatic storylines to our social history. How we interpret those stories is related to how we see divorce in general as a personal drama and as a social issue.

The first celebrity divorce in the United States covered by national media—in this case, newspapers and magazines—involved silent-movie star Charlie Chaplin, renowned for his portrayal of the downtrodden everyman figure known as the Tramp. In 1927, Chaplin's second wife, Lita Grey, sued him for divorce.

Grey was to have been the lead actress in Chaplin's new movie, *The Gold Rush*, but the actor/director, himself the product of divorced parents, hurriedly married her—and replaced her in the cast—when she became pregnant. The young actress was just 16 years old and he was 35 when they crossed the border into Mexico to get married. Because of her age, he feared he could be charged with statutory rape unless they married. It was Chaplin's second divorce (the first was also from an actress under 18), and it created a national sensation, with charges and countercharges aired in the press, breaking on page 1 of the *New York Times* on January 11, 1927, with the subheadline, "Film Star's Wife Makes Sensational Charges of Infidelity and Threats on Her Life."

The divorce settlement that Lita Grey received was itself sensational: at $625,000, it was the largest monetary settlement in the United States at that time. (However, at just $8 million in today's dollars, it was skimpy compared with the celebrity settlements we've grown accustomed to since; and had their marriage not cut short her career, she might have ended up even richer.) Despite the scandal, Chaplin's career continued on an upward trajectory, and he remains a cultural icon today. Today's celebrity divorces may feature scandalous accusations, but that's less common now that such charges are not necessary to gain court approval for a legal divorce.

Changing Attitudes

A century ago, advocates for women's equality argued that liberalizing divorce law was essential to women's equal rights, and most people assumed that divorce promoted equality between the sexes (Smock 2004). Later critics, concerned about the rising number of single mothers living in poverty, feared that divorce was not just expanding women's rights but also contributing to the "feminization of poverty," since few women received anything like the large settlement that Lita Grey received from Chaplin (Klawitter and Garfinkel 1992). Still, feminists consider access to divorce essential for gender equality.

Today, acceptance of divorce is widespread but not universal. As of 2016, when asked whether divorce is "morally acceptable" versus "morally wrong," 72 percent of Americans told the Gallup poll that they thought it was morally acceptable (Gallup 2016). But the pattern of support closely follows divisions between conservative and liberal political views (as you can see in Figure 10.1). The idea that easy access to divorce is weakening families in America and causing harm to children in particular is common among social conservatives (Coontz 1992). Social conservatives tend to combine views in favor of "traditional" family structure with support for traditional religious authority as well. That explains why those who attend religious activities more often are so much more likely to oppose loose divorce laws (Stokes and Ellison 2010).

How acceptable—or reasonable—divorce is in response to relationship problems reflects the way people are raised and their cultural attitudes in general. However, people's attitudes also reflect a practical response to their own experiences and the experiences of those around them. In an interesting example of that social process, a study of one community over time found that divorce tends to appear in clusters of friends, coworkers, and siblings (McDermott, Fowler, and Christakis 2013). And although most people favor nonrestrictive divorce laws and believe that divorce is a morally acceptable solution to serious marital problems, in some liberal communities divorced people experience feelings of failure and find themselves the subject of gossip. That was the experience of the women quoted in a feature story about divorced Brooklyn

Figure 10.1 **Attitudes toward divorce**

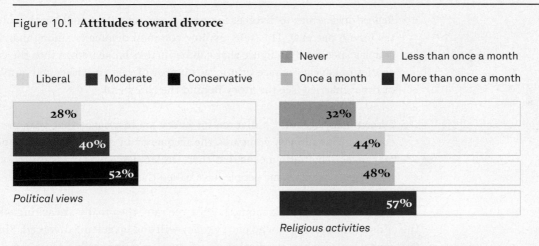

Percent of people who say that divorce in the United States "should be more difficult to obtain than it is now." People with more conservative political views and those who participate in more religious activities have a more negative view of permissive divorce laws.

SOURCE: Author's graph from the General Social Survey data, 2014–2016 (Smith et al. 2017).

mothers (Paul 2011). "I've definitely experienced judgment," said Priscilla Gilman, a writer quoted in the story. "Everyone said: 'Isn't there anything more you can do? Your kids need you to be together. They're so little.'"

These cultural skirmishes, occurring in the personal lives of many people as they make their way through a lifetime of family decisions, reflect the unresolved nature of our cultural attitudes toward families. In this case, the competitive attitude toward parenting—which encourages parents to put their children above all else and judges them harshly when they do not (as we saw in Chapter 9)—clashes with the individualist view that marriage must be self-fulfilling and rewarding (as described in Chapter 8).

produce several different divorce rates, depending on what other information we have (England and Kunz 1975):

- *Crude divorce rate*: 3.9 divorces for every 1,000 people in the country. This simply indicates how common divorce is in the whole country. We can report this if all we know is the number of divorces and the size of the entire population. That is why we use it for long-term trends, going back to years before there was good available data. As Figure 10.2 shows (using a different data source), the crude divorce rate rose from the earliest national estimate almost continuously for most of the twentieth century, until about 1981, from which time it has been falling almost continuously.

- *Refined divorce rate*: 16 divorces for every 1,000 married couples in the country (or 1.6 percent). This tells us how common divorce is among married couples specifically, a figure that can be further broken down into the categories of education, race/ethnicity, number of years married, and number of times married (see the Story Behind the Numbers).

- *Divorce-marriage ratio*: 1 divorce for every 2.2 marriages that year in the country. This directly compares the frequency of divorces to that of new marriages. That ratio means that there are 46 percent as many divorces as marriages—which some people have called the "divorce rate."

When most people ask about the divorce rate, they really are asking what the odds are that a couple who marry *today* will end up getting divorced. Since that question involves predicting the future, it's impossible to answer, of course, but that won't stop us from trying. There are two helpful ways of going about it. First, we can look at the marriage and divorce history of older people today. For example, a study in 2009 showed that, of all the people who got married in the 1950s, about 40 percent were divorced after 50 years. Among the group that married later, at the height of divorce in the late 1970s,

Figure 10.2 Crude divorce rate, 1860–2015

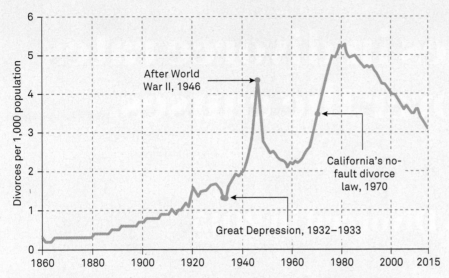

A consistent rise from 1860 to 1981, except for some major events that disrupted the trend: a dip during the Great Depression, when many people postponed divorce because they couldn't afford to move out on their own; and a spike after World War II, when many people who had rushed into marriage before the war divorced.

SOURCES: Statistical Abstracts; National Vital Statistics of the United States; Jacobson (1959). Note: For 1920–present these are official counts from the National Center for Health Statistics, and they do not exactly match those from the American Community Survey.

a higher percentage—46 percent—were already divorced after only 30 years of marriage. Although many people believe that 50 percent of marriages end in divorce, no cohort of couples has yet (quite) achieved that high of a rate (Kreider and Ellis 2011).

Second, we can estimate how many of today's marriages will end in divorce by calculating what would happen if some recent year (in this case, 2012) happened over and over again—that is, if everyone lived through today's divorce rates for their entire marriages (Preston 1975). That way of estimating future events predicts that 53 percent of new marriages will eventually end in divorce, with the other 47 percent ending with the eventual death of one of the spouses (Cohen 2016). Using recent history to predict the future is complicated by the aging of the population. It turns out divorce rates have been rising for older people but falling for younger people, and we can't know what will happen to today's young people when they become tomorrow's old people (Kennedy and Ruggles 2014). We will return to divorce at older ages in this chapter's Trends to Watch.

In summary, regardless of which numbers we use, we can safely say that divorce rates are a lot higher than they were 150 years ago, and they peaked around 1980 before starting to decline. But if we want to know what percentage of new marriages will end in divorce, we can only make an educated guess, but it will probably be about half.

Differences in divorce rates help uncover the causes.

% Divorced in 2015

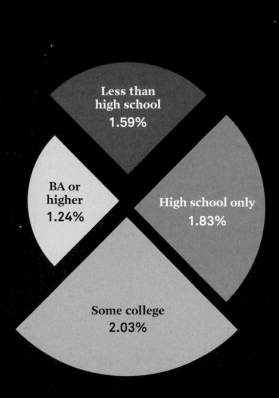

Less than high school
1.59%

BA or higher
1.24%

High school only
1.83%

Some college
2.03%

Education

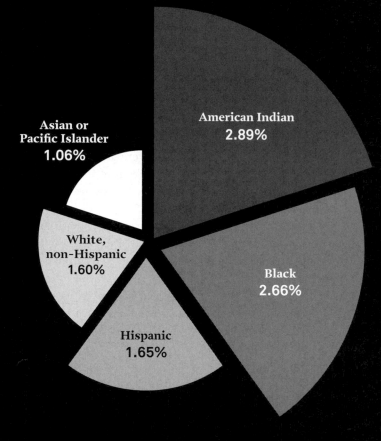

Asian or Pacific Islander
1.06%

American Indian
2.89%

White, non-Hispanic
1.60%

Black
2.66%

Hispanic
1.65%

Race/ethnicity

There were 1.1 million divorces in the U.S. in 2015, which means just less than 2 percent of all married people per year get divorced. Divorce rates are higher for people who have been married multiple times, and even higher in the first 10 years of marriage. Regarding education, divorces are less common for college graduates than everyone else. Among the racial-ethnic groups, American Indians and African Americans have the highest divorce rates, while Asian and Pacific Islanders have the lowest rates, and Whites and Hispanics are in the middle.

Source: Author's tabulation of data from the 2015 American Community Survey via Ruggles et al. 2016.

http://wwnpag.es/sbtn10

Go to this link for an animation narrated by the author.

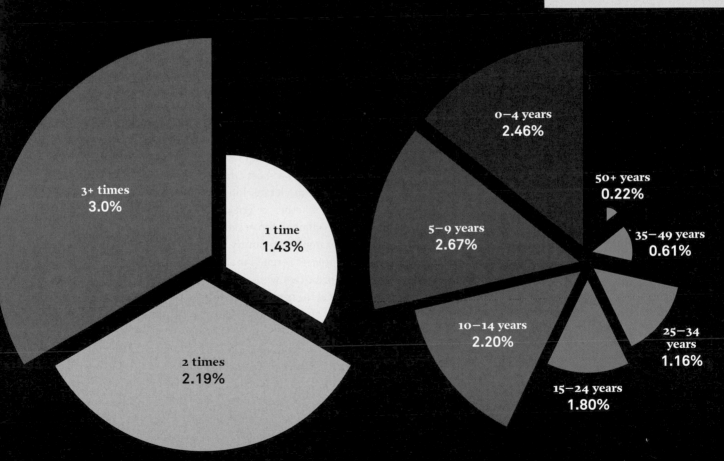

Times married

Years married

The Divorce Revolution

Let's return to the years 1960–1980, when there was a dramatic increase in divorce that came to be called the "divorce revolution" (Weitzman 1985). What happened? Many people associate that rise with the liberalization of family law, which started permitting easier, "no-fault" divorces. Under the new laws, which spread across most of the country in the 1970s, couples could get a legal divorce without an accusation of wrongdoing, such as infidelity, abuse, or desertion. More important, in most states, either spouse could *unilaterally* demand a divorce. In other words, the law took on the reality that marriage was a voluntary arrangement between free individuals. Although not specifically written to privilege women, the new divorce laws were part of a tide of reforms in the legal system, inspired by the feminist movement, aimed at liberating women from traditional discriminatory laws (Strebeigh 2009).

Divorce reform was probably the most radical change ever in the law governing families. But did such a dramatic break with the legal past really cause the number of divorces to skyrocket? Yes and no. As Figure 10.2 shows, divorce had been increasing for decades, and the rate was increasing rapidly even before 1970, when the first no-fault divorce law took effect in California. In fact, even prior to 1970, although the law mandated an adversarial divorce process based on finding one spouse at fault, many couples and their lawyers were able to work around the legality to arrange divorces even when no legal breach of the marriage vows had occurred (Cherlin 2010).

And yet, there is no doubt that the more liberal legal environment made divorce easier. By studying the trends in different states as they adopted the new laws, researchers have determined that no-fault divorce did in fact lead to a sharp spike in divorces, but only for a short time (Wolfers 2006). After that, the divorce rate returned to a more moderate, long-run upward trend (Schoen and Canudas-Romo 2006). Thus, whether or not changes in the law were directly responsible, the divorce rate climbed for decades and eventually reached levels high enough to have a major impact on family life.

By the time the baby boomers reached marriage age, their attitudes toward family commitments and priorities were unique in American history. People born in the late 1950s—during the baby boom—had the highest divorce rate ever recorded. About one-third of them had experienced a divorce as early as age 40 (Kreider and Ellis 2011).

The fact that divorce was so common affected the decisions people made about whether to get married, whom to marry, whether and when to have children—and everything in between. By the 1970s, divorce achieved a critical level of momentum, generating ripple effects throughout society. For example, the later age at marriage and the practice of cohabitation, which we discussed in Chapter 8, are related to this reality. People fearful of divorce may postpone or forgo marriage altogether.

Finally, the divorce revolution has proved to be multigenerational (Wolfinger 2005). Whether the effects of divorce on children are positive or negative—and as we will see, either outcome is possible—one consequence is that the children of divorced parents are substantially more likely to get divorced themselves (Goodwin, Mosher, and Chandra 2010). In the view of some children of baby boomer parents—the so-called Generation X, born between 1965 and 1979—their parents' divorces were the defining experiences of their generation.

"It is a hard truism that every generation is shaped by its war," wrote Susan Thomas in her memoir *In Spite of Everything* (2011:xvi). Previous generations were marked by life during World War II or the Vietnam War, for example. But "Generation X's war," she believes, "was the ultimate war at home: divorce." Thomas, who was determined never to put her kids through the same thing she experienced, nevertheless eventually got divorced herself.

Causes of Divorce

Our sociological perspective is useful for organizing ideas about the causes of divorce. Like other family behavior, divorce is intimate and personal, but also the product of larger social forces. This description of the causes of divorce can't cover everything, but it provides a framework for thinking about what contributes to couples breaking up (Lyngstad and Jalovaara 2010).

In the Story Behind the Numbers we can see some of the larger patterns: divorces are relatively common for people with less education, for African Americans and American Indians, for those earlier in their marriages, and for those who have been married before. Some of that is not surprising given what we have learned earlier. For example, we saw in Chapter 8 that White marriages are reported to be somewhat happier than Black marriages (Broman 2005). And indeed, the higher rate of divorce among Black couples, compared with White and Latino couples, is a long-standing pattern (Bulanda and Brown 2007). But by looking more closely at the various aspects of marriage, we can learn much more about the nature and causes of divorce.

The Matching Process

When people join into couples, through marriage or cohabitation, the nature of the relationship is affected by the way they come together and by what they each bring to the union. The clearest way to see this is by comparing those who cohabit and those who marry: cohabiting couples break up more than married couples—they're more likely to eventually split up and more likely to do so quickly. This may be because people get married when their relationships are already better or their commitments stronger. Or getting married may change relationships in ways that make them stronger.

For cohabitors who do get married, there are contrasting views on how living together before marriage might affect the chance of the relationship surviving. One perspective is that people who live together first get to know each other better. As a result, they make more informed decisions about marrying and their marriages are stronger. On the other hand, living together outside the bond of marriage might undermine their sense of commitment, making divorce more likely.

Cohabitation is a practical question for many people who are considering whether to move in with someone they are planning eventually to marry. However, several problems complicate the goal of resolving it. People who live together before marriage have more liberal family views in general and a more accepting attitude toward divorce in particular. They also tend to have less stable lives—for example, in their work experience and history of moving around the country. So if they get divorced more, it might be as a result of these factors. Moreover, the "relationship clock" has already started for couples that live together before marrying. So comparing couples after, say, five years of marriage might be misleading, since those who lived together already have been in the relationship longer (Lyngstad and Jalovaara 2010). Careful analysis, taking these complications into account, shows that living together with a partner does not affect the chance of divorcing if the couple eventually marry (Manning and Cohen 2012). However, one important distinction is between those who are *engaged*

Figure 10.3 **Chance of divorce within the first 10 years, by wife's age at marriage**

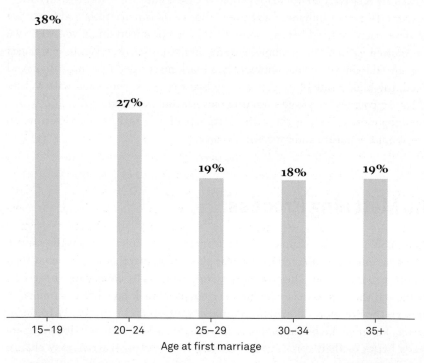

Almost 40 percent of marriages in which the wife is under age 20 when they marry end in divorce within 10 years, about twice the rate of those who are over age 25 when they first marry.

SOURCE: Author calculations from the 2015 American Community Survey.

when they start cohabiting and those who aren't. People who move in together when they're engaged are less likely to get divorced—maybe because their relationship commitment was stronger all along (Goodwin et al. 2010).

Another important element of the matching process is the age at which couples marry. People who are older when they first marry are less likely to divorce, and this could help explain falling divorce rates (Rotz 2016). As Figure 10.3 shows, people who marry before age 20 are about twice as likely as people who marry after age 25 to divorce within the first 10 years. Again, this could be because older people make more sensible decisions about marriage or because those who marry later are more mature emotionally, more financially secure, and better educated (Lehrer and Chen 2013).

Relationship Dynamics

Divorce usually follows unhappiness and conflict within marriage, which is not surprising. But when researchers study marriage dynamics, some other key issues emerge as risk factors for divorce (Bulanda and Brown 2007). Couples are more likely to divorce when they:

- describe themselves as unhappy in their marriages;

- spend less time alone with each other;

- disagree frequently about household tasks, money, time together, sex, and their in-laws; or

- have heated arguments, shout at, or hit each other.

However, these problematic relationship dynamics have many sources. And other influences within the family work against these risk factors (Kamp Dush and Taylor 2012). For example, religion may be a source of stability, as churchgoing couples are less likely to divorce. But religious disagreement is a source of strife for many couples as well, and couples where the husband and wife have different levels of religious commitment or belief are more likely to divorce (Vaaler, Ellison, and Powers 2009).

The most important consideration for many couples is their children, as even those couples who can't agree about much often share a goal of minimizing their children's unhappiness in a divorce. In fact, couples with children—especially young children—are less likely to divorce (Lillard and Waite 1993). Ironically, married people with young children also are less happy in their marriages, perhaps making a happiness sacrifice during the early childbearing years on behalf of their long-term commitment to each other and their children (Twenge, Campbell, and Foster 2003).

Some difficulties with parents and children, however, clearly contribute to relationship stress and increase the chance of divorce. Infertility problems, children's health disabilities, and the presence of stepchildren all have been shown to increase the likelihood of divorce (Reichman, Corman, and Noonan 2004; Teachman 2008). However, I should stress here that for each couple who divorce under such circumstances, there are many who do not—and who might actually describe the stress they endured together as an experience that made their family bonds stronger.

Employment and Independence

If you look carefully at Figure 10.2, you can see that the divorce rate was already increasing in the late nineteenth century. Without knowing how high the rate would eventually get, many people at that time were concerned. And some were already connecting the rise of divorce with the increased liberties of women, who could not even legally vote yet. Writing in 1889, the sociologist Carroll Wright (1889:169) asked, "Would the perfect independence of woman, her perfect equality before the law as a voter, accelerate divorce?" Soberly, he concluded that even if expanding women's rights did increase the number of divorces, that was a necessary price to pay to preserve the sanctity of marriage—which, he believed, should always and only be freely chosen.

By the time of the divorce revolution, it was not women's voting rights that drew attention, but rather the growing tendency of women to hold their own paying jobs. Surely, thought analysts in the 1970s and 1980s, if more women could support themselves, they would be more likely to get divorces and strike out on their own. After all, the majority of divorces are initiated by women. But surprisingly, the role of women's economic independence in accelerating the "divorce revolution" remains unclear. That is because independence actually works two ways (Sayer and Bianchi 2000).

First, it is true that when women (or men, for that matter) have the economic means to survive on their own, they are more likely to leave unhappy marriages. This has been called the *independence effect* of women's employment (Teachman 2010). Careful research—which tracks couples over time—has shown that women with jobs are more likely to seek divorces than they would otherwise, but only if they are dissatisfied with their marriage. There is no evidence that employment increases the tendency of women to leave happy marriages (Sayer et al. 2011). However, it may be that women who are considering divorce get jobs in anticipation of needing to support themselves and their children later on (Oezcan and Breen 2012). Still, the bottom line is that the rise of women's employment, and the independence it provides, have contributed to the upward trend in divorce.

On the other hand, ironically, independence also works to strengthen many marriages (Cooke et al. 2013). Couples in which both spouses have higher education and earn more are actually less likely to divorce. This is called the *income effect* of employment, because higher income within the couple serves as a source of stability and reduces stress between spouses. In fact, this tendency of high-earning couples to stay together has increased in the last several decades, with a clear gap opening up in the divorce rates between those with more education—who divorce relatively rarely—and those with less education, whose marriages are more prone to break up (Martin 2006). In combination, the independence and income effects of employment mean that employed people are freer to leave unhappy marriages, and people with higher incomes are more stable in their marriages—maybe because richer people leave marriages that don't satisfy them. That's part of the explanation for the pattern seen in Figure 10.4, which shows happiness levels to be higher for those with more family income.

We also see how important employment is in providing stability and reducing relationship stress when we study people who *lose* their jobs (Hardie and Lucas 2010). Couples in which one member experiences a job loss often have relationship problems as a result and are more likely to divorce. This pattern is especially pronounced when it is the husband who is out of a job. That suggests that it is not just couples' financial well-being that matters, but also a continued cultural expectation that husbands will provide income for their families (Killewald 2016). However, that norm may be weakening, as it is no longer the case that couples are more likely to divorce when the wife has more education than her husband (Schwartz and Han 2014).

There is one final consideration about the place of employment—and unemployment—in understanding divorce. With the severe economic recession

Figure 10.4 **Marital happiness by family income**

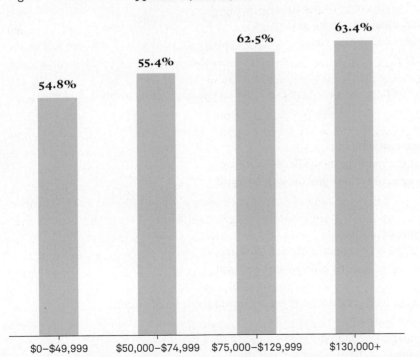

When asked how they would describe their marriage, more than half of all married people answered "very happy." But those whose family incomes are higher are even more likely to say that they are "very happy."

SOURCE: Author's calculations from the General Social Surveys, 2016 (Smith et al. 2017).

When Is Enough, Enough?

In response to a series of sex scandals involving married politicians, the Gallup polling organization asked more than 500 married Americans whether they would forgive their spouse if she or he had a sexual affair with another person. Figure 10.5 shows the breakdown of the responses.

In addition, 62 percent told Gallup they would get a divorce if they discovered such an affair—about the same percentage as the no-forgivers. Where to draw that line for divorce is not automatic. It is a product of a person's attitudes, upbringing, and the wider cultural context. Historian Stephanie Coontz (2007:14) writes, "But for better or worse, people decide what they will and will not put up with in a relationship today on a totally different basis than they used to."

So, what's a good reason to divorce—or not to divorce? In this exercise, individual students, small groups, or the whole class should ask themselves two sets of questions:

Figure 10.5 **Would you forgive your spouse if you found out s/he was having a sexual affair?**

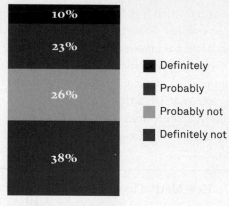

- ■ Definitely
- ■ Probably
- ■ Probably not
- ■ Definitely not

SOURCE: J. Jones (2008).

1. How strongly do you feel divorce is or is not morally acceptable? Think about it this way: Is divorce okay...
   a. With kids
      i. always, if someone wants to
      ii. sometimes, if the marriage is really not working
      iii. rarely, in the case of serious problems or betrayal
      iv. never
   b. Without kids
      i. always, if someone wants to
      ii. sometimes, if the marriage is really not working
      iii. rarely, in the case of serious problems or betrayal
      iv. never
2. If divorce is ever okay, which conditions or events would justify a divorce?
   a. Unhappiness in the marriage
   b. Couple growing apart, love fading
   c. Social lives incompatible, friends not getting along
   d. Poor sex life
   e. One spouse disrespectful to or unable to get along with extended family

f. Irresponsible spouse not carrying own weight in the marriage
g. Religious differences irresolvable
h. Career situation impossible to resolve for both spouses
i. One instance of infidelity
j. Repeated infidelity or long-running affair
k. Neglecting children or failing to care for them property
l. Abuse or violence within the family
m. Others?

In a group discussion, small group session, or individual writing, compare your answers to the first set of questions—how strongly you feel that divorce is okay or not okay—with your answers to the second set of questions about specific situations that might justify getting a divorce.

Compare your responses with those of others. What is the range of differences within the class? What do you think is the source of the differences of opinion? You may want to consider the role of upbringing, family experience, and religious or political views.

that occurred at the end of the 2000s, many people were concerned that divorce rates would increase—which is what we might expect if job loss puts marriages at higher risk of divorce (Amato and Beattie 2011). However, divorce rates continued to fall after the crisis (Cohen 2014b). Why? Future research may provide a definite answer, but I suspect that the recession both caused some divorces and prevented some divorces. Some were caused by the stress and disruption of job loss, especially when people lost their homes as a result. But because divorce is often expensive, other divorces were prevented by the same factors. At minimum, divorce requires legal fees and the costs of one spouse moving out—and it may require selling the family home to split up the proceeds, something that was very difficult during the recession of the late 2000s. So some unhappy couples may have been stuck together by the recession as well.

Consequences of Divorce

Divorce isn't the outcome people look forward to when they get married. So we usually think of divorce as a bad outcome. However, once people are in an unhappy marriage, divorce may be a better option than staying married, so we should consider the potential positive as well as negative aspects of the experience. There are also different parties to a divorce to consider—the adults, the children, and anyone else involved. In this section, I will introduce a few ways of looking at the question.

Adults' Happiness

Divorced people are generally less happy than married people, but that doesn't mean that divorce caused their unhappiness. Not surprisingly, unhappy people are more likely to get divorced in the first place (Lucas 2005). But at least for a time, the process of divorce increases the odds of those involved experiencing symptoms of depression or unhappiness (Kamp Dush 2013). Still, among those who get divorced, the differences in experience are more important than trying to identify a single common result.

For example, a study of several thousand British couples asked a series of questions to measure people's level of mental stress, such as whether they had recently had trouble with concentration, sleep, making decisions, feeling under strain, feeling helpless or worthless, or feeling depressed. The researchers tracked these couples over time and compared those who divorced or separated with those who didn't (Gardner and Oswald 2006). As Figure 10.6 shows, two years before a marital dissolution, those headed for a breakup clearly showed a higher level of stress, which rose until the year of the separation or divorce and then fell back down to a lower level than before (although it was still slightly higher than the stress experienced by stably married adults). This suggests that there is at least some benefit to divorcing for these relatively stressed-out people.

Figure 10.6 **Mental stress levels in the years surrounding divorce or separation**

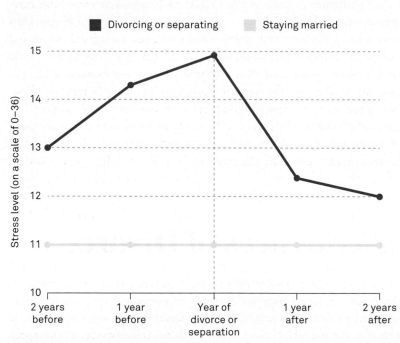

Stress levels are higher, and rising, before divorce or separation, but then fall back to a level near that of stably married adults.

SOURCE: Adapted from Gardner and Oswald (2006).

On the other hand, because divorce is so widely considered a "failure," many people experience a stigma after they divorce, which makes them less happy. Even though it has become more common, more permissible, and less universally condemned socially, divorced people still often want to keep their divorced status private due to feelings of failure or self-disapproval, and they may fear people are judging them negatively. This actually contributes to the desire many divorced people have to remarry; remarrying removes their "status" as a divorced person (Cohen 2010b).

Economic Status

Consider a simple divorce scenario, shown in Figure 10.7. In a typical married-couple family with two children in 2016, a husband employed full-time earns about $60,000 and a wife about $40,000. That means that the total of $100,000 works out to $25,000 per person. If they divorce and each spouse keeps earning the same amount—and the children live with their mother—then the mother and children will be in a household with $40,000 and three people (or, $13,333 per person) while the father is on his own with $60,000. His per-person income goes up, hers and the children's goes down. If she doesn't have (or keep) her full-time job, the scenario will be worse for them.

The lower incomes of women and the tendency for them to live with their children after divorce are the reasons courts often order fathers to pay child support after a divorce (Oldham 2008). Unfortunately, this does not close the income gap that opens up after divorce. That is because the poorer people were before their divorce, the less money the parent who lives with the children gets in child support—and the more likely they are not going to receive their child support payments at all (Grall 2016).

The divorce revolution, from 1960 to 1980, undoubtedly contributed to what became known as the "feminization of poverty" in the 1980s (Hill 1985). By the end of the 1970s, about 60 percent of all poor families with children were led by single mothers. In fact, these mostly involved women who had never been married, but the dire economic consequences experienced by many divorced women were an important part of the story as well. The breakup of cohabiting couples is also a common situation, and because many cohabiting women are poor to start with, the demise of those relationships is very costly for them as well (Avellar and Smock 2005).

However, because most women now have work experience when they're married, and their education levels have increased, these losses are not as bad as they were in decades past (McKeever and Wolfinger 2001). Financially, it is also helpful that families have fewer children now than they did in decades past (Bengtson, Biblarz, and Roberts 2002). Nevertheless, women are more than twice as likely as men to be below the poverty line (discussed in Chapter 4) in the year after a divorce (see Figure 10.8). This gender disparity in poverty rates remains one of the important features of divorce's fallout, especially for children.

Figure 10.7 **Breaking up a household**

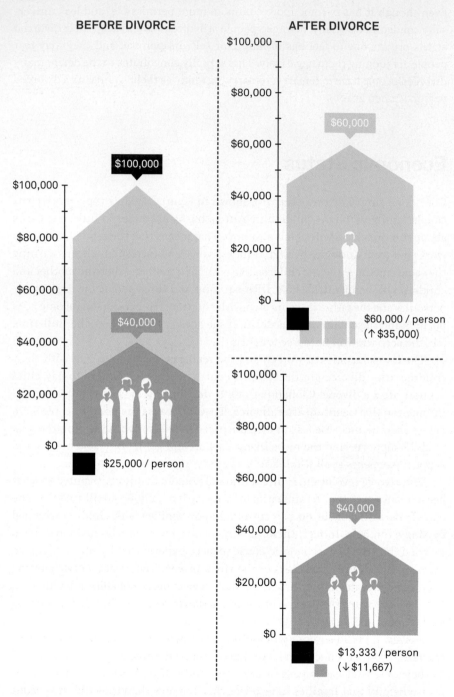

Using typical incomes for married men and women with full-time jobs, this illustration shows the increase in available income for men—and the decrease for women and children—if the children go live with their mother and the spouses' incomes remain the same.

SOURCE: Author's analysis of data from the March 2016 Current Population Survey.

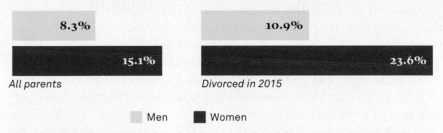

Figure 10.8 **Poverty and divorce: percentage in poverty for all parents and for those who divorced in 2015**

8.3%

10.9%

15.1%

23.6%

All parents

Divorced in 2015

☐ Men   ■ Women

Overall, mothers are about 7 percent more likely to be in poverty than fathers. But among those who divorced in the last year, women are more than twice as likely to be poor.

SOURCE: Author's calculations from the 2015 American Community Survey (Ruggles et al. 2016). Note: Includes parents ages 18–59, living with children.

Children's Well-Being

When Rachelle and Stephen planned their wedding, there were some practical questions to resolve. Both the bride and groom had divorced parents. Rachelle wondered:

> How do you include one mother in the processional when the other does not want to walk down the aisle, much less alone, and there's no clear answer for who should escort her? How do you figure out the seating for the ceremony for the mothers, fathers, second wives, stepsiblings and half-siblings so that everyone feels honored but no one is forced to sit next to someone who causes them pain to be near? This is the tip of the iceberg, my friends, and it feels never-ending.

Long before they considered marriage, Rachelle wrote, their relationship was marked by their histories of divorce:

> We dated tentatively. We fell in love tentatively. We talked about moving in together "one day" for over a year before we finally felt comfortable doing so. Every move forward was risking getting hurt bigger, more spectacularly. We had almost no one to model a healthy and happy relationship for us. We didn't have any way to know that we weren't doing it completely wrong, doomed to fail miserably at some inevitable future point. ("Planning a Wedding with Divorced Parents" 2011)

Rachelle's experience, which she described anonymously online, shows how, as with any major life event, marital dissolution creates ripples—or waves—that have many effects on children's lives. In the short run, the stress of a divorce may negatively affect school performance and children's happiness (Kim 2011). In the long run, the experience can threaten the mental health of its survivors and undermine their relationships with their parents. There is no simple way to generalize about these consequences, however, and researchers recognize that divorce may have positive effects as well (Amato and Anthony 2014).

Divorce is an "uncoupling process" rather than a single event—including the time leading up to the legal divorce or separation and the period of adjustment that follows. It is potentially a stressful process for everyone involved, but in different ways (Kelly and Emery 2003). For example, older children may be more aware of the divorce as it is happening, while younger children might not be seriously affected until they move into a new household without one of their parents. For those who are aware of the unhappiness in the marriage, its dissolution may cause immediate feelings of relief. The ambiguity about parents breaking up is even more pronounced when they weren't married before splitting, which means that there is no definitive moment provided by a legal divorce, and the relationships that follow are less clearly defined (Allen 2007).

Sociologist Paul Amato (2010) has divided the potential factors that affect children's experience of divorce into three categories: stressful aspects of the divorce process, protective factors to help prevent negative effects, and post-divorce outcomes.

These aspects of the divorce experience increase stress for those children involved:

- Less parental time and energy—or patience—for the normal aspects of parenting, and sometimes less time with parents altogether (Cooper et al. 2009)

- Losing contact with one parent for periods of time

- Witnessing or being part of conflicts, such as arguing or shouting (especially having to do with the children), which may continue for years after the divorce

- Residential moves, job and school transitions, and economic hardship

These factors offer protection for children from the negative consequences of divorce:

- Coping skills, interpersonal skills, and self-confidence

- Economic, educational, or other resources that help families buffer children from stressors

- Attentive parenting, diminished conflict, and continued involvement of both parents after the divorce

These are common outcomes that children may experience as a result of divorce:

- Short-term emotional or behavioral reactions or school problems

- Permanent emotional changes

- New roles and identities in the family or social environment

We saw in Chapter 9 that many more children are born to unmarried parents than was the case several decades ago. Trying to build or improve the relationships between children and the parents they don't live with—usually their fathers—has become increasingly important as their numbers have grown (Holt 2016). This is naturally even more challenging when fathers had little to do with the children in the first place (Edin, Tach, and Mincy 2009). But when fathers remain more involved in their children's lives after divorce, the effects generally are beneficial (Carlson and Magnuson 2011). Children who live with their mothers are better off psychologically, behaviorally, and academically when they remain involved with their fathers (Adamsons and Johnson 2013).

Still, the expectations for how, and how much, fathers should remain involved in their children's lives by spending time together, contributing money, and making important family decisions are often not clear. As we will see, the complications only increase when parents start forming new blended families after a divorce.

As the number of children of divorced parents has increased—and as those children have grown up—we have been able to learn more about the consequences of divorce for children. (In fact, I found more than 1,000 published studies about divorce and children.) One of the most important developments in this research has been the discovery that much of what looks like a consequence of divorce is actually related to which parents get divorced in the first place (Amato 2010). The people who divorce are more likely to be relatively poor, unstable or depressed, or unable to manage relationships—and their children simply reflect some of these problems. And some of the negative outcomes seen among children of divorce are also found among the children of parents in unhappy marriages who *don't* divorce.

Nevertheless, divorce is a major transition for most children (Brown, Stykes, and Manning 2016). And transitions themselves—moving, changing schools and neighborhoods, gaining and losing family members—pose challenges to children's development. So divorce remains an important milestone in the development of many children and their families (see Changing Law, "Who Gets the Kids?").

Remarriage and Blended Families

The story of American marriage is increasingly the story of remarriage. Most people who divorce eventually remarry, and my analysis of the American Community Survey finds that about 40 percent of new marriages involve at least one

Who Gets the Kids?

If parents weren't married before they had children, the children almost always live with the mother after the relationship breaks up. In those cases, the father may pay—or be ordered to pay—child support, as long as his paternity is established. If he is unable to pay, he may provide other kinds of support to help care for the kids (Kane, Nelson, and Edin 2015). On the other hand, when parents are married, the law no longer assumes that the children will live with the mother; that's a matter for the separation or divorce agreement or for the couple and their children to work out informally as they split up.

There are no comprehensive national statistics on legal child custody arrangements after divorce. And the legal arrangements might not be an accurate reflection of the messy reality of families' daily lives in any event. However, it is clear that the great majority of children of divorced parents live primarily with their mothers. The 2015 American Community Survey shows, for example, that 67 percent of children whose parents got divorced in the previous year are now living in single-mother households.

Why is this an important sociological issue? Here are three reasons. First, the care and nurturing of children is an important part of gender inequality. Because the parent who has custody of the children provides the bulk of their care, the tendency of children to live with their mothers means that the labor and expense fall mostly to women (Folbre 1994b).

Second, disputes over custody arrangements—over contact with the children (visitation rights) and payments of child support in particular—are one of the painful legacies of many divorces that have negative consequences for children and their parents and stepparents. So if the arrangements are not consensual or if they are a source of conflict, then the negative effects of divorce will be amplified. And third, research shows that maintaining good relationships and close contact between separated parents and children can be good for both parents and children (Choi, Palmer, and Pyun 2014).

Changing Assumptions

Judges in divorce cases—and the state legislatures that make the rules for them to follow—face a complex task of balancing interests. One goal is for children to maintain good relationships with both parents. Another goal is to promote a stable family life for children's development. This balance is not easily achieved, but it is one reason why many divorces today result in joint custody arrangements, in which children live alternately with both parents, with the mother and father sharing the costs and responsibilities of child rearing (Warshak 2014).

Among fathers who do not live with their children, it is difficult to maintain close, supportive parenting relationships. When joint custody is successful, it improves fathers' involvement with their children, which benefits their development. If, on the other hand, it is assumed that children belong with their mothers, then the economic losses associated with divorce will be more concentrated among women and children, and men who want custody may feel bitter and left out.

Partly in realization of these facts, in the last several decades many states have changed their laws from instructing judges to evaluate custody cases based on "the best interests of the child"—which usually meant the mother—to a legal "presumption" that joint custody is the best outcome (Allen and Brinig 2011). More fathers now actively seek custody of their children—and they have higher incomes, which makes a favorable impression on judges—so shared custody and even father-only custody seems more attractive as a solution. As a result, many more divorces are leading to joint custody agreements (Cancian et al. 2014).

Still, one recurring pattern in post-divorce disputes relates to the linking of child support with child custody or visitation rights. In an effort to reduce poverty among mothers and children and decrease the number of single-parent families receiving welfare, states and local governments have increased their enforcement of child support orders. This includes restricting visitation rights, garnishing the wages of parents who don't make payments, suspending their driver's licenses, and even arresting them for failure to pay. That approach has not been successful with fathers who have low incomes or poor employment prospects (including those who go to prison). As a result, millions of relatively poor fathers owe large debts of child support that they will never be able to repay, placing them in legal jeopardy and undermining relationships with their children and former partners (Pao 2015).

Ironically, even as more men have gained custody of their children after divorce, the perception that men's rights are harmed by these legal arrangements has only increased. This sense of being wronged has led some men to join the "men's rights" movement (Flood 2012). This situation has also given rise to a new cultural genre—the custody rant. Both men and women have taken to complaining publicly about their ex-spouses and the disputes that followed their divorces. I found one man's 8-minute "rant" (his term), which included this passage:

> I don't feel I should be paying for children, who I'm not seeing—you're alienating me from their lives, I want to be in their lives—you say I'm not good enough but my money is.... I feel

Alec Baldwin and Kim Basinger's custody battle over their daughter Ireland (pictured) lasted for years after their divorce.

my ex-wife tries to punish me. She tries to totally alienate the children from me, yet I have done *nothing* wrong.... I used to love seeing the children all the time. Then all of a sudden it stops. She meets somebody. She gets married. The game now changed. I don't wanna play the game. I wanna see my kids. You want my child support and I want my visitation.

Regardless of the form the rants take, bitter divorces are likely to generate bitter custody disputes. And children's relationships with their parents—and their family stability—will suffer as a result.

spouse who has been married before. The more ex-spouses and children from previous relationships there are when a couple gets married, the more everyone involved has the challenge—or opportunity—of rethinking their family lives (Sweeney 2010).

Traditionally, the prefix "step" was added to various family terms to indicate a relationship by marriage rather than by "blood" or adoption. So, for example, a "stepparent" was married to a child's parent. Over time, as cohabitation and other informal relationships became more common, people also started using the terms to refer to relationships that did not include marriage. As a result, these definitions are a little complicated, but they are necessary nonetheless before we can go much further.

Defining Ambiguity

First let's consider the parent-child relationships. A **stepparent** is the spouse or committed partner of one's biological or adoptive parent. On the flip side, a **stepchild** is the child of one's spouse or committed partner. Thus, step-relations have no biological relationship, but are related by the marriage or similar commitments of adults.

Next let's consider the sibling relationships. Following the logic of "step" as a marital (or marriage-like) connection, a **stepsibling** (stepbrother or stepsister) is the child (son or daughter) of one's stepparent. Again, stepsiblings are not biologically related. In contrast, a **half-sibling** is the biological child of one's parent and another person. That is, half-siblings share only one biological parent. From the children's point of view, families often include both stepsiblings and half-siblings—for example, when their mother and stepfather have a new child in addition to the stepsibling that came to the marriage.

Unfortunately, these definitions are becoming even more complicated in several ways. First, some stepparents eventually adopt their stepchildren legally.

stepparent

The spouse or committed partner of one's biological or adoptive parent.

stepchild

The child of one's spouse or committed partner.

stepsibling (stepbrother/ stepsister)

The child (son/daughter) of one's stepparent.

half-sibling (half-brother/ half-sister)

The biological child of one's parent and another person.

Second, some states have recently created legal definitions of stepparent-child relationships, with rights and obligations attached to them, so that such informal terms may not be legally accurate (Pollet 2010). Finally, although I have included unmarried partners in the definition of stepparents and stepsiblings, without a formal marriage it may not be clear whether such a partner is actually a stepparent. Family members might not agree on whether the partner actually lives in the household (for example, does he still have another apartment?). And they may not agree on the partner's relationship to or responsibility for the children, which often develops gradually over time (Ganong 2004).

Here is one telling example of such confusion. A large survey interviewed adolescents (7th grade through 12th grade) and the biological mothers with whom they lived. The children and their mothers were asked about the other people in the household. In the responses, 2.7 percent of adolescents said that their mother's partner lived in the household. But almost twice as many mothers—5.2 percent—said that they were living with a partner. In other words, mothers were more likely to say that their boyfriends were actually living in the household (Brown and Manning 2009).

Such "cohabiting stepparent families" are just one example of the ambiguity that many people experience in attempting to define and name their family type and its members as people come and go. For our purposes, any family that includes stepparents, stepsiblings, or half-siblings is a **blended family** (Kreider and Ellis 2011b). The word *blended* implies that more than one family is mixed together, with at least one outside family member whose relationship is not shared with everyone. By one way of counting them, which I show in Figure 10.11, 13 percent of children now live in blended families (but this is probably an undercount, since the survey I used doesn't show whether the children living with single parents are full- or half-siblings).

As we discussed in Chapter 1, knowing who is and who is not a family member is an important aspect of children's healthy development. Most important are the parent (or other caregiver) relationships, since these are the adults children need to trust in order to feel safe and secure, especially at the youngest ages. Beyond that, however, it is important for family members to agree on the boundaries of the family, the limits of the intimate family space on the inside, versus the more public social space on the outside. In blended families, the condition of **boundary ambiguity** occurs when family members do not know or do not agree on who is in the family and what role each person plays (Carroll, Olson, and Buckmiller 2007). This is more complicated the more people who are involved, and the more fluid living arrangements undermine the physical sense of family. Positive outcomes depend on the quality of the relationships as well. For example, teens who have a better relationship with their stepfathers were more likely than those who felt more distant to report feeling a sense of family belonging (King, Boyd, and Thorsen 2015).

The attempt to reduce such ambiguity in family relations was an important motivation for those who spent years attempting to achieve legal recognition for same-sex marriage. Because many gay and lesbian couples have children from previous marriages, the inherent ambiguity in their families was exacerbated by uncertain legal status (Carpenter and Gates 2008). When gay and lesbian

blended family

Any family that includes stepparents, stepsiblings, or half-siblings.

boundary ambiguity

The situation in which family members do not know or do not agree on who is in the family and what role each person plays.

Modern Family's diverse family structures mirror those in the United States today: divorce, remarriage, children from previous relationships, same-sex marriage, and adoption are all common reasons our ideas of "family" are changing.

marriages were not legally recognized, these families faced more difficulty establishing family roles that are clear to people both inside and outside their families. Marriage hasn't eliminated these unique challenges for same-sex couples, but it has made an important difference in their lives (Baumle and Compton 2017).

Interestingly, the rules of appropriate sexual intimacy are related to these boundaries. Almost everyone opposes sex between siblings or half-siblings, a taboo that usually extends to stepsiblings as well. However, when the stepparents are not married, or the children were not raised together, or even when two teenagers are dating before their parents become romantic partners, the informal rules are not clear. The following excerpt is from a young woman, speaking anonymously in an Internet discussion board, attempting to justify having sex with the son of her parent's unmarried partner. I have slightly edited the text and withheld the web address to protect the user's identity:

> I [had sex with] my stepbrother. Well, he's not really a stepbrother. Well he is, but our parents aren't married, and I'd only met him like four times. I couldn't date him or be with him, but it was just the once.... Dating your brother or sister or cousin that you share the same DNA with is sick. A stepsibling that you have absolutely no relation to, strange, but not sick. Maybe if you grew up together, but not in this case.

In the absence of a clear legal rule or strict social convention, these boundaries are worked out over time in countless conversations such as this. Eventually, perhaps, new rules emerge. By the end of that conversation, the woman was slightly ashamed of what she had done (and mentioned it was under the influence of alcohol), even though others reassured her that it was not "sick" or "wrong."

Who Remarries?

The short answer is: most people. America's high divorce rate—compared with that of the rest of the world—is complemented by a high remarriage rate. Or, as sociologist Andrew Cherlin jokes, "We seem to love marriage so much we do it over and over again." It may seem funny, but it does reflect the high value Americans place on marriage—although the tendency toward divorce and remarriage suggests that Americans care as much about being married as they do about maintaining marriages.

The pattern of remarriage seems to be changing, however, as both cultural attitudes about remarriage and the nation's demographics shift with the big baby boomer generation moving through its middle-aged years. As you can see in Figure 10.9, the group with the most remarriages is ages 55 to 64. Almost 30 percent of that group has been married more than once. Most of them married

Figure 10.9 **Number of times married, by age, 2015**

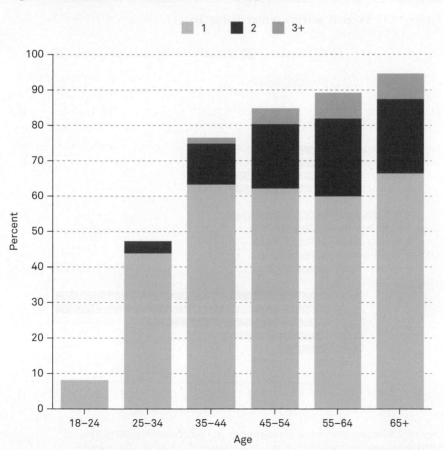

Multiple marriages are most common among people ages 55 to 64, of whom 29 percent have been married more than once.

SOURCE: Author's calculations from the 2015 American Community Survey (Ruggles et al. 2017).

for the first time in the late 1970s, and their marriages were the most likely to end in divorce. Thus, this generation—which also introduced the United States to the highest rates of cohabitation—has led the growth of remarriage as well as the growth of divorce. The effect of their family behavior on future generations remains to be seen (see Trend to Watch).

The rapid changes evident in this pattern make it difficult to make predictions, but it is likely that two-thirds of those who are divorcing now will eventually remarry (Sweeney 2010). Ironically, if divorce is seen by some people as a stigma, it doesn't apparently harm their chances of remarriage, at least for the majority of those who want to remarry. It helps that with so many divorced people in the "marriage market," they often end up marrying each other—maybe because they are willing to accept marriage to a person who has been divorced.

While fairly common after divorce, remarriage is much less common after widowhood. That is because divorced people tend to be younger and also because they more actively seek remarriage. In fact, people may choose to initiate a

Figure 10.10 **Percent getting remarried in 2015**

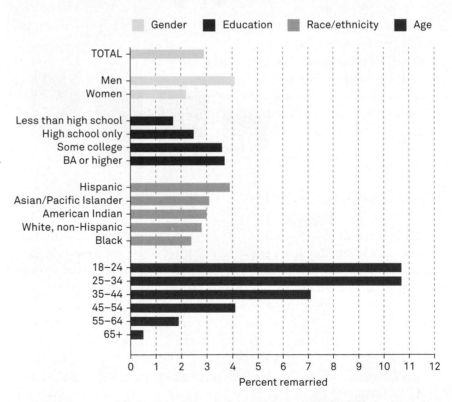

Overall, 2.9 percent of divorced or widowed adults got remarried in 2015. The differences between racial-ethnic groups are relatively small, but there are big differences by gender, education, and especially age.

SOURCE: Author's calculations from the 2015 American Community Survey (Ruggles et al. 2017).

divorce partly based on their perception that they have a good chance of remarriage (Sweeney 2010).

For a snapshot of the general pattern in remarriage, Figure 10.10 shows remarriage rates for 2015—that is, the percentage of previously married people in each group who got married again in that year. Overall, almost 3 percent remarried, but the differences between groups are significant. Most prominent, men are almost twice as likely as women to remarry in a given year. Children play a large role in that disparity (Goldscheider and Sassler 2006). Women with children are less likely to remarry; since most divorced mothers live with their children, this suggests that many men seek to avoid marriages with stepchildren. On the other hand, few divorced men live with children, and if they do, it actually increases their chance of remarrying (possibly because it increases their desire to find a new spouse).

Figure 10.10 also extends our understanding of the inequalities we have seen in the rates of marriage and divorce. The lower likelihood of remarriage for African Americans is a longstanding pattern (Furstenberg et al. 1983). And now we can see that people with lower levels of education are also less likely to remarry (McNamee and Raley 2011). This has unfortunate consequences for economic inequality. Remarriage can help families recover from the financial losses they suffered in a divorce—especially women with children (Morrison and Ritualo 2000). But those who are having trouble financially are much less likely to remarry successfully.

As with first marriages, the dynamics of remarriage are affected by the situation of the couple at the start. For example, most people who remarry today have already lived together with their new spouse (Teachman 2008). Their age, their relationship experience, and, especially, their children all shape the blended families that remarriage creates.

Challenges for Blended Families

As blended families have become more common, the problems of definition and boundary ambiguity noted earlier have become more prominent. In fact, these issues are a part of the social change underway for families in general, in which growing diversity has created increasing challenges of identity for each generation. The potential benefits of such change, however, include growing freedom for people to choose how to live their family lives—and growing acceptance of the diversity that results. In addition, increased independence for women and the trend toward smaller families make today's families better prepared to handle challenging transitions than were families in the past (Bengtson et al. 2002).

Today's children are certainly experiencing blended families at higher rates than those in the past. Even though divorce rates have declined since the 1980s, remarriage remains very common, and there are more children living with unmarried parents who cohabit with a partner, who may have children as well.

Figure 10.11 Children living in blended families

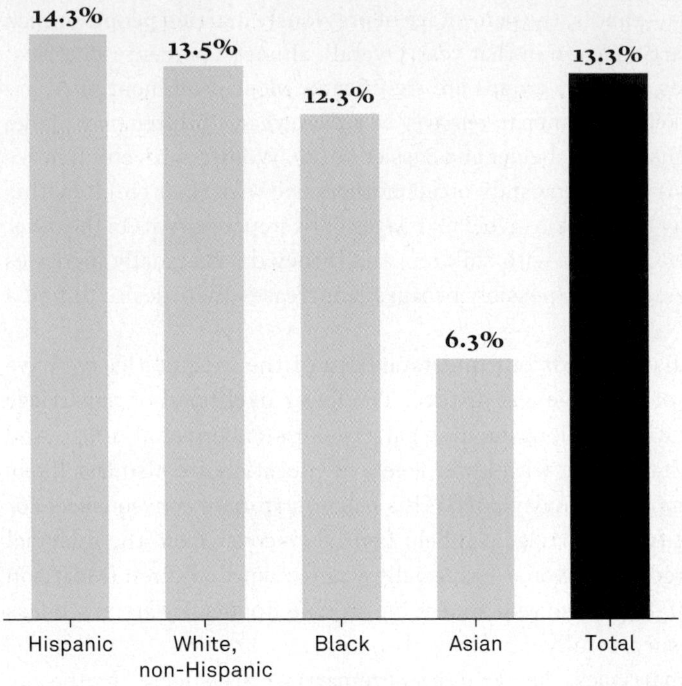

SOURCE: Author calculations from the 2016 Current Population Survey.

But blended families are not equally common in different groups in the United States. Figure 10.11 shows that Hispanic children most often experience blended families. Even though Latino couples have relatively low divorce rates, they are quite likely to remarry. The opposite is true for African Americans: although they have high divorce rates, relatively few children live in blended families because the remarriage rate is low.

From the perspective of broader social change, blended families are ahead of the curve in several respects. For one thing, remarried adults tend to preserve their individual autonomy more than those in first marriages—they are less inclined to give up their career interests for their spouses, for example. That more independent orientation makes sense once you consider that most of them are managing complex sets of relationships with multiple families. Also, they may have learned from their divorce experiences—for better or worse—to protect their independence. For children, that means growing up in a family with parents who are more individually oriented than those in first marriages. Not surprisingly, children of divorced parents seem to be more individualistic than those whose parents remain married (Bengtson et al. 2002).

Conflicts within blended families often reflect the problem of overlapping family boundaries. For example, stepparents face the challenge of integrating different parenting strategies, as each biological parent may attempt to preserve his or her parenting style. That causes conflict when the two parenting styles differ: Which parent makes (and enforces) the rules for which child? Other common problems include money disputes having to do with the partners' previous spouses and arguments over how to manage relations with the partners' extended families (Coleman et al. 2005).

Finally, what about intergenerational support in and around blended families? Here, again, the informal rules and customs are being figured out as we go (Curran, McLanahan, and Knab 2003). It may seem clear that a stepfather who marries a child's mother when the child is young has the same support obligations as any other parent—including, if possible, to pay for the child's college education. And the child, in turn, might be expected to help care for him when he's old if that becomes necessary. But does it matter if the stepfather and mother aren't married but are merely cohabiting partners? What if the stepfather enters the family when the child is 17—or 27? And what about the children from his previous marriage?

The law may provide some guidance for the complicated situations and dilemmas posed by blended families, but the legal rules remain tentative and often unclear (Mahoney 2006). Beyond that, the questions remain up in the air—part of the cultural remaking taking place in American families—with no destination in sight. The different approaches people take to working out these issues form a vital part of the family diversity we experience today.

Trend to Watch: Gray Divorce

The baby boom generation, born in the years 1946–1964, is in the age range 54–72 as of 2018. Besides being so numerous as to skew the whole population upward in age (see Chapter 13), what will be the impact of this generation's journey through senior citizenship? These are the people who brought us the rise of cohabitation before marriage, then delayed their first marriages until their middle or late 20s, and then ushered in the divorce revolution. So maybe we should not have been startled to learn that this generation is also bringing us a boom in divorce after age 50. Over the two decades leading up to 2010, the divorce rate over age 50 doubled, in what researchers call the "gray divorce revolution" (Brown and Lin 2012). And that was as divorces were becoming less common among younger people.

You might think the baby boomers had gotten divorce out of their system over the previous decades, and that is partly true; many of them divorced from their first marriages before age 50. However, today's divorce-after-50 is likely to be ending a second or third marriage. In fact, half of those over 50 who divorced in 2015 were married two or more times, compared with just one in four of those under 50. Cohabitation, later marriage, divorce, remarriage, and divorce again—that is a marriage life history introduced to modern society by the generation born after World War II.

While the previous debates about divorce concerned the well-being of young children whose lives were disrupted by divorce, the conversation about older-age divorce will likely be about pensions and savings, how to arrange caring for older people, and the personal relationships of grown children with their divorced older parents. The question for the future is whether this generation is unique, or whether divorce at older ages will become a more permanent or even increasing feature of the family landscape. It's too early to say. However, as noted above, divorce has a multigenerational pattern, in which people often emulate the behavior of their parents. If that is the case, we may expect relatively high divorce rates at older ages to persist.

KEY TERMS:

marital dissolution   separation

divorce   annulment of marriage

stepparent   stepchild

stepsibling (stepbrother/stepsister)

half-sibling (half-brother/half-sister)

blended family   boundary ambiguity

Questions for Review

1. Explain how the increase in divorces and remarriages is related to family diversity, social class inequality, and social change.

2. Contrast the historical marriage based on the authority of the Christian church with the modern institution of marriage based on the authority of the state.

3. How is an annulment different from a divorce?

4. What are some of the ways to interpret the question, "What is the divorce rate?" What do people probably mean when they ask that question?

5. What are two methods you might use to predict the odds of divorce for a couple marrying today?

6. Describe some ways that the "divorce revolution" benefited women in particular.

7. Discuss the connections between the divorce revolution and the "independence effect" and "income effect."

8. How might have the Great Recession both caused and prevented some divorces?

9. Who is most likely to remarry after a divorce, and why?

10. Why is it often difficult to define relationships and roles in blended families?

11

Work and Families

In Laura Ingalls Wilder's literary classic *Little House on the Prairie*, a family of nineteenth-century American settlers lives a self-sufficient lifestyle on the Kansas plains (Wilder 1935). For breakfast, the children drink milk from the family cow and eat stew made with rabbits they hunt, accompanied by corn hauled on the family's wagon. Their food is produced and prepared within the family, by the parents and children. In that setting, the relationships between people, and between people and their work, seemed relatively straightforward. Everyone could see whom they were feeding and where the food came from.

As the process of feeding children has grown more complicated in modern society, so has the relationship between work and families (DeVault 1991). Today, the work done within families and the work that people do outside their family home occur in very different social settings. Sorting out these complications will help us understand work and family today.

Consider the breakfast experiences of some contemporary children:

- Walker Harrison, a teenager who lives with his upper-middle-class parents in Brooklyn, New York, has a baseball game on Sunday. He starts the morning with breakfast cooked by his father, who is a writer and editor: four eggs, three pieces of bacon, and honey toast (Wilson 2009).

- Gloria Castillo's boys, ages 7 and 8, eat breakfast from a McDonald's drive-through in Dallas, Texas. Their mother takes them there on the way to school—after her night shift at work ends and her husband leaves for his day shift. They split sausage, eggs, bacon, biscuits, hash browns, and orange juice and get to school by 7:45 a.m. (LeDuff 2006).

The types of food we eat and how it's prepared reflect changes in family structure and the economy. Many children now eat breakfast at school, a meal provided to them for free or at reduced cost by the government.

- Christopher, a 14-year-old boy from Manassas, Virginia, eats a free breakfast in the school cafeteria, along with 460 other children (paid for by a combination of government programs). "I eat it every day. I love the pancakes," he said (Robotham 2017).

These scenarios illustrate three institutional arenas in which we feed and care for children: the family, the market, and the state. As we saw in Chapter 2, the transformation of the American family over the last century and a half has been closely related to the growing influence of the market and the state. In recent decades, the most important change has been the movement of women's work from their families to the paid labor market (Thistle 2006). Day care centers, nursing homes, restaurants, cleaning services—all these are market locations for work that was once primarily done within families.

Today, the 24-hour service economy both serves the demand for prepared meals and provides many people with the jobs that help pay their bills (Presser 2003). In fact, Gloria Castillo bought her children breakfast at McDonald's because she was rushing to get them to school after her night shift at Burger King. Most women and men—even those with young children—have paid jobs. For all the benefits that people get from their jobs—including not just money but also a chance at personal independence and a sense of identity in the world—the tensions between paid work and family obligations have only grown more severe. That means that the work-related decisions that people face as individuals and as families have grown more important.

The sociological perspective on work, as with families, is somewhat different from common notions. As you can tell from the earlier examples, we pay careful attention not only to what kind of work people do—the *content* of the work—but also to the relations between people involved—the social *context* of the work. Combining content and context provides us with the perspective on work that we need for this chapter.

Work in Institutional Arenas

work

The exertion of effort to produce or accomplish something.

care work

Work performed face-to-face for the purpose of enhancing the capabilities of another person.

housework

Work to maintain a household's functions.

In its simplest definition, **work** is the exertion of effort to produce or accomplish something. However, I will use three terms to identify different kinds of work. The first is the most directly relevant for this chapter because it is the most clearly identified with families. **Care work** is work performed face-to-face for the purpose of enhancing the capabilities of another person (England, Budig, and Folbre 2002). The quintessential care work is child care, which is usually hands-on, intimate work to provide children with the material, intellectual, and emotional support they need.

On the other hand, **housework** is work to maintain a household's functions. Most housework is devoted to cleaning and cooking, but maintenance, working in the yard, shopping, and paying bills are housework as well. Compared with the direct, interpersonal qualities of care work, housework is often seen as solitary drudgery. Sometimes care work and housework overlap or are done together, such as when a parent both cooks a meal and feeds it to the children at home, something many parents find especially stressful (Offer and Schneider 2011).

In modern society, these tasks increasingly are performed by people outside of the family. Some work is done for pay, in the service sector of the market economy. And some work is done by (or with the help of) machines, from refrigerators to vacuum cleaners and washing machines (see Changing Technology, "Laborsaving Devices," in Chapter 2). Thus, more and more of the care work and housework in society is performed as **market work**—that is, work done by employees for pay.

To organize our thinking about how these different kinds of work are related, we can use the term **system of care** to describe how a society accomplishes the necessary care work and housework (Ferree 2010). Although the system doesn't have a central coordinator or a master plan, we can see it as a system when we step back and look at the patterns of decisions and interactions it entails. In the framework of this book, we want to understand where such work takes place in terms of institutional arenas. Figure 11.1 shows how housework and care work partly overlap within families and how either kind of work can be done in the market for pay or at home without pay.

The overlapped areas in Figure 11.1 represent some of the interesting challenges for the study of work and family. Here are some of the decisions modern families must face (Hartmann 1981):

- *How to divide the housework and care work within the family.* For couples, this is often a contentious issue, which shows us that it is not really "families" that make decisions, but the individuals within them. That decision making may be cooperative, but it isn't always, especially when economic pressures make the choices increasingly difficult (Legerski and Cornwall 2010).

- *When to pay for household services instead of doing the housework themselves.* Based on their budgets and their personal preferences, people have to decide which housework to "outsource" to the market—for example, whether to hire a lawn-mowing service or eat their meals at restaurants (Craig and Baxter 2016).

- *When to take care of children at home versus using child-care services.* Parents must compare the costs of high-quality child care with the benefits of parents' employment. Government policy affects these decisions—for example, by subsidizing (or not) child-care costs (Ha and Miller 2015).

Each of these modern dilemmas involves the overlap among the institutional arenas we discussed in Chapter 1. The prospects people face in one arena (such as their potential earnings from market work) need to be weighed against their relationships and expectations in another (such as the feelings of love and obligation

market work

Work done by employees for pay.

system of care

How a society accomplishes the necessary care work and housework.

Figure 11.1 **Institutional settings for different kinds of work**

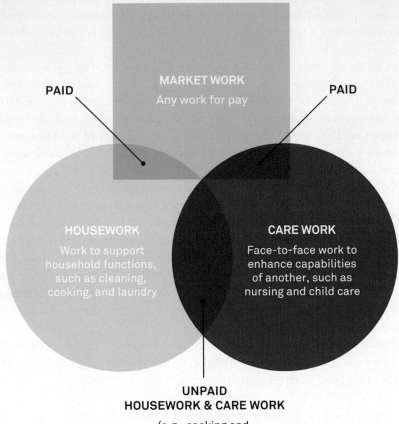

within the family). When something changes in one area—for example, a new job opportunity—people may have to reevaluate their decisions.

In addition to the relocation of work from within the family household to paid workplaces, another, less visible change has taken place. The state redistributes much of the product of our labor. That is, the government takes taxes to pay benefits and provide services for people in certain categories, such as old people, children, the sick, and the poor. That redistribution has taken the place of direct support for many people, which means that when we work, the beneficiaries of our labor often are not personally known to us. For example, you could say that a young worker in a coffee shop in Florida is paying for the health care of a low-income retiree in California, although the two will never meet. As a result, our personal contribution to caring for others has become more abstract and hard to observe. This transition—from the face-to-face nature of family-centered care work to the more impersonal system of care associated with the market and the welfare state—has had a far-reaching impact on both families and society.

In the last half century or so, the main story in the realm of work and family has been the growth of market work in the system of care. That involved the majority of women taking paid jobs outside their homes for the first time in history. And it transformed both paid work and family life.

Paid Work

In Chapter 2, we saw the transformation of work in the nineteenth and twentieth centuries, with men increasingly working away from home, in urban factories and offices, while women worked in increasing isolation at home without pay. But women's movement into the paid workforce grew as well—it just started later (Goldin 1990). First single women, then married women without children, and eventually even most married women with young children took paid jobs outside the home. The most rapid period of change occurred in the three decades after 1960 as the proportion of women in the labor force increased from about one-third to three-quarters (Cohen and Bianchi 1999).

Figures 11.2 and 11.3 show how widespread and dramatic this change was. At

Figure 11.2 **Percentage of women in the labor force, by education and presence of children in the home, 1950−2015**

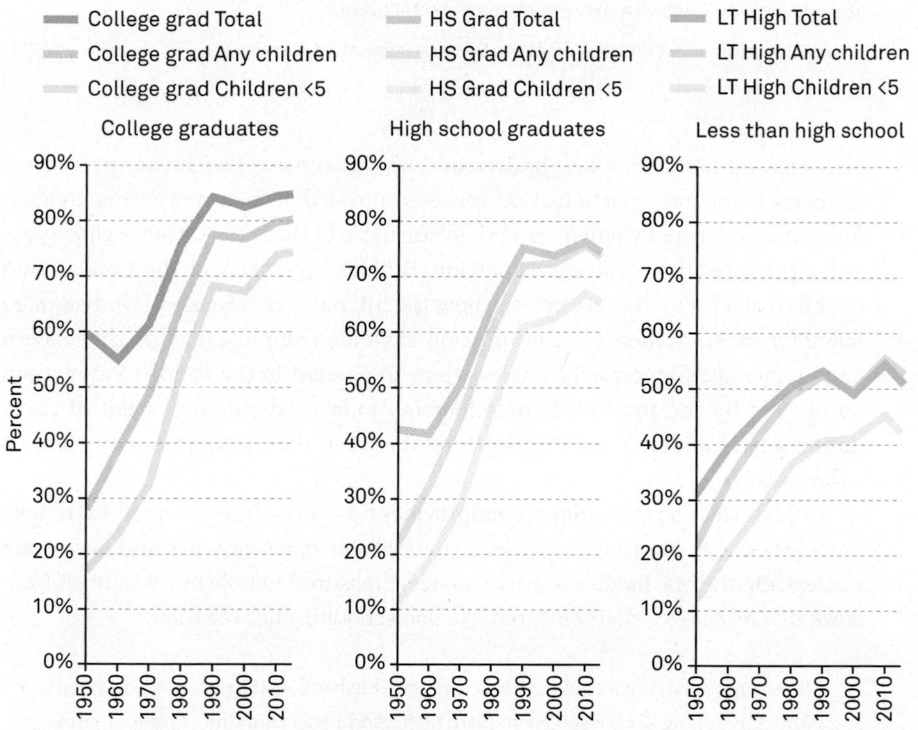

SOURCE: Author's calculations from U.S. Census Bureau sources. Includes women ages 25–54.

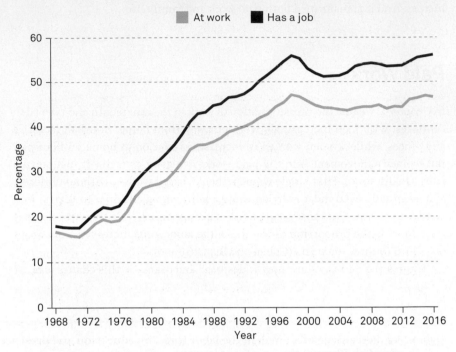

Figure 11.3 **Percentage of women with a child less than one year old who are employed, 1968-2016**

The percentage of women with a child under age 1 increased rapidly from the 1960s to the 1990s but has not increased since then. (Note some women have a job but are not at work, probably because they are taking parental leave.)

SOURCE: Author's calculations from the Current Population Survey.

all levels of education, with children or without, and even with young children, women's labor force participation rocketed upward. The increase was greatest for college-educated women—and there are more of them than ever—whose participation rates have reached 85 percent. By looking closely at the time around the birth of a first child, we can see how the intensive child-care period has *narrowed* for most mothers. The proportion of women employed while they have a child under age 1 increased from less than 20 percent in the 1960s to more than 50 percent by the 1990s, where it remains today. (About 10 percent of these mothers have a job but weren't working the week they were interviewed; they were on leave.)

In historical terms, women's employment patterns have evolved extremely quickly—so quickly that the expectations people have for work and family are unclear. On the one hand, some women feel pressured to take more time off from work for the sake of their children. As one schoolteacher recalled,

"I remember having a conversation with [my husband's] sister. She said, 'What! Oh! Only taking six weeks? Blah, blah, blah.' And I was thinking, 'I am not going to put us in debt so that I can stay home for six more weeks!' I'm just not going to do it. It's ridiculous. The baby's not going to remember if I was there or not. You know? She'll be fine!" (Barnes 2013:13)

On the other hand, some women feel guilty when they *do* take time off from their jobs for maternity leave:

"I thought I was sort of a bad person because I had got pregnant at this juncture," said one woman. "And now I was already on maternity leave." (Sevón 2005:472)

Even though the growth has stalled since the 1990s, the movement of women into paid work left a profound mark on today's families. The baby boom children—those born between the end of World War II and the mid-1960s—are most of today's grandparents. It was their lives that changed so suddenly during that postwar period. For them, the whole sweep of changes described in this book—including not just women's education and employment but also delayed marriage, falling birth rates, and rising single parenthood and divorce—were felt as a great wave of social transformation. But the movement of women's work out of the home was perhaps the most profound, and many people see it as the precursor of—or the driving force behind—the other changes of the era (Bianchi 1995).

While women's behavior was changing so dramatically, with paid employment becoming a permanent, lifelong aspect of most American women's lives, what happened with men? I did not include men in the various graphs because the lines would be boring. Men's employment rates have declined a small amount, as some retire earlier and some have been squeezed out by economic changes that left them jobless. But in the 25- to 54-year-old age range covered in the women's graphs, employment for men remains above 80 percent. In that sense, what some people call a "revolution" in work behavior has in fact been quite lopsided (England 2010).

Occupational Segregation

Women's employment became acceptable within the cultural mainstream so rapidly in part because of the kinds of paid work women did. The U.S. labor force was (and remains) marked by **occupational gender segregation**, with men and women having jobs in separate occupations. The kind of paid work most women do is closely related to their work within the family. Occupational segregation, together with the way men and women divide unpaid care work and housework, make up the **gender division of labor**—the allocation of work between men and women in society. Women at home do the lion's share of housework and care work (discussed shortly), and as we saw in Chapter 5, their paid work is also concentrated in these areas—for example, nursing, child care and teaching, food service, and cleaning. Figure 11.4 provides a closer look at

occupational gender segregation

Men and women having jobs in separate occupations.

gender division of labor

The allocation of work between men and women in society.

Figure 11.4 Annual earnings and gender composition in jobs traditionally performed by women when done at home, 2015

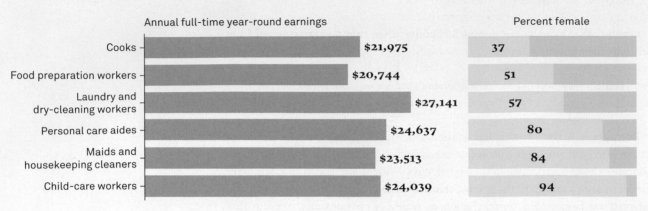

These are some of the lowest-paid jobs in the economy, and (except for cooking) they are all female dominated in the paid workforce.

SOURCE: Author's graph from 2015 American Community Survey data via American FactFinder 2017.

some jobs that involve tasks similar to those mothers are most likely to perform at home.

In the paid market, naturally, jobs are very different. Some of women's traditional work is now done in nursing, for example, which is a professional occupation with tasks much different from the care women historically provided to sick family members at home. But among professionals, the tendency of women and men to specialize in different educational fields—for women to train in psychology, for example, while men become engineers—maintains the traditional divisions. This segregation meant that as women entered the workforce, even if some men were uncomfortable with their own wives leaving home every morning, most did not feel that their jobs were threatened by women's presence in the workforce.

Popular attitudes toward the appropriate divisions between men and women have gradually shifted. Both men and women express support for gender equality, especially regarding work, much more than in the past. For example, in the late 1970s, only one-third of Americans told the General Social Survey that mothers' employment was *not* harmful for their preschool-aged children; 40 years later, that has risen to three-quarters. As attitudes shifted, occupational segregation declined, and women came to occupy positions in formerly male-dominated occupations, especially in white-collar jobs such as school and health care administration, real estate, and human resources (Cotter, Hermsen, and Vanneman 2004). However, it remains the case that most Americans labor alongside coworkers of the same gender—and most women work in the female-dominated occupations that have grown as the service sector has become more prominent in the economy (Cohen 2013c).

Housework and Child Care

Women's movement into the workforce has increased their independence and their own incomes. But does it also represent more work for them, as they are still stuck with a "second shift" (Hochschild and Machung 1989) of seemingly endless housework and child care on top of their hours working for pay? Men's employment patterns haven't changed very much, but have they changed their role at home—or do men still leave the great majority of housework and child care to their wives, girlfriends, and mothers?

Beneath these questions lies a larger issue: Who decides? Are families making decisions cooperatively, dividing work and rewards according to a common purpose, as the consensus perspective suggests (see Chapter 1)? Or are household members acting as individuals, making decisions in their own economic and emotional interest, according to the expectations of conflict theory? Before addressing these issues directly, I will describe a method for studying unpaid work and other informal activities that has greatly enhanced the ability of sociologists and other social scientists to understand how families work: time use studies.

Time Use Studies

In the market arena, most relationships are formal, and payments are handled with currency (dollars), which is easily measured. That makes paid work relatively straightforward to study, with consistent national statistics. In the family arena, on the other hand, where most work is not paid, there is no formal accounting of who does what for whom and how they are compensated (see Changing Culture, "Valuing Unpaid Work"). Moreover, the benefits of this unpaid work sometimes take years to appear (for example, when children grow up). As a result, family-based housework and care work often seem invisible, especially to people outside the family (Folbre 2001). Because of this difficulty, time use studies are a way for researchers to investigate how people fill their days with activities (see Chapter 1). The most prominent of these is the American Time Use Survey, conducted each year by the federal government.

Using data collected in 2015, Figure 11.6 shows the breakdown of activities for American men and women in a typical day. I have organized the activities so that the work tasks are all grouped together at the bottom. Adding up the paid work, housework and cooking, shopping, lawn and garden care, and care work, you can see that men spend an average of 8 hours and 04 minutes per day working, almost the same as the 8 hours and 22 minutes women work. (Note that this "typical day" includes weekends as well as weekdays, and it includes people who are employed as well as those who aren't, so these are very general averages.) Thus, the greater hours of paid work for men are, on average, balanced out by the greater hours of unpaid work for women (Bianchi, Robinson, and Milkie 2006).

Valuing Unpaid Work

Consider two hypothetical families, the Smiths and the Johnsons (see Figure 11.5). In the Smith family, the husband and wife divide work pretty equally. They both work full-time jobs at $15 per hour. In addition, they each do some unpaid work—housework and child care. Let us say that Mr. Smith does about 1 hour of unpaid work each day, and Mrs. Smith does 2 hours—not too unusual. In the Johnson family, on the other hand, the division of labor is more traditional, and Mr. Johnson has a higher-paying job. At his full-time job he earns $30 per hour, but he does no unpaid work around the house. Mrs. Johnson works the same number of total hours as Mrs. Smith, 10 hours, but all of it is unpaid work. Which family is better off?

In terms of income, the two families are equal. Each earns $240 per day. But in terms of total economic gain, the Johnson family has a clear advantage. In addition to the same amount of money, the Johnsons have the benefit of 7 additional hours of unpaid work. Maybe their house is cleaner, their children are better cared for, or their meals are more delicious. On the other hand, maybe the Smiths have to spend some of their $240 per day for frozen dinners, takeout meals, child care, and a housecleaner. At a glance, then, in the short run at least, it appears that the Johnson family comes out ahead—but what they gain doesn't show up directly in their bank balance. (This example is modified from one offered by Nancy Folbre [2009].)

Figure 11.5 **Paid and unpaid work in married-couple families**

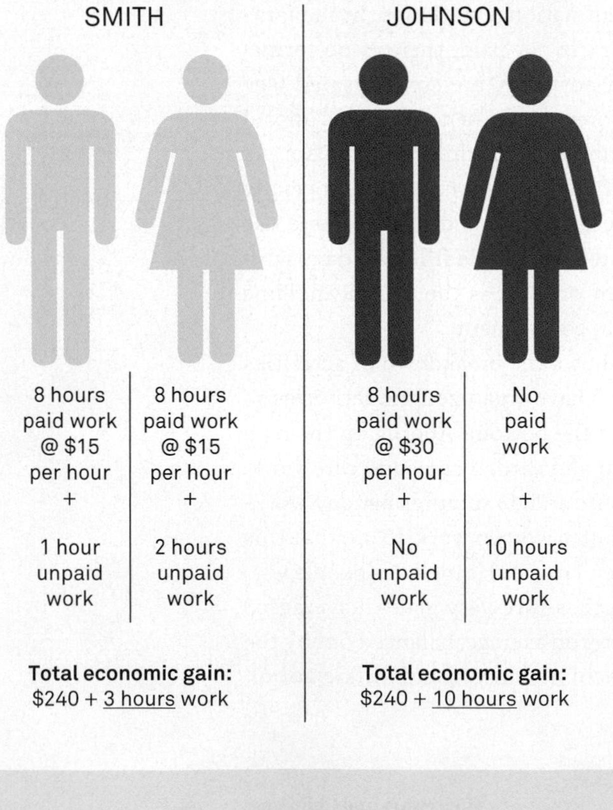

SMITH		JOHNSON	
8 hours paid work @ $15 per hour	8 hours paid work @ $15 per hour	8 hours paid work @ $30 per hour	No paid work
+	+	+	+
1 hour unpaid work	2 hours unpaid work	No unpaid work	10 hours unpaid work

Total economic gain: $240 + <u>3 hours</u> work

Total economic gain: $240 + <u>10 hours</u> work

But what about the spouses considered separately? Mr. and Mrs. Smith share the benefits of their relationship pretty equally. Mrs. Smith does more unpaid work, but that is not uncommon, and the couple can probably rationalize it without too much conflict. On the other hand, Mr. and Mrs. Johnson depend on each other more directly. If they were to split up, each would have to face the problem of replacing what the other had provided. Mr. Johnson either would need a new partner or would have to spend some of his money replacing Mrs. Johnson's labor. Mrs. Johnson would need a new source of income, either by getting a job or finding a new breadwinning partner. But the Johnson situation is not really equal, because Mr. Johnson is gaining work experience and seniority, so if he ends up on his own, he will be in a position to earn more money. Mrs. Johnson is not gaining new job skills and experience, and her abilities as a homemaker are not likely to be highly rewarded in the labor market if she ends up needing a job. In short, she is taking a greater economic risk in their marriage.

The extra unpaid work and the imbalance in the marriage create two problems. The first is that unpaid work is not recognized because it has no direct dollar value—and dollars is how we usually measure value in a market economy. And the second is the unequal implications for Mr. and Mrs. Johnson.

Wages for Housework?

There are a lot of other differences between families like this, with many pros and cons to each arrangement. The spouses may be happy, or not, for a variety of other reasons beyond the simple economics. But this comparison raises a challenge. Some economists believe that the gross domestic product (GDP) and other common measures of economic activity are seriously flawed because they do not take into account the value of work done without pay (Folbre 2001). And politically, some feminists believe that the lack of compensation for unpaid work is a systematic means by which male domination is perpetuated.

In the 1970s, in an effort to empower women, a group of feminists organized to demand that housewives be paid wages for their labor (MacKinnon 1991). If housewives' labor was paid, they could freely choose between a job outside the home and working at home for pay, without sacrificing income or independence. They would also have public recognition for the value of their work because it would become part of the formal economy. It could be taxed, they could receive pensions based on their pay when they retire, and they could organize labor unions with the option of going on strike to demand better pay or working conditions. "If women were paid for all they do," went one slogan, "there'd be a lot of wages due" (Edmond and Fleming 1975:5).

How much would really be due for all that unpaid work? We don't know for sure. But we can make some guesses. At the time of the "wages for housework" campaign, wives did about seven times more housework than their husbands, so it made sense for feminists to treat it as a women's issue. Now the balance is much more equal, so husbands would have about 40 percent of this money coming to them as well. By my calculations, using the unpaid work time shown in Figure 11.6, it would cost $10,643 at $12 per hour to hire someone to do the typical man's unpaid work for a year (2 hours, 26 minutes per day) and $22,207 to hire someone for the typical woman's workload (5 hours, 4 minutes per day). Of course, $12 per hour might not be high enough to hire qualified people to do all the unpaid tasks we do, so that might be a low estimate.

In any event, we are talking about a lot of money. In the big picture, by one government economic estimate, the total value of all unpaid household work is equal to 26 percent of the country's GDP, which is the total value of all the goods and services the economy produces in a given year (Bridgman et al. 2012).

The campaign to gain wages for housework ultimately was not successful. Instead, the great majority of women entered the paid labor force, and the struggle to achieve equality in unpaid work mostly remained within the private sphere of the family home. However, as women's work contributions outside the home increased, the unfairness of the division of labor at home became more apparent for all to see. As a result, more couples have wrestled with the balance in their relationships, and the gender gap has narrowed.

Figure 11.6 **Time use in a typical day, 2015**

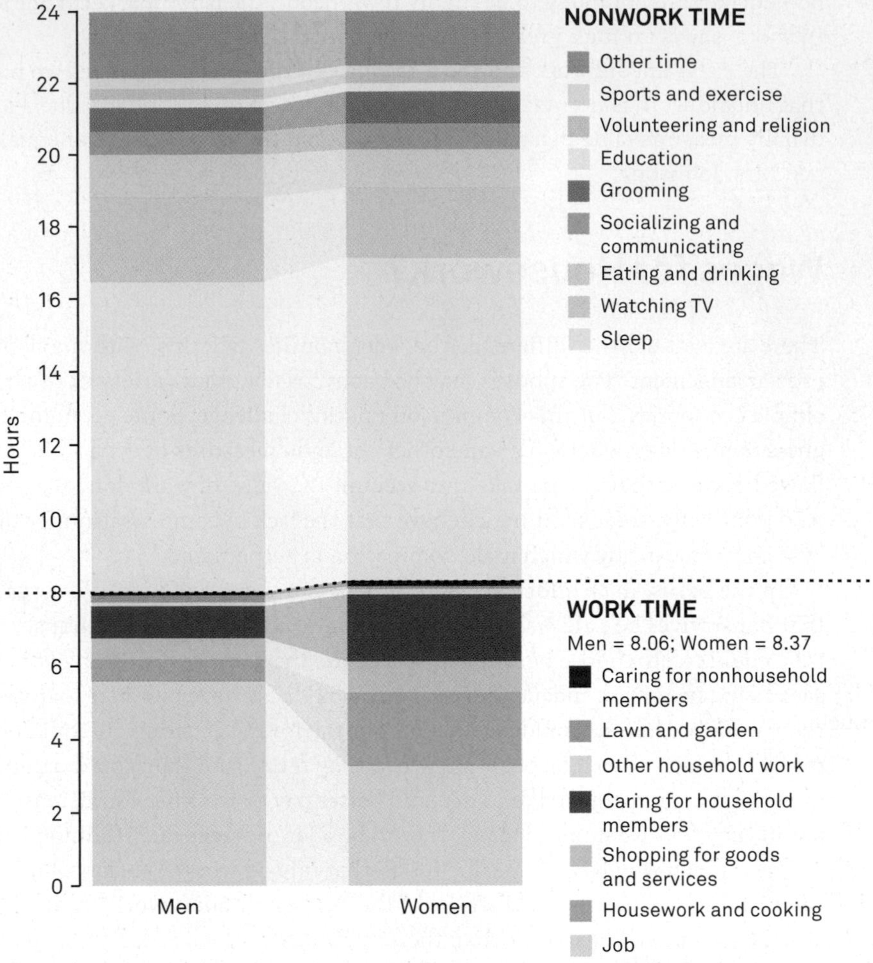
24
22
20
18
16
14
12
10
8
6
4
2
0
Hours
Men
Women
NONWORK TIME
Other time
Sports and exercise
Volunteering and religion
Education
Grooming
Socializing and communicating
Eating and drinking
Watching TV
Sleep
WORK TIME
Men = 8.06; Women = 8.37
Caring for nonhousehold members
Lawn and garden
Other household work
Caring for household members
Shopping for goods and services
Housework and cooking
Job

SOURCE: Author's figure from U.S. Bureau of Labor Statistics (2016d).

Toward Gender Balance

Time use studies have also made it possible for us to track the other side of the rapid change in employment patterns—unpaid work at home. For decades, feminist social scientists have argued that the division of unpaid work within families is a fundamental source of gender inequality (Hartmann 1981). On the other hand, some analysts counter that the division of labor represents a rational, cooperative response of families to the demands on their time and money (Becker 1981). There are elements of truth in both perspectives, as we will see.

Time use data show that married women have cut their housework time roughly in half over the last half-century, while married men have doubled theirs (see the Story Behind the Numbers). As a result, where married women once spent seven times as many hours on housework as their husbands, the difference is now less than 2 to 1. The figure also shows how the gender difference eroded not just because the balance between men and women shifted, but because the *total* amount of time spent on housework by married couples declined. Married couples do less housework, and husbands do a greater share of it. When we focus on child care, we see a similar narrowing of the gender gap among married couples with children: Mothers did about four times as much child care in 1965, but only twice as much in 2015. But the child-care change since the 1970s did not result from a decline in total child care. Instead, both men and women *increased* their time with children (Bianchi 2000). With those basic trends in mind, we can discuss the reasons couples divide their labors the way they do. Examining these patterns will help us understand the nature of the social change that has occurred, as well as the dynamics of families today in our system of care.

The division of unpaid labor within families follows certain common patterns that have been identified by those researchers trying to understand why there is such a persistent gender gap. (Note that this section mostly concerns families that are living together, partly because that is what our data reflect and partly because it simplifies the issues for purposes of discussion.) There are three main factors within couples that seem to account for the fact that women perform so much more of this work than men: time, resources, and gender (Lachance-Grzela and Bouchard 2010).

First, the partner with greater obligations away from home tends to do less housework and child care because that person has less time available. Since men's employment rates are higher than women's, they are more likely to be away from home and not available to do unpaid work (Sayer 2005). This reasoning is somewhat circular, however. The decisions about which partner will work for pay and which will concentrate on unpaid work may be made at the same time: Maybe the husband does not do housework because he is busy working for pay, and maybe the woman does not have a job because she is busy doing housework. In fact, research shows that women whose husbands work especially long hours are more likely to quit their jobs altogether than are those whose husbands work regular full-time hours (Shafer 2011).

Second, although some people enjoy housework and child care, most prefer to avoid at least the more onerous aspects of these responsibilities (and it's hard to separate the fun parts, such as playing peekaboo or reading together, from the less pleasant tasks). Therefore, as couples negotiate over who does what work, partners with greater personal resources are more likely to take the upper hand in the negotiation and do less unpaid labor. This is where the apparent equality between the total work time of husbands and wives becomes problematic. If one partner's work is paid and the other's is unpaid, the partner who has the earnings controls more resources and usually has more decision-making power in the relationship (Sayer, Bianchi, and Robinson 2004).

Division of labor within married couples

Housework
Number of weekly hours

4.7	1965	33.9
6.7	1975	26.1
10.4	1985	21.9
10.4	1996	19.4
10.5	2005	18.8
10.2	2015	18.3

Time use surveys show that married women have cut their housework time almost in half, while married men have doubled theirs. As a result, where married women once spent seven times as many hours on housework as their husbands, the difference is now less than 2 to 1. We also see a narrowing of the gender gap in child care among married couples with children. Mothers performed four times as much child care in 1965, but only twice as much in 2015.

Source: Bianchi et al. (2012) and author calculations from the American Time Use Survey.

Gender of spouse in married couple

■ Men   ■ Women

http://wwnpag.es/sbtn11

Go to this link for an animation narrated by the author.

Child care
Number of weekly hours

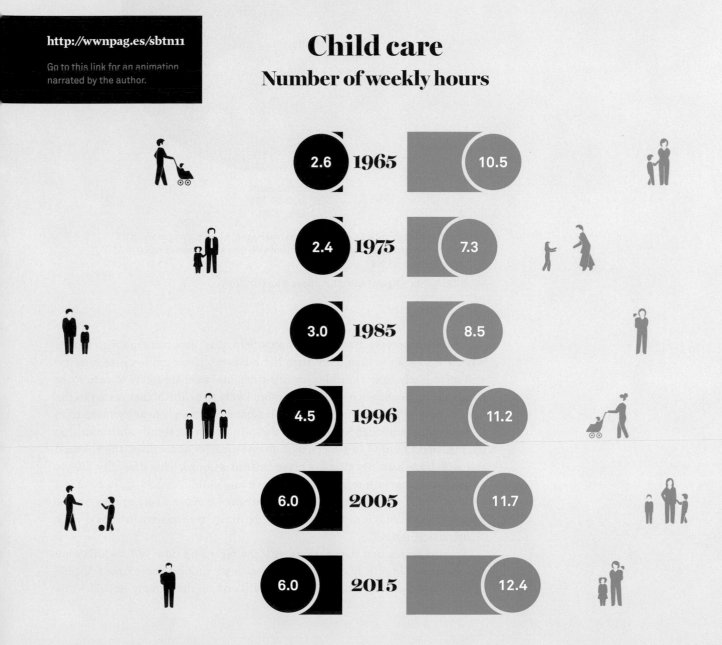

2.6	1965	10.5
2.4	1975	7.3
3.0	1985	8.5
4.5	1996	11.2
6.0	2005	11.7
6.0	2015	12.4

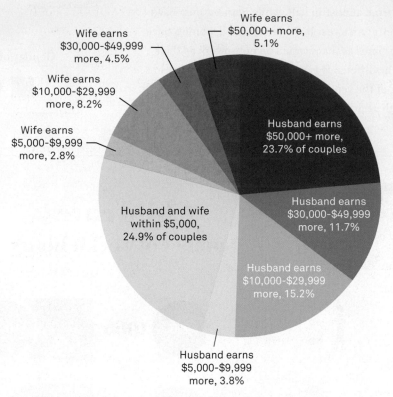

Figure 11.7 **Relative earnings of husbands and wives, 2016**

Wife earns $50,000+ more, 5.1%

Wife earns $30,000-$49,999 more, 4.5%

Wife earns $10,000-$29,999 more, 8.2%

Wife earns $5,000-$9,999 more, 2.8%

Husband earns $50,000+ more, 23.7% of couples

Husband earns $30,000-$49,999 more, 11.7%

Husband and wife within $5,000, 24.9% of couples

Husband earns $10,000-$29,999 more, 15.2%

Husband earns $5,000-$9,999 more, 3.8%

Husbands earned more in 54 percent of the marriages; wives earned more in 21 percent of the marriages; and husband and wife earnings were about equal in 25 percent of the marriages.

SOURCE: Author's figure from U.S. Census data (2017c).

With the increase in women's employment, it is more common than it once was for a woman to earn more than her husband. However, because men are still more likely to work, and work full-time, and men are likely to earn more than women, husbands remain much more likely to be the higher earner in the family. As you can see in Figure 11.7, husbands earn significantly more than their wives in more than half of all couples, while the wife significantly outearns the husband in only 1 in 5 marriages. In one-quarter of families, the husband and wife have earnings that are close (within $5,000). This disparity affects decision making with regard to housework and child care and again creates a cycle in which the spouse with higher earnings is more likely to stay on the job and the one with lower earnings is more likely to specialize in unpaid work (Schneider 2011).

Finally, notice that the previous patterns regarding time and resources are gender neutral in principle. That is, whichever partner has more time available or less resources with which to bargain will end up doing more unpaid work.

However, gender dynamics also affect couples' internal interactions directly. For example, men and women in couples often act out the socialization they experienced growing up, which tends to pass the division of unpaid labor from one generation to the next. And people who express adherence to traditional gender expectations and attitudes are more likely to arrange their household labor in the traditional way. (I use *traditional* in this section as shorthand for the separate spheres ideal, as described in Chapter 2.) Thus, much of the pattern we see is the result of cultural attitudes—or gender ideology—lived out in daily life (Greenstein 2000). Socialization is not a simple blueprint of adult behavior, however. The lessons learned in childhood are applied in relation to the situations in which people find themselves as adults. Thus, men who grew up with an employed mother do more housework when they grow up themselves. But they still also negotiate and bargain along the lines of the time and resource principles (Gupta 2006).

In addition to the factors described here, research has identified some groups as having either more traditional divisions of household labor or less traditional divisions. For example, Christians with a conservative interpretation of the Bible follow a more traditional gender division of labor than average (Ellison and Bartkowski 2002), especially for the less pleasant tasks of infant care (DeMaris, Mahoney, and Pargament 2011). On the other hand, there is evidence that lesbian and gay male couples share housework and child care somewhat more equally than male-female couples, although the research in this area remains quite limited (Civettini 2016). And with regard to race/ethnicity, White and Black couples share housework more equally than Latino and Asian couples. That is partly because Hispanic and Asian women are in general less likely to be in the workforce, but also because of other factors, such as attitudes toward gender (Wright, Bianchi, and Hunt 2013).

Putting these factors together, we can create profiles of couples and how they divide their unpaid labor. Equal divisions are more likely (though still rare) where both partners are employed, where the demands on their time are lower (such as those who have no children), where their earning potential is equal, and where they share a set of beliefs that encourages equality between men and women (Deutsch 1999). On the other hand, couples in which the husband works more outside the home and earns more, where there are heavy care work demands, and where the partners do not share a commitment to equality are likely to assign a much greater share of the unpaid labor to the female partner (Milkie, Raley, and Bianchi 2009).

Social Change

Even among the more traditional families, a sense of generational change pervades U.S. society in the area of housework. One baby boomer—a 50-year-old, working-class, conservative Christian woman whose husband had recently lost his factory job—described the changes she saw:

I'm from a different generation than the young girls, and I still feel that my job is in the home and the meals. I think that the new generation is more like, "I work, you work." I know that my girls do that. They'll come home and my son-in-law will come home and she hasn't fixed supper and she goes, "If you want something, fix it." My generation just didn't do that. (Legerski and Cornwall 2010:461)

Interestingly, this woman expressed such a traditional perspective even though at the time of the interview she was employed full-time herself. In fact, it is common for spouses to rationalize unequal divisions of labor. For example, they might attribute women's housecleaning to men's longer work hours, even when the housework inequality is larger than the paid work difference. Thus, although inequality is a source of serious conflict in many families, many spouses also justify the division of labor in order to avoid conflict. That is probably because expressing a commitment to equality in relationships has become culturally expected (van Hooff 2011).

Although these patterns concern housework and care work performed within families, the institutional setting surrounding families is crucial as well (Pedulla and Thébaud 2015). That setting includes a number of social factors:

- A labor market where men usually earn more than women, which encourages couples to decide that wives should stay home with the children (Lincoln 2008)

- A relatively low-wage (and therefore low-cost) service economy that permits those women who have their own earnings to avoid housework that their husbands are unwilling to do (Craig et al. 2016)

- A variety of government policies that affect work-family balance, such as offering paid leave or public child care, which can also affect how couples divide their labor (Altintas and Sullivan 2017)

- A pattern of gender socialization—primarily through families, schools, and the media (see Chapter 5)—that affects how men and women feel about the division of labor within their families, their ambitions, and their ideals for family life

Once again, we see that although family decisions often seem highly individual and feel intimate, they are influenced in many ways, large and small, by the broader social situation.

Conflicts and Solutions

In preindustrial America, work and family were not separate realms with competing time demands. In the *Little House on the Prairie* scenario that opened this chapter, care work, housework, and market work were interwoven throughout the activities of fathers, mothers, and children. However, in the system of care established with industrialization—and under the separate spheres ideal—women's and men's work were divided, hers mostly at home and his mostly in the labor market (Thistle 2006).

In the last half-century, however, the growth of women's employment contributed to conflicts between family and paid work obligations. The system in which women's unpaid work combined with men's income to provide essential goods and services for families was disrupted. The system did not work for single parents, who could not combine the paid and unpaid work of two spouses. And among married couples, who spent more time and energy away from home, getting housework and child care done was increasingly difficult. At the same time, employers found themselves attempting to manage employees with more demanding obligations outside the workplace. In fact, more than 80 percent of American parents report that they would like to have more time with their families, according to the General Social Survey.

As researchers came to examine this tension systematically, they identified the problem of **work-family conflict**, which occurs when the time demands, strains, or obligations of work or family roles make it difficult for people to fulfill their obligations in either role (Greenhaus and Beutell 1985). Work-family conflict has become a pervasive and costly experience (Kelly, Moen, and Tranby 2011). It harms workplaces when employees can't be productive, and it harms families by increasing their stress and hardship (Offer and Schneider 2011). Many of the work-related problems that families experience today arise from work-family conflict.

work-family conflict

The conflict that occurs when the time demands, strains, or obligations of work or family roles make it difficult to fulfill obligations in either role.

Single Parents

Although married couples seem to get most of the attention, the growing number of single mothers experience the most severe work-family crunch (Nomaguchi 2012). Not surprisingly, research now finds that single mothers are more likely to feel stressed and fatigued while spending time with their children (Meier et al. 2016). For those without the ability to earn higher incomes, there simply are not enough hours in the day to earn money, do housework, and take care of children without a time conflict erupting between those obligations. Most, but not all, of these single parents are women, who lead 82 percent of poor single-parent households (Proctor, Semega, and Kollar 2016). Besides being fewer in number, single fathers are better off for a number of reasons. They are more likely to have high-paying jobs, more likely to live with a partner who can help care for the children, and less likely to have very young children, for whom care work is most demanding (Coles 2015).

From the 1930s to the 1990s, federal welfare policy was designed to supplement the incomes of single mothers who were poor so that they would not need to have jobs—or at least not full-time jobs—while caring for their children alone. This policy recognized that most married mothers were supported by employed husbands. By the same token, its supporters argued, single mothers and their children should be supported by the state—that is, welfare should supplement the system of care to plug the hole left by absent fathers (Mink 1998). That system was far from perfect, and many single mothers experienced poverty and hardship anyway. But when the welfare system was reformed in 1996, policymakers abandoned the assumption that the government would provide income support instead of full-time work. Instead, single parents were expected to maintain a job while receiving temporary support and then transition to full-time work with no cash welfare benefit as soon as possible (Greenberg et al. 2002).

That new policy approach has not worked well, however. As we saw in Chapter 4, the number of single mothers living in poverty increased over the decade of the 2000s. Under the new welfare rules, the federal government's cash assistance program did not keep up with that increase. At the same time, employment problems for single mothers also mounted, both because of the 2000s economic recession and because of work-family conflicts that made it difficult for them to get and hold jobs. In 2016, only 70 percent of single mothers were employed— no more than had jobs when welfare reform was implemented in the late 1990s. Declining welfare support, and stagnant employment prospects, together add up to intensified hardship for single mothers and their families over the last two decades (Eamon and Wu 2011).

The "Motherhood Penalty"

Another cost of work-family conflict is the "motherhood penalty," the loss of earnings women experience after they have children. At first glance, this may appear to be the simple result of the choices mothers make: They take time out of the labor force for childbirth, child care, and housework, and they select jobs with flexible or part-time hours or jobs that are closer to home so they have time for child care and housework. And that is all true to some extent. However, even after taking work experience into account, women earn less if they have children (Budig and England 2001). And research shows that their occupational choices aren't the explanation for their lower earnings either (Glauber 2012).

In fact, many mothers lose earnings because of employer discrimination, as employers believe that mothers will be less devoted to their jobs, so they should be paid less or passed over for jobs altogether (Correll, Benard, and Paik 2007). Further, the time and energy that women expend on their family obligations end up hurting their careers. Ironically, it is women with the highest earnings potential who lose the most in terms of future wages when they take time out of the labor force to have children (England et al. 2016). Despite their best efforts, then, modern mothers pay a price at work for their children, while fathers generally do not. In fact, fathers seem to earn a "fatherhood premium" against the motherhood penalty—that is, they earn more than men who aren't fathers—partly because (when they are married) the labor and support of their wives helps them get ahead at work (Killewald 2013).

What Gives?

Given the prevalence of work-family conflict, the time and money demands of intensive parenting, and the tensions over the gender division of unpaid labor at home, what choices do people have? To alleviate these problems, something has to change: work has to change, families have to change, or people have to alter the balance between work and family in their lives (Damaske 2011). Each possibility has shown some promise, and each raises its own obstacles.

Work One of the major goals of the U.S. labor movement of the late nineteenth century was a limit to the length of the working day. Through a series of hard-fought legal reforms over several decades, the federal government eventually established a standard 40-hour workweek for most workers (Whaples 1990). One of the movement's early slogans was "Eight hours for work, eight hours for rest, eight hours for what we will" (Rosenzweig 1983). Thus, balancing work, rest, and leisure has long been an aspiration for American workers.

In recent years, some employers have adapted to the work-family conflicts of their workers. They may offer flexible or part-time schedules, for example. But the progress has been slow, and even though some businesses are able to recruit and retain good workers with such policies, other employers view them as costly sacrifices that put their companies at a disadvantage in the competitive marketplace (Glass and Estes 1997). In fact, there is an ongoing debate over who is responsible for creating policies to ease the relationship between work and family demands: employers or the government (Esping-Andersen 2009). To reduce work-family conflict, a number of work-based reforms would help:

- Work hours could simply be reduced, permitting workers greater equality in the work-family balance. In the United States, the standard full-time workweek is 40 hours, but the typical employed person works 34 hours per week including breaks and leave, which is still substantially more than in most wealthy countries. For example, Germans and Norwegians work an average of 27 hours per week (see Figure 11.8 below).

- Work hours could be more flexible across the day or the week, allowing workers to arrange schedules to meet the competing demands on their time (Kelly, Moen, and Tranby 2011). Ironically, although flexible scheduling—or "flextime"—has become more common, it is workers in the highest-paid jobs who have so far benefited most from this trend (Glauber 2011). On the other hand, it seems that flexibility in work time often benefits employers more than workers, as American workers are much more likely than those in Europe to work on nights and weekends (Hamermesh and Stancanelli 2014).

- Finally, family supports by employers—such as child-care benefits or time off for family care—would reduce the strains associated with work-family conflict (Boushey 2016). Unfortunately, many of the workers who take advantage of these benefits, mostly women, find that their careers suffer as a result (Glass 2004). The federal government does require some unpaid time off for family care obligations, but it is often not adequate to the needs of modern families (see Changing Law, "Family Leave").

Naturally, reform in any of these areas would entail costs as well as benefits. For example, allowing reduced hours or scheduling flexibility might reduce employee turnover, which saves employers money in the hiring and training process. But if employers are responsible for paying health insurance and other benefits for each worker, it may be more cost-effective for them to have fewer employees working longer hours each. Because of the difficulty in implementing such reforms—and the powerful interests of business leaders who oppose reforms that might reduce profits—workplace change is not a simple prospect.

Family If U.S. workplaces are inflexible, is it up to families to respond? As sociologist Judith Lorber puts it, "Workplace pressures are thought to be unchangeable, so the burden of innovation falls on the family" (2005:40). We have seen that housework and care work patterns have changed, with men doing more and women doing less. But the gender balance that remains is still quite unequal. And the cost of replacing unpaid work with paid services is too high for most families (Craig and Baxter 2016). Ironically, as some wealthier families have reduced their work-family conflicts by employing service workers—either directly as nannies and housecleaners or indirectly by relying more on restaurants or dry cleaners—this has increased the number of low-wage workers who work long hours or odd hours, exacerbating their own work-family conflicts (Presser 2003).

Many families strive to reduce work-family conflict by changing the dynamics or arrangements within the family (Hansen 2005). For example, they may arrange for extended family members to move in with them, contributing rent, child care, or housework support (Cohen 2002). Or they may take alternate shifts, like the woman who told researcher Sarah Damaske how she and her husband split their time: "He worked nights and I worked days. He had a shift where he would work sometimes from eleven o'clock at night to seven o'clock in the morning. So, I slept along with the kids. And that's the way we had to do it in order to balance out the babysitting" (Damaske 2011:84). Arrangements like this are not available to or practical for all families. And some people—such as single parents or those without extended kin—don't have this option.

To achieve a more complete solution to the imbalances and inequalities within families, Lorber proposes "degendering" families, so that gender differences in the responsibilities of men and women are gradually erased. In the process, she believes, parents will gain more high-quality time to care for their children, and the conflicts between paid and unpaid work will be reduced.

Although hardly anyone has removed gender from the division of labor entirely, some families have successfully divided their parenting work evenly by making deliberate efforts to ensure balance through ongoing negotiation—and through a shared commitment to equality. The families that practice what Francine Deutsch (1999) calls "equally shared parenting" have succeeded best by

Family Leave

When Congress passed the Family and Medical Leave Act (FMLA) in 1993, then vice president Al Gore declared, "American families will no longer have to choose between their families and their jobs" (Clymer 1993). That was a goal that many people sought, but achieving it was not as simple as it was for Democratic president Bill Clinton to put his signature on the bill the next day.

Under the law, American workers now are entitled to unpaid leave if they become too sick to perform on the job or if they need to care for family members in the event of a birth, adoption, or illness. This leave can extend up to 12 weeks per year. The guarantee means, in effect, that the employer must hold workers' jobs for them while they are away (and continue their health insurance, if they have it). However, not everyone is covered by this guarantee. It generally applies to all government workers and to those in the private sector who have worked for at least a year at a workplace with at least 50 employees (U.S. Department of Labor description: http://www.dol.gov/whd/fmla/). Those restrictions translate into about half of all workers.

Business leaders were afraid that FMLA would drive up employment costs and reduce profits—which is why Republican president George H. W. Bush had vetoed the law two times before 1993. Many family and women's advocates, on the other hand, feared that the law did not go far enough and provided too many exemptions and exceptions.

Whether it has been effective or not, however, FMLA represented an increased level of regulation of the American economy, an intervention by the state into the delicate balance of work and family life.

How U.S. Law Compares with Other Countries

In the United States, care work is much more market based than it is in many other countries, which tend to have more state-based solutions. For example, children here spend more time in the care of their parents or informal caregivers, paid for by their own families. In Europe, children spend more time in professional day care centers, and the expense is much more often borne by the government (Esping-Andersen 2009). Even though it was a government act, however, FMLA did not really change all that. Rather, the law attempted to protect the family's role in the system of care by protecting workers' ability to spend time caring for their family members.

A quarter of a century later, the United States is the only wealthy country that still does not guarantee any *paid* leave to parents to care for their children—and most countries provide more unpaid leave as well. Figure 11.8 shows a comparison of 20 wealthy industrialized countries, in which the United States ranked at the bottom in terms of paid parental leave guarantees. (Most of these countries don't guarantee full pay during the leave time, but all include a substantial portion.)

At the other extreme, Finland guarantees more than three years of paid leave. But in many countries it is common for parents to be provided with a year or more of paid leave to care for their children. In some countries, the policy is motivated in large part by the desire to promote

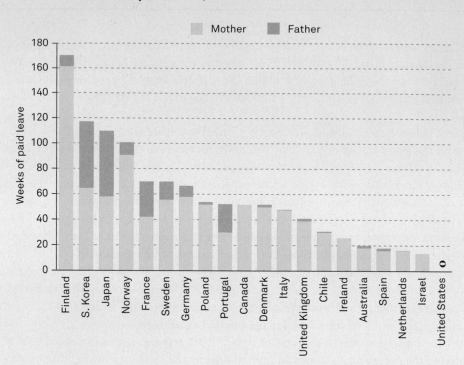

Figure 11.8 **Total paid family leave guaranteed to parents with children: 20 wealthy countries, 2016**

Legend: Mother | Father

Y-axis: Weeks of paid leave (0 to 180)

Countries (X-axis): Finland, S. Korea, Japan, Norway, France, Sweden, Germany, Poland, Portugal, Canada, Denmark, Italy, United Kingdom, Chile, Ireland, Australia, Spain, Netherlands, Israel, United States

SOURCE: Organisation for Economic Co-operation and Development (OECD) (2017X).

childbearing. The governments hope that by making child rearing more compatible with pursuing a career, they will encourage young couples to have more children.

In addition to the shorter leave provided in the United States, researchers have identified three major limitations to the protections offered by the Family and Medical Leave Act (Gerstel and McGonagle 1999):

- *Leave is unpaid.* That makes leave hard, or even impossible, for many people to afford, even if they are covered by the law. And many families are in a bind because they have to choose between giving up their salary to take care of their children and remaining at work and attempting to arrange high-quality child care.

- *Many people aren't covered.* With only about half of the workforce covered, FMLA is not really a national policy. Further, those who are covered tend to be people who have better jobs already, such as those who have worked for their employers longer and those who work for larger companies.

- *Many employers offer leave only grudgingly.* Although it may be required by law, many workers feel pressured not to take leave when they have children, for fear that they will anger or disappoint their employers. Those who do take leave may find themselves punished informally in the future when it comes to wage increases or promotions.

The extent of inequality in the availability of parental leave is starkly illustrated in Figure 11.9. It shows, for example, that half of all women with less than a high school education quit their jobs when they have their first child, compared with about 1 in 8 of those with a college degree or higher. On the other hand, about two-thirds of college graduates take some paid leave when they have their first child, which may include formal maternity leave, vacation leave, or paid sick leave. Compare that with less than 20 percent of women who have not graduated from high school who take paid leave. Some workers also use disability leave for childbirth, and the figure shows that this option is more available to those with higher education as well.

Thus, the quality of one's job appears to play a large role in the options available for balancing work and family, at least around the issue of time off for having children. FMLA may help provide a basic level of leave to many workers, but clearly it does not resolve work-family conflicts for most workers or alleviate the inequality between workers with better or worse job opportunities.

Figure 11.9 **Type of leave used by employed women for their first birth, by education level, 2006–2008**

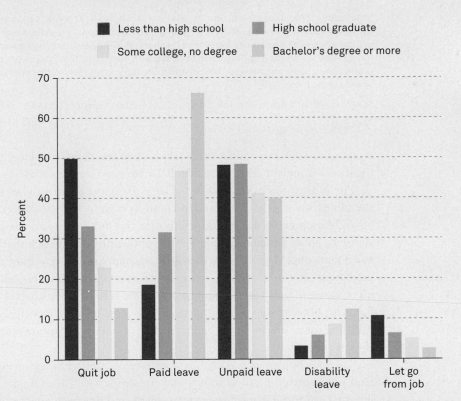

Women with lower levels of education are much more likely to quit their jobs or to be let go when they have a first child, and those with more education more often take paid leave from work.

SOURCE: Author's figure from Laughlin (2011).

Figure 11.10 Time spent in primary activities for adults with a child under age 6 in the family, 2015

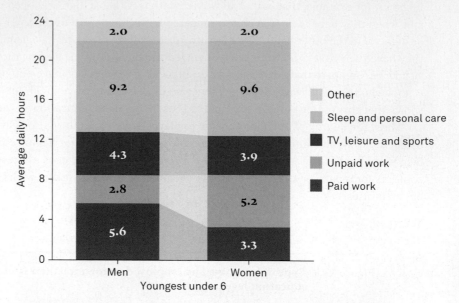

Note: Paid work includes travel time. Unpaid work includes housework, child care, caring for others, yard work, repairs, shopping, and procuring services. Personal care includes grooming and other private time (such as sex). The paid and unpaid work for men and women add up very close to equal, with men doing more paid work and women doing more unpaid work. Men spend more time on TV, leisure, and sports, while women sleep more.

SOURCE: Author's figure from U.S. Bureau of Labor Statistics data (2016d).

focusing on the early childbearing years, when the division of labor tends to be the most strongly marked by gender (Glauber and Gozjolko 2011).

Figure 11.10 shows the division of time use between men and women, using the same time use data I showed in Figure 11.6 but now focusing on those who have children under age 6. You will notice that both men and women average about 8.5 hours per day of work. But the gender division is such that women do much more unpaid work, while men do much more paid work. Although this may seem equal in terms of total hours, it leaves women disadvantaged in several ways: because they earn less money, they are less likely to control the family finances; because they get out of the house less, they are less likely to have a fulfilling social life; because their own careers stagnate, they are more at risk in the case of a divorce.

To find couples who truly share housework and child care equally often requires identifying people in unusual circumstances. For example, researcher Bonnie Fox (2009) identifies a couple—Ross and Rosa—in which the wife was the primary earner before their baby was born, the husband believed strongly in sharing work equally, and they were financially secure enough that they could both take six months off after the baby arrived. Under those rather unique circumstances, and with a commitment from both partners, they were able to share child rearing and housework responsibilities evenly. Instead of the birth of their child exacerbating gender inequality, then, it became an opportunity to rebalance. For example, when Rosa was breastfeeding, Ross found himself spending more time doing housework.

In contrast to a deliberate decision to divide care work evenly, some couples find their roles suddenly reversed—or at least upended—by economic crises. In fact, the most common reason for families to adopt an at-home father arrangement is because the father has lost his job or is unable to work (Kramer, Kelly, and McCulloch 2013). In such cases, it is common for the father's unemployment to cause resentment and unhappiness or even a stronger commitment to traditional gender roles (Legerski and Cornwall 2010). That resistance partly results from the discomfort people feel in a role that may not be socially recognized. As one stay-at-home dad told researcher Beth Latshaw, "On some level, I see a stay-at-home dad and think, what's wrong with you? I know what's wrong with me, but what's wrong with you? I joke about it, but honestly, I have that reaction, so if I'm having that reaction, everyone's having that reaction" (Latshaw 2011:138).

Sometimes, however, we find that stay-at-home fathers do embrace their new role as primary caretaker of the children (Chesley 2011). But this is quite uncommon and has not caught on as a social trend. For example, the U.S. Census Bureau asks families in which the wife was employed who has primary responsibility for taking care of the children. In 2011, only 10 percent of fathers in working-mother families were the primary caretakers for their children (Laughlin 2013:20).

Balance From what we have seen, families may be as difficult to change as workplaces. One unintended consequence of this logjam may be a solution that people choose reluctantly: reducing the role of family in their lives. As we saw in Chapter 9, women are having fewer children—and having them later in life—than they did in the 1960s. Delaying marriage also reduces housework burdens, at least for women. That is because, deliberately or not, over time marriage increases the tendency of couples to fall into a traditional division of labor (Baxter, Hewitt, and Haynes 2008). However, it is hard to tell how much people are delaying their marriage and childbearing as a strategy to manage work-family conflict or for other reasons, because people often can't explain their own motivations objectively to researchers (Damaske 2011).

The barriers to rebalancing work and family are substantial (Damaske and Frech 2016). Most people need their jobs to pay their bills, and they need their own labor at home to stretch their paychecks enough to make ends meet. But we can still learn something about what people say they would *like* to do. Research shows that many people who experience work-family conflicts would like to reduce their work hours, and this is especially the case when people have children (Reynold and Johnson 2012). When the Pew Research Center asked women what their ideal work situation would be, they found that a majority of American mothers would prefer *not* to work a full-time job (see Figure 11.11). Half of those with jobs would prefer a part-time job, and another 11 percent would rather have no job at all. Among mothers without jobs, however, a majority would like to

Figure 11.11 Ideal working situations for U.S. mothers

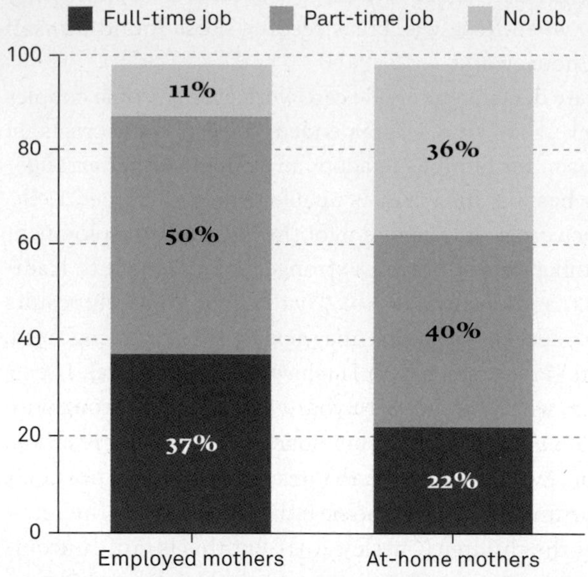

Legend: ■ Full-time job   ■ Part-time job   ■ No job

Employed mothers: Full-time job 37%, Part-time job 50%, No job 11%

At-home mothers: Full-time job 22%, Part-time job 40%, No job 36%

When asked what their "ideal" work situation would be, half of employed mothers say they prefer part-time work. On the other hand, most mothers without jobs would prefer to have one, at least part-time.

SOURCE: Parker and Wang (2013).

have either a part-time or full-time job. Clearly, ideals are not matching reality in many families. (Interestingly, three-quarters of fathers think a full-time job is ideal for them, and this figure has remained stable for many years.)

Working part-time is a popular preference among employed mothers who feel the pull of parenting and the demands of unpaid work, whether because they are single or because their partners won't—or can't—do more at home. But part-time work is not an easy choice. Those who are employed full-time and want to drop down to part-time hours often face uncooperative employers. For example, some of the successful businesswomen that sociologist Pamela Stone (2007) interviewed looked into working part-time rather than dropping out of their jobs to take care of their children. But they found that it was simply not an option in their fast-track careers. And many of those who manage to arrange part-time schedules find that their career progress stalls as a result (Bertrand, Goldin, and Katz 2010).

People who are not employed and seek to enter the workforce (or reenter it after taking time off) find that part-time jobs don't offer the same career potential and opportunities. Still, even a part-time job with limited career potential can provide an important sense of independence and personal value.

> "I can't wait to get out of this house," said one woman, who worked part-time as a pharmacist. "Just to have some time to myself. You know, just dress up and

get out [chuckling]....I think working gives you a higher self-esteem, like you're qualified to do something that you're good at. When you know you're good at it, it's rewarding." (Damaske 2011:110)

The problems of work-family conflict are certainly complex, as are the potential solutions we might consider. On the one extreme, some people have too much work. Professional careers are increasingly demanding extra-long workweeks, creating harried parents who, when they finally make it home, are frequently interrupted by their ever-present mobile communication devices (Conley 2009). On the other extreme, some people have too little work. Working-class parents often string together a series of overlapping part-time or temporary jobs—interrupted by periods of no job at all—trying to bring in enough earnings and benefits to keep their households afloat (Kalleberg 2011). Many such parents report that they would like to have more time to do housework (Stanczyk, Henly, and Lambert 2017). In between these extremes are millions of American families and individuals with one or the other of these problems—or both—to varying degrees. As a result, time itself has become an increasingly central piece of America's inequality puzzle (Jacobs and Gerson 2004).

Government Action

Despite the tenor of the previous section, there is a lot of good news in the story of work and family in the United States. Increased women's employment has brought new levels of independence and individual self-fulfillment to several generations of women. Workplaces, colleges and universities, and families themselves have seen many benefits from tapping into the much larger pool of potential that resulted from women gaining more education and joining the workforce in such great numbers. Children have grown up with wider horizons and more potential opportunities.

Nevertheless, the underlying issues discussed in this chapter often lead to seeing work and family as a series of problems that remain to be solved. To summarize, these problems may be put into three categories:

- The inequality between men and women that persists in the workplace is mirrored in most families as well. The gender division of labor is associated with a gender hierarchy in which men have more power and more options than do women.

- The balance between work and family—or rather the imbalance—creates stress for men, women, families, and workplaces that undermines the potential benefits of the social changes we have seen in the last half-century.

- Raising children to be happy and successful, and raising them in a way that offers equal opportunity to all regardless of the status of their parents, seems impossible to many people under the current arrangements that dominate the U.S. scene. Most parents are under too much stress, are too busy, and face too many irreconcilable choices to achieve the parenting they want for their children.

We have seen that people have tried—in workplaces and in families—to find new sources of balance in the work-family relationship. But in each arena, the challenges remain formidable. Given the apparent state of impasse, some analysts believe that strong government action is needed.

The theory that the state can jumpstart change in both the workplace and the family arises from the belief that government can create incentives for reform that are more universal, and more equalizing, than either families or the market can achieve on their own. This is especially the case with regard to workplaces, because many employers believe that they would be at a competitive disadvantage if they took steps on their own to improve their employees' work-family balance (Baum 2003). Companies are especially concerned about losing their investments in hiring and training when workers leave the job. However, if the government requires certain practices by all companies, and if everyone has to comply with them, then companies are not going out on a limb alone by implementing a new, family-friendly policy.

What are the most important policies? The economist Heather Boushey, in her book *Finding Time* (2016), suggests four areas in which relatively small policy changes could make a big difference for work-family balance (although she prefers the term work-*life* balance). By implementing changes in the areas she calls Here, There, and Care, Boushey argues we can help people to earn a living, care for their families, and reduce inequality between men and women, all while fostering the healthy development of children—and boosting the economy as well.

Here Workers need time to be "here," at home, without jeopardizing their jobs, which means guaranteed paid family and sick leave. One of the biggest problems that parents face is the disruption in their careers caused by the demands of caring for children or other family members. Many parents cannot afford to take unpaid leave, especially if there is no guarantee that their job will be waiting for them when they come back—and many American workers can't even call in sick from their jobs without losing pay, or worse. This prevents people from making the contributions they could at home and at work. If the government required this from all employers, no one would be at a disadvantage for offering such benefits. To help reduce costs for employers, the government can provide some of the compensation to workers from payroll taxes, as it does for unemployment insurance.

There When to be "there," at work, is a major challenge as well. Some people have hours that are too short, others have jobs that demand too much—and hours on the job are increasing overall (Miller 2015). Boushey calls for regulations that would permit worker flexibility to arrange their schedules, while providing an assurance of predictability so they can plan their schedules in advance instead

Figure 11.12 **Average annual hours worked per worker, selected countries, 2015**

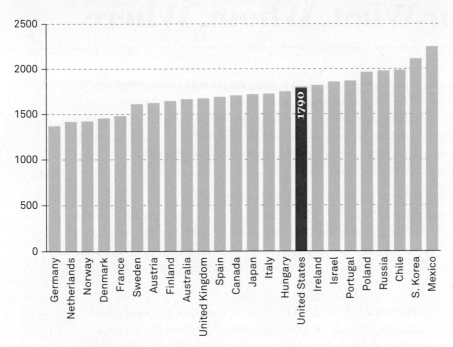

The differences between countries reflect different rates of part-time work, differences in the length of the standard workweek, and different levels of time off from work.

SOURCE: OECD (2017b).

of being forced to respond to employer demands on short notice. We have as examples a number of countries that have reduced their working hours through shortening the workweek altogether, increasing the number of part-time workers, or offering more time off from work (see Figure 11.12). Employers are reluctant to embrace such changes alone if it means they must train and provide benefits to more workers. But if all companies are required to implement these changes, it is not as costly for them.

Care Securing high-quality, affordable care for both young children and adults who can't live on their own is a problem for almost all families at one time or another. Addressing that squeeze will be expensive at first, but experts insist the long-run payoff will be worth it both socially and economically. In the United States, it is common for children to have only informal child care or family-based child care until age 4 or even 5; only 29 percent of U.S. four-year-olds attend public preschools (National Institute for Early Education Research 2016). Those who support expanding education to children at earlier ages argue that the cost of child care and the time required to manage it are a major impediment to parents' careers in the early years of parenthood. And many American parents find

Work for What, Whom, Where

At the start of the chapter, I described the work of feeding children in three different institutional arenas: home (family), school (state), and fast-food restaurant (market). In this workshop, we dig deeper into the principle that the social setting or context of work often is as important as its content. To help understand the importance of this point, let's consider specifically the rewards, rules, and relationships of work in different situations.

Consider growing tomatoes in three settings:

- *Urban balcony garden.* A couple named Kyla and Peter started a blog called "Adventures in Clueless Urban Balcony Gardening." They described it as "a little diary by two younguns who like the idea of growing at least some of their own food." For them, the rewards are mostly aesthetic—they enjoy the work and the feeling of satisfaction it provides, and they like the tomatoes. They might save a little money by growing their own tomatoes, but that's not the point.

- *Family farm.* The Pritt family farm in northern Ohio grows tomatoes as well (Podolak 2012). Owner Artie Pritt and the family support themselves by selling the produce grown on 70 acres, with the help of children, grandchildren, and great-grandchildren. "It's wonderful to have our four generations working together," said his daughter Rhonda. "The kids learn about a work ethic, customer service, and having pride in something they've helped to grow." For the children, those life lessons may be all they earn for a day's work: According to U.S. labor law, children can work on their family's farm without pay, as long as it is outside of school hours and the work is not hazardous.

- *Commercial farms.* In Florida, there are more than 30,000 tomato-farm workers, who earn about $17,000 per year—paid by the pound as they hand-carry some two tons of tomatoes per day. As farmworkers, they have less legal protection under labor laws than the rest of the labor force. Most are immigrants or migrant workers from Central or South America, earning a wage to feed their families (who are either in Florida or back in their home countries). In recent years, they have organized a series of successful protests and boycotts to increase their wages and improve working conditions, but they remain among the lowest-paid workers in the country (Ríos 2011).

One Task, Different Settings

For this exercise, working individually or in groups, decide on a single task that you know is performed in different social contexts. Make a list of the different settings in which the work is done and compare the rewards, rules, and relationships in the different situations. (This can be a simple brainstorming exercise or a research project outside of class.)

When you buy produce, do you think about where it comes from or who harvests it?

For each social context, trace the impact of the rewards, rules, and relationships you uncover back to the families of whoever does the work. And ask questions such as the following: Does having the work done in different settings have different implications for the families of workers? Do you see a pattern of change, with one setting becoming more or less common than another? What is causing such a change, and what is the effect?

Here are some sample tasks to consider:

Task	Setting 1	Setting 2	Setting 3
Cleaning toilets	Unpaid at home	By a custodian at an airport	By an inmate in a prison
Reading to children	Parents at home	In a private school	In a public library
Caring for sick elderly people	In the home of their grown children	With a spouse in their own home	In a private nursing home

it impossible to afford higher-quality child care at all. In response, several states and cities have moved to expand pre-kindergarten education in recent years, most notably New York City (see Trend to Watch). In contrast with the United States, most European countries start education at a younger age, with children expected to attend a public school by age 3. Many economists believe that providing more universal high-quality early childhood education will go far toward equalizing opportunities for children as they grow up (Heckman 2006). At the other end of the age spectrum, the problem of providing care to old people who need it causes emotional and economic problems for a growing share of families. As the population ages (see Chapter 13), this challenge will only grow more acute.

How people and their families decide who will do which work, and for what rewards, remains a dilemma not only for individuals but also for families, workplaces, and the government (Jacobs and Gerson 2016). The stakes are high, as the outcome of these decisions will affect everything from the stability of marriage to the equality between men and women, from the productivity of our workplaces to the potential of our children. For sociologists, this subject tests our understanding of how major institutional arenas interact in everyday life. As busy as we are researching these issues—and there are dozens of new sociology articles published every year with the words *work* and *family* in the title—there is little chance that we researchers will put ourselves out of work anytime soon.

Trend to Watch: Local Policy Innovation

From marijuana to the minimum wage, and many other issues, state and local law is often where important policy innovations emerge. And work-family policy is no exception. Consider early childhood education, a key part of extending state support to reduce family work burdens. In 2013, then president Obama called for the government to "make high-quality preschool available to every single child in America" (Rich 2013). But with Republicans controlling Congress, Obama had little chance to create a big federal program during the remainder of his presidency. It was different in New York City, however, where Bill de Blasio, then running for mayor, took up Obama's call and made it part of his winning campaign (Kirp 2016). Now the city has a successful program that enrolls tens of thousands of children every year, and the mayor wants to expand it to include three-year-olds as well (Taylor 2017). New York's popular effort may become a model for other local governments, or someday inspire a federal policy.

There is a similar story with paid family leave. After the federal Family and Medical Leave Act failed to provide paid leave, the California state government took up the challenge and implemented a paid leave program in 2004. Now a number of states and cities have moved to develop their own family leave laws, and a handful of states have implemented paid policies as well (National

Conference of State Legislatures 2016). California, still the biggest, offers six weeks of paid leave to all workers who have spent at least one year working more than half time at their current employer (Milkman and Appelbaum 2013). The program is funded by a payroll tax on all workers, and it provides about half pay for workers with a new child or ill family member. The result in California has been more mothers taking leave from their jobs around the time of childbirth, and returning to the same job later in the year. (Fathers have used the program much less, however [Baum and Ruhm 2016].) With California's success, other states are following (including New York and New Jersey), and some cities are trying as well (such as Washington, D.C.).

Progressive work-family policies seem to be getting little attention at the federal level, so these state and local initiatives may represent a way forward for advocates of work-family balance and policies that support care work. A patchwork of policies across the country might be confusing and inefficient. And maybe people will start thinking more about such policies when they decide where to move for work or family reasons, which could further polarize the country between places that embrace such programs and those that don't. On the other hand, local successes might lead to national gains by creating successful policy examples, eventually shaping federal policy. That question is one of many uncertainties on today's political horizons.

Questions for Review

1. Think of your typical breakfast experience. Is it the same as when you were a child? How might differences in family background result in different breakfast experiences?

2. What is the "second shift"?

3. Why is it easier to quantify paid work done outside the home over unpaid housework and child care? What have been some suggestions for measuring the amount of housework and child care performed?

4. Think about how your parents spent their time each day when you were a child, whether performing housework, doing child care, enjoying leisure time, etc. How do you think your time use patterns will differ if you have children, or how do they differ already?

5. How is the division of unpaid housework and care work affected by gender, upbringing, and income?

6. Describe ways that employers could reduce work-family conflict.

7. What are the three major limitations of the Family and Medical Leave Act?

8. Discuss Janet Gornick and Marcia Meyers's policy suggestions. How would a legislator try to get these suggestions passed (or rejected)?

12 Family Violence and Abuse

By the time Bernadette Powell was 22, she had been married to Herman Smith for several years and they had two children. It was the early 1970s, and Powell, an African American, was living in upstate New York. Her mother had not finished high school; her father was a truck driver. She hadn't finished high school either, and her husband was unsuccessfully trying to make it as an auto mechanic. But poverty and its hardships were only part of Powell's problem. Smith was an abusive alcoholic who beat her repeatedly. The police were called to their home 19 times. After the attacks, sometimes he would apologize and the couple would reconcile. But by 1977, when Powell was 25, the marriage was over.

Then one night in 1978, Smith showed up at Powell's house in Ithaca, New York, and took her—abducted her, she said—to a motel on the edge of town. There she killed him in what she said was an act of self-defense: When he fell asleep, she stole his gun and shot him when he woke up suddenly.

At Powell's trial, the prosecutor, a White man named Joseph Joch, accused her of planning the murder and going to the motel purposively to carry it out. When her defense counsel brought up the years of abuse, Joch turned the tables on her. "Do you know what a masochist is?" he demanded to know. "Are you a person who likes to be hurt?" If she had really been unhappy in the marriage, he charged, she could have simply left Smith years earlier.

The jury of 12 local citizens—all White, 9 of them men—found her guilty, and she was sentenced to prison. Interviewed after the trial, one of the jurors said: "We wondered why, if it was as bad as she said it was, she didn't just leave a whole lot sooner. Personally I think she asked for a lot of it. But even if she didn't deserve it, she didn't have to make such a big thing out of it."

Even though Powell went to prison, the story continued, as told in Ann Jones's book *Everyday Death* (1985). In the 1970s, there was a growing awareness about

Decades after Bernadette Powell's case, more people are aware of violence within families thanks in large part to feminists campaigning for social change.

family violence, reflecting the activism of a new feminist generation. A new local group was staffing a telephone hotline for what were then known as "battered women," and some of them organized to help Bernadette Powell's appeal.

Although the appeal ultimately was not successful, and Powell served 15 years in prison (where she earned a college degree), the feminists who came to her aid raised issues that would become more important in later years. They argued that with a history of violent abuse in her marriage, Powell could not have been expected simply to walk away from Herman Smith; his violence was successfully controlling her. Further, leaving an abusive relationship without proper support or protection can actually increase the danger (Rezey 2017). Powell's supporters also pointed out that Joch himself had been accused of violence by his wife while he was in the prosecutor's office. In essence, they accused the legal system of blaming the victim in Powell's case and of looking the other way when the abuser was a successful White male prosecutor.

Since then, as we will see, both the cultural and the political climate have changed on the issue of violence within families. Awareness has increased, new kinds of intervention and assistance are available to help people who are abused within their families, and the amount of family violence appears to have declined substantially. However, serious systematic problems remain.

Family Violence: An Institutional Perspective

The subject of family violence and abuse is personal and painful. Instructors and students should pause at this point to consider the possible effects of discussing these topics, especially for those who have experienced abuse in their own lives (van der Kolk 2000). Because this kind of victimization still is so common in the United States, most of us will know someone who has been touched by it in one way or another. However, because families often are protected by a cultural—and sometimes legal—expectation of privacy and a shroud of secrecy, those who suffer usually do so in isolation. That leaves us with the complexity of a problem that is widespread but experienced alone and often invisibly.

Such isolation can make the experience of abuse even worse. One benefit of addressing the issue in this book is that we can help pierce that isolation and encourage victims to realize that they are not alone. That goes for the perpetrators of violence and abuse as well. In many cases, their harmful acts are not the mere outcome of bad personalities or evil intentions—individual traits—but also the product of systemic features of our society for which no one person is responsible alone.

In this chapter, we will attempt to develop an appreciation of how prevalent family violence and abuse are and consider some of their causes and consequences. We will also consider why family violence has grown less common in the last several decades. And we will explore some of the legal and policy challenges that these issues pose for the future.

To put the story of Bernadette Powell—and the broader facts—in perspective, we will need to shake one common way of thinking about the problem of violence and abuse within families. We should not think that there is a correct way that families are "supposed" to work. Yes, families are part of the system of care that enhances the lived experience and survival of most people. But we should not leap from that observation to the idea that when family members abuse each other, it means that their families are *not* working. That idea is related to the functionalist approach discussed in Chapter 1, based on the assumption that if something is common in society, it must serve some positive function. To this way of thinking, the "normal" functions of the family are positive, and harmful acts or outcomes are deviations from that normal mode.

The family is an institutional arena, and the relationships between people within that arena include all kinds of interactions, good and bad. The way families work is the outcome of many processes—the kind of cultural, legal, technological, and political changes described in this book. And while one family member may view the family as not working—a child suffering abuse at the hands of a trusted caretaker, for example—from the point of view of the abuser, the family may in fact be working quite well, regarding the family as a safe place to carry out abuse without getting caught or punished. Similarly, some kinds of abuse—such as the harsh physical punishment of children or the sexual abuse of wives—may be expected outcomes of a family system in which adults have much more power than children and men (usually) have more power than women. In such cases, what looks like abuse to the victims (or the law) may seem to the abuser like a person just doing his or her job of running the family.

As we discussed in Chapter 1, the family arena is linked to the arenas of the state and market, and much of what happens within families is associated with these connections. For example, although the state sometimes cares for people directly—such as feeding children school lunch or providing medical care to military veterans—it is more common for the state to provide support to family members so that they can care for each other.

Consider children specifically. The federal government gives poor parents food stamps or housing assistance and expects them to feed and house their children. The state operates public schools but assumes that parents will facilitate their children's participation in the school system, from getting them to school every day to helping them with their homework. And the legal system holds parents responsible for their children's behavior, essentially requiring parents to discipline their children. In all these ways, the state increases the authority of parents over their children. That is usually helpful for parents and children. But when parents abuse that privilege, they may do so with relative impunity, since their behavior occurs within the context of their legal authority. That makes it difficult to prevent, detect, or punish parental abuse—and sometimes even to define it.

In these circumstances, abuses of power, however morally or even criminally objectionable, are not mere aberrations or misbehavior. They are an outcrop of a set of institutional relations that creates the context for such abuse.

What Is Family Violence?

Family violence and abuse include a broad array of problems, defined by the relationship between victim and perpetrator. Just as there are different definitions of families, and not all family members share a common perception of who is included in every family, defining family violence also is sometimes ambiguous.

We can classify the victims of family violence into three categories:

- *Intimate partners:* Spouses, cohabiting partners, romantic or sexual partners (or former partners after a breakup)

- *Children:* Biological children, stepchildren, foster children, or adopted children—that is, any child who relies on an adult for intimate care, generally at home

- *Elders:* Older family members, usually parents or in-laws, who may or may not rely on their children for care and support

Two elements are usually present in the relationship between victims and perpetrators. First, there is **intimacy,** meaning that the people involved love or at least know each other very well and interact in private. Second, there is a **care relationship**, in which one person is responsible for another person's care. That means that what happens between them is within the family arena and may be complicated by its invisibility to those outside the family. The relationships not only are close but also generally private. And when the relationships include dependencies of support and caring, the emotional stakes of violence and abuse may be higher, causing long-term psychological damage (Meng and D'Arcy 2016).

Family violence and *abuse* can be used as umbrella terms to refer to several kinds of harm caused by family members against each other. In this chapter, I include under the category of "violence" some acts that are not directly violent but rather are threats of force or intimidation (just as the law treats a holdup at gunpoint as a "violent" crime even if no shots are fired). And in the category of "abuse," I include neglect that rises to the level of abuse when it is directly harmful to the people involved. Some behavior, such as sexual assault, constitutes both violence and abuse. Clearly, it is not always possible to separate acts of violence and acts of abuse into neat categories (Tolan, Gorman-Smith, and Henry 2006). Nevertheless, these are important distinctions that we need to keep in mind as we examine specific facts and patterns.

intimacy

A type of relationship in which people love or at least know each other very well and interact in private.

care relationship

A relationship in which one person is responsible for another's care.

Child Abuse and Neglect

Child maltreatment involves a range of behaviors, including both deliberate acts against children and the failure to protect or provide for children. The federal government's definition of **child abuse and neglect** provides a general perspec-

child abuse and neglect

The act or failure to act on the part of a parent or caretaker that results in (or puts children at imminent risk for) physical or emotional harm, sexual abuse, or exploitation.

Lauren Kavanaugh was horrifically abused by her mother and stepfather from age 2 until 8. Other family members and officials failed to see what was happening. She miraculously survived but more than a decade later still struggles with normal life.

tive on this issue: the act or failure to act on the part of a parent or caretaker that results in (or puts children at imminent risk for) physical or emotional harm, sexual abuse, or exploitation (U.S. Department of Health and Human Services 2017). Besides directly harming children, then, abuse and neglect may occur when parents leave their young children unattended, fail to take them to school or to the doctor, or don't keep them clean, fed, and clothed (Gaudin 1993).

This definition is easier to work with in cases of abuse rather than neglect, because abuse is more often physically observable, especially when children are seriously injured (Leventhal and Gaither 2012). Neglect is more difficult to identify. First, we may not all agree on what supervision or care is necessary (Dubowitz 2014). Basic nutrition and safety are not controversial, but in other areas, there is much more ambiguity. For example, there is an ongoing, lively debate about the appropriate age at which it is okay to leave children unattended, and local laws vary in how they set rules for this. Or, to choose an example that seems more trivial, consider bathing. American parents are expected to bathe their children much more now than they were in the past, in part because we better understand the health benefits of hygiene but also because cultural standards have changed regarding what is considered normal and attractive (Bushman and Bushman 1988). When common practices change or different cultural groups interact, not everyone agrees on where to draw the line between family preferences and neglect.

Second, we do not always agree on who is responsible for caring for particular people. When caring is shared between two parents who don't live together, for example, or between a school and a foster family, pinning blame on one actor or another may be difficult. (It's a good bet that if we can't tell who is responsible for caring for someone, that person is at risk of being neglected, or worse.)

The Convention on the Rights of the Child

Who determines the standards for children's care? What is considered right or wrong, necessary or evil, in the treatment of the vulnerable is a social construction—that is, the product of social interaction, with outcomes that vary from time to time and place to place. For example, consider that the Ten Commandments of the Judeo-Christian Bible, which cover the most egregious crimes, order children to respect their parents, but not parents to respect their children.

A social construction of more modern times, the Convention on the Rights of the Child, was adopted by the United Nations in 1989. It specifies a number of rights and protections for children as well as obligations for those who care for them (Office of the High Commissioner for Human Rights n.d.). The Convention is the world's most widely accepted human rights treaty, with 193 countries so far having ratified it—as close as we get to an international consensus (Blanchfield 2013).

The Convention's preamble includes a strong statement of support for families as the primary social location for raising children. The rights it describes are based on agreement with these principles:

> Convinced that the family, as the fundamental group of society and the natural environment for the growth and well-being of all its members and particularly children, should be afforded the necessary protection and assistance so that it can fully assume its responsibilities within the community,
>
> Recognizing that the child, for the full and harmonious development of his or her personality, should grow up in a family environment, in an atmosphere of happiness, love and understanding,
>
> Considering that the child should be fully prepared to live an individual life in society, and brought up in the spirit of the ideals proclaimed in the Charter of the United Nations, and in particular in the spirit of peace, dignity, tolerance, freedom, equality and solidarity.

As of early 2014, of all of the members of the United Nations, only the United States and Somalia have not ratified the treaty. In the United States, there has been a campaign of opposition to the treaty led by religious conservatives who say it would lead to government control over their rights as parents, possibly prohibiting religious education and corporal punishment. Among other things, the treaty's opponents take issue with Article 19, which states:

> Parties shall take all appropriate legislative, administrative, social and educational measures to protect the child from all forms of physical or mental violence, injury or

abuse, neglect or negligent treatment, maltreatment or exploitation, including sexual abuse, while in the care of parent(s), legal guardian(s) or any other person who has the care of the child.

This passage could be interpreted to mean that corporal punishment—including spanking—is prohibited as a form of "violence." Further, critics say that under the Convention, children would be free to choose their own religion or get abortions—and sue their parents if they tried to intervene. (In reality, the treaty contains no enforcement provisions, so its rules would not be legally binding in the United States.)

The debate shows how definitions of child abuse have evolved over time and how they remain uneven across cultures. Opponents object to the Convention's framing of children's development as a process of individualization and independence. In the view of most American religious conservatives, humans are born sinful, and therefore harsh punishment of children is acceptable or even desirable (Ellison and Sherkat 1993). But that seems to have become the minority view worldwide.

One original objection to the treaty from the U.S. government was over a provision against the death penalty for children convicted of murder. At the time, U.S. states could legally execute people for crimes committed when they were younger than 18 years old. However, that practice is no longer allowed by the Supreme Court, in accordance with the *Roper v. Simmons* decision of 2005. In that case, the Court deferred to the international community's moral standards, finding that the almost universal prohibition of the death penalty for minors added to the weight of evidence that the practice is "cruel and unusual" ("The Debate over Foreign Law in *Roper v. Simmons*" 2005).

Much of what we call "child abuse" is easily agreed on as abuse. But to enforce that definition requires drawing the line between parental and state authority. On the one hand, it is the responsibility of parents to care for and discipline their children. On the other hand, the state has an obligation to step in when parents abuse their children. That requires defining the relationship between the state and the family as institutional arenas, which makes it a complicated—and contentious—issue in modern society.

Michael Pearl is a preacher and author of the popular book *To Train Up a Child*, which instructs parents on how to use corporal punishment. But others argue that corporal punishment is child abuse.

More generally, is there a broader social responsibility to care for children (see Changing Politics, "The Convention on the Rights of the Child")? Caring for vulnerable family members requires resources to which not everyone has access. For example, parents who have had their children removed from their care for neglect and placed in the foster care system may object that poverty is the real reason their children are neglected. In fact, it is true that if they can't afford to buy adequate nutrition, shelter, clothing, and medical care—or arrange to get them from charities or the government—parents may lose custody of their children despite their earnest efforts to care for them (Rosenfeld et al. 1997). In such cases, we may think of the children as neglected, but not because of neglectful actions by their caretakers; rather, they are neglected by the larger social structures that block them from getting the resources they need.

Child abuse challenges our perceptions of what is commonly experienced or expected. And it can—and should—lead us to question our own assumptions. For example, most people consider the family home to be the safest place for a child. But when children are abused at home, that expectation may be turned on its head. One woman who was abused as a child, interviewed later, remembered school as a place to get away from her family: "I loved it because that was eight hours out of the day that I knew I was safe," she remembered, "and that was a great feeling" (Thomas and Hall 2008:154).

Patterns of Abuse and Neglect

A clear pattern in the research on child abuse is that most of the harmful and dangerous acts perpetrated against children occur in the family home at the hands of their parents or other caregivers. That doesn't mean that families are bad for children. On the contrary, we may think of all the safe families as places where children are protected from the abusive adults in the dangerous families. So rather than think of the family as an institution that simply protects—or harms—children, we need to think of it as an institutional arena in which the safety of children is determined, for better and for worse.

However, beyond the problems of definition, the study of child abuse and neglect is plagued by inadequate information. Many cases—probably most cases—are never reported to authorities. For example, a review of national data on confirmed cases of child maltreatment (neglect and abuse) found that 12.5 percent or one-in-eight children suffer maltreatment at some point during childhood (Wildeman et al. 2014). However, social scientists using sample surveys find higher rates. Asking people to recall experiences from their own childhood, one major survey, with interviews of about 15,000 young adults, found that 28 percent had experienced physical assault by parents or caregivers during their childhood, while 12 percent had experienced physical neglect and 5 percent had experienced sexual abuse (Hussey, Chang, and Kotch 2006).

Even if there are shortfalls in the formal reporting of abuse and neglect, state

Figure 12.1 **Percentage of reported child abuse and neglect cases by perpetrator relationship, 2015**

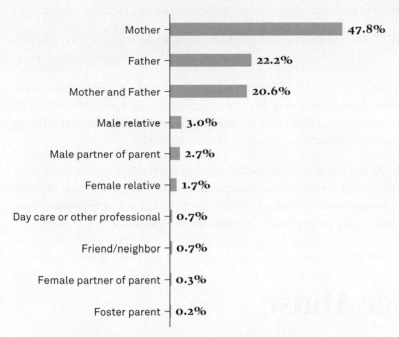

SOURCE: U.S. Department of Health and Human Services (2017).

and federal governments do collect a lot of data that can be useful. For example, it is probably safe to assume that cases of abuse within families are even less likely to be reported than those in schools or other institutions, which operate more in the public eye. So the fact that the vast majority of *reported* cases come from family members reinforces that notion that families are the source of most abuse. Figure 12.1 shows the percentage of reported abuse and neglect cases (those that are substantiated by official investigations) attributed to different categories of relationship to the child.

Mothers and fathers together account for 90 percent of child abuse cases, with most of the remainder attributed to other family members or romantic partners of the parents. (Note that the high representation of mothers acting alone partly reflects the fact that so many children in single-parent families live with their mothers rather than their fathers.) With such a large portion of people experiencing violent child abuse at some time in their lives, and that abuse so heavily concentrated within families, we need to think of this problem as a systematic, though not universal, feature of American families, rather than an individual experience.

From a combination of surveys and official records, we have some good information about which children are most likely to experience child abuse, as reviewed by Tolan, Gorman-Smith, and Henry (2006):

- Those who live with parents who have their own mental health problems, especially poor impulse control and low self-esteem or a history of violence.

- Those in households where domestic violence occurs between adults.

- Those in poor families or poor neighborhoods. Most analysts trace this pattern to the stresses and resource deprivation that poor parents experience.

- Those in families with weak support networks. When parents have fewer relatives, friends, and neighbors to whom they may turn during difficult times, the stresses that build up increase the chance that the parents—or others in the household—will abuse their children.

Thus, the risks that children face are connected to other problems in their families, especially poverty, social isolation, and violence. Some of that violence occurs between parents or among married couples or romantically involved couples. We will return to that issue after discussing elder abuse.

Elder Abuse

elder abuse

The physical, sexual, or emotional abuse of old people by someone with whom they share an intimate or caring relationship.

As the U.S. population grows older, due to increasing life expectancy and the aging of the baby boom generation, the issue of elder abuse has attracted more attention from researchers, policymakers, and social service agencies (Dong 2015). We define **elder abuse** as the physical, sexual, or emotional abuse of old people by someone with whom they share an intimate or caring relationship. As with child abuse and neglect, elder abuse is difficult to identify and prevent because it often takes place in isolated, intimate settings, mostly within families or in institutional care facilities.

Difficult as it is to measure, however, we have some concrete information. One large national survey asked Americans ages 70 and older whether they had been abused in the previous year by a friend, romantic partner, family member, or caregiver (Rosay and Mulford 2017). Researchers found that 14 percent of this population had experienced elder abuse (see Figure 12.2). The most common experiences were "coercive control" (including threats, keeping them from leaving home, or controlling their money without consent) and "expressive aggression" (such as acting so angry that it felt dangerous, or severely insulting or humiliating them).

Violent crime against old people is quite rare compared with the rates experienced by young adults. Just under 2 percent of people 70 and older reported physical or sexual violence from intimate partners or caregivers, as Figure 12.2 shows. Overall, people ages 18 to 24 are about five times more likely to be the victim of a violent crime than are people over age 65 (Truman and Morgan 2016). However, abuse and neglect are serious problems for a substantial portion of the older population, and most of this mistreatment takes place at the hands of family members or caregivers.

Figure 12.2 **Percentage of Americans age 70 and older reporting abuse in the previous year, by type of abuse**

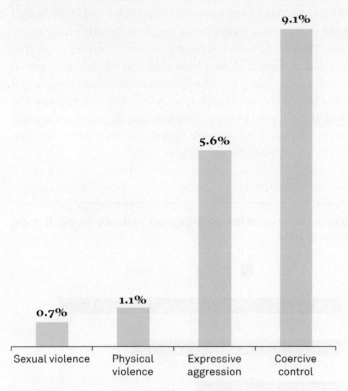

SOURCE: Rosay and Mulford (2017).

Intimate Partner Violence

Researchers and statistical agencies in recent years have grouped together the violence between adults. Because family boundaries are difficult to define, they have used the concept of "intimate partners," which includes married spouses as well as romantic partners and people who are dating. As a result, what is known as **intimate partner violence** refers to violence between partners who are (or were) involved in a sexual or romantic relationship. This includes completed as well as threatened physical violence (from slapping to murder), rape or sexual assault, and stalking (Black et al. 2011).

Several other terms are common among researchers in this area, as well as among social service and activist organizations. *Domestic violence* has long been used to refer to any violence within families. Although that term is less common now, many organizations—such as emergency shelters for women seeking refuge from abuse—were created with the words "domestic violence" in their names. And among feminists, the term *violence against women* usually refers to intimate partner violence committed by men (Jordan, Campbell, and Follingstad 2010). I

intimate partner violence

Violence between partners who are (or were) involved in a sexual or romantic relationship.

use *intimate partner violence*, which is now used by the federal government in its data collection and related programs.

As with child abuse and elder abuse, many cases of intimate partner violence are not reported. To get an idea of the amount of such violence, then, social scientists again have used sample surveys to ask people to describe their experiences confidentially. The results from one large government survey show that 37 percent of women and 17 percent of men have experienced "contact" sexual violence (which includes rape, being forced to penetrate someone else, sexual coercion, or unwanted sexual contact [Smith et al. 2017]). Not surprisingly, the less extreme forms of violence are the most common. But the numbers are still large: About 10 percent of women, for example, report that they have ever been choked or suffocated by an intimate partner (Figure 12.3).

Figure 12.3 **Lifetime occurrence of intimate partner violence for adult men and women, 2010**

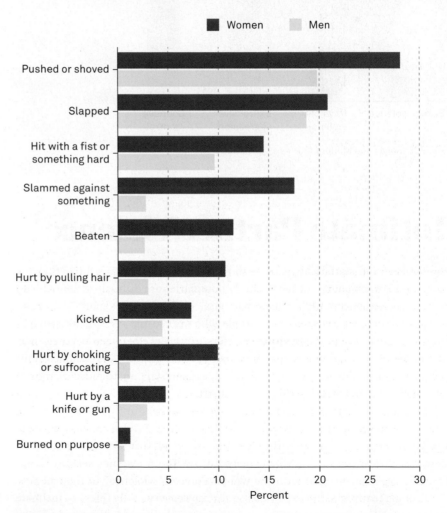

SOURCE: Black et al. (2011).

Figure 12.4 **Reason why intimate partner violent crime wasn't reported to police, 2006–2010**

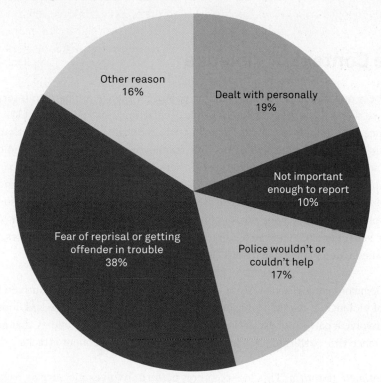

Other reason
16%

Dealt with personally
19%

Not important
enough to report
10%

Fear of reprisal or getting
offender in trouble
38%

Police wouldn't or
couldn't help
17%

SOURCE: Catalano (2012).

In the single year 2015—rather than over a whole lifetime—women were more than 10 times more likely than men to be the victims of intimate partner violence, according to the government's Crime Victimization Survey. In that year, 5.4 out of every 1,000 women told the survey that they had such an experience, compared with 0.5 out of every 1,000 men (U.S. Bureau of Justice Statistics 2017). And yet, only 54 percent of the violent crime suffered at the hands of intimate partners is reported to police, according to that same survey.

The reasons for not reporting intimate partner violent crime are shown in Figure 12.4. The most common reason is fear of the consequences—either that the perpetrator would punish the victim for reporting it or that the perpetrator would get in too much trouble. For example, women who depend on their husband or partner for financial support might not want him to go to jail or lose his job. Another 17 percent of those surveyed believed that the police would be either powerless or unwilling to help. What people do when they experience family violence is the product of how they view their relationships, what they think their alternatives are, and what they think the outcome of reporting the violence might be. Reporting a crime can itself be traumatic, and this is especially the case with regard to sexual violence. This problem is confounded by the fear, often realized, that police or other authorities will not believe the story told by the victim, especially if she is in a relationship with her attacker (Miller et al. 2011). To understand those dynamics, it is helpful to think more systematically about the contexts in which such violence takes place.

The Context of Violence

Numbers on the prevalence of intimate partner violence are hard to interpret, because they reflect many different kinds of relationships and different kinds of violence. Researchers have made some important distinctions, however, that will help us understand what's going on. One framework, devised by the sociologist Michael Johnson (2006), involves putting acts of violence into a broader pattern within the relationship. For example, does violence occur frequently, at random, or only in response to certain triggers? Does it serve a specific purpose, such as controlling a spouse's behavior, or is it more an uncontrolled lashing out? What about self-defense? After analyzing survey data on violence, researchers have identified three principal patterns (Johnson 2008):

- *Common couple violence.* As the name suggests, this is the most common form of violence. It results from specific arguments within a couple and does not involve a pattern of escalating violence over time. Most couples that experience this pattern do not suffer severe injuries or frequent attacks.

- *Intimate terrorism.* This less common pattern involves violence as part of a campaign for control or domination within a relationship (Johnson, Leone, and Xu 2014). This is more likely to involve escalating violence and serious injury as well as psychological abuse. As seen in the Bernadette Powell story at the beginning of the chapter, this pattern was part of what motivated feminists to organize for social and legal services to protect women.

- *Violent resistance.* When a spouse or partner is the victim of a pattern of violence, she or he may lash out in response. This may or may not meet the legal definition of self-defense, which requires an immediate threat. But it should be seen as part of a generally defensive pattern of standing up for oneself and possibly preparing to leave the relationship.

This set of categories allows us to see the social meaning and consequences of violence more clearly—to see the context of violence. In particular, as Johnson (2011) points out, when we look at the severity, frequency, and uses of violence, we find that men are much more likely than women to perpetrate long-term, serious violence as a means of domination within their relationships. That pattern is sometimes mistaken for a simple escalation of mutual violence rather than an exercise of domination, especially when the perpetrator has a good reputation or high status, as in the case of White male celebrities (Pepin 2016).

As a result of these patterns, women are much more likely to be seriously

Figure 12.5 **Intimate partner homicides, 2015**

Note: Includes only victims age 18 or older, in homicides for which the perpetrator was known to police.

SOURCE: Author analysis of the 2015 FBI Uniform Crime Reporting Supplemental Crime Reports.

injured or killed than are men. Government figures on homicide reveal this gender disparity very well (Cooper and Smith 2011). In one year, 2015, three times as many women as men were killed by intimate partners, as shown in Figure 12.5. Put another way, 43 percent of women who were murdered were killed by their intimate partners, compared with just 3 percent of men who were murdered, and women were three-quarters of all victims in intimate partner homicides (U.S. Department of Justice 2015).

Who Is at Greatest Risk?

Research shows a number of complicated patterns in the occurrence of intimate partner violence. Although some breakdowns are not controversial, others reflect a variety of causes that are not easy to unravel. Here are some of the clearest findings (Jordan, Campbell, and Follingstad 2010):

- Women, especially younger women, are at much greater risk of rape and of violence that causes serious injury.

- Women in families that experience economic hardship are more likely to suffer intimate partner violence (Lucero, Lim, and Santiago 2016). When couples have less economic security, they are more likely to take their stress out on each other through common couple violence (Cunradi, Caetano, and Schafer 2002).

- Relationships that involve drug and alcohol abuse are more likely to be violent (Wiersma et al. 2010).

- Women in cohabiting relationships are more likely to experience violence than those who are married (Copp et al. 2016).

- For serious violence, women face higher risks shortly after they have left their abusers (as was illustrated by the Bernadette Powell case; she was kidnapped after leaving her husband).

In addition to these patterns, there are differences between racial-ethnic groups. Reported violence is more common among American Indians and African Americans than among Whites and Asians, as shown in Figure 12.6. Intimate

Figure 12.6 **Lifetime prevalence of intimate partner violence, by race/ethnicity**

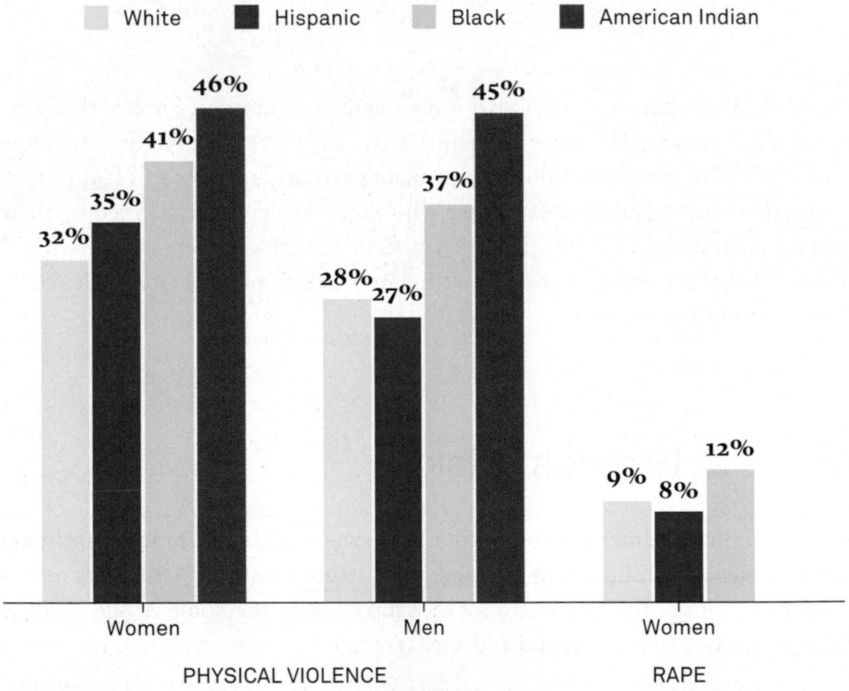

Note: The sample of Asians and the number of rapes among American Indians were too small to calculate rates accurately.

SOURCE: Walters, Chen, Breiding (2013).

partner violence rates are lower among Asian Americans than in the general population, but there were not enough of them in the National Intimate Partner and Sexual Violence Survey to include in Figure 12.6 (Chang, Shen, and Takeuchi 2009). Although this is important information for understanding who is most likely to experience intimate partner violence, the cause of these differences is not always clear. We do know that poverty and substance abuse, which contribute to family violence, are more common in American Indian communities than in the general population (Arbuckle et al. 1996). And Blacks on average live in disadvantaged neighborhoods compared with Whites, which affects their ability to access resources or networks of employed friends and relatives and to get jobs themselves. When Blacks and Whites in similar social settings are compared, the rate of domestic violence in the two groups is virtually the same (Li et al. 2010).

As the differing experiences of Blacks and Whites illustrate, along with the stresses and conflicts that produce intimate partner violence, we should also consider the availability of help to prevent or end violence. One reason some groups have higher violence rates than others is that they are less likely to benefit from resources directed at the problem (Boba and Lilley 2009). For example, research shows that there are more domestic violence shelters, hotlines, and counseling services in some areas than in others. Specifically, wealthier areas, college towns, and places with a higher percentage of Whites all have more services available to help prevent violence within relationships (Tiefenthaler, Farmer, and Sambira 2005).

Sexual Violence

As in the case of intimate partner violence generally, the nature of sexual violence is partly defined by the relationships between the people involved. And that may involve subjective perceptions that are hard to measure. Nevertheless, the concepts are clearly defined, even if describing particular incidents is not always easy.

In most legal systems, including the United States, rape has a specific definition that involves three elements: penetration, force, and lack of consent (MacKinnon 2007). In general terms, **rape** is the forced vaginal, anal, or oral penetration or attempted penetration of a person without his or her consent. Rape by definition involves penetration, but that is only one form of sexual violence. The more general term **sexual assault** refers to unwanted penetration or touch, by force or threat of force, without consent (Jordan, Campbell, and Follingstad 2010). This is a broader category of violence that includes rape but also, for example, sexually grabbing or fondling people—in fact, "any type of sexual contact or behavior"—against their will (U.S. Department of Justice 2017). Whether sex is forced or not, it is also illegal if it meets the definition of **incest**, which is sex between close relatives, primarily involving parents, children, and siblings, but in some places also including aunts and uncles and the spouses of close relatives.

In legal cases involving rape or sexual assault, the conflict often involves

rape

Forced vaginal, anal, or oral penetration or attempted penetration of a person without his or her consent.

sexual assault

Unwanted penetration or touch, by force or threat of force, without consent.

incest

Sex between close relatives.

determining whether the victim consented to the behavior, as this is based on the perceptions of the people involved and the communication between them. In real relationships, much of the communication is unspoken. And to make matters more complicated, people often make assumptions about the consent between people based on their relationship status—for example, assuming that a man's girlfriend is always willing to have sex with him.

In practice, the legal ambiguity around consent arises from the long-standing tendency to disbelieve female victims of rape and assault—to discount their stories in favor of the men's (Lisak et al. 2010). A few examples will help illustrate the problem. In the last several decades, the law has evolved to permit prosecution when the rape victim does not consent but also does not actively resist or explicitly reject sex. The most common of these cases occur when the victim is incapacitated by drugs or alcohol, whether taken voluntarily or not (Falk 2002).

That was apparently the situation with Brock Turner (as we saw in Chapter 7). Turner was a student at Stanford University and champion swimmer, who was convicted in 2016 of sexual assault for the penetration and attempted rape of a woman who had been at a fraternity party with him, and who was passed out drunk and unable to resist. Because she was incapacitated and did not resist, the law allowed the judge (also a Stanford graduate) to give Turner a very lenient sentence, and he ended up serving only three months in jail. In response to the outrage that followed, California amended the law to require a stiffer minimum sentence even if the victim does not physically resist (Chokshi 2016).

As in cases of a victim who is mentally disabled, or physically helpless, incapacitated victims are now usually considered unable to offer their consent to sex. (The same reasoning applies in cases of statutory or underage rape, as discussed in Chapter 6.) Surprisingly, such cases were not always considered "rape" at all, legally speaking, until the law was changed to account for the *inability* to consent. In North Carolina, for instance, in 1977 it was conceivable for a man to argue in his defense that he was not guilty of rape because the woman he had sex with was passed out and did not resist—because he choked her into unconsciousness! Fortunately, his appeal was denied, and the precedent was set that active resistance was not necessary to justify a rape prosecution, at least in North Carolina (*State of North Carolina v. Rosco William Hall*, 1977).

If the victim and perpetrator are in a relationship—dating, living together, or married—it has historically been difficult to prove that a rape occurred unless the victim is seriously injured; and the closer (the more familiar) the relationship, the harder the case is to make. Research shows that men are more likely than women to blame the victim of a rape for what happened, especially in cases where the man and woman know each other (Grubb and Harrower 2009). Deference to husbands and boyfriends—especially by male prosecutors, judges, and jurors—makes these cases hard to win. Marriage has posed the hardest problem for the law regarding rape (see Changing Law, "Marital Rape"). Before the 1970s, most cases of marital rape—a husband forcing sex on his wife—were not even covered by rape laws. Husbands were legally exempt, because it was assumed that by the very act of marriage, wives permanently consented to sex (Strebeigh 2009). In the decades that followed, most states changed their laws to permit the prosecution of husbands for raping their wives (Sitton 1993).

Marital Rape

In his book *The Subjection of Women* (1869), the British philosopher John Stuart Mill wrote that in one way at least, wives were worse off than slaves, since men could not (legally) rape their slaves. But for wives,

> however brutal a tyrant she may unfortunately be chained to—though she may know that he hates her, though it may be his daily pleasure to torture her, and though she may feel it impossible not to loathe him—he can claim from her and enforce the lowest degradation of a human being, that of being made the instrument of an animal function contrary to her inclinations.

In other words, wives were presumed to have consented to sex for their entire lives at the moment of their marriage. At the time of Mill's writing, wives in the United States were generally governed under the legal standard of *coverture*, in which they did not exist under the law separate from their husbands (see Chapter 2). With regard to sex, wives had no legal right to protection from rape by their husbands. That law came from England, where the seventeenth-century chief justice Matthew Hale wrote, "the husband cannot be guilty of a rape committed by himself upon his lawful wife, for by their mutual matrimonial consent and contract the wife hath given up herself in this kind unto her husband, which she cannot retract" (Martin, Taft, and Resick 2007:331).

That state of affairs persisted until the late 1970s, or even later in some places (Martin, Taft, and Resick 2007). (At that time, some lawyers used to joke, "If you can't rape your wife, who can you rape?"; Strebeigh 2009:329.) In North Carolina, for example, the law prohibiting rape included this caveat until 1993: "A person may not be prosecuted under this Article if the victim is the person's legal spouse at the time of the commission of the alleged rape or sexual offense unless the parties are living separate and apart." In 1993, that law was finally changed to this: "A person *may* be prosecuted under this Article *whether or not* the victim is the person's legal spouse at the time of the commission of the alleged rape or sexual offense."

Rape within marriage is illegal now, but convictions are still hard to come by. The concept of lifelong consent is a difficult one to shake. Often,

John Stuart Mill

lawyers or judges suspect that an accusing wife is making a false claim for personal gain, such as winning a child custody case (Lazar 2015).

In a creative study to investigate this issue, Mercedes Duran and colleagues (Duran, Moya, and Megias 2011) asked 75 Spanish college students to read the following story:

> Andres is married to Ana. They have been married for 15 years. A few days ago, Andres and Ana had an argument over some "minor problems." Andres seemed to have forgotten the incident but Ana was still angry at him and refused to have sex with her husband since the argument. After a week, things seemed to have improved between the couple, so Andres and Ana went out for dinner and both enjoyed the evening. When they came back home, Andres insisted again on having sex with his wife, but she said "no." He insisted once more.

Then the researchers asked: "If Andres forced his wife to have sex, to what extent would you consider it rape?" On a scale of 1 to 5, with 3 indicating neutrality and 5 indicating that students "strongly agreed" that they would consider it rape, the average score was 2.9 for men and 4.1 for women. That is, the average male student was neutral on whether the husband forcing his wife to have sex should be considered rape.

The researchers also compared the opinions of those students according to how strongly they held "benign" sexist views. Those are attitudes reflected by such sentiments as "In a disaster, women ought to be rescued before men" or "Women have a quality of purity few men possess." Students who held such views were less likely to consider Andres's actions to be rape; they took the traditional view that a wife's duties include complying with her husband's sexual desires, even against her will.

This research suggests that although it is a very old idea that rape within marriage is impossible, the notion persists in modern culture as well. It is part of a set of beliefs about marriage that may not seem overtly sexist yet preserve a traditional image of marriage as a male-dominated institution.

In addition to male biases in the courts, the place of the family in the legal system has been a further complication. Within families, the privacy from outside scrutiny and the intimacy of relationships between family members make both preventing and prosecuting sexual violence difficult. And as we will see shortly, the consequences of such violence—enhanced by the privacy and intimacy of family life—often are profound.

How Common Are Rape and Sexual Assault?

In 2010, the federal government conducted the National Intimate Partner and Sexual Violence Survey (NISVS), a large, confidential telephone survey, which

Figure 12.7 How common is rape, compared with other experiences?

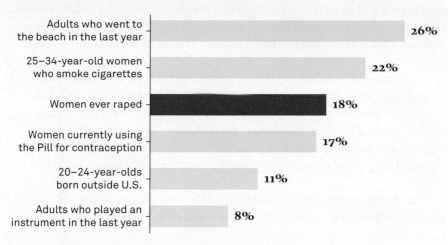

Adults who went to the beach in the last year — **26%**

25–34-year-old women who smoke cigarettes — **22%**

Women ever raped — **18%**

Women currently using the Pill for contraception — **17%**

20–24-year-olds born outside U.S. — **11%**

Adults who played an instrument in the last year — **8%**

SOURCE: Walters, Chen, Breiding (2013); Statistical Abstract of the United States.

now provides the best estimates we have of the prevalence of rape and sexual assault. The survey found that 18 percent of women and 1 percent of men in the United States have been raped at some time in their lives (Black et al. 2011). In college, the rates appear to be higher, with about one-fifth of female students experiencing an attempted or completed rape while they are in college (Anderson and Clement 2015).

Rape for men remains quite rare, and for them rape within families most likely occurs when they are children. For women, rape is much more common. To get a sense of how common it is, in Figure 12.7 I compare women's lifetime experience of rape (18 percent) with some other occurrences, ranging from relatively unusual events (playing an instrument, 8 percent) to more common events (going to the beach, 26 percent). The point is not to equate rape as an experience with these other characteristics or behaviors, but rather to put the frequency of rape in perspective with these more mundane statistics.

As further evidence of the normalcy of rape—"normal" in the sense that it commonly occurs within typical life experiences—we also need to consider the perpetrators of rape and their relationships to their victims. Based on women's reports in the National Intimate Partner and Sexual Violence Survey, we know that rape most often occurs within intimate relationships (including marriage) or within families (Figure 12.8). Although for many women rape by strangers is a source of fear and concern—and reasonably so—as a social problem it is much more prevalent in families and relationships than it is on the streets.

The main reason rape and sexual assault are more common on college campuses than in the general population is because of assaults by dates and acquaintances, especially in the context of fraternity and sorority parties where drugs and alcohol are heavily used, what Lisa Wade calls "party rape." Thus, this violence occurs within a peer group setting, where many young people are looking for sex, and some are developing relationships, which makes reporting the crimes

Figure 12.8 Women's relationship to the perpetrator in cases of rape

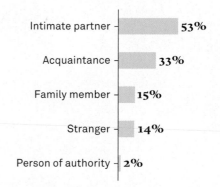

Intimate partner — **53%**

Acquaintance — **33%**

Family member — **15%**

Stranger — **14%**

Person of authority — **2%**

Percentages sum to more than 100 because some women reported more than one incident of rape. Acquaintances include first dates.

Note: Based on lifetime experience.

SOURCE: Walters, Chen, Breiding (2013).

socially difficult for women. Unless they qualify as the "perfect victim"—having acted, dressed, and resisted "right," and reported the crime immediately—women feel they will not be believed, and reporting the assault seems futile (Wade 2017). One woman told researchers that she woke up alone and naked after blacking out drunk at a fraternity party. She believed she had been raped, but didn't report it:

> I was scared and wanted to get the hell out of there. I didn't know who it was, so how am I supposed to go to the hospital and say someone might've raped me? It could have been any one of the hundred guys that lived in the house....I was also thinking like, you know, I just got to school, I don't want to start off on a bad note with anyone, and now it happened so long ago, it's just one of those things that I kind of have to live with. (Armstrong, Hamilton, and Sweeney 2006:491)

The prevalence of rape within intimate relationships and families is the reason this subject is so important for studies related to the family.

Violence in Lesbian and Gay Relationships

Most of the features of family violence discussed so far may apply to lesbian and gay couples as well. These include common risk factors for intimate partner violence, such as a history of family violence, and substance abuse (Badenes-Ribera et al. 2016). However, there are several unique aspects of same-sex relationships as well (Edwards, Sylasky, and Neal 2015).

Until the 1990s, when lesbian and gay relationships became more widely recognized, the problem of violence within these couples remained hidden. In fact, when Claire Renzetti wrote *Violent Betrayal* (1992), a book about partner abuse among lesbians, one of the problems she uncovered was that victims had a hard time convincing people that their partners were abusive.

The federal government has begun collecting data on violence that identify the sexual orientation of those involved (Walters, Chen, and Breiding 2013). This evidence shows that the lifetime occurrence of intimate partner violence is similar for homosexuals and heterosexuals—that is, lesbian and straight women are both more likely to experience violence than gay and straight men. However, lifetime occurrence is difficult to interpret, as about a third of lesbians who report having experienced intimate partner violence say that it was perpetrated by a male partner. The limited research on gay male couples shows similar rates of violence as are found among straight couples (Houston and McKirnan 2007). Unfortunately, despite advances in research, our detailed knowledge of same-sex intimate partner violence remains limited (Finneran and Stephenson 2013).

When it comes to preventing or punishing violence among same-sex couples, the situation is complicated by the ambiguous—even hostile—stance taken toward homosexuality in the laws of most states. Specific services for the victims of violence may not be available to those in same-sex relationships, and in some cases, legal protections were written into the law specifically *excluding* gays and lesbians (Pattavina et al. 2007). As a result, although the problems of violence in some ways are similar between straight and gay or lesbian couples, the experiences differ in important ways related to the marginal status of homosexuality, and the solutions are not readily applicable across groups.

Regardless of the causes, if the occurrence of family violence is different among different sectors of the population, so, too, are its consequences. Given the large proportion of people who have experienced family violence at some time in their lives, this is an important piece of the puzzle in understanding how people's backgrounds affect their future lives. But before turning to that issue, we need to understand that violence within families has declined dramatically in the last several decades.

Declining Violence

Since the 1990s, the United States—along with many other wealthy countries— has experienced steep declines in the level of criminal violence (Tonry 2014). Violence within families seems to have followed this trend as well. Although the reasons for this welcome change are not fully understood, it is so dramatic that it requires further examination.

The drop in violence appears in both official reports to police and confidential surveys (Truman and Morgan 2016). There was a rise in violence starting in the mid-1960s, which accelerated in the 1980s spurred in part by increases in concentrated poverty and the illegal drug trade in America's major cities. Since then, the decline has been most apparent in urban areas, but it has also occurred in small towns and rural areas (Schwartz and Gertseva 2010). Intimate partner violence, especially against women, fell sharply, dropping more than 50 percent in the 1990s and about another 20 percent since then—despite an increase during the economic recession of the late 2000s (see the Story Behind the Numbers). This trend occurred at all ages and among all racial-ethnic groups (Catalano 2012). For children the drop in family violence has been especially dramatic: Serious violence committed against them by intimate partners and family members dropped by about four-fifths since the early 1990s (see Figure 12.9).

Because so many crimes are not reported, it is possible that these numbers do not reflect such a big drop in actual violence. However, we can be confident that the trend is real for two reasons. First, the trend is apparent in both official crime reports and surveys. For example, since 1990, the rate of rape in the population dropped rapidly in both the National Crime Victimization Survey (about 70 percent) and official police reports (about 50 percent). And second, the decline is apparent in homicides, which are counted very accurately (Reckdenwald and Parker 2012). As Figure 12.10 shows, the homicide rate for both men and women

Figure 12.9 Violent victimization rates for children ages 12–17, by intimates or other relatives, 1993–2015

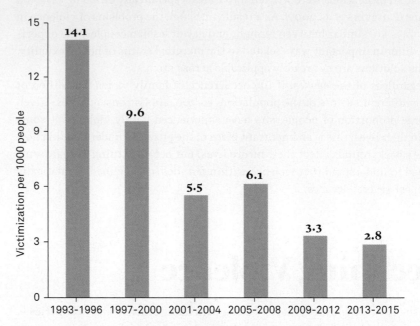

Children experience serious violence at the hands of their family members much less than they did two decades ago, which coincides with a general decline in violent crime.

SOURCE: Author analysis of National Crime Victimization Survey. Includes nonfatal violence only.

dropped, and it dropped both for homicides committed by family members and those not committed by family members. Children's homicide is an especially accurate indicator of family violence, because almost all young children are killed by family members (mostly their parents), friends, or acquaintances (such as mothers' boyfriends). From its peak in the mid-1990s, there was almost a 20 percent drop in the rate of homicide among children under age 5—and this trend, too, occurred for children in different racial-ethnic groups (Cooper and Smith 2011).

If we conclude that violence decreased throughout society, then we might not need a special explanation for what has happened within families. And explaining the broad decline in violence is beyond the scope of this book. However, there are some factors we should consider that may have contributed to the trend within families (Reckdenwald and Parker 2012):

- The increase in shelters and hotlines for abused women and children and in domestic violence legal services may have made it easier for women to gain protection or distance from their abusive partners (Dugan, Nagin, and Rosenfeld 2003).

- Women's increased economic independence and the greater acceptance of divorce—as well as recognition of the harm caused by family violence—have

Figure 12.10 **Homicide rates by relationship to perpetrator, 1994–2014**

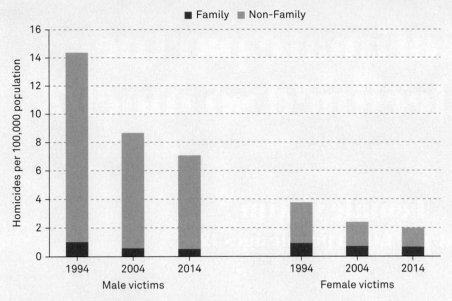

Note: Unknown perpetrators are counted as non-family members.

SOURCE: Federal Bureau of Investigation. Supplementary Homicide Reports and U.S. Census Bureau data.

made women more willing and able to leave abusive relationships, which could reduce the risk of violence.

- A decline in the number of married or cohabiting adults may have reduced violence simply by reducing the number of people exposed to potentially violent partners.

All of these may be factors in the decline of family violence, but we cannot say for certain which, if any, are most important. (We return to this issue in this chapter's Trend to Watch.)

Consequences of Family Violence

Despite declines in family violence, it remains distressingly pervasive, and its consequences remain serious, or even devastating, for too many people. The consequences of family violence stem from a unique constellation of factors. Such violence is usually intimate, often sexually so (as in the case of incest), and

Why has intimate partner violence declined so much?

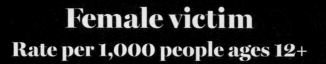

Female victim
Rate per 1,000 people ages 12+

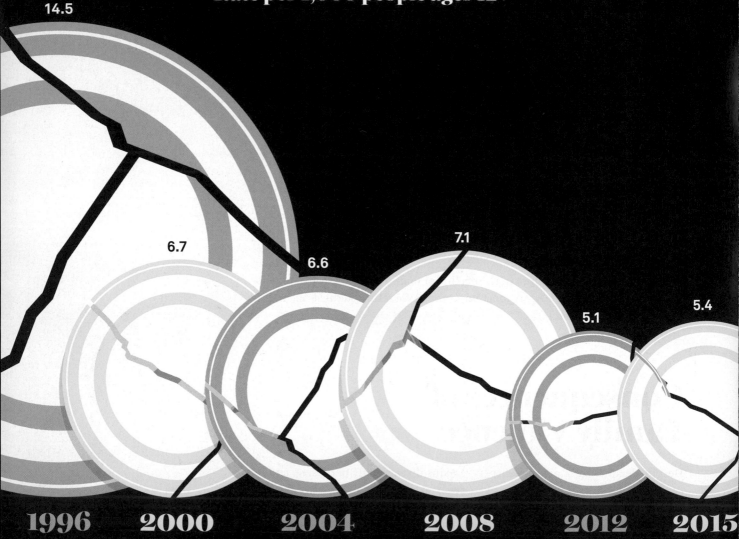

14.5

6.7

6.6

7.1

5.1

5.4

1996   2000   2004   2008   2012   2015

Along with a general decrease in violent crime in the U.S., intimate partner violence, especially against women, fell sharply starting in the 1990s. It dropped more than 50 percent in the 1990s and about another 25 percent since then—despite an increase during the recession of the late 2000s. Violence against male partners has fallen as well, although the levels were already much lower. These trends show that, as serious as this problem remains, we have been able to make progress. And that suggests we could do even better.

Source: National Crime Victimization Survey (U.S. Bureau of Justice Statistics 2017).

Male victim
Rate per 1,000 people ages 12+

http://wwnpag.es/sbtn12

Go to this link for an animation narrated by the author.

1.9

1.1

1.8

1.5

1.0

0.5

1996

2000

2004

2008

2012

2015

may be repeated over a long period of time. In addition, it is often experienced beginning in childhood, which causes a cascade of effects throughout the life course of its victims, starting with adolescent development. As a result, family violence leaves a trail of shame and stigma as well as physical hurt, and it has particularly painful effects on future intimate relationships (Nguyen, Karney, and Bradbury 2017).

The ripple effects of family violence spread not only across time but also through families. The long-term legacy of child abuse includes children who witness the abuse of others and who themselves experience trauma. One woman told an interviewer:

> "My sister and I slept in the same bedroom in bunk beds. I slept on the top bunk and my sister on the bottom. Every night for as long as I can remember, my father would come to my sister's bed and force her to have sex with him. I laid there and listened quietly" (Cherlin et al. 2004:776)

For children, the effects of abuse and neglect often are first seen in their behavior (Woodruff and Lee 2011). Both children who have been abused themselves and those who have lived with violence between other family members are at risk for behavior problems in adolescence (Peisch et al. 2016). As they age, the survivors of child abuse are more likely than other children to abuse alcohol or drugs, suffer from weight or sleep problems, and be depressed (Thomas and Hall 2008). In extreme cases, they may suffer from a form of anxiety known as posttraumatic stress disorder, which can cause flashbacks, memory problems, fear of common situations, and feelings of guilt for past events (Jordan, Campbell, and Follingstad 2010).

For adults who experience family violence—especially women who suffer violence at the hands of their partners or spouses—depression and anxiety are common outcomes (Trevillion et al. 2012). And the next generation is affected as well, as mothers who have experienced domestic violence have higher rates of postpartum depression—the specific form of depression that occurs in some mothers after they give birth (Kornfeld et al. 2012). In summary, although the specific experience of violence affects the kinds of outcome researchers find, it is clear that family violence, and especially sexual violence, contributes to painful mental health consequences (Wadsworth and Records 2013).

Future Intimate Relationships

We have seen that family violence causes harm to the mental well-being of its victims. We should understand, however, that people with mental health problems before they enter relationships also are more likely to end up in bad relationships. The result is a potentially endless cycle of violence and unhappiness.

In a detailed study of low-income women from three U.S. cities, Andrew Cherlin and his colleagues (2004) explored the long-term effects of physical and sexual abuse on subsequent marriage and cohabitation experiences. Prior research had shown that the survivors of abuse have higher rates of risky sexual behavior and have a harder time in relationships, partly because they have difficulty trusting people. But Cherlin and his colleagues tried to figure out how women's relationship histories unfolded as a result. Did they live in long-term stable relationships, remain single for many years, or go through a series of transitory relationships?

The experience of abuse clearly reduced the odds of establishing long-term, stable relationships. Women with a history of childhood abuse or sexual abuse most often had transitory relationship patterns. For example, those who were sexually abused in childhood were much more likely to cohabit with a man instead of marrying. Interestingly, those women who had been abused physically but not sexually often seemed to avoid relationships altogether. The study showed the complexity of trying to understand how personal history shapes family formation and development.

One contributing factor to the relationship problems of abuse victims is sexuality itself. The victims of sexual violence in particular may avoid sex and may have difficulty developing enjoyable sexual relationships for years after their own abuse occurs (Vaillancourt-Morel et al. 2016).

But there is good news amid the bad news or at least some positive trends working against the negative cycles described here. Women are no longer as trapped in abusive relationships as they once were (Cherlin et al. 2004). Not only is divorce more available legally than it was before the 1980s, but it has become more acceptable to end relationships when one's partner is abusive. At one time, women might have been expected to silence themselves for fear of embarrassing their families and children—and endure abuse without end. But the current cultural climate expects women to leave abusive men, for the sake of their children as well as themselves. So while the long-term increase in divorce and separation may seem like bad news for families, this is one way that those trends are positive.

Despite the negative outcomes described here, researchers also find that some people are wiser as a result of their abuse experiences and are appropriately cautious about their relationships. One Black woman with a history of abuse reported that she would never have ended up with her husband if she had suspected he would ever become abusive. Now she and her husband are both secure in their knowledge that violence is not an option for them:

> We never worried about violence, like hitting each other, because we weren't raised that way. We worked together and built up savings and then we got married. It's forever for us. Fighting and slapping each other around is not how we do business. No matter how hard it is, we just don't roll like that.

Stories like hers remind us that families are both sources of suffering and pain—as in her abusive childhood—and sources of strength and resilience. By relying on and trusting each other, she and her husband have been able to break the cycle of violence that might otherwise have continued through generations.

Feminist Perspectives

How can the problem of violence and abuse—including sexual violence—be so common, and so common within families, when the family is almost universally respected as a good thing in society? Can the deliberate infliction of pain and suffering be a systematic part of an institution almost everyone loves?

Notice that we have a capitalist economy that produces income and wealth for most people, even while some people are always poor and unemployed (Wright and Rogers 2011). And we have a democratic state that responds to popular interests through elections, even though powerful elites have much more influence than the common person (Domhoff 2009). In the same way, we have a family system that produces essential caring, love, and support for many people, even though it also produces bad outcomes for a substantial number of people. To understand this paradox, feminist explanations for family violence and abuse may be helpful.

The problem of family violence and abuse involves overlapping institutional arenas. In Chapter 11, we saw that work has shifted historically, with more now taking place in the arena of the market rather than the family. That movement created opportunities for individuals to make a different set of choices—for example, whether to work at home or for pay, and whether to care for children at home or place them in child care. In the case of family violence, the most important overlapping is between the family and the state. This is clearly seen in the problem of reporting violence to the police: Should one call the authorities or handle it within the family?

For students of society, this raises important questions. Does the state provide protections to women and children that help alleviate the problem of male domination within the family? On the other hand, does the state's intervention into the family arena—through policing, child welfare agencies, and schools—impose on families and weaken their role as core elements of the social order?

Male Domination

Feminists have long argued that the prevalence of male violence against women—especially rape and sexual assault—is the result of male domination more broadly (Anderson 1997). As explained in Chapter 1, feminists see male power within families as part of their overall domination of society. Because men have more power in the economy, the political system, and the family, they are able to commit violence against women to achieve their ends. In fact, violence against women is one of the most important ways men maintain their greater power, according to this view.

The feminist perspective on family violence has been controversial, partly because some research shows that many women also use violence against their intimate partners and children. However, the violence that men use is much more likely to cause serious injury or death and is more often part of a pattern of control within the family or relationship. For example, men are more likely to use violence when their partners are economically dependent on them and feel unable to leave the relationship (Anderson 2010).

Sociologist Carrie Yodanis (2004:656) summarized the feminist theory like this: "The more unequal women are compared to men in a society, the more likely men are to be violent toward women." To demonstrate this pattern, she compared data from 27 countries and found that there is more sexual violence against women in countries where men have greater advantages in occupations and education.

Systematic Abuse A crucial aspect of the feminist perspective on sexual violence is its systematic approach. Although not all men commit rape and not all women are its victims, the experience is common enough, feminists argue, that it constitutes a structural part of male domination (MacKinnon 1991). Beyond fear of not being believed, many women are afraid that if people find out they have been raped, they will be disrespected as "damaged goods." This concern is not unfounded, as many people still believe that women who have been raped are themselves at fault (Suarez and Gadalla 2010). This might help explain why 35 years elapsed between the first time Bill Cosby allegedly drugged and then sexually assaulted a woman and the first time someone reported it to the police, in 2000—and it would take another 15 years for the story to become a major scandal (Wade 2017).

But attitudes have changed. In 1988, the feminist magazine *Ms.* published a report on the widespread experience of date and acquaintance rape (Warshaw and Koss 1994). The report drew on surveys from the 1980s, which showed that 17 percent of female college students reported experiencing a rape or attempted rape in the previous year. In 84 percent of the cases, the woman knew her attacker, and in a little more than half of the cases, the victim was on a date with the man. Despite disagreements over details in the research methods, a consensus emerged that rape was largely underreported.

The feminist message, which has since become much more widely accepted, is that rape is not principally a problem of strangers attacking women in isolation, but rather a much more common feature of relationships between men and women—including within families and romantic relationships—in which men often act with threats or mild violence rather than extreme violence and women often do not report being raped because they think it was their fault or that no one will believe them. Feminists' efforts to raise awareness about the potential for systematic violence in relationships have led to improved data collection and a more robust legal response to the problem of rape and sexual assault, especially concerning date rape and marital rape (Rozee and Koss 2001).

Religious Authority To consider how male domination contributes to sexual abuse, we might consider the sexual abuse scandal in the Catholic Church—dramatized to chilling effect in the 2015 movie *Spotlight*, which told the story of the *Boston Globe* reporters who exposed the scandal. Over a five-decade period, thousands of Catholic priests in the United States—and even more worldwide—sexually abused children. Three-quarters of the victims were ages 11 to 17, and about 80 percent were boys (John Jay College of Criminal Justice 2004). The

The sexual abuse scandal in the Catholic Church revealed that individual priests committed crimes against boys and young men, while the institution covered up the crimes to protect its own interests.

Church is probably the world's largest institution that is formally ruled by men: From the Pope down to local bishops and priests, the rules of the institution dictate that authority is held by men (Shupe 2007).

Although the great majority of priests did not sexually abuse children, local bishops routinely covered up complaints of abuse; they quietly retired priests or transferred them to different regions where the local parishioners didn't know their history. Because this implicated the Church hierarchy, the institution has paid billions of dollars for treatment, compensation, and settlements to victims worldwide (White and Terry 2008).

The abuse of children often occurred in situations where the Church had assumed some caring responsibility for them, most often at the priest's home or when traveling on Church events or at homes for troubled boys (for example, Carroll 2002). In many cases, parents had been happy that their children received special attention from the priests. One mother said that she appreciated the priest taking the children on outings to help keep them "in line." Her son, years later, recalled why he felt powerless to resist the sexual abuse: "You cannot leave it to a young boy to object to sexual advances," he wrote. "The desire to please family and authority figures, in addition to a strong sense of fear, makes this impossible. That is what happened to me" (Levitz 2002).

In another case, Morning Star Ranch, a home for boys founded by the Catholic Diocese of Spokane, Washington, cared for more than 1,000 boys over several decades. The priest who directed it beat boys violently to discipline them, and another priest was accused of raping them. Here, too, the Church was responsible for caring for the boys, who had records of misbehavior (Shors 2009).

Although there have been many cases of sexual abuse in male-dominated institutions, I focus on the Catholic Church scandal because it illustrates several important points:

- It shows the institutional nature of sexual violence. For decades, Catholic authorities were aware of the problem. But rather than involve state legal authorities, they usually transferred priests away from their victims, arranged for their psychiatric care, or silenced the victims.

- The scandal illuminates the difficulty of identifying who is responsible for the care of children. Children with weak family supports, or no families at all, were especially vulnerable. In most cases, parents willingly turned their children over to the care of the Church, but in other cases the government paid the Church for their care. As is the case with parents or teachers, when people have authority over those weaker than them, there is a risk that they will abuse that power.

The U.S. military is another male-dominated institution plagued by sexual abuse. Military leaders admit there is an ongoing problem but have resisted legislators' attempts to reform the institution.

- Finally, it demonstrates other key elements necessary for understanding the effects of sexual abuse: the long-term consequences for the health and happiness of the victims, the shame and stigma felt by those reporting their own suffering, and the difficulty getting through the veils of privacy surrounding sexuality and the family to hold the right people accountable.

Another male-dominated institution in which sexual abuse has attracted considerable attention is the U.S. military. Women in the military—under the command of men, greatly outnumbered by men among the ranks, and isolated from civilian authorities—experience high rates of sexual harassment and assault (Barth et al. 2016). In recent years, top military leaders have taken steps intended to curb sexual assault and harassment within the military (Stander and Thomsen 2016). Advocates have also urged the Veterans Health Administration to improve treatment and intervention programs for veterans who have experienced intimate partner violence (Gerber et al. 2014).

Intersectionality

Feminists have helped reshape the national dialogue about family violence and sexual assault. But the experiences of violence and abuse, which clearly are related to gender inequality, also are complicated by their intersection with issues of race and social class (Crenshaw 1991). For example, I said earlier that the higher rates of intimate partner violence experienced by Black women are partly attributable to their relatively high rates of poverty, concentration in resource-poor neighborhoods, and other factors. That is important to stress, because it helps refute the assumption that African American men are inherently more prone to committing acts of violence. However, although the causes of this pattern are complex, the fact remains that Black women are more likely to experience intimate partner violence as well as sexual assault. Such complexities are the subject of "intersectionality" studies, the attempt to untangle overlapping problems of inequality (McGuffey 2013).

Black women specifically are more likely to experience violence, but they also are less able on average to protect themselves with the resources available to other women. In particular, domestic violence relief and prevention agencies are more readily available in wealthier communities, and Black women often have reason to distrust the police or other authorities in their communities (Kingsnorth and MacIntosh 2004). As a result of such distrust, perhaps, some minority women employ different strategies to respond to abuse, including fighting back physically (Potter 2008).

Black women also face the dilemma that even when they need protection by the police, they might not want to contribute to the problem of incarceration that affects so many men in their communities (Wakefield and Wildeman 2013). Losing a spouse or partner to prison also represents the loss of a potentially vital source of economic support for them and their children (Richie 2012). (We saw in Chapter 3 that mass incarceration has contributed to a marriage squeeze for Black women.) Among Latinas as well, a minority of women may not want to go to the authorities when they experience intimate partner violence because they fear provoking immigration authorities to investigate them or their families (Gonzalez-Guarda et al. 2013).

These issues serve as an important reminder that a problem as widespread and complicated as family violence and abuse cannot have simple solutions. To help people in diverse social situations requires diverse forms of intervention or assistance. We turn next to some strategies for intervention and prevention of violence and abuse.

Interventions

Partly in response to feminist political pressure through the legal system, local and state governments have tried a variety of criminal justice approaches to the problem of domestic violence, especially targeting intimate partner violence (Koss 2000). Although, as noted, the level of family violence has declined in the last several decades, we cannot say that progress is the result of any one of these efforts. But we can learn a lot from careful studies of what has been tried. Here are some of the more popular programs and policies from recent years:

- *Civil protection orders.* After a spouse or partner has experienced physical abuse, she or he may be able to obtain a protection order from a judge (Jordan et al. 2010). These either threaten the abuser with harsher punishment if he or she commits violence again or in some cases order the abuser not to have any contact with the victim. Research shows that these measures may be effective in preventing future attacks, but only when they are adequately enforced and provide thorough protection (Klein 2009).

- *Mandatory arrest or pro-arrest rules.* Police often leave the scene of domestic violence without making an arrest, because one or both spouses tell the police that the incident is over or asks them not to get involved. To separate couples and increase the chance that police can convince the victim to press charges, some communities have instituted mandatory arrest policies, requiring (or strongly encouraging) police to make an arrest and separate a couple experiencing violence. Unfortunately, policies to promote or require arrests on the scene have not proven effective at reducing intimate partner violence (Xie, Lauritsen, and Heimer 2012). It's possible that rules requiring an arrest actually deter victims from calling the police if they don't want the family broken up or they fear retribution (Broidy, Albright, and Denman 2016).

- *Court-ordered treatment.* Many courts have required domestic violence perpetrators to undergo psychological counseling or other treatment as part of their punishment. These programs have a low success rate—and sometimes lead to greater violence—either because they are of low quality or because the offenders are so resentful of being required to participate (Klein 2009).

- *Domestic violence courts.* Some feminists are committed to the idea of reforming the legal system to prevent domestic violence. One way they have been able to work with the justice system has been on specialized "domestic violence courts." Such courts employ specially trained staff, including judges and advocates for victims, and take a problem-solving approach rather than a strictly punitive one (Cissner, Labriola, and Rempel 2015).

- *Services for domestic violence victims.* As I mentioned earlier, the feminist movement has created a variety of services to help women deal with or prevent family violence. These include hotlines for people in danger, shelters for people who need to leave their homes, and legal counseling for people who need help navigating the justice system (Dugan, Nagin, and Rosenfeld 2003). In addition to preventing family violence or punishing the perpetrators, there are many approaches to assisting or treating those who are affected, including individual psychological counseling and treatment and community-based services (Jordan, Campbell, and Follingstad 2010).

Responsibility Frames

When it comes to the people we know and love—or ourselves—it's sometimes easy to give advice: Eat right, exercise, avoid dangerous situations, study hard, treat others with respect. We all have to do our best to take care of ourselves.

But when it comes to analyzing society, we can't simply apply the same logic to responsibility. When something bad happens, we might be able to identify an individual who is to blame. But when bad things happen systematically—when they are part of the "normal" workings of society—then we need to think about responsibility systematically as well. We can think of these as two different frames—ways to draw the border around an issue that defines how we think about it: a *personal responsibility* frame and a *social responsibility* frame.

The scenarios presented here are composites from the research that I read in preparing this chapter. For each one, try to construct personal versus social responsibility frames. Working individually or in groups, in writing or in class discussion, use the following guidelines:

1. *List* both individual and social causes of the problem that occurs. There can be multiple causes—it's okay to speculate.

2. *Suggest* alternative approaches or solutions implied by each frame. You might think of these as advice you would give to your friend *personally* versus a policy you want the government (or some other larger actor) to adopt *socially*.

3. *Discuss* the two frames: What are the advantages or disadvantages of adopting either frame to address the problem? Are they mutually exclusive?

Scenarios

Child neglect. A young boy has an inadequate diet and doesn't sleep enough. As a result, he has a low energy level, has trouble paying attention in school, and sometimes doesn't attend. Since he mostly sits quietly at school, the teacher in his crowded classroom usually ignores him, and he falls further and further behind. When no parent shows up for a parent-teacher conference, a counselor contacts his family and discovers that his mother works several jobs at irregular hours with long commutes. They live in a neighborhood considered dangerous, and the boy isn't allowed outside unsupervised. He is mostly cared for by his older sister, but she often leaves him home alone or ignores him while she hangs out with her friends.

Child abuse. A single mother with two preteen sons lives in a small town with no other family around and struggles to raise her boys on her own. In the summer, she hears about a free program for "at-risk" boys, run by a local church, which promises to provide them with activities ranging from outdoor games to light volunteer work like brush clearing. Over the course of the summer, she sees her older son become withdrawn and start to look for ways to avoid the day program. Eventually, he tells her he has been sexually abused by the director of the program.

Incapacitation rape. A first-year female college student goes with some of her new friends to a fraternity party. The fraternity was suspended by the university a few years ago, and they hold their parties in a private house off-campus. At the party, she has a good time, but she drinks too much. Her friends are staying and she doesn't have a ride home. Eventually, she passes out. She wakes up naked and alone in an upstairs bedroom, knowing she has been raped, but doesn't remember what happened.

One important lesson learned is that a variety of services may be necessary at once. For example, we may need legal advice and protection, counseling, and social support all at the same time. Consider the story of one immigrant woman interviewed about her long experience emerging from a violent marriage (Ting and Panchanadeswaran 2009:831):

> I left three times. Each time I file papers for protection, then I come back because he promises to change. I did not have anyone to tell me men like him don't change; I didn't know about this "cycle of abuse," this honeymoon period. Each time it would be better for a while, then start again. Now I know, I have people, my counselor, my women's group, I can call when I need to talk. It is hard in the beginning, but I have some new friends. They all believe me, that I do the right thing.

In this case, the woman benefited from legal protection, education, counseling, a support group, and a group of supportive friends aware of her predicament—without any one of which, she suggests, she might not have escaped her abusive situation.

Despite the decline in violence, and even though the justice system (along with other institutions, such as the Catholic Church and the U.S. military) has increased its attention to the problems of family violence and abuse, these problems remain widespread. That reality highlights the distinct social location of the family in relation to the institutions of the state and the market. Although social life across these arenas is interrelated, the doors of the family home at times remain closed to the outside social world. That seems wonderful when families are happy, protective, supportive, and loving. But when they are locations of violence and abuse—when the power wielded within the family arena is used to oppress its members, usually women and children—then the separateness of family life can become a prison for its victims.

We conclude in the next chapter with a projection of family trends into the future. In that future, both sides of family life—its supporting and loving side and its oppressive or exploitative side—will figure importantly.

Trend to Watch: A Less Violent Future?

Are we headed toward a less violent future? And if we are, how will this change family life in our society? Earlier I described the decline in violence after the 1980s. However, if you look at the trends over a much longer period, it's clear that the United States has become a much less violent place over the last few centuries (Fischer 2010). In that light, the improvement over the last quarter century is part of a much longer trend.

Despite the horrific wars and genocides of the last century, there is good evidence that modernity has been a period of reduced interpersonal violence. This overall pattern has been the subject of a long history of social science research, including Philippe Ariès (1962), who proposed that modernity introduced the concept of childhood as a life stage, along with the imperative to protect and nurture children in safety. Ariès followed the German sociologist Norbert Elias (1939), who argued that modern society steered people to restrain their impulses—especially the violent impulse as a way of resolving conflicts—and instead to rely on the governments and economic institutions to manage more and more of social life. Finally, the psychologist Steven Pinker (2011) has proposed that the post-Enlightenment embrace of reason has led to a greater tendency to study and understand the experience of people different from ourselves, resulting in greater empathy and less violence.

A continued reduction in violence generally—and within families and intimate relationships—would obviously be good news. And there is some reason to believe it could become a virtuous cycle, reinforcing itself over time. For example, according to the National Crime Victimization Survey, the proportion of U.S. children living in a household in which anybody experienced a violent attack dropped from more than 12 percent in the early 1990s to less than 4 percent by 2010, signifying a decline in violence as a presence in children's lives (Walters, Chen, and Breiding 2013). Because experiencing violence as a child is a clear risk factor for committing violence as an adult, maybe this trend will lead to less violence in the next generation (Eriksson and Mazerolle 2015). If that is the case, it might also contribute to a reduction in divorce. And it might help motivate people to press for institutional change, such as that occurring within the Catholic Church after its widespread child abuse was exposed.

Questions for Review

1. How do sociologists and government groups attempt to collect more accurate statistics about abuse, neglect, and rape?

2. Why might someone be reluctant to report abuse, neglect, or rape to the authorities?

3. Why is neglect more difficult to identify than abuse?

4. What are some reasons why the United States has not ratified the Convention on the Rights of the Child?

5. Which children are more likely to experience child abuse?

6. After reading the story of Andres and Ana (see Changing Law, "Marital Rape"), what number would you assign on the scale of 1 to 5?

7. Explain the evolution of marital rape laws.

8. Why are people more inclined to believe that rape has occurred when it involves a stranger, even though more rapes are committed by acquaintances/partners?

9. What are some factors that have contributed to the decline in violence within families?

13 The Future of the Family

With all of the changes that have occurred in modern families, it is perhaps not surprising that some people have jumped to the conclusion that the family as an institution is doomed. A report commissioned by several conservative foundations expressed this apocalyptic perspective (Longman et al. 2011):

> A turning point has occurred in the life of the human race. The sustainability of humankind's oldest institution, the family...is now an open question. On current trends, we face a world of rapidly aging and declining populations, of few children—many of them without the benefit of siblings and a stable, two-parent home—of lonely seniors living on meager public support, of cultural and economic stagnation.

Of course, the social changes described in this book present daunting challenges for the future of family life. Not only has inequality between rich and poor widened, but with the decline in the number of children born after the baby boom, it will be a struggle for the next generation of workers to support their elders in retirement.

However, we also have seen unprecedented opportunities flowing from the expansion of equal rights and the growing acceptability of diverse ways of arranging our family lives and interacting within them. Interracial marriage has grown more acceptable and more common, gay and lesbian rights have advanced (although unevenly), and gender inequality within families and in the wider world has decreased.

In this chapter, we will discuss the changes in family life with regard to diversity, inequality, and social change more broadly. Without being able to predict the future, we may nevertheless imagine where the family is headed as a result of changes already underway. I will then conclude the chapter by offering some responses to these changes.

Some people interpret lower birth and marriage rates as a sign that the family as an institution is on the brink of collapse. One response among Evangelical Christians like the Jeub family has been to have as many children as God allows. They have 16 children.

Diversity

Most discussions of diversity in the United States concentrate on the issue of race/ethnicity (Lee and Bean 2010). However, diversity has increased in many other areas of family life in the United States. We have seen evidence of this throughout the book, but here I will present some summary descriptions to put the trends in perspective. First, however, I will discuss how diversity can be defined and measured.

Diversity in the simplest terms means difference or variance—the presence of different things or qualities of things. But in sociology, we think of differences among people, so I will use the following definition: **Social diversity** is the condition of difference in experiences or characteristics of people in a population. At the extremes, we can think of circumstances with no diversity (in which everyone is the same in some way) or complete diversity (in which everyone is different).

In Pakistan, for example, 94 percent of people in a recent large survey said that their religious identity was Sunni Muslim. That is, Pakistan has little religious diversity. In contrast, one of the most religiously diverse societies is New Zealand, where the survey recorded 19 different religious denominations, only three of which claimed more than 12 percent of the population each: Anglican, Presbyterian, and Roman Catholic (World Values Survey 2015).

We can describe social diversity with a single number, called a *diversity index*. It tells us the probability that if we select two people at random, we will find individuals who differ according to the characteristic we are interested in (Haughton and Mukerjee 1995). In Pakistan, your chance of picking two people with different religions is only 12 percent, but in New Zealand, it's more than 80 percent. The level of diversity is something that affects people in their daily lives and interactions whether they recognize it or not. The next time you walk down the street, look around your classroom, or attend a weekend party, ask yourself if you see people who are alike or different from each other (and from you).

Social diversity depends on the number of categories we use to describe people. For example, if the Anglicans, Presbyterians, and Catholics in New Zealand all thought of themselves merely as "Christians," that society would suddenly be much less religiously diverse. In some cases, breaking ourselves into more categories is divisive and leads to conflict between people in different categories—for example, ethnicity, religion, or political affiliation (Cannadine 2013). At other times, however, recognizing differences—and labeling them—is liberating because it allows people to express their identities more honestly. Clearly, the construction of social categories—including race/ethnicity, religion, and family experience—is an important process in society. And it has important implications for the future of families.

social diversity

The condition of difference in experiences or characteristics of people in a population.

Race and Ethnicity

As we saw in Chapter 3, immigration to the United States has led to the growth of the Latino and Asian populations in particular. This is partly because most immigrants come from Latin America and Asia and partly because those immigrants and their children have higher rates of marriage and childbearing and thus spur growth within those groups (Lichter et al. 2012). These developments are especially important to the study of families, because we see different family dynamics and childbearing patterns within and across racial-ethnic groups.

There are several reasons that immigrants have higher rates of fertility. First, most people who migrate from one country to another are relatively young, healthy, and ambitious. Although many people migrate for work or to increase their income, their plans also often include having children. Second, many of the countries of origin for today's immigrants are places where birth rates are higher than they are in the United States. That means that many migrants were raised in a culture that encourages having more children than is the average in the United States.

However, how many children immigrants have depends on such factors as their level of integration into the mainstream culture and the economic and health conditions they experience in the United States. For example, one Mexican immigrant woman told an interviewer that her family's economic situation might alter their expectations about children: "We wanted to have three in the beginning and we still have the idea of three kids. But, if we see that there are a lot of expenses, and if our finances don't allow more children, then just two" (Wilson and McQuiston 2006:314).

When this woman was a child in Mexico, it was expected that healthy couples would have four or more children. But immigrants from Mexico face pressures that lead many people to trim their expectations. Another woman in the same study had four daughters. She and her husband really wanted a son, but they were reluctant to try again:

> It wasn't clear at first how many we were going to have. . . . After the first child it was all happiness, everything was so easy. But now that they are growing, they need more, and we are starting to see that it is not so easy to raise a family . . . to really provide what they need, it's not easy. (Wilson and McQuiston 2006:314)

If immigrants, and maybe even their children, continue to have more children than the average in the United States, then the ethnic groups to which they belong will grow relative to the general population. However, if they adopt the lower fertility rates that prevail here, then we would not expect as much change in their populations. And of course, the frequency of intermarriage between groups will have an impact on this as well: A quarter of Latinos who got married in 2015 married someone who did not identify as Latino (see Figure 8.6).

The future of American racial and ethnic diversity partly depends on the politics and policies of the government with regard to immigration, partly on the economic and social conditions that encourage or discourage immigration, and partly on the nature of social life and family life for the immigrants themselves and their children (Rodríguez-García et al. 2015). Clearly, predicting the future in this area is not going to be easy. However, we may be sure that the issue will remain an important one for years to come.

Religion

Religious identity is important for families because so many of the traditions and practices associated with religion affect how people behave and interact within families. This is apparent at every stage of family life. Consider a few examples:

- *At birth.* Traditional Jewish practice requires circumcision—removing the foreskin of the male child's penis in the first few days of life. Although as a surgical procedure this is very common among both Jews and others, the orthodox Jewish tradition makes it a family affair (Silverman 2006). Family members attend the event, with the baby being passed from one person to another before the procedure, during which he is held down by male relatives or family honorees. Other religions have their own birth-related customs, such as baptism in some branches of Christianity.

- *At marriage.* From the choice of a spouse to the wedding ceremony itself, marriage as a transition into a new, adult stage of the life course often is an opportunity for people to reassert their family's religious heritage (Bengston 2017).

A mohel prepares to circumcise a baby boy at an Orthodox Jewish synagogue with many family members and friends in attendance.

- *As parents.* From corporal punishment of children, which is often practiced by American conservative Christians (Hoffmann, Ellison, and Bartkowski 2017), to simply modeling good behavior for their children, parents often base their parenting practices on religious teachings and traditions.

- *End of life.* Religious ritual is perhaps no more visible than at funerals, when grieving relatives turn to religious authority to facilitate their grief and attend to the practicalities of interment and burial. Perhaps in anticipation of an afterlife, many people place high significance on the religious aspects of a funeral. When her Catholic parents found out that actor Julia Sweeney was an atheist, she remembered in her monologue *Letting Go of God,* "My dad said, 'I don't even think you should come to my funeral.' After I hung up I thought, Just try and stop me!" (She did attend her father's funeral.)

The United States has become more religiously diverse in the past several decades (Merino 2010). In 1972, the General Social Survey found that 90 percent of Americans identified as either Protestant or Catholic. By 2016, those two dominant groups had shrunk to 71 percent, and a number of smaller groups had proliferated—mostly Muslims, Hindus, and Buddhists—as a result of immigration from countries where those religions are popular. However, there has also been a large increase in people identifying as having no religion (Pew Research Center 2015e). And more people now proclaim an unaffiliated "Christian" identity. These trends partly reflect the decline in the power of religious authorities, as more people make religious institutions less central in their lives or choose not to participate altogether. (The increase in religious diversity, using a reduced number of categories because of data limitations, is shown in the Story Behind the Numbers.)

Family Paths and Types

In addition to racial/ethnic and religious diversity, we have also seen in the previous chapters an increasing diversity in the structure of American families and in the pathways to family formation and family outcomes (Smock and Greenland 2010). To illustrate this pattern, let us compare 1960 with 2010, two moments half a century apart. The end of the 1950s was the peak of American family conformity. In that decade more than any other, great majorities of Americans married early, lived in isolated nuclear families, and had high numbers of children by historical standards. Since then, family life has become more diverse.

If you knocked on a door at random in 1960, you would most likely have encountered a (heterosexually) married couple living with no one else other than their children. That arrangement was behind two-thirds of all household doors in 1960. But by 2015, that number had dropped below 45 percent. Married couples

Increased diversity in American family life

http://wwnpag.es/sbtn13

Go to this link for an animation narrated by the author.

Using a diversity index, we can calculate the probability that, if we select two people at random, we will find individuals who differ according to the characteristic we are interested in. If the score is 0, everyone is the same, if the score is 1 everyone is unique. In household types; there was a decline in married-couple households, and a growth of different kinds of living arrangements—the diversity index increased from .51 to .71. Age at marriage, racial ethnicity, and religious preference have also become more diverse in the last half century. Increasing diversity means more people in the population differ according to family structure, marital status, race/ethnicity, or religion. That's the new, modern world of the family.

Sources: Author's calculations from U.S. Census Bureau data provided by IPUMS (Ruggles et al. 2017), the General Social Survey (Smith et al. 2016), and National Center for Health Statistics (1964).

Household types

- Married couples
- Extended households
- Individual
- Single parent
- Non-family group

Racial-ethnic identity

- White
- Latino
- Black
- Asian/Pacific Islander
- Other
- American Indian

Age at first marriage, men only

- 15–19
- 20–24
- 25–29
- 30–34
- 35–39
- 40–49
- 50+

Religious preference

- Protestant
- Catholic
- Jewish
- None
- Other

1960
Diversity score: .52

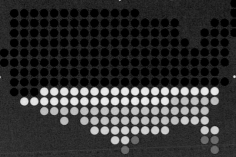

2015
Diversity score: .70

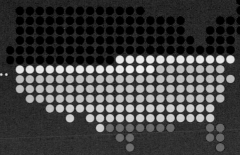

1970
Diversity score: .29

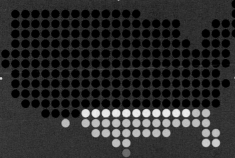

2015
Diversity score: .57

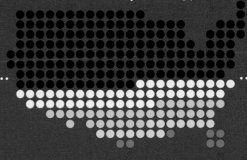

1960
Diversity score: .67

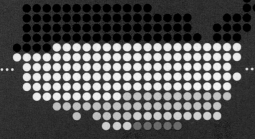

2015
Diversity score: .79

1972
Diversity score: .53

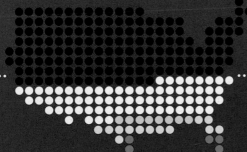

2016
Diversity score: .67

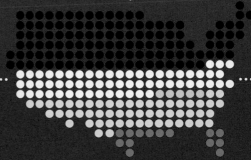

are still common, but now they represent less than half the total number of families. Extended households, single-parent families, individuals living alone, and groups of unrelated individuals have all become more common arrangements, together now making up more than half of all households.

In Chapter 2, we saw that the average age at which Americans first marry has risen from the early 20s to the late 20s in the last half-century. However, the change in marriage age is not just an increase in the average but also an increase in the *range* of ages at which people marry. Consider the Story Behind the Numbers, which shows that in the 1960s, more than half of people who married for the first time did so in the narrow range of ages 20 to 24. In contrast, among people who married for the first time in 2015, less than one-third married in the most popular age range (now 25 to 29), with the rest spread across the age spectrum from 20 to 50 or older. In 1960, if you heard of someone getting married, it was a pretty safe bet he or she was under age 30—a 90 percent chance, actually. Today, guessing the age of a person getting married for the first time is much more difficult.

Age at marriage is just one important source of diversity in family paths. Single people, divorced people, unmarried parents, and same-sex—to name some of the most prominent examples—all represent different kinds of diversity as well. Even when their numbers are small, as in the case of people who are transgender, their visibility in the media and popular conversation can amplify the diversity that they help create, and increase our perception that families today are growing ever more varied and complicated.

The concept of diversity relates to the level of difference in society according to the categories we use. But it does not necessarily reflect the level of inequality. Social differences often are not between equals but rather between groups with unequal amounts of important resources. We can think of rich, middle class, and poor, for example, as three different groups, but if we don't recognize that there is a hierarchy between them, we won't be able to understand the real dynamics of society. And that makes it more difficult to respond to the challenges that rising inequality brings.

Inequality

The rise of economic inequality in the United States—and many other countries around the world—in the last half-century is one of the most important social developments we face (Stiglitz 2013). As we saw in Chapter 4, this has resulted in a bigger income gap between richer and poorer families. This means that the poor suffer more hardships, but people in the middle class also experience more insecurity, or "fear of falling" (Ehrenreich 1989)—because their risk of falling has increased.

In this concluding chapter, I will expand on the discussion of inequality to describe four types of inequality that challenge people and their families. These four inequalities will play a key role in defining the future of the family.

Between Families

The increase in inequality in the United States has not affected all families equally. One major divide has opened up along educational lines. Compared with people who haven't completed college, college graduates are more likely to get married, marry each other, and stay married—and the wives in these families are more likely to be employed than they were in the past (McLanahan and Jacobsen 2015). On the other hand, those with less education are increasingly less likely to get married. What this means for inequality is crucial: More families with two high earners, on the one hand, and more families with one low earner on the other.

This pattern is illustrated in Figure 13.1, which shows the rising fortunes of married-couple families compared with single-parent families. Since the 1970s, the median income for single-mother and single-father families, adjusted for inflation, has been relatively flat. However, the income of married-couple families has increased from around $63,000 per year to more than $94,000 per year. As a result, we see that married-couple families had a median income about $41,000 higher than that of single-mother families in 1975, and that gap is now about $64,000. Further, people with less education have more children, on average, than those with more education (see Chapter 9). As a result, high-income couples

Figure 13.1 **Median family income in families with children, by family type, 1974–2016**

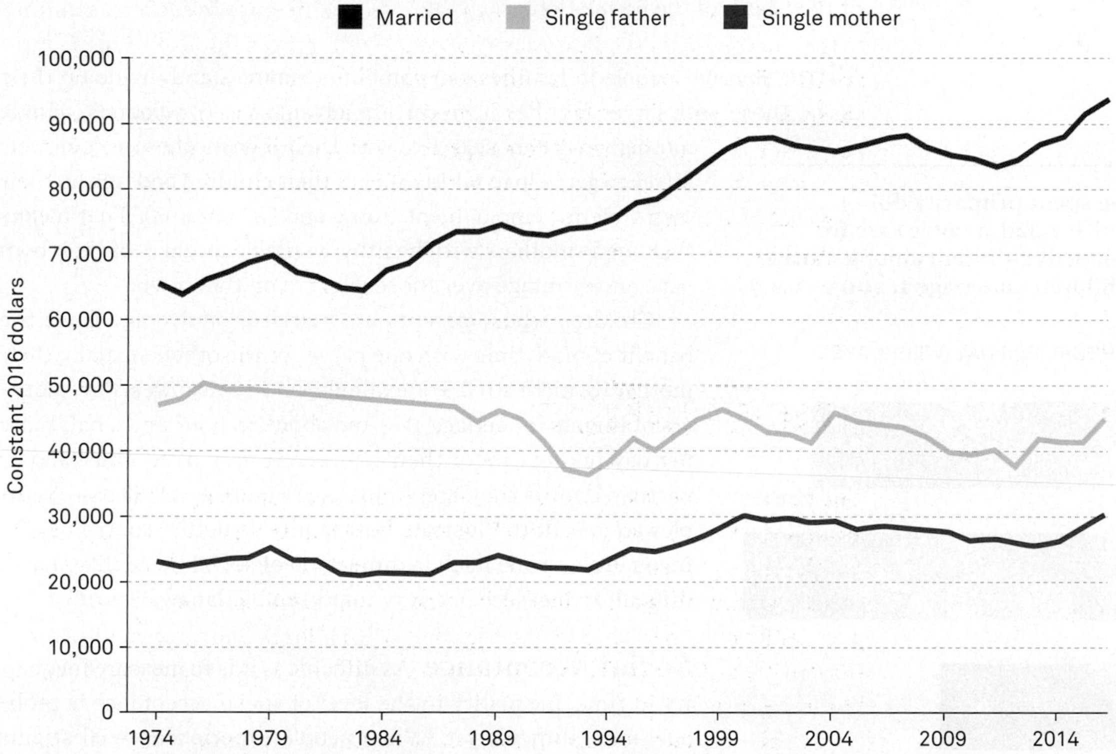

Note: Incomes adjusted for inflation to 2016 dollars.
Source: U.S. Census Bureau historical income tables.

have more money to invest in a smaller number of children, while low-income families are falling further behind in caring for and educating their children (Duncan and Murnane 2011).

Income may be the simplest indicator of inequality to measure and describe. But there are other assets and advantages that set people in some family structures above others.

Health Because people's well-being is wrapped up in their social situation—who cares for them, who they care for, and the web of their intimate interactions—it is not surprising that their health is associated with the kind of family they live in. The clearest example of this is the large body of research showing that married people are healthier than those who are not married (Zheng and Thomas 2013). That also means that children whose parents are married gain the benefits of having parents who are healthier (Bianchi et al. 2004).

There are three reasons for the health advantage of married people. The first is simply that healthier people are more likely to get married in the first place (Kane 2016). The second is that marriage leads people to alter their behavior in ways that make them healthier—for example, reducing their alcohol use (Staff et al. 2014). Finally, married people also take care of each other in many ways, big and small, from encouraging healthy behavior to caring for each other in the face of serious illness. Sadly, people with health problems—and people whose children have health problems—are also more likely to get divorced (Cohen and Petrescu-Prahova 2006). Clearly, society cannot count on marriage to take care of the health of the population.

Time Because people in families can combine resources and divide up their tasks, those with larger families have certain advantages. For example, single mothers may choose to live with their own mothers or other relatives to get help in taking care of their children and free up their own time for employment (Kang and Cohen 2015). That means that single mothers with healthy, available mothers of their own have an advantage over those who are on their own.

Children whose parents are married, on average, have the benefit of more time with one parent or the other—usually their mother (Bianchi 2011). For example, on a typical weekday, mothers of infants (under age 1) spend about an hour and a half more per day taking care of their children if they have a husband or partner than if they are single (see Figure 13.2). These examples are meant to illustrate how family structure contributes to inequality in time itself, a dimension of social inequality that is difficult to measure but very important (Zilanawala 2016).

Social Acceptance As difficult as it is to measure inequality in time, inequality in the level of social acceptance is probably more difficult yet. When people experience social stigma or isolation as a result of the structure of their families, it may lead to negative outcomes ranging from unhappiness to extreme

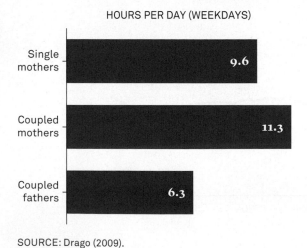

Figure 13.2 **Time spent primarily doing activities that involve care for dependent children, among mothers of children under age 1, 2003–2007**

HOURS PER DAY (WEEKDAYS)

Single mothers 9.6

Coupled mothers 11.3

Coupled fathers 6.3

SOURCE: Drago (2009).

financial and legal difficulties. Although attitudes toward family diversity certainly have evolved in the last several decades, there are still common stigmas around certain family types, especially in regard to adoption, single parenthood, and parenting by same-sex couples (Fisher 2003). For example, in the United States before the 1980s, adoption was usually practiced in secret, with adoptive parents attempting to keep anyone—including their children—from knowing that the children were adopted. Telling a child he or she was adopted was considered an insult, and children suffered as a result (Miall and March 2005).

When someone's family structure runs up against state definitions tied to older traditions, the consequences may be costly in monetary terms as well. For example, when Edith Windsor and her wife Thea Spyer got married in Canada in 2012, their marriage was recognized by the state of New York but not by the federal government (Applebome 2012). They were quite wealthy: When Spyer died, Windsor had to pay $600,000 in inheritance taxes that she would not have paid if same-sex marriage had been legal under federal law. (Windsor's case eventually was decided in her favor by the U.S. Supreme Court in *Windsor v. United States*, which overturned the federal law against recognizing same-sex marriage.)

The flip side of stigma and the denial of acceptance is the rewards associated with an acceptable or widely admired family structure. A good example of this is the discrimination in favor of married men in the workplace, or against men who aren't married (Killewald 2013). Because men are often expected to provide for their wives and children, some employers believe they have an obligation to protect married men from lower wages or layoffs. Although this may seem like doing the "family man" a favor, it amounts to discrimination against others who don't get such consideration.

Within Families

Not every kind of inequality is increasing. In fact, inequality *within* families is lower now than it was half a century ago. That is mostly because women have increased the amount of income they earn by spending more hours in the labor force and making inroads into higher-paying jobs, while many men have had no real increase in wages. In addition, husbands and wives now share their housework and child-care responsibilities more equally than they did in the past (Sayer 2016). Finally, the preferential treatment of sons over daughters has diminished as well, reducing the advantages that boys have over girls within their families (Raley and Bianchi 2006). In all of these ways, families are less internally divided by inequality than they used to be.

Nevertheless, inequality within families remains a pressing challenge for the future. As we saw in Chapter 5, men continue to command higher incomes in the labor force and work longer hours. Partly for that reason, and partly because of traditional attitudes, women continue to do a larger share of housework and child care. This contributes to women's lower average earning power and more limited career opportunities. Of course, it is not necessary for everyone within a family to have equal incomes—or do the same jobs—for the family members to be happy and successful. But when marriages are unhappy and couples divorce, the consequences of the breakup are worse when one spouse, usually the wife, finds herself on her own without a high income or the ability to earn one.

From Generation to Generation

In Chapter 2, we learned that families have been the conduit for social status across the generations for centuries. Prior to the modern era, there was no better predictor of a child's future than the social standing of his or her parents. And traditional marriage practices merely exacerbated this pattern, as parents usually arranged for their children to marry within their social class.

Family background still has a powerful influence on children's social class destinations (Reeves 2017). But modern capitalism and the expansion of public education and social welfare policies made it increasingly possible for children to move up relative to the economic fortunes of their parents. This was especially the case during periods of rapid economic growth for the United States, when the number of high-paying jobs was increasing faster than the number of low-paying jobs (Hout 2015). As the modern manufacturing economy created good jobs for the children of parents with low levels of education, many young adults found themselves able to marry and start their families with a good and stable job. However, after the 1970s, as the manufacturing economy declined, those opportunities dwindled. In their place, the economy offered jobs that were highly dependent on education (Levy 1998). People with higher education have done well in the service economy, especially in the health, information, and financial sectors, while those with less education have found themselves tracked toward the bottom, where insecure jobs with poor benefits offer little promise of advancement for workers or their children (Kalleberg 2011).

As the level of economic inequality in American society has increased, the stakes for children have risen as well. Children who merely do as well as their parents today may find themselves far behind in the competition for security, stability, and financial well-being. In fact, as we saw in Chapter 4, despite its self-image as a can-do society in which opportunity is open to all, the United States now has lower levels of social mobility than many of its highly developed peer countries. That is, children in the United States are more likely to end up in the same social class position as their parents than are children in most other advanced democratic countries. Although that poses a challenge for U.S. social policy, it also offers the opportunity for us to learn (if we choose to) from the policies of other countries (Mazumder 2015).

No Families

In most descriptions of people in this book, I have assumed that they are in a family. I write about children and their parents, parents and their children, extended families, and so on. That is reasonable in a book about families. But perhaps neglected in this approach is the story of people without families—and that is an important part of how families fit in the society at large, as we saw in Chapter 2.

People come to be without families in a variety of ways. The most dramatic case is children who are orphans, children who because they do not have living parents lack the family bonds that normally extend from parents outward—aunts and uncles, grandparents, cousins, and so on. Many such children today are adopted into happy and loving families. About 2 percent of children in the United States live in adoptive families, and a much smaller fraction live with foster parents—together about 1.7 million. Some of those live in the foster care system throughout their childhoods. For them, the benefits of parental love and investment, both for their childhood and for their future, are elusive or absent.

But there are still other ways we may think of people as living without families—or at least without the families of their choosing. For example, some people are separated from their parents (or children) by incarceration (Wakefield and Wildeman 2013). As the United States pursued a policy of "mass incarceration" starting in the 1970s, which imprisoned millions of people, this affected Black families especially dramatically (Coates 2015). In other cases, immigrants may be deported from the United States to their home countries if they do not have legal status in the country, leaving their children to live with relatives or even in the foster care system in the United States (Dreby 2012). (Remember that any child born in the country is automatically a citizen.) The exact numbers are not known, but it is safe to say that several hundred thousand immigrants with U.S.-citizen children (mostly their fathers) have been deported in the last decade. Some of these parents were apprehended at the border as they entered illegally in an attempt to rejoin their families. The children in these families often experience a trauma, and the instability of having to change residences and caregivers and losing income, which contributes to problems such as behavioral issues and trouble at school (Koball et al. 2015).

One 12-year-old girl told researcher Joanna Dreby that her parents were detained by immigration officials in the Walmart parking lot. "[My uncle] came in my room and he woke me up and he said that 'Your mom is . . . the police got her.' I don't know, like—my head almost exploded. . . . It look like it exploded 'cause that's, like, my mom" (Dreby 2012:829). On the other hand, even without legal problems, some immigrants live in the United States with long distances and months or years separating them from their families back home.

Still another way we may think of people without families involves those whose family choices are limited by harsh demographic realities. As we saw in Chapter 3, incarceration, joblessness, and mortality all have combined to limit the marriage options for many African American women. Then there are those who reach old age with no or few children—or whose children simply live far away—and find themselves without loving family care in their time of need later in life (Aykan 2003). The practice of adult children caring for their elderly parents has become less common. And because the average number of children in each family has declined, those who do provide such care are increasingly doing it without the support of siblings or other relatives (Wolff and Kasper 2006).

All of these examples serve as cautionary tales for those who study families. Most of us celebrate the contributions of family members to each other's well-being. And we often devise social policies that presume that people's families are there for them. Social Security spousal support, welfare, education, and private pensions, for example, all provide ways for family members to harness the resources of the state or the market for the benefit of their family members. But as we consider the high levels of inequality we currently face in this society, one important challenge of the future will be how to assist and care for those without families to help them (Klinenberg 2012).

Social Change

The future of the family will be affected by social changes both within families and in the larger society. Some of these changes have been going on for a very long time, and some are more recent. We can never be sure what the future will hold, but there are some trends that have a certain social momentum, which means that they will be important for at least the next several generations. The most obvious of these is the changing age structure of the population, because no matter what happens in the next 100 years, we cannot have more 100-year-olds then than there are babies born this year (unless they immigrate in the intervening years).

Aging and Fertility

To understand one set of social changes affecting families—those involving the population—we need to return to the demographic perspective introduced in Chapter 1, which emphasizes how family processes affect the larger population. In the nineteenth and twentieth centuries, the world experienced what came to be known as the **demographic transition**, the historical change from a society with low life expectancy and high birth rates to one with high life expectancy and low birth rates. Although it has not occurred identically in all societies, this transition is in fact a defining feature of modern society (Kirk 1996). Before the transition, high rates of mortality, especially for children, triggered high birth rates, because parents needed a family labor force—and needed children to be their own future caretakers. But then clean water, sanitation, and vaccinations helped prevent many diseases, and medical care cured or treated many others (Cutler and Miller 2005). Child mortality declined, and eventually people started to have fewer children. As a result, even as modern medicine extended the lives of old people, the smaller number of children per family guaranteed slower population growth.

The result of these trends was a long-term change in the **age structure**, the relative number of people of each age in a population. The most common way of

demographic transition

The historical change from a society with low life expectancy and high birth rates to one with high life expectancy and low birth rates.

age structure

The relative number of people of each age in a population.

visualizing the age structure is with a population pyramid, a graph that shows how many people there are at each age. When there are a lot of children born and people do not live to be very old, the graph looks like a pyramid (which is where it got its name). But when relatively few children are born and many people live to old age, the graph looks more like a pillar.

Figure 13.3 shows the population pyramids for the United States from 1900, 1960, and 2016, about 60 years apart. Notice how many more children there were in 1900—about 12 percent of the population was under age 5. Now that number is about 6 percent, and the percentage of people at older ages has increased dramatically. In fact, the proportion of people age 85 and over, sometimes called the "oldest old," has increased by 10 times, from 0.2 percent to 2 percent of the population—and that group will only grow in the future (see Trend to Watch).

The consequences of the demographic transition and the change in the age structure are quite profound, even if they develop slowly, over generations. The first is that with fewer children, society invests more in each child, just

Figure 13.3 **Percent distribution of population by age and sex, 1900, 1960, and 2016**

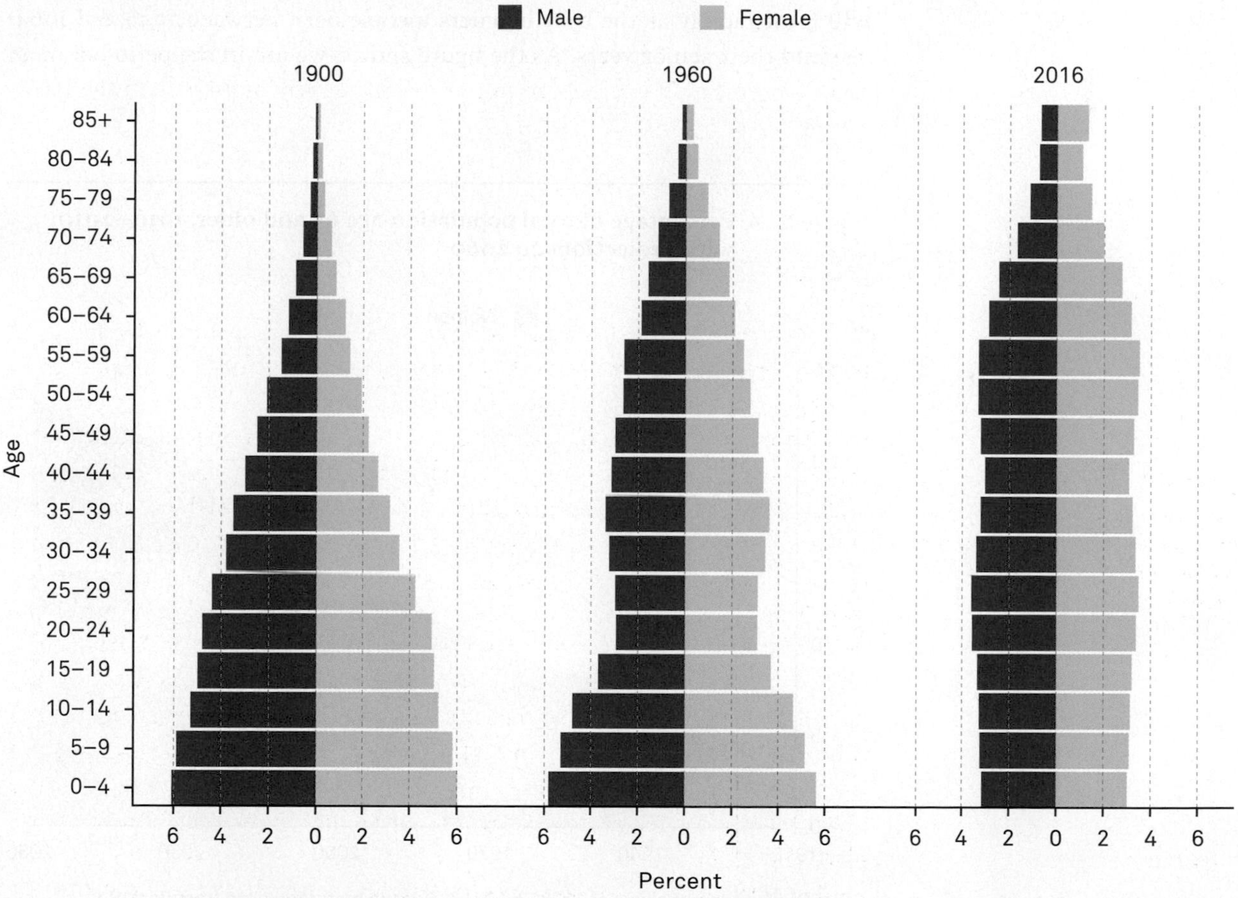

SOURCE: Author analysis of U.S. Census data.

as families with fewer children do. This change is reflected in the rise of public (and private) education systems, so that formal education now stretches into adulthood for most people. The trend of devoting more resources to each child has contributed to our changing view of children as precious individuals rather than as generic future adults (Zelizer 1985).

The second consequence of demographic transition is the increase in the number of elderly people. For those of us who hope to grow old one day, this is good news. But it poses serious economic challenges if we expect old people to retire at some point and continue to live without working. It means that we need to either increase savings over the life course—so that old people can pay for their own retirement—or devote more of our national income to caring for old people. In practical terms, that means that the costs of two major social insurance programs for older people—Medicare and Social Security—are likely to increase in the coming decades. (The aging population poses social challenges for families as well, as described in Changing Culture, "65-Plus: Aging Relationships.")

Figure 13.4 shows the growing percentage of the total population that is age 65 or older, using census data and then government projections to estimate the population up to the year 2060. In 2016, 15 percent of the U.S. population was age 65 or older (22 million men and 27 million women). That elderly population will grow rapidly as the baby boomers (people born between 1946 and 1964) age into their senior years. As the figure shows, we are in the period of most

Figure 13.4 **Percentage of total population age 65 and older, 1910–2010, with projections to 2060**

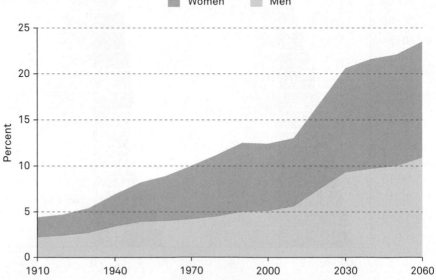

SOURCE: Author's analysis of 1910–2010 U.S. Census historical data from IPUMS (Ruggles et al. 2014), U.S. Census (2014b).

rapid change now. Fortunately, there are two trends that will help us confront this challenge.

- *The rising labor force participation of women.* Over the last half-century, we have seen many more women working for pay, and that includes those age 55 and older. The percentage of women in the age group 55 to 74 who are not in the labor force fell from more than 82 percent in 1950 to 56 percent in 2010. That means that women have generated a lot more income and savings—and paid a lot more into our social insurance programs.

- *Longer healthy life.* People aren't just living longer; they are also living healthy longer (Crimmins et al. 2009). That means they are more able (and willing) to delay their retirement and lengthen their economically active lives. This is an especially important change for men's work. In the past most older men experienced declining health and dropped out of the labor force in their 60s (or sooner). Since the 1990s, however, older men are increasingly remaining in the labor force—some out of necessity and some by choice. That means that they are contributing income to their families and to the country's social insurance programs. Further, as we saw in Chapter 9, grandparents are playing an increasing role in caring for their grandchildren.

The federal government is in the process of raising the age at which people are eligible to receive their full Social Security benefits, a change intended to lengthen their careers. People born in 1960 or later won't get their full benefits unless they retire at age 67 or older; if they retire earlier, they get reduced benefits. However, even with the increase in women's employment and the rising retirement age, we still face the challenge of caring for a growing population of even older people. We will need to find ways to transfer more resources generated from the working population to the care of people in their retirement years, which will require expensive (and therefore controversial) policy decisions.

Modern Identities

The demographic changes described here are related to cultural changes that have reshaped the way people think of themselves and their family lives. There is no simple description of the wide sweep of cultural change, but we can draw some generalizations that help explain what is happening with families. For this I will return to the discussion of modernity theory introduced in Chapter 1.

Modernity theory describes the emergence of the individual as an actor in society (Beck and Lau 2005). Although individuals have always existed, the modern era has produced an individual identity that is historically new. In the state arena, the individual identity is that of a citizen. In the market arena, it is that of a worker and consumer. And in the family arena, modern individuality emerges in the form of a freely acting family member who chooses his or her family members—and how to relate to them (Giddens 1992).

65-Plus: Aging Relationships

The historical trend toward longer life expectancy (see Chapter 2) has meant that most grandparents have relationships with their grandchildren that last years longer than in the past. And the trend toward lower birth rates means that there are fewer grandchildren, so the relationships may be emotionally closer (Bengtson 2001). That emotional quality may be more important now than it was in decades past partly because more old people are living independently, so their family relationships are more voluntary, less determined by necessity (Phillipson and Allan 2004). On the other hand, for families with young children who face economic hardship, caregiving by grandparents often plays a crucial role.

The web of family relationships has grown increasingly diverse. Over a lifetime, the cumulative effect of cohabitation, divorce, and remarriage—for oneself and one's grown children—means that many people reach old age embedded in a dizzying array of emotionally and practically complicated relationships. Ironically, while old people today may have fewer direct biological relatives—children and grandchildren—they are likely to have more nonbiological or ambiguous relatives. In many cases, there are no established customs for how people should interact in the midst of this complexity. For example, should one offer to babysit for a former stepgrandchild? Are adults comfortable inviting both of their divorced parents (and maybe a boyfriend or girlfriend, too) to a young child's birthday party? Such dilemmas and the conflicts they cause are not merely socially awkward. Lack of clearly defined relationships may undermine the ability of families to marshal their intergenerational networks of care and support (Seltzer and Bianchi 2013).

Figure 13.5 provides one scheme for representing the diversity of living arrangements among men and women in early, middle, and late old age. The figure shows that in the younger group, ages 65 to 74, 58 percent of men and 45 percent of women are living in what many would consider an ideal retirement-age arrangement: in their own, married-couple households, without any of their own children present. (This number is higher for men than for women because women are more likely to have been widowed, and if divorced they are less likely to have remarried.)

About 12 percent of people ages 65–74 live in their own households (married or not), but with one or more of their children present—what is known as "hosting" a multigenerational family (Cohen and Casper 2002). As old age advances, however, the proportion of people hosting declines, and more people are living in the homes of their children. In the 85-and-older age group, 9 percent of men and 17 percent of women are living with their children. By that age as well, more people are living in institutions (primarily nursing homes), reaching 11 percent of women age 85 or older.

Declining health among the survivors to older ages tends to lead them into the homes of others or the care of institutions. But most people's preference is to live in a married-couple household, and the last choice is to live in a nursing home. In between are many divorced, widowed, or never-married people who are healthy enough to live alone independently—perhaps with limited assistance—if they can afford to. Living independently, many people believe,

Figure 13.5 **Living arrangements of Americans age 65 and older, by age and sex, 2015**

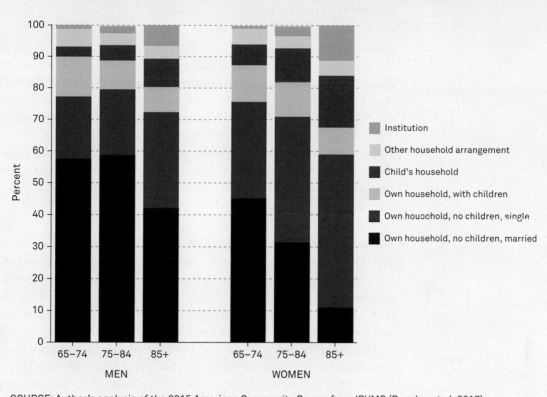

SOURCE: Author's analysis of the 2015 American Community Survey from IPUMS (Ruggles et al. 2017).

allows them to maintain healthy, voluntary relationships with their family members without compromising their privacy and personal autonomy. As the sociologist Eric Klinenberg (2012) has written, one of the challenges for our system of care—and even for the urban design of our cities—is to find ways to enable old people to live independently in community settings that allow for healthy social contact with friends and neighbors. As the (healthy) elderly population grows, this challenge will only become more acute.

Individual actors in modern family life face an institutionalized expectation of choice, which means, paradoxically, that freely making individual choices is not optional! In our culture, this freedom of choice takes several forms:

- *Diversity and choices.* As noted earlier, the variety of family structures and choices people make (and their timing) has become increasingly diverse.

There are simply more culturally acceptable lifestyles to choose from than there were, especially compared with the highly constrained period around the 1950s. As a result, people have many patterns to reflect on as models—positive or negative—for their own choices.

- *Evaluating and reflecting.* Faced with a diverse array of choices, people find themselves forced to actively investigate—and justify—the choices they make. This is most clearly seen in the popular media, such as reality TV shows, psychology programs such as *Ellen* and *Dr. Phil*, and countless magazines and websites. In these media, individuals publicly defend their lifestyles while millions of viewers look on, comparing themselves with the subjects displayed. Then people act out their own miniature versions of these debates in their daily lives. Social science research also plays a role in this process, especially when the news media report on research showing positive or negative outcomes from family choices.

- *Live and let live?* There is no shortage of judgmental commentary on the lifestyles of everyone from celebrities and politicians to criminals and other individuals who briefly appear in the media spotlight for one reason or another. However, the cultural expectation that everyone will make their own family choices has helped produce a popular attitude that the law should not restrict such choices. From interracial marriage to divorce, from gay and lesbian relationships to adoption and reproductive technology, the law has relaxed its regulation of family life and put the onus on individuals to choose their own way. But that transformation is far from complete, as the strong opposition that persists among some Americans to same-sex marriage demonstrates.

These features of modern thinking help set the stage not only for our own decisions but also for how we evaluate the social changes we observe around us (and read about in social science textbooks).

Responses to Family Change

In politics and culture, there is a wide spectrum of responses to family change. This includes organized responses, such as when political groups or activists lobby, bring lawsuits, or campaign for elections. And it includes the informal responses of people in their families and communities, lending social acceptance, criticism, or even shame to particular family practices as well as to the notion of change in general.

Consider these results from a 2010 poll of the American public. The Pew Research Center asked almost 3,000 people if they thought that the "growing variety in the types of family arrangements" is "a good thing, a bad thing, or don't you think it makes a difference?" The responses were pretty evenly split, as you can see in Figure 13.6. However, the responses followed strong patterns according to age, religious adherence, and political affiliation. People over 55, those who attend religious services more often, and people who consider themselves Republicans are much more likely to view family diversity as a bad thing for society. Interestingly, younger people, those who don't attend religious services as much, and Democrats are pretty evenly split between those who think diversity is a good thing and those who say it makes no difference.

I consider those "no difference" people to be an important group for the future of family change. Rather than just an intermediate position, this view represents the modern trend toward live and let live described earlier. To put that in context, it is worth taking a few moments to consider these three attitudes—change is bad, change is okay, change is good—in more detail.

Figure 13.6 **Attitudes toward growing family diversity, 2010**

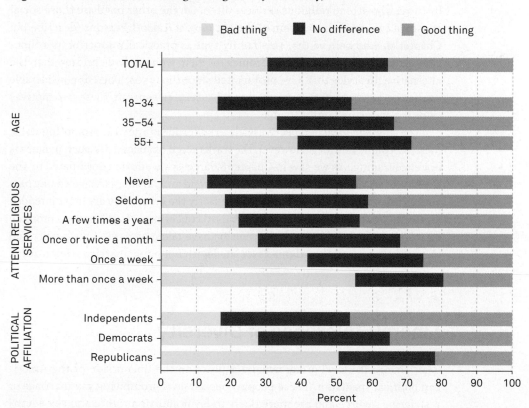

SOURCE: Author's analysis of data from Pew Research Center (2010).

Conservative: The Singular Ideal

In the "change is bad" category are those who believe that married couples (man and woman) with their own biological children are the ideal family type toward which we should strive. That is, our policies, laws, and regulations should encourage this arrangement by rewarding those who achieve it and maybe even penalizing (legally, symbolically, or monetarily) those who do not.

I refer to this position as the "singular ideal" because it goes against the trend of diversity and promotes its opposite: conformity. For those holding this position, the major trends of the last half-century—including the spread of no-fault divorce, nonmarital cohabitation, unmarried parenthood, and same-sex marriage—all represent the decline of "the family" and are problems to be addressed. In that way, this perspective is similar to the structural functionalist orientation described in Chapter 1 and is most often expressed by people on the political right of the American scene. As the conservative pundit Bradford Wilcox (2011) put it, "The intact, biological, married family remains the gold standard for family life in the United States."

Within this perspective, however, there are two major strands of thought. One is religious, expressing the view of some Jewish, Christian, and Muslim believers that the "gold standard" family type was dictated by God and should be practiced according to God's wishes. That's why this view is so strongly held by those who attend religious services often. On the other hand are those social conservatives more in the vein of the sociologist Talcott Parsons (described in Chapter 1), who believe that this family type is practically superior as a functional form, leading to better outcomes for men, women, and children than the alternative lifestyles that have proliferated since the 1950s. There is considerable overlap between these two groups, but it is useful to separate these two motivations for opposing family change.

The singular-ideal perspective leads to policy ideas aimed at promoting stable married-couple families. However, the track record of success for such policies is not encouraging. As we saw in Chapter 8, large-scale efforts coordinated by the federal government have failed to alter the trend away from marriage among parents with less than a college education—exactly the group they are most intended to affect. Some researchers have also raised concerns that attempts to promote marriage through behavioral intervention have taken on a religious quality and have only increased the stigma associated with not being married (Heath 2012).

Liberal: Tolerance of Diversity

The "change is okay" group usually appears on the liberal side of the American political spectrum. These people opposed laws prohibiting gay marriage or restricting divorce and are more likely to favor abortion rights and sex education. But they are not against the "traditional" American family any more than they are for the growing new family structures. Rather, they prefer a hands-off approach that does not interfere with the family decisions of other people.

For example, consider how former president Barack Obama described his decision to change his mind and support same-sex marriage. He did not say he opposed the traditional family or wanted to see more different kinds of families, but rather expressed belief in equal treatment of everyone, which he called "the golden rule—you know, treat others the way you would want to be treated" (Calmes and Baker 2012).

The terms *tolerance* and *diversity* go well together, because neither specifies what kind of differences are being recognized or how they are to be recognized. Rather, according to this perspective, it is difference itself that is a value to be accepted with tolerance. And tolerance does not imply a strong endorsement, but rather a simple welcoming. In short, tolerance and diversity together reflect live-and-let-live modern values. That may be why even Donald Trump, who has opposed marriage rights for same-sex couples as a policy matter, has also tried to indicate his tolerance. In a 2011 interview he said about his hometown: "New York is a place with lots of gays, and I think it's great. But I'm not in favor of gay marriage" (Summers 2011).

The liberal attitude toward tolerating family diversity has mostly promoted policies of relaxing restrictions on family behavior. Historically, these efforts have included permitting birth control use among unmarried couples, allowing divorce without a finding of fault on the part of one spouse or the other, and most recently permitting the marriage of same-sex couples. Liberal supporters celebrate these reforms as efforts to extend equal rights to people in all families. However, some critics believe that by loosening the rules surrounding marriage and family structure, liberal tolerance has contributed to the deinstitutionalization of marriage (Cherlin 2004).

Critical: Embrace of Change

There is a more active attitude toward change, however, adopted by the people who see the growing diversity of family life not merely as okay but as a good thing. Although many people who offered the "good thing" response to the survey would not call themselves feminists, feminism promotes the view that the "traditional" family *should* decline. That is because that family arrangement usually involves a husband who makes more money (and has more power) than his wife and a social attitude that gives privileges to (straight) married-couple families over those in other arrangements. The breakdown of that dominant family form, in this view, was the result of hard-fought advances by women that made it possible for them to survive—and thrive—outside of the protective dominance of a breadwinner husband.

One proponent of this perspective is the sociologist Judith Stacey, who wrote a famous essay called "Good Riddance to 'The Family'" (1993). Stacey argued that people who believe that family diversity represents the decline of "the family" are trying to protect a family form that exacerbates inequality and blocks the emergence of diversity. She concluded: "Family sociologists should take the lead in burying the ideology of 'the family' and in rebuilding a social environment in which diverse family forms can sustain themselves with dignity and mutual respect."

For people who share this critical perspective, the policy agenda has revolved around freeing people (especially women) from the need to rely on their families for survival. Chief among these policies are a variety of welfare supports for poor women and their children, whether through tax policy or direct monetary support (Christopher 2002). But advocates support a wider array of policies as well. These range from paid family leave from work to giving credit in pension retirement programs for unpaid care work performed over the life of a worker. Together, such policies are sometimes known as "defamilialization," because they are seen to free people from family dependency and make family relationships more voluntary (Saraceno 2015). This goal unites critical family advocates with the broader feminist aim of promoting women's independence (Orloff 2009).

Time will tell the future of these three competing perspectives. Although younger people are more prone to supporting—or at least not opposing—family change, their attitudes may change as they age. And the environment within which diverse families operate may have an effect as well. People like to embrace successful changes more than unsuccessful ones. If our society's laws and policies support and protect people in the full variety of family types, family diversity may become even more widely accepted.

Families in the Face of Inequality

We have seen many instances in which families are the sites where inequality is experienced or produced. That includes inequality between spouses, between parents and children, and between families as well. Families also are sites of caring, cooperation, and resilience in the face of inequality. As we think about addressing the challenges that inequality poses to us in the future, we need to consider how people in families respond—or fail to respond—in support of each other.

In Chapter 2, we saw an example of complex family bonds from prehistoric times: village members of an extended family buried in a way that seemed to honor their relationships. Living together is the most recognizable expression of familial cooperation. Today, most people choose to live independently—either alone or in a nuclear family—rather than in extended households, if they can afford to (Kahn, Goldscheider, and García-Manglano 2013). But although multigenerational families remain less common than they were a century ago, the tendency of people to live together across generational lines has rebounded in the last several decades. To illustrate this trend, I will describe two common patterns.

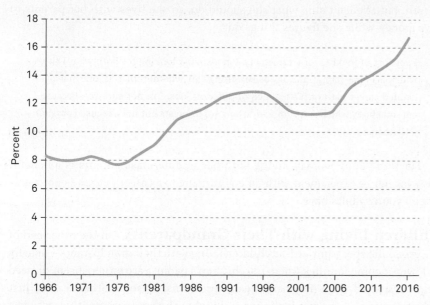

Figure 13.7 **Percentage of adults ages 25 to 34 living with their parents (or in-laws), 1966–2016**

NOTE: Three-year averages shown.

SOURCE: Author's analysis of Current Population Survey data from IPUMS (Flood et al. 2017).

Young Adults Living with Their Parents As the marriage age has increased and more people are attending school into their 20s, the number of young people who are dependent on—and living with—their parents has increased (Furstenberg 2010). The percentage of young adults, ages 25 to 34, living with their parents has doubled since the 1960s, rising especially dramatically after the recession of the late 2000s (see Figure 13.7). This has sparked popular concern that children are "taking so long to grow up" (Henig 2010). Financial hardship is part of the explanation for this change, as young adults with shaky career prospects lean on the support of their parents to help them strike out on their own.

When young adults live with their parents, the line of financial support usually runs from the parents to their children (Seltzer and Bianchi 2013). That is most clear when we look at whose home it is. When multiple generations of adults live together, the people whose home it is earn 70 percent of the household's income, on average. That is because people who can afford to usually run their own households, and their less financially stable relatives join them, often on a temporary basis (Kochhar and Cohn 2011). So when we see larger families living together, we often assume that someone is financially dependent or struggling to get by on their own—for example, immigrants trying to get started, young people who haven't gotten good jobs after leaving school, single mothers raising children with their parents' support, or young adults living at home while they go to college.

The support received by young adults is not just financial, however. In her book *The Accordion Family*, sociologist Katherine Newman quotes a young woman in her late 20s who has graduated from an elite college and could be supporting herself, but she isn't sure what she should do, so she lives with her parents to save money while she figures things out:

> I am sort of looking for a career, but I'm also just looking for both what I think will make me happy and be contributing. So whether that is one narrowly defined career path or it's a bunch of different jobs, I'm not sure yet, because I am somebody who has sort of a wide range of interests but not a focused passion. (Newman 2012:10)

For this young woman, living with her middle-class parents is a benefit, allowing her to experiment without committing to a career path. It is not a luxury all young adults have.

Children Living with Their Grandparents On the other end of the economic spectrum we find children living with their grandparents—usually in lower-income families where the children's parents are either absent or need help because of unemployment, health problems, or some other reason. Just as with young adults moving in (or staying) with their parents, this, too, is a

Figure 13.8 **Percentage of people age 55 and older who live with and are responsible for a grandchild, by poverty level, 2015**

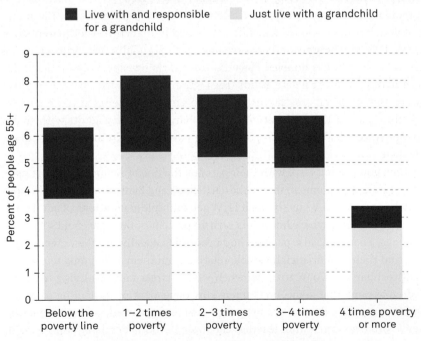

SOURCE: Author's calculations from the 2015 American Community Survey data provided by IPUMS (Ruggles et al. 2017).

growing trend (see Chapter 9). Although a small fraction of wealthy grandparents live with their grandchildren, this is much more common among those with low incomes. The pattern is shown in Figure 13.8. At the low end of the income scale, about 6 percent of people age 55 or older live with a grandchild, and about 4 percent are "responsible for most of the basic needs" of their grandchildren. The group most likely to live with grandchildren, however, are those with just enough income to be above the poverty line, but not much, as the figure shows. These are grandparents who may have enough income to help, but also have poorer relatives in need of help.

Why do grandparents take in their needy relatives? This is a reversal from the more common historical condition in which old people lived with their grown children in order to be cared for after their retirement or when they became disabled. Research suggests that they do it out of a sense of family loyalty. Consider the explanation of Samuel, a 76-year-old African American man caring for his three great-grandchildren after his wife and daughter died and the children's mother became too irresponsible to be trusted with them: "There ain't no other way. I have to raise these babies else the service people will take 'em away. This is my family. Family has to take care of family else we won't be no more" (Stack and Burton 1993:161).

Taking care of his family members was a self-evident obligation to Samuel. Instead of letting "the service people" take care of them (in the foster care system), he devoted himself to their needs because they were his family members. Not everyone has this reaction. In the same study, Stack and Burton (1993) report on family members who refuse to be put in such a situation and instead assert their independence. But stories of survival in harsh conditions more often than not include such relatives stepping in to help when needed.

Conclusion

The family as an institutional arena in the modern era is a showcase for the increasing diversity in American society. The arrangements people choose—or have chosen for them—have proliferated under the influence of cultural, demographic, and legal changes. Not only are more people living in a greater variety of family situations than in the past, but they are moving through the stages of family life according to different time sequences, and sometimes in different directions, than in the past.

This growing family diversity is accompanied by growing economic inequality. What is happening in families is not the only factor—or even the most important factor—behind the increasing inequality in the United States and many other societies. But families play a role in contributing to inequality, especially by passing on their privileges—and disadvantages—to the next generation. On the other hand, families also provide relief from the afflictions that accompany our modern era. Relatives care for each other. Families open their doors to make room for their less fortunate parents, siblings, children, and grandchildren.

Conservative, Liberal, and Critical Responses

Social reality is messy and complicated. To study it—to ask questions of social life and see if they are supported by evidence—social scientists need to create categories out of the mess and hold them up to scrutiny. The classical social scientist Max Weber used the term *ideal type* to define this process of categorization (Bruun 2007). Ideal types are somewhat fictional; they don't exist as real distinctions with clear boundaries, but rather as concepts used to simplify our descriptions.

The three perspectives on family change that I described in this chapter—conservative opposition, liberal tolerance, and critical embrace—are ideal types. I invented them to try to capture the different views on family change. Do they work? To put them into practice, let's take a family trend and hold it up to their light.

Working alone, in groups, or as a whole class, choose a topic to consider, such as one of these:

- Unmarried parenthood

- Divorce

- Remarriage

- Same-sex marriage

- Open adoption

Then split up to devise arguments about the trend and its impact on society from each of the three proposed perspectives. You can prepare reports, write short essays, or just make a list of arguments to present verbally to illustrate the views you think people from each perspective would put forward.

In writing, group discussion, or class presentations, pitch your perspective to the class. Then ask questions such as these:

- Is this position logically consistent?

- Does it represent a coherent perspective you can see in American political or cultural debates?

- Does the ideal-type category work to capture a real perspective, or does it create an artificial distinction?

Finally, what do you think? Has categorizing the perspectives related to this issue helped you to come to a conclusion yourself—and is it different from what you started with?

In the last few decades, the older generation, which came of age during a time of economic growth and prosperity after World War II, has provided much-needed support to the less secure children of the baby boom. Now, as the population ages, the savings of retirees will be stretched thinner, and a greater share of our income will need to go toward their care. What the family and the market cannot provide to that end, the state may have to arrange.

How American society will respond to the ongoing changes in family structure and relationships remains to be seen. Conflicting cultural attitudes toward family diversity, changing laws and political debates, and even new technologies will all affect how new family forms emerge and develop. We can't predict that future; trying to figure out how the past got us here has been difficult enough. But if we apply our knowledge and skills to the task, I think we can at least make a fair attempt at understanding the present while it's upon us.

Trend to Watch: The Limits of Longevity

The people who will turn 100 at the end of the twenty-first century are already 18 years old, the youngest members of what some people call the Millennial generation. We have no way of knowing how many of these survivors there will

New ideas in society, along with changing laws, modern technology, and shifting demographics, have altered the meaning of "family" into something that Americans would not have imagined even 50 years ago. How do you think the idea of the "family" will change for the next generation?

be, or which members of this generation will live to be our oldest elders at the end of the century. But we have every reason to hope their chances of surviving that long will be greater than they were for the first people to come of age in the twentieth century.

In the last few decades the population of centenarians—people age 100 or older—has grown almost twice as fast as the total population and is now approaching 60,000 (U.S. Census Bureau 2012g). Demographers only began using the term **oldest old**, meaning people ages 85 and older, in the early 1980s, when it became clear that simply lumping all "old" people over age 65 into one category would no longer represent the diversity of that population (Suzman and Riley 1985). The oldest old are now 2 percent of the U.S. population, and the Census Bureau projects that will rise to 5 percent by 2060 (U.S. Census Bureau 2014b). Baby boomers (who were born in 1946–1964) are starting to dominate the older population, swelling the ranks of those age 65 to 75. But if advances in survival continue, those who are entering the "oldest old" group will continue to live longer, so that when the baby boomers reach 85 their chances of living to 100 will be greater than ever.

How much further can human longevity go? We don't know. Only two people are known to have lived past their 118th birthdays. One of them, the Frenchwoman Jeanne Calment, lived to 122 in 1997, making her the oldest person ever recorded (Goldenberg 2015). All of the demographic projections about the future in this book are based on assumptions about how long people will live in the future. But if scientific research leads to medical breakthroughs to stop the basic processes of aging, or prevent or cure some of the diseases of old age, the survival ceiling may be dramatically raised, and our demographic projections could be way off. If that happens, we will have a lot of new research to do!

oldest old

People ages 85 and older.

KEY TERMS:

social diversity

demographic transition

age structure **oldest old**

Questions for Review

1. Think of significant events in your family life: Has your religion influenced how you marked the occasion? How might someone from a different family/religious background have marked the occasion?

2. Look around your classroom. How are other students like you? How are they different? Do you experience more diversity in your class or in other areas of your life?

3. What is the demographic transition? How does it affect government programs, society, and family relationships?

4. What are the two trends that could mitigate the challenges of a growing elderly population?

5. Explain the conservative, liberal, and critical viewpoints on family diversity.

6. What are the advantages of living with family members? How does not having a family prevent a person from having these advantages?

7. Describe various scenarios in which multigenerational households come together. How many people do you know who live with their parents and/or grandparents?

8. What are the three reasons married people tend to be healthier?

Glossary

acculturation: The acquisition of a new culture and language.

adolescence: The period of development between childhood and adulthood.

adoptive parents: Parents to a child they did not produce biologically.

age structure: The relative number of people of each age in a population.

androgynous: Neither exclusively masculine nor exclusively feminine.

annulment of marriage: A legal or religious determination that the marriage was never valid.

assimilation: The gradual reduction of ethnic distinction between immigrants and the mainstream society.

baby boom: The period of high birth rates in the United States between 1946 and 1964.

bias: The tendency to impose previously held views on the collection and interpretation of facts.

big data: Data collections large enough to require special computing resources, and complex enough to require customized computer applications.

biological parents: The adults whose bodies—including the father's sperm and the mother's egg—produce a child.

blended family: Any family that includes stepparents, stepsiblings, or half-siblings.

boundary ambiguity: The situation in which family members do not know or do not agree on who is in the family and what role each person plays.

breadwinner-homemaker family: An employed father, a nonemployed mother, and their children.

care relationship: A relationship in which one person is responsible for another's care.

care work: Work performed face-to-face for the purpose of enhancing the capabilities of another person.

census: A periodic count of people in a population and their characteristics, usually performed as an official government function.

child abuse and neglect: The act or failure to act on the part of a parent or caretaker that results in (or puts children at imminent risk for) physical or emotional harm, sexual abuse, or exploitation.

class identity: The awareness of, and sense of belonging to, a specific social class.

cohabitation: Living together as a sexual or romantic couple without being married.

cohort: A group of people who experience an event together at the same point in time.

coming out: The process of revealing one's gay sexual orientation to the significant people in one's life.

companionate marriage: A view of marriage as a companionship, a friendship, and a romance, rather than as a practical platform for cooperation and survival.

companionship family: An ideal type of family characterized by the mutual affection, equality, and comradeship of its members.

conflict perspective: The view that opposition and conflict define a given society and are necessary for social evolution.

consensus perspective: A perspective that projects an image of society as the collective expression of shared norms and values.

courtship: The mate selection process in which couples begin a relationship with supervised contact in public, then proceed to additional dates in the woman's home and then to marriage if the parents approve.

coverture: A legal doctrine that lasted until the late nineteenth century, under which wives were incorporated into their husbands' citizenship.

dating: The mate selection process in which young adults spend time with a variety of partners before making a long-term commitment.

demographic perspective: The study of how family behavior and household structures contribute to larger population processes.

demographic transition: The historical change from a society with low life expectancy and high birth rates to one with high life expectancy and low birth rates.

division of labor: The social process of determining who does what work and for what rewards.

divorce: The legal dissolution of marriage according to the laws of the state.

elder abuse: The physical, sexual, or emotional abuse of old people by someone with whom they share an intimate or caring relationship.

endogamy: Marriage and reproduction within a distinct group.

ethnicity: A group of people with a common cultural identification, based on a combination of language, religion, ancestral origin, or traditional practices.

exchange theory: The theory that individuals or groups with different resources, strengths, and weaknesses enter into mutual relationships to maximize their own gains.

exogamy: Marriage and reproduction outside one's distinct group.

exploitation: The process by which the labor of some produces wealth that is controlled by others.

extended families: Family households in which relatives beyond parents and their children live together.

families: Groups of related people, bound by connections that are biological, legal, or emotional.

familism: A personal outlook that puts family obligations first, before individual well-being.

family arena: The institutional arena where people practice intimacy, childbearing and socialization, and caring work.

family wage: The amount necessary for a male earner to provide subsistence for his wife and children without their having to work for pay.

feminist theory: A theory that seeks to understand and ultimately reduce inequality between men and women.

fertility: The number of children born in a society or among a particular group.

gender: The social realization of biological sex.

gender division of labor: The allocation of work between men and women in society.

gender expression: One's pattern of outward behavior in relation to common standards of a gender category.

gender identity: The identification with the social category boy/man or girl/woman.

genealogy: The study of ancestry and family history.

Gini index: A measure of inequality in which 0 represents complete equality and 1 represents complete inequality.

half-sibling (half-brother/half-sister): The biological child of one's parent and another person.

heterogamy: Marriage between a man and a woman.

homophily: The principle by which similar people have more of a given kind of contact than dissimilar people.

homogamy: Marriage between two people of the same sex.

homophobia: Fear of or antipathy toward homosexuality in general and gays and lesbians in particular.

hooking up: A casual sex or romantic encounter without explicit commitment or exclusivity.

household: A group of people that lives and eats separately from other groups.

housework: Work to maintain a household's functions.

incest: Sex between close relatives.

infertility: The failure of a couple to have a successful pregnancy despite deliberately having sex without contraception.

institutional arena: A social space in which relations between people in common positions are governed by accepted rules of interaction.

intensive motherhood: Cultural pressure on women to devote more time, energy, and money to raising their children.

intermarriage: Marriage between members of different racial or ethnic groups.

intersex: A condition in which a person's chromosomal composition doesn't correspond with his or her sexual anatomy at birth, or the anatomy is not clearly male or female.

intimacy: A type of relationship in which people love or at least know each other very well and interact in private.

intimate partner violence: Violence between partners who are (or were) involved in a sexual or romantic relationship.

involved father ideal: The father as an emotional, nurturing companion who bonds with his children as well as providing for them.

legal family: A group of individuals related by birth, marriage, or adoption.

life chances: The practical opportunity to achieve desired material conditions and personal experiences.

life course perspective: The study of the family trajectories of individuals and groups as they progress through their lives, in social and historical context.

longitudinal surveys: A research method in which the same people are interviewed repeatedly over a period of time.

love: A deep affection and concern for another, with whom one feels a strong emotional bond.

male provider ideal: The father as an economic provider and authority figure for his children.

marital dissolution: The end of a marriage through permanent separation or divorce.

market: The institutional arena where labor for pay, economic exchange, and wealth accumulation take place.

market work: Work done by employees for pay.

marriage market: The social space in which people search for potential marriage partners.

mate selection: The process by which people choose each other for sexual or romantic relationships.

minority group: A racial or ethnic group that occupies a subordinate status in society.

modernity theory: A theory of the historical emergence of the individual as an actor in society and how individuality changed personal and institutional relations.

monogamy: A family system in which each person has only one spouse.

nuclear family: A married couple living with their own (usually biological) children and no extended family members.

occupational gender segregation: Men and women having jobs in separate occupations.

oldest old: People ages 85 and older.

opportunity cost: The price one pays for choosing the less lucrative of the available options.

parent: An adult intimately responsible for the care and rearing of a child.

parenting: The activity of raising a child.

patriarchy: The system of men's control over property and fathers' authority over all family members.

peers: People in a similar social situation and of similar status with whom an individual interacts.

personal family: The people to whom we feel related and who we expect to define us as members of their family as well.

polygamy: A family system in which one person has more than one spouse, usually one man and multiple women.

poverty line: The level of income below which the federal government defines a family or individual as poor.

race: A group of people believed to share common descent, based on perceived innate physical similarities.

racial ethnicity: An ethnic group perceived to share physical characteristics.

rape: Forced vaginal, anal, or oral penetration or attempted penetration of a person without his or her consent.

romantic love: The passionate devotion and attraction one person feels for another.

romantic relationships: Mutually acknowledged, ongoing interactions featuring heightened affection and intensity.

sample survey: A research method in which identical questions are asked of many different people and their answers gathered into one large data file.

selection effect: The problem that occurs when the cause being studied has already been determined by the outcome that is under investigation.

separate spheres: The cultural doctrine under which women were to work at home, to make it a sanctuary from the industrial world in which their husbands worked for pay.

separation: The formal or informal separation of married spouses into different households.

sex: One's biological category, male or female, based on anatomy and physiology.

sexual assault: Unwanted penetration or touch, by force or threat of force, without consent.

sexual double standard: The practice of applying stricter moral or legal controls to women's sexual behavior than to men's.

sexual identity: The recognition, or internalization, of a biological sex category.

sexual orientation: The pattern of romantic or sexual attraction to others in relation to one's own gender identity.

social capital: The access to resources one has by virtue of relationships and connections within a social network.

social distance: The level of acceptance that members of one group have toward members of another group.

social diversity: The condition of difference in experiences or characteristics of people in a population.

social mobility: The movement, up or down, between social classes.

social script: A commonly understood pattern of interaction that serves as a model of behavior in familiar situations.

socialization: The process by which individuals internalize elements of the social structure in their own personalities.

state: The institutional arena where, through political means, behavior is legally regulated, violence is controlled, and resources are redistributed.

stem family: The household formed by one grown child remaining in the family home with his or her parents.

stepchild: The child of one's spouse or committed partner.

stepparent: The spouse or committed partner of one's biological or adoptive parent.

stepsibling (stepbrother/stepsister): The child (son/daughter) of one's stepparent.

stigma: A quality that is perceived as undesirable and that sets a person apart from others in his or her social category.

symbolic interactionism: A theory concerned with the ability of humans to see themselves through the eyes of others and to enact social roles based on others' expectations.

system of care: How a society accomplishes the necessary care work and housework.

time use studies: Surveys that collect data on how people spend their time during a sample period, such as a single day or week.

total fertility rate: The number of children born to the average woman in her lifetime.

transgender: A term to describe individuals whose gender identity does not match their assigned sex.

utilitarian love: The practical, rational dedication of one person to another based on shared understanding and emotional commitment.

work: The exertion of effort to produce or accomplish something.

work-family conflict: The conflict that occurs when the time demands, strains, or obligations of work or family roles make it difficult to fulfill obligations in either role.

Bibliography

60 Minutes, Vanity Fair. 60 Minutes/Vanity Fair Poll, Aug. 2011 [survey question]. USCBS.201108DVF.Q64. CBS News [producer]. Cornell University, Ithaca, NY: Roper Center for Public Opinion Research, iPOLL [distributor], accessed October 9, 2016.

Abma, Joyce C., and Gladys M. Martinez. 2006. "Childlessness among Older Women in the United States: Trends and Profiles." *Journal of Marriage and Family* 68(4):1045–1056.

Abrams, Kerry. 2013. "The End of Annulment." *The Journal of Gender Race and Justice* 16 (Summer).

Adamsons, Kari, and Sara K. Johnson. 2013. "An Updated and Expanded Meta-Analysis of Nonresident Fathering and Child Well-Being." *Journal of Family Psychology* 27 (4): 589–99. doi:10.1037/a0033786.

Adimora, Adaora A., Victor J. Schoenbach, and Michelle A. Floris-Moore. 2009. "Ending the Epidemic of Heterosexual HIV Transmission among African Americans." *American Journal of Preventive Medicine* 37(5):468–471.

Adler, Patricia A., Steven J. Kless, and Peter Adler. 1992. "Socialization to Gender Roles: Popularity among Elementary School Boys and Girls." *Sociology of Education* 65(3):169–187.

Adorno, Theodor W. 1994. *Adorno: The Stars Down to Earth and Other Essays on the Irrational in Culture*. London; New York: Routledge.

Afifi, T. O., N. P. Mota, P. Dasiewicz, H. L. MacMillan, and J. Sareen. 2012. "Physical Punishment and Mental Disorders: Results From a Nationally Representative US Sample." *Pediatrics*, 2011–2947.

AIGA. 2013. The Professional Association for Design. http://www.aiga.org. Accessed July 18, 2013.

Akers, Aletha Y., Cheryl P. Lynch, Melanie A. Gold, Judy C. Chang, Willa Doswell, Harold C. Wiesenfeld, Wentao Feng, and James Bost. 2009. "Exploring the Relationship among Weight, Race, and Sexual Behaviors among Girls." *Pediatrics* 124(5):e913–e920.

Alba, Richard D., and Victor Nee. 2003. *Remaking the American Mainstream: Assimilation and Contemporary Immigration*. Cambridge, MA: Harvard University Press.

Albelda, Randy. 2011. "Time Binds: U.S. Antipoverty Policies, Poverty, and the Well-Being of Single Mothers." *Feminist Economics* 17(4):189–214.

Albrecht, Carol Mulford, Mark A. Fossett, Cynthia M. Cready, and K. Jill Kiecolt. 1997. "Mate Availability, Women's Marriage Prevalence, and Husbands' Education." *Journal of Family Issues* 18(4):429–452. doi:10.1177/019251397018004004.

Alexander, Michelle. 2010. *The New Jim Crow: Mass Incarceration in the Age of Colorblindness*. New York; Jackson, TN: New Press.

Allegretto, Sylvia A. 2011. "The State of Working America's Wealth, 2011." Economic Policy Institute. http://www.epi.org/publication/the_state_of_working_americas_wealth_2011/. Accessed June 18, 2014.

Allen, Douglas W., and Margaret Brinig. 2011. "Do Joint Parenting Laws Make Any Difference?" *Journal of Empirical Legal Studies* 8(2):304–324.

Allen, Katherine R. 2007. "Ambiguous Loss After Lesbian Couples with Children Break Up: A Case for Same-Gender Divorce." *Family Relations* 56(2):175–183.

Allen, Lisa. 2009. "Disorders of Sexual Development." *Obstetrics and Gynecology Clinics of North America* 36(1):25–45.

Allison, Paul D. 1978. "Measures of Inequality." *American Sociological Review* 43(6): 865–880.

Altintas, Evrim. 2016. "The Widening Education Gap in Developmental Child Care Activities in the United States, 1965–2013." *Journal of Marriage and Family* 78 (1): 26–42. doi:10.1111/jomf.12254.

Altintas, Evrim, and Oriel Sullivan. 2017. "Trends in Fathers' Contribution to Housework and Childcare under Different Welfare Policy Regimes." *Social Politics: International Studies in Gender, State and Society* 24 (1): 81–108.

Altschul, Inna, Shawna J. Lee, and Elizabeth T. Gershoff. 2016. "Hugs, Not Hits: Warmth and Spanking as Predictors of Child Social Competence." *Journal of Marriage and Family* 78: 695–714.

Amato, Paul R. 2010. "Research on Divorce: Continuing Trends and New Developments." *Journal of Marriage and Family* 72(3):650–666. doi:10.1111/j.1741-3737.2010.00723.x.

Amato, Paul R., and Brett Beattie. 2011. "Does the Unemployment Rate Affect the Divorce Rate? An Analysis of State Data 1960–2005." *Social Science Research* 40(3):705–715.

Amato, Paul R., and Christopher J. Anthony. 2014. "Estimating the Effects of Parental Divorce and Death with Fixed Effects Models." *Journal of Marriage and Family* 76: 370–86.

Amato, Paul R., and Frieda Fowler. 2002. "Parenting Practices, Child Adjustment, and Family Diversity." *Journal of Marriage and Family* 64(3):703–716.

American FactFinder. 2014. U.S. Census Bureau. Available at factfinder2.census.gov.

———. 2016. U.S. Census Bureau. Available at factfinder2.census.gov.

American Library Association. 2016. Top Ten Most Frequently Challenged Books. http://www.ala.org/bbooks/frequentlychallengedbooks/top10.

American Psychiatric Association. 2000. "313.89 Reactive Attachment Disorder of Infancy or Early Childhood," in *DSM-IV-TR: Diagnostic and Statistical Manual of Mental*

Disorders (4th ed.). Washington, DC: American Psychiatric Association.

The American Society for Aesthetic Plastic Surgery. 2016. "Cosmetic Surgery National Data Bank Statistics: 2015." http://www.surgery.org/sites/default/files/Stats2015.pdf.

Anderson, Kristin L. 1997. "Gender, Status, and Domestic Violence: An Integration of Feminist and Family Violence Approaches." *Journal of Marriage and Family* 59(3):655–669. doi:10.2307/353952.

———. 2010. "Conflict, Power, and Violence in Families." *Journal of Marriage and Family* 72(3):726–742. doi:10.1111/j.1741-3737.2010.00727.x.

Anderson, N., and S. Clement. 2015. Poll shows that 20 percent of women are sexually assaulted in college. *Washington Post* June 12. http://www.washingtonpost.com/sf/local/2015/06/12/1-in-5-women-say-they-were-violated/.

Anderson, Sarah E., and Robert C. Whitaker. 2010. "Household Routines and Obesity in U.S. Preschool-Aged Children." *Pediatrics* 125(3):420–428.

Angel, Jacqueline L. 2008. *Inheritance in Contemporary America: The Social Dimensions of Giving across Generations.* Baltimore, MD: Johns Hopkins University Press.

Ansari, Aziz, and Eric Klinenberg. 2016. *Modern Romance.* Penguin Books.

Applebome, Peter. 2012. "Reveling in Her Supreme Court Moment." *New York Times*, December 11, p. A24.

Arbuckle, Justin, Lenora Olson, Mike Howard, Judith Brillman, Carolyn Anctil, and David Sklar. 1996. "Safe at Home? Domestic Violence and Other Homicides among Women in New Mexico." *Annals of Emergency Medicine* 27(2):210–215.

Arias, E. 2015. United States Life Tables, 2011. *National Vital Statistics Reports* 64(11). Hyattsville, MD: National Center for Health Statistics.

Ariès, Philippe. 1962. *Centuries of Childhood: A Social History of Family Life.* Vintage Books.

Armstrong, Elizabeth A., and Suzanna M. Crage. 2006. "Movements and Memory: The Making of the Stonewall Myth." *American Sociological Review* 71(5):724–751.

Armstrong, Elizabeth A., Paula England, and Alison C. K. Fogarty. 2010. "Orgasm in College Hookups and Relationships." In *Families as They Really Are*, edited by B. J. Risman, pp. 362–377. New York: W.W. Norton.

Armstrong, Elizabeth A., Laura Hamilton, and Brian Sweeney. 2006. "Sexual Assault on Campus: A Multilevel, Integrative Approach to Party Rape." *Social Problems* 53(4):483–499.

Associated Press. 2015. "Obama on Same-Sex Marriage Ruling." *New York Times*, June 26. http://www.nytimes.com/video/us/politics/100000003766147/obama-on-same-sex-marriage-ruling.html. Accessed June 27, 2015.

———. 2017. "Transcript: Donald Trump's News Conference at White House." *New York Times*, February 17. https://www.nytimes.com/aponline/2017/02/17/us/ap-us-trump-transcript.html.

Atkins, David C., and Deborah E. Kessel. 2008. "Religiousness and Infidelity: Attendance, but Not Faith and Prayer, Predict Marital Fidelity." *Journal of Marriage and Family* 70(2):407–418.

Augustine, Jennifer March, Timothy Nelson, and Kathryn Edin. 2009. "Why Do Poor Men Have Children? Fertility Intentions among Low-Income Unmarried U.S. Fathers." *The Annals of the American Academy of Political and Social Science* 624(1):99–117. doi:10.1177/0002716209334694.

Avellar, Sarah, and Pamela J. Smock. 2005. "The Economic Consequences of the Dissolution of Cohabiting Unions." *Journal of Marriage and Family* 67(2):315–327.

Avenilla, Frank, Emily Rosenthal, and Pete Tice. 2006. *Fathers of U.S. Children Born in 2001: Findings from the Early Childhood Longitudinal Study, Birth Cohort.* Washington, DC: U.S. Department of Education, National Center for Education Statistics.

Aykan, Hakan. 2003. "Effect of Childlessness on Nursing Home and Home Health Care Use." *Journal of Aging and Social Policy* 15(1):33–53.

Baca Zinn, Maxine. 2000. "Feminism and Family Studies for a New Century." *Annals of the American Academy of Political and Social Science* 571(September):42–56.

Baca Zinn, Maxine, and Angela Y. H. Pok. 2002. "Tradition and Transition in Mexican-Origin Families." In *Minority Families in the United States: A Multicultural Perspective*, edited by R. L. Taylor, pp. 79–100. Upper Saddle River, NJ: Prentice Hall.

Baca Zinn, Maxine, and Barbara Wells. 2000. "Diversity within Latino Families: New Lessons for Family Social Science." In *Handbook of Family Diversity*, edited by David H. Demo, Katherine R. Allen, and Mark A. Fine, pp. 252–273. New York: Oxford University Press.

Badenes-Ribera, L., A. Bonilla-Campos, D. Frias-Navarro, G. Pons-Salvador, and H. Monterde-i-Bort. 2016. "Intimate Partner Violence in Self-Identified Lesbians: A Systematic Review of Its Prevalence and Correlates." *Trauma Violence & Abuse* 17(3): 284–297. https://doi.org/10.1177/1524838015584363.

Bagemihl, Bruce. 1999. *Biological Exuberance: Animal Homosexuality and Natural Diversity.* New York: St. Martin's Press.

Bailey, Beth L. 1988. *From Front Porch to Back Seat: Courtship in Twentieth-Century America.* Baltimore, MD: Johns Hopkins University Press.

Baker, Regina S. 2015. "The Changing Association among Marriage, Work, and Child Poverty in the United States, 1974–2010." *Journal of Marriage and Family* 77:1166–78.

Bankrate. 2016. "2016 Presidential Candidates: Their Kids' Net Worth." *http://www.bankrate.com/finance/savings/presidential-candidates-kids-net-worth-2.aspx*.

Banton, Michael. 1998. *Racial Theories*. Cambridge, UK: Cambridge University Press.

Barber, Nigel. 1995. "The Evolutionary Psychology of Physical Attractiveness: Sexual Selection and Human Morphology." *Ethology and Sociobiology* 16(5):395–424.

Bardasi, Elena, and Mark Taylor. 2008. "Marriage and Wages: A Test of the Specialization Hypothesis." *Economica* 75(299):569–591.

Barnes, Medora W. 2013. "Having a First versus a Second Child: Comparing Women's Maternity Leave Choices and Concerns." *Journal of Family Issues* 34(1):85–112. doi:10.1177/0192513X12440089.

Barth, S. K., R. E. Kimerling, J. Pavao, S. J., McCutcheon, S. V. Batten, E. Dursa, and A. I. Schneiderman. 2016. "Military Sexual Trauma Among Recent Veterans." *American Journal of Preventive Medicine* 50(1): 77–86.

Batalova, Jeanne A., and Philip N. Cohen. 2002. "Premarital Cohabitation and Housework: Couples in Cross-National Perspective." *Journal of Marriage and Family* 64(3):743–755.

Bauer, Greta R., and Jennifer A. Jairam. 2008. "Are Lesbians Really Women Who Have Sex with Women (WSW)? Methodological Concerns in Measuring Sexual Orientation in Health Research." *Women and Health* 48(4):383–408.

Baum, Charles L., II. 2002. "A Dynamic Analysis of the Effect of Child Care Costs on the Work Decisions of Low-Income Mothers with Infants." *Demography* 39(1):139–164.

Baum, Charles L., and Christopher J. Ruhm. 2016. "The Effects of Paid Family Leave in California on Labor Market Outcomes." *Journal of Policy Analysis and Management* 35(2):333–U135. doi:10.1002/pam.21894.

Baumeister, Roy F. 1986. *Identity: Cultural Change and the Struggle for Self*. New York: Oxford University Press.

Baumle, Amanda K., and D'Lane R. Compton. 2017. "Love Wins?" *Contexts* 16(1):30–35. doi:10.1177/1536504217696061.

Baxter, Janeen, Belinda Hewitt, and Michele Haynes. 2008. "Life Course Transitions and Housework: Marriage, Parenthood, and Time on Housework." *Journal of Marriage and Family* 70(2):259–272.

Bayer, Ronald. 1981. *Homosexuality and American Psychiatry: The Politics of Diagnosis*. Princeton, NJ: Princeton University Press.

Bean, Frank D., and Marta Tienda. 1987. *The Hispanic Population of the United States*. New York: Russell Sage Foundation.

Bearman, Peter S., and Hannah Brückner. 2002. "Opposite-Sex Twins and Adolescent Same-Sex Attraction." *American Journal of Sociology* 107(5):1179–1205.

Beatie, Thomas. 2008. *Labor of Love: The Story of One Man's Extraordinary Pregnancy*. Berkeley, CA: Seal Press.

Beatty, Barbara, Emily D. Cahan, and Julia Grant. 2006. *When Science Encounters the Child: Education, Parenting, and Child Welfare in 20th-Century America*. New York: Teachers College Press.

Beck, Ulrich, and Christoph Lau. 2005. "Second Modernity as a Research Agenda: Theoretical and Empirical Explorations in the 'Meta-Change' of Modern Society." *British Journal of Sociology* 56(4):525–557.

Beck, Ulrich, and Elisabeth Beck-Gernsheim. 2004. "Families in a Runaway World." In *The Blackwell Companion to the Sociology of Families*, edited by Jacqueline Scott, Judith Treas, and Martin Richards, pp. 499–514. Malden, MA: Blackwell.

Becker, Gary S. 1973. "A Theory of Marriage: Part I." *The Journal of Political Economy* 81(4): 813–846.

——. 1981. *A Treatise on the Family*. Cambridge, MA: Harvard University Press.

Beckett, Megan K., Marc N. Elliott, Steven Martino, David E. Kanouse, Rosalie Corona, David J. Klein, and Mark A. Schuster. 2010. "Timing of Parent and Child Communication about Sexuality Relative to Children's Sexual Behaviors." *Pediatrics* 125(1):34–42. doi:10.1542/peds.2009-0806.

Beecher, Catharine E., and Harriet B. Stowe. 1869. *The American Woman's Home: Or, Principles of Domestic Science; being a Guide to the Formation and Maintenance of Economical, Healthful, Beautiful, and Christian Homes*. New York: J. B. Ford.

Beller, Emily, and Michael Hout. 2006. "Intergenerational Social Mobility: The United States in Comparative Perspective." *Future of Children* 16(2):19–36.

Belluck, Pam. 2016. "W.H.O. Weighs Dropping Transgender Identity From List of Mental Disorders." *The New York Times*, July 26, 2016. http://www.nytimes.com/2016/07/27/health/who-transgender-medical-disorder.html.

Ben-Shalom, Yonatan, Robert A. Moffitt, and John Karl Scholz. 2011. "An Assessment of the Effectiveness of Anti-Poverty Programs in the United States." National Bureau of Economic Research Working Paper No. 17042. http://nber.org/papers/w17042.pdf. Accessed September 2, 2013.

Bengtson, Vern L. 2001. "Beyond the Nuclear Family: The Increasing Importance of Multigenerational Bonds." *Journal of Marriage and Family* 63(1):1–16.

——. 2017. *Families and Faith: How Religion Is Passed Down Across Generations*. New York: Oxford University Press.

Bengtson, Vern L., Timothy J. Biblarz, and Robert E. L. Roberts. 2002. *How Families Still Matter: A Longitudinal Study of Youth in Two Generations*. Cambridge, UK: Cambridge University Press.

Berg, Kate, Vence Bonham, Joy Boyer, Larry Brody, Lisa Brooks, Francis Collins, Alan Guttmacher, Jean McEwen, Max Muenke, Steve Olson, Vivian O. Wang, Laura L. Rodriguez, Nadarajen Vydelingum, Esther Warshauer-Baker, and Race Ethnicity Genetics Working. 2005. "The Use of Racial, Ethnic, and Ancestral Categories in Human Genetics Research." *American Journal of Human Genetics* 77(4):519–532.

Berge, Jerica M., Tai J. Mendenhall, Gretchen M. Wrobel, Harold D. Grotevant, and Ruth G. McRoy. 2006. "Adolescents' Feelings about Openness in Adoption: Implications for Adoption Agencies." *Child Welfare* 85(6):1011–1039.

Berlet, Chip, and Matthew N. Lyons. 2000. *Right-Wing Populism in America: Too Close for Comfort*. New York: Guilford Press.

Bernard, Jessie. 1982. *The Future of Marriage*. New Haven, CT: Yale University Press.

Bernstein, Jacob. 2015. "For Some in Transgender Community, It's Never Too Late to Make a Change." *The New York Times*, March 6. http://www.nytimes.com/2015/03/08/fashion/for-some-in-transgender-community-its-never-too-late-to-make-a-change.html.

Berry, John W. 1997. "Immigration, Acculturation, and Adaptation." *Applied Psychology: An International Review* 46(1):5–34.

Bertrand, Marianne, Claudia Goldin, and Lawrence F. Katz. 2010. "Dynamics of the Gender Gap for Young Professionals in the Financial and Corporate Sectors." *American Economic Journal: Applied Economics* 2(3):228–255.

Bianchi, Suzanne M. 1995. "Changing Economic Roles of Women and Men." Pp. 107–154 in Reynolds Farley, ed., *State of the Union: America in the 1990s, Vol. I*. New York: Russell Sage Foundation.

———. 2000. "Maternal Employment and Time with Children: Dramatic Change or Surprising Continuity?" *Demography* 37(4):401–414.

———. 2011. "Family Change and Time Allocation in American Families." *Annals of the American Academy of Political and Social Science* 638:21–44.

Bianchi, Suzanne, Philip N. Cohen, Sara Raley, and Kei Nomaguchi. 2004. "Inequality in Parental Investment in Child-Rearing: Expenditures, Time, and Health." In *Social Inequality*, edited by K. M. Neckerman, pp. 189–219. New York: Russell Sage Foundation.

Bianchi, Suzanne M., John P. Robinson, and Melissa A. Milkie. 2006. *Changing Rhythms of American Family Life*. New York: Russell Sage Foundation.

Bianchi, Suzanne M., Liana C. Sayer, Melissa A. Milkie, and John P. Robinson. 2012. "Housework: Who Did, Does, or Will Do It and How Much Does It Matter?" *Social Forces* 91(1):55–63.

Biblarz, Timothy J., and Evren Savci. 2010. "Lesbian, Gay, Bisexual, and Transgender Families." *Journal of Marriage and Family* 72(3):480–497.

Biblarz, Timothy J., and Judith Stacey. 2010. "How Does the Gender of Parents Matter?" *Journal of Marriage and Family* 72(1):3–22.

Billingsley, Andrew. 1992. *Climbing Jacob's Ladder: The Enduring Legacy of African-American Families*. New York: Simon and Schuster.

Bittman, Michael, Paula England, Liana Sayer, Nancy Folbre, and George Matheson. 2003. "When Does Gender Trump Money? Bargaining and Time in Household Work." *American Journal of Sociology* 109(1):186–214.

Bittman, Michael, James M. Rice, and Judy Wajcman. 2004. "Appliances and Their Impact: The Ownership of Domestic Technology and Time Spent on Household Work." *British Journal of Sociology* 55(3):401–423.

Black, Michele C., Kathleen C. Basile, Matthew J. Breiding, Sharon G. Smith, Mike L. Walters, Melissa T. Merrick, Jieru Chen, and Mark R. Stevens. 2011. *The National Intimate Partner and Sexual Violence Survey (NISVS): 2010 Summary Report*. National Center for Injury Prevention and Control, Centers for Disease Control and Prevention. http://www.cdc.gov/violenceprevention/pdf/nisvs_report2010-a.pdf. Accessed October 24, 2013.

Blackwell, Debra L., and Daniel T. Lichter. 2000. "Mate Selection among Married and Cohabiting Couples." *Journal of Family Issues* 21(3):275–302.

Blanchard, Ray, and Doug P. VanderLaan. 2015. "Commentary on Kishida and Rahman (2015), Including a Meta-Analysis of Relevant Studies on Fraternal Birth Order and Sex-ual Orientation in Men." *Archives of Sexual Behavior* 44 (5): 1503–9. doi:10.1007/s10508-015-0555-8.

Blanchfield, Louisa. 2013. "The United Nations Convention on the Rights of the Child." Congressional Research Service. http://www.fas.org/sgp/crs/misc/R40484.pdf. Accessed October 25, 2013.

Bluestone, Barry, and Bennett Harrison. 1982. *The Deindustrialization of America: Plant Closings, Community Abandonment, and the Dismantling of Basic Industries*. New York: Basic Books.

Blum, Linda M. 2015. *Raising Generation Rx: Mothering Kids with Invisible Disabilities in an Age of Inequality*. New York: NYU Press.

Blume, Libby Balter, and Thomas W. Blume. 2003. "Toward a Dialectical Model of Family Gender Discourse: Body, Identity, and Sexuality." *Journal of Marriage and Family* 65(4):785-794.

Boba, R., and D. Lilley. 2009. "Violence Against Women Act (VAWA) Funding A Nationwide Assessment of Effects on Rape and Assault." *Violence Against Women* 15(2): 168-85. https://doi.org/10.1177/1077801208329146.

Bogle, Kathleen A. 2008. *Hooking Up: Sex, Dating, and Relationships on Campus.* New York: New York University Press.

Bongaarts, John. 2015. "Global Fertility and Population Trends." *Seminars in Reproductive Medicine* 33(01):005-010. doi:10.1055/s-0034-1395272.

Bonilla-Silva, Eduardo. 2013. *Racism without Racists: Color-Blind Racism and the Persistence of Racial Inequality in America.* 4th ed. Lanham: Rowman & Littlefield Publishers.

Boone, Jon. 2010. "Afghan Feminists Fighting from under the Burqa." *Guardian.* April 30.

Bourdieu, Pierre. 1986. "The Forms of Capital." In *Handbook of Theory and Research for the Sociology of Education,* edited by J. G. Richardson, pp. 46-58. New York: Greenwood Press.

Boushey, Heather. 2016. *Finding Time: The Economics of Work-Life Conflict.* Cambridge, MA: Harvard University Press.

Bowden, Sue, and Avner Offer. 1994. "Household Appliances and the Use of Time: The United States and Britain since the 1920s." *The Economic History Review* 47(4):725-748.

Bozick, Robert, and Angela Estacion. 2014. "Do Student Loans Delay Marriage? Debt Repayment and Family Formation in Young Adulthood." *Demographic Research* 30(69):1865-91. doi:10.4054/DemRes.2014.30.69.

Brady, Sonya S., and Bonnie L. Halpern-Felsher. 2007. "Adolescents' Reported Consequences of Having Oral Sex versus Vaginal Sex." *Pediatrics* 119(2):229-236.

Braithwaite, Dawn O., Loreen N. Olson, Tamara D. Golish, Charles Soukup, and Paul Turman. 2001. "'Becoming a Family': Developmental Processes Represented in Blended Family Discourse." *Journal of Applied Communication Research* 29(3):221-247.

Brecher, Edward M., and Jeremy Brecher. 1986. "Extracting Valid Sexological Findings from Severely Flawed and Biased Population Samples." *The Journal of Sex Research* 22(1, Methodology in Sex Research):6-20.

Breen, Richard. 2010. "Educational Expansion and Social Mobility in the 20th Century." *Social Forces* 89(2):365-388.

Brettell, Rachel, Peter S. Yeh, and Lawrence W. M. Impey. 2008. "Examination of the Association between Male Gender and Preterm Delivery." *European Journal of Obstetrics Gynecology and Reproductive Biology* 141(2):123-126.

Bridgman, Benjamin, Andrew Dugan, Mikhael Lal, Matthew Osborne, and Shaunda Villones. 2012. "Accounting for Household Production in the National Accounts, 1965-2010." *Survey of Current Business* 92(5):23-36.

Brody, Leslie. 1999. *Gender, Emotion, and the Family.* Cambridge, MA: Harvard University Press.

Brodzinsky, David M., and Abbie E. Goldberg. 2016. "Contact with Birth Family in Adoptive Families Headed by Lesbian, Gay Male, and Heterosexual Parents." *Children and Youth Services Review* 62 (March):9-17. doi:10.1016/j.childyouth.2016.01.014.

Broidy, L., D. Albright, and K. Denman. 2016. "Deterring Future Incidents of Intimate Partner Violence: Does Type of Formal Intervention Matter?" *Violence Against Women* 22(9):1113-1133. https://doi.org/10.1177/1077801215617552.

Broman, Clifford L. 2005. "Marital Quality in Black and White Marriages." *Journal of Family Issues* 26(4):431-441.

Brotto, Lori A., Johannes Bitzer, Ellen Laan, Sandra Leiblum, and Mijal Luria. 2010. "Women's Sexual Desire and Arousal Disorders." *Journal of Sexual Medicine* 7(1):586-614. doi:10.1111/j.1743-6109.2009.01630.x.

Brotto, Lori A., and Morag Yule. 2016, August. "Asexuality: Sexual Orientation, Paraphilia, Sexual Dysfunction, or None of the Above?" *Archives of Sexual Behavior* 46(3):1-9. doi:10.1007/s10508-016-0802-7.

Broussard, Danielle L., William M. Sappenfield, and David A. Goodman. 2012. "The Black and White of Infant Back Sleeping and Infant Bed Sharing in Florida, 2004-2005." *Maternal and Child Health Journal* 16(3):713-24. doi:10.1007/s10995-011-0768-y.

Brown, Patricia L. 2009. "Invisible Immigrants, Old and Left with 'Nobody to Talk To'." *New York Times*, August 30.

Brown, Stephen L., Brandye D. Nobiling, James Teufel, and David A. Birch. 2011. "Are Kids Too Busy? Early Adolescents' Perceptions of Discretionary Activities, Overscheduling, and Stress." *Journal of School Health* 81(9):574-580.

Brown, Susan L. 2000. "Fertility Following Marital Dissolution: The Role of Cohabitation." *Journal of Family Issues* 21(4):501-524.

———. 2006. "Family Structure Transitions and Adolescent Well-Being." *Demography* 43(3):447-461.

Brown, Susan L., and Sayaka Kawamura. 2010. "Relationship Quality among Cohabitors and Marrieds in Older Adulthood." *Social Science Research* 39(5):777-786.

Brown, Susan L., and I.-Fen Lin. 2012. "The Gray Divorce Revolution: Rising Divorce Among Middle-Aged and Older Adults, 1990-2010." *The Journals of Gerontology: Series B* 67(6):731-41. doi:10.1093/geronb/gbs089.

Brown, Susan L., and Wendy D. Manning. 2009. "Family Boundary Ambiguity and the Measurement of Family Structure: The Significance of Cohabitation." *Demography* 46(1):85-101.

Brown, Susan L., J. Bart Stykes, and Wendy D. Manning. 2016. "Trends in Children's Family Instability, 1995–2010." *Journal of Marriage and Family* 78(5):1173–83. doi:10.1111/jomf.12311.

Bruni, Frank. 2009. "A Sapphic Victory, but Pyrrhic." *New York Times*, November 15, Week in Review. http://www.nytimes.com/2009/11/15/weekinreview/15bruni.html. Accessed June 18, 2014.

Brunsma, David L. 2005. "Interracial Families and the Racial Identification of Mixed-Race Children: Evidence from the Early Childhood Longitudinal Study." *Social Forces* 84(2):1129–1155.

Bruun, Hans H. 2007. *Science, Values, and Politics in Max Weber's Methodology*. Aldershot, UK: Ashgate.

Budig, Michelle J., and Paula England. 2001. "The Wage Penalty for Motherhood." *American Sociological Review* 66(2):204–225.

Bulanda, Jennifer R., and Susan L. Brown. 2007. "Race-Ethnic Differences in Marital Quality and Divorce." *Social Science Research* 36(3):945–967.

Burdette, Amy M., Christopher G. Ellison, Terrence D. Hill, and Norval D. Glenn. 2009. "'Hooking Up' at College: Does Religion Make a Difference?" *Journal for the Scientific Study of Religion* 48(3):535–551.

Bureau of Consular Affairs. 2014. "Understanding the Hague Convention." Washington, DC: U.S. Department of State. https://travel.state.gov/content/adoptionsabroad/en/hague-convention/understanding-the-hague-convention.html. Accessed March 22, 2017.

Burgess, E. W. 1963. *The Family: From Institution to Companionship*. New York: American Book Co.

Burton, Linda M., and M. B. Tucker. 2009. "Romantic Unions in an Era of Uncertainty: A Post-Moynihan Perspective on African American Women and Marriage." *The Annals of the American Academy of Political and Social Science* 621:132–148.

Bush, Andrew S. 2004. *TANF Information Memorandum (TANF-ACF-IM-2004-02)*. Washington, DC: U.S. Department of Health and Human Services.

Bushman, Richard L., and Claudia L. Bushman. 1988. "The Early History of Cleanliness in America." *Journal of American History* 74(4):1213–1238.

Byers, E. S. 2005. "Relationship Satisfaction and Sexual Satisfaction: A Longitudinal Study of Individuals in Long-Term Relationships." *Journal of Sex Research* 42(2):113–18.

Calmes, Jackie, and Peter Baker. 2012. "Obama Endorses Same-Sex Marriage, Taking Stand on Charged Social Issue." *New York Times,* May 10, p. A1.

Cancian, Francesca M. 1987. *Love in America: Gender and Self-Development*. New York: Cambridge University Press.

Cancian, M., D. R. Meyer, P. R. Brown, and S. T. Cook. 2014. "Who Gets Custody Now? Dramatic Changes in Children's Living Arrangements After Divorce." *Demography* 51(4):1381–96. doi:10.1007/s13524-014-0307-8.

Cannadine, David. 2013. *The Undivided Past: Humanity Beyond Our Differences*. New York: Random House.

Card, Claudia. 1996. "Against Marriage and Motherhood." *Hypatia* 11(3):1–23.

Carlson, M. J. 2006. "Family Structure, Father Involvement, and Adolescent Behavioral Outcomes." *Journal of Marriage and Family* 68(1):137–54. doi:10.1111/j.1741-3737.2006.00239.x.

Carlson, Marcia J., and Katherine A. Magnuson. 2011. "Low-Income Fathers' Influence on Children." *Annals of the American Academy of Political and Social Science* 635:95–116.

Carpenter, Christopher, and Gary J. Gates. 2008. "Gay and Lesbian Partnership: Evidence from California." *Demography* 45(3):573–590.

Carr, Deborah, and Sara M. Moorman. 2011. "Social Relations and Aging." In *Handbook of Sociology of Aging*, edited by R. A. Settersten and J. L. Angel, 145–60. New York: Springer.

Carrasquillo, Hector. 2002. "The Puerto Rican Family." In *Minority Families in the United States: A Multicultural Perspective*, edited by R. L. Taylor, pp. 101–113. Upper Saddle River, NJ: Prentice Hall.

Carroll, Jason S., Chad D. Olson, and Nicolle Buckmiller. 2007. "Family Boundary Ambiguity: A 30-Year Review of Theory, Research, and Measurement." *Family Relations* 56(2):210–230.

Carroll, Matt. 2002. "State Action on Priest Fell Short, DYS Team Says." *Boston Globe*, March 25.

Carter, Susan B., Scott Sigmund Gartner, Michael R. Haines, Alan L. Olmstead, Richard Sutch, and Gavin Wright (eds). 2006. *Historical Statistics of the United States, Earliest Times to the Present: Millennial Edition*. New York: Cambridge University Press.

Casper, Lynne M., and Philip N. Cohen. 2000. "How Does POSSLQ Measure Up? Historical Estimates of Cohabitation." *Demography* 37(2):237–45.

Catalano, Shannan. 2012. *Intimate Partner Violence, 1993–2010*. Washington, DC: Bureau of Justice Statistics.

Cataldi, Emily F., Jennifer Laird, and Angelina KewalRamani. 2009. *High School Dropout and Completion Rates in the United States: 2007*. Washington, DC: National Center for Education Statistics, U.S. Department of Education.

Caulfield, Mina D. 1985. "Sexuality in Human Evolution: What Is 'Natural' in Sex?" *Feminist Studies* 11(2):343–363.

Centers for Disease Control and Prevention. 2013. "Strategies to Prevent Obesity and Other Chronic Diseases." Atlanta: U.S. Department of Health and Human Services.

———. 2016a. "NSFG—About the National Survey of Family Growth." https://www.cdc.gov/nchs/nsfg/about_nsfg.htm.

_____. 2016b. "Trends in the Prevalence of Sexual Behaviors and HIV Testing National YRBS: 1991–2015." https://www.cdc.gov/healthyyouth/data/yrbs/pdf/trends/2015_us_sexual_trend_yrbs.pdf. Accessed January 11, 2017.

_____. 2016c. "HIV Surveillance Report, 2015." Vol. 27. http://www.cdc.gov/hiv/library/reports/hiv-surveillance.html.

_____. 2016d. Compressed Mortality File 1999-2015, Series 20 No. 2U. Accessed March 23, 2017. http://wonder.cdc.gov/cmf-icd10.html.

_____. 2016e. National Immunization Surveys. Table at https://www.cdc.gov/breastfeeding/data/nis_data/rates-any-exclusive-bf-socio-dem-2013.htm. Accessed March 20, 2017.

Cesar, Mary-Lynn. 2016. "Of Love and Money: The Rise of the Online Dating Industry." NASDAQ.com, February 13. http://www.nasdaq.com/article/of-love-and-money-the-rise-of-the-online-dating-industry-cm579616.

Cha, Youngjoo. 2010. "Reinforcing Separate Spheres." American Sociological Review 75(2):303–329.

Chambers, Alan. 2013. "I Am Sorry." Orlando, FL: Exodus International. http://exodusinternational.org/2013/06/i-am-sorry/. Accessed August 16, 2013.

Chang, Doris F., Biing-Jiun Shen, and David T. Takeuchi. 2009. "Prevalence and Demographic Correlates of Intimate Partner Violence in Asian Americans." International Journal of Law and Psychiatry 32(3):167–175.

Chao, Ruth K. 1995. "Chinese and European American Cultural Models of the Self Reflected in Mothers' Childrearing Beliefs." Ethos 23(3):328–354.

Chao, Ruth, and Vivian Tseng. 2002. "Parenting of Asians." In Handbook of Parenting: Vol. 4. Social Conditions and Applied Parenting (2nd ed.), edited by M. H. Bornstein, pp. 59–93. Mahwah, NJ: Lawrence Erlbaum.

Chemerinsky, Erwin. 2015. "Symposium: A Landmark Victory for Civil Rights." SCOTUSblog. http://www.scotusblog.com/2015/06/symposium-a-landmark-victory-for-civil-rights/. Accessed June 27, 2015.

Cheng, Siwei. 2016. "The Accumulation of (Dis)advantage: The Intersection of Gender and Race in the Long-Term Wage Effect of Marriage." American Sociological Review 81:29–56.

Cherlin, Andrew J. 2004. "The Deinstitutionalization of American Marriage." Journal of Marriage and Family 66(4):848–861.

_____. 2005. "American Marriage in the Early Twenty-First Century." The Future of Children 15(2, Marriage and Child Wellbeing):33–55.

_____. 2009. The Marriage-Go-Round: The State of Marriage and the Family in America Today. New York: Alfred A. Knopf.

_____. 2010. "Demographic Trends in the United States: A Review of Research in the 2000s." Journal of Marriage and Family 72(3):403–419.

Cherlin, Andrew J., Linda M. Burton, Tera R. Hurt, and Diane M. Purvin. 2004. "The Influence of Physical and Sexual Abuse on Marriage and Cohabitation." American Sociological Review 69(6):768–789.

Cherlin, Andrew J., and Frank F. Furstenberg. 1986. The New American Grandparent: A Place in the Family, a Life Apart. New York: Basic Books.

Chesley, Noelle. 2011. "Stay-at-Home Fathers and Breadwinning Mothers: Gender, Couple Dynamics, and Social Change." Gender and Society 25(5):642–664.

Chetty, Raj, and Nathaniel Hendren. 2016. "The Equality of Opportunity Project." http://www.equality-of-opportunity.org/. Accessed December 9, 2016.

Chetty, Raj, Nathaniel Hendren, Patrick Kline, and Emmanuel Saez. 2014. "Where Is the Land of Opportunity? The Geography of Intergenerational Mobility in the United States." Working Paper 19843. National Bureau of Economic Research. http://www.nber.org/papers/w19843.

Chew, Kenneth S. Y., and John M. Liu. 2004. "Hidden in Plain Sight: Global Labor Force Exchange in the Chinese American Population, 1880–1940." Population and Development Review 30(1):57–78.

Chodorow, Nancy. 1978. The Reproduction of Mothering: Psychoanalysis and the Sociology of Gender. Berkeley, CA: University of California Press.

Choi, Jeong-Kyun, Robert J. Palmer, and Ho-Soon Pyun. 2014. "Three Measures of Non-Resident Fathers' Involvement, Maternal Parenting and Child Development in Low-Income Single-Mother Families." Child & Family Social Work 19(3):282–91. doi:10.1111/cfs.12000.

Chokshi, N. 2016. "After Stanford Case, California Governor Signs Bill Toughening Penalties for Sexual Assault." New York Times, September 30. https://www.nytimes.com/2016/10/01/us/sentencing-law-california-stanford-case.html.

Christopher, Karen. 2002. "Welfare State Regimes and Mothers' Poverty." Social Politics: International Studies in Gender, State, and Society 9(1):60–86.

Chua, Amy. 2011. Battle Hymn of the Tiger Mother. New York: Penguin Press.

Cissner, A. B., M. Labriola, and M. Rempel. 2015. "Domestic Violence Courts: A Multisite Test of Whether and How They Change Offender Outcomes." Violence Against Women 21(9):1102–1122. https://doi.org/10.1177/1077801215589231.

Civettini, Nicole. 2016. "Housework as Non-Normative Gender Display Among Lesbians and Gay Men." Sex Roles 74(5–6):206–19. doi:10.1007/s11199-015-0559-9.

Clark-Stewart, K. and Alison. 1978. "Popular Primers for Parents." *American Psychologist* 33(4):359–69. doi:10.1037/0003-066X.33.4.359.

Cleveland, David A. 1991. "Migration in West Africa: A Savanna Village Perspective." *Africa: Journal of the International African Institute* 61(2):222–246.

Clymer, Adam. 1993. "Congress Passes Measure Providing Emergency Leaves." *New York Times*, February 5, p. A1.

CNN. 2008a. "Busy Moms Staying Afloat." http://edition.cnn.com/SPECIALS/2008/busy.moms/. Accessed January 6, 2014.

———. 2008b. "Lou Dobbs Tonight." June 6, 2008. http://transcripts.cnn.com/TRANSCRIPTS/0806/06/ldt.01.html. Accessed November 6, 2013.

Coakley, Timothy W. 1906. *The American Race: Its Origin, Fusion of Peoples; Its Aim, Fraternity.* Boston, MA: Municipal Printing Office.

Cocks, H. G. 2006. "Modernity and the Self in the History of Sexuality." *Historical Journal* 49(4):1211–1227.

Cohen, Philip N. 1998. "Replacing Housework in the Service Economy: Gender, Class, and Race-Ethnicity in Service Spending." *Gender and Society* 12(2):219–231.

———. 2002. "Extended Households at Work: Living Arrangements and Inequality in Single Mothers' Employment." *Sociological Forum* 17(3):445–463.

———. 2004. "The Gender Division of Labor: 'Keeping House' and Occupational Segregation in the United States." *Gender and Society* 18(2):239–252.

———. 2007. "Confronting Economic Gender Inequality." *Review of Radical Political Economics* 39(1):132.

———. 2010a. "Parenting through the (Only Very Recent) Ages." Blog post. http://familyinequality.wordpress.com/2010/12/17/parenting-through-the-only-very-recent-ages/. Accessed October 30, 2013.

———. 2010b. *Scripting Diversity.* Workshop on Family Change, Institute of European and American Studies, Academia Sinica, Taipei.

———. 2011. "Homogamy Unmodified." *Journal of Family Theory and Review* 3(1):47–51. doi:10.1111/j.1756-2589.2010.00080.x.

———. 2012. "Do Asians in the U.S. Have High Incomes?" *Family Inequality.* http://familyinequality.wordpress.com/2012/06/25/do-asians-in-the-u-s-have-high-incomes/. Accessed January 6, 2014.

———. 2013a. "Children's Gender and Parents' Color Preferences." *Archives of Sexual Behavior* 42(3):393–397.

———.2013b. "The End of Men Is Not True: What Is Not and What Might Be on the Road toward Gender Equality." *Boston University Law Review* 93:1159.

———. 2013c. "The Persistence of Workplace Gender Segregation in the US." *Sociology Compass* 7(11):889–99. doi:10.1111/soc4.12083.

———. 2014a. "Divergent Responses to Family Inequality." Chapter 2 in *Families in an Era of Increasing Inequality: Diverging Destinies.* Eds. Paul Amato, Alan Booth, Susan McHale, and Jennifer Van Hook. New York: Springer.

———. 2014b. "Recession and Divorce in the United States, 2008–2011." *Population Research and Policy Review.* February 5, 2014. http://link.springer.com/article/10.1007/s11113-014-9323-z. Print edition forthcoming.

———. 2015. "How Troubling Is Our Inheritance? A Review of Genetics and Race in the Social Sciences." *The ANNALS of the American Academy of Political and Social Science* 661(1):65–84. doi:10.1177/0002716215587673.

———. 2016. "Multiple-Decrement Life Table Estimates of Divorce Rates." Open Science Framework. June 8. osf.io/zber3.

———.2018. *Enduring Bonds: Inequality, Marriage, Parenting, and Everything Else That Makes Families Great and Terrible.* Berkeley, CA: University of California Press.

Cohen, Philip N., and Suzanne M. Bianchi. 1999. "Marriage, Children, and Women's Employment: What Do We Know?" *Monthly Labor Review* 122(12):22–31.

Cohen, Philip N., and Lynne M. Casper. 2002. "In Whose Home? Multigenerational Families in the United States, 1998–2000." Sociological Perspectives 45(1):1–20.

Cohen, Philip N., and Matt L. Huffman. 2003. "Individuals, Jobs, and Labor Markets: The Devaluation of Women's Work." *American Sociological Review* 68(3):443–463. doi:10.2307/1519732.

Cohen, Philip N., and Miruna Petrescu-Prahova. 2006. "Gendered Living Arrangements among Children with Disabilities." Journal of Marriage and Family 68(3):630–638. doi:10.1111/j.1741-3737.2006.00279.x.

Cohn, D'Vera. 2016. "Federal Officials May Revamp How Americans Identify Race, Ethnicity on Census and Other Forms." Pew Research Center. October 4. *http://www.pewresearch.org/fact-tank/2016/10/04/federal-officials-may-revamp-how-americans-identify-race-ethnicity-on-census-and-other-forms/.*

Coleman, James S. 1988. "Social Capital in the Creation of Human Capital." *American Journal of Sociology* 94:S95–S120.

Coles, Roberta L. 2006. *Race and Family: A Structural Approach.* Thousand Oaks, CA: Sage.

———. 2015. "Single-Father Families: A Review of the Literature." *Journal of Family Theory & Review* 7(2):144–66. doi:10.1111/jftr.12069.

Coleman, Marilyn, Lawrence H. Ganong, Jason D. Hans, Elizabeth A. Sharp, and Tanja C. Rothrauff. 2005. "Filial

Obligations in Post-Divorce Stepfamilies." *Journal of Divorce and Remarriage* 43(3–4):1–27. doi:10.1300/J087v43n03_01.

Collins, Lauren. 2016. "The Model American." *New Yorker*, May 9. http://www.newyorker.com/magazine/2016/05/09/who-is-melania-trump.

Collins, Patricia H. 1994. "Shifting the Center: Race, Class and Feminist Theorizing about Motherhood." In *Mothering: Ideology, Experience, and Agency*, edited by E. N. Glenn, G. Chang, and L. R. Forcey, pp. 45–66. New York: Routledge.

Collins, Randall. 1975. *Conflict Sociology: Toward an Explanatory Science*. New York: Academic Press.

Collins, W. Andrew, Deborah R. Welsh, and Wyndol Furman. 2009. "Adolescent Romantic Relationships." *Annual Review of Psychology* 60:631–652.

Colson, Eve R., Denis Rybin, Lauren A. Smith, Theodore Colton, George Lister, and Michael J. Corwin. 2009. "Trends and Factors Associated with Infant Sleeping Position: The National Infant Sleep Position Study 1993–2007." *Archives of Pediatrics & Adolescent Medicine* 163 (12):1122–28. doi:10.1001/archpediatrics.2009.234.

Coltrane, Scott. 1996. *Family Man: Fatherhood, Housework, and Gender Equity*. New York: Oxford University Press.

Comfort, Alex. 1972. *The Joy of Sex: A Gourmet Guide to Lovemaking*. New York: Crown.

Common Sense Media. 2013. *Zero to Eight: Children's Media Use in America 2013*. http://www.commonsensemedia.org/file/zero-to-eight-2013pdf-0/download. Accessed December 8, 2016.

Condron, Dennis J. 2007. "Stratification and Educational Sorting: Explaining Ascriptive Inequalities in Early Childhood Reading Group Placement." *Social Problems* 54(1):139–160.

Congressional Budget Office. 2016. "The Distribution of Household Income and Federal Taxes, 2013." https://www.cbo.gov/publication/51361.

Conley, Dalton. 2009. *Elsewhere, U.S.A.* New York: Pantheon Books.

Connell, R. W., and James W. Messerschmidt. 2005. "Hegemonic Masculinity: Rethinking the Concept." *Gender and Society* 19(6):829–859.

Cooke, Lynn Prince, Jani Erola, Marie Evertsson, Michael Gahler, Juho Harkonen, Belinda Hewitt, Marika Jalovaara, et al. 2013. "Labor and Love: Wives' Employment and Divorce Risk in Its Socio-Political Context." *Social Politics* 20(4):482–509. doi:10.1093/sp/jxt016.

Coontz, Stephanie. 1992. *The Way We Never Were: American Families and the Nostalgia Trap*. New York: Basic Books.

———. 2000. "Historical Perspectives on Family Studies." *Journal of Marriage and Family* 62(2):283–297. doi:10.1111/j.1741-3737.2000.00283.x.

———. 2005. *Marriage, a History: From Obedience to Intimacy, or How Love Conquered Marriage*. New York: Viking.

———. 2007. "The Origins of Modern Divorce." *Family Process* 46(1):7–16.

———. 2010. "Why American Families Need the Census." *Annals of the American Academy of Political and Social Science* 631:141–149.

Coontz, Stephanie, and Nancy Folbre. 2010. "Briefing Paper: Marriage, Poverty, and Public Policy." In *Families as They Really Are*, edited by B. J. Risman, pp. 185–193. New York: W. W. Norton.

Cooper, Alexia, and Erica L. Smith. 2011. Homicide Trends in the United States, 1980–2008. NCJ 236018. Bureau of Justice Statistics. https://www.bjs.gov/content/pub/pdf/htus8008.pdf.

Cooper, Michael. 2012. "Election Result Proves a Victory for Pollsters and Other Data Devotees." *New York Times*, November 8, Section P, p. 8.

Copen C. E., and Chandra A. Febo-Vazquez. 2016. "Sexual Behavior, Sexual Attraction, and Sexual Orientation among Adults Aged 18–44 in the United States: Data from the 2011–2013 National Survey of Family Growth." National Health Statistics Reports, no. 88. Hyattsville, MD: National Center for Health Statistics. https://www.cdc.gov/nchs/data/nhsr/nhsr088.pdf.

Copp, Jennifer E., Peggy C. Giordano, Wendy D. Manning, and Monica A. Longmore. 2016. "Couple-Level Economic and Career Concerns and Intimate Partner Violence in Young Adulthood." *Journal of Marriage and Family* 78(3):744–58. doi:10.1111/jomf.12282.

Corra, Mamadi, Shannon K. Carter, J. S. Carter, and David Knox. 2009. "Trends in Marital Happiness by Gender and Race, 1973 to 2006." *Journal of Family Issues* 30(10):1379–1404.

Correll, Shelley J, Stephen Benard, and In Paik. 2007. "Getting a Job: Is There a Motherhood Penalty?" *The American Journal of Sociology* 112(5):1297–1339.

Cott, Nancy F. 1976. "Divorce and the Changing Status of Women in Eighteenth-Century Massachusetts." *The William and Mary Quarterly* 33(4):586–614.

———. 2000. *Public Vows: A History of Marriage and the Nation*. Cambridge, MA: Harvard University Press.

Cotter, David A., Joan M. Hermsen, and Reeve Vanneman. 2004. *Gender Inequality at Work*. New York: Russell Sage Foundation.

———. 2011. "The End of the Gender Revolution? Gender Role Attitudes from 1977 to 2008." *American Journal of Sociology* 117(1):259–289.

Cousineau, Tara M., and Alice D. Domar. 2007. "Psychological Impact of Infertility." *Best Practice and Research Clinical Obstetrics and Gynaecology* 21(2):293–308.

Cowan, Ruth S. 1976. "The 'Industrial Revolution' in the Home: Household Technology and Social Change in the 20th Century." *Technology and Culture* 17(1):1–23.

Craig, Lyn, and Janeen Baxter. 2016. "Domestic Outsourcing, Housework Shares and Subjective Time Pressure: Gender Differences in the Correlates of Hiring Help." *Social Indicators Research* 125(1):271–88. doi:10.1007/s11205-014-0833-1.

Craig, Lyn, and Killian Mullan. 2011. "How Mothers and Fathers Share Childcare: A Cross-National Time-Use Comparison." *American Sociological Review* 76(6):834–61. doi:10.1177/0003122411427673

Craig, Lyn, Francisco Perales, Sergi Vidal, and Janeen Baxter. 2016. "Domestic Outsourcing, Housework Time, and Subjective Time Pressure: New Insights from Longitudinal Data." *Journal of Marriage and Family* 78(5):1224–36. doi:10.1111/jomf.12321.

Crawford, Mary, and Danielle Popp. 2003. "Sexual Double Standards: A Review and Methodological Critique of Two Decades of Research." *Journal of Sex Research* 40(1):13–26.

Crenshaw, Kimberle. 1991. "Mapping the Margins: Intersectionality, Identity Politics, and Violence against Women of Color." *Stanford Law Review* 43(6):1241–1299.

Crimmins, Eileen M., Mark D. Hayward, Aaron Hagedorn, Yasuhiko Saito, and Nicolas Brouard. 2009. "Change in Disability-Free Life Expectancy for Americans 70 Years Old and Older." *Demography* 46(3):627–646.

Crissman, Halley P., Mitchell B. Berger, Louis F. Graham, and Vanessa K. Dalton. 2016. "Transgender Demographics: A Household Probability Sample of US Adults, 2014." *American Journal of Public Health*, December, e1–3. doi:10.2105/AJPH.2016.303571

Croft, Darren P., Rufus A. Johnstone, Samuel Ellis, Stuart Nattrass, Daniel W. Franks, Lauren J. N. Brent, Sonia Mazzi, Kenneth C. Balcomb, John K. B. Ford, and Michael A. Cant. 2017. "Reproductive Conflict and the Evolution of Menopause in Killer Whales." *Current Biology* (online first). doi:10.1016/j.cub.2016.12.015.

Crosnoe, Robert, and Shannon E. Cavanagh. 2010. "Families with Children and Adolescents: A Review, Critique, and Future Agenda." *Journal of Marriage and Family* 72(3):594–611.

Cross, Gary S. 2004. *The Cute and the Cool: Wondrous Innocence and Modern American Children's Culture.* New York: Oxford University Press.

Crowder, Kyle, and Scott J. South. 2003. "Neighborhood Distress and School Dropout: The Variable Significance of Community Context." *Social Science Research* 32(4):659–698.

Crowder, Kyle D., and Stewart E. Tolnay. 2000. "A New Marriage Squeeze for Black Women: The Role of Racial Intermarriage by Black Men." *Journal of Marriage and Family* 62(3):792–807.

Cruz, Julissa. 2013. "Marriage Rate in the U.S., 2011." National Center for Marriage and Family Research. http://ncfmr.bgsu.edu/pdf/family_profiles/file130942.pdf. Accessed September 14, 2013.

Cummings, Steven R., Xu Ling, and Katie Stone. 1997. "Consequences of Foot Binding among Older Women in Beijing, China." *American Journal of Public Health* 87(10):1677–1679.

Cunradi, Carol B., Raul Caetano, and John Schafer. 2002. "Socioeconomic Predictors of Intimate Partner Violence among White, Black, and Hispanic Couples in the United States." *Journal of Family Violence* 17(4):377–389. doi:10.1023/A:1020374617328.

Currie, Glenne. 1981. "Charles Is Taller." United Press International, June 11.

Cutler, David, and Grant Miller. 2005. "The Role of Public Health Improvements in Health Advances: The Twentieth-Century United States." Demography 42(1):1–22.

Cutright, Phillips, Michael Hout, and David R. Johnson. 1976. "Structural Determinants of Fertility in Latin America: 1800–1970." *American Sociological Review* 41(3):511–527.

Curran, Sara R., Sara McLanahan, and Jean Knab. 2003. "Does Remarriage Expand Perceptions of Kinship Support among the Elderly?" *Social Science Research* 32(2):171–190. doi:10.1016/S0049-089X(02)00046-7.

Currie, Janet, and Hannes Schwandt. 2014. "Short- and Long-Term Effects of Unemployment on Fertility." *Proceedings of the National Academy of Sciences* 111(41):14734–39. doi:10.1073/pnas.1408975111.

Dalla, Rochelle L., and Wendy C. Gamble. 1998. "Social Networks and Systems of Support among American Indian Navajo Adolescent Mothers." In *Resiliency in Native American and Immigrant Families*, edited by H. I. McCubbin, E. A. Thompson, A. I. Thompson, and J. E. Fromer, pp. 183–198. Thousand Oaks, CA: Sage.

Damaske, Sarah. 2011. *For the Family? How Class and Gender Shape Women's Work.* Cambridge UK: Oxford University Press.

Damaske, Sarah, and Adrianne Frech. 2016. "Women's Work Pathways Across the Life Course." *Demography* 53:365–91.

Daniels, Kimberly, William D. Mosher, and Jo Jones. 2013. "Contraceptive Methods Women Have Ever Used: United States, 1982–2010." *National Health Statistics Reports* 62. Hyattsville, MD: National Center for Health Statistics.

Danziger, Sandra K. 2010. "The Decline of Cash Welfare and Implications for Social Policy and Poverty." *Annual Review of Sociology* 36:523–530, C1–C3, 531–545.

Danziger, Sheldon, and David Ratner. 2010. "Labor Market Outcomes and the Transition to Adulthood." *Future of Children* 20(1):133–158.

Darroch, Jaqueline E., Susheela Singh, Jennifer J. Frost, and Study Team. 2001. "Differences in Teenage Pregnancy Rates among Five Developed Countries: The Roles of Sexual Activity and Contraceptive Use." *Family Planning Perspectives* 33(6):244–250, 281.

Davis, Georgiann. 2015. *Contesting Intersex: The Dubious Diagnosis.* New York: NYU Press.

Davis, Georgiann, Jodie M. Dewey, and Erin L. Murphy. 2016. "Giving Sex: Deconstructing Intersex and Trans Medicalization Practices." *Gender & Society* 30:490–514.

Davis, Kingsley, and Wilbert E. Moore. 1945. "Some Principles of Stratification." *American Sociological Review* 10(2):242–249.

Dawkins, Richard. 2006. *The Selfish Gene.* Oxford, UK: Oxford University Press.

"The Debate over Foreign Law in *Roper v. Simmons*." 2005. *Harvard Law Review* 119(1):103–108.

DeLamater, John. 2012. "Sexual Expression in Later Life: A Review and Synthesis." *The Journal of Sex Research* 49(2–3): 125–41. doi:10.1080/00224499.2011.603168.

DeMallie, Raymond J. 1994. "Kinship and Biology in Sioux Culture." In *North American Indian Anthropology: Essays on Society and Culture*, edited by Raymond J. DeMallie and Alfonso Ortiz, pp. 125–146. Norman, OK: University of Oklahoma Press.

DeMaris, Alfred, Annette Mahoney, and Kenneth I. Pargament. 2011. "Doing the Scut Work of Infant Care: Does Religiousness Encourage Father Involvement?" *Journal of Marriage and Family* 73(2):354–368. doi:10.1111/j.1741-3737.2010.00811.x.

Denton, Melinda L. 2004. "Gender and Marital Decision Making: Negotiating Religious Ideology and Practice." *Social Forces* 82(3):1151–1180.

Denton Flanagan, Kristin, and Cameron McPhee. 2009. *The Children Born in 2001 at Kindergarten Entry: First Findings from the Kindergarten Data Collections of the Early Childhood Longitudinal Study, Birth Cohort (ECLS-B).* Washington, DC: National Center for Education Statistics.

Desmond, Matthew. 2016a. *Evicted: Poverty and Profit in the American City.* New York: Crown.

———. 2016b. "Milwaukee Area Renters Study (MARS)." Harvard Dataverse, V3. doi:10.7910/DVN/BLUU3U

Deutsch, Francine. 1999. *Halving It All: How Equally Shared Parenting Works.* Cambridge, MA: Harvard University Press.

DeVault, Marjorie L. 1991. *Feeding the Family: The Social Organization of Caring as Gendered Work.* Chicago: University of Chicago Press.

Dilworth-Anderson, Peggye, Linda M. Burton, and David M. Klein. 2005. "Contemporary and Emerging Theories in Studying Families." In *Sourcebook of Family Theory and Research*, edited by Vern L. Bengtson, Alan C. Acock, Katherine R. Allen, Peggye Dilworth-Anderson, and David M. Klein, pp. 35–58. Thousand Oaks, CA: Sage.

DiPrete, Thomas A., and Claudia Buchmann. 2013. *The Rise of Women: The Growing Gender Gap in Education and What It Means for American Schools.* New York: Russell Sage Foundation.

Dixon, Suzanne. 1992. *The Roman Family.* Baltimore, MD: Johns Hopkins University Press.

Dodds, Peter Sheridan, Kameron Decker Harris, Isabel M. Kloumann, Catherine A. Bliss, and Christopher M. Danforth. 2011. "Temporal Patterns of Happiness and Information in a Global Social Network: Hedonometrics and Twitter." *PLOS ONE* 6(12): e26752. doi:10.1371/journal.pone.0026752

Doering, Nicola M. 2009. "The Internet's Impact on Sexuality: A Critical Review of 15 Years of Research." *Computers in Human Behavior* 25 (5): 1089–1101. doi:10.1016/j.chb.2009.04.003.

Dollahite, David C., and Nathaniel M. Lambert. 2007. "Forsaking All Others: How Religious Involvement Promotes Marital Fidelity in Christian, Jewish, and Muslim Couples." *Review of Religious Research* 48(3):290–307.

Domhoff, G. William. 2009. *Who Rules America? Challenges to Corporate and Class Dominance.* Boston: McGraw-Hill.

Dong, Xin Qi. 2015. "Elder Abuse: Systematic Review and Implications for Practice." *Journal of the American Geriatrics Society* 63 (6): 1214–38. doi:10.1111/jgs.13454.

Do Rozario, Rebecca-Anne C. 2004. "The Princess and the Magic Kingdom: Beyond Nostalgia, the Function of the Disney Princess." *Women's Studies in Communication* 27(1):34–59.

Doucet, Andrea. 2006. *Do Men Mother? Fathering, Care, and Domestic Responsibility.* Toronto, Canada: University of Toronto Press.

Dow, Dawn Marie. 2016. "The Deadly Challenges of Raising African American Boys: Navigating the Controlling Image of the 'Thug'." *Gender & Society* 30(2):161–88. doi:10.1177/0891243216629928.

Doyle, Leonard. 2009. "Segregated High School Proms Divide Georgia's Students." *Daily Telegraph,* June 21, 2009. http://www.telegraph.co.uk/news/worldnews/northamerica/usa/5586617/Segregated-high-school-proms-divide-Georgias-students.html. Accessed June 24, 2010.

Drago, Robert. 2009. "The Parenting of Infants: A Time-Use Study." *Monthly Labor Review* 132(10):33–43.

Dreby, Johanna. 2010. *Divided by Borders: Mexican Migrants and Their Children.* Berkeley, CA: University of California Press.

———. 2012. "The Burden of Deportation on Children in Mexican Immigrant Families." *Journal of Marriage and Family* 74(4):829–845.

Dreger, Alice. 2015. *Galileo's Middle Finger: Heretics, Activists, and One Scholar's Search for Justice.* Penguin Books.

Drouin, Michelle, Daniel Miller, Shaun M. J. Wehle, and Elisa Hernandez. 2016. "Why Do People Lie Online? 'Because Everyone Lies on the Internet.'" *Computers in Human Behavior* 64(November);134–42. doi:10.1016/j.chb.2016.06.052.

Du Bois, W. E. B. 1942. "A Chronicle of Race Relations." *Phylon (1940–1956)* 3(3):320–334.

Duberman, Martin. 1978. "Male Impotence in Colonial Pennsylvania." *Signs* 4(2):395–401.

Dubowitz, Howard. 2014. "Child Neglect." *Pediatric Annals* 43(11):444–45. doi:http://dx.doi.org/10.3928/00904481-20141022-07.

Dufour, Lynn R. 2000. "Sifting through Tradition: The Creation of Jewish Feminist Identities." *Journal for the Scientific Study of Religion* 39(1):90–106.

Dugan, Laura, Daniel S. Nagin, and Richard Rosenfeld. 2003. "Exposure Reduction or Retaliation? The Effects of Domestic Violence Resources on Intimate-Partner Homicide." *Law and Society Review* 37(1):169–198.

Duncan, Greg J., and Richard J. Murnane. 2011. *Whither Opportunity? Rising Inequality, Schools, and Children's Life Chances.* New York: Russell Sage Foundation

Duncan, Greg J., Bessie Wilkerson, and Paula England. 2006. "Cleaning Up Their Act: The Effects of Marriage and Cohabitation on Licit and Illicit Drug Use." *Demography* 43(4):691–710.

Duncan, Greg J., W. J. Yeung, Jeanne Brooks-Gunn, and Judith R. Smith. 1998. "How Much Does Childhood Poverty Affect the Life Chances of Children?" *American Sociological Review* 63(3):406–423.

Duran, Mercedes, Miguel Moya, and Jesus L. Megias. 2011. "It's His Right, It's Her Duty: Benevolent Sexism and the Justification of Traditional Sexual Roles." *Journal of Sex Research* 48(5):470–478.

Durand, John D. 1946. "Married Women in the Labor Force." *The American Journal of Sociology* 52(3):217–223.

Durkheim, Émile. 1897 [1951]. *Suicide: A Study in Sociology.* New York: Free Press.

———. 1893 [1997]. *The Division of Labor in Society.* New York: Simon and Schuster.

Eamon, Mary K., and Chi-Fang Wu. 2011. "Effects of Unemployment and Underemployment on Material Hardship in Single-Mother Families." *Children and Youth Services Review* 33(2):233–241.

eAstrolog.com. 2013. "Leo Sign Compatibility with Virgo." http://www.eastrolog.com/zodiac-sign-compatibility/leo-virgo-sign-compatibility.php. Accessed September 8, 2013.

Eckholm, Erik. 2013. "Federal Judge Rules That Same-Sex Marriage Is Legal in Utah." *New York Times*, December 20. http://www.nytimes.com/2013/12/21/us/utahs-gay-marriage-ban-is-ruled-unconstitutional.html. Accessed June 27, 2015.

———. 2014. "Access to Abortion Falling as States Pass Restrictions." *New York Times*, January 3. http://www.nytimes.com/2014/01/04/us/women-losing-access-to-abortion-as-opponents-gain-ground-in-state-legislatures.html. Accessed June 18, 2014.

Edin, Kathryn, and Maria Kefalas. 2005. *Promises I Can Keep: Why Poor Women Put Motherhood before Marriage.* Berkeley, CA: University of California Press.

Edin, Kathryn, and Rebecca J. Kissane. 2010. "Poverty and the American Family: A Decade in Review." *Journal of Marriage and Family* 72(3):460–479.

Edin, Kathryn, and Timothy J. Nelson. 2013. *Doing the Best I Can: Fatherhood in the Inner City.* Berkeley, CA: University of California Press.

Edin, Kathryn, and Joanna M. Reed. 2005. "Why Don't They Just Get Married? Barriers to Marriage among the Disadvantaged." *Future of Children* 15(2):117–137.

Edin, Kathryn, Laura Tach, and Ronald Mincy. 2009. "Claiming Fatherhood: Race and the Dynamics of Paternal Involvement among Unmarried Men." *Annals of the American Academy of Political and Social Science* 621:149–177.

Edmond, Wendy, and Suzie Fleming. 1975. *All Work and No Pay: Women, Housework, and the Wages Due.* Bristol, UK: Power of Women Collective; Falling Wall Press.

Edwards, K. M., K. M. Sylaska, and A. M. Neal. 2015. "Intimate Partner Violence Among Sexual Minority Populations: A Critical Review of the Literature and Agenda for Future Research." *Psychology of Violence* 5(2): 112–21. https://doi.org/10.1037/a0038656.

Effron, Lauren. 2013. "Miley Cyrus Talks Ending Relationship with Liam Hemsworth." ABC News. December 16. http://abcnews.go.com/blogs/entertainment/2013/12/miley-cyrus-talks-ending-relationship-with-hemsworth-fears-of-being-alone/.

Egan, James F. X., Winston A. Campbell, Audrey Chapman, Alireza A. Shamshirsaz, Pad-malatha Gurram, and Peter A. Benn. 2011. "Distortions of Sex Ratios at Birth in the United States; Evidence for Prenatal Gender Selection." *Prenatal Diagnosis* 31(6):560–565. doi:10.1002/pd.2747.

Egan, Susan K., and David G. Perry. 2001. "Gender Identity: A Multidimensional Analysis with Implications for Psychosocial Adjustment." *Developmental Psychology* 37(4):451–463.

Eggan, Frederick R. 1967. "The Kinship Behavior of the Hopi Indians." In *North American Indians: A Sourcebook*, edited by Roger C. Owen, James Deetz, and Anthony D. Fisher, pp. 429–443. New York: Macmillan.

Ehrenreich, Barbara. 1989. Fear of Falling: The Inner Life of the Middle Class. New York: Pantheon Books.

Elder, Glen H., Jr. 1975. "Age Differentiation and the Life Course." *Annual Review of Sociology* 1:165–190.

Elias, Norbert. 1939. *The Civilizing Process: The History of Manners*. Urizen Books.

Elizabeth, Vivienne. 2003. "To Marry, or Not to Marry: That Is the Question." *Feminism and Psychology* 13(4):426–431.

Ellis, Renee R., and Tavia Simmons. 2014. "Coresident Grandparents and Their Grandchildren: 2012," Current Population Reports, pp. 20–576, U.S. Census Bureau, Washington, DC.

Ellison, Christopher G., and John P. Bartkowski. 2002. "Conservative Protestantism and the Division of Household Labor among Married Couples." *Journal of Family Issues* 23(8):950–985. doi:10.1177/019251302237299.

Ellison, Christopher G., and Darren E. Sherkat. 1993. "Conservative Protestantism and Support for Corporal Punishment." *American Sociological Review* 58(1):131–144.

Emory, Allison Dwyer. 2015. "What Children Experience When Mothers, Fathers, or Both Parents Are Sent to Jail or Prison." Scholars Strategy Network. Retrieved from http://thesocietypages.org/ssn/2015/06/08/parental-incarceration

Endendijk, Joyce J., Marleen G. Groeneveld, Marian J. Bakermans-Kranenburg, and Judi Mesman. 2016. "Gender-Differentiated Parenting Revisited: Meta-Analysis Reveals Very Few Differences in Parental Control of Boys and Girls." *PLOS ONE* 11(7):e0159193. doi:10.1371/journal.pone.0159193

Engelhardt, Gary V., and Jonathan Gruber. 2004. "Social Security and the Evolution of Elderly Poverty." National Bureau of Economic Research Working Paper No. 10466. http://www.nber.org/papers/w10466.pdf. Accessed June 18, 2014.

England, J. Lynn, and Phillip R. Kunz. 1975. "The Application of Age-Specific Rates to Divorce." *Journal of Marriage and Family* 37(1):40–46.

England, Paula. 2010. "The Gender Revolution Uneven and Stalled." *Gender and Society* 24(2):149–166.

———. 2016. "Sometimes the Social Becomes Personal: Gender, Class, and Sexualities." *American Sociological Review* 81(1):4–28. doi:10.1177/0003122415621900.

England, Paula, Jonathan Bearak, Michelle J. Budig, and Melissa J. Hodges. 2016. "Do Highly Paid, Highly Skilled Women Experience the Largest Motherhood Penalty?" *American Sociological Review* 81(6):1161–89. doi:10.1177/0003122416673598.

England, Paula, Michelle Budig, and Nancy Folbre. 2002. "Wages of Virtue: The Relative Pay of Care Work." *Social Problems* 49(4):455–473. doi:10.1525/sp.2002.49.4.455.

England, Paula, Emma Mishel, and Monica L. Caudillo. 2016. "Increases in Sex with Same-Sex Partners and Bisexual Identity across Cohorts of Women (but Not Men)." *Sociological Science* 3(November):951–70. doi:10.15195/v3.a42.

Epstein, Marina, Jerel P. Calzo, Andrew P. Smiler, and L. M. Ward. 2009. "'Anything from Making Out to Having Sex': Men's Negotiations of Hooking Up and Friends with Benefits Scripts." *Journal of Sex Research* 46(5):414–424.

Eriksson, Li, and Paul Mazerolle. 2015. "A Cycle of Violence? Examining Family-of-Origin Violence, Attitudes, and Intimate Partner Violence Perpetration." *Journal of Interpersonal Violence* 30 (6): 945–64. doi:10.1177/0886260514539759.

Ermisch, John, Markus Jäntti, and Timothy M. Smeeding. 2012. *From Parents to Children: The Intergenerational Transmission of Advantage*. New York: Russell Sage Foundation.

Eskridge, William N. 1993. "A History of Same-Sex Marriage." *Virginia Law Review* 79(7):1419–1513.

Esping-Andersen, Gøsta. 2009. *Incomplete Revolution: Adapting Welfare States to Women's New Roles*. Cambridge, UK: Polity Press.

Esteve, Albert, Ron J. Lesthaeghe, Antonio López-Gay, and Joan García-Román. 2016. "The Rise of Cohabitation in Latin America and the Caribbean, 1970–2011." In *Cohabitation and Marriage in the Americas: Geo-Historical Legacies and New Trends*, edited by Albert Esteve and Ron J. Lesthaeghe, pp. 25–57. Springer International Publishing.

Ethics Committee of the American Society for Reproductive Medicine. 2015. "Use of Reproductive Technology for Sex Selection for Nonmedical Reasons." *Fertility and Sterility* 103(6):1418–1422. doi:10.1016/j.fertnstert.2015.03.035

Facebook Diversity. 2015. Status update. https://www.facebook.com/facebookdiversity/posts/774221582674346. Accessed December 21, 2016.

Falk, Patricia J. 2002. "Rape by Drugs: A Statutory Overview and Proposals for Reform." *Arizona Law Review* 44(Spring):131–212.

Farley, Reynolds, and John Haaga. 2005. *The American People: Census 2000*. New York: Russell Sage Foundation.

Feliciano, Cynthia, Belinda Robnett, and Golnaz Komaie. 2009. "Gendered Racial Exclusion among White Internet Daters." *Social Science Research* 38(1):41–56.

Ferree, Myra Marx. 1990. "Beyond Separate Spheres: Feminism and Family Research," *Journal of Marriage and Family* 52(4):866–884.

——. 2010. "Filling the Glass: Gender Perspectives on Families." *Journal of Marriage and Family* 72(3):420–439.

Ferrie, Joseph P. 2005. "History Lessons: The End of American Exceptionalism? Mobility in the United States since 1850." *The Journal of Economic Perspectives* 19(3):199–215.

Fernandez, Roberto M., and Marie L. Mors. 2008. "Competing for Jobs: Labor Queues and Gender Sorting in the Hiring Process." *Social Science Research* 37(4):1061–1080.

Fetner, Tina. 2016. "U.S. Attitudes Toward Lesbian and Gay People Are Better than Ever." *Contexts* 15(2):20–27. doi:10.1177/1536504216648147.

Fields, Barbara J. 1982. "Ideology and Race in American History." In *Region, Race, and Reconstruction: Essays in Honor of C. Vann Woodward*, edited by J. M. Kousser and J. M. McPherson, pp. 143–147. New York: Oxford University Press.

Finer, Lawrence B. 2007. "Trends in Premarital Sex in the United States, 1954–2003." *Public Health Reports* 122(1):73–78.

Finer, Lawrence B., Lori F. Frohwirth, Lindsay A. Dauphinee, Susheela Singh, and Ann M. Moore. 2005. "Reasons U.S. Women Have Abortions: Quantitative and Qualitative Perspectives." *Perspectives on Sexual and Reproductive Health* 37(3):110–118. doi:10.1111/j.1931-2393.2005.tb00045.x.

Finer, Lawrence B., and Mia R. Zolna. 2016. "Declines in Unintended Pregnancy in the United States, 2008–2011." *New England Journal of Medicine* 374(9):843–52. doi:10.1056/NEJMsa1506575.

Fink, Bernhard, Nick Neave, Gayle Brewer, and Boguslaw Pawlowski. 2007. "Variable Preferences for Sexual Dimorphism in Stature (SDS): Further Evidence for an Adjustment in Relation to Own Height." *Personality and Individual Differences* 43(8):2249–2257.

Finneran, C., and R. Stephenson. 2013. "Intimate Partner Violence Among Men Who Have Sex With Men: A Systematic Review." *Trauma Violence & Abuse* 14(2):168–85. https://doi.org/10.1177/1524838012470034.

Fischer, Claude. 2010. "A Crime Puzzle: Violent Crime Declines in America." The Berkeley Blog. June 16. http://blogs.berkeley.edu/2010/06/16/a-crime-puzzle-violent-crime-declines-in-america/.

Fisher, Allen P. 2003. "Still 'Not Quite as Good as Having Your Own'? Toward a Sociology of Adoption." *Annual Review of Sociology* 29:335–361.

Flannery, Kent V. 2002. "The Origins of the Village Revisited: From Nuclear to Extended Households." *American Antiquity* 67(3):417–433.

Flentje, Annesa, Nicholas C. Heck, and Bryan N. Cochran. 2013. "Sexual Reorientation Therapy Interventions: Perspectives of Ex-Ex-Gay Individuals." *Journal of Gay and Lesbian Mental Health* 17(3):256–277.

Flood, Michael. 2012. "Separated Fathers and the 'Fathers' Rights' Movement." *Journal of Family Studies* 18(2–3):235–45.

Flood, Sarah, Miriam King, Steven Ruggles, and J. Robert Warren. 2017. "Integrated Public Use Microdata Series, Current Population Survey: Version 4.0." [dataset]. Minneapolis, MN: University of Minnesota.

Folbre, Nancy. 1994a. "Children as Public Goods." *The American Economic Review* 84(2):86–90.

——. 1994b. *Who Pays for the Kids? Gender and the Structures of Constraint*. London: Routledge.

——. 2001. *The Invisible Heart: Economics and Family Values*. New York: New Press.

——. 2009. "Valuing Unpaid Work Matters, Especially for the Poor." Blog post. http://economix.blogs.nytimes.com/2009/09/21/valuing-unpaid-work-matters-especially-for-the-poor/. Accessed October 11, 2013.

Foley, Jodie. 2004. "From Liverpool to Cut Bank: The Story of Montana War Bride Ruth Poore Batchen." *Montana: The Magazine of Western History* 54(3):71–73.

Fomby, Paula, and Cynthia Osborne. 2010. "The Influence of Union Instability and Union Quality on Children's Aggressive Behavior." *Social Science Research* 39(6):912–924.

Foner, Eric. 1995. *Free Soil, Free Labor, Free Men: The Ideology of the Republican Party before the Civil War*. New York: Oxford University Press.

Fong, Timothy P. 2008. *The Contemporary Asian American Experience: Beyond the Model Minority*. Upper Saddle River, NJ: Prentice Hall.

Food and Nutrition Service. 2013. WIC Income Eligibility Guidelines 2013–2014. http://www.fns.usda.gov/wic/howtoapply/incomeguidelines.htm. Accessed September 2, 2013.

Forhan, Sara E., Sami L. Gottlieb, Maya R. Sternberg, Fujie Xu, S. D. Datta, Geraldine M. McQuillan, Stuart M. Berman, and Lauri E. Markowitz. 2009. "Prevalence of Sexually Transmitted Infections among Female Adolescents Aged 14 to 19 in the United States." *Pediatrics* 124(6):1505–1512.

Foster, Brooke Lea. 2016. "For Interracial Couples, Growing Acceptance, With Some Exceptions." *New York Times*, November 26. http://www.nytimes.com/2016/11/26/fashion/weddings/for-interracial-couples-growing-acceptance-with-some-exceptions.html.

Fox, Bonnie J. 2009. *When Couples Become Parents: The Creation of Gender in the Transition to Parenthood*. Toronto, Canada: University of Toronto Press.

Fox, Greer Litton, and Velma McBride Murry. 2000. "Gender and Families: Feminist Perspectives and Family Research." *Journal of Marriage and Family* 62(4):1160–1172. doi:10.1111/j.1741-3737.2000.01160.x.

Francis, Andrew M. 2008. "Family and Sexual Orientation: The Family-Demographic Correlates of Homosexuality in Men and Women." *Journal of Sex Research* 45(4):371–377.

Franklin, Donna L. 1997. *Ensuring Inequality: The Structural Transformation of the African-American Family.* New York: Oxford University Press.

Frankowski, Barbara L. 2004. "Sexual Orientation and Adolescents." *Pediatrics* 113(6):1827–1832.

Frassanito, Paolo, and Benedetta Pettorini. 2008. "Pink and Blue: The Color of Gender." *Child's Nervous System* 24(8):881–882. doi:10.1007/s00381-007-0559-3.

Frazier, E. Franklin. 1930. "The Negro Slave Family." *The Journal of Negro History* 15(2):198–259.

———. 1939. *The Negro Family in the United States.* Notre Dame, IN: University of Notre Dame Press.

Freund, David M. P. 2007. *Colored Property: State Policy and White Racial Politics in Suburban America.* Chicago, IL: University of Chicago Press.

Fricke v. Lynch. 1980. Civil Action No. 80-214:381. 491 F.Supp. 381 (D.R.I. 1980).

Friedersdorf, Conor. 2014. "Hillary Clinton's Gay-Marriage Problem." *The Atlantic*, June 13. http://www.theatlantic.com/politics/archive/2014/06/hillary-clintons-gay-marriage-problem/372717/. Accessed June 27, 2015.

Friedman, Allison L., Rachel E. Kachur, Seth M. Noar, and Mary McFarlane. 2016. "Health Communication and Social Marketing Campaigns for Sexually Transmitted Disease Prevention and Control: What Is the Evidence of Their Effectiveness?" *Sexually Transmitted Diseases* 43(February): S83–101.

Frietson, Galis, Clara M. A. Ten Broek, Stefan Van Dongen, and Liliane C. D. Wijnaendts. 2010. "Sexual Dimorphism in the Prenatal Digit Ratio (2D:4D)." *Archives of Sexual Behavior* 39(1):57–62. doi:10.1007/s10508-009-9485-7.

Frost, Joe L. 2010. *A History of Children's Play and Play Environments: Toward a Contemporary Child-Saving Movement.* New York: Routledge.

Fuentes, Agustin. 1998. "Re-evaluating Primate Monogamy." *American Anthropologist* 100(4):890–907.

Fujimura, Joan H. 2006. "Sex Genes: A Critical Sociomaterial Approach to the Politics and Molecular Genetics of Sex Determination." *Signs* 32(1, Autumn):49–82. doi:10.1086/signs.2006.32.issue-1.

Furstenberg, Frank F. 2000. "The Sociology of Adolescence and Youth in the 1990s: A Critical Commentary." *Journal of Marriage and Family* 62(4):896–910.

———. 2007. "The Making of the Black Family: Race and Class in Qualitative Studies in the Twentieth Century." *Annual Review of Sociology* 33:429–448.

———. 2010. "On a New Schedule: Transitions to Adulthood and Family Change." *The Future of Children* 20(1):67–87.

Furstenberg, Frank F., James L. Peterson, Christine Winquist Nord, and Nicholas Zill. 1983. "The Life Course of Children of Divorce: Marital Disruption and Parental Contact." *American Sociological Review* 48(5):656–668.

Gaby, Sarah, and Neal Caren. 2012. "Occupy Online: How Cute Old Men and Malcolm X Recruited 400,000 US Users to OWS on Facebook." *Social Movement Studies* 11(3–4): 367–74. doi:10.1080/14742837.2012.708858

Gallagher, Sally K. 2003. *Evangelical Identity and Gendered Family Life.* New Brunswick, NJ: Rutgers University Press.

Gallup. 2016. "Birth Control, Divorce Top List of Morally Acceptable Issues." Gallup.com. June 8. http://www.gallup.com/poll/192404/birth-control-divorce-top-list-morally-acceptable-issues.aspx.

———. 2017a. "Most Admired Man and Woman." Gallup.com. Accessed January 6. *http://www.gallup.com/poll/1678/Most-Admired-Man-Woman.aspx.*

———. 2017b. "Abortion." http://www.gallup.com/poll/1576/abortion.aspx. Accessed March 22, 2017.

Gammon, Katharine. 2015. "Playboy's Image of the Ideal Woman Sure Has Changed." Wired.com, October 15. https://www.wired.com/2015/10/playboy-playmates-bmi/.

Gamson, Joshua. 1990. "Rubber Wars: Struggles Over the Condom in the United States." *Journal of the History of Sexuality* 1(2):262–282.

Gamson, Joshua, and Dawne Moon. 2004. "The Sociology of Sexualities: Queer and Beyond." *Annual Review of Sociology* 30:47–64.

Ganong, Lawrence H. 2004. *Stepfamily Relationships: Development, Dynamics, and Interventions.* New York: Kluwer Academic/Plenum Publishers.

Gans, Herbert J. 2007. "Acculturation, Assimilation and Mobility." *Ethnic and Racial Studies* 30(1):152–164.

Gardner, Jonathan, and Andrew J. Oswald. 2006. "Do Divorcing Couples Become Happier by Breaking Up?" *Journal of the Royal Statistical Society Series A: Statistics in Society* 169:319–336.

Garrett-Peters, Raymond, and Linda M. Burton. 2015. "Reframing Marriage and Marital Delay among Low-Income Mothers: An Interactionist Perspective." *Journal of Family Theory & Review* 7(3):242–64. doi:10.1111/jftr.12089.

Gaudin, James M. 1993. *Child Neglect: A Guide for Intervention.* Washington, DC: U.S. Department of Health and Human Services.

Gearing, Frederick O. 1958. "The Structural Poses of 18th-Century Cherokee Villages." *American Anthropologist* 60:1148–1157.

George, Robert P., and John B. Londregan. 2009. "Princeton and the Hookup Culture." *Princeton Alumni Weekly*, March 4. http://paw.princeton.edu/issues/2009/03/04/pages/7001/. Accessed September 6, 2013.

Gerber, M. R., K. M. Iverson, M. E. Dichter, R. Klap, and R. E. Latta. 2014. "Women Veterans and Intimate Partner Violence: Current State of Knowledge and Future Directions." *Journal of Women's Health*, 23(4), 302–09.

Gerson, Kathleen. 2010. *The Unfinished Revolution: How a New Generation Is Reshaping Family, Work, and Gender in America.* New York: Oxford University Press.

Gerstel, Naomi, and Katherine McGonagle. 1999. "Job Leaves and the Limits of the Family and Medical Leave Act: The Effects of Gender, Race, and Family." *Work and Occupations* 26(4):510–534. doi:10.1177/0730888499026004006.

Geyer-Ryan, Helga. 1996. "From Morality to Mortality: Women and the Violence of Political Change, or Law and (b) Order." *Philosophy Social Criticism* 22(4):1–11.

Gibbons, Ann. 2008. "The Birth of Childhood." *Science* 322(5904):1040–1043.

Gibson-Davis, Christina M., Kathryn Edin, and Sara McLanahan. 2005. "High Hopes but Even Higher Expectations: The Retreat from Marriage among Low-Income Couples." *Journal of Marriage and Family* 67(5):1301–1312.

Giddens, Anthony. 1992. *The Transformation of Intimacy: Sexuality, Love, and Eroticism in Modern Societies.* Stanford, CA: Stanford University Press.

Gierisch, Jennifer M., Remy R. Coeytaux, Rachel Peragallo Urrutia, Laura J. Havrilesky, Patricia G. Moorman, William J. Lowery, Michaela Dinan, et al. 2013. "Oral Contraceptive Use and Risk of Breast, Cervical, Colorectal, and Endometrial Cancers: A Systematic Review." *Cancer Epidemiology Biomarkers & Prevention* 22(11):1931–43. doi:10.1158/1055-9965.EPI-13-0298.

Gilje, Paul A., and Howard B. Rock. 1994. "'Sweep O! Sweep O!': African-American Chimney Sweeps and Citizenship in the New Nation." *The William and Mary Quarterly* 51(3, Mid-Atlantic Perspectives): 507–538.

Gilley, Brian J. 2006. *Becoming Two-Spirit: Gay Identity and Social Acceptance in Indian Country.* Lincoln, NE: University of Nebraska Press.

Gillman v. School Board for Holmes County. 2008. 567 F.Supp. 2d 1359 (N.D. Fla. 2008).

Gilroy, Marilyn. 2002. "Operation Pedro Pan: Memories and Accolades 40 Years Later." *The Hispanic Outlook in Higher Education* 12(20):8.

Ginsburg, Kenneth R. 2007. "The Importance of Play in Promoting Healthy Child Development and Maintaining Strong Parent-Child Bonds." *Pediatrics* 119(1):182–91. doi:10.1542/peds.2006-2697.

Giordano, Peggy C. 2003. "Relationships in Adolescence." *Annual Review of Sociology* 29:257–281.

Glass, Jennifer. 2004. "Blessing or Curse? Work-Family Policies and Mother's Wage Growth Over Time." *Work and Occupations* 31(3):367–394.

Glass, Jennifer L., and Sara Beth Estes. 1997. "The Family Responsive Workplace." *Annual Review of Sociology* 23:289–313.

Glauber, Rebecca. 2011. "Limited Access: Gender, Occupational Composition, and Flexible Work Scheduling." *Sociological Quarterly* 52(3):472–494.

———. 2012. "Women's Work and Working Conditions: Are Mothers Compensated for Lost Wages?" *Work and Occupations* 39(2):115–138.

Glauber, Rebecca, and Kristi L. Gozjolko. 2011. "Do Traditional Fathers Always Work More? Gender Ideology, Race, and Parenthood." *Journal of Marriage and Family* 73(5):1133–1148.

Glenn, Evelyn N. 1985. "Racial Ethnic Women's Labor: The Intersection of Race, Gender and Class Oppression." *Review of Radical Political Economics* 17(3):86–108.

———. 1986. *Issei, Nisei, Warbride: Three Generations of Japanese American Women in Domestic Service.* Philadelphia, PA: Temple University Press.

Glenn, Evelyn N., and Stacey G. H. Yap. 2002. "Chinese American Families." In *Minority Families in the United States: A Multicultural Perspective*, edited by R. L. Taylor, pp. 134–163. Upper Saddle River, NJ: Prentice Hall.

Glover, Jenna A., Renee V. Galliher, and Trenton G. Lamere. 2009. "Identity Development and Exploration among Sexual Minority Adolescents: Examination of a Multidimensional Model." *Journal of Homosexuality* 56(1):77–101.

Godwin, John. 2010. *Legal Environments, Human Rights and HIV Responses among Men Who Have Sex with Men and Transgender People in Asia and the Pacific.* Bangkok, Thailand: United Nations Development Programme.

Goffman, Erving. 1963. *Stigma: Notes on the Management of Spoiled Identity.* Englewood Cliffs, NJ: Prentice Hall.

Goldenberg, David. 2015. "Why the Oldest Person in the World Keeps Dying." FiveThirtyEight. May 26. https://fivethirtyeight.com/features/why-the-oldest-person-in-the-world-keeps-dying/.

Goldin, Claudia. 1990. *Understanding the Gender Gap: An Economic History of American Women.* New York: Oxford University Press.

———. 1991. "The Role of World War II in the Rise of Women's Employment." *The American Economic Review* 81(4):741–756.

Goldin, Claudia D., and Lawrence F. Katz. 2002. "The Power of the Pill: Oral Contraceptives and Women's Career and Marriage Decisions." *The Journal of Political Economy* 110(4):730–770.

———. 2003. "The 'Virtues' of the Past: Education in the First Hundred Years of the New Republic." National Bureau of Economic Research Working Paper No. 9958. http://www.nber.org/papers/w9958.pdf. Accessed June 18, 2014.

Goldman, David, Gabor Oroszi, and Francesca Ducci. 2006. "The Genetics of Addictions: Uncovering the Genes." *Focus* 4(3):401–415.

Goldscheider, Frances K., Dennis Hogan, and Regina Bures. 2001. "A Century (Plus) of Parenthood: Changes in Living with Children, 1880–1990." *The History of the Family,* 6(4):477–494.

Goldscheider, Frances, and Sharon Sassler. 2006. "Creating Stepfamilies: Integrating Children into the Study of Union Formation." *Journal of Marriage and Family* 68(2):275–291. doi:10.1111/j.1741-3737.2006.00252.x.

Goldrick-Rab, Sara. 2016. *Paying the Price: College Costs, Financial Aid, and the Betrayal of the American Dream.* Chicago, IL: University of Chicago Press.

Golombok, Susan, John Rust, Karyofyllis Zervoulis, Tim Croudace, Jean Golding, and Melissa Hines. 2008. "Developmental Trajectories of Sex-Typed Behavior in Boys and Girls: A Longitudinal General Population Study of Children Aged 2.5–8 Years." *Child Development* 79(5):1583–1593.

Gonzalez-Guarda, R. M., A. M. Cummings, M. Becerra, M. C. Fernandez, and I. Mesa. 2013. "Needs and Preferences for the Prevention of Intimate Partner Violence Among Hispanics: A Community's Perspective." *The Journal of Primary Prevention* 34(4): 221–35.

Goode, William J. 1959. "The Theoretical Importance of Love." *American Sociological Review* 24(1):38–47.

Gooding, Gretchen, and Rose Kreider. 2010. "Women's Marital Naming Choices in a Nationally Representative Sample." *Journal of Family Issues* 31(5):681–701.

Goodman, Ellen. 1996. "A Criminal Record—or a Wedding Band?" *Boston Globe*, September 12.

Goodwin, Paula Y., William D. Mosher, and Anjani Chandra. 2010. "Marriage and Cohabitation in the United States: A Statistical Portrait Based on Cycle 6 (2002) of the National Survey of Family Growth." *Vital Health Statistics* 23(28). Hyattsville, MD: National Center for Health Statistics.

Gordon, Linda. 1994. *Pitied but Not Entitled: Single Mothers and the History of Welfare, 1890–1935.* New York: Free Press.

Gordon, Milton M. 1964. *Assimilation in American Life: The Role of Race, Religion, and National Origins.* New York: Oxford University Press.

Gould, Stephen J. 1996. *The Mismeasure of Man.* New York: W. W. Norton.

Graefe, Deborah Roempke, and Daniel T. Lichter. 1999. "Life Course Transitions of American Children: Parental Cohabitation, Marriage, and Single Motherhood." *Demography* 36(2):205–217. doi:10.2307/2648109.

Grall, Timothy. 2016. "Custodial Mothers and Fathers and Their Child Support: 2013." *Current Population Reports* (P60-255). U.S. Census Bureau.

Gray, Jo A., Jean Stockard, and Joe Stone. 2006. "The Rising Share of Nonmarital Births: Fertility Choice or Marriage Behavior?" *Demography* 43(2):241–253.

Gray, Peter B., and Kermyt G. Anderson. 2010. *Fatherhood: Evolution and Human Paternal Behavior.* Cambridge, MA: Harvard University Press.

Green, Robert-Jay. 2010. "From Outlaws to In-Laws: Gay and Lesbian Couples in Contemporary Society." In *Families as They Really Are*, edited by B. J. Risman, pp. 197–213. New York: W.W. Norton.

Greenberg, Mark H., Jodie Levin-Epstein, Rutledge Q. Hutson, Theodora J. Ooms, Rachel Schumacher, Vicki Turetsky, and David M. Engstrom. 2002. "The 1996 Welfare Law: Key Elements and Reauthorization Issues Affecting Children." *Future of Children* 12(1):27–57.

Greenhaus, Jeffrey H., and Nicholas J. Beutell. 1985. "Sources of Conflict between Work and Family Roles." *The Academy of Management Review* 10(1):76–88.

Greenstein, Theodore N. 2000. "Economic Dependence, Gender, and the Division of Labor in the Home: A Replication and Extension." *Journal of Marriage and Family* 62(2):322–335.

Greenwood, Jeremy, Ananth Seshadri, and Mehmet Yorukoglu. 2005. "Engines of Liberation." *Review of Economic Studies* 72(1):109–133.

Griswold, Robert L. 1993. *Fatherhood in America: A History.* New York: Basic Books.

Grubb, Amy Rose, and Julie Harrower. 2009. "Understanding Attribution of Blame in Cases of Rape: An Analysis of Participant Gender, Type of Rape and Perceived Similarity to the Victim." *Journal of Sexual Aggression* 15(1):63–81. doi:10.1080/13552600802641649.

Guilmoto, Christophe Z. 2009. "The Sex Ratio Transition in Asia." *Population and Development Review* 35(3):519–549.

Gupta, Sanjiv. 2006. "The Consequences of Maternal Employment during Men's Childhood for Their Adult Housework Performance." *Gender and Society* 20(1):60–86.

———. 2007. "Autonomy, Dependence, or Display? The Relationship between Married Women's Earnings and Housework." *Journal of Marriage and Family* 69(2):399–417.

Gutman, Herbert G. 1975. "Persistent Myths about the Afro-American Family." *Journal of Interdisciplinary History* 6(2, The History of the Family, III):181–210.

———. 1976. *The Black Family in Slavery and Freedom, 1750–1925.* New York: Pantheon Books.

Guttmacher Institute. 2013. *State Policies in Brief: Sex and HIV Education.* http://www.guttmacher.org/statecenter/spibs/spib_SE.pdf. Accessed August 28, 2013.

_____. 2006. *U.S. Teenage Pregnancy Statistics: National and State Trends and Trends by Race and Ethnicity.* New York: Allan Guttmacher Institute.

_____. 2016. "Abortion Bans in Cases of Sex or Race Selection or Genetic Anomaly." December 1. https://www.guttmacher.org/state-policy/explore/abortion-bans-cases-sex-or-race-selection-or-genetic-anomaly. Accessed December 18, 2016.

_____. 2017a. "Sex and HIV Education." January 1. https://www.guttmacher.org/state-policy/explore/sex-and-hiv-education.

_____. 2017b. "Target Regulation of Abortion Providers: State Laws and Policies as of March 1, 2017." https://www.guttmacher.org/state-policy/explore/targeted-regulation-abortion-providers. Accessed March 22, 2017.

Guzzo, Karen, and Frank Furstenberg. 2007. "Multipartnered Fertility among American Men." *Demography* 44(3):583–601.

Ha, Yoonsook, and Daniel P. Miller. 2015. "Child Care, Subsidies and Employment Outcomes of Low-Income Families." *Children and Youth Services Review* 59 (December): 139–48. doi:10.1016/j.childyouth.2015.11.003.

Haak, Wolfgang, Guido Brandt, Hylke N. de Jong, Christian Meyer, Robert Ganslmeier, Volker Heyd, Chris Hawkesworth, Alistair W. G. Pike, Harald Meller, and Kurt W. Alt. 2008. "Ancient DNA, Strontium Isotopes, and Osteological Analyses Shed Light on Social and Kinship Organization of the Later Stone Age." *Proceedings of the National Academy of Sciences* 105(47):18226–18231.

Haider-Markel, Donald, and Mark R. Joslyn. 2008. "Beliefs about the Origins of Homosexuality and Support for Gay Rights: An Empirical Test of Attribution Theory." *Public Opinion Quarterly* 72(2):291–310.

Haines, Michael R. 2006. "Total Fertility Rate and Birth Rate, by Race and Age: 1800–1998." In *Historical Statistics of the United States, Earliest Times to the Present: Millennial Edition,* edited by S. B. Carter, S. S. Gartner, M. R. Haines, A. L. Olmstead, R. Sutch and G. Wright, Table Ab52-117. New York: Cambridge University Press.

Hamermesh, Daniel S., and Elena Stancanelli. 2014. "Long Workweeks and Strange Hours." Working Paper 20449. National Bureau of Economic Research. doi:10.3386/w20449.

Hamilton B. E., J. A. Martin, M. J. K. Osterman, et al. 2015. Births: Final Data for 2014. *National Vital Statistics Reports* 64(12). Hyattsville, MD: National Center for Health Statistics.

Hamilton, Laura, Simon Cheng, and Brian Powell. 2007. "Adoptive Parents, Adaptive Parents: Evaluating the Importance of Biological Ties for Parental Investment." *American Sociological Review* 72(1):95–116.

Hamplova, Dana, and Céline Le Bourdais. 2009. "One Pot or Two Pot Strategies? Income Pooling in Married and Unmarried Households in Comparative Perspective." *Journal of Comparative Family Studies* 40(3):355–386.

Hancock, Jeffrey T., and Catalina L. Toma. 2009. "Putting Your Best Face Forward: The Accuracy of Online Dating Photographs." *Journal of Communication* 59(2):367–386.

Handy, Bruce, and Elizabeth L. Bland. 1997. "Roll Over, Ward Cleaver." *Time* 149(15, April 14):78.

Hansen, Hans-Tore. 2005. "Unemployment and Marital Dissolution: A Panel Data Study of Norway." *European Sociological Review* 21(2):135–148.

Hardie, Jessica H., and Amy Lucas. 2010. "Economic Factors and Relationship Quality among Young Couples: Comparing Cohabitation and Marriage." *Journal of Marriage and Family* 72(5):1141–1154.

Harris, Henry P. 1906. "Divorce and Remarriage." *The Arena* 35(April):337–448.

Harrison, Rea J. 2007. "Black and White Prom Nights: The Unconstitutionality of Racially Segregated High School Proms in the 21st Century." *Journal of Gender, Race and Justice* 10:505.

Harmon, Amy. 2003. "Online Dating Sheds Its Stigma as Losers.com." *New York Times,* June 29. http://www.nytimes.com/2003/06/29/us/online-dating-sheds-its-stigma-as-loserscom.html. Accessed March 3, 2014.

_____. 2007. "Stalking Strangers' DNA to Fill In the Family Tree." *New York Times,* April 2, p. A1.

Harper, Gary W., Christine Gannon, Susan E. Watson, Joseph A. Catania, and M. Margaret Dolcini. 2004. "The Role of Close Friends in African American Adolescents' Dating and Sexual Behavior." *Journal of Sex Research* 41(4):351–362.

Hartmann, Heidi I. 1981. "The Family as the Locus of Gender, Class, and Political Struggle: The Example of Housework." *Signs* 6(3):366–394.

Hasbany, Richard. 1989. *Homosexuality and Religion.* New York: Haworth Press.

Haughton, Dominique M. A., and Swati Mukerjee. 1995. "The Economic Measurement and Determinants of Diversity." *Social Indicators Research* 36(3):201–225.

Hays, Sharon. 1996. *The Cultural Contradictions of Motherhood.* New Haven, CT: Yale University Press.

Hayslip, Bert, Jr, and Patricia L. Kaminski. 2005. "Grandparents Raising Their Grandchildren: A Review of the Literature and Suggestions for Practice." *The Gerontologist* 45(2):262–269.

Healy, Patrick. 2012. "How Celebrities Come Out Now." *New York Times*, June 9, Sunday Review.

Heath, Melanie. 2012. *One Marriage under God: The Campaign to Promote Marriage in America.* New York: New York University Press.

Heckman, James J. 2006. "Skill Formation and the Economics of Investing in Disadvantaged Children." *Science* 312(5782):1900–1902.

Hegewisch, Ariane, and Asha DuMonthier. 2016. "The Gender Wage Gap: 2015." Institute for Women's Policy Research. http://www.iwpr.org/publications/pubs/the-gender-wage-gap-2015-annual-earnings-differences-by-gender-race-and-ethnicity. Accessed December 24, 2016.

Hemez, Paul, and Wendy D. Manning. 2017. "Over Twenty-Five Years of Change in Cohabitation Experience in the U.S., 1987–2013." Family Profiles, FP-17-02. National Center for Family & Marriage Research. http://www.bgsu.edu/content/dam/BGSU/college-of-arts-and-sciences/NCFMR/documents/FP/hemez-manning-25-years-change-cohab-fp-17-02.pdf.

Henig, Robin M. 2010. "What Is It about 20-Somethings?" *New York Times Magazine,* August 18.

Henretta, John C., Douglas A. Wolf, Matthew F. Van Voorhis, and Beth J. Soldo. 2012. "Family Structure and the Reproduction of Inequality: Parents' Contribution to Children's College Costs." *Social Science Research* 41(4):876–887.

Hergovich, Andreas, and Sophie Süssenbach. 2015. "The Time Trend of Beauties: Detection of Cross-Cultural Invariance in Playboy Centerfolds." *Current Psychology* 34(4):666–71. doi:10.1007/s12144-014-9279-5.

Herman, Ellen. 2008. *Kinship by Design: A History of Adoption in the Modern United States.* Chicago, IL: University of Chicago Press.

Hertz, Rosanna. 2006. *Single by Chance, Mothers by Choice: How Women Are Choosing Parenthood without Marriage and Creating the New American Family.* New York: Oxford University Press.

Heywood, Wendy, Kent Patrick, Anthony M. A. Smith, and Marian K. Pitts. 2015. "Associations Between Early First Sexual Intercourse and Later Sexual and Reproductive Out-comes: A Systematic Review of Population-Based Data." *Archives of Sexual Behavior* 44(3):531–69. doi:10.1007/s10508-014-0374-3.

Hill, Mark E. 2002. "Skin Color and the Perception of Attractiveness among African Americans: Does Gender Make a Difference?" *Social Psychology Quarterly* 65(1):77. doi:10.2307/3090169.

Hill, Martha S. 1985. "The Changing Nature of Poverty." *Annals of the American Academy of Political and Social Science* 479(May):31–47.

Hill, Shirley A. 2005. *Black Intimacies: A Gender Perspective on Families and Relationships.* Walnut Creek, CA: AltaMira Press.

Hindman, Hugh D. 2002. *Child Labor: An American History.* Armonk, NY: M. E. Sharpe.

Hirsch, Jennifer S., Miguel Muñoz-Laboy, Christina M. Nyhus, Kathryn M. Yount, and José A. Bauermeister. 2009. "They 'Miss More Than Anything Their Normal Life Back Home': Masculinity and Extramarital Sex among Mexican Migrants in Atlanta." *Perspectives on Sexual and Reproductive Health* 41(1):23–32.

Hobbs, Frank, and Nicole Stoops. 2002. *Demographic Trends in the 20th Century.* Washington, DC: U.S. Census Bureau, U.S. Government Printing Office. http://www.census.gov/prod/2002pubs/censr-4.pdf. Accessed February 18, 2014.

Hochschild, Arlie R., and Anne Machung. 1989. *The Second Shift.* New York: Avon Books.

Hodges, Quincy. 2015. "Monroe, La. High School Reverses Decision, Will Now Allow Lesbian Student to Wear Tuxedo to Prom." NOLA.com, April 7. http://www.nola.com/news/baton-rouge/index.ssf/2015/04/monroe_la_high_school_reverses.html.

Hoffmann, J. P., C. G. Ellison, and J. P. Bartkowski. 2017. "Conservative Protestantism and Attitudes toward Corporal Punishment, 1986–2014." *Social Science Research* 63, 81–94. https://doi.org/10.1016/j.ssresearch.2016.09.010.

Hoffman, Saul D. 1998. "Teenage Childbearing Is Not So Bad After All…or Is It? A Review of the New Literature." *Family Planning Perspectives* 30(5):236–243.

Hofstadter, Richard. 1944. *Social Darwinism in American Thought.* Boston: Beacon Press.

Hollingsworth v. Perry. 2013. 570 U.S. __.

Holt, Stephanie. 2016. "'Quality' Contact Post-Separation/Divorce: A Review of the Literature." *Children and Youth Services Review* 68(September):92–99. doi:10.1016/j.childyouth.2016.07.001.

Horowitz, Irving Louis. 1962. "Conflict and Cooperation: A Sociological Inventory." *Social Forces* 41(2):177–188.

Houston, Eric, and David J. McKirnan. 2007. "Intimate Partner Abuse among Gay and Bisexual Men: Risk Correlates and Health Outcomes." *Journal of Urban Health: Bulletin of the New York Academy of Medicine* 84(5):681–690.

Hout, M. 2015. "A Summary of What We Know about Social Mobility." The ANNALS of the American Academy of Political and Social Science 657(1):27–36. http://doi.org/10.1177/0002716214547174.

Hoxie, Frederick E. 1991. "Searching for Structure: Reconstructing Crow Family Life during the Reservation Era." *American Indian Quarterly* 15(3):287.

Hoyert, Donna L., and Jiaquan Xu. 2012. "Deaths: Preliminary data for 2011." *National Vital Statistics Reports* 61(6):1–52. Hyattsville, MD: National Center for Health Statistics.

Hoyt, Helen. 1923. "Flower and Flame." *Poetry* 23(1):5–6.

Huffman, Matt L., Philip N. Cohen, and Jessica Pearlman. 2010. "Engendering Change: Organizational Dynamics and Workplace Gender Desegregation, 1975–2005." *Administrative Science Quarterly* 55(2, June):255–277.

Human Rights Watch. 2016. "Shut Out: Restrictions on Bathroom and Locker Room Access for Transgender Youth in US Schools." *https://www.hrw.org/report/2016/09/13/shut-out/restrictions-bathroom-and-locker-room-access-transgender-youth-us-schools.* ISBN: 978-1-6231-34037. Accessed December 21, 2016.

Humane Society of the United States. 2016. "Pets by the Numbers." http://www.humanesociety.org/issues/pet_overpopulation/facts/pet_ownership_statistics.html.

Humes, Karen R., Nicholas A. Jones, and Roberto R. Ramirez. 2011. "Overview of Race and Hispanic Origin: 2010." Census 2010 Brief (March). Washington, DC: U.S. Census Bureau.

Hurt, Tera R. 2010. *Toward a Deeper Understanding of the Meaning of Marriage among Black Men.* Working Paper Series WP-10-12. Bowling Green, OH: National Center for Family and Marriage Research.

Hussey, Jon M., Jen Jen Chang, and Jonathan B. Kotch. 2006. "Child Maltreatment in the United States: Prevalence, Risk Factors, and Adolescent Health Consequences." *Pediatrics* 118(3):933–942. doi:10.1542/peds.2005-2452.

Hvistendahl, Mara. 2011. *Unnatural Selection: Choosing Boys over Girls, and the Consequences of a World Full of Men.* New York: Public Affairs.

Iceland, John. 2003. *Poverty in America: A Handbook.* Berkeley, CA: University of California Press.

Igartua, Karine, Brett D. Thombs, Giovani Burgos, and Richard Montoro. 2009. "Concordance and Discrepancy in Sexual Identity, Attraction, and Behavior among Adolescents." *Journal of Adolescent Health* 45(6):602–608.

Ignatiev, Noel. 1995. *How the Irish Became White.* New York: Routledge.

Illouz, Eva. 1997. *Consuming the Romantic Utopia: Love and the Cultural Contradictions of Capitalism.* Berkeley, CA: University of California Press.

Illouz, Eva, and Shoshannah Finkelman. 2009. "An Odd and Inseparable Couple: Emotion and Rationality in Partner Selection." *Theory and Society* 38(4):401–422.

Indian Health Service. 2003. *Trends in Indian Health.* Rockville, MD: U.S. Department of Health and Human Services.

Ingraham, Chrys. 2008. *White Weddings: Romancing Heterosexuality in Popular Culture.* New York: Routledge.

Inhorn, Marcia C., and Pasquale Patrizio. 2015. "Infertility around the Globe: New Thinking on Gender, Reproductive Technologies and Global Movements in the 21st Century." *Human Reproduction Update* 21(4):411–26. doi:10.1093/humupd/dmv016.

Inniss, Leslie B., and Joe R. Feagin. 1995. "The Cosby Show: The View from the Black Middle Class." *Journal of Black Studies* 25(6):692–711.

Inter-Parliamentary Union. 2016. "Women in National Parliaments (as of December 1)." http://www.ipu.org/wmn-e/arc/classif011216.htm. Accessed December 24, 2016.

Internal Revenue Service. 2012. "2010 Earned Income Tax Credit (EITC)—Can I Claim It?" http://apps.irs.gov/app/eitc2010/SetLanguage.do. Accessed January 8, 2014.

International Association of Athletics Federations. 2014. "World Records." http://www.iaaf.org/records/by-category/world-records. Accessed March 3, 2014.

IPUMS-CPS. 2016. University of Minnesota, www.ipums.org.

Irvine, Janice M. 2002. *Talk about Sex: The Battles over Sex Education in the United States.* Berkeley, CA: University of California Press.

Irwin, Sarah. 2009. "Locating Where the Action Is: Quantitative and Qualitative Lenses on Families, Schooling and Structures of Social Inequality." *Sociology: The Journal of the British Sociological Association* 43(6):1123–1140.

Isay, Richard A. 1996. *Becoming Gay: The Journey to Self-Acceptance.* New York: Pantheon Books.

Jacobs, Jerry A., and Kathleen Gerson. 2016. "Unpacking Americans' Views of the Employment of Mothers and Fathers Using National Vignette Survey Data: SWS Presidential Address." *Gender & Society* 30(3):413–41. doi:10.1177/0891243215597445.

Jacobson, Darien B., Brian G. Raub, and Barry W. Johnson. 2011. *The Estate Tax: Ninety Years and Counting.* Washington, DC: Internal Revenue Service.

Jacobson, Paul H. 1959. *American Marriage and Divorce.* New York: Rinehart, Table 42, p. 90.

Jankowiak, William R., and Edward F. Fischer. 1992. "A Cross-Cultural Perspective on Romantic Love." *Ethnology* 31(2):149–155.

Jatlaoui, T. C., Ewing, A., Mandel, M. G., et al. 2016. "Abortion Surveillance: United States, 2013." *Morbidity and Mortality Weekly Report* 65(No. SS-12):1–44.

Jena, Anupam B., Dana P. Goldman, and Seth A. Seabury. 2015. "Incidence of Sexually Transmitted Infections after Human Papillomavirus Vaccination among Adolescent Females." *JAMA Internal Medicine* 175(4):617–23. doi:10.1001/jamainternmed.2014.7886.

Jeong, Yu-Jin, and Hyun-Kyung You. 2008. "Different Historical Trajectories and Family Diversity among

Chinese, Japanese, and Koreans in the United States." *Journal of Family History* 33(3):346–356.

Jerman, Jenna, Rachel K. Jones, and Tsuyoshi Onda. 2016. *Characteristics of U.S. Abortion Patients in 2014 and Changes since 2008*. New York: Guttmacher Institute.

Jerolmack, Colin, and Shamus Khan. 2014. "Talk Is Cheap Ethnography and the Attitudinal Fallacy." *Sociological Methods & Research* 43(2):178–209. doi:10.1177/0049124114523396

John Jay College of Criminal Justice. 2004. *The Nature and Scope of Sexual Abuse of Minors by Catholic Priests and Deacons in the United States 1950–2002*. Washington, DC: U.S. Conference of Catholic Bishops.

Johnson, Matthew D. 2012. "Healthy Marriage Initiatives: On the Need for Empiricism in Policy Implementation." *The American Psychologist* 67(4):296–308. doi:10.1037/a0027743.

Johnson, Michael P. 1995. "Patriarchal Terrorism and Common Couple Violence: Two Forms of Violence against Women." *Journal of Marriage and Family* 57(2, May):283–294.

———. 2006. "Conflict and Control Gender Symmetry and Asymmetry in Domestic Violence." *Violence Against Women* 12(11):1003–1018. doi:10.1177/1077801206293328.

———. 2008. *A Typology of Domestic Violence: Intimate Terrorism, Violent Resistance, and Situational Couple Violence*. Boston : Hanover, NH: Northeastern.

———. 2011. "Gender and Types of Intimate Partner Violence: A Response to an Anti-Feminist Literature Review." *Aggression and Violent Behavior, Current Controversies on the Role of Gender in Partner Violence*, 16(4):289–96.

Johnson, Norman J., Eric Backlund, Paul D. Sorlie, and Catherine A. Loveless. 2000. "Marital Status and Mortality: The National Longitudinal Mortality Study." *Annals of Epidemiology* 10(4):224–238.

Johnston, Deirdre D., and Debra H. Swanson. 2006. "Constructing the 'Good Mother': The Experience of Mothering Ideologies by Work Status." *Sex Roles* 54(7–8):509–519.

Jones, Ann. 1985. *Everyday Death: The Case of Bernadette Powell*. New York: Holt, Rinehart and Winston.

Jones, Jacqueline. 2010. *Labor of Love, Labor of Sorrow: Black Women, Work and the Family, from Slavery to the Present*. New York: Basic Books.

Jones, Meredith. 2009. "Pygmalion's Many Faces." In *Cosmetic Surgery: A Feminist Primer*, edited by Cressida J. Heyes and Meredith Jones, pp. 171–190. Surrey, UK: Ashgate.

Jones, Rachel K., and Jenna Jerman. 2017. "Abortion Incidence and Service Availability in the United States, 2014." *Perspectives on Sexual and Reproductive Health* 49(1):17–27. doi:10.1363/psrh.12015.

Jordan, Carol E., Rebecca Campbell, and Diane Follingstad. 2010. "Violence and Women's Mental Health: The Impact of Physical, Sexual, and Psychological Aggression." *Annual Review of Clinical Psychology* 6:607–628. doi:10.1146/annurev-clinpsy-090209-151437.

Jordan, C. E., A. J. Pritchard, D. Duckett, and R. Charnigo. 2010. "Criminal Offending Among Respondents to Protective Orders: Crime Types and Patterns That Predict Victim Risk." *Violence Against Women* 16(12):1396–1411. https://doi.org/10.1177/1077801210389680.

Kahn, Joan R., Frances Goldscheider, and Javier García-Manglano. 2013. "Growing Parental Economic Power in Parent–Adult Child Households: Coresidence and Financial Dependency in the United States, 1960–2010." *Demography* 50(4):1449–1475.

Kalleberg, Arne L. 2011. *Good Jobs, Bad Jobs: The Rise of Polarized and Precarious Employment Systems in the United States, 1970s to 2000s*. New York: Russell Sage Foundation.

Kalmijn, Matthijs. 2004. "Marriage Rituals as Reinforcers of Role Transitions: An Analysis of Weddings in the Netherlands." *Journal of Marriage and Family* 66(3):582–594.

———. 2010. "Comment: Educational Inequality, Homogamy, and Status Exchange in Black-White Intermarriage." *The American Journal of Sociology* 115(4):1252–1263.

Kamp Dush, Claire M. 2013. "Marital and Cohabitation Dissolution and Parental Depressive Symptoms in Fragile Families." *Journal of Marriage and Family* 75(1):91–109.

Kamp Dush, Claire M., and Miles G. Taylor. 2012. "Trajectories of Marital Conflict across the Life Course: Predictors and Interactions with Marital Happiness Trajectories." *Journal of Family Issues* 33(3):341–368.

Kane, J. B. 2016. "Marriage Advantages in Perinatal Health: Evidence of Marriage Selection or Marriage Protection?" *Journal of Marriage and Family* 78(1), 212–229. https://doi.org/10.1111/jomf.12257.

Kane, Jennifer B., Timothy J. Nelson, and Kathryn Edin. 2015. "How Much In-Kind Support Do Low-Income Nonresident Fathers Provide? A Mixed-Method Analysis." *Journal of Marriage and Family* 77:591–611.

Kang, J., and P. N. Cohen. 2015. "Household Extension and Employment Among Asian Immigrant Women in the United States." *Journal of Family Issues*. https://doi.org/10.1177/0192513X15606489

Kanin, Eugene J. 1957. "Male Aggression in Dating-Courtship Relations." *The American Journal of Sociology* 63(2):197–204.

Kasarda, John D. 1989. "Urban Industrial Transition and the Underclass." *Annals of the American Academy of Political and Social Science* 501(The Ghetto Underclass: Social Science Perspectives):26–47.

Katz, Michael B. 1986. *In the Shadow of the Poorhouse: A Social History of Welfare in America*. New York: Basic Books.

Keister, Lisa A. 2014. "The One Percent." *Annual Review of Sociology* 40:347–367.

Keita, Shomarka O. Y., Rick A. Kittles, Charmaine D. M. Royal, George E. Bonney, Paulette Furbert-Harris, Georgia M. Dunston, and Charles N. Rotimi. 2004. "Conceptualizing Human Variation." *Nature Genetics* 36(11):S17–S20.

Kelly, Erin L., Phyllis Moen, and Eric Tranby. 2011. "Changing Workplaces to Reduce Work-Family Conflict Schedule Control in a White-Collar Organization." *American Sociological Review* 76(2):265–290. doi:10.1177/0003122411400056.

Kelly, Gail P. 1986. "Coping with America: Refugees from Vietnam, Cambodia, and Laos in the 1970s and 1980s." *Annals of the American Academy of Political and Social Science* 487(September):138–149.

Kelly, Joan B., and Robert E. Emery. 2003. "Children's Adjustment following Divorce: Risk and Resilience Perspectives." *Family Relations* 52(4):352–362.

Kendig, Sarah M., and Suzanne M. Bianchi. 2008. "Single, Cohabitating, and Married Mothers' Time with Children." *Journal of Marriage and Family* 70(5):1228–1240.

Kennedy, G. E. 2005. "From the Ape's Dilemma to the Weanling's Dilemma: Early Weaning and Its Evolutionary Context." *Journal of Human Evolution* 48(2):123–145.

Kennedy, S., and S. Ruggles. 2014. "Breaking Up Is Hard to Count: The Rise of Divorce in the United States, 1980–2010." *Demography* 51(2):587–598.

Kennedy, Sheela, and Larry Bumpass. 2008. "Cohabitation and Children's Living Arrangements: New Estimates from the United States." *Demographic Research* 19:1663–1692.

Khan, Shamus R. 2011. *Privilege: The Making of an Adolescent Elite at St. Paul's School.* Princeton, NJ: Princeton University Press.

———. 2012. *Privilege: The Making of an Adolescent Elite at St. Paul's School.* Princeton, NJ: Princeton University Press.

Kiley, Jessica, and Cassing Hammond. 2007. "Combined Oral Contraceptives: A Comprehensive Review." *Clinical Obstetrics and Gynecology* 50(4):868–877.

Kilgannon, Corey. 2007. "At a Harlem Reunion, a Rancher from Missouri Meets His 'DNA Cousins.'" *New York Times*, March 14, p. E3.

Killewald, Alexandra. 2013. "A Reconsideration of the Fatherhood Premium: Marriage, Coresidence, Biology, and Fathers' Wages." *American Sociological Review* 78(1):96–116. doi:10.1177/0003122412469204.

———. 2016. "Money, Work, and Marital Stability: Assessing Change in the Gendered Determinants of Divorce." *American Sociological Review* 81(4):696–719. doi:10.1177/0003122416655340.

Kim, Chigon, and Pyong G. Min. 2010. "Marital Patterns and Use of Mother Tongue at Home among Native Born Asian Americans." *Social Forces* 89(1):233–256.

Kim, Christine, and Robert Rector. 2008. *Abstinence Education: Assessing the Evidence.* Washington, DC: Heritage Foundation.

Kim, Hyoun K., and Pattrick C. McKenry. 2002. "The Relationship between Marriage and Psychological Well-Being: A Longitudinal Analysis." *Journal of Family Issues* 23(8):885–911.

Kim, Hyun S. 2011. "Consequences of Parental Divorce for Child Development." *American Sociological Review* 76(3):487–511.

Kimbro, Rachel T., and Ariela Schachter. 2011. "Neighborhood Poverty and Maternal Fears of Children's Outdoor Play." *Family Relations* 60(4):461–475.

King, Deborah K. 1988. "Multiple Jeopardy, Multiple Consciousness: The Context of a Black Feminist Ideology." *Signs* 14(1):42–72.

King, V., L. M. Boyd, and M. L. Thorsen. 2015. "Adolescents' Perceptions of Family Belonging in Stepfamilies." *Journal of Marriage and Family* 77(3): 761–74. http://doi.org/10.1111/jomf.12181.

King, Valarie, and Mindy E. Scott. 2005. "A Comparison of Cohabiting Relationships among Older and Younger Adults." *Journal of Marriage and Family* 67(2):271–285.

Kingsnorth, Rodney F., and Randall C. Macintosh. 2004. "Domestic Violence: Predictors of Victim Support for Official Action." *Justice Quarterly* 21(2):301–328.

Kinsey, Alfred C., Wardell B. Pomeroy, and Clyde E. Martin. 1948. *Sexual Behavior in the Human Male.* Philadelphia, PA: W. B. Saunders.

Kirk, Dudley. 1996. "Demographic Transition Theory." *Population Studies* 50(3):361–387.

Kirp, David L. 2016. "How New York Made Pre-K a Success." *New York Times*, February 13. https://www.nytimes.com/2016/02/14/opinion/sunday/how-new-york-made-pre-k-a-success.html.

Klawitter, Marieka. 2008. "The Effects of Sexual Orientation and Marital Status on How Couples Hold Their Money." *Review of Economics of the Household* 6(4):423–446.

Klawitter, Marieka M., and Irwin Garfinkel. 1992. "Child Support, Routine Income Withholding, and Postdivorce Income." *Contemporary Policy Issues* 10(1):52–64.

Klein, Andrew R. 2009. *Practical Implications of Current Domestic Violence Research: For Law Enforcement, Prosecutors and Judges.* Washington, DC: National Institute of Justice.

Klinenberg, Eric. 2012. *Going Solo: The Extraordinary Rise and Surprising Appeal of Living Alone.* New York: Penguin Press.

Koball, Heather, Randy Capps, Sarah Hooker, Krista Perreira, Andrea Campetella, Juan Manuel Pedroza, William Monson, and Sandra Huerta. 2015. "Health and Social Service Needs of U.S.-Citizen Children with Detained or

Deported Immigrant Parents." Washington, D.C.: Migration Policy Institute.

Kobrin, Frances E., and Linda J. Waite. 1984. "Effects of Childhood Family Structure on the Transition to Marriage." *Journal of Marriage and Family* 46(4):807–816.

Kochanek K. D., S. L. Murphy, J. Q. Xu, and B. Tejada-Vera. 2016. Deaths: Final Data for 2014. *National Vital Statistics Reports* 65(4). Hyattsville, MD: National Center for Health Statistics.

Kochhar, Rakesh, and D'Vera Cohn. 2011. "Fighting Poverty in a Tough Economy, Americans Move in with Their Relatives." Washington, DC: Pew Research Center.

Kohn, Melvin L. 1977. *Class and Conformity: A Study in Values, with a Reassessment, 1977*. Chicago, IL: University of Chicago Press.

Kornfeld, Benjamin D., Megan Bair-Merritt, Emily Frosch, and Barry S. Solomon. 2012. "Postpartum Depression and Intimate Partner Violence in Urban Mothers: Co-Occurrence and Child Healthcare Utilization." *The Journal of Pediatrics* 161(2):348–353.e2.

Korzeniewicz, Roberto P., and Timothy P. Moran. 2009. *Unveiling Inequality: A World-Historical Perspective*. New York: Russell Sage Foundation.

Koss, Mary P. 1992. "The Underdetection of Rape: Methodological Choices Influence Incidence Estimates." *Journal of Social Issues* 48(1):61–75.

_____. 2000. "Blame, Shame, and Community: Justice Responses to Violence against Women." *American Psychologist* 55(11):1332–1343.

Kramer, Adam D. I., Jamie E. Guillory, and Jeffrey T. Hancock. 2014. "Experimental Evidence of Massive-Scale Emotional Contagion through Social Networks." *Proceedings of the National Academy of Sciences* 111(24):8788–90. doi:10.1073/pnas.1320040111

Kramer, Karen Z., Erin L. Kelly, and Jan B. McCulloch. 2013. "Stay-at-Home Fathers: Definition and Characteristics Based on 34 Years of CPS Data." *Journal of Family Issues*. doi: 10.1177/0192513X13502479.

Kravdal, Øystein, and Ronald R. Rindfuss. 2008. "Changing Relationships between Education and Fertility: A Study of Women and Men Born 1940 to 1964." *American Sociological Review* 73(5):854–873.

Kreager, Derek A., and Jeremy Staff. 2009. "The Sexual Double Standard and Adolescent Peer Acceptance." *Social Psychology Quarterly* 72(2):143–64. doi:10.1177/019027250907200205.

Kreider, Rose M. 2007. "Interracial Adoptive Families in the U.S., 2000." In *Adoption Factbook IV*, edited by Thomas C. Atwood, pp. 155–172. Alexandria,VA: National Council for Adoption.

_____. 2010. *Increase in Opposite-Sex Cohabiting Couples from 2009 to 2010 in the Annual Social and Economic Supplement to the Current Population Survey*. Washington, DC: U.S. Census Bureau.

Kreider, Rose M. and Renee Ellis. 2011. *Number, Timing, and Duration of Marriages and Divorces: 2009*.Washington, DC: U.S. Census Bureau.

_____. 2011b. "Living Arrangements of Children: 2009." *Household Economic Studies* (P70-126). U.S. Census Bureau.

Kreider, Rose M., and Daphne A. Lofquist. 2015. "Matching Survey Data with Administrative Records to Evaluate Reports of Same-Sex Married Couple Households." U.S. Census Bureau SEHSD Working Paper #: 2014-36. http://www.census.gov/hhes/samesex/files/Kreider-Lofquist-Working-Paper.pdf. Accessed February 20, 2017.

Kreider, Rose M., and Elizabeth Raleigh. 2017. "Comparison of Black and White Adoptive Parents of Black Children." SEHSD Working Paper #2017-10. U.S. Census Bureau.

Kuperberg, Arielle. 2014. "Age at Coresidence, Premarital Cohabitation, and Marriage Dissolution: 1985–2009." *Journal of Marriage and Family* 76:352–69.

Lachance-Grzela, Mylène, and Genevieve Bouchard. 2010. "Why Do Women Do the Lion's Share of Housework? A Decade of Research." *Sex Roles* 63(11 12):767–780.

Lacy, Karyn R. 2007. *Blue-Chip Black: Race, Class, and Status in the New Black Middle Class*. Berkeley, CA: University of California Press.

Lamont, Ellen. 2014. "Negotiating Courtship Reconciling Egalitarian Ideals with Traditional Gender Norms." *Gender & Society* 28:189–211.

Lamont, Michèle. 1992. *Money, Morals, and Manners: The Culture of the French and the American Upper-Middle Class*. University of Chicago Press.

Lamont, Michèle, Jason Kaufman, and Michael Moody. 2000. "The Best of the Brightest: Definitions of the Ideal Self among Prize-Winning Students." *Sociological Forum* 15(2):187–224.

Lampert, Ada. 1997. *The Evolution of Love*. Westport, CT: Praeger.

Landale, Nancy S., and R. S. Oropesa. 2007. "Hispanic Families: Stability and Change." *Annual Review of Sociology* 33:381–405.

Landale, Nancy S., Kevin J. A. Thomas, and Jennifer Van Hook. 2011. "The Living Arrangements of Children of Immigrants." *Future of Children* 21(1):43–70.

Landers, Ann. 1974. "He Plays with Dolls," in Alexandra Tweten, "From the Stacks: He Plays with Dolls." *Ms. Magazine*, May 5, 2010. http://msmagazine.com/blog/2010/05/05/from-the-stacks-he-plays-with-dolls/. Accessed January 8, 2014.

Landry, Bart, and Kris Marsh. 2011. "The Evolution of the New Black Middle Class." *Annual Review of Sociology* 37:373–394.

Laner, Mary Riege, and Nicole A. Ventrone. 2000, "Dating Scripts Revisited." *Journal of Family Issues* 21(4):488–500.

Langdon, Carol A., and Nick Vesper. 2000. "The Sixth Phi Delta Kappa Poll of Teachers' Attitudes toward the Public Schools." The Phi Delta Kappan 81(8):607–611.

Lange, Jennifer. 2003. "Some Residents Say Prom Gives Wrong Image of Community." *Columbus Ledger-Enquirer,* May 12.

Laqueur, Thomas W. 1990. *Making Sex: Body and Gender from the Greeks to Freud.* Cambridge, MA: Harvard University Press.

Lareau, Annette. 2011. *Unequal Childhoods: Class, Race, and Family Life, 2nd edition with an Update a Decade Later.* Berkeley, CA: University of California Press.

Lareau, Annette, and Dalton Conley. 2008. *Social Class: How Does It Work?* New York: Russell Sage Foundation.

Latshaw, Beth A. 2011. "Is Fatherhood a Full-Time Job? Mixed Methods Insights into Measuring Stay-at-Home Fatherhood." *Fathering: A Journal of Theory, Research, and Practice about Men as Fathers* 9(2):125–149.

Lauer, Sean, and Carrie Yodanis. 2010. "The Deinstitutionalization of Marriage Revisited: A New Institutional Approach to Marriage." *Journal of Family Theory and Review* 2(1):58–72.

Laughlin, Lynda. 2011. *Maternity Leave and Employment Patterns of First-Time Mothers: 1961–2008.* Current Population Reports P70–128, Household Economic Studies. Washington, DC: U.S. Census Bureau.

———. 2013. *Who's Minding the Kids? Child Care Arrangements: Spring 2011.* Current Population Reports P70–135. Washington, DC: U.S. Census Bureau. http://www.census. gov/prod/2013pubs/p70-135.pdf. Accessed February 14, 2014.

Laumann, Edward O. 1994. *The Social Organization of Sexuality: Sexual Practices in the United States.* Chicago, IL: University of Chicago Press.

Lavner, Justin A., and Thomas N. Bradbury. 2010. "Patterns of Change in Marital Satisfaction over the Newlywed Years." *Journal of Marriage and Family* 72(5):1171–1187.

Lazar, Ruthy Lowenstein. 2015. "The Vindictive Wife: The Credibility of Complainants in Cases of Wife Rape." *Southern California Review of Law and Social Justice* 25:[i]–38.

Lazer, David, and Jason Radford. 2017. "General Introduction to Big Data." *Annual Review of Sociology* 43. doi:10.1146/ annurev-soc-060116-053457

LeDuff, Charlie. 2006. "Dreams in the Dark at the Drive-Through Window." *New York Times,* November 27.

Lee, Gary R., and Krista K. Payne. 2010. "Changing Marriage Patterns since 1970: What's Going On, and Why?" *Journal of Comparative Family Studies* 41(4):537–555.

Lee, James Z., and Wang Feng. 1999. *One Quarter of Humanity: Malthusian Mythology and Chinese Realities, 1700–2000.* Cambridge, MA: Harvard University Press.

Lee, Jennifer, and Frank D. Bean. 2004. "America's Changing Color Lines: Immigration, Race/Ethnicity, and Multiracial Identification." *Annual Review of Sociology* 30:221–242.

———. 2010. *The Diversity Paradox: Immigration and the Color Line in Twenty-First Century America.* New York: Russell Sage Foundation.

Lee, Jennifer, and Min Zhou. 2015. *The Asian American Achievement Paradox.* New York: Russell Sage Foundation.

Lee v. Randolph County Board of Education. 1995. Civil Action No. 847-E:642. 885 F.Supp. 1526, 1532 (M.D. Ala.1994).

Legerski, Elizabeth M., and Marie Cornwall. 2010. "Working-Class Job Loss, Gender, and the Negotiation of Household Labor." *Gender and Society* 24(4):447–474.

Lehrer, Evelyn L., and Yu Chen. 2013. "Delayed Entry into First Marriage and Marital Stability: Further Evidence on the Becker-Landes-Michael Hypothesis." *Demographic Research* 29(September):521–41. doi:10.4054/DemRes.2013.29.20.

Lemay, Helen R. 1984. "Guido Bonatti: Astrology, Society and Marriage in Thirteenth-Century Italy." *Journal of Popular Culture* 17(4):79–90.

Lenhart, Amanda. 2015. "Teens, Social Media & Technology Overview 2015." Pew Research Center: Internet, Science & Tech. April 9. http://www.pewinternet.org/2015/04/09/ teens-social-media-technology-2015/.

Leonard, Jack, Harriet Ryan, and Doug Smith. 2009. "Sentencing Evolution Doesn't Favor Polanski; Statutory-Rape Terms Tend to Be Quadruple What He Faced in 1978." *Los Angeles Times,* December 4, Metro Desk; Part A.

Lerner, Gerda. 1973. *Black Women in White America: A Documentary History.* New York: Vintage Books.

Leventhal, John M., and Julie R. Gaither. 2012. "Incidence of Serious Injuries Due to Physical Abuse in the United States: 1997 to 2009." *Pediatrics* 130(5):e847–e852.

Levine, David I., and Gary Painter. 2003. "The Schooling Costs of Teenage Out-of-Wedlock Childbearing: Analysis with a Within-School Propensity-Score-Matching Estimator." *Review of Economics and Statistics* 85(4):884–900.

Levitz, Jennifer. 2002. "Father Lamountain: 'Can You Ever Forgive Me?' James Egan: 'NO.'" *Providence Journal-Bulletin,* June 2.

Levy, Frank. 1998. *The New Dollars and Dreams: American Incomes and Economic Change.* New York: Russell Sage Foundation.

Lewis, Jamie M. 2012. "Fathering Attitudes and Father Involvement." PhD dissertation, University of North Carolina.

Li, Qing, Russell S. Kirby, Robert T. Sigler, Sean-Shong Hwang, Mark E. LaGory, and Robert L. Goldenberg. 2010. "A Multilevel Analysis of Individual, Household, and Neighborhood Correlates of Intimate Partner Violence among Low-Income Pregnant Women in Jefferson County, Alabama." *American Journal of Public Health* 100(3):531–539. doi:10.2105/AJPH.2008.151159.

Liben, Lynn S., Rebecca S. Bigler, and Holleen R. Krogh. 2001. "Pink and Blue Collar Jobs: Children's Judgments of Job Status and Job Aspirations in Relation to Sex of Worker." *Journal of Experimental Child Psychology* 79(4):346–363.

Lichter, Daniel T., Kenneth M. Johnson, Richard N. Turner, and Allison Churilla. 2012. "Hispanic Assimilation and Fertility in New U.S. Destinations." *International Migration Review* 46(4):767–791.

Lichter, Daniel T., Diane K. Mclaughlin, and David C. Ribar. 2002. "Economic Restructuring and the Retreat from Marriage." *Social Science Research* 31(2):230–256.

Lichter, Daniel T., and Zhenchao Qian. 2008. "Serial Cohabitation and the Marital Life Course." *Journal of Marriage and Family* 70(4):861–878.

Lieberson, Stanley. 2000. *A Matter of Taste: How Names, Fashions, and Culture Change.* New Haven, CT: Yale University Press.

Lillard, Lee A., and Linda J. Waite. 1993. "A Joint Model of Marital Childbearing and Marital Disruption." *Demography* 30(4):653–681.

———.1995. "'Til Death Do Us Part: Marital Disruption and Mortality." *American Journal of Sociology* 100(5):1131–1156.

Lin, Nan. 1999. "Social Networks and Status Attainment." *Annual Review of Sociology* 25:467–487.

Lincoln, Anne E. 2008. "Gender, Productivity, and the Marital Wage Premium." *Journal of Marriage and Family* 70(3):806–814.

Lindau, Stacy Tessler, L. Philip Schumm, Edward O. Laumann, Wendy Levinson, Colm A. O'Muircheartaigh, and Linda J. Waite. 2007. "A Study of Sexuality and Health among Older Adults in the United States." *New England Journal of Medicine* 357(8):762–74. doi:10.1056/NEJMoa067423.

Lindberg, Laura D., John S. Santelli, and Susheela Singh. 2006. "Changes in Formal Sex Education: 1995–2002." *Perspectives on Sexual and Reproductive Health* 38(4):182–189.

Lindholm, Charles. 1998. "Love and Structure." *Theory Culture Society* 15(3):243–263.

Lino, M., Kuczynski, K., Rodriguez, N., and Schap, T. 2017. "Expenditures on Children by Families, 2015." Miscellaneous Publication No. 1528-2015. U.S. Department of Agriculture, Center for Nutrition Policy and Promotion.

Liptak, Adam. 2015. "Supreme Court Ruling Makes Same-Sex Marriage a Right Nationwide." *New York Times*, June 26. http://www.nytimes.com/2015/06/27/us/supreme-court-same-sex-marriage.html. Accessed June 27, 2015.

Lisak, David, Lori Gardinier, Sarah C. Nicksa, and Ashley M. Cote. 2010. "False Allegations of Sexual Assualt: An Analysis of Ten Years of Reported Cases." *Violence Against Women* 16(12):1318–1334. doi:10.1177/1077801210387747.

Livingston, Gretchen, and Kim Parker. 2011. "A Tale of Two Fathers." Pew Research Center's Social & Demographic Trends Project. June 15. http://www.pewsocialtrends.org/2011/06/15/a-tale-of-two-fathers/. Accessed February 1, 2017.

The Local. 2009. "Swedish Parents Keep 2-Year-Old's Gender Secret." June 24. http://www.thelocal.se/20090623/20232. Accessed November 3, 2013.

Loftus, Jeni. 2001. "America's Liberalization in Attitudes toward Homosexuality, 1973 to 1998." *American Sociological Review* 66(5):762–782.

Longman, Phillip, Paul Corcuera, Laurie DeRose, Marga Gonzalvo-Cirac, Andres Salazar, Claudia Tarud Aravena, and Antonio Torralba. 2011. "The Empty Cradle: How Contemporary Family Trends Undermine the Global Economy." In *The Sustainable Demographic Dividend*, pp 4–23. New York: Social Trends Institute.

Loving v. Virginia. 1967. 388 U.S. 1.

Lowrie, Samuel H. 1948. "Dating, a Neglected Field of Study." *Marriage and Family Living* 10(4, Fall):90–95.

Lucas, Richard E. 2005. "Time Does Not Heal All Wounds: A Longitudinal Study of Reaction and Adaptation to Divorce." *Psychological Science* 16(12):945–950.

Lucero, Jessica L., Sojung Lim, and Anna Maria Santiago. 2016. "Changes in Economic Hardship and Intimate Partner Violence: A Family Stress Framework." *Journal of Family and Economic Issues* 37(3):395–406. doi:10.1007/s10834-016-9488-1.

Luker, Kristin. 1984. *Abortion and the Politics of Motherhood.* Berkeley, CA: University of California Press.

———. 2006. *When Sex Goes to School: Warring Views on Sex—and Sex Education—since the Sixties.* New York: W. W. Norton.

Lundquist, Erika, JoAnn Hsueh, Amy E. Lowenstein, Kristen Faucetta, Daniel Gubits, Charles Michalopoulos, and Virginia Knox. 2014. *A Family-Strengthening Program for Low-Income Families: Final Impacts from the Supporting Healthy Marriage Evaluation.* OPRE Report 2014-09A. Washington, DC: Office of Planning, Research and Evaluation, Administration for Children and Families, U.S. Department of Health and Human Services.

Luoma, Jason B., and Jane L. Pearson. 2002. "Suicide and Marital Status in the United States, 1991–1996: Is

Widowhood a Risk Factor?" *American Journal of Public Health* 92(9):1518–22.

Lyngstad, Torkild H., and Marika Jalovaara. 2010. "A Review of the Antecedents of Union Dissolution." *Demographic Research* 23:257–291.

Maccoby, E.E.; Martin, J.A. 1983. "Socialization in the context of the family: Parent-child interaction". In Mussen, P.H.; Hetherington, E.M. *Manual of child psychology*, Vol. 4: Social development. New York: John Wiley and Sons.

Machalek, Richard, and Michael W. Martin. 2004. "Sociology and the Second Darwinian Revolution: A Metatheoretical Analysis." *Sociological Theory* 22(3):455–476.

MacKinnon, Catharine A. 1991. *Toward a Feminist Theory of the State*. Cambridge, MA: Harvard University Press.

———. 2007. *Sex Equality*. 2nd ed. New York: Foundation Press; St. Paul: Thomson/West.

Macmillan, R., and R. Copher. 2005. "Families in the Life Course: Interdependency of Roles, Role Configurations, and Pathways." *Journal of Marriage and Family* 67(4):858–879.

Mahoney, Margaret M. 2006. "Stepparents as Third Parties in Relation to Their Stepchildren." *Family Law Quarterly* 40(1):81–108.

Manlove, Jennifer, Heather Fish, and Kristin Anderson Moore. 2015. "Programs to Improve Adolescent Sexual and Reproductive Health in the US: A Review of the Evidence." *Adolescent Health, Medicine and Therapeutics* 6:47–79. doi:10.2147/AHMT.S48054.

Manning, Christel. 1999. *God Gave Us the Right: Conservative Catholic, Evangelical Protestant, and Orthodox Jewish Women Grapple with Feminism*. New Brunswick, NJ: Rutgers University Press.

Manning, Wendy D., Susan L. Brown, and Krista K. Payne. 2014. "Two Decades of Stability and Change in Age at First Union Formation." *Journal of Marriage and Family* 76:247–60.

Manning, Wendy D., Susan L. Brown, and J. Bart Stykes. 2016. "Same-Sex and Different-Sex Cohabiting Couple Relationship Stability." *Demography* 53(4):937–53. doi:10.1007/s13524-016-0490-x.

Manning, Wendy D., and Jessica A. Cohen. 2012. "Premarital Cohabitation and Marital Dissolution: An Examination of Recent Marriages." *Journal of Marriage and Family* 74 (2): 377–387. doi:10.1111/j.1741-3737.2012.00960.x

Manning, Wendy D., and Pamela J. Smock. 2005. "Measuring and Modeling Cohabitation: New Perspectives from Qualitative Data." *Journal of Marriage and Family* 67(4):989–1002.

Manzoli, Lamberto, Paolo Villari, Giovanni M. Pirone, and Antonio Boccia. 2007. "Marital Status and Mortality in the Elderly: A Systematic Review and Meta-Analysis." *Social Science and Medicine* 64(1):77–94.

Marcus, Kenneth, and R. Alexander Acosta. 2005. "Dear Colleague Letter: Addressing the Issue of Civil Rights Violations Inherent in Racially Separate Proms or Dances." December 19. http://www2.ed.gov/about/offices/list/ocr/letters/segprom-2004.html. Accessed January 24, 2014.

Marsh, Kris, William A. Darity Jr, Philip N. Cohen, Lynne M. Casper, and Danielle Salters. 2007. "The Emerging Black Middle Class: Single and Living Alone." *Social Forces* 86(2):735–762.

Marsiglio, W., and K. Roy. 2012. *Nurturing Dads: Social Initiatives for Contemporary Fatherhood*. New York: Russell Sage Foundation.

Martin, Carol Lynn, and Diane N. Ruble. 2010. "Patterns of Gender Development." *Annual Review of Psychology* 61:353–381.

Martin, Elaine K., Casey T. Taft, and Patricia A. Resick. 2007. "A Review of Marital Rape." *Aggression and Violent Behavior* 12(3):329–347.

Martin, J. A., Hamilton, B. E., Osterman, M. J. K., et al. 2017. "Births: Final data for 2015." National vital statistics report; 6(1). Hyattsville, MD: National Center for Health Statistics.

Martin, Karin A. 1998. "Becoming a Gendered Body: Practices of Preschools." *American Sociological Review* 63(4, August):494. doi:10.2307/2657264.

———. 2009. "Normalizing Heterosexuality: Mothers' Assumptions, Talk, and Strategies with Young Children." *American Sociological Review* 74(2):190–207.

Martin, Patricia Yancey. 2004. "Gender as Social Institution." *Social Forces* 82(4):1249–1273.

Martin, Steven P. 2006. "Trends in Marital Dissolution by Women's Education in the United States." *Demographic Research* 15(20):537–560.

Martin, Steven P., and John P. Robinson. 2007. "The Income Digital Divide: Trends and Predictions for Levels of Internet Use." *Social Problems* 54(1):1–22.

Marx, Karl. 1867 [1990]. *Capital: A Critique of Political Economy*. London, UK: Penguin Books.

Mastekaasa, Arne. 1994. "Psychological Well-Being and Marital Dissolution: Selection Effects." *Journal of Family Issues* 15(2):208–228.

May, Elaine T. 1988. *Homeward Bound: American Families in the Cold War Era*. New York: Basic Books.

May, Martha. 1982. "The Historical Problem of the Family Wage: The Ford Motor Company and the Five Dollar Day." *Feminist Studies* 8(2, Women and Work):399–424.

Mayer, Susan E. 1997. *What Money Can't Buy: Family Income and Children's Life Chances*. Cambridge, MA: Harvard University Press.

Mazumder, B. 2015. "Intergenerational Mobility: A Cross-National Comparison." In *Emerging Trends in the Social and*

Behavioral Sciences. John Wiley & Sons, Inc. https://doi.org/10.1002/9781118900772.etrds0192.

McBride, Dorothy E. 2008. *Abortion in the United States: A Reference Handbook*. Santa Barbara, CA: ABC-CLIO.

McCarthy, Justin. 2015. "More Americans Say Low-Income Earners Pay Too Much in Taxes." Gallup.com, April 15, 2015. http://www.gallup.com/poll/182426/americans-say-low-income-earners-pay-taxes.aspx.

McClintock, E. A. 2014. "Beauty and Status: The Illusion of Exchange in Partner Selection?" *American Sociological Review.* http://doi.org/10.1177/0003122414536391

McClintock, Elizabeth A. 2010. "When Does Race Matter? Race, Sex, and Dating at an Elite University." *Journal of Marriage and Family* 72(1):45–72.

McDermott, Monica, and Frank L. Samson. 2005. "White Racial and Ethnic Identity in the United States." *Annual Review of Sociology* 31:245–261.

McDermott, Rose, James Fowler, and Nicholas Christakis. 2013. "Breaking Up Is Hard to Do, Unless Everyone Else Is Doing It Too: Social Network Effects on Divorce in a Longitudinal Sample." *Social Forces* 92 (2): 491–519.

McDowell, Margaret A., Cheryl D. Fryar, Cynthia L. Ogden, and Katherine M. Flegal. 2008. "Anthropometric Reference Data for Children and Adults: United States, 2003–2006." National Health Statistics Reports 10. Hyattsville, MD: National Center for Health Statistics.

McFarlane, Jessica, Carol Lynn Martin, and Tannis MacBeth Williams. 1988. "Mood Fluctuations: Women Versus Men and Menstrual Versus Other Cycles." *Psychology of Women Quarterly* 12(2):201–223.

McGuffey, C. S. 2013. "Rape and Racial Appraisals: Culture, Intersectionality, and Black Women's Accounts of Sexual Assault." *Du Bois Review-Social Science Research on Race,* 10(1):109–30.

McHale, Susan M., Ann C. Crouter, and Shawn D. Whiteman. 2003. "The Family Contexts of Gender Development in Childhood and Adolescence." *Social Development* 12(1):125–148.

McKeever, Matthew, and Nicholas H. Wolfinger. 2001. "Reexamining the Economic Costs of Marital Disruption for Women." *Social Science Quarterly* 82(1):202–217.

———. 2011. "Thanks for Nothing: Income and Labor Force Participation for Never-Married Mothers since 1982." *Social Science Research* 40(1):63–76.

McKie, Raymond M., Robin R. Milhausen, and Nathan J. Lachowsky. 2017. "'Hedge Your Bets': Technology's Role in Young Gay Men's Relationship Challenges." *Journal of Homosexuality* 64(1):75–94. doi:10.1080/00918369.2016.1172883.

McLanahan, S., and W. Jacobsen. 2015. "Diverging Destinies Revisited." In P. R. Amato, A. Booth, S. M. McHale, and J. V. Hook (Eds.), *Families in an Era of Increasing Inequality* pp. 3–23. Springer International Publishing. https://doi.org/10.1007/978-3-319-08308-7_1.

McLanahan, Sara, and Christine Percheski. 2008. "Family Structure and the Reproduction of Inequalities." *Annual Review of Sociology* 34(1):257–276.

McLanahan, Sara, and Gary D. Sandefur. 1994. *Growing Up with a Single Parent: What Hurts, What Helps*. Cambridge, MA: Harvard University Press.

McMillen v. Itawamba County School District. 2010. 1:10-cv-61, 2010 WL 1172429 (N.D. Miss. Mar. 23, 2010).

McNamee, Catherine B., and R. K. Raley. 2011. "A Note on Race, Ethnicity and Nativity Differentials in Remarriage in the United States." *Demographic Research* 24:293–312.

McPherson, Miller, Lynn Smith-Lovin, and James M. Cook. 2001. "Birds of a Feather: Homophily in Social Networks." *Annual Review of Sociology* 27:415–444.

Meier, Ann, Kelly Musick, Sarah Flood, and Rachel Dunifon. 2016. "Mothering Experiences: How Single Parenthood and Employment Structure the Emotional Valence of Parenting." *Demography* 53(3):649–74. doi:10.1007/s13524-016-0474-x.

Mele, C. 2016. "Oregon Court Allows a Person to Choose Neither Sex." June 13. *New York Times*. http://www.nytimes.com/2016/06/14/us/oregon-nonbinary-transgender-sex-gender.html.

Meng, Xiangfei, and Carl D'Arcy. 2016. "Gender Moderates the Relationship between Childhood Abuse and Internalizing and Substance Use Disorders Later in Life: A Cross-Sectional Analysis." Bmc Psychiatry 16(November): 401. doi:10.1186/s12888-016-1071-7.

Merino, Stephen M. 2010. "Religious Diversity in a 'Christian Nation': The Effects of Theological Exclusivity and Interreligious Contact on the Acceptance of Religious Diversity." *Journal for the Scientific Study of Religion* 49(2):231–246.

Miall, Charlene E., and Karen March. 2005. "Open Adoption as a Family Form: Community Assessments and Social Support." *Journal of Family Issues* 26(3):380–410.

Milbrath, Constance, Brightstar Ohlson, and Stephen L. Eyre. 2009. "Analyzing Cultural Models in Adolescent Accounts of Romantic Relationships." *Journal of Research on Adolescence* 19(2):313–351.

Milkie, Melissa A. 2002. "Contested Images of Femininity: An Analysis of Cultural Gatekeepers' Struggles with the 'Real Girl' Critique." *Gender and Society* 16(6):839–859.

Milkie, Melissa A., Sara B. Raley, and Suzanne M. Bianchi. 2009. "Taking on the Second Shift: Time Allocations and Time Pressures of U.S. Parents with Preschoolers." *Social Forces* 88(2):487–517.

Milkman, Ruth, and Eileen Appelbaum. 2013. *Unfinished Business: Paid Family Leave in California and the Future of U.S. Work-Family Policy.* Ithaca, NY: Cornell University Press.

Mill, John Stuart. 1869. *The Subjection of Women.* London, UK: Longmans, Green, Reader, and Dyer.

Miller, Audrey K., Erika J. Canales, Amanda M. Amacker, Tamika L. Backstrom, and Christine A. Gidycz. 2011. "Stigma-Threat Motivated Nondisclosure of Sexual Assault and Sexual Revictimization: A Prospective Analysis." *Psychology of Women Quarterly* 35(1):119–28. doi:10.1177/0361684310384104.

Miller, Claire Cain. 2015. "The 24/7 Work Culture's Toll on Families and Gender Equality." *New York Times,* May 28. https://www.nytimes.com/2015/05/31/upshot/the-24-7-work-cultures-toll-on-families-and-gender-equality.html.

Mills, C. Wright. 1959 [2000]. *The Sociological Imagination.* New York: Oxford University Press.

Mink, Gwendolyn. 1998. *Welfare's End.* Ithaca, NY: Cornell University Press.

Mintz, Steven. 1998. "From Patriarchy to Androgyny and Other Myths: Placing Men's Family Roles in Historical Perspective." In *Men in Families: When Do They Get Involved? What Difference Does It Make?,* edited by A. Booth and A. C. Crater, pp. 3–30. Mahwah, NJ: Lawrence Erlbaum Associates.

Mohr, Jonathan J., and Christopher A. Daly. 2008. "Sexual Minority Stress and Changes in Relationship Quality in Same-Sex Couples." *Journal of Social and Personal Relationships* 25(6):989–1007.

Mokyr, Joel. 2000. "Why 'More Work for Mother?' Knowledge and Household Behavior 1870–1945." *Journal of Economic History* 60(1):1–41.

Mongeau, Paul A., Janet Jacobsen, and Carolyn Donnerstein. 2007. "Defining Dates and First Date Goals Generalizing from Undergraduates to Single Adults." *Communication Research* 34(5):526–47. doi:10.1177/0093650207305235.

Monte, Lindsay M. 2017. "Multiple Partner Fertility Research Brief." Current Population Reports, P70BR-146. U.S. Census Bureau.

Moore, Justin Xavier, Brice Lambert, Gabrielle P. Jenkins, and Gerald McGwin. 2015. "Epidemiology of High-Heel Shoe Injuries in U.S. Women: 2002 to 2012." *The Journal of Foot and Ankle Surgery* 54(4):615–19. doi:10.1053/j.jfas.2015.04.008.

Moran, Jeffrey P. 2000. *Teaching Sex: The Shaping of Adolescence in the 20th Century.* Cambridge, MA: Harvard University Press.

Moran, Rachel F. 2001. *Interracial Intimacy: The Regulation of Race and Romance.* Chicago, IL: University of Chicago Press.

Morning, Ann. 2005. "Race." *Contexts* 4(4):44–46.

Morrison, Donna Ruane, and Amy Ritualo. 2000. "Routes to Children's Economic Recovery after Divorce: Are Cohabitation and Remarriage Equivalent?" *American Sociological Review* 65(4):560–580. doi:10.2307/2657383.

Moynihan, Daniel P. 1965. "The Negro Family: The Case for National Action." Washington, DC: Office of Policy Planning and Research.

Moynihan, Ray, Iona Heath, and David Henry. 2002. "Selling Sickness: The Pharmaceutical Industry and Disease Mongering." *British Medical Journal* 324(7342):886–890.

Mukherjee, Siddhartha. 2010. *The Emperor of All Maladies: A Biography of Cancer.* New York: Scribner.

Murray, Charles A. 1984. *Losing Ground: American Social Policy, 1950–1980.* New York: Basic Books.

Musick, Kelly, Paula England, Sarah Edgington, and Nicole Kangas. 2009. "Education Differences in Intended and Unintended Fertility." *Social Forces* 88(2):543–572.

Musick, Kelly, and Robert D. Mare. 2006. "Recent Trends in the Inheritance of Poverty and Family Structure." *Social Science Research* 35(2):471–499.

Musick, Kelly, and Katherine Michelmore. 2015. "Change in the Stability of Marital and Cohabiting Unions Following the Birth of a Child." *Demography* 52:1463–85.

Mutchler, Jan E., Lindsey A. Baker, and SeungAh Lee. 2007. "Grandparents Responsible for Grandchildren in Native-American Families." *Social Science Quarterly* 88(4):990–1009.

Myers, Scott M. 1996. "An Interactive Model of Religiosity Inheritance: The Importance of Family Context." *American Sociological Review* 61(5):858–866.

———. 2006. "Religious Homogamy and Marital Quality: Historical and Generational Patterns, 1980–1997." *Journal of Marriage and Family* 68(2):292–304.

National Alliance to End Homelessness. 2016. "The State of Homelessness in America: 2016." http://www.endhomelessness.org/library/entry/SOH2016. Accessed December 9, 2016.

National Center for Children in Poverty. 2014. Basic Needs Budget Calculator. http://nccp.org/tools/frs/budget.php. Accessed January 8, 2014.

National Center for Education Statistics. 2015. "Postsecondary Attainment: Differences by Socioeconomic." http://nces.ed.gov/programs/coe/indicator_tva.asp.

National Center for Health Statistics. 1968. "Marriage Statistics Analysis, 1963." Vital and Health Statistics 21(16). http://www.cdc.gov/nchs/data/series/sr_21/sr21_016acc.pdf. Accessed September 14, 2013.

———. 2010. "Cohort Fertility Tables." http://www.cdc.gov/nchs/nvss/cohort_fertility_tables.htm. Accessed October 30, 2009.

———. 2013. "Deaths: Final Data for 2010." *National Vital Statistics Reports* 61(4).

———. 2016. "Key Statistics from the National Survey of Family Growth." https://www.cdc.gov/nchs/nsfg/key_statistics.htm.

———. 2017. Key Statistics from the National Survey of Family Growth. https://www.cdc.gov/nchs/nsfg/key_statistics.htm. Accessed March 22, 2017.

National Conference of State Legislatures. 2013. "Defining Marriage." http://www.ncsl.org/issues-research/human-services/same-sex-marriage-overview.aspx. Accessed September 25, 2013.

———. 2016. "State Family and Medical Leave Laws." http://www.ncsl.org/research/labor-and-employment/state-family-and-medical-leave-laws.aspx.

National Indian Gaming Commission. 2013. Various reports. Washington, DC.

National Institute for Early Education Research. 2016. "The State of Preschool: 2015." http://nieer.org/state-preschool-yearbooks/the-state-of-preschool-2015. Accessed April 20, 2017.

Nelson, Margaret. 2010a. "Helicopter Moms, Heading for a Crash." *Washington Post,* July 4, Opinion.

Newman, Katherine S. 1999. *No Shame in My Game: The Working Poor in the Inner City.* New York: Alfred A. Knopf and the Russell Sage Foundation.

———. 2012. *The Accordion Family: Boomerang Kids, Anxious Parents, and the Private Toll of Global Competition.* Boston, MA: Beacon Press.

Newport, Frank, and Igor Himelfarb. 2013. "In U.S., Record-High Say Gay, Lesbian Relations Morally OK." Washington, DC: Gallup.

Nguyen, T. P., B. R. Karney, and T. N. Bradbury. 2017. "Childhood Abuse and Later Marital Outcomes: Do Partner Characteristics Moderate the Association?" *Journal of Family Psychology* 31(1):82–92. https://doi.org/10.1037/fam0000208.

Noack, Turid, Eva Bernhardt, and Kenneth Aarskaug Wiik. 2013. "Cohabitation or Marriage? Contemporary Living Arrangements in the West." In *Contemporary Issues in Family Studies*, edited by Angela Abela and Janet Walker, pp. 16–30. John Wiley & Sons.

Nock, Steven L. 2005. "Marriage as a Public Issue." *Future of Children* 15(2):13–32.

Nomaguchi, Kei M. 2012. "Marital Status, Gender, and Home-to-Job Conflict among Employed Parents." *Journal of Family Issues* 33(3):271–294.

Norris, Tina, Paula L. Vines, and Elizabeth M. Hoeffel. 2012. "The American Indian and Alaska Native Population: 2010." Washington, DC: U.S. Census Bureau.

Norton, Kevin I., Timothy S. Olds, Scott Olive, and Stephen Dank. 1996. "Ken and Barbie at Life Size." *Sex Roles* 34(3–4):287–294.

Nostrand, Richard L. 1975. "Mexican Americans Circa 1850." *Annals of the Association of American Geographers* 65(3):378–390.

O'Brien, Kelsie. 2015. "5 Habits for a Healthy Marriage (Faith-Based)." BetterMarriages.org. http://www.bettermarriages.org/communication/5-habits-for-a-healthy-marriage/.

Obergefell v. Hodges. 2015. 576 U.S. __.

Ochsner, Nick. 2016. "Matthews School Punishes Boy for Having Long Hair." WBTV. August 30. http://www.wbtv.com/story/32816460/matthews-school-punishes-boy-for-having-long-hair.

OECD, Family Database. 2017a. "Table PF2.1 Key Characteristics of Parental Leave Systems." http://www.oecd.org/els/soc/PF2_1_Parental_leave_systems.pdf

———. 2017b. "Hours Worked (indicator)." doi:10.1787/47be1c78-en. Accessed May 6, 2017.

OED Online. "homosexual." 2013. December 2013. New York: Oxford University Press. http://www.oed.com/view/Entry/88110?redirectedFrom=homosexual. Accessed January 17, 2014.

Oezcan, Berkay, and Richard Breen. 2012. "Marital Instability and Female Labor Supply." *Annual Review of Sociology* 38:463–81.

Offer, Shira, and Barbara Schneider. 2011. "Revisiting the Gender Gap in Time-Use Patterns: Multitasking and Well-Being among Mothers and Fathers in Dual-Earner Families." *American Sociological Review* 76(6):809–833.

Office of the High Commissioner for Human Rights. N.d.. Convention on the Rights of the Child. http://www.ohchr.org/en/professionalinterest/pages/crc.aspx. Accessed May 30, 2017.

Oldham, J. Thomas. 2008. "Changes in the Economic Consequences of Divorces, 1958–2008." *Family Law Quarterly* 42(3):419–447.

Olsen, Emily O'Malley, Laura Kann, Alana Vivolo-Kantor, Steve Kinchen, and Tim McManus. 2014. "School Violence and Bullying Among Sexual Minority High School Students, 2009–2011." *Journal of Adolescent Health* 55(3):432–38. doi:10.1016/j.jadohealth.2014.03.002.

Oppenheimer, Valerie K. 1994. "Women's Rising Employment and the Future of the Family in Industrial Societies." *Population and Development Review* 20(2):293–342.

Orloff, Ann S. 2009. "Gendering the Comparative Analysis of Welfare States: An Unfinished Agenda." *Sociological Theory* 27(3):317–343.

Osborne, Horace W. 1945. "Your Daughter Gets Married Only Once." *Saturday Evening Post*, May 26, p. 41.

Osterman, Paul. 1979. "Sex Discrimination in Professional Employment: Case-Study." *Industrial and Labor Relations Review* 32(4):451–464.

Owen, Patricia R., and Erika Laurel-Seller. 2000. "Weight and Shape Ideals: Thin Is Dangerously In." *Journal of Applied Social Psychology* 30(5):979–990.

"Planning a Wedding with Divorced Parents." 2011. Anonymous blog post, May 26. *A Practical Wedding.* http://apracticalwedding.com/2011/05/planning-a-wedding-with-divorce-parents-part-i/. Accessed October 10, 2013.

Pagnini, Deanna L., and S. Philip Morgan. 1990. "Intermarriage and Social Distance among U.S. Immigrants at the Turn of the Century." *The American Journal of Sociology* 96(2):405–432.

———. 1996. "Racial Differences in Marriage and Childbearing: Oral History Evidence from the South in the Early Twentieth Century." *American Journal of Sociology* 101(6):1694–1718.

Painter, Nell I. 2010. *The History of White People.* New York: W.W. Norton.

Panel Study of Income Dynamics, public use dataset. 2013. Produced and distributed by the Survey Research Center, Institute for Social Research. Ann Arbor, MI: University of Michigan.

Pao, Maureen. 2015. "How America's Child Support System Failed to Keep Up with the Times." *NPR.* November 19. http://www.npr.org/2015/11/19/456632896/how-u-s-parents-racked-up-113-billion-in-child-support-debt.

Paoletti, Jo B. 1987. "Clothing and Gender in America: Children's Fashions, 1890–1920." *Signs* 13(1, Women and the Political Process in the United States):136–143.

———. 2012. *Pink and Blue: Telling the Boys from the Girls in America.* Bloomington, IN: Indiana University Press.

Parker, Kim, and Wendy Wang. 2013. *Modern Parenthood: Roles of Moms and Dads Converge as They Balance Work and Family.* Washington, D.C.: Pew Research Center.

Parker-Pope, Tara. 2010. "Is Marriage Good for Your Health?" *New York Times*, April 18, MM; Magazine Desk.

Parks, Casey. 2016. "Oregon Court Allows Person to Change Sex from 'Female' to 'Non-Binary.'" *Oregonian*, June 10. http://www.oregonlive.com/portland/index.ssf/2016/06/oregon_court_allows_person_to.html.

Parnell, Allan M., Gray Swicegood, and Gillian Stevens. 1994. "Nonmarital Pregnancies and Marriage in the United States." *Social Forces* 73(1):263–287.

Parry, Diana C. 2005. "Women's Experiences with Infertility: The Fluidity of Conceptualizations of 'Family'." *Qualitative Sociology* 28(3):275–291.

Parsons, Talcott. 1954. "The Incest Taboo in Relation to Social Structure and the Socialization of the Child." *British Journal of Sociology* 5(2):101–117.

Parsons, Talcott, and Robert F. Bales. 1955. *Family, Socialization and Interaction Process.* Glencoe, IL: Free Press.

Pascoe, C. J., and Tristan Bridges. 2016. *Exploring Masculinities : Identity, Inequality, Continuity, and Change.* New York: Oxford University Press.

Passel, Jeffrey S., Wendy Wang, and Paul Taylor. 2010. *Marrying Out: One-in-Seven U.S Marriages Is Interracial or Interethnic.* Washington, DC: Pew Research Center.

Pattavina, April, David Hirschel, Eve Buzawa, Don Faggiani, and Helen Bentley. 2007. "A Comparison of the Police Response to Heterosexual Versus Same-Sex Intimate Partner Violence." *Violence Against Women* 13(4):374–394.

Patterson, Charlotte J. 1992. "Children of Lesbian and Gay Parents." *Child Development* 63(5):1025–1042. doi:10.1111/j.1467-8624.1992.tb01679.x.

Paul VI. 1968. "Encyclical Letter Humanae Vitae of the Supreme Pontiff Paul VI to His Venerable Brothers the Patriarchs, Archbishops, Bishops and Other Local Ordinaries in Peace and Communion with the Apostolic See, to the Clergy and Faithful of the Whole Catholic World, and to All Men of Good Will, on the Regulation of Birth." http://www.vatican.va/holy_father/paul_vi/encyclicals/documents/hf_p-vi_enc_25071968_humanae-vitae_en.html. Accessed November 3, 2013.

Paul, Pamela. 2011. "How Divorce Lost Its Groove." *New York Times*, June 17, Fashion and Style.

Pawłowski, Bogusław. 1999. "Loss of Oestrus and Concealed Ovulation in Human Evolution: The Case against the Sexual-Selection Hypothesis." *Current Anthropology* 40(3):257–276.

Payne, Krista K. 2014. "Demographic Profile of Same-Sex Couple Households with Minor Children, 2012 (FP-14-03)." National Center for Family & Marriage Research.

Pearce, Lisa D., and Arland Thornton. 2007. "Religious Identity and Family Ideologies in the Transition to Adulthood." *Journal of Marriage and Family* 69(5):1227–1243.

Pedulla, David S., and Sarah Thébaud. 2015. "Can We Finish the Revolution? Gender, Work-Family Ideals, and Institutional Constraint." *American Sociological Review* 80:116–39.

Peisch, Virginia, Justin Parent, Rex Forehand, Andrew Golub, Megan Reid, and Mathew Price. 2016. "Intimate Partner Violence in Cohabiting Families: Reports by Multiple Informants and Associations with Adolescent Outcomes." *Journal of Family Violence* 31(6):747–57. doi:10.1007/s10896-016-9808-0.

Peiss, Kathy. 1986. *Cheap Amusements: Working Women and Leisure in Turn-of-the-Century New York.* Philadelphia, PA: Temple University Press.

Penner, Andrew M. 2008. "Gender Differences in Extreme Mathematical Achievement: An International Perspective on Biological and Social Factors." *American Journal of Sociology* 114:S138–S170.

People. 2016. "Chrissy Teigen Shares Why She Chose to Have a Daughter: John 'Deserves That Bond.'" February 24. http://celebritybabies.people.com/2016/02/24/chrissy-teigen-john-legend-picked-girl-embryo/.

Pepin, Joanna Rae. 2016. "Nobody's Business? White Male Privilege in Media Coverage of Intimate Partner Violence." *Sociological Spectrum* 36(3):123–41. doi:10.1080/02732173.2015.1108886.

Peplau, Letitia Anne, and Adam W. Fingerhut. 2007. "The Close Relationships of Lesbians and Gay Men." *Annual Review of Psychology* 58:405–424. doi:10.1146/annurev.psych.58.110405.085701.

Perry v. Schwarzenegger. 2010. 704 F. Supp. 2d 921. Dist. Court, ND California.

Perry, Samuel L. 2016. "From Bad to Worse? Pornography Consumption, Spousal Religiosity, Gender, and Marital Quality." *Sociological Forum* 31(2):441–64. doi:10.1111/socf.12252.

Peters, Jeremy W. 2008. "New York to Back Same-Sex Unions from Elsewhere." *New York Times,* May 29, p. A1.

Pettit, Becky, and Bruce Western. 2004. "Mass Imprisonment and the Life Course: Race and Class Inequality in U.S. Incarceration." *American Sociological Review* 69(2):151–169.

Pew Research Center. 2006. "Guess Who's Coming to Dinner." Washington, DC: Pew Research Center.

———. 2007a. "From 1997 to 2007: Fewer Mothers Prefer Full-Time Work." Washington, DC: Pew Research Center.

———. 2007b. "Muslim Americans: Middle Class and Mostly Mainstream." Washington, DC: Pew Research Center.

———. 2009. "Eastern, New Age Beliefs Widespread: Many Americans Mix Multiple Faiths." http://www.pewforum.org/files/2009/12/multiplefaiths.pdf. Accessed October 9, 2016.

———. 2010. "The Decline of Marriage and Rise of New Families." Washington, DC: Pew Research Center.

———. 2011. "Muslim Americans: No Signs of Growth in Alienation or Support for Extremism." Pew Research Center for the People and the Press. August 30. http://www.people-press.org/2011/08/30/muslim-americans-no-signs-of-growth-in-alienation-or-support-for-extremism/.

———. 2013. "Changing Attitudes on Gay Marriage." http://features.pewforum.org/same-sex-marriage-attitudes/. Accessed September 23, 2013.

———. 2015a. "Parenting in America." http://www.pewsocialtrends.org/2015/12/17/parenting-in-america/. Accessed September 28, 2016.

———. 2015b. "U.S. Public Becoming Less Religious." http://www.pewforum.org/2015/11/03/u-s-public-becoming-less-religious/. Accessed January 10, 2017.

———. 2015c. "Changing Attitudes on Gay Marriage." http://features.pewforum.org/same-sex-marriage-attitudes/. Accessed June 27, 2015.

———. 2015d. "Parenting in America." Washington, D.C. http://www.pewsocialtrends.org/files/2015/12/2015-12-17_parenting-in-america_FINAL.pdf. Accessed February 1, 2017.

———. 2015e. "America's Changing Religious Landscape." Washington, D.C.

———. 2016a. "Unauthorized Immigration." http://www.pewresearch.org/topics/unauthorized-immigration/. Accessed November 25.

———. 2016b. "Changing Attitudes on Gay Marriage." Pew Research Center's Religion & Public Life Project. http://www.pewforum.org/2016/05/12/changing-attitudes-on-gay-marriage/.

Philips, Benjamin T., and Sylvia B. Fishman. 2006. "Ethnic Capital and Intermarriage: A Case Study of American Jews." *Sociology of Religion* 67(4):487–505.

Phillipson, Chris, and Graham Allan. 2004. "Aging and the Life Course." In *The Blackwell Companion to the Sociology of Families*, edited by Jacqueline Scott, Judith Treas, and Martin Richards, pp. 126–141. Malden, MA: Blackwell Publishing.

Piketty, Thomas, Emmanuel Saez, and Gabriel Zucman. 2016. "Distributional National Accounts: Methods and Estimates for the United States." http://gabriel-zucman.eu/files/PSZ2016.pdf.

Pink Stinks. 2013. "About Us." http://www.pinkstinks.org.uk/about-us.html. Accessed July 23, 2013.

Pinker, Steven. 2011. *The Better Angels of Our Nature: Why Violence Has Declined.* New York: Viking.

Podolak, Janet. 2012. "Tomatoes Ripening a Month Early at Pritt Family Farm." *News-Herald,* July 5. http://www.news-herald.com/articles/2012/07/05/life/nh5684531.txt. Accessed June 18, 2014.

Pollet, Susan L. 2010. "Still a Patchwork Quilt: A Nationwide Survey of State Laws Regarding Stepparent Rights and Obligations." *Family Court Review* 48(3):528–540. doi:10.1111/j.1744-1617.2010.01327.x.

Popenoe, David. 1993. "American Family Decline, 1960–1990: A Review and Appraisal." *Journal of Marriage and Family* 55(3):527–542.

Portes, Alejandro. 1998. "Social Capital: Its Origins and Applications in Modern Sociology." *Annual Review of Sociology* 24:1–24.

———. 2005. "Introduction: The Second Generation and the Children of Immigrants Longitudinal Study." *Ethnic and Racial Studies* 28(6):983–999.

Portes, Alejandro, and Rubén G. Rumbaut. 2001. *Legacies: The Story of the Immigrant Second Generation.* Berkeley, CA:

University of California Press; New York: Russell Sage Foundation.

Potter, Hillary. 2008. *Battle Cries: Black Women and Intimate Partner Abuse.* New York: New York University Press.

Potterat, John J., Stephen Q. Muth, Richard B. Rothenberg, Helen Zimmerman-Rogers, David L. Green, Jerry E. Taylor, Mandy S. Bonney, and Helen A. White. 2002. "Sexual Network Structure as an Indicator of Epidemic Phase." *Sexually Transmitted Infections* 78:i152–i158.

Powell, Brian, Catherine Bolzendahl, Claudia Geist, and Lala C. Steelman. 2010. *Counted Out: Same-Sex Relations and Americans' Definitions of Family.* New York: Russell Sage Foundation.

Presser, Harriet B. 1998. "Decapitating the U.S. Census Bureau's 'Head of Household': Feminist Mobilization in the 1970s." *Feminist Economics* 4(3):145–158.

———. 2003. *Working in a 24/7 Economy: Challenges for American Families.* New York: Russell Sage Foundation.

Preston, Julia. 2013. "Forced to Choose: Love or Country." *New York Times,* February 17, p. A8.

Preston, Samuel H. 1975. "Estimating the Proportion of American Marriages That End in Divorce." *Sociological Methods and Research* 3(4):435–460.

Preston, Samuel, Patrick Heuveline, and Michel Guillot. 2000. *Demography: Measuring and Modeling Population Processes.* Malden, MA: Wiley-Blackwell.

Preston, Samuel H., Suet Lim, and S. P. Morgan. 1992. "African-American Marriage in 1910: Beneath the Surface of Census Data." *Demography* 29(1):1–15.

Prickett, Kate C., Alexa Martin-Storey, and Robert Crosnoe. 2015. "A Research Note on Time with Children in Different- and Same-Sex Two-Parent Families." *Demography* 52(3): 905–18. doi:10.1007/s13524-015-0385-2.

Pujazon-Zazik, Melissa, and M. J. Park. 2010. "To Tweet, or Not to Tweet: Gender Differences and Potential Positive and Negative Health Outcomes of Adolescents' Social Internet Use." *American Journal of Men's Health* 4(1):77–85.

Putnam, Robert D. 2000. *Bowling Alone: The Collapse and Revival of American Community.* New York: Simon and Schuster.

Puts, David A., Cynthia L. Jordan, and S. M. Breedlove. 2006. "O Brother, Where Art Thou? The Fraternal Birth-Order Effect on Male Sexual Orientation." Proceedings of the National Academy of Sciences of the United States of America 103(28):10531–10532.

Pyke, Karen. 2004. "Immigrant Families in the U.S." In *The Blackwell Companion to the Sociology of the Family,* edited by J. L. Scott, J. Treas, and M. P. M. Richards, pp. 253–269. New York: Blackwell.

Qian, Zhenchao, and Daniel T. Lichter. 2007. "Social Boundaries and Marital Assimilation: Interpreting Trends in Racial and Ethnic Intermarriage." *American Sociological Review* 72(1):68–94.

Queen, Stuart A. 1985. *The Family in Various Cultures.* New York: Harper and Row.

Quinn, Graham E., Chai H. Shin, Maureen G. Maguire, and Richard A. Stone. 1999. "Myopia and Ambient Lighting at Night." *Nature* 399(6732):113–14. doi:10.1038/20094.

Rahilly, Elizabeth P. 2015. "The Gender Binary Meets the Gender-Variant Child Parents' Negotiations with Childhood Gender Variance." *Gender & Society* 29:338–61.

Raleigh, Elizabeth. 2016. "An Assortative Adoption Marketplace: Foster Care, Domestic, and Transnational Adoptions." *Sociology Compass* 10(6):506–17. doi:10.1111/soc4.12371.

Raley, R. Kelly. 1996. "A Shortage of Marriageable Men? A Note on the Role of Cohabitation in Black-White Differences in Marriage Rates." *American Sociological Review* 61(6):973–983.

Raley, Sara, and Suzanne Bianchi. 2006. "Sons, Daughters, and Family Processes: Does Gender of Children Matter?" *Annual Review of Sociology* 32(1):401–421.

Raley, Sara, and Suzanne Bianchi. 2006. "Sons, Daughters, and Family Processes: Does Gender of Children Matter?" *Annual Review of Sociology* 32(1):401–421.

Ramey, Valerie A. 2009. "Time Spent in Home Production in the Twentieth-Century United States: New Estimates from Old Data." *Journal of Economic History* 69(1):1–47.

Randles, Jennifer M. 2016. *Proposing Prosperity?: Marriage Education Policy and Inequality in America.* New York: Columbia University Press.

Rankin, Bruce H., and James M. Quane. 2002. "Social Contexts and Urban Adolescent Outcomes: The Interrelated Effects of Neighborhoods, Families, and Peers on African-American Youth." *Social Problems* 49(1):79–100.

Ransome, David R. 1991. "Wives for Virginia, 1621." *The William and Mary Quarterly* 48(1):3–18.

Rasmussen, Kyler. 2016. "A Historical and Empirical Review of Pornography and Romantic Relationships: Implications for Family Researchers." *Journal of Family Theory & Review* 8 (2):173–91. doi:10.1111/jftr.12141.

Read, Jen'nan G. 2004. "Family, Religion, and Work among Arab American Women." *Journal of Marriage and Family* 66(4):1042–1050.

Read, Jen'nan G., and John P. Bartkowski. 2000. "To Veil or Not to Veil? A Case Study of Identity Negotiation among Muslim Women in Austin, Texas." *Gender and Society* 14(3):395–417.

Reardon, Sean F. 2011. "The Widening Academic Achievement Gap between the Rich and the Poor." In *Whither Opportunity?,* edited by Greg Duncan and Richard Murnane, pp. 91–116. New York: Russell Sage Foundation.

Reckdenwald, Amy, and Karen F. Parker. 2012. "Understanding the Change in Male and Female Intimate Partner Homicide over Time: A Policy- and Theory-Relevant Investigation." *Feminist Criminology* 7(3):167–195.

Reeves, R. V. 2017. *Dream Hoarders: How the American Upper Middle Class Is Leaving Everyone Else in the Dust, Why That Is a Problem, and What to Do about It.* Brookings Institution Press.

Reeves, Terrance, and Claudette E. Bennett. 2004. "We the People: Asians in the United States." Washington, DC: U.S. Dept. of Commerce, Economic and Statistics Administration, U.S. Census Bureau.

Reichman, Nancy E., Hope Corman, and Kelly Noonan. 2004. "Effects of Child Health on Parents' Relationship Status." *Demography* 41(3):569–584.

Reiss, Ira L. 1965. "Social Class and Campus Dating." *Social Problems* 13(2):193–205.

Remnick, David. 2010. *The Bridge: The Life and Rise of Barack Obama.* New York: Alfred A. Knopf.

Renzetti, Claire M. 1992. *Violent Betrayal: Partner Abuse in Lesbian Relationships.* Newbury Park, CA: Sage.

Resnick, Michael D., Peter S. Bearman, Robert W. Blum, Karl E. Bauman, Kathleen M. Harris, Jo Jones, Joyce Tabor, Trish Beuhring, Renee E. Sieving, Marcia Shew, Marjorie Ireland, Linda H. Bearinger, and J. Richard Udry. 1997. "Protecting Adolescents from Harm: Findings from the National Longitudinal Study on Adolescent Health." *Journal of the American Medical Association* 278(10):823–832.

Reynolds, Jeremy, and David R. Johnson. 2012. "Don't Blame the Babies: Work Hour Mismatches and the Role of Children." *Social Forces* 91(1):131–55. doi:10.1093/sf/sos070.

Rezey, Maribeth L. 2017. "Separated Women's Risk for Intimate Partner Violence: A Multiyear Analysis Using the National Crime Victimization Survey." *Journal of Interpersonal Violence*, February. doi:10.1177/0886260517692334.

Rhoades, Galena K., Scott M. Stanley, and Howard J. Markman. 2009. "Couples' Reasons for Cohabitation Associations with Individual Well-Being and Relationship Quality." *Journal of Family Issues* 30(2):233–258.

Rich, Adrienne. 1980. "Compulsory Heterosexuality and Lesbian Existence." *Signs* 5(4, Women: Sex and Sexuality):631–660.

Rich, Motoko. 2013. "Few States Look to Extend Preschool to All 4-Year-Olds." *New York Times*, February 14, p. A19.

Richie, Beth. 2012. *Arrested Justice: Black Women, Violence, and America's Prison Nation.* New York: New York University Press.

Ríos, Kristofer. 2011. "After Long Fight, Farmworkers in Florida Win an Increase in Pay," *New York Times*, January 18. http://www.nytimes.com/2011/01/19/us/19farm.html. Accessed November 3, 2013.

Risman, Barbara J. 2004. "Gender as a Social Structure: Theory Wrestling with Activism." *Gender and Society* 18(4):429–450.

Risman, Barbara, and Rachel Allison. 2014. "Not Everybody Is Hooking Up at college—Here's Why." Council on Contemporary Families. http://www.contemporaryfamilies.org/commuter-hookups/. Accessed January 25, 2014.

Risman, Barbara, and Pepper Schwartz. 1988. "Sociological Research on Male and Female Homosexuality." *Annual Review of Sociology* 14:125–147.

Ritzer, George. 2000. *Sociological Theory.* New York: McGraw-Hill.

Roberts, Andrea L., Margaret Rosario, Natalie Slopen, Jerel P. Calzo, and S. Bryn Austin. 2013. "Childhood Gender Nonconformity, Bullying Victimization, and Depressive Symptoms Across Adolescence and Early Adulthood: An 11-Year Longitudinal Study." *Journal of the American Academy of Child and Adolescent Psychiatry* 52(2):143–52. doi:10.1016/j.jaac.2012.11.006

Roberts, Donald F., and Ulla G. Foehr. 2008. "Trends in Media Use." *Future of Children* 18(1):11–37.

Robotham, Rojan. 2017. "Manassas Students Fill up on 'Second-Chance Breakfast.'" *Potomac Local.* April 28. http://potomaclocal.com/2017/04/28/manassas-students-fill-up-on-second-chance-breakfast/.

Rodríguez-García, D., D. T. Lichter, Z. Qian, and D. Tumin. 2015. "Whom Do Immigrants Marry? Emerging Patterns of Intermarriage and Integration in the United States." *The ANNALS of the American Academy of Political and Social Science* 662(1):57–78. https://doi.org/10.1177/0002716215594614.

Rogers, Katie. 2016. "Bride Is Walked Down Aisle by the Man Who Got Her Father's Donated Heart." *New York Times*, August 8. http://www.nytimes.com/2016/08/09/fashion/weddings/bride-is-walked-down-aisle-by-the-man-who-got-her-fathers-donated-heart.html.

Roksa, Josipa, and Daniel Potter. 2011. "Parenting and Academic Achievement." *Sociology of Education* 84(4):299–321.

Roof, Wade C. 1999. *Spiritual Marketplace: Baby Boomers and the Remaking of American Religion.* Princeton, NJ: Princeton University Press.

Roots, Charles R. 1998. *The Sandwich Generation: Adult Children Caring for Aging Parents.* New York: Garland.

Rosay, Andre B., and Carrie F. Mulford. 2017. "Prevalence Estimates and Correlates of Elder Abuse in the United States: The National Intimate Partner and Sexual Violence Survey." *Journal of Elder Abuse & Neglect* 29(1):1–14. doi:10.1080/08946566.2016.1249817.

Rose, Suzanna, and Irene Hanson Frieze. 1993. "Young Singles Contemporary Dating Scripts." *Sex Roles* 28(9–10):449–509.

Rosenbaum, Janet E. 2009. "Patient Teenagers? A Comparison of the Sexual Behavior of Virginity Pledgers and Matched Nonpledgers." *Pediatrics* 123(1):E110–E120.

Rosenfeld, Alvin A., Daniel J. Pilowsky, Paul Fine, Marilyn Thorpe, Edith Fein, Mark D. Simms, Neal Halfon, Martin Irwin, Jose Alfaro, Ronald Saletsky, and Steven Nickman. 1997. "Foster Care: An Update." *Journal of the American Academy of Child and Adolescent Psychiatry* 36(4):448–457.

Rosenfeld, Michael J. 2005. "A Critique of Exchange Theory in Mate Selection." *American Journal of Sociology* 110(5):1284–1325.

———. 2007. *The Age of Independence: Interracial Unions, Same-Sex Unions, and the Changing American Family.* Harvard University Press.

———. 2008. "Racial, Educational and Religious Endogamy in the United States: A Comparative Historical Perspective." *Social Forces* 87(1):1–31.

———. 2014. "Couple Longevity in the Era of Same-Sex Marriage in the United States." *Journal of Marriage and Family* 76:905–18.

———. 2015. "Revisiting the Data from the New Family Structure Study: Taking Family Instability into Account." *Sociological Science* 2(September):478–501. doi:10.15195/v2.a23.

Rosenfeld, Michael J., and Reuben J. Thomas. 2012. "Searching for a Mate: The Rise of the Internet as a Social Intermediary." *American Sociological Review* 77(4):523–547.

Rosenfeld, Michael J., Reuben J. Thomas, and Maja Falcon. 2011. "How Couples Meet and Stay Together, Waves 1, 2, and 3." Public version 3.04 [computer file]. Stanford, CA: Stanford University Libraries.

Rosenzweig, Roy. 1983. *Eight Hours for What We Will: Workers and Leisure in an Industrial City, 1870–1920.* Cambridge, UK: Cambridge University Press.

Ross, Louie E. 1997. "Mate Selection Preferences among African American College Students." *Journal of Black Studies* 27(4):554–569.

Rossi, Alice S. 1984. "Gender and Parenthood." *American Sociological Review* 49(1):1–19.

Rotz, Dana. 2016. "Why Have Divorce Rates Fallen? The Role of Women's Age at Marriage." *Journal of Human Resources* 51(4):961–1002. doi:10.3368/jhr.51.4.0214-6224R.

Roughgarden, Joan. 2004. *Evolution's Rainbow: Diversity, Gender, and Sexuality in Nature and People.* Berkeley, CA: University of California Press.

Rowe, K. E. 1979. "Feminism and Fairy-Tales." *Womens Studies—An Interdisciplinary Journal* 6(3):237–257.

Rozee, Patricia D., and Mary P. Koss. 2001. "Rape: A Century of Resistance." *Psychology of Women Quarterly* 25(4):295–311. doi:10.1111/1471-6402.00030.

Rubin, Gayle. 1975. "The Traffic in Women: Notes on the 'Political Economy' of Sex." In *Toward an Anthropology of Women*, edited by R. R. Reiter, pp. 157–210. New York: Monthly Review Press.

Rudder, Christian. 2009. "How Your Race Affects the Messages You Get." http://blog.okcupid.com/index.php/your-race-affects-whether-people-write-you-back/. Accessed September 8, 2013.

Ruggles, Steven. 1994. "The Transformation of American Family Structure." *American Historical Review* 99:103–128.

Ruggles, Steven, J. Trent Alexander, Katie Genadek, Ronald Goeken, Matthew B. Schroeder, and Matthew Sobek. 2013. "The Census of 1880." *Integrated Public Use Microdata Series,* Census Enumeration Forms. Minneapolis, MN: Minnesota Population Center. https://usa.ipums.org/usa/voliii/items1880.shtml. Accessed December 26, 2013.

———. 2014. *Integrated Public Use Microdata Series.* Minneapolis, MN: Minnesota Population Center. https://usa.ipums.org/usa/index.shtml. Accessed January 7, 2014.

———. 2016. *Integrated Public Use Microdata Series.* Minneapolis, MN: Minnesota Population Center. https://usa.ipums.org/usa/index.shtml.

Ruggles, Steven, and Susan Brower. 2003. "Measurement of Household and Family Composition in the United States, 1850–2000." *Population and Development Review* 29(1):73–101.

Rumbaut, Rubén G. 2004. "Ages, Life Stages, and Generational Cohorts: Decomposing the Immigrant First and Second Generations in the United States." *International Migration Review* 38(3):1160–1205.

Russell, John. 2016. "For Lilly's Cialis, Glory Days are Over." *Indianapolis Business Journal*, February 2. http://www.ibj.com/articles/57284-for-cialis-glory-days-are-over.

Russell, Stephen T., Katerina O. Sinclair, V. Paul Poteat, and Brian W. Koenig. 2012. "Adolescent Health and Harassment Based on Discriminatory Bias." *American Journal of Public Health* 102(3):493–95. doi:10.2105/AJPH.2011.300430.

Rust, Paula C. 1993. "'Coming Out' in the Age of Social Constructionism: Sexual Identity Formation among Lesbian and Bisexual Women." *Gender and Society* 7(1):50–77.

Rutherford, Markella B. 2009. "Children's Autonomy and Responsibility: An Analysis of Childrearing Advice." *Qualitative Sociology* 32(4):337–353.

Ryan, William. 1976. *Blaming the Victim.* New York: Vintage Books.

Sabia, Joseph J., and Daniel I. Rees. 2008. "The Effect of Adolescent Virginity Status on Psychological Well-Being." *Journal of Health Economics* 27(5):1368–1381.

_____. 2009. "The Effect of Sexual Abstinence on Females' Educational Attainment." *Demography* 46(4):695–715

Sanchez, George J. 1993. *Becoming Mexican American: Ethnicity, Culture, and Identity in Chicano Los Angeles, 1900–1945.* New York: Oxford University Press.

Sandoval, Daniel A., Mark R. Rank, and Thomas A. Hirschl. 2009. "The Increasing Risk of Poverty across the American Life Course." *Demography* 46(4, November):717–737.

Saraceno, Chiara. 2015. "A Critical Look to the Social Investment Approach from a Gender Perspective." *Social Politics: International Studies in Gender, State and Society* 22(2):257–69

Saraceno, Chiara, and Wolfgang Keck. 2011. "Towards an Integrated Approach for the Analysis of Gender Equity in Policies Supporting Paid Work and Care Responsibilities." *Demographic Research* 25:371–405.

Sarche, Michelle, and Paul Spicer. 2008. "Poverty and Health Disparities for American Indian and Alaska Native Children: Current Knowledge and Future Prospects." *Reducing the Impact of Poverty on Health and Human Development: Scientific Approaches* 1136:126–136.

Sassler, Sharon. 2010. "Partnering across the Life Course: Sex, Relationships, and Mate Selection." *Journal of Marriage and Family* 72(3):557–575.

Savage, Charlie. 2009. "On Nixon Tapes, Ambivalence over Abortion, Not Watergate." *New York Times*, June 24, U.S./Politics. http://www.nytimes.com/2009/06/24/us/politics/24nixon.html. Accessed June 18, 2014.

_____. 2013. "V.A. to Provide Spousal Benefits to Gays, Administration Says." *New York Times*, September 4. http://www.nytimes.com/2013/09/05/us/va-to-provide-spousal-benefits-to-gays-administration-says.html. Accessed September 23, 2013.

Sax, Leonard. 2002. "How Common Is Intersex? A Response to Anne Fausto-Sterling." *The Journal of Sex Research* 39(3):174–178.

Sayer, Liana C. 2005. "Gender, Time and Inequality: Trends in Women's and Men's Paid Work, Unpaid Work and Free Time." *Social Forces* 84(1):285–303.

_____. 2016. "Trends in Women's and Men's Time Use, 1965–2012: Back to the Future?" In S. M. McHale, V. King, J. V. Hook, and A. Booth (Eds.), *Gender and Couple Relationships* (pp. 43–77). Springer International Publishing. https://doi.org/10.1007/978-3-319-21635-5_2.

Sayer, Liana C., and Suzanne M. Bianchi. 2000. "Women's Economic Independence and the Probability of Divorce: A Review and Reexamination." *Journal of Family Issues* 21(7):906–943.

Sayer, Liana C., Suzanne M. Bianchi, and John P. Robinson. 2004. "Are Parents Investing Less in Children? Trends in Mothers' and Fathers' Time with Children." *American Journal of Sociology* 110(1):1–43.

Sayer, Liana C., Paula England, Paul Allison, and Nicole Kangas. 2011. "She Left, He Left: How Employment and Satisfaction Affect Men's and Women's Decisions to Leave Marriages." *American Journal of Sociology* 116(6):1982–2018.

Schalet, Amy T. 2011. *Not Under My Roof: Parents, Teens, and the Culture of Sex.* Chicago: University of Chicago Press.

Scherrer, Kristin. 2013. "Culturally Competent Practice with Bisexual Individuals." *Clinical Social Work Journal* 41(3):238–48. doi:10.1007/s10615-013-0451-4.

Schilt, Kristen, and Laurel Westbrook. 2015. "Bathroom Battlegrounds and Penis Panics." *Contexts* 14(3):26–31. doi:10.1177/1536504215596943

Schnabel, L. 2015. "Religion and Gender Equality Worldwide: A Country-Level Analysis." *Social Indicators Research*, pp. 1–15. doi:10.1007/s11205-015-1147-7

Schneider, Daniel. 2011. "Market Earnings and Household Work: New Tests of Gender Performance Theory." *Journal of Marriage and Family* 73(4):845–860.

Schneider, Daniel, and Orestes P. Hastings. 2015. "Socioeconomic Variation in the Effect of Economic Conditions on Marriage and Nonmarital Fertility in the United States: Evidence from the Great Recession." *Demography* 52:1893–1915.

Schoen, Robert. 1983. "Measuring the Tightness of a Marriage Squeeze." *Demography* 20(1):61–78.

Schoen, Robert, and Vladimir Canudas-Romo. 2006. "Timing Effects on Divorce: 20th Century Experience in the United States." *Journal of Marriage and Family* 68(3):749–758.

Schoen, Robert, Young J. Kim, Constance A. Nathanson, Jason Fields, and Nan Marie Astone. 1997. "Why Do Americans Want Children?" *Population and Development Review* 23(2):333–358.

Schumm, Walter R., Cynthia A. Akagi, and Kathy R. Bosch. 2008. "Relationship Satisfaction for Heterosexual Women Compared to Lesbians and Men in a Sample of Faith Communities from Topeka, Kansas." *Psychological Reports* 102(2):377–388.

Schumm, Walter R., Farrell J. Webb, and Stephan R. Bollman. 1998. "Gender and Marital Satisfaction: Data from the National Survey of Families and Households." *Psychological Reports* 83(1):319–327.

Schwartz, Christine R. 2010. "Earnings Inequality and the Changing Association between Spouses' Earnings." *American Journal of Sociology* 115(5):1524–1557.

Schwartz, Christine R., and Hongyun Han. 2014. "The Reversal of the Gender Gap in Education and Trends in Marital Dissolution." *American Sociological Review* 79(4):605–29. doi:10.1177/0003122414539682.

Schwartz, Christine R, and Robert D. Mare. 2005. "Trends in Educational Assortative Marriage from 1940 to 2003." *Demography* 42(4):621–646.

Schwartz, Jennifer, and Arina Gertseva. 2010. "Stability and Change in Female and Male Violence across Rural and Urban Counties, 1981–2006." *Rural Sociology* 75(3):388–425. doi:10.1111/j.1549-0831.2010.00016.x.

Seaver, Maggie. 2017. "The National Average Cost of a Wedding Hits $35,329." Theknot.com. https://www.theknot.com/content/average-wedding-cost-2016.

Seltzer, Judith A., and Suzanne M. Bianchi. 2013. "Demographic Change and Parent-Child Relationships in Adulthood." *Annual Review of Sociology* 39(1):275–290. doi:10.1146/annurev-soc-071312-145602.

Selvin, Elizabeth, Arthur L. Burnett, and Elizabeth A. Platz. 2007. "Prevalence and Risk Factors for Erectile Dysfunction in the U.S." *The American Journal of Medicine* 120(2):151–157.

Sevón, Eija. 2005. "Timing Motherhood: Experiencing and Narrating the Choice to Become a Mother." *Feminism and Psychology* 15(4):461–482.

Shafer, Emily Fitzgibbons. 2011. "Wives' Relative Wages, Husbands' Paid Work Hours, and Wives' Labor-Force Exit." *Journal of Marriage and Family* 73(1):250–263.

Sharp, Elizabeth A., and Lawrence Ganong. 2007. "Living in the Gray: Women's Experiences of Missing the Marital Transition." *Journal of Marriage and Family* 69(3):831–844.

Shattuck, Kathryn. 2010. "Men's Engagement Rings Proclaim, 'He's Taken'." *New York Times*, August 1, ST; Society Desk.

Shelach, Gideon. 2006. "Economic Adaptation, Community Structure, and Sharing Strategies of Households at Early Sedentary Communities in Northeast China." *Journal of Anthropological Archaeology* 25(3):318–345.

Sherkat, Darren E. 2000. "'That They Be Keepers of the Home': The Effect of Conservative Religion on Early and Late Transitions into Housewifery." *Review of Religious Research* 41(3):344–358.

———. 2004. "Religious Intermarriage in the United States: Trends, Patterns, and Predictors." *Social Science Research* 33(4):606–625.

Sherman, Arloc. 2011. "Hardship in America, Part 1: Majority of Poor Children Live in Households with Major Hardships." Off the Charts Blog | Center on Budget and Policy Priorities. http://www.offthechartsblog.org/hardship-in-america-part-1-majority-of-poor-children-live-in-households-with-major-hardships/. Accessed January 6, 2014.

Shilts, Randy. 1987. *And the Band Played On: Politics, People, and the AIDS Epidemic.* New York: St. Martin's Press.

Shipp, Thomas D., Diane Z. Shipp, Bryann Bromley, Robert Sheahan, Amy Cohen, Ellice Lieberman, and Beryl Benacerraf. 2004. "What Factors Are Associated with Parents' Desire to Know the Sex of Their Unborn Child?" *Birth—Issues in Perinatal Care* 31(4):272–279.

Shors, Benjamin. 2009. "Ranch Accused of Abuse; Boys' Home Allowed Mistreatment for Years, Say Residents, Records." *Spokesman Review*, May 26.

Short, Kathleen. 2011. "The Research Supplemental Poverty Measure: 2010." Washington, DC: U.S. Census Bureau.

Shupe, Anson D. 2007. *Spoils of the Kingdom: Clergy Misconduct and Religious Community.* Urbana, IL: University of Illinois Press.

Sidel, Ruth. 1998. *Keeping Women and Children Last: America's War on the Poor.* New York: Penguin Books.

Silva, Tony. 2017. Forthcoming. "Constructing Normative Masculinity among Rural Straight Men That Have Sex With Men." *Gender and Society.* doi:10.1177/0891243 216679934.

Silverman, Eric K. 2006. *From Abraham to America: A History of Jewish Circumcision.* Lanham, MD: Rowman and Littlefield.

Simmons, Tavia, and Jane L. Dye. 2003. "Grandparents Living with Grandchildren: 2000." Washington, DC: U.S. Census Bureau.

Simon, William, and John H. Gagnon. 1984. "Sexual Scripts." *Society* 22(1):53–60.

Singh, Devendra, Peter Renn, and Adrian Singh. 2007. "Did the Perils of Abdominal Obesity Affect Depiction of Feminine Beauty in the Sixteenth to Eighteenth Century British Literature? Exploring the Health and Beauty Link." Proceedings of the Royal Society B—Biological Sciences 274(1611):891–894.

Sitton, Jaye. 1993. "Old Wine in New Bottles: The Marital Rape Allowance." *North Carolina Law Review* 72(November):261–289.

Skocpol, Theda. 1992. *Protecting Soldiers and Mothers: The Political Origins of Social Policy in the United States.* Cambridge, MA: Belknap Press of Harvard University Press.

Sleddens, Ester F. C., Sanne M. P. L. Gerards, Carel Thijs, Nanne K. de Vries, and Stef P. J. Kremers. 2011. "General Parenting, Childhood Overweight and Obesity-Inducing Behav-iors: A Review." *International Journal of Pediatric Obesity* 6(2Part2):e12–27. doi:10.3109/17477166.2011.566339.

Smart, Carol. 2006. "Children's Narratives of Post-Divorce Family Life: From Individual Experience to an Ethical Disposition." *Sociological Review* 54(1):155–170.

Smith, Aaron. 2016. "15% of American Adults Have Used Online Dating Sites or Mobile Dating Apps." Pew Research Center, February 11. http://www.pewinternet.org/2016/02/11/15-percent-of-american-adults-have-used-online-dating-sites-or-mobile-dating-apps/.

Smith, Dinitia. 2004. "Love That Dare Not Squeak Its Name." *New York Times*, February 7, B; Arts and Ideas/Cultural Desk.

Smith, Euclid O., and Whitney S. Helms. 1999. "Natural Selection and High Heels." *Foot and Ankle International* 20(1):55–57.

Smith, Jack C., James A. Mercy, and Judith M. Conn. 1988. "Marital Status and the Risk of Suicide." *American Journal of Public Health* 78(1):78–80.

Smith, S.G., J. Chen, K. C. Basile, L. K. Gilbert, M. T. Merrick, N. Patel, M. Walling, and A. Jain. 2017. "The National Intimate Partner and Sexual Violence Survey (NISVS): 2010–2012 State Report." Atlanta, GA: National Center for Injury Prevention and Control, Centers for Disease Control and Prevention.

Smith, Tom W, Peter Marsden, Michael Hout, and Jibum Kim. 2014. "General Social Surveys, 1972–2012 [machine-readable data file]." Principal Investigator, Tom W. Smith; Co-Principal Investigator, Peter V. Marsden; Co-Principal Investigator, Michael Hout; Sponsored by National Science Foundation. NORC ed. Chicago: National Opinion Research Center [producer]; Storrs, CT: The Roper Center for Public Opinion Research, University of Connecticut [distributor].

———. 2015. "General Social Surveys, 1972–2014 [machine-readable data file]." Principal Investigator, Tom W. Smith; Co-Principal Investigator, Peter V. Marsden; Co-Principal Investigator, Michael Hout; Sponsored by National Science Foundation. NORC ed. Chicago: National Opinion Research Center [producer]; Storrs, CT: The Roper Center for Public Opinion Research, University of Connecticut [distributor].

———. 2016. General Social Surveys, 1972–2014 [machine-readable data file]/Principal Investigator, Tom W. Smith; Co-Principal Investigator, Peter V. Marsden; Co-Principal Investigator, Michael Hout; Sponsored by National Science Foundation. -NORC ed.- Chicago: NORC at the University of Chicago [producer and distributor].

Smock, Pamela J. 2000. "Cohabitation in the United States: An Appraisal of Research Themes, Findings, and Implications." *Annual Review of Sociology* 26:1–20.

———. 2004. "The Wax and Wane of Marriage: Prospects for Marriage in the 21st Century." *Journal of Marriage and Family* 66(4):966–973.

Smock, Pamela J., and Fiona R. Greenland. 2010. "Diversity in Pathways to Parenthood: Patterns, Implications, and Emerging Research Directions." *Journal of Marriage and Family* 72(3):576–593.

Snipp, C. Matthew. 2003. "Racial Measurement in the American Census: Past Practices and Implications for the Future." *Annual Review of Sociology* 29(1):563–588.

———. 2006. "American Indian Population: Number of Tribes, Average Size, and Number Extinct, by Region: 1600–1990." In *Historical Statistics of the United States, Earliest Times to the Present: Millennial Edition,* edited by Susan B. Carter, Scott S. Gartner, Michael R. Haines, Alan L. Olmstead, Richard Sutch, and Gavin Wright. New York: Cambridge University Press.

Social Explorer. 2014. http://socialexplorer.com/. Accessed January 7, 2014.

Social Security Administration. 2014. "Top 10 Baby Names For 2015." http://www.ssa.gov/OACT/babynames/.

Sommer, Volker, and Paul L. Vasey. 2006. *Homosexual Behaviour in Animals: An Evolutionary Perspective.* Cambridge, UK: Cambridge University Press.

Sonfield, Adam. 2016. "The Women's Health Amendment Is Getting an Update. What Should It Include?" *Health Affairs.* September 14. http://healthaffairs.org/blog/2016/09/14/the-womens-health-amendment-is-getting-an-update-what-should-it-include/.

Soons, Judith P. M., and Matthijs Kalmijn. 2009. "Is Marriage More Than Cohabitation? Well-Being Differences in 30 European Countries." *Journal of Marriage and Family* 71(5):1141–1157.

Soule, Sarah A. 2004. "Going to the Chapel? Same-Sex Marriage Bans in the United States, 1973–2000." *Social Problems* 51(4):453–477.

Spencer, Ruth. 2015. "These Photographs Helped Integrate Proms in Montgomery, Georgia." *The Guardian*, May 15. https://www.theguardian.com/music/2015/may/15/integrated-proms-race-georgia-gillian-laub-photographs.

Spillman, Brenda C., and Liliana E. Pezzin. 2000. "Potential and Active Family Caregivers: Changing Networks and the 'Sandwich Generation.'" *The Milbank Quarterly* 78(3):347–374.

Spriggs, Aubrey L., and Carolyn T. Halpern. 2008. "Sexual Debut Timing and Depressive Symptoms in Emerging Adulthood." *Journal of Youth and Adolescence* 37(9):1085–1096.

Stacey, Judith. 1993. "Good Riddance to the Family: Response." *Journal of Marriage and Family* 55(3):545–547

Stack, Carol B., and Linda M. Burton. 1993. "Kinscripts." *Journal of Comparative Family Studies* 24(2):157–170.

Stack, Liam. 2016. "In Stanford Rape Case, Brock Turner Blamed Drinking and Promiscuity." *New York Times*, June 8. https://www.nytimes.com/2016/06/09/us/brock-turner-blamed-drinking-and-promiscuity-in-sexual-assault-at-stanford.html.

Staff, J., K. M. Greene, J. L. Maggs, and I. Schoon. 2014. "Family Transitions and Changes in Drinking from Adolescence through Mid-life." *Addiction* 109(2):227–236. https://doi.org/10.1111/add.12394.

Stanczyk, Alexandra B., Julia R. Henly, and Susan J. Lambert. 2017. "Enough Time for Housework? Low-Wage Work and

Desired Housework Time Adjustments." *Journal of Marriage and Family* 79(1):243–60. doi:10.1111/jomf.12344.

Stander, V. A., and C. J. Thomsen. 2016. "Sexual Harassment and Assault in the U.S. Military: A Review of Policy and Research Trends." *Military Medicine* 181(1S).

Stanford, Eleanor. 2016. "13 Questions to Ask Before Getting Married." *New York Times*, March 24. https://www.nytimes.com/interactive/2016/03/23/fashion/weddings/marriage-questions.html.

Stanley, Scott M., Galena K. Rhoades, and Howard J. Markman. 2006. "Sliding versus Deciding: Inertia and the Premarital Cohabitation Effect." *Family Relations* 55(4):499–509.

Stanton, Elizabeth C. 1898 [1993]. *Eighty Years and More: Reminiscences, 1815–1897.* Boston, MA: Northeastern University Press.

Steadman, Sharon R. 2004. "Heading Home: The Architecture of Family and Society in Early Sedentary Communities on the Anatolian Plateau." *Journal of Anthropological Research* 60(4):515–558.

Stearns, Peter N. 1990. "The Rise of Sibling Jealousy in the Twentieth Century." *Symbolic Interaction* 13(1):83–101.

———. 2003. *Anxious Parents: A History of Modern Childrearing in America.* New York: New York University Press.

Stevens, Gillian, Mary E. M. McKillip, and Hiromi Ishizawa. 2006. "Intermarriage in the Second Generation: Choosing between Newcomers and Natives." *The Migration Information Source.* http://www.migrationinformation.org/Feature/display.cfm?id=444. Accessed January 6, 2014.

Stiglitz, Joseph E. 2013. *The Price of Inequality: How Today's Divided Society Endangers Our Future.* New York: W. W. Norton.

Stokes, Charles E., and Christopher G. Ellison. 2010. "Religion and Attitudes Toward Divorce Laws among U.S. Adults." *Journal of Family Issues* 31(10):1279–1304. doi:10.1177/0192513X10363887.

Stolberg, Michael. 2000. "The Monthly Malady: A History of Premenstrual Suffering." *Medical History* 44(3):301–322.

Stone, Pamela. 2007. *Opting Out? Why Women Really Quit Careers and Head Home.* Berkeley, CA: University of California Press.

Strasser, Susan. 1982. *Never Done: A History of American Housework.* New York: Pantheon Books.

Strebeigh, Fred. 2009. *Equal: Women Reshape American Law.* New York: W.W. Norton.

Streib, Jessi. 2015. *The Power of the Past: Understanding Cross-Class Marriages.* Oxford University Press.

Stryker, Sheldon. 1968. "Identity Salience and Role Performance: The Relevance of Symbolic Interaction Theory for Family Research." *Journal of Marriage and Family* 30(4):558–564.

Stulp, G., Buunk, A. P., Pollet, T. V., Nettle, D., & Verhulst, S. 2013. "Are Human Mating Preferences with Respect to Height Reflected in Actual Pairings?" *PLoS* ONE 8(1), e54186. http://doi.org/10.1371/journal.pone.0054186

Suarez, Eliana, and Tahany M. Gadalla. 2010. "Stop Blaming the Victim: A Meta-Analysis on Rape Myths." *Journal of Interpersonal Violence* 25(11):2010–2035. doi:10.1177/0886260509354503.

Sullivan, Laura, and Amy Walters. 2011. "Incentives and Cultural Bias Fuel Foster System." *NPR.* October 25. http://www.npr.org/2011/10/25/141662357/incentives-and-cultural-bias-fuel-foster-system. Accessed January 5, 2014.

Summers, Juana. 2011, February 14. "Trump: Gays Yes, Gay Marriage No." *Politico.* http://www.politico.com/story/2011/02/trump-gays-yes-gay-marriage-no-049527.

Sunderam, S., Kissin, D.M., Crawford, S.B., et al. 2017. "Assisted Reproductive Technology Surveillance: United States, 2014." *Morbidity and Mortality Weekly Report* 66(No. SS-6):1–24.

Suzman, Richard, and Matilda White Riley. 1985. "Introducing the 'Oldest Old'." The Milbank Memorial Fund Quarterly. *Health and Society* 63(2):175–86.

Svensen, Stuart, and Ken White. 1995. "A Content-Analysis of Horoscopes." *Genetic Social and General Psychology Monographs* 121(1):5–38.

Sweeney, Megan M. 2010. "Remarriage and Stepfamilies: Strategic Sites for Family Scholarship in the 21st Century." *Journal of Marriage and Family* 72(3):667–684.

Sweeney, Megan M., and Maria Cancian. 2004. "The Changing Importance of White Women's Economic Prospects for Assortative Mating." *Journal of Marriage and Family* 66(4):1015–1028.

Sweet, Elizabeth. 2014. "Toys Are More Divided by Gender Now Than They Were 50 Years Ago." *The Atlantic,* December 9. http://www.theatlantic.com/business/archive/2014/12/toys-are-more-divided-by-gender-now-than-they-were-50-years-ago/383556/.

Swidler, Ann. 2001. *Talk of Love: How Culture Matters.* Chicago, IL: University of Chicago Press.

Swift, Art. 2016. "Birth Control, Divorce Top List of Morally Acceptable Issues." Gallup.com. June 8. http://www.gallup.com/poll/192404/birth-control-divorce-top-list-morally-acceptable-issues.aspx.

Szelenyi, Szonja. 2001. "The 'Woman Problem' in Stratification Theory and Research." In *Social Stratification: Class, Race and Gender in Sociological Perspective,* edited by D. Grusky, pp. 681–688. Boulder, CO: Westview Press.

Tarman, Christopher, and David O. Sears. 2005. "The Conceptualization and Measurement of Symbolic Racism." *Journal of Politics* 67(3):731–761.

Tavernise, Sabrina, Jason Deparle, and Robert Gebeloff. 2011. "Voices of the Near Poor." Economix blog post. http://economix.blogs.nytimes.com/2011/11/19/voices-of-the-near-poor/. Accessed June 18, 2014.

Taylor, Alan C., and Aparna Bagdi. 2005. "The Lack of Explicit Theory in Family Research: A Case Analysis of the *Journal of Marriage and Family*." In *Sourcebook of Family Theory and Research*, edited by Vern L. Bengston, Alan C. Acock, Katherine R. Russell, Peggye Dilworth-Anderson, and David M. Klein, pp. 22–25. Thousand Oaks, CA: Sage.

Taylor, Kate. 2013. "She Can Play That Game, Too." *New York Times*, July 14, p. ST1.

_____. 2017. "New York City Will Offer Free Preschool for All 3-Year-Olds." *New York Times*, April 24. https://www.nytimes.com/2017/04/24/nyregion/de-blasio-pre-k-expansion.html.

Taylor, Ronald L. 2000. "Diversity within African American Families." In *Handbook of Family Diversity*, edited by David H. Demo, Katherine R. Allen, and Mark A. Fine, pp. 232–251. New York: Oxford University Press.

Teachman, Jay D. 2008. "Complex Life Course Patterns and the Risk of Divorce in Second Marriages." *Journal of Marriage and Family* 70(2):294–305.

_____. 2010. "Wives' Economic Resources and Risk of Divorce." *Journal of Family Issues* 31(10):1305–1323.

Thistle, Susan. 2006. *From Marriage to the Market: The Transformation of Women's Lives and Work*. Berkeley, CA: University of California Press.

Thomas, Sandra P., and Joanne M. Hall. 2008. "Life Trajectories of Female Child Abuse Survivors Thriving in Adulthood." *Qualitative Health Research* 18:149–166.

Thomas, Susan G. 2011. *In Spite of Everything: A Memoir of Divorce, My Messed-Up Childhood, and the Fight to Make Everything Right*. New York: Random House.

Thompson, A., C. Hollis, and D. Richards. 2003. "Authoritarian Parenting Attitudes as a Risk for Conduct Problems: Results from a British National Cohort Study." *European Child & Adolescent Psychiatry* 12(2):84–91. doi:10.1007/s00787-003-0324-4.

Thornton, Arland, William G. Axinn, and Yu Xie. 2007. *Marriage and Cohabitation*. Chicago, IL: University of Chicago Press.

Thyen, Ute, Kathrin Lanz, Paul-Martin Holterhus, and Olaf Hiort. 2006. "Epidemiology and Initial Management of Ambiguous Genitalia at Birth in Germany." *Hormone Research* 66(4):195–203.

Tiefenthaler, Jill, Amy Farmer, and Amandine Sambira. 2005. "Services and Intimate Partner Violence in the United States: A County-Level Analysis." *Journal of Marriage and Family* 67(3):565–578.

Tilly, Charles. 1998. *Durable Inequality*. Berkeley, CA: University of California Press.

Timmons, B. F. 1939. "The Cost of Weddings." *American Sociological Review* 4(2):224–33. doi:10.2307/2084209.

Ting, Laura, and Subadra Panchanadeswaran. 2009. "Barriers to Help-Seeking among Immigrant African Women Survivors of Partner Abuse: Listening to Women's Own Voices." *Journal of Aggression, Maltreatment and Trauma* 18(8):817–838.

Tolan, Patrick, Deborah Gorman-Smith, and David Henry. 2006. "Family Violence." *Annual Review of Psychology* 57:557–583.

Tolnay, Stewart E. 1997. "The Great Migration and Changes in the Northern Black Family, 1940 to 1990." *Social Forces* 75(4):1213–1238.

Tolnay, Stewart E., and E. M. Beck. 1995. *A Festival of Violence: An Analysis of Southern Lynchings, 1882–1930*. Urbana, IL: University of Illinois Press.

Toma, Catalina L., and Mina Choi. 2015. "The Couple Who Facebooks Together, Stays Together: Facebook Self-Presentation and Relationship Longevity Among College-Aged Dating Couples." *Cyberpsychology, Behavior, and Social Networking* 18(7):367–72. doi:10.1089/cyber.2015.0060.

Tonry, M. 2014. "Why Crime Rates Are Falling throughout the Western World." In M. Tonry (Ed.), *Crime and Justice, Vol 43: Why Crime Rates Fall, and Why They Don't* pp. 1–63. Chicago, IL: University of Chicago Press.

Torche, Florencia, and Peter Rich. 2017. "Declining Racial Stratification in Marriage Choices? Trends in Black/White Status Exchange in the United States, 1980 to 2010." *Sociology of Race and Ethnicity* 3(1):31–49. doi:10.1177/2332649216648464.

Traister, Rebecca. 2016. *All the Single Ladies: Unmarried Women and the Rise of an Independent Nation*. New York: Simon & Schuster.

Treas, Judith. 2004. "Sex and Family: Changes and Challenges." In *The Blackwell Companion to the Sociology of Families*, edited by Jacqueline Scott, Judith Treas, and Martin Richards, pp. 397–415. Malden, MA: Blackwell.

_____. 2008. "Transnational Older Adults and Their Families." *Family Relations* 57(4):468–478.

Trevillion, Kylee, Siân Oram, Gene Feder, and Louise M. Howard. 2012. "Experiences of Domestic Violence and Mental Disorders: A Systematic Review and Meta-Analysis." *PLoS ONE* 7(12):e51740.

Trexler, Richard C. 2002. "Making the American Berdache: Choice or Constraint?" *Journal of Social History* 35(3):613–636.

Trussell, James, and Charles F. Westoff. 1980. "Contraceptive Practice and Trends in Coital Frequency." *Family Planning Perspectives* 12(5):246–249.

Tucker, M. Belinda. 2000. "Marital Values and Expectations in Context: Results from a 21-City Survey." In *The Ties That Bind*, edited by Linda J. Waite, pp. 187–197. New York: Aldine de Gruyter.

Twenge, Jean M., W. Keith Campbell, and Craig A. Foster. 2003. "Parenthood and Marital Satisfaction: A Meta-Analytic Review." *Journal of Marriage and Family* 65(3):574–583.

Umberson, Debra, Robert Crosnoe, and Corinne Reczek. 2010. "Social Relationships and Health Behavior across the Life Course." *Annual Review of Sociology* 36:139–157.

United Nations. 2004. *Levels and Trends of Contraceptive Use as Assessed in 2002.* New York: United Nations.

United Nations Statistics Division. 2012. "Social Indicators." New York: United Nations. http://unstats.un.org/unsd/demographic/products/socind/. Accessed July 23, 2013.

United States v. Windsor. 2013. 570 U.S. ___.

U.S. Bureau of Justice Statistics. 2017. National Crime Victimization Survey. Special tabulation from the NCVS Victimization Analysis Tool. http://www.bjs.gov/index.cfm?ty=nvat. Washington, DC: Office of Justice Programs. Accessed May 25, 2017.

U.S. Bureau of Labor Statistics. 2006. Current Employment Statistics. http://www.bls.gov/ces/. Accessed October 30, 2013.

_____. 2011. American Time Use Survey—2010 Results. http://www.bls.gov/news.release/archives/atus_06222011.htm. Accessed February 14, 2014.

_____. 2013. Labor Force Statistics from the Current Population Survey. Table 39: "Median Weekly Earnings of Full-Time Wage and Salary Workers by Detailed Occupation and Sex." http://www.bls.gov/cps/cpsaat39.htm. Accessed July 21, 2013.

_____. 2014a. Current Employment Statistics Survey. http://www.bls.gov/ces/. Accessed January 5, 2014.

_____. 2014b. Labor Force Statistics from the Current Population Survey (Household data, annual averages). http://www.bls.gov/cps/cpsaat03.htm. Accessed March 16, 2014.

_____. 2016a. Table 5. Employment status of the population by sex, marital status, and presence and age of own children under 18, 2014–2015 annual averages. http://www.bls.gov/news.release/famee.t05.htm. Accessed September 29, 2016.

_____. 2016b. Employment Situation (August). http://www.bls.gov/news.release/empsit.toc.htm. Accessed October 1, 2016.

_____. 2016c. "Median Weekly Earnings of Full-Time Wage and Salary Workers by Detailed Occupation and Sex." Accessed December 24, 2016. https://www.bls.gov/cps/cpsaat39.htm.

_____. 2016d. "American Time Use Survey: 2015 Results." June 24. https://stats.bls.gov/news.release/pdf/atus.pdf. Accessed May 4, 2017.

U.S. Census Bureau. 1975. *Historical Statistics of the United States: Colonial Times to 1970.* Washington, DC: U.S. Department of Commerce.

_____. 1996. *Statistical Abstract of the United States.* Washington, DC: U.S. Dept. of Commerce, Economics and Statistics Administration, Bureau of the Census.

_____. 2001. "Population by Age, Sex, Race, and Hispanic or Latino Origin for the United States: 2000." http://www.census.gov/population/www/cen2000/briefs/phc-t9/. Accessed October 30, 2013.

_____. 2007–2011a. American Factfinder, Table DP02 and DP03 for Geographic area: Navajo Nation Reservation and Off-Reservation Trust Land, AZ—NM—UT, 2007–2011 5-year estimates.

_____. 2007–2011b. "Selected Economic Characteristics: ACS 5-year Estimates." http://factfinder2.census.gov/faces/nav/jsf/pages/index.xhtml. Accessed November 3, 2013.

_____. 2007–2011c. "Selected Social Characteristics in the United States: ACS 5-year Estimates." http://factfinder2.census.gov/faces/nav/jsf/pages/index.xhtml. Accessed November 3, 2013.

_____. 2008. *Statistical Abstract of the United States: 2009* (128th edition). Washington, DC. http://www.census.gov/compendia/statab/2009/. Accessed June 18, 2014.

_____. 2010a. *America's Families and Living Arrangements: 2010.* http://www.census.gov/hhes/families/data/cps2010.html. Accessed October 30, 2013.

_____. 2010b. "Census Questionnaire Form." U.S. Department of Commerce. http://www.census.gov/2010census/partners/pdf/langfiles/2010_Questionnaire_Info_Copy.pdf. Accessed January 5, 2014.

_____. 2011a. Press release: "Census Bureau Releases Estimates of Same-Sex Married Couples." http://www.census.gov/newsroom/releases/archives/2010_census/cb11-cn181.html. Accessed December 5, 2013.

_____. 2011b. Current Population Survey, Annual Social and Economic Supplement. Table FINC-01. Selected Characteristics of Families by Total Money Income in 2010. http://www.census.gov/hhes/www/cpstables/032011/faminc/new01_001.htm. Accessed January 13, 2014.

_____. 2011c. *Families and Living Arrangements.* "Table MS-2. Estimated Median Age at First Marriage, by Sex: 1890 to the Present." http://www.census.gov/hhes/families/data/marital.html. Accessed January 6, 2014.

_____. 2011d. *Fertility of American Women.* http://www.census.gov/hhes/fertility/data/cps/2010.html. Accessed September 25, 2013.

_____. 2011e. "Selected Population Profile in the United States: 2011 ACS 1-year Estimates." http://factfinder2.census.gov/faces/nav/jsf/pages/index.xhtml. Accessed November 3, 2013.

_____. 2012a. *America's Families and Living Arrangements: 2012*. Table A2. http://www.census.gov/hhes/families/data/cps2012.html. Accessed June 14, 2013.

_____. 2012b. *America's Families and Living Arrangements: 2012*. Table FG3. Updated annually. http://www.census.gov/hhes/families/data/cps2012.html. Accessed February 2, 2014.

_____. 2012c. Historical Poverty Tables—Families. http://www.census.gov/hhes/www/poverty/data/historical/families.html. Accessed February 11, 2014.

_____. 2012d. "Poverty." Table POV01. http://www.census.gov/hhes/www/cpstables/032013/pov/pov01_100.htm. Accessed March 16, 2014.

_____. 2012e. "Race: FAQ." http://www.census.gov/population/race/about/faq.html. Accessed July 1, 2013.

_____.2012f. Poverty Statistics. http://www.census.gov/hhes/www/cpstables/032012/pov/toc.htm. Accessed September 2, 2013.

_____. 2012g. "2010 Census Special Reports, Centenarians: 2010." Washington, DC: U.S. Department of Commerce.

_____. 2013a. "American Community Survey Data on Same Sex Couples." http://www.census.gov/hhes/samesex/data/acs.html. Accessed September 23, 2013.

_____. 2013b. *America's Families and Living Arrangements: 2013*. Family groups table series. http://www.census.gov/hhes/families/data/cps2013FG.html. Accessed January 28, 2013.

_____. 2013c. *America's Families and Living Arrangements: 2013*. Households (H table series). http://www.census.gov/hhes/families/data/cps2013H.html. Accessed January 28, 2014.

_____. 2013d. Historical Poverty Tables—People. Table 2. Poverty Status of People by Family Relationship, Race, and Hispanic Origin: 1959 to 2011. http://www.census.gov/hhes/www/poverty/data/historical/people.html. Accessed September 2, 2013.

_____. 2013e. "Income, Poverty and Health Insurance in the United States." http://www.census.gov/hhes/www/poverty/data/incpovhlth/index.html. Accessed September 2, 2013.

_____. 2013f. *Living Arrangements of Children*. Table CH-2: Living Arrangements of White Children Under 18 Years Old: 1960 to Present. Table CH-3: Living Arrangements of Black Children under 18 Years Old: 1960 to Present. Table CH-4: Living Arrangements of Hispanic Children under 18 Years Old: 1960 to Present. https://www.census.gov/hhes/families/data/children.html. Accessed February 3, 2014.

_____. 2013g. *Living Arrangements of Children*. Table CH-7. Grandchildren under Age 18 Living in the Home of Their Grandparents: 1970 to Present. https://www.census.gov/hhes/families/data/children.html. Accessed February 3, 2014.

_____. 2013h. 2012 National Population Projections: Summary Tables (Middle Series). https://www.census.gov/population/projections/data/national/2012/summarytables.html. Accessed February 18, 2014.

_____. 2013i. Poverty. Table POV03. http://www.census.gov/hhes/www/cpstables/032013/pov/pov03_000.htm. Accessed January 28, 2014.

_____. 2013j. Survey of Income and Program Participation. Table 2. http://www.census.gov/sipp/tables/quarterly-est/household-char/hsehld-char-11.html. Accessed September 2, 2013.

_____. 2014a. "Computer and Internet Use." *http://www.census.gov/topics/population/computer-internet/data/tables.html*. Accessed December 8, 2016.

_____. 2014b. National Population Projections. https://www.census.gov/population/projections/data/national/2014/summarytables.html. Accessed June 10, 2017.

_____. 2015a. *America's Families and Living Arrangements: 2015*. http://www.census.gov/hhes/families/data/cps2015.html. Accessed September 28, 2016.

_____. 2015b. *Fertility of American Women*. http://www.census.gov/hhes/fertility/data/cps/2010.html. Accessed March 20, 2017.

_____. 2015c. "Fertility of Women in the United States: 2014." https://www.census.gov/hhes/fertility/data/cps/2014.html. Accessed March 18, 2017.

_____. 2016a. 2016 Census Test: Self and Enumerator Response. http://www.reginfo.gov/public/do/PRAViewIC?ref_nbr=201604-0607-003&icID=218769. Accessed October 22, 2016.

_____. 2016b. Annual Estimates of the Resident Population by Single Year of Age and Sex for the United States: April 1, 2010 to July 1, 2015. Factfinder.census.gov (table PEPSYASEXN). Accessed October 1, 2016.

_____. 2016c. *Families and Living Arrangements*. "Table MS-2. Estimated Median Age at First Marriage, by Sex: 1890 to the Present." http://www.census.gov/hhes/families/data/marital.html.

_____. 2016d. Population Estimates; Current Estimates Data. *http://www.census.gov/popest/data/index.html*. Accessed November 20, 2016.

_____. 2016e. American FactFinder. Table S0501: Selected Characteristics of the Native and Foreign-Born Populations, 2015. http://factfinder2.census.gov.

_____. 2016f. Income Distribution to $250,000 or More for Families (Table FINC-07). http://www.census.gov/data/tables/time-series/demo/income-poverty/cps-finc/finc-07.html. Accessed December 4, 2016.

_____. 2016g. Historical Poverty Tables: People and Families. Table 2. "Poverty Status of People by Family Relationship, Race, and Hispanic Origin." http://www.census.gov/data/tables/time-series/demo/income-poverty/historical-poverty-people.html. Accessed December 6, 2016.

_____. 2016h. Historical Poverty Tables: People and Families. Table 3. "Poverty Status of People, by Age, Race, and Hispanic Origin: 1959 to 2015." http://www.census.gov/data/tables/time-series/demo/income-poverty/historical-poverty-people.html. Accessed December 6, 2016.

_____. 2016i. "Current Population Survey Detailed Tables for Poverty." http://www.census.gov/data/tables/time-series/demo/income-poverty/cps-pov.html. Accessed December 13, 2016.

_____. 2016j. Survey of Income and Program Participation. Table 2. http://www.census.gov/programs-surveys/sipp/publications/tables/hsehld-char.html. Accessed December 5, 2016.

_____. 2016k. *America's Families and Living Arrangements: 2016*. Family groups table series. http://www.census.gov/hhes/families/data/cps2016FG.html. Accessed February 20, 2017.

_____. 2017a. Table MS-1. Marital Status of the Population 15 Years Old and Over, by Sex, Race and Hispanic Origin: 1950 to Present. https://www.census.gov/hhes/families/data/marital.html. Accessed February 18, 2017.

_____. 2017b. Living Arrangements of Children. https://www.census.gov/hhes/families/data/children.html. Accessed March 19, 2017.

_____. 2017c. *America's Families and Living Arrangements: 2016*. Table FG3. https://www.census.gov/data/tables/2016/demo/families/cps-2016.html. Accessed May 5, 2017.

U.S. Department of Agriculture. 2013. "National School Lunch Program." http://www.fns.usda.gov/sites/default/files/NSLPFactSheet.pdf. Accessed January 8, 2014.

U.S. Department of Health and Human Services. 2011. *Child Maltreatment 2010*. Washington, DC: Administration for Children and Families, Administration on Children, Youth and Families, Children's Bureau.

_____. 2012. *Child Maltreatment 2011*. Washington, DC: Administration for Children and Families, Administration on Children, Youth and Families, Children's Bureau. http://www.acf.hhs.gov/programs/cb/research-data-technology/statistics-research/child-maltreatment. Accessed October 23, 2013.

_____. 2017. *Child Maltreatment 2015*. Washington, D.C. Administration for Children and Families, Administration on Children, Youth and Families, Children's Bureau. https://www.acf.hhs.gov/sites/default/files/cb/cm2015.pdf.

United States Department of Justice. 2015. Federal Bureau of Investigation. Uniform Crime Reporting Program Data: Supplementary Homicide Reports, 2015. ICPSR36790-v1.

Ann Arbor, MI: Inter-university Consortium for Political and Social Research [distributor], 2017-05-04. https://doi.org/10.3886/ICPSR36790.v1.

_____. 2017. "Sexual Assault." https://www.justice.gov/ovw/sexual-assault.

U.S. Department of Labor. 2014. Family Medical Leave Act: Overview. http://www.dol.gov/whd/fmla/. Accessed February 14, 2014.

U.S. Department of State. 2014. Intercountry Adoption Statistics. Bureau of Consular Affairs. http://adoption.state.gov/about_us/statistics.php. Accessed May 5, 2014.

_____. 2016a. "#RefugeesWelcome: U.S. Admits 10,000 Syrian Refugees This Year." August 30. http://blogs.state.gov/stories/2016/08/30/refugeeswelcome-us-admits-10000-syrian-refugees-year.

_____. 2016b. Intercountry Adoption Statistics. Bureau of Consular Affairs. https://travel.state.gov/content/adoptionsabroad/en/about-us/statistics.html. Accessed March 18, 2017.

USCIS. 2016. "Form I-821D Deferred Action for Childhood Arrivals." USCIS. Accessed November 25, 2016. https://www.uscis.gov/tools/reports-studies/immigration-forms-data/data-set-form-i-821d-deferred-action-childhood-arrivals.

Vaaler, Margaret L., Christopher G. Ellison, and Daniel A. Powers. 2009. "Religious Influences on the Risk of Marital Dissolution." *Journal of Marriage and Family* 71(4):917–934.

Vaidyanathan, Rajini. 2009. "Fifty Years of Barbie." *BBC News,* March 9, 2009. http://news.bbc.co.uk/2/hi/americas/7931700.stm. Accessed September 7, 2013.

Vaillancourt-Morel, M.-P., N. Godbout, S. Sabourin, J. Briere, Y. Lussier, and M. Runtz. 2016. "Adult Sexual Outcomes of Child Sexual Abuse Vary According to Relationship Status." *Journal of Marital and Family Therapy* 42(2), 341–356. https://doi.org/10.1111/jmft.12154.

Van der Kolk, Bessel. 2000. "Posttraumatic Stress Disorder and the Nature of Trauma." *Dialogues in Clinical Neuroscience* 2(1):7–22.

Van Hooff, Jenny H. 2011. "Rationalising Inequality: Heterosexual Couples' Explanations and Justifications for the Division of Housework along Traditionally Gendered Lines." *Journal of Gender Studies* 20(1):19–30.

Vandivere, Sharon, Karin Malm, and Laura Radel. 2009. *Adoption USA: A Chartbook Based on the 2007 National Survey of Adoptive Parents.* Washington, DC: U.S. Department of Health and Human Services.

Vespa, Jonathan. 2014. "Historical Trends in the Marital Intentions of One-Time and Serial Cohabitors." *Journal of Marriage and Family* 76(1):207–17. doi:10.1111/jomf.12083.

Vickery, Clair. 1977. "The Time-Poor: A New Look at Poverty." *The Journal of Human Resources* 12(1):27–48.

Wade, Lisa. 2013. "The New Science of Sex Difference." *Sociology Compass* 7(4):278–93. doi:10.1111/soc4.12028
———. 2017. *American Hookup: The New Culture of Sex on Campus*. New York: W. W. Norton.

Wadsworth, P., and K. Records. 2013. "A Review of the Health Effects of Sexual Assault on African American Women and Adolescents." *Jognn-Journal of Obstetric Gynecologic and Neonatal Nursing* 42(3): 249–73. https://doi.org/10.1111/1552-6909.12041.

Wakefield, S., and C. Wildeman. 2013. *Children of the Prison Boom: Mass Incarceration and the Future of American Inequality*. Oxford University Press.

Waldfogel, Jane. 2006. *What Children Need*. Cambridge, MA: Harvard University Press.

Walters, Mikel L., Jieru Chen, and Matthew J. Breiding. 2013. *The National Intimate Partner and Sexual Violence Survey (NISVS): 2010 Findings on Victimization by Sexual Orientation*. National Center for Injury Prevention and Control, Centers for Disease Control and Prevention. http://www.cdc.gov/violenceprevention/pdf/nisvs_sofindings.pdf. Accessed October 24, 2013.

Walvoord, Emily C. 2010. "The Timing of Puberty: Is It Changing? Does It Matter?" *Journal of Adolescent Health* 47(5):433–39. doi:10.1016/j.jadohealth.2010.05.018.

Wang, Jennifer. 2016. "Donald Trump's Fortune Falls $800 Million to $3.7 Billion." *Forbes*. http://www.forbes.com/sites/jenniferwang/2016/09/28/the-definitive-look-at-donald-trumps-wealth-new/. Accessed October 2, 2016.

Warikoo, Natasha, and Prudence Carter. 2009. "Cultural Explanations for Racial and Ethnic Stratification in Academic Achievement: A Call for a New and Improved Theory." *Review of Educational Research* 79(1):366–394.

Warner, Michael. 1999. "Normal and Normaller: Beyond Gay Marriage." *GLQ: A Journal of Lesbian and Gay Studies* 5(2):119–171.

Warshak, Richard A. 2014. "Social Science and Parenting Plans for Young Children: A Consensus Report." *Psychology Public Policy and Law* 20(1):46–67. doi:10.1037/law0000005.

Warshaw, Robin, and Mary P. Koss. 1994. *I Never Called It Rape: The Ms. Report on Recognizing, Fighting, and Surviving Date and Acquaintance Rape*. New York: HarperPerennial.

Washington Post. 2016. "Part 2: Donald Trump Jr. Testifies in Zakarian Lawsuit." September 30. http://www.washingtonpost.com/video/politics/part-2-donald-trump-jr-testifies-in-zakarian-lawsuit/2016/09/30/f5e797dc-873e-11e6-b57d-dd49277af02f_video.html. Accessed October 1, 2016.

Waters, Mary C., and Tomás R. Jimenez. 2005. "Assessing Immigrant Assimilation: New Empirical and Theoretical Challenge." *Annual Review of Sociology* 31:105–125.

Weaver, Hilary N., and Barry J. White. 1997. "The Native American Family Circle: Roots of Resiliency." In *Cross-Cultural Practice with Couples and Families*, edited by Philip M. Brown and John S. Shalett, pp. 67–80. Binghamton, NY: Haworth Press.

Weber, Max. 1946. *From Max Weber: Essays in Sociology*, edited by C. Wright Mills, translated by Hans Heinrich Gerth. New York : Oxford University Press. https://archive.org/stream/frommaxweberessa00webe/frommaxweberessa00webe_djvu.txt. Accessed January 13, 2014.

Weeden, Jason, and John Sabini. 2005. "Physical Attractiveness and Health in Western Societies: A Review." *Psychological Bulletin* 131(5):635–653.

Weeks, Jeffrey. 2000. *Making Sexual History*. Cambridge, UK: Polity Press; Blackwell Publishers.

Weeks, John R. 2011. *Population: An Introduction to Concepts and Issues*. Belmont, CA: Wadsworth Publishing.

Weitzman, Lenore J. 1985. *The Divorce Revolution: The Unexpected Social and Economic Consequences for Women and Children in America*. New York: Free Press.

Welch, Charles E., III, and Paul C. Glick. 1981. "The Incidence of Polygamy in Contemporary Africa: A Research Note." *Journal of Marriage and Family* 43(1):191–193.

Wells-Barnett, Ida B. 1892. *Southern Horrors: Lynch Law in All Its Phases*. Pamphlet. Originally published in New York by *The New York Age*.

Wery, A., and J. Billieux. 2017, January. "Problematic Cybersex: Conceptualization, Assessment, and Treatment." *Addictive Behaviors* 64:238–46. doi:10.1016/j.addbeh.2015.11.007.

West, Candace, and Don H. Zimmerman. 1987. "Doing Gender." Gender and Society 1(2):125–151.

Western, Bruce, Deirdre Bloome, Benjamin Sosnaud, and Laura Tach. 2012. "Economic Insecurity and Social Stratification." *Annual Review of Sociology* 38:341–359.

Whaples, Robert. 1990. "Winning the Eight-Hour Day, 1909–1919." *The Journal of Economic History* 50(2):393–406. doi:10.1017/S0022050700036512.

Whisman, Mark A., and Douglas K. Snyder. 2007. "Sexual Infidelity in a National Survey of American Women: Differences in Prevalence and Correlates as a Function of Method of Assessment." *Journal of Family Psychology* 21(2):147–154.

Whitbeck, Les B., Ronald L. Simons, and Meei-Ying Kao. 1994. "The Effects of Divorced Mothers' Dating Behaviors and Sexual Attitudes on the Sexual Attitudes and Behaviors of Their Adolescent Children." *Journal of Marriage and Family* 56(3):615–621.

White, Lynn, and Stacy J. Rogers. 2000. "Economic Circumstances and Family Outcomes: A Review of the 1990s." *Journal of Marriage and Family* 62(4):1035–1051.

White, Michael D., and Karen J. Terry. 2008. "Child Sexual Abuse in the Catholic Church: Revisiting the Rotten Apples Explanation." *Criminal Justice and Behavior* 35(5):658–678.

Whiteford, Linda M., and Lois Gonzalez. 1995. "Stigma: The Hidden Burden of Infertility." *Social Science and Medicine* 40(1):27–36.

Whiteman, Shawn D., Julia M. B. Bernard, and Susan M. McHale. 2010. "The Nature and Correlates of Sibling Influence in Two-Parent African American Families." *Journal of Marriage and Family* 72(2):267–281.

Whyte, Martin K. 1992. "Choosing Mates—the American Way." *Society* 29(3):71–77.

Whyte, Stephen, and Benno Torgler. 2017. "Things Change with Age: Educational Assortment in Online Dating." *Personality and Individual Differences* 109(April):5–11. doi:10.1016/j.paid.2016.12.031.

Wienke, Chris, and Gretchen J. Hill. 2009. "Does the "Marriage Benefit" Extend to Partners in Gay and Lesbian Relationships? Evidence from a Random Sample of Sexually Active Adults." *Journal of Family Issues* 30(2):259–289.

Wiersma, Jacquelyn D., H. Harrington Cleveland, Veronica Herrera, and Judith L. Fischer. 2010. "Intimate Partner Violence in Young Adult Dating, Cohabitating, and Married Drinking Partnerships." *Journal of Marriage and Family* 72(2):360–374.

Wight, Vanessa R., Suzanne M. Bianchi, and Bijou R. Hunt. 2013. "Explaining Racial/Ethnic Variation in Partnered Women's and Men's Housework: Does One Size Fit All?" *Journal of Family Issues* 34(3):394–427. doi:10.1177/0192513X12437705

Wilcox, Melissa M. 2003. *Coming Out in Christianity: Religion, Identity, and Community.* Bloomington, IN: Indiana University Press.

Wilcox, W. Bradford. 2011. "Why Marriage Matters: Thirty Conclusions from the Social Sciences." New York: Institute for American Values.

Wildeman, Christopher. 2009. "Parental Imprisonment, the Prison Boom, and the Concentration of Childhood Disadvantage." *Demography* 46(2):265–280.

Wildeman, C., N. Emanuel, J. M. Leventhal, E. Putnam-Hornstein, J. Waldfogel, and H. Lee. 2014. "The Prevalence of Confirmed Maltreatment among US Children, 2004 to 2011." *JAMA Pediatrics.* http://doi.org/10.1001/jamapediatrics.2014.410.

Wilder, Laura I. 1935. *Little House on the Prairie.* New York: Harper and Brothers.

Wildsmith, Elizabeth, Myron P. Gutmann, and Brian Gratton. 2003. "Assimilation and Intermarriage for U.S. Immigrant Groups, 1880–1990." *The History of the Family* 8(4):563–584.

Wilgoren, Jodi, and Jacques Steinberg. 2000. "Even for Sixth Graders, College Looms." *New York Times,* July 3.

Williams, Alex. 2006. "Trump Jr.: Finally Trading on a Famous Name." *New York Times,* November 21. http://www.nytimes.com/2006/11/21/arts/21iht-trump.3611735.html.

———. 2010. "The New Math on Campus." *New York Times,* February 7, Style.

Wilson, Elizabeth. 1990. "Deviant Dress." *Feminist Review* (35):67–74.

Wilson, Ellen K., and Chris McQuiston. 2006. "Motivations for Pregnancy Planning among Mexican Immigrant Women in North Carolina." *Maternal and Child Health Journal* 10(3):311–320.

Wilson, Michael. 2009. "Eggs, Bacon and a Baseball Cap." *New York Times,* August 16, Metro, p. 2.

Wilson, William J. 1987. *The Truly Disadvantaged: The Inner City, the Underclass, and Public Policy.* Chicago, IL: University of Chicago Press.

———. 1997. *When Work Disappears: The World of the New Urban Poor.* New York: Vintage Books.

———. 2009. *More Than Just Race: Being Black and Poor in the Inner City.* New York: W.W. Norton.

Winthrop, John. 1853. "The History of New England." Vols. 1 and 2. In *The History of New England from 1630 to 1649,* edited by J. Savage. Boston, MA: Little, Brown. http://press-pubs.uchicago.edu/founders/documents/v1ch13s1.html. Accessed March 24, 2009.

Witt, Susan D. 1997. "Parental Influence on Children's Socialization to Gender Roles." *Adolescence* 32(126):253–259.

Wolff, Edward N., and Maury Gittleman. 2011. "Inheritances and the Distribution of Wealth, or Whatever Happened to the Great Inheritance Boom? Results from the SCF and PSID." National Bureau of Economic Research Working Paper No. 16840. http://www.nber.org/papers/w16840.pdf. Accessed June 18, 2014.

Wolff, Jennifer L., and Judith D. Kasper. 2006. "Caregivers of Frail Elders: Updating a National Profile." *The Gerontologist* 46(3):344–356.

Wolfinger, Nicholas H. 2005. *Understanding the Divorce Cycle: The Children of Divorce in Their Own Marriages.* Cambridge, UK: Cambridge University Press.

Wolfers, Justin. 2006. "Did Unilateral Divorce Laws Raise Divorce Rates? A Reconciliation and New Results." *The American Economic Review* 96(5):1802–1820.

Woodruff, Kristen, and Bethany Lee. 2011. "Identifying and Predicting Problem Behavior Trajectories among Pre-

School Children Investigated for Child Abuse and Neglect." *Child Abuse and Neglect* 35(7):491–503.

World Values Survey. 2015. WVS Wave 6 2010-2014. World Values Survey Association. www.worldvaluessurvey.org. Accessed June 1, 2017.

Wright, Carroll D. 1889. *A Report on Marriage and Divorce in the United States, 1867–1886*. Washington, DC: U.S. Government Printing Office.

Wright, Erik O. 1997. *Class Counts: Comparative Studies in Class Analysis*. Cambridge, UK: Cambridge University Press.

Wright, Erik O., and Joel Rogers. 2011. *American Society: How It Really Works*. New York: W.W. Norton.

Wright, Paul J., Robert S. Tokunaga, and Ashley Kraus. 2016. "Consumption of Pornography, Perceived Peer Norms, and Condomless Sex." *Health Communication* 31(8):954–63. doi:10.1080/10410236.2015.1022936.

Xie, M., J. L. Lauritsen, and K. Heimer. 2012. "Intimate Partner Violence in US Metropolitan Areas: The Contextual Influences of Police and Social Services." *Criminology* 50(4): 961–92. https://doi.org/10.1111/j.1745-9125.2012.00284.x.

Yahr, Emily. 2015. "Bruce Jenner's in-Depth Interview: 'For All Intents and Purposes, I Am a Woman.'" *The Washington Post*, April 24. https://www.washingtonpost.com/news/arts-and-entertainment/wp/2015/04/24/bruce-jenner-for-all-intents-and-purposes-i-am-a-woman/.

Yardley, Jim, and Elisabetta Povoledo. 2015. "Pope Francis Announces Changes for Easier Marriage Annulments." *New York Times*, September 8. https://www.nytimes.com/2015/09/09/world/europe/pope-francis-marriage-annulment-reforms.html.

Ybarra, Michele L., and Kimberly J. Mitchell. 2014. "'Sexting' and Its Relation to Sexual Activity and Sexual Risk Behavior in a National Survey of Adolescents." *Journal of Ado-lescent Health* 55(6):757–64. doi:10.1016/j.jadohealth.2014.07.012.

Yen, Hope. 2013. "US Stopping Use of Term 'Negro' for Census Surveys." February 25. Associated Press. http://bigstory.ap.org/article/us-stopping-use-term-negro-census-surveys. Accessed January 5, 2014.

Yodanis, Carrie L. 2004. "Gender Inequality, Violence against Women, and Fear: A Cross-National Test of the Feminist Theory of Violence against Women." *Journal of Interpersonal Violence* 19(6):655–675.

Zadnik, Karla. 2000. "Vision: Myopia and Ambient Night-Time Lighting." *Nature* 404(March 9):143–144.

Zaretsky, Eli. 1976. *Capitalism, the Family, and Personal Life*. London, UK: Pluto Press.

Zelizer, Viviana A. Rotman. 1985. *Pricing the Priceless Child: The Changing Social Value of Children*. Princeton, NJ: Princeton University Press.

Zheng, Hui, and Patricia A. Thomas. 2013. "Marital Status, Self-Rated Health, and Mortality: Overestimation of Health or Diminishing Protection of Marriage?" *Journal of Health and Social Behavior* 54(1):128–143.

Zilanawala, A. 2016. "Women's Time Poverty and Family Structure: Differences by Parenthood and Employment." 37(3):369–392. https://doi.org/10.1177/0192513X14542432.

Zimmer, Carl. 2016. "A Single Migration From Africa Populated the World, Studies Find." *New York Times*, September 21. http://www.nytimes.com/2016/09/22/science/ancient-dna-human-history.html.

Zong, Jie, and Jeanne Batalova. 2015. "Middle Eastern and North African Immigrants in the United States." Migrationpolicy.org. June 2. http://www.migrationpolicy.org/article/middle-eastern-and-north-african-immigrants-united-states.

Zrenchik, Kyle, and Shonda M. Craft. 2016. "The State of GLBT Family Research: An Opportunity to Critically Reflect." *Journal of GLBT Family Studies* 12(2):138–59. doi:10.1080/1550428X.2015.1011817.

Photo Credits

Index

In this index, page references in *italics* refer to illustrative material.

A

Abolition of slavery, 53

Abortion
  patterns in America, 330–332, *331*
  sex-selective, 157
  teenage pregnancy and, 224

Abrahamic religions, 180. *See also specific religion*

Abstinence
  as birth control method, 46
  hooking up *vs.*, 248
  in sex education, *228–229*

Abuse and violence. *See* Child abuse and neglect; Family
  violence and abuse

Accomplishment of natural growth, in parenting, 150,
  153

The Accordion Family (Newman), 502

Accountability, 25

Acculturation
  assimilation *vs.*, 108
  definition of, 107

Activities, gender-typed, 184–185, *184*

Adam and Eve story, 164

Adolescence
  changing sexual norms, 221
  definition of, 221

Adoption
  informal, 6
  legal definition of family and, 8
  stigma of, 487
  trends and issues, 327–329, *328*

Adoptive parents, 327–329, *328*
  definition of, 321

Adorno, Theodor, *268*

Adventures in Clueless Urban Balcony Gardening, *430*

The Adventures of Ozzie and Harriet, *58*

African Americans, 90–97. *See also* Black population;
  Blacks
  blended families data, 394, *394*
  Census Bureau data on, *80, 81, 82*
  dating views, 244
  death rates among men, 92

decline in marriage rates and, 53, 95, *95, 98–99*
deindustrialization and, 94
divorce and, 53, 91, 95, *370–371*
emerging modern family (1820-1900), 52, 53
families enslaved, 44
family profile, 94
family resilience and, 91–92
grandparents as family caregivers, 70
incarceration and, 96, *96,* 98
infant mortality rate, *48*
informal marriages and, 91, 92
intimate partner violence and, 452–453, *452*
lynching of, 110
marriage demographics, 284–285
marriage gap between Whites and, 24–25
mate selection patterns, 262–266
poverty and, 135
retreat from marriage and, 95–97
sibling relationships and, 178
slavery's legacy and, 90–91
urban poverty and, 92–95
voting rights for, 68
women's employment and, 64

Age
  divorce and, 374–375, *374*
  of first marriage, 55, *55, 482–483,* 484

Age structure
  definition of, 490
  for United States, 490–491, *491*

Aging
  childbearing patterns and, 323, 326–327, *326*
  cohabitation patterns, 300–301, *300*
  divorce trends with, 395–396
  fertility and, 490–493, *491, 492*
  future trends and challenges, 491–493, *492*
  sexual behaviors, 219–220, *220,* 232–233, *232*

Agriculture. *See* Farms

Aid to Dependent Children, 57

Aid to Families with Dependent Children, 64, 308

AIDS, trends and impacts, 225–226, *226*

Airbnb, 74

Alaska Natives, Census Bureau data on, *80*

Alger, Horatio, 142

All the Single Ladies (Traister), 303

Almshouses, 52

Alternative lifestyles, traditional virtues as, 239

Amato, Paul, 384

E

H

K

Katz, Lawrence, 214
Kavanaugh, Lauren, *441*
Kennedy, Anthony, *312*
Kinsey, Alfred, 211
Kinsey Reports, 211
Kohn, Melvin, 150
Korea, preference for sons in, 157
Korean War, War Brides Act and, 106

L

Labor. *See also* Division of labor
   of African Americans, 53
   of Asian Americans, 53–54, *53*
   by gender. *See* Gender division of labor
   laborsaving devices for housework, 62–63, *62*
   of Mexican Americans, 54
   women's entry into force (1950s-now), 403–405, *403*,
      404
Laborsaving devices, 62–63
Ladies' Home Journal, 177
Ladies' Magazine, 48
Landers, Ann, 170, 171
Language acquisition, children of immigrants and, 108
Lareau, Annette, 28, 150, 153
Latin America, undocumented immigrants from, 114
Latino population, 84, 97, 100–101
   average number of family members living together, *101*
   Census Bureau data on, *80, 81, 82*
   culture and diversity in, 97, 100
   decline in marriage rate and, 101
   familism and, 100–101
   family profile of, by national origin, *100*
   fertility rate of, 87, 323–324, *324*
   in future of family, 479
   generational change and, 108
   intermarriage rates and, 111
   median age of, 97
   in Milwaukee, Wisconsin, 93
   poverty and, 135
   U.S. race-ethnic composition, 1970-2050, *86*, 87

Latinos/Latinas
   children's living arrangements, 336–337, *337*
   division of labor patterns, 415
   in emerging modern period, 54
   family violence and, 469–470
   fertility rates, 87, 323–324, *324*
   in future of family, 479
   infertility rates, 332–333, *333*
   intermarriage and, 111, *113*
   marriage demographics, 111, 286, *286*
Latshaw, Beth, 424–425
Lee v. Randolph County Board of Education, 255–256
Legal family, 7–8
   defined by U.S. Census, 10
   definition of, 7
Legal issues. *See also* Divorce
   of blended families, 388–390, 395
   children's rights, 442–443
   child support and custody, *386–388*
   civil rights, 68, 255
   family leave, *421–423*
   family violence, 470–471, 473
   gender diversity, 169
   high school proms, 255–256
   in immigration, 104, 105–107
   interracial marriage, 110
   landholding rights, 51
   local policy initiatives, 432–433
   rape and sexual assault, 453–456
   same-sex marriage, *311–314*
   voting rights, 68
Legend, John, 157
Lesbians. *See* Gay rights; Homosexuality
Letting Go of God, 481
LGBT (lesbian, gay, bisexual, or transgender), use of
   term, 200
Liberal political views
   on divorce, 367
   on family diversity, 498–499, *504*
Lieberson, Stanley, 72
Life chances, definition of, 122
Life course perspective
   definition of, 23
   family and, 23–24
Life expectancy, gender and, 164
Lincoln, Abraham, 50

V

W

X

X chromosomes, 160

Y

Y chromosomes, 160